MIDDLE EAST
PATTERNS

THIRD EDITION

MIDDLE EAST PATTERNS

Places, Peoples, and Politics

Colbert C. Held

Baylor University

With the assistance of
Mildred McDonald Held

Cartography by John V. Cotter

Westview Press
A Member of the Perseus Books Group

The calligraphy on pp. ii, 1, and 239 (which means "Over every learned one is one more learned") is taken from Mohamed U. Zakariya, *The Calligraphy of Islam: Reflections on the State of the Art* (Washington, D.C.: Center for Contemporary Arab Studies, Georgetown University, 1979) and is used by permission of the Center.

All photos are by the author unless otherwise attributed.

Published in 2000 in the United States of America by Westview Press, 5500 Central Avenue, Boulder, Colorado 80301–2877, and in the United Kingdom by Westview Press, 12 Hid's Copse Road, Cumnor Hill, Oxford OX2 9JJ

Find us on the World Wide Web at www.westviewpress.com

A CIP catalog record for this book is available from the Library of Congress.

ISBN 0-8133-3488-8

The paper used in this publication meets the requirements of the American National Standard for Permanence of Paper for Printed Library Materials Z39.48–1984.

10   9   8   7   6   5   4   3   2

CONTENTS

PART ONE
PHYSICAL AND CULTURAL GEOGRAPHY

1 Tricontinental Junction: An Introduction   3

Middle East Preview, 3
The Middle East: Definition, 7
Regional Unity of Empires, 9
Aims and Concepts: A Glance, 10

2 Patterns of Time: Historical-Geographical Foundations   13

Persistence of Patterns, 13
Early Patterns, 15
Historical-Political Evolution, 18
Some Inferences: Power Cores, 31

3 The Lands and the Waters   35

An Overview, 35
Survey of Landforms, 38
Middle East Seas, 46
Middle East Lakes, 49
Major River Systems, 50
Groundwater, 53

PART TWO
REGIONAL GEOGRAPHY

Iranian Economic Patterns, 500
Regional and Global Relations, 509

TABLES AND ILLUSTRATIONS

Illustrations (photographs)

PREFACE AND ACKNOWLEDGMENTS TO THE THIRD EDITION

Even during a time of global transformation, the Middle East region has changed remarkably, both quantitatively and qualitatively; and in 2000, as this third edition of *Middle East Patterns* is prepared, the region is greatly refashioned from that of only a decade ago, when the first edition was published. The metamorphosis has increased manyfold from the slowly emerging area to which I was introduced in early 1957 as a young Foreign Service Officer. Thus, I have monitored the changing Middle East for 43 years, as resident (1957–1966 and 1969–1975), as academic scholar (after 1975), and as periodic field worker (1979, 1990, and 1997). Each revisit was a literal revelation both of the vigorous dynamics driving the general area and of the transformation they had wrought. Despite change and modernization, however, the Middle East preserves some of its persistent character and fascinations. It is this persistent traditional character and fascination, as well as the dynamics and manifestations of change in this region, that I have attempted to capture and to present to the reader.

The peace process, in its initial phases when the second edition appeared, has progressed more slowly than the Oslo Agreements presaged. Nevertheless, the Palestinian Authority has emerged and is evolving, probably the most significant political phenomenon since the 1994 edition, and is holding out the logical promise of a Palestinian state. The early enthusiasm about the peace process after the election of Prime Minister Ehud Barak soon faced a reality check, and, on the Syrian track, the Golan problem was still on dead center in July 2000. One bright spot was southern Lebanon, from which Israel withdrew in May 2000. On the Palestinian track, a summit meeting in July 2000 at Camp David grappled unsuccessfully with problems of a final settlement. Relevant sections of this edition deal with other major developments—political extremism by several Muslim groups and Jewish groups; Yemen civil war in 1994; reform in Iran and signs of U.S.-Iranian détente; increasingly close alliance between Israel and Turkey; disastrous earthquakes in Turkey; peace treaty between Israel and Jordan in 1994; death of King Husayn of Jordan in 1999 and of President al-Asad of Syria in 2000 and the succession of their sons; stagnation of the situation in Iraq; continuing difficulties of the Kurds; immigration and high-tech developments in Israel; settlement of political boundaries on the Arabian Peninsula; fall and rise of oil prices; improvements in transportation in many countries; major projects in Egypt; and other profound changes in the region.

To accommodate the changes and the new developments, this third edition has been completely revised. Every statistic has been updated, and entire sections have been rewritten. Included in this edition are 65 maps, 7 completely new and 37 that have been updated or otherwise modified, especially to depict newly delineated boundaries; 126 photographs, 80 that are new and most of which I took during my 1997 field work; 14 tables, all of which have been completely updated; and 3 new graphs. The bibliography and notes have again been appreciably expanded in recognition of the explosion of materials on the Middle East. One major addition is a number of Web sites that offer significant information regarding many aspects of the region.

It is a pleasure to acknowledge the generous help and support from many people and agencies in the preparation of this volume, especially those who contributed to the success of the field work that my wife and I conducted in 1997 in thirteen of the sixteen countries in the region. As in the past, support came from American and local government officials, oil company representatives, and academicians and others. Foreign Service colleagues, including some friends from 40 years ago, were especially helpful. I should like to express particularly profound gratitude to Ambassador to Yemen David Newton and his wife, Christa, for help and warm hospitality, and to his staff members Angela R. Dickey, political officer; Lynn Donovan, economic officer; and Lt.-Col. Ted Seel, defense attaché. I am also grateful to Ambassador and Mrs. Patrick Theros, Doha. In other posts, I very much appreciate informative briefings by political officer Stephen Kimmel and economic officer Christopher H. Jones, Consulate General Istanbul; political officer Marc Sievers, economic officer Virginia Morris, agricultural attaché Mark Sloan, and defense attaché Col. Michael Carlin, as well as long-time local employee Meral Ishakbeyoğlu-Yemez, Embassy Ankara; commercial assistant M. Sohad Atassi and agricultural engineer M. Jaber Dalati, both veteran local employees in Embassy Damascus; political counselor Roberta Newell, economic chief Gary A. Grappo, and Col. Mike Anthony, defense attaché, Amman; economic officer Thomas A. Kelsey, political-military affairs officer Thomas E. Williams, Jr., Kuwait; political chief Denise Valois and economic officer Karen L. Malzahn, Manama; political-economic chief Daniel Goodspeed, economic officer Alan Oslick, and defense attaché Col. Ronald A. Edwards, Muscat; several Embassy officers in Cairo; political officers Gerald Anderson and Edgard D. Kagan, economic officer John Fennerty, and army attaché Col. Richard G. Reynolds, Tel Aviv; and deputy chief of mission Deborah E. Graze and public affairs officer Dr. Judith R. Baroody, Nicosia. I also appreciate significant support by Douglas Silliman and Elizabeth Jones in the Department of State, Washington.

Local government officials, academicians, and intellectuals in every country were extraordinarily helpful with briefings, materials, and support. Although not all can be listed, I cannot neglect Taner Ercömert of the Turkish State Hydraulic Works (DSİ); long-time friends Dr. and Mrs. Munir Shamrnaa, AUB Hospital, Beirut; Shaykh Abdillah M. A. al-Thor, Sana, and Tammam M. Ali Bashraheel, managing editor, *al-Ayyam* newspaper, Aden; and others.

Several oil companies continued to extend courtesies that afforded unusual visits and insights. Yemen Hunt Oil Company provided excellent briefings and a dramatic helicopter trip for my wife and me from Sana to the floating storage and offloading facility *Safir,* for which I extend thanks to A. W. "Bill" Lewis, vice-president and general manager, and his helpful staff. I am likewise grateful for the generous field support given once again by Crescent Oil Company president and friend of many years, Hamid Jafar, and his staff, including John Boreta. Ron E. Rutherford, president of Dubai Petroleum Company, gave an excellent briefing and useful materials. Vice president and manager of exploration Denis Mascardelli of Amoco Egypt gave generously of his time and extensive knowledge for a rewarding briefing in Cairo.

Bradford Thomas, formerly of the Office of the Geographer, Department of State, went the extra mile in giving several evaluations of my discussions and maps of boundaries and other coverage. I cannot thank him enough. At Baylor University, Dr. John Wilson, Documents Librarian, was unstinting in making available exotic items of great use, and other librarians were also helpful. Political Science colleagues Dr. William Mitchell and Dr. Linda Adams made helpful critical assessments of the chapters on Turkey and Jordan respectively. Baylor head photographer Chris Hansen made the excellent black-and-white prints from my Kodachrome slides that have appeared in all three editions. Cori Rhodes and Kimberly Combs of the Information Technology Center supported such computer skills as I possess. Peter Speers, Arabic language and Arabian affairs guru, continued to advise on transliterations and other abstruse matters. Westview Press staff members were patient and reassuring during the eighteen-month delay in completion of the manuscript caused by lung-cancer surgery—completely successful, fortunately.

My profoundest gratitude is extended with deepest affection to my wife, Milly, for her faithful support during Middle East illnesses and the lung surgery, as well as for her indispensable assistance in preparation of all editions of this study. Both of our daughters, Joanne Cummings and Melinda Brunger, also gave vital support during both the illness and the book preparation, as did their respective husbands, John and Bill.

Regardless of the briefings and materials and help given by the many generous persons mentioned above, any mistakes or errors in this volume are my complete responsibility. Any corrections or other comments by readers will be appreciated.

Colbert Held

A NOTE
ON TRANSLITERATION

For transliteration of place-names from Arabic, Hebrew, and Greek, I have generally followed the recommendations of the U.S. Board on Geographic Names (BGN), except that I elected to omit diacritical marks on transliterations from those three languages. (I retained diacritics in Turkish words, since Turkish uses a basically Roman alphabet in which diacritics are an integral part of the written language.) Indicating the *ain* and the *hamza* in Arabic words merely confuses the general reader who knows no Arabic and adds little of essence for readers who do. I have deliberately accepted inconsistency in using conventional forms and spellings for certain names—Cairo (rather than al-Qahirah), Damascus (al-Dimashq), Yemen (al-Yaman), Bab el-Mandeb (Bab al-Mandab), Dubai (Dubayyah), Medina (al-Madinah), Doha (al-Dawhah), Bekaa (Biqa), and others. I have also dropped the definite article (*al*) in many names: Aqabah, Riyadh, Qatif; and where I have retained it I have used it only in the basic form, not in the form modified by "sun letters" (Sharm al-Shaykh, not Sharm ash-Shaykh; Jabal al-Ruwaq, not Jabal ar-Ruwaq). I have also retained certain spellings that have become ingrained through use by oil companies.

Some names create certain problems. For example, the Gulf is called the Persian Gulf by Iran and many other countries and the Arabian Gulf by Arab states and some other countries. Many names in former Palestine—and the use of the name *Palestine* itself—imply particular biases: West Bank versus Samaria and Judea, Gulf of Aqabah versus Gulf of Elat, al-Quds or Jerusalem versus Yerushalayyem, and others. Jordan's disengagement from the West Bank in July–August 1988 has rendered even the applicability of the term *West Bank* a question mark. Revolutionary Iran has changed dozens of place-names because they connoted the Pahlavi royal family: for example, Bandar-e Pahlavi is now Bandar-e Anzali, Rezaiyeh is Urumiyeh (conventional: Urmia), and Bandar-e Shahpur is Bandar-e Khomeyni. I have used the new names that have been publicly announced.

C. C. H.

PART ONE

Physical and
Cultural Geography

1

Tricontinental Junction:
An Introduction

Middle East Preview

Located at the tricontinental hub of Europe, Asia, and Africa, the Middle East possesses unique geopolitical significance. It is the cradle of civilization, birthplace of the three great monotheistic religions, crossroads of movement and trade, base of extensive empires, resource area for 65 percent of the world's petroleum, home to 289.5 million people in sixteen countries, fountain of political and ideological ferment, and locus of some of the most persistently explosive conflicts since World War II. No country on earth can be unconcerned with the course of major developments in the region.

The Middle East has been in the news, often treated at length, almost daily since 1947. It was the center of attention of the world media not only during the wars of 1956, 1967, 1973, 1980–1988, 1982, and especially 1990–1991 but also during the protracted peace process through most of the 1990s. Yet the vast amount of routine reporting has rarely included in-depth objective background information about the area's complex patterns of regions, peoples, and problems—until the 1990–1991 Gulf war. Even then, the almost continuous detailed coverage naturally focused on news—the hour-by-hour events in the Gulf and, often, in Israel. Background information was often more pejorative than objective, not only concerning Iraq, the aggressor, but also regarding many members of the coalition. Fortunately, the media responsibly displayed maps of relevant areas, so that the world—especially the U.S. public—was generally better informed about the Middle East after the Gulf war than ever before. Nevertheless, much of the public

perception of the fundamental nature of the Middle East continued to be sketchy at best and continued to include stereotypes and prejudices that have roots as far back as the Crusades.

Every year after 1991, a more balanced and analytical media focus was devoted to the painful pursuit of regional peace. Many long-neglected aspects of the region and its profound problems received intensive attention from many quarters as each major accord signaled another small step forward. For almost the first time, spokesmen for all sides had the opportunity to present full, undistorted, and uncensored viewpoints. The sometimes seemingly interminable peace process demonstrated the many complexities of the problems involved.

Rational decisions and actions on the part of governments, as well as intelligent participation by citizens in those decisions and actions, require objective knowledge and understanding of the interactions among the basic enduring patterns in this vital region of the world. Decision makers and citizens must depend on sources other than the three-minute sound bites of the daily news for the background information necessary to comprehend an area with the complexity and significance of the Middle East.

The fate of much of the world, including that of the industrialized countries, is inextricably bound up with developments in the Middle East. It is important, therefore, to recognize that the region's peoples and states have their own histories, aspirations, value systems, problems of development and change, regional and global relationships, and agendas. With the transformation of the former Soviet realm in the early

1990s and the shuffling of transnational relationships in Eurasia, the Middle East assumes a changed and perhaps increasingly significant role. It is the aim of this book to examine the natural and cultural patterns of the Middle East and their influence on political and economic developments, to analyze and interpret the more significant regional and global relations, and thus to afford a greater knowledge of and insights into this crucial region.

Political and religious confrontations, military conflicts, and economic influence have given the Middle East an increasingly central role in world affairs. Because of its tricontinental location (Map 1-1) and its central position in the World-Island (see Chap. 11), the region has historically been a world crossroads, and the late Professor George B. Cressey titled his 1960 study of Middle East geography *Crossroads* to emphasize that important function.

However, the region is often perceived in particularistic terms—of petroleum or the Islamic resurgence or Israel or Arab nationalism or other single issues—which clouds the greater significance of this exceedingly complex area. Short-term and simplistic perceptions are also misleading—for example, that the Middle East has only recently become important or that it is typified by the Iranian revolution of the late 1970s, by the Iraqi aggression of 1990, or by rich oil *shaykhs* (sheikhs) in desert kingdoms. In fact, the Middle East blends diverse geographical elements, rich historical traditions, and complex cultural and national groupings to produce kaleidoscopic patterns that continue to evolve and change. Inevitably, the impact of rapid change and of the continued search for legitimacy and identity induces stress and resultant antagonisms. The maps and photographs in this book depict some of these complexities and contrasts (see, for example, Figs. 1-1 and 1-2).

The significance of the location of the Middle East derives partly from its irregular shape. Seas penetrate deeply into the land and alternate with peninsulas and land bridges around the Syrian-Mesopotamian core. These seas, including the Red, Mediterranean, Black, and

MAP 1-1   The Middle East as tricontinental hub, centrally located in the heart of the World-Island.

Caspian (actually an inland lake), and the Persian/Arabian Gulf have made maritime movements of the peoples of the area relatively easy for more than 5,000 years, provide access to the region, and conversely, serve as natural insulation between regional cultural groups.

The Middle East is commonly known as the "cradle of civilization." Evidence of the earliest known humans has been found in East Africa, and very old human skeletons and tools have been found in other areas; but the Middle East had human inhabitants very early and seems to have produced the earliest integrated civilizations, agricultural villages and developed towns, and religious-political systems. These civilizations evolved in the Fertile Crescent, an arc of fertile land that extends from the Mediterranean around the Syrian Desert to the Gulf, and particularly the Mesopotamian Basin, the depression occupied by the Tigris and Euphrates rivers. From this geographical core, the ideas, techniques, and implements of the Fertile Crescent diffused to other similar environments—westward to the Nile Valley in Egypt, eastward to the Indus Valley in present-day Pakistan, and beyond—and mixed with impressive civilizations in those areas.

More than 5,000 years ago, this seminal culture hearth of Mesopotamia produced the earliest known writing and high levels of science

FIGURE 1-1   Barren, wind-rippled dunes in Saudi Arabia's Rub al-Khali (Empty Quarter).

and mathematics. The Middle East thus became a matrix for later Western and Oriental civilizations. The cultural complex that spread outward from the Mesopotamian core also gave rise to successive confrontations among expanding ancient empires. The high level of civilization achieved by successive empires suggests a resilience and capacity for adaptation that is still evident in the region. Several power foci, which will be discussed later in this book, emerged through the centuries and have persisted for more than 4,500 years to the present.

In addition to the clashes between successive empires, there also evolved in the Middle East the three major monotheistic religions—Judaism, Christianity, and Islam. Each is rooted in earlier religions, yet each is distinctive. Their respective origins within the region provide one measure of the cultural richness and unique significance of the Middle East.

Just as Christianity gave rise through the centuries to a general civilization referred to as Christendom, so Islam engendered the Islamic

civilization. The cradle of both the religion of Islam and the culture of Islam, the Middle East remains the heartland of the Islamic culture realm, the original core area of which—Mecca and Medina in western Saudi Arabia—is the goal of the annual Muslim hajj, or pilgrimage, and is a religious focus for most Muslims.

The Islamic civilization is the single most pervasive unifying factor in the Middle East, and the correlation between religion and culture on the one hand and geographical area and environment on the other is a major element in any study of the region. Two important functions of the Middle East region during medieval times relate to the bond between the area and Islam. During the centuries of the so-called Dark Ages in Europe, and while the Byzantine Empire was absorbed in political and theological disputes, the Islamic Middle East was translating and interpreting classical writings—literary, philosophical, and scientific—thus preserving the classical heritage, much of which might otherwise have been lost. Also, contemporaneously, the Middle East was a remarkable

FIGURE 1-2   Village surrounded by green fields of corn (maize) and well-forested slopes in Turkey's Pontic Mountains, an area of moderately heavy precipitation just south of the Black Sea.

commercial crossroads, maintaining contacts with potent East Asian civilizations, partly through Muslim missionaries, and later linking those civilizations with a revived Mediterranean area and Renaissance Europe.

Significant as the foregoing traditional aspects of the Middle East are, four contemporary aspects dominate the world's perception of the area: enormous petroleum resources, the political tensions arising from the Arab-Israeli confrontation, the bewildering rivalries among leaders and states, and the extremism among zealous Muslims, Jews, and Christians. Most of the petroleum—two-thirds of the world's known reserves—lies along a broad depression extending southeastward from near Elazığ, Turkey, along the axis of the Gulf, to the Arabian Sea coast of Oman. Of the 65 million barrels of petroleum produced daily in the world in 1999, 19 million barrels, or more than 29 percent, originated in the countries on the Gulf. In 1979, at the height of Middle East production, the region's percentage of the

world's total was more than half. In addition to selling oil to the West, the Middle East oil-producing countries depend heavily upon imports of goods and technical/managerial expertise from the industrialized countries. The resultant interdependence between industrialized countries and oil-producing countries has increased as the former grow more concerned with stable energy supplies and as the latter continue to require Western technology for development.

The Arab-Israeli wars in 1948–1949, 1956, 1967, 1973, and 1982 resulted in thousands of casualties and the diversion to armaments of billions of dollars needed for development. The consequent oil boycott in 1973, periodic outbreaks of fighting in the Levant, and regional and international obsession with the Arab-Israeli problem all attest to the destabilizing effects of the Arab-Israeli conflict. Although less protracted, the internecine Gulf wars of 1980–1988 and 1990–1991 resulted in many more casualties than the earlier battles in the Levant and were immeasurably more devastating.

The Middle East: Definition

That the Fertile Crescent is the core of the Middle East is universally accepted, and that the region comprises the general area from northeast Africa to south Asia is also widely approved. There is, moreover, a broad consensus that the Middle East extends from the western border of Egypt to the eastern border of Iran and from the Black Sea to the Arabian Sea. However, the precise limits of the region are still variously conceived by scholars and media. All the attention devoted to the region has not ended the uncertainty about what the Middle East includes, and only recently has the area's name been generally accepted. What is the proper designation of the Middle East? What is its actual extent? And what criteria best determine the region's name and limits?

Nomenclature

Changes in terminology in recent decades reflect underlying changes in Western perceptions of the region. Earlier toponyms implied a Eurocentric viewpoint: the East, Orient (Latin for "east"), Levant (also "east"), Near East, or Nearer East. Thus, the East was obviously named by the West, specifically Western Europe. During the thirteenth century, the Italians, at the beginning of the Renaissance the most active European traders with the Mediterranean lands, referred to the eastern Mediterranean as the Levant—the "rising" (of the sun), signifying the East. Levant was taken into other European languages and has long been used to designate the lands near the coasts of the eastern Mediterranean and is used in that sense in this book.

Increasing contacts between Western Europe and the Ottoman Empire during the sixteenth and seventeenth centuries—as a consequence of voyages of discovery, increased commercial ties, and later, European imperialism—produced a new name for the eastern Mediterranean region. "East" applied to lands of the Ottoman Empire, from the Balkan Peninsula eastward and southeastward, whereas "Far East" designated the newly opening lands of China, Japan, and Indo-China. Later in the nineteenth century, with increasing involvement in Persia and India by Britain and France, "Near East" became the designation for Ottoman territories, including those in the Balkans, and "East" applied to India and adjacent areas. The breakup of the Ottoman Empire after World War I disrupted the political unity of the Near East, as it had come to be defined by Europeans, and thus the term lost its geographical exactness.

In 1902, the advocate of expanded U.S. sea power, Captain Alfred T. Mahan, employed the name "Middle East" for an indefinite area around the Gulf. Potential applicability of the designation was reinforced in the late 1930s when the British government applied "Middle East Command" to military forces in the area that extended from the central Mediterranean into the Indian subcontinent. Gradually, especially after the Middle East Command Headquarters was moved to Cairo, the designation for the military command came to be applied to the area itself. Books, journals, and organizations showed a growing preference for Middle East, as did the Washington-based Middle East Institute and its *Middle East Journal,* founded in 1946.

The National Geographic Society entitled its map of the area in the early 1960s "Lands of the Eastern Mediterranean (Called the Near East or the Middle East)." By the mid-1970s, however, the society's maps of the region carried unqualified "Middle East" titles. The official designation of the U.S. Department of State geographic bureau responsible for the area is Bureau of Near Eastern Affairs (NEA), but informal usage favors Middle East. The U.S. military services followed the British precedent and used Middle East after World War II, and the Central Intelligence Agency has long used that designation in its public reports. Current British usage is predominantly Middle East, and the United Nations generally uses that designation, although some UN statistical series use Near East.

MAP 1-2   Map delineating the Middle East as defined for this book. Map shows only international boundaries, country names, capital cities, and seas. Radius of the circle is 1,250 miles/2,012 km.

In an effort to avoid the implication of a Eurocentric perspective, some specialists have sought more objective terminology, favoring the designation "Southwest Asia." Taking this effort one step further, Cressey urged use of the portmanteau word "Swasia," as short for Southwest Asia.[1] Southwest Asia is used to some extent, but Swasia is rarely employed. The toponym "Middle East" is used in this book, both because it is well accepted in international usage and also because "middle" connotes the region's central location, its function as a tricontinental hub, and its role as a strategic bridge. Moreover, Egypt, an essential part of the region, lies in northeast Africa.

Delimitation

The geographical limits of the region are more debatable than is its toponym, and areas accepted as integral elements of the Middle East vary somewhat from study to study. The problem is periodically explored if not settled.[2]

Following the reasoning of the Department of State geographer in the 1950s, this book defines the Middle East as shown in Map 1-2, which includes sixteen countries. However, Cressey added Afghanistan, to the east of Iran; Fisher also included part of Libya, to the west of Egypt;[3] and Beaumont, Blake, and Wagstaff included all of Libya.[4] The sixteen countries that are the focus of this book are considered as the Middle East on the latest maps published by the National Geographic Society, Department of State, Central Intelligence Agency, John Bartholomew (leading British map agency), and other international agencies.

Current histories of the Middle East vary still more in coverage. A few include not only Libya but also the Sudan, and like some geographers and anthropologists, some historians include all of North Africa.

There is appreciable validity in including the countries of North Africa, as since the early years of Islam, that region has been linked in many ways with the Near East. This link has meant inter alia that North Africa is also Arab and Muslim. Arabs often refer to the area of northwestern Africa as the Maghrib (Maghreb, west) and to the Arab lands east of Libya as the Mashriq (east). Even Turkey has past links with the Maghrib because of onetime Ottoman holdings in North Africa, and Iranian lands were a core area of the Abbasid Empire when it controlled the Maghrib. If land links between the Maghrib and the Mashriq faltered, maritime links along the Mediterranean could sustain the commercial and cultural ties.

Nevertheless, despite the religious and historical links, certain differences have existed between northwestern Africa and the Middle East proper. The Mashriq has had more intimate relations with Turks and Persians, given that Byzantine and then Ottoman political control was both stronger and lasted longer in the Mashriq than in the Maghrib. Christian influence has persistently been appreciable in the Fertile Crescent, much less so in the Maghrib. Lands west of the Nile have had their own regional influences and, unlike the Mashriq realm, were subject to direct European colonization in the nineteenth century. Especially since World War II, the Arab states of the Mashriq have been increasingly interactive with

one another, despite periodic divisive influences; and although each is locked in hostility rather than cooperation with its Arab neighbors, Israel on the west and Iran on the east are increasingly involved in the region. Turkey is similarly becoming interlinked with its pre-1918 imperial provinces.

Although the Middle East is the core of the Islamic culture realm, the "Muslim world" must be clearly differentiated from the Middle East and from the Middle East-North Africa area. Lands in which the Islamic religion and civilization are dominant extend well into West Africa on the west and far into central and southern Asia and Australasia on the east. Central Asia, with its famous Islamic urban centers of Samarkand, Tashkent, Merv (Mary), Bukhara, and Balkh, was more closely linked with Middle East core areas from the seventh to the eighteenth centuries than was the Maghrib. However, conquest of central Asia by Russia during the late nineteenth century broke virtually all of the links, and the five new (since 1991) independent states of Kazakhstan, Kyrghyzstan, Tajikistan, Turkmenistan, and Uzbekistan—even though Muslim—cannot categorically be included in the current Middle East region. It is, nevertheless, noteworthy that these five states are being cultivated by—and are responding to—such Middle East governments as Turkey, Iran, Saudi Arabia, the UAE, and also Israel. Similarly, Azerbaijan in the Caucasus, the only Muslim state of the three newly independent polities in the isthmus, is being courted by its southern neighbors.

Regional Unity of Empires

Interwoven historical-political-geographical developments have, over many centuries, exercised integrating influences on the region. For 4,000 years, up to the end of World War I, the Middle East experienced varying degrees of control by a series of great empires centered in several power cores or foci in the region. The empires echo many familiar names: Babylonian, Hittite, Egyptian, Assyrian, Chaldean, Persian, Seleucid, Ptolemaic, Roman, Byzantine,

Parthian, Sassanian, Umayyad, Abbasid, and Ottoman. A score of other smaller empires are less familiar: Aramaean, Phoenician, Sabaean, Nabataean, and others.

Except for the Roman Empire, which was governed from outside the Middle East, the major empires centered successively in four focal points of power: Mesopotamia, Asia Minor, Nile Valley, and Iranian Plateau, with the Syrian realm a possible fifth. Each of the power foci has functioned two or three times as an imperial power center over the millennia, and at one time or another, each major part of the Middle East has controlled most or much of the rest of the region; conversely, almost every part of the Middle East has been controlled by each of the other major parts. During periods of close political unity, an interchange of ideas, mores, goods, and people among areas added to a unifying cultural identity. The roles of these power foci and of additional minor cores are a major theme of this book and will be analyzed in both their historical and geopolitical contexts (see Chaps. 2 and 11).

Aims and Concepts: A Glance

In recognition of the reciprocal relationships between geography and history, this book integrates historical highlights with a geographical analysis of patterns, particularly cultural patterns. These cultural patterns, very much emphasized in this study, are especially influenced by time, so that process becomes an essential element in the analysis. Biophysical patterns generally change less slowly but likewise yield to noteworthy processes. We shall, therefore, examine the interaction of people and biophysical phenomena not only in the context of their spatial relations but also in the context of their historical processes.

Further, geography emphasizes the complementary character of the patterns of human activity and natural elements, revealing its dual character—cultural and physical. Human or cultural elements include both people (their number, distribution, ethnic types, and other

group characteristics, including their sense of identity) and their great variety of works (settlements, agriculture and related facilities, transportation routes and facilities, industries, and other cultural features). Major biophysical or natural elements include landforms, water resources, climate, soils, vegetation, animal life, and mineral resources.

After a discussion of the historical foundations (Chap. 2), the patterns of the foregoing elements are examined from both a systematic and a regional perspective. Chapters 3 through 11 examine the area from a broad systematic or topical perspective, examining a succession of element patterns, both natural and cultural. Chapters 12 through 22 then shift perspective and examine the regions of the Middle East. In this regional approach, the overall Middle East region is subdivided into meaningful segments (subregions or minor regions) that are interpreted both as individual units and as interrelated parts of the whole. For the purposes of this book, the main regional unit of analysis is the sovereign nation or state (Map 1-3). Thus, we shall study the Middle East not only as a whole, in terms of the elements or topics, but also as sixteen state/regions. Within each state (or country), the component "landscapes" or third-order regions (that is, sub-subregions) receive attention and are clearly numbered on the respective country maps.

Perceptions of environment vary from one cultural group to another and change over time. For example, to the Bedouins of eastern Saudi Arabia during the early twentieth century, their habitat was a typical desert area in which they, as nomadic pastoralists, could wander with their flocks in search of pasturage. By contrast, the petroleum geologists and engineers at midcentury, concentrating on subsurface features, perceived that same desert as an area of potential petroleum resources. This book also gives consideration to such varying environmental perceptions.

In summary, this geographical study of the Middle East focuses on spatial relations among peoples, human activities, and biophysical elements—their overall configuration

MAP 1-3   Reference map showing most of the names frequently used in this book. Note latitudes and inter-penetration of land and water.

and also microlevel interactions. In the process, the analysis reveals both variations and similarities within the region, its unity and diversity, with a focus on those factors that are most influential in giving the contemporary Middle East its remarkable mosaic of interacting patterns.

Notes

1. Cressey 1960.

2. See especially Pearcy 1964 (Pearcy was geographer, U.S. Department of State, at the time). Also relevant are Davison 1960 and Keddie 1972.

3. William B. Fisher 1978.

4. Beaumont, Blake, and Wagstaff 1988.

2

Patterns of Time: Historical-Geographical Foundations

Persistence of Patterns

A Succession of Landscapes

Having evolved over thousands of years and a wide range of environments, the Middle East's cultural mosaic and political patterns are exceedingly complex. Chronologically successive cultures and empires have partially erased and yet partially preserved preceding patterns, creating by this long development a geographical palimpsest. This sequential development and its traces in the modern Middle East are the themes of this chapter, which deals with the historical political geography of the region.

Evidence of sequent occupance,[1] or the settlement and exploitation of the same region by successive cultures, dates from prehistoric times and characterizes many Middle Eastern landscapes. In the narrow coastal plain of southern Lebanon, for example, a modern oil pipeline extends along or over Ottoman Turkish buildings, medieval Muslim mosques, a Crusader castle, Byzantine mosaics, Roman tombs, ruins of the Phoenician port of Sidon, Bronze Age pottery shards, and Neolithic flints (Fig. 2-1). The wrinkled hand of the past has fashioned much of the landscape of the Middle East.

Even if ruins and artifacts from the distant past are not visible on the surface, they are often stratified in successively older layers beneath the surface. In the more favorable environments of the Middle East, few excavations fail to yield some kind of evidence of ancient human occupation or use of the land. The past is nearly always present.

Heritage of Patterns

Prior to surveying the evolution of the regional palimpsest, we can gain appreciation of the significance of the region's long heritage by glancing at six selected topics as examples of that heritage. These examples underscore the relevance of even the distant past to present-day patterns and problems.

1. Religion. Certain sites and towns settled in ancient times had religious motivations or gained religious importance for later groups. Many of the centers have retained their significance or have achieved even greater emotional impact, so that they attract hundreds of thousands of pilgrims and secular tourists annually, thereby maintaining major economic importance. For example, before the development of Saudi Arabia's oil fields, pilgrims to Mecca and Medina provided the major basis for the kingdom's economy. Similarly, control over Jerusalem generated foreign exchange for the Ottoman Empire, later for Jordan, and after 1967 for Israel. Religious sites often hold significance for multiple religious groups, leading to disputes over which historical "layer" is to be recognized or preserved or excavated. Such controversies center on several sites in and around Jerusalem.

2. Infrastructure. Infrastructural features—basic facilities that support other development, including irrigation systems, caravan routes, and hillside terracing to facilitate farming—have evolved over many centuries. Numerous ancient infrastructures still survive and continue to enhance the value of particular areas and to influence relative levels of prosperity in

FIGURE 2-1 Excavated ruins of Byblos, Lebanon, one of the most significant archaeological sites in the Middle East. Finds date from the Neolithic and include Egyptian, Amorite, Phoenician, Persian, Roman, and Crusader ruins.

the region. The middle and lower Tigris-Euphrates Valley, the Nile Valley and Delta, and the Jordan Valley, for example, have been developed over thousands of years into productive irrigated farming areas. Such development required enormous efforts by earlier peoples to achieve the clearing of dense vegetation, drainage, leveling, cultivation, irrigation by means of an elaborately engineered system of canals, and restoration after periodic flooding. Thus, modern economies rely on ancient infrastructures and on the cultural heritage of ancient technologies.

3. *Natural Resources.* Settlements and human activities have long correlated with patterns of natural resources in the Middle East, notably those of water, fertile soils, and more recently, oil. Natural resource sites often show signs of a remarkable sequent occupance, exhibiting infrastructural elements from Roman aqueducts to modern pipelines. In addition, however, certain ecological problems

persist. Increasingly serious difficulties are associated with salt-impregnated soils resulting from faulty irrigation of poorly drained areas or from soil erosion caused by improperly cultivated steep slopes or by overgrazing. Stone implements found along former lakeshores in deserts of the Arabian Peninsula signal later environmental deterioration. Meanwhile, new areas have become habitable, with oil providing an economic base and with new technologies such as pumping and desalination providing the necessary water. The long history of civilization in the Middle East yields practical information about the area's patterns of natural resources and their evolution over time.

4. *Strategic Features.* The strategic significance of Middle East seas, straits, coastal plains, mountain passes, river valleys, and major trade and invasion routes was displayed in ancient times and persists at the beginning of the twenty-first century despite modern technology. For example, the Strait of Hormuz and

the Gulf are both still important despite sophisticated military aircraft and missiles.

5. Culture and Art. Virtually every contemporary city in the Middle East has developed on the site of an ancient town. Excavations for foundations of modern buildings commonly uncover statues, monuments, or ruins of earlier occupation. Logically enough, certain locational factors exercise a persistent attraction for human occupation and certain cross-country routes. Ruins of monuments and other structures, found by the thousands throughout the settled Middle East, have become major sources of tourist revenues for many countries in the region, and transportable artifacts, inscriptions on stone and clay, documents on papyrus and vellum, and other antiquities are preserved in museums both within and outside the Middle East. Such items are valuable for research, their economic benefits, and understanding of the historical evolution of the area.

6. Conflict. Sequent occupance over the millennia has resulted in competing claims to the same lands and pressure on inhabited areas to accommodate high population growth, refugees, and new immigrants. The founding of the modern state of Israel, in which a Jewish population has largely displaced a Palestinian—primarily Muslim—one, exemplifies this type of conflict. The war between Iran and Iraq in the 1980s echoed numerous territorial and religious conflicts of earlier periods. Thus, any analysis of modern conflicts in the region must take cognizance of the roots of those conflicts in the area's historical political geography.

Early Patterns

Primitive People and Pristine Environments

The more favorable Middle East environments attracted human habitation as early as the Paleolithic, or Old Stone Age, contemporary with Pleistocene glaciation (about 1.6 million years ago to 12,000 BC). Primitive Paleolithic human (or humanoid) groups were environmentally bound to sites that offered fresh water, easily

gathered food, and natural shelters, especially caves. Particularly favorable sites were found in the areas marked by the western and eastern limbs of the Fertile Crescent (Map 2-1). The earliest known humanoid occupance site in the region, dating from more than one million years ago, is in northern Saudi Arabia, near the village of Shuwayhitiyah. The study of this site in the mid-1980s introduced an entirely new concept of human migration from the area of hominid origin in East Africa into Asia. Stone tools from several of these extremely ancient sites in Arabia have now been found.[2] Until the 1980s, the earliest site studied dated from 600,000 years ago and is at Ubaydiyah, on an ancient lakeshore in the Jordan Valley just south of the Sea of Galilee. Numerous Paleolithic sites more than 100,000 years old are scattered from the Nile Valley to the piedmont arc around Mesopotamia.

Climatic changes that caused the northward retreat of the last ice sheets in Eurasia about 15,000 years ago also modified the regional ecology of the Middle East. Open woodlands and grasslands soon characterized the Fertile Crescent, in contrast to the damp forests that invaded Eurasian areas uncovered by the melting and retreating glaciers. As one consequence, the Fertile Crescent population increased and developed, ushering in the Mesolithic period, or Middle Stone Age—sometimes called Epipaleolithic—which began about 12,000 BC.

Neolithic Revolution in a Special Environment

Ameliorating climatic conditions after 9000 BC brought further steady improvements in the Fertile Crescent environment, which encouraged not only an increase in the number of Mesolithic peoples but also the growth and spread of wild plants and animals that constituted the humans' food supply. This favorable environment of grasslands with scattered trees became the native habitat of early forms of wheat and barley, varieties of which still grow along field borders in the northern Fertile

MAP 2-1   Selected major ancient sites. The Fertile Crescent (stippled) is often referred to in the text.

Crescent.[3] After wild varieties of the two cereals had been widely harvested for many centuries, they were gradually domesticated and cultivated along with other major food plants, including vegetables and nut trees. At about the same time, animals that still dominate the farm scene were domesticated—sheep, goats, cattle, pigs, and dogs. Hence, in about 8000 BC, in the arc from the Levant to the western Zagros, there occurred the Agricultural Revolution, or Agricultural Transformation, the most important single innovation in human history.

Thus, a particular environment, a special plant community, and an adaptive population combined to initiate the Neolithic—the New Stone Age. Heralded especially by the agricultural

revolution, the Neolithic period also saw the systematic development of organized settlements. Such settlements were not feasible prior to the planned cultivation of plants and domestication of animals, so that the agricultural and urban revolutions functioned reciprocally. Moreover, these stimulated, or at least were accompanied by, a further complex of cultural processes: political administration, organized religion, trade, and finally writing in both Mesopotamia and Egypt.

The Archaeological Tell

Giving mute, fascinating, and vital testimony regarding Neolithic and later settlements is the archaeological mound, a common feature of the

Middle East landscape. Usually referred to by the Semitic name *tell*,[4] an archaeological mound marks an ancient site on which successive settlements were established on the debris of earlier ones. Typical mounds, or tells, contain layers of cultural remains accumulated over thousands of years, the height of the mound generally indicating the length of time the site was occupied. With characteristically flat tops and sharply sloping sides, tells are prime targets for archaeological excavations. Correlation of finds among tells reveals patterns of cultures and settlement, including economic and political relations, that existed more than 5,000 years ago.

Of the thousands of tells scattered over the Middle East, several score are world renowned and attract hundreds of scholars and tourists annually. Familiar examples include: Troy, in northwestern Asia Minor; Babylon, in central Mesopotamia; and Jericho, in the Jordan Valley (all shown on Map 2-1).

Agriculture, Cities, and Civilization

The human advance from food gathering to food producing about 7000 BC[5] and the consequent expansion of the food supply accompanied a great increase in population in more favorable areas. As well as providing a more balanced diet, agriculture also permitted production of a food surplus for nonproductive seasons and famines. In addition, farming permitted and encouraged experimentation, cooperative planning, and a concentration of people into villages, which resulted in a widening of social exchange, organization, and trade within and among settlements. Food-storage facilities, key evidence of early agriculture, and food-preservation techniques required group planning.

About 5500 BC, Fertile Crescent farmers took another giant step forward and minimized their dependence on local rainfall: They extended, then gradually shifted, farming from the Zagros piedmonts above the Tigris-Euphrates Basin down to the Mesopotamian plain along the river-banks. The new agriculture was irrigated cultivation, utilizing a system of canals to feed river water to the cultivated fields.

Along with the earlier rain-fed farming advances, irrigation farming accompanied or had a "feedback" effect on key social developments in Mesopotamia: cooperative planning; organized engineering; expanded storage facilities for harvest surpluses; trade relations to exchange excess food for other items; cities to accommodate people, goods, and expanded activities, as well as to permit specialization of labor; defenses for the protection of food supplies, irrigation works, settlements, and temples; centralized administration to apportion water and to coordinate activities; and for inventories and trade, a system of writing, the basis for future law, literature, and long-distance communication.

Evidence of origins of agriculture in areas outside Mesopotamia is contradictory. Rather than having been borrowed from the Tigris-Euphrates Basin, systematic agriculture in the Nile Valley may have had independent beginnings. Certainly, farming began very early in Egypt, as it did also in Southeast Asia. However, evidence for Mesopotamia as the source area for the diffusion of settled agriculture remains strong.

Specific innovations developed as Mesopotamian irrigation agriculture evolved. The plow appeared about 3000–4000 BC; the wheel was well known in Mesopotamia by 3500 BC, but apparently not in Egypt until 1700 BC; and stamp and cylinder seals (possibly ancestors of writing) had appeared in some quantity by 3500 BC. Impressive temples had been constructed in Uruk (Erech of the Old Testament, Warka in modern Iraq) by 3300 BC; earliest evidences of writing also appeared about 3300 BC, and cuneiform (wedge-shaped) writing on clay was common by 2400 BC;[6] and a dozen major Sumerian cities, and many more villages, existed in Mesopotamia by 2700 BC.

Excavated remains of some of the early Mesopotamian cities reveal cultural achievements that were remarkably advanced for their time (4000–3500 BC). Areal extents and estimated populations of the cities, as well as the architecture and artistic decorations of temples and palaces, have fascinated both specialists and casual observers. The ruins of Uruk, visible under a mantle of sand southeast of present-day Baghdad (Map 2-1), suggest an ancient population of 50,000, and the outline of the walls extends for 5.6 miles/9 km. Impressive temples, some on stepped platforms, and terraced towers, or ziggurats, dominated several of the cities on the Mesopotamian plain, and the Hanging Gardens of Babylon and the Tower of Babel of the Old Testament were almost certainly ziggurats. The building of terraced or stepped towers in Mesopotamia was generally contemporary with pyramid construction in Egypt, and the stepped design of the Pyramid of Zoser at Saqqara, the oldest known pyramid along the Nile, suggests that it was borrowed from the Mesopotamian ziggurat concept.

Thus, evidence from 5,000 years ago clearly shows a remarkable interaction between people and environment in the Tigris-Euphrates Basin. Irrigation farming and urban development were twin manifestations of the evolving and expanding early culture.[7]

One major factor in the human-environmental relationship was the availability of building materials for the growing number of structures erected in Mesopotamia. In the southern part of the basin, only the clays and silts laid down by the Tigris and Euphrates rivers on their lower alluvial plain were directly available for use as building materials. Unshaped river mud (*tawf*) supplied the material for the earlier structures in the area, and it is still a common construction material for houses in villages of southern Iraq. Later structures were of sun-dried mud brick, and still later buildings were faced with fired brick. Southern Mesopotamian ziggurats, temples, and palaces of the third and second millennia are, therefore, less well preserved than are the massive Egyptian temples and pyramids, which were constructed of the limestone that was plentiful along the Nile Valley (Fig. 2-2). Similarly, Assyrian palaces in northern Mesopotamia, built of limestone from nearby quarries, have survived wonderfully well.

Historical-Political Evolution

The rise and expansion of Middle East empires after 4000 BC display pattern dynamics that are still relevant to the modern region. For this reason, the following condensed survey of the evolution of ancient and medieval patterns serves as a prelude to studying the modern region.

Early Mesopotamian States

Middle East recorded history begins in the fourth millennium BC in southern Mesopotamia with the Sumerians, whose origins are unknown and whose written language is unrelated to any other known language. The earliest records show them in control of the irrigation works and related settlements in ancient Sumer, whether or not they built the impressive installations. (Sumer is remembered as Shinar in the biblical account—Genesis, Chaps. 10 and 11.) Functioning as city-states, the major cities of Sumer in the middle of the third millennium BC were Eridu, Uruk, Ur (later Ur of the Chaldees, home of Abraham of both the Old Testament and the Quran [Koran]), and others shown on Map 2-2. The partially excavated ruins of these famous settlements of 4,500–5,000 years ago now lie well away from any river, but the towns were originally established along the banks of the Euphrates, which later changed course. The banks of the slower and more manageable Euphrates offered greater advantages for the siting of Sumerian cities and fields than did the banks of the more rapidly flowing Tigris, advantages that are still factors in urban locations in the late twentieth century.

North of the Sumerians lived the Akkadians, first of numerous Semitic groups to enter Mesopotamia. They probably originated in the Arabian Peninsula, a source region for successive waves of Semitic peoples into the Fertile Crescent for 3,000 years. The Akkadians overwhelmed the Sumerians about 2335 BC, unified the former city-states, and developed the first known empire. The Akkadian Empire quickly spread into the Zagros Mountains on the east and to the Mediterranean Sea on the west, and

FIGURE 2-2 Temple of Hatshepsut (Dayr al-Bahari) in ancient Thebes, Egypt. The temple (fifteenth century BC) faces east toward the Nile and Karnak and Luxor on the east bank of the river. Behind the cliff, to the west, is the Valley of the Kings.

the Akkadian language became the lingua franca, or common language, of the civilized Middle East for several centuries. After a short but productive period, the Akkadian heartland was overrun about 2200 BC by the Gutians from the Zagros Mountains. A precursor of many later invasions of Mesopotamia from the mountains and plateau east of the Tigris—the latest in the 1980s—the Gutian adventure collapsed after less than a century.

Reemerging as a culturally mixed people, the Sumerians established a United Sumer and Akkad with a capital at Ur. This Sumerian Empire reached its peak of brilliance about 2000 BC, developing a thriving trade with the Indus Valley peoples and establishing ports of trade on the sea route to the Indus. Ruins of such ports have been found along the shores of the modern UAE and Oman and on islands in the Gulf, especially on Bahrain. There excavations

have uncovered well-preserved ruins of what is believed to have been the Dilmun referred to in Sumerian records.[8]

The first Babylonian Empire emerged soon after 2000 BC and absorbed Sumer. It was created by another Semitic group, the Amorites ("westerners"), who immigrated into central Mesopotamia from the Syrian Desert about 2000 BC. Having established a power center in Babylon, they expanded their control over all of Mesopotamia. Between 1792 and 1750 BC, Babylonia was ruled by one of the most famous kings in oriental history, Hammurabi the Great. Hammurabi's famous legal code collected and systematized Sumerian and Akkadian laws from earlier centuries and brought a new sophistication to political administration and control. Babylon and Babylonia played important roles in Mesopotamia for more than 2,000 years.[9]

MAP 2-2   Mesopotamia and adjacent lands, showing earliest known states as well as earliest known cities—Uruk, Eridu, Ur, Lagash, and others. Dashed line indicates approximate limits of the Old Babylonian Empire.

Other noteworthy power centers evolved and expanded in several parts of the Middle East and adjacent areas after 1700 BC, emphasizing the persistence of the ebb and flow of imperial realms. Mesopotamia lost its isolated self-sufficiency as peoples with new languages and new cultures immigrated into Asia Minor, the Iranian Plateau, the Levant, and the Caucasus. Such groups included the Indo-European Hittites, who controlled Asia Minor for more than 400 years from their stronghold of Hattusa on the Anatolian Plateau. The Hittites destroyed Babylon during an incursion in the sixteenth century BC, after which the Indo-European Kassites emerged from the Zagros Mountains to rule the weakened Babylonian area for more than four centuries. Another group, the Hurrians (biblical Horites), spoke a language that was neither Semitic nor Indo-European and relied on an

Indo-European warrior aristocracy and horse-drawn chariots to build the Kingdom of Mitanni about 1500 BC. Hurrian military power pushed the borders of Mitanni control westward to the Mediterranean and eastward to the Zagros.

However, of all the ancient Middle East civilizations and empires outside Mesopotamia, none could match the fabled culture of the Nile, the Pharaonic kingdoms of Upper and Lower Egypt.

Early Egypt

The steadily evolving Mesopotamian culture of the late Neolithic and early Bronze Age diffused not only eastward to the Indus Valley and beyond but also westward to the Nile Valley. Ancient cultures to which the Nile was already host adapted Mesopotamian influences and made them distinctly "Egyptian." For example, writing developed in Sumer as a practical method of recording inventories and trade transactions, and the relatively simple technique required quick incisions with a reed stylus on damp clay, both the reed and the clay being widely available. This concept of writing was apparently borrowed by the Egyptians, who used their own familiar materials, a bronze chisel and stone, to carve elaborate hieroglyphics for religious or royal inscriptions. Indeed, "hieroglyphic" means "sacred carving."[10]

Basic environmental differences between Mesopotamia and Egypt influenced other historical and cultural differences. Both rivers of Mesopotamia, Tigris and Euphrates, have irregular flow regimes, flow in shallow beds, flood unpredictably (or did so especially before the hydraulic works of the twentieth century), shift courses, and generally lack dependable rhythm. The Nile, in contrast, has eroded a wall-bounded valley in the rock desert, has a regular floodplain and flood time (late summer), seldom shifts course, and follows a regular rhythm documented over centuries.

Although links between culture and environment can be overstated, certain correlations can be drawn for the early Nile civilization. Egyptian cultural stability followed the rhythm of

the river and was influenced by the relative isolation enforced by the desert beyond the Nile
Valley. The Nile's physical unity facilitated early
political unity after a certain cultural level
developed along the river (Map 2-3). Well
before 3000 BC sailboats proceeded upstream,
blown by the northeast trade winds, and downstream, carried by the river's current. Only limited east-west traffic left the Nile Valley, since
regular commercial movement over the deserts
flanking the valley was hazardous.

Also, unified administration coordinated
efforts to construct and maintain major canals,
allocate water, protect riparian rights of access
to the Nile, re-survey fields after the annual
floods that deposited the fertile silt, and maintain a god-king leadership figure.[11] The continuity and stability of the cosmos was a
dominant concept among the ancient Egyptians; their perception of life as a benevolent
rhythm was influenced by their observing
preservation of wood, cloth, and papyrus, even
the desiccated remains of people and animals,
in their hot, dry climate.

The Egyptians constructed advanced architectural works in the form of tombs and temples. They created sophisticated jewelry, inlaid
ornaments, vases, and sculpture. To obtain such
materials as gold, ebony, cedar, and turquoise,
the Egyptians carried on an active trade, especially in the eastern Mediterranean, northern
Red Sea, and upper Nile. Trade relations among
Egyptians, Minoans on Crete, Mycenaeans in
several locations, Hittites in Asia Minor,
Canaanites along the Levant coast, and other
peoples in the Sinai and to the south engendered
a cross-fertilization of ideas and techniques.
Enriched by contacts with Mesopotamia, Anatolia, and the Levant, Egyptian culture in its turn
influenced Greek and Roman development, and
thereby Western civilization.

Egyptian power declined after about 1090 BC
and surrendered to outside control as Libyans,
Ethiopians, and Assyrians imposed their
respective dynasties. The Persians then conquered Egypt in 525 BC and held it, with only a
brief interruption, for 200 years until it was
seized by Alexander the Great in 332 BC. Under

MAP 2-3 Ancient Egypt and the Levant, showing
major ancient sites. Dashed line shows approximate
maximum limit of the New Kingdom control.

Alexander's Hellenistic successors, the Greek-
Macedonian Ptolemies, Egypt achieved independence again for 250 years. It experienced a
cultural resurgence before passing to Roman
control in 30 BC after the suicide of Cleopatra,
last of the Ptolemaic line. Although it enjoyed
long periods of autonomy under several hege-
mons, Egypt was not to be completely independent again under indigenous regimes for
almost 2,000 years, until after World War II.

Mesopotamia to the Roman Conquests

Assyrian Empire. Along with Babylonia,
Assyria was one of the most persistent of Fertile
Crescent imperial states. It emerged in the mid-
1350s BC, centered in the upper Tigris Basin, and
dominated the Middle East for 300 years after

935 BC as the prototypal oriental monarchy (Map 2-4A). Although exaggerated, Assyrian cruelty is legend, but the empire also maintained control by means of its organization, efficiency, engineering, commerce, communications, and record keeping. During its eighth-century expansion, Assyria mastered the Levant, conquered the biblical kingdom of Israel, and in the latter case dispersed the population, a practice the Assyrians often followed with conquered peoples. The Assyrians themselves disappeared from history after being overwhelmed by Babylonians and Medes, who took Nineveh in 612 BC. Modern-day Assyrians are a religious group and are not known to have any connection with the ancient Assyrians.

Discoveries in the ruins of Assyrian capitals and other cities—Assur, Nineveh, and the palace complexes at Khorsabad and Nimrud—in the early nineteenth century launched modern systematic archaeology. They also stimulated an appreciation of ancient Mesopotamian history as it emerged from the translation of some of the 22,000 clay tablets found in the palace library at Nineveh.

Neo-Babylonian (Chaldean) Empire. With Assyria destroyed, Babylonia once again became the dominant power in Mesopotamia. This Neo-Babylonian Empire was led for almost a century by the Chaldeans, a Semitic people from the Syrian Desert, like the Semitic Amorites of the Old Babylonian Empire 1,400 years earlier. The great imperial capital, Babylon, was revitalized by the Chaldean king Nebuchadrezzar the Great (also known as Nebuchadnezzar), who reigned 604–562 BC. Its Hanging Gardens (a ziggurat with planted terraces) were considered one of the Seven Wonders of the Ancient World, and the Ishtar Gate remains impressive even in ruins. The extensive ruins of Nebuchadrezzar's palace were very impressive but were somewhat depreciated by unduly extensive reconstruction by the Iraqi government during the 1980s. In any case, Babylon's excavated ruins afford significant insight into the life of 2,000 to 4,000 years ago. The biblical account of the destruction of Jerusalem and other Judean cities by Nebuchadrezzar and of the deportation of the Judeans into Babylonian exile in 586 BC provided an enduring record of this monarch and his empire.

Persian (Achaemenid) Empire. After its brilliant Chaldean revival, Babylonia fell to the Persian king Cyrus the Great in 539 BC. The city of Babylon itself, captured without a struggle, survived for another six centuries—Alexander the Great died there in 323 BC—but by AD 100 it had been abandoned. The Chaldean Babylonian Empire was the last native Mesopotamian state of antiquity. The Tigris-Euphrates Basin was ruled by outside powers for the next 2,500 years, well into the twentieth century, although the strategic narrow interfluve (area between the rivers) between Babylon on the west and Baghdad on the east served repeatedly as a location for successive imperial capitals.

The Persians were members of an Indo-European tribe who swept down on Babylonia from their stronghold on the Iranian Plateau. The plateau had already disgorged the Gutians and the Indo-European Kassites and Medes, and from it later erupted other conquering Persians and Persian-related groups—Parthians, Sassanians, and Safavids. Thus, the Iranian Plateau has been the source area for Indo-European conquerors and immigrants into the Fertile Crescent as the Arabian Peninsula has been for Semitic invaders.

Having merged with the Medes, the Persians during the Achaemenid dynasty swiftly established an empire that was more extensive than any of its predecessors. Their territories reached from the Balkan Peninsula-Aegean Sea and Nile Valley on the west to the Indus Valley and Turanian Basin on the east (Map 2-4A). Thus, for the first time, one Middle East power center controlled all the other power centers, excepting only the barren and inaccessible Arabian Peninsula.

In addition, Persia profited from, inherited, and improved on Assyrian efficiency and communications. The Persian Royal Road from Susa (in southwestern Iran) to Sardis (in western Asia Minor, see Map 2-4A) permitted the rapid transportation of goods and messages

MAP 2-4   Major Middle East-Mediterranean empires from
before 1000 BC to the rise of Islam.

FIGURE 2-3   Persepolis in modern Iran. Wonderfully detailed bas-reliefs on staircase and platform of the Apadana (fifth century BC), built by Darius the Great and his son Xerxes, depict representatives of subject peoples and reveal much about the social and political situation of the time.

and served as an early Middle Eastern Pony
Express. Some already established cities played
more powerful roles, especially Susa, Ecbatana
(modern Hamadan), and the legendary Persepolis. Modern excavations, reconstructions,
and studies of Persepolis are especially revealing (Fig. 2-3). The Persian Empire continued
for more than 200 years until it was conquered
by Alexander the Great between 334 and 326
BC. Although Persia never regained the territorial dominion of Achaemenid times, Iranian
peoples again controlled the plateau within a
century after Alexander's death. They have
shown themselves for 2,300 years to be a culturally and politically significant power.

Empire of Alexander.   Leaving his small Mace-
donian home base in northern Greece in 334 BC,
Alexander the Great had conquered the entire
Persian Empire by 326 BC and had established

his eastern frontier beyond the Indus (Map 2-
4B). Alexander founded cities, brought about
cultural interchange, and spread Hellenistic
ideas and practices in the process of expanding
his own empire beyond the limits of the preceding Persian borders. His death in Babylon at
the age of 33 left a power vacuum that disrupted the carefully crafted unity of the Hellenistic Empire, and imperial lands were
parceled out among Alexander's top generals.
Ultimately, a threefold division emerged that,
alongside revived Persian power, survived for
250 years.

Seleucid and Ptolemaic Empires.   With slightly
shifting boundaries, the two most important
Hellenistic states in the Middle East were the
Seleucid and the Ptolemaic (Map 2-4C), and
ruins and other vestiges of these empires are still
evident in scores of sites in Egypt and the Levant.

Asia Minor fragmented into a complex mosaic of kingdoms. An Armenian state persisted for centuries and became the base for an Armenian national identity that still endures. The northeastern Iranian Plateau area embraced the Iranian Parthian kingdom, and a Hellenized Greco-Bactrian kingdom dominated lands farther east.

Hellenistic cultural influences continued into the Roman and Byzantine empires in the Middle East, spanning a period of almost 1,000 years. Two Hellenistic cities in the Middle East are noteworthy: Antioch (contemporary Antakya, Turkey) became a prominent city and regional center in the Seleucid realm; and in the Ptolemaic kingdom, Alexandria, founded in 331 BC by Alexander near the mouth of the Nile, became a brilliant center of Hellenism with a large Greek population. Alexandria's lighthouse (Pharos), built about 300 BC, was one of the Seven Wonders of the Ancient World and aided navigation for 1,600 years. The Ptolemaic Empire ended with Cleopatra's suicide in 30 BC, when Egypt entered 673 years of control by the Roman and eastern Roman empires. During the late 1990s, archaeologist-scuba divers discovered and delineated a large sector of ancient Alexandria that was destroyed and submerged in an earthquake more than 1,600 years ago; what were believed to be parts of palaces and the lighthouse from Cleopatra's time were among the finds. The Seleucid Empire also collapsed before the advancing Romans, and Syria became a Roman province in 64 BC.

Smaller Semitic Kingdoms. Other noteworthy cultures contemporaneous with the extensive empires just reviewed include those of the Canaanite-Phoenicians, Hebrews, and Aramaeans. The Hebrews, a Semitic tribe, appear to have emerged from the Arabian Desert, as did other Semites mentioned earlier. Legends of their early culture and migrations, typical of many tribal groups of the time, are recorded in the book of Genesis. These accounts include the exodus from Egypt, generally dated in the thirteenth century BC, and the entry into southern Canaan. The accounts yield valuable insights into both the Hebrew culture and also many of the attitudes of the time. In Canaan, the Hebrews not only confronted the native Canaanites in the hill country; they also were long kept from the southern coast by other recent arrivals—the Sea Peoples, especially the Philistines, from the Aegean region. Archaeological discoveries have now shown that theirs was not the uncouth, retarded culture that we traditionally associate with the name *Philistine,* but was, indeed, generally superior to that of their Israelite neighbors.[12] It was from Philistia, land of the Philistines, that the later name Falastina, or Palestine, was derived.

The biblical record indicates that a unified Israelite kingdom finally emerged (about 1020 BC) and lasted almost a century, dividing in 922 BC after the death of Solomon. The northern kingdom, Israel, lasted less than 200 years and was conquered by Assyrians in 722 BC, its people dispersed as the ten lost tribes. Judah, the southern kingdom, with Jerusalem as its capital, survived Israel by 136 years but fell to Nebuchadrezzar in 586 BC, when thousands of Judeans were deported to Babylon. Many returned to Judea after the 50 years of the Babylonian captivity, but hundreds remained, to form a thriving Jewish colony in Mesopotamia that lasted 2,500 years. For the returnees, Judea became a core of territorial contention among Ptolemaic Egypt, the Seleucids, Rome, and local kingdoms. It is interesting to note that from 922 BC until the present time, the Palestine area was a sovereign state under a native administration in de jure control of a unified territory for only a few decades under the Hasmoneans (Maccabees), a reign that was ended by the Romans in 63 BC. Most of the Jews of Palestine had been dispersed over the Mediterranean Basin and the Middle East by the middle of the second century after Christ.[13]

The "land of Canaan" comprised the general area of the western Syria-Palestine realm. Although the individualistic Canaanite city-states maintained active common cultural and economic relations, including language, religion, and trade, they failed to unify politically or militarily. Thus, because they were vulnerable to invading Egyptians, Amorites, Israelites, Assyrians, and others, the more extended Canaanite civilization declined after about the eleventh century BC.

Canaanite artistic genius, however, long stimulated and diversified through interaction with the advanced Egyptian civilization, now became concentrated among the northern coastal Canaanites, who became known as Phoenicians. These extraordinary innovators developed remarkable city-states around ports at Tyre, Sidon, Beirut, Byblos, Tripoli, and Aradus. Because they were compacted into an isolated coastal plain with limited agricultural land, the Phoenicians turned to the sea and developed an aggressive maritime trade, which reached as far as the western Mediterranean, and founded colonies over a wide area. Their most powerful colony, Carthage, founded about 800 BC, challenged Rome itself for supremacy in the three Punic (Phoenician) Wars of the second and third centuries BC. While conducting their wide-ranging trade, the Phoenicians simplified and carried with them the first true alphabet, developed by Semitic peoples in the Levant. This alphabet was subsequently adapted by the Greeks, Etruscans, and Romans.[14]

The Aramaeans, who—like the neighboring Canaanites—were long indigenous, were inland traders who diffused their culture along with their Semitic language. The Aramaic tongue spread along land trading routes and became the lingua franca of commerce and diplomacy from Egypt to Mesopotamia. It was still spoken in Syria and Palestine at the time of Christ. According to Old Testament accounts, Damascus and other Aramaean city-states, the biblical Aram, were overcome by the Hebrew King David. However, they regained their independence and continued as Aramaean centers until conquered by the Assyrians in 732 BC. The Aramaean culture gradually faded, but dialects of the Aramaic language continued into the twentieth century in several church liturgies as well as in villages north of Damascus.

Roman and Successor Empires

Roman.   Although Hellenistic control over much of the Middle East originated from an outside area (Macedonia), Rome was the first power from outside the region to maintain hegemony over large areas of the Middle East for a lengthy period. However, extensive as it was, Roman territorial control in the Middle East never equaled that of the Persian and Hellenistic empires (Map 2-4). Even so, Egypt and Syria-Palestine felt the lingering Roman influence until the seventh century after Christ, and Asia Minor did so for several centuries longer.

Roman legions failed to venture beyond Mesopotamia. They contended with Iranian-based armies along the Euphrates and in Armenia but were never successful in sustained desert operations. To symbolize their military presence, however, the Romans constructed lines of forts and boundary markers to form the Limes Arabicus (Arabian Boundary), similar to the Roman *limes* constructed in central Europe. In northwestern Syria, well-preserved stretches of Roman roads still exist, a part of ancient infrastructure underlying the modern Middle East. Hundreds of vestiges of Roman occupation—roads, forts, theaters, temples, aqueducts, baths—are prominent features in the landscapes of Asia Minor, the Levant, and parts of Egypt, partly because Roman construction in those areas was monumental and well engineered (Fig. 2-4). Some structures combine Hellenistic, Roman, and Byzantine construction from different periods, and these Greco-Roman ruins attract many visitors to areas from Istanbul in the northwest to Dura Europos on the upper Euphrates in the east.[15]

Parthian.   Although Alexander destroyed the Persian Empire, the Iranian identity reasserted itself a century later through the Iranian Parthians. Emerging as a native kingdom in 248 BC, the Parthian Kingdom became an empire within 75 years, extending over the Iranian Plateau and Mesopotamia. Observing the

FIGURE 2-4 Two famous Graeco-Roman ruins in the Middle East: the dramatic amphitheater on a cliffside in Pergamum (modern Bergama, Turkey) *(top)*, and colonnaded street in the ruins of Jerash, north of Amman, Jordan *(bottom)*, a great Roman provincial city. Note the well-paved street, which has a well-engineered storm drain underneath.

historic strategic value of the narrowest width of the middle Tigris-Euphrates interfluve, the Parthians established twin capital cities—Seleucia and Ctesiphon—near the location of modern Baghdad in Iraq.

Sassanian. The Parthian Empire was overthrown and was succeeded in AD 226 by another Iranian empire, the Sassanian. The powerful Sassanians expanded northeastward across the Oxus River (modern Amu Darya, between the post-1991 republics of Turkmenistan and Uzbekistan) and eastward to the Indus, as well as across the Gulf into the Qatif area of Arabia and into Oman (Map 2-4D). They maintained Ctesiphon as a capital (Fig. 2-5) and also inherited Rome as a perennial territorial adversary in Syria-Mesopotamia. The Sassanian Empire collapsed entirely under the assault of invading Arab Muslims in the 630s and 640s.

Byzantine. Although the western Roman Empire and its formerly great capital declined after the fourth century, the eastern empire and its capital thrived. Founded by the first eastern emperor, Constantine, and named after its founder, Constantinople was earlier Byzantium and later Istanbul. Steadily orientalized, the eastern empire became less Latin and more Greek and after the fall of Rome in 476 was referred to as the Byzantine Empire. Holding extensive lands for many centuries (Map 2-4D), it gradually contracted until the only remaining territory was Constantinople and its environs, which fell to the Ottomans in the watershed year of 1453. Allowing for its expansions and contractions, the Byzantine Empire survived for 1,123 years, longer than any other empire in the Middle East.[16]

Having battled the Sassanians to a standstill for control of the Fertile Crescent, the weakened Byzantines lost Egypt and the Levant in the 630s to the same Arab assault that overwhelmed the Sassanians. The Byzantines, however, were able to hold on to their Anatolian stronghold while the Sassanians lost not only Mesopotamia but also their entire Iranian

Plateau power base. The Middle East had entered a new era, that of Islam.

Islamic Empires

The Arab eruption into Mesopotamia and Syria-Palestine in AD 633 was another in the series of Semitic waves from interior Arabia extending back over 3,000 years. This particular Arab invasion, however, involved many more people and far more territory than had previous incursions, and it had incalculably greater ramifications. With this invasion, the present cultural patterns of the Middle East began to emerge.

The founder of Islam, the Prophet Muhammad, had unified the Arabs of the Hijaz (western Arabia) and then of the Arabian Peninsula. He achieved unification on three levels: a new religion (whose adherents were called Muslims—see Chap. 6), a political organization (virtually a theocracy), and ethnic identity. Precepts for all three are found in the Muslim scriptures, the Quran. After Muhammad's death in 632, dedicated Muslims poured northward to spread the faith and to seize new lands for its flowering. Within a century, Muslim forces appeared before Tours in France, the high point of their westward spread, and other Muslims held central Asia. At its maximum extent in the eighth century AD, the Arab Empire exceeded in size all previous Middle East empires and compared with the Roman Empire at its maximum (compare Maps 2-4 and 2-5). The Muslim invasion marked the first Semitic conquest of the Iranian Plateau, although the conquerors imposed only the religion of Islam and their alphabet, not their Semitic language, Arab identity, or racial (physical) characteristics.

However, even more than the Roman Empire, the Arab Empire and its successor Muslim empires and kingdoms shifted capitals and cores, broke into parts, recombined in different patterns, and changed composition. But unified or fragmented, the region retained one enduring characteristic—Islam as religion and culture. The development of Islam and the

FIGURE 2-5 Ruins of the great vaulted hall (*al-Madain*) in Ctesiphon, Sassanian capital (Map 2-4D) on left bank of the Tigris River southeast of Baghdad. The brick vault of the third century is one of the highest freestanding brick arches ever constructed. Note two figures standing right of lower center.

Muslim state were two highly integrated aspects of the same phenomenon. These aspects not only still thrive, but, having been remolded in the contemporary state system, they have become resurgent traditions.

With the founding of the Umayyad Empire in AD 661, power shifted from the Hijaz to Syria, with the new capital in Damascus. The character of the Muslim state altered accordingly, from a religion-centered theocracy to an empire imitative of Byzantine and Persian courts.

In AD 750, the Abbasid dynasty seized control of the Arab Empire and moved the center from Damascus to Mesopotamia. The Abbasids built their new capital, Baghdad, on the Tigris-Euphrates interfluve, which had been occupied earlier by a succession of imperial capital cities. The next century brought the reign of the Abbasid caliph, Harun al-Rashid, of *Arabian*

Nights fame.[17] During the same century, however, evidence of the decline of the Abbasids appeared, as the court weakened and breakaway kingdoms rose, expanded, and were absorbed.[18]

Seljuks, Crusaders, Mongols

Seljuks. Besides the breakaway states, several other kingdoms were established by invaders from outside the Middle East. During the tenth century, Seljuk Turks from central Asia moved onto the Iranian Plateau. The Seljuks entered Baghdad in 1055 but left the Abbasid caliphs as figureheads; from Mesopotamia they forced their way westward and, in the watershed battle of Manzikert north of Lake Van (1071), defeated Byzantine armies and carried Islam into inner Anatolia for the first time. Islam gradually expanded over all of Asia Minor and

MAP 2-5   Arab Empire at its maximum extent, late eighth century. Arabs never succeeded in conquering Asia Minor.

has remained entrenched there ever since. With the way open into Anatolia, the Seljuks established the Sultanate of Rum and indirectly paved the way for the later expansion of the Turkish Ottoman Empire.

Crusaders.   The second group of states established by outside invaders arose primarily because of the Seljuk incursions and their threat to the Byzantines. After their defeat at Manzikert and with Seljuk territorial control continuing to expand, the Byzantines petitioned for help from the Roman Catholic feudal states of western Europe. Successive waves of Christians— French, English, German, Italian, and other Europeans, all labeled "Franks" by the Middle East Muslims—were sent in response to the Byzantine request. The human waves became known as the Crusades, the first beginning in 1096, succeeding ones in 1147, 1189, 1202, 1218, and 1228, and there were others unconnected with the original purpose. The First Crusade established the Crusader kingdoms, which occupied a relatively small area along a coastal strip at the eastern end of the Mediterranean.

The last Crusader foothold fell in 1291. Although the Crusades had only a modest impact on the Middle East at the time, the reverse effects were momentous, since they were a major stimulus for the European Renaissance. In the Levant, numerous ruined Crusader castles remain as romantic symbols of early European imperialism in the Middle East. Some castles, like other more ancient Middle East monuments, served military purposes intermittently into the twentieth century because of their massive walls and strategic sites.[19]

Mongols.   In the thirteenth century, invading horse-mounted Mongol and Tatar-Mongol archers made far-ranging territorial conquests in the Middle East to add to their vast empires in Asia. Generally short-lived, the conquests nevertheless yielded the Il-Khanid dynasty in Persia (1256–1349) through Genghis Khan's grandson, Hulagu. Genghis Khan, Hulagu (who sacked Baghdad in 1258), and Tamerlane (Timur Leng, who took Baghdad in 1393) all laid waste extensive areas of the Middle East. So devastating was Hulagu's ravaging of Mesopotamia that the centuries-old complex irrigation system and the road system were not restored to their former efficiency until the twentieth century.

Ottoman Empire and Contemporaries

Like the Seljuks, the Ottomans were a Turkish tribe who converted to Islam in central Asia and then migrated onto the plateaus of Iran and Anatolia. Beginning in the early fourteenth century, the Ottomans expanded from a small principality in northwestern Asia Minor until they controlled a vast area from the Danube to Yemen. The Ottoman Middle East holdings remained fairly constant from the early 1600s until World War I—with the notable exception of Egypt, which gradually disengaged itself. Like the Byzantines, whom they displaced, the Ottomans gained and lost territories but were remarkable for their political longevity, as an unbroken dynasty held the sultanate for 600 years.

Reviving Persian political organization once again, a kingdom under the Safavids emerged in the Iranian Plateau in 1500. With changes in dynasty in 1736 (Afshars), 1750 (Zands), 1794 (Qajars), and 1925 (Pahlavis), Persia survived—periodically contending with the Ottomans over Mesopotamia—as a monarchy until early 1979 (its name was changed to Iran in 1935) and still survives as a dynamic Islamic republic.

Thus, from about 1500 until World War I, two major Middle East powers, each based in one of the two strongest power foci, contended with each other, primarily along the line of the Zagros piedmont: the Ottoman Empire, based in Anatolia, and the Persian Empire or Kingdom, based on the Iranian Plateau. Still occupying a third power focus, but with limits on its former greatness, Egypt gradually eased away from direct Ottoman control during the early nineteenth century and had passed under British protection by World War I. The interior of the Arabian Peninsula escaped Ottoman control and remained tribally fragmented until most of the peninsula was unified as Saudi Arabia in the 1930s.

Some Inferences: Power Cores

The foregoing review of the evolution of political-geographical patterns of the Middle East suggests several general observations. Lessons to be drawn from the review are vitally significant and relevant not only as a basis for the rest of this book but also as guidelines for determining practical foreign policies in the region.

1. Four major power foci or cores and two minor ones have appeared and reappeared in the Middle East throughout history: The Anatolian Plateau (Asia Minor), Iranian Plateau, Mesopotamia (Tigris-Euphrates Basin), and Nile Valley are the four major cores, and the western Fertile Crescent and central and western Arabian Peninsula are the two minor cores. The Yemen and Oman areas have also served as centers of strength (Map 2-6).
2. The two most persistently powerful foci, and the two from which the greatest geographical areas have usually been controlled, have been the two intermontane plateaus, Anatolia and Iran. These two centers now host two of the three most populous states—which are also among the most powerful states—in the Middle East: Turkey, Iran, and Egypt.
3. No one power has ever succeeded in conquering and occupying the entire Middle East as the region is defined in Chapter 1. Regardless of the existing imperial power during any given period, some other part of the region maintained its independence.
4. The one area that has always been able to maintain its independence, or at least its separateness from outside powers, is the interior of the Arabian Peninsula (Najd). The peninsula was a center of imperial territorial control during the middle of the seventh century, but otherwise the area has maintained its separateness except as a source of migrants who appeared in Syria and Mesopotamia between 2500 BC and AD 700.

MAP 2-6 Middle East power foci or cores. Each of the four major power centers has controlled most of the Middle East at some time, but none has controlled all other centers simultaneously.

5. Although Mesopotamia was the earliest power focus and remained the main core for 1,700 years, it gradually weakened as a separate center and later functioned as a focus of power only when connected to the Iranian Plateau center. Under the sovereignty of Iraq, Mesopotamia demonstrated renewed potency beginning in the 1980s.

6. The political-geographical history of the Middle East has, to a great extent, revolved around the cyclic interaction of the powers occupying Asia Minor and the Iranian Plateau. Each power often sought control

of Mesopotamia, with Mesopotamia sometimes being used as a springboard against the power on the other side of the basin.

7. Powers centered in the three northern foci have controlled the Nile Valley at various times, but never has the Nile Valley power controlled any one of the three major northern foci. Rather, Egyptian control outside Egypt has been limited to the western limb of the Fertile Crescent (Syria-Palestine realm) plus some brief inroads into southeastern Anatolia by Egyptian forces in the 1830s.

Neither history nor geography can dictate the future. Changing technology, outside influences, or other developments might alter the relative significance of the several power foci in the Middle East. Since the 1950s, the emergence of Israel and the rise of the Middle East's petroleum age have unquestionably reorchestrated political, military, and economic influences. Yet to consider historical and geographical factors in the region's role as mere academic curiosities is to misread vital lessons and to risk repetition of the mistakes of the past. The roles of the centers in the twentieth century are considered in Chapter 11, which examines contemporary Middle East political-geographical development.

Notes

1. Whittlesey 1929.

2. Whalen and Pease 1992. In line with the Arabian discoveries was the finding of a humanoid jawbone in 1991 near Tbilisi, Georgia, that was dated to 900,000 years ago. Another dating gave the bone an age of 1.6 million years. *New York Times,* Feb. 3, 1992.

3. See Redman 1978. Recent additional evidence is given in Heun et al. 1997 and is covered in the *New York Times,* Nov. 18, 1997.

4. A *tell* is termed a *tepe* or *chega* in Persian, *hüyük* in Turkish, and *kom* in Egyptian usage.

5. The Wendorf team found evidence that indicated, through laboratory dating, much earlier cultivation in the Nile Valley. See Wendorf and Schild 1980.

6. See Schmandt-Bessarat 1978 and other articles by her. See also the readable but scholarly Redman 1978, with its attention to environmental factors. See also Robinson 1995, 8–13 and 58–87, and *New York Times,* Apr. 6, 1999.

7. See Redman 1978, along with his article, Redman 1994; Burenhult 1993; and Saggs 1989.

8. See Bibby 1969.

9. Among scores of accounts of Mesopotamian prehistory and early historical geography, many are in scarce technical journals. Available accounts are in Redman 1978, Saggs 1995, and Burenhult 1994, 16–59.

10. German archaeologists claimed in late 1989 that some inscriptions found at Abydos gave radiocarbon dates of 3200 3400 BC, thus predating Mesopotamian writing. The claims met with general skepticism.

11. See Butzer 1976, which has its critics but is informative and stimulating.

12. See Tubb 1998, chaps. 7 and 8, and *New York Times,* Sept. 29, 1992, and July 23, 1996.

13. Among myriad books and articles on ancient Israel, see Aharoni 1967, Baly 1957 and 1987, and Smith 1935 for consideration of geographical factors. A readable history is Grant 1984.

14. For detailed treatment, see Moscati 1968.

15. Kennedy and Derrick 1990 has fascinating aerial photographs of Roman roads and ruins in the region.

16. Among several excellent accounts of the Byzantines, see Shaw 1976, Shaw and Shaw 1977, and the recent Norwich 1997.

17. The original title of *Tales of the Arabian Nights* was *The Thousand and One Nights.* These charming stories, which include such familiar tales as those about Sindbad the Sailor and Ali Baba and the Forty Thieves, reveal many aspects of medieval Islamic culture. For good historical coverage of this period see Fisher and Ochsenwald 1990 and Hourani 1991.

18. Many good histories cover the Islamic Arab empires and later developments. The older classic is Brockelmann 1949. A useful recent one is Hourani 1991.

19. The standard work on the Crusades is Runciman 1954.

3
The Lands and
the Waters

An Overview

A basic tenet of geography is that physical features on the earth's surface and their related bioclimatic elements mutually interact with patterns of population, peoples, and human activities. This chapter and Chapters 4 and 5 focus on the biophysical elements of the Middle East; Chapters 6–11 consider peoples and their activities. Since the related factors of geomorphology (landforms) and climate (see Chap. 4) have the broadest effects on cultural and economic patterns, they are examined first.

Map 3-1 reveals that land and sea areas alternate like broad spokes around the Middle East hub, with four land areas forming great promontories into the seas and, conversely, four seas penetrating into the land. In the northwest, Asia Minor, embracing the Anatolian Plateau, comprises a peninsular bridge to southeastern Europe. Southeastward from eastern Anatolia, the Iranian Plateau extends into Asia proper. Continuing clockwise, there is a massive rectangular Arabian Peninsula, which split from Africa along the axis of the Red Sea. The southwestern quadrant of the Middle East is occupied by Egypt, the square northeastern corner of the continent of Africa. Finally, the regional hub consists of the Fertile Crescent area, which occupies the zone between the northern (Anatolian-Iranian) and southern (Egyptian-Arabian) belts of the region.

Alternately, five bodies of water touch or reach far into the Middle East land area. The deep Mediterranean Sea on the west washes the shores of six of the Middle East states. The Black Sea, to the north of Asia Minor, lies between Turkey and the other five littoral states and overflows to the Mediterranean through the straits of the Bosporus and Dardanelles. The Caspian Sea to the northeast is really an inland lake with no outlet to the sea, and its surface is well below sea level. The Persian/Arabian Gulf— or simply "the Gulf"—occupies the drowned, downbuckled tectonic trough between Arabia and Iran. The Red Sea, with its two extensions to the north and the related Gulf of Aden to the south, floods the great rift that separates the Arabian Peninsula from Africa (Fig. 3-1).

Penetration of seas into the land has several major consequences. Physically, the seas—the Mediterranean especially—intersperse sources of moisture in areas that would be far more desertic without the seas. In addition, penetration of the seas means a great deal more coastline, which increases the number of outlets to and contacts with the outside world. The seaways provide, as they have for millennia, major routes for trade and movement of peoples, and the sailing of tankers up and down the Gulf, even during conflicts of the 1980s and 1990s, exemplifies one utility of Middle East seas.

Major landform provinces and features of the Middle East originated generally because of a shifting of large segments of the earth's outermost shell over millions of years. These earth crust parcels, or "plates," in the lithosphere[1] jostle one another periodically and in so doing profoundly affect one another's adjacent edges. According to the theory of plate tectonics,[2] at least four and perhaps six or more plates have collided or pulled apart to create the present pattern of the Middle

MAP 3-1 Middle East: Major geomorphic (landform) features.

East (Map 3-2). Typically, several plate contact borders are marked by major fault zones, some of which are still active and periodically cause destructive earthquakes. Other contact areas have resulted in compression-folded mountain ranges (the Zagros, for example) or downfolded troughs (the Gulf).

Although most of the gross landforms of the Middle East have evolved directly or indirectly from regional plate movements, smaller and more local forms have been shaped by other factors. Local earth movements, erosion by water or wind, and combined wind erosion and deposition are some typical factors. For example, some of the extensive sand deserts of Arabia are reshaped deposits of sand blown in from appreciable distances, sometimes hundreds of miles.

Elsewhere are broad plains areas of "desert pavement." Here the surface is blanketed with a layer of pebbles that lag behind after finer particles have been blown away by persistent winds. This pavement of pebbles serves as an armor for the underlying sand particles so long as the deceptively delicate ecological balance is undisturbed. Unfortunately, that equilibrium has been completely upset in extensive areas by modern development, with its wheeled vehicles,

FIGURE 3-1   Looking northeast across the Sinai Peninsula, with Gulf of Suez on the west and the Gulf of Aqabah on the east. Note rugged, dark basement rocks in southern Sinai and along eastern coast of the Gulf of Aqabah. (Photograph courtesy of National Aeronautics and Space Administration)

construction equipment, bulldozers, and—most destructive of all—military tanks and the installation of trenches and bunkers. Wartime operations in Sinai and in northeastern Arabia, Kuwait, and southern Iraq especially destroyed the protective pebble pavement, exposing the underlying sand to wind erosion and the new evolution of sand dunes.[3]

Running water, even though relatively limited in the vast arid realms that dominate the region, has profoundly altered some of the desert areas. However, many forms shaped by streams were developed in earlier geological ages when rainfall was higher and streams were much larger. Weathering and erosion of rock in arid areas produce a greater angularity and sharpness of outline than are typically found in more humid areas, such as northern Turkey, where the silhouettes are more rounded. Such angularity can be seen on a small scale in many places where thin lava flows have mechanically weathered into a rugged cover of sharp boulders, one type of hamadah (Fig. 3-2).

Usually the result of tectonic plate shifts, significant seismic activity and the effects of volcanism are widespread in the Middle East. The map of earthquakes (later in this chapter) both indicates zones of actively colliding plates and illustrates the high incidence of seismic events in Anatolia, Iran, and Cyprus. Colliding plates, separating plates, and some shearing plates generate outpourings of lava either explosively from volcanoes or quietly through vents and fissures. Anatolia especially has numerous classic volcanic cones, including Mount Ararat; and extensive areas of southwestern Syria, central Jordan, western Yemen, and especially western Saudi Arabia are buried under extensive lava flows (Fig. 3-3).

MAP 3-2   Generalized tectonic map of the Middle East. Note the concentration of tectonic zones in eastern Anatolia. Symbols: 1 = collision zone apparently involving subduction of seafloor along arcuate plate contacts; 2 = collision zone involving continental overthrusting (western Iran); 3 = horizontal displacement along transform faults (arrows indicate left-lateral or right-lateral); 4 = seafloor spreading, the pulling apart of the ocean's crust.

Survey of Landforms

On a broad scale, the landform patterns of the Middle East may be grouped into three general structural and macro landform provinces: the Stable Interior Province, the Mobile Belt, and intermediate between the two, the Median Trough (see Map 3-2). This threefold division serves as a basis for a survey of major Middle Eastern landforms that will, in turn, aid in understanding the region's cultural patterns. Maps 3-1 and 3-2 show most of the features

mentioned below, but a more detailed map is recommended for the study of this chapter. The features mentioned below interact significantly with cultural aspects, including economy and politics, an important concept that will be examined in later chapters.

Stable Interior Province

The Stable Interior Province lies in the southwest of the Middle East, its core an extensive area of ancient metamorphic basement rock

FIGURE 3-2   Rock-strewn steppe landscape in southwestern Syria—one type of hamadah. A thin lava flow has broken down to produce this type of surface. The angularity of the boulders is typical of weathering in a dry climate area.

FIGURE 3-3   The extensive volcanic fields of the Western Arabian Shield include many explosion craters, such as al-Wahbah shown here, and hundreds of cinder cones such as that next to al-Wahbah crater.

composing the Nubian-Arabian Shield. Planed down during millions of years, the shield is primarily plateau in character but displays many remarkable volcanic features as well as mountain ridges along ancient sutures. A prominent uptilt has created mountains on either side of the Red Sea rift.

The shield's ancient basement rocks, some more than 1 billion years old but most 890–560 million years old by radiometric dating, have split open along the Red Sea axis and are exposed along both uptilted coasts of this slowly widening rift. The shield was depressed around its flanks except to the southwest, and the flanks were covered by thousands of feet of sedimentary rocks, principally limestones. These sedimentaries now outcrop in and underlie the great arc of territory sweeping from northern Egypt through the Fertile Crescent countries and around the eastern and southeastern flanks of the Arabian Peninsula.

Egyptian Deserts. Between the Red Sea and the Nile Valley, the Eastern Desert of Egypt culminates in the Red Sea Hills, a moderately rugged and barren mountain mass of dominantly basement rocks of the Nubian Shield. West of the Nile, in the Western Desert, the shield is blanketed with relatively thin sedimentary strata to the south and additional, thicker, younger strata to the north. Depressions along the contact between the two different sets of thicknesses of sedimentary cover cradle five oases, and the deep Qattara Depression reaches 436 ft./133 m below sea level. The significance of these depressions is examined in Chap. 20. The Nile River flows along the separation between the two major deserts, and its great delta lies in a former embayment of the Mediterranean coast.

Arabian Peninsula. A narrow coastal plain, Tihamah, extends virtually the full length of the peninsula's Red Sea coast and is backed by a formidable mountain range. This linear barrier, the Hijaz Mountains, averages 7,000 ft./2,135 m and forms the uptilted western edge of the Arabian Shield. Back of the Hijaz, the ancient basement rocks of the shield extend in a semicircle concave westward, to the heart of the Arabian Peninsula. There the Central Arabian Arch bowed up the shield, causing increased erosion to force an eastward retreat of the edge of the older sedimentary cover that formerly blanketed much of western Arabia millions of years ago.

The opening of the Red Sea rift occurred in two stages, the first in the late Oligocene-early Miocene (about 25 million years ago), the second during the Pliocene (about 4–5 million years ago). This sea-floor spreading, plus faulting along the edges, induced the extrusion of several extensive flows of basaltic lava—one as large as 7,720 miles^2/20,000 km^2—from both fissures and vents in the shield (Fig. 3-3). Successive older lava series reach thousands of feet in thickness in the peninsula's southwestern corner and constitute the rugged mountains that give the High Yemen its character (shown in Chaps. 10 and 19).

To the north, northeast, and southeast of central Arabia, the basement is depressed and is buried under layers of sedimentary rock, the Arabian Shelf. These sedimentaries have a vital significance in the world economy, since around and under the Gulf they contain the world's greatest known oil resources.

Sand, wind, aridity, and open space have combined to create three large and several small sand deserts in the Arabian Peninsula. In the south center lies the Rub al-Khali (Empty Quarter), the world's largest single sand dune area (see Fig. 1-1). In the north is the Nafud (or the Great Nafud), one-fifth the size of the Rub al-Khali. Extending in a great arc from the Nafud to the Rub al-Khali through eastern Arabia is a belt of red sand known as the Dahna.

At the southeastern corner of the Arabian Peninsula are the rugged and curious Oman Mountains (or Jabal al-Hajar), with elevations typically around 5,000 ft./1,525 m but peaking at 10,000 ft./3,048 m. Also a product of collision between the Arabian Plate and the Iranian subplate, the range is more related structurally and petrologically to the mountains of southwestern Iran than to neighboring parts of Arabia.

FIGURE 3-4   The Jordan River meandering across its floodplain (*al-Zor*), flowing sluggishly from upper right (from the Sea of Galilee, just out of picture) to lower left. The higher terrace level is *al-Ghor* (*al-Gawr*).

At their northern end, the Oman Mountains culminate in the Musandam Peninsula, informally, and aptly, referred to as the Horn of Arabia.[4]

Syrian Desert.   The same general sedimentary sequence found in the eastern Arabian Peninsula overlies the basement rocks in the Syrian Desert area in the heart of the Middle East. However, the dip of the strata in the central area is gentler, and large expanses of eastern Jordan, eastern and southern Syria, and western Iraq show level to undulating surfaces of Cretaceous limestones.

Jordan Valley and Related Features.   A major geomorphic feature of the western Fertile Crescent is the Levant Rift System, a great trench that extends from the northwestern end of the Red Sea up the Gulf of Aqabah and along the axis of the Wadi al-Arabah, Dead Sea, Jordan Valley, and Bekaa of Lebanon to the Ghab Depression in northwestern Syria (Fig. 3-4). It

thus extends through or along parts of Egypt, Saudi Arabia, Israel, Jordan, Lebanon, and Syria. This feature is considered to be primarily a transform fault, similar to the San Andreas Fault in California, that resulted chiefly from rotation of the Arabian Plate away from the African Plate, as described earlier.

The system, called by several other names—Dead Sea Fault, Jordan-Dead Sea Rift, West Arabian Fault Zone, and others—is a left-lateral fault (showing a leftward shear when viewed across the fault line) that resulted in a total horizontal displacement of 66.5 miles/107 km during two main stages. Thus, the igneous and metamorphic rocks north of Aqabah were formerly adjacent to the center of the east coast of the Sinai Peninsula. The four deeper basins along the fault—the Gulf of Aqabah, Dead Sea, Sea of Galilee, and Huleh Basin—are "pull-apart zones" in which elongated depressions were formed as local grabens. The bottom of the trench is below sea level from north of the

Sea of Galilee to well south of the Dead Sea, with the Dead Sea the lowest body of water on the globe (see "Middle East Lakes" section later in this chapter).

The first of the rift system's three main segments comprises the trench and related features extending from the Gulf of Aqabah north to and including the Huleh Basin. A second segment begins at the southern border of Lebanon, where the Levant Rift bends to the northeast. This segment consists of a less profound trench but still constitutes a prominent linear depression through eastern Lebanon, the Bekaa. This segment of the Levant Rift is the Yammunah Fault, which exhibits a significant vertical displacement along its western side that is still continuing, creating frequent but minor earthquakes. In the third segment, beginning at the northern border of Lebanon, the fault zone turns north again and finally disappears just beyond the Ghab Depression in northwestern Syria, the northernmost feature of the system (pictured in Chap. 7).

The belt west of the three-segment fault is upwarped along a north-south axis for most of its length and is considered by some geologists to be a sliver subplate related to the African Plate. The highlands formed by the upfolded and faulted structures west of the Levant Rift include, from south to north, the Judean and Samarian hills, the upper Galilee highlands, Mount Lebanon, and the Jabal al-Nusayriyah (sometimes Jabal al-Ansariyah, but officially Jabal al-Sahiliyah). East of the Bekaa are the Anti-Lebanon Mountains, beyond which extend the prominent splayed ridges of the Palmyra Folds, crumpled up and faulted by rotation of the Arabian Plate.

Mobile Belt

The Mobile Belt (or Fold Belt) is a continuous band of folded and faulted mountains extending from western to eastern Anatolia and then southeastward across Iran and eastward into the Himalayas. This belt, the middle segment of the vast Alpine-Himalayan mountain system, makes Turkey, northeastern Iraq, and Iran structurally extraordinarily complex.

Asia Minor (Anatolia). South of and generally parallel to the Black Sea coast, the Pontic Mountains (5,000–13,000 ft./1,524–3,962 m) stretch virtually the full length of Turkey. For much of their extent, they lie north of the great North Anatolian Transform Fault (Map 3-2), the eastern end of a 4,000-mile/6,440-km fault zone that begins at the Mid-Atlantic Rift. Periodic slippage along this right-lateral fault has produced devastating earthquakes, the most disastrous of which occurred south of Istanbul on August 17, 1999.

Rimming the southern side of Asia Minor are the Taurus Mountains (7,000–9,000 ft./2,135–2,745 m), whose complexity reflects the severity of the compression that formed them. The slightly offset Anti-Taurus Mountains extend eastward to merge with folds that in turn bend southeastward to become the Zagros Mountains. The Anti-Taurus generally parallel the East Anatolian Transform Fault, which in turn partially parallels the Southeast Anatolian Suture Zone between the former northern edge of the Arabian Plate and the southeastern edge of the Anatolian subplate (see Map 3-2).

At its southwestern end, the East Anatolian Transform Fault links with both the northern end of the Levant Rift System and the eastern end of the Cyprus Subduction Zone. At its northeastern end, it intersects the North Anatolian Fault. The proximity of these several seismic belts results in frequent and severe earthquakes (Map 3-3), such as the three catastrophic quakes in the Erzincan area in 1938, 1983, and 1992. South of the suture zone is a complex foreland in which moderate Border Folds merge into the Harran Plain along the Turkish-Syrian boundary.

Extreme western Anatolia is an area of block mountains, alternating uplifted and down-dropped masses (horsts and grabens). These structures have produced a series of rugged east-west promontories and deeply indented bays on the Aegean coast, which beckoned

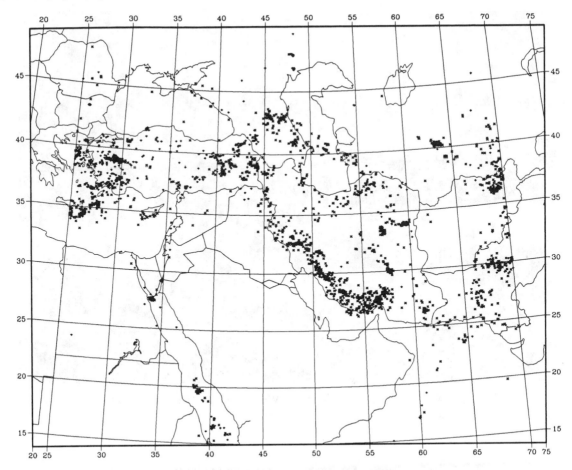

MAP 3-3   Major Middle East earthquakes 1966–1986 (magnitude of more than 4.5 and depth less than 31 miles/50 km). Note the concentration of seismicity along the Zagros Fold and Overthrust Belt and in western and eastern Anatolian Turkey. Compare with Map 3–2. Boundaries as shown on NEIC compilation. (Map by special courtesy of National Earthquake Information Center, U.S. Geological Survey)

Ionian Greeks to settle in the sixth century BC. In the northwest, a large foundered block flooded to form the Sea of Marmara. More than 600 miles/965 km to the east, the East Anatolian Accretionary Complex is a jumble of mountains and tilted plateaus (Fig. 3-5), the area where the junction of plates and compression create severe seismic movements. Volcanic vents have also opened and are now marked by massive volcanoes (Mount Ararat near the Turkish-Iranian border reaches 16,948 ft./ 5,166 m), lava flows, and crater lakes. Mineralization along these various plate contacts gives Turkey more nonfuel mineral wealth than any

other country in the Middle East, although Iran is similarly wealthy for the same geological reasons. In between this East Anatolian complex and the western mountains is the exceedingly complex central Anatolian intermontane plateau, with its lowest part an almost flat-floored basin occupied by the shallow Tuz Gölü ("salt lake").

Off the Mediterranean coast of Turkey, the island of Cyprus is believed to have been formed as a result of the same plate collision that produced the Taurus range on the mainland. An exposed granitic intrusion forms the core of the Troodos (6,407 ft./1,953 m), the

FIGURE 3-5   Eastern Anatolian mountains west of Lake Van—rugged, snow-covered, cloud-shrouded, and geologically very complex. Heavy precipitation makes this mountain area a major hydrographic center spawning such important rivers as the Tigris and Euphrates.

highly mineralized mountain mass of southern Cyprus, whereas a linear limestone reef was uplifted to produce the narrow Kyrenia range (3,360 ft./1,025 m), which parallels the northern coast of the island. The depression between the Troodos and Kyrenia highlands is a sediment-filled basin, the Mesaoria, Cyprus's breadbasket.

Iranian Plateau. Complex folding in the Mobile Belt extends farther eastward and southeastward into the Iranian mountain and intermontane plateau regions. From the junction of Turkey, Iran, and Iraq to the Arabian Sea, compression between the Arabian Plate and the Iranian subplate has crumpled, faulted, and thrust-faulted mostly sedimentary rocks along the longest and most prominent fold belt in the Middle East, the Zagros Mountains

(10,000–14,000 ft./3,000–4,300 m) (Fig. 3-6). In the southern Zagros, scores of salt plugs have been pushed to or near the surface, creating stratigraphic structures that in many instances have entrapped large quantities of petroleum and natural gas. Farther southeast, the Makran range, which lies behind Iran's coast on the Gulf of Oman, is the result of uplift of oceanic crust and exhibits forms that are distinctly different from the Zagros geomorphology and that are related to the Oman Mountains.

Compressed between the rigid core blocks of Iran and the Russian Platform of the Eurasian Plate, high linear ridges were folded sharply upward across northern Iran. The Elburz Mountains south of the Caspian Sea and the series of ridges in the Kopet Mountains along the Iran-Turkmenistan border reach elevations of 12,000–15,000 ft./3,660–4,575 m in the

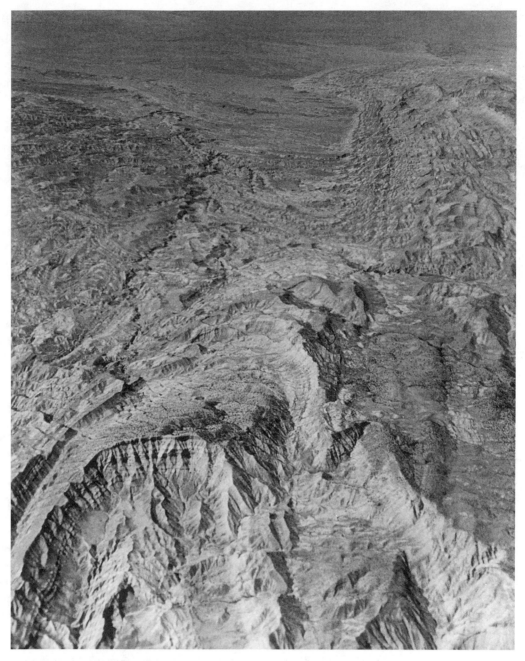

FIGURE 3-6   Denuded pitching anticline in typical structures of the Folded Zagros Mountains of western Iran. In such subsurface folds are found the great petroleum reservoirs of the area. Compare with Figure 11-5, which shows salt domes that also form oil-reservoir structures.

Elburz and somewhat less in the Kopet. As in eastern Turkey, plate collision in the Elburz belt squeezed lava out of the vent of the Mt. Damavand volcano (18,600 ft./5,669 m, the highest point in the entire Middle East). Along the eastern Iranian border, near Pakistan, scattered volcanoes—including Iran's only recently active vent—and complex fold mountains around the Zahedan Plateau enclose the third side of the triangular Iranian Plateau core. As in central Anatolia, the lowest part of Iran's inner basin contains ephemeral salt lakes (playas), known in Iran as *kavirs*.

Median Trough

The Mesopotamian-Gulf trough, which is technically the northeastern edge of the Stable Interior Province, lies along the median axis between the Arabian Plate and the Iranian subplate and is a major geomorphic feature of the Middle East. The world's greatest petroleum province, it is a zone of downbuckling and subsidence on the flanks of the Arabian Shield. The northwestern half of the trough is above sea level and is partly a low plateau northwest of Baghdad and an alluvial-deltaic plain from Baghdad to the Gulf. The southeastern half of the structural trough has been invaded by the shallow waters of the Gulf, entering from the Indian Ocean through the Strait of Hormuz. The strait is thus as significant physically as it is economically and strategically.

Middle East Seas

Even after the sea basins of the main water bodies of the Middle East reached their approximate present contours, major modifications occurred in response to slight crustal adjustments and to climatic variations. Especially during the Pleistocene glacial period, sea level fell more than 395 ft./120 m below its current level during periods of ice advance, when millions of cubic meters of ocean water were frozen into the ice sheets. During those same periods of glacial maxima, the Middle East enjoyed pluvial

periods, when precipitation increased appreciably. The increased rainfall charged the regional aquifers and induced environmental conditions more favorable for human cultural development during the long Paleolithic period. Eustatic (sea level) changes during glacial retreats, when the melting of the ice sheets freed water that had been previously locked in the glaciers, brought seas 180–195 ft./55–60 m higher than at present, giving a total differential of more than 590 ft./180 m over the 1.3 million years of the glacial Pleistocene.

The great drop in sea level during glacial maxima dried up the Strait of Gibraltar, connecting the Mediterranean and the Atlantic; the Bosporus and Dardanelles, connecting the Mediterranean and the Black Sea; and the Strait of Hormuz, connecting the Gulf and the Indian Ocean. With their main water supplies cut off, the basins of the three inland seas became extensive desert basins, large-scale versions of today's Death Valley in California. Some of the salt deposited during the periods of evaporation still affects the chemical composition of rocks, water, and soil in the region. As the interglacial thaw induced a rise in sea level, the mounting water crested the dried-up straits and roared into the empty basins in thunderous cascades, refilling the huge depressions to their former, and approximately present, configurations.

Red Sea and the Gulf of Aden

The Red Sea occupies an elongated, escarpment-bounded depression 1,220 miles/1,965 km long and 155–280 miles/250–450 km wide. Rifting opened the Red Sea in two phases, one 30 million–15 million years ago and a more recent one beginning 5 million years ago and still continuing along the sea's entire length. South of 21° N Lat, the sea's main trough, 2,000–3,000 ft./600–1,000 m deep, is bisected by a deeper axial trough, which is usually less than 30 miles/50 km wide and about 6,500 ft./2,000 m deep, formed by seafloor spreading during the past 4 million years. By contrast, north of 25° N Lat, the inner axial trough is lacking, and the floor has an irregular, faulted surface. Between the shores and the center axis, narrow continental shelf extends all along both coasts.

Seafloor spreading, especially in a series of eighteen deeps in the transition zone between 24° and 21°, brings molten lava into the bottom of the trench. The lava heats the seawater above it and stimulates the formation of hot brines and the development of a sludge with high concentrations of zinc, copper, silver, gold, and other metals. Facing each other across these deeps, Saudi Arabia and Sudan formed a Red Sea Commission in 1975 to consider exploitation of the metals. The sludge is not a commercially feasible source at present, but it will be a major source for the metals in the future.

Rifting along both branches of the Red Sea at the northern end, along the Gulf of Suez west of the Sinai Peninsula and the Gulf of Aqabah east of the Sinai (Fig. 3-1), is of two different types and ages. With great depths, exceeding 5,900 ft./1,800 m, the Gulf of Aqabah is a pull-apart zone associated with the Levant Rift and is morphogenetically related to the Dead Sea, Sea of Galilee, and Huleh Basin. Much shallower, only about 150 ft./45 m, and a much older structure, the Gulf of Suez split from the Red Sea Hills to the West and subsided over a long period.

Opening by seafloor spreading along a rift at right angles to the one widening the southern Red Sea, the Gulf of Aden has proceeded further and can be considered as an example of a young ocean basin. It exhibits well-defined continental margins, small ocean basins, an oceanic crust floor, an active midocean ridge (Sheba Ridge), and a spreading center characterized by a rift valley and transverse fracture zones. This triple junction of the rifts (see Map 3-2) creates a magnificent laboratory for observing the mechanics and processes of active seafloor spreading.

Persian/Arabian Gulf

Lying in a tectonic basin of Late Pliocene to Pleistocene age, the shallow Gulf is a marginal sea that exhibits striking contrasts with the Red Sea and the Gulf of Aden. It covers approximately 87,000 miles^2/226,000 km^2 and is about 620 miles/1,000 km long and 125–185 miles/201–300 km wide. Although it reaches depths of more than 330 ft./100 m near the Strait of Hormuz, its average depth is only 115 ft./35 m. Since the floor slope and depth are greater on the Iranian side, the basin has a marked bathymetric asymmetry across its axis, reflecting the downfolding between the Arabian Plate and Iranian subplate. Because the Gulf's elongated axis defines this separation between two different geomorphic provinces, the opposite coasts, Arabia to the west and Iran to the east, reflect the contrasting structures. The low surface of the eastern half of the stable Arabian Shelf is a generally level coastal area that slopes gently under the shallow Gulf waters and is fringed with offshore sand islands and sand spits. One such sand spit is Ras Tanura, location of three large oil installations. To the east of the anticlinal Qatar Peninsula is a broad, shallow area 33–66 ft./10–20 m deep studded with numerous shoals and salt-dome islands, around which huge petroleum accumulations are exploited. Formerly the world's greatest natural-pearl fishing area, the Great Pearl Bank Barrier extends eastward across this embayment. The concave southern coast of the Gulf is typified by low, evaporitic, supratidal flats (*sabkhahs*), some of which, along the coast of the United Arab Emirates, are more than 6 miles/10 km wide. On the east, in contrast, the Iranian coast rises steeply and quickly merges with the folded ridges of the Zagros Foreland.

The Gulf shows a wide variation in temperature and salinity because of its shallowness and limited connection with the ocean. In summer, the surface waters are warm and evaporation is high. Even in winter, water temperature is about 68°F/20°C. Salinity varies from 7 percent (twice that of average seawater) in protected Arabian lagoons to less than 3.7 percent near the Strait of Hormuz. The major freshwater influx into the Gulf is that of the Shatt al-Arab (the combined Tigris and Euphrates rivers), but water also enters from the Karun River in Iran and from short streams descending the western ridges of the Zagros Foreland. Tidal ranges in the western Gulf are moderate, with average maximums of about 8 ft./2.5 m. When the sea level fell during the later Pleistocene glaciation to empty the Gulf, the Tigris-Euphrates river system flowed across the dry basin and emptied into the Arabian Sea through the Strait of Hormuz. Seawater began to pour back into the basin about 18,000 years ago, and the present level was reached about 5,000 years ago.

With more than a score of major oil export terminals in operation in the Gulf virtually around the clock, and with 40 to 50 large tankers sailing up or down the Gulf daily, pollution of the waters and beaches has long been a grave concern around the littoral. Despite government monitoring and caveat, and despite appreciable care taken by oil companies and shippers, as many as a quarter of a million barrels of oil pollute the Gulf annually. The rapidly growing population around the littoral discards many tons of waste into the water daily. However, the greatest blow to the Gulf came in January 1991, when Iraqis occupying Kuwait dumped several million barrels of crude oil (the exact amount is uncertain) into the Gulf off the coast of the amirate. This oil spill, the largest ever in the world, spread to cover more than 600 miles^2/1,554 km^2 of sea surface and to foul 300 miles/483 km of the Gulf's west coast. With the Gulf's counterclockwise circulation, the slick spread south to the Qatar coast within 60 days, killing countless fish, shrimp, crabs, and birds, as well as fouling sea-grass beds and beaches and posing a threat to desalination plant intakes. Fortunately, reasonable revival took take place in less time than the more pessimistic predictions in 1990–1991.

Caspian Sea

Unlike the other "seas," the inland Caspian has no outlet, and its surface averages about 92 ft./28 m below sea level. The Caspian bottom has two basins connected by a channel east of the Baku Peninsula. The shallower of the basins lies at the northern end and eastern side; the greatest depth is in the southwestern quadrant, 3,363 ft./

1,025 m. With most of the fluviatile inflow coming from the Volga at the northern end, the level of the Caspian slowly dropped until the late 1970s as the Russians increasingly utilized Volga water for irrigation. The trend reversed in 1977, and by 1995 the Caspian had risen by 8 ft./2.4 m before slowly receding. A railroad ferry crosses from Baku to Krasnovodsk, and other freight and passenger vessels utilize the sea; however, most boats on the Caspian are fishing vessels, seeking especially the famous Caspian sturgeon, source of the valuable Russian and Iranian caviar. As in the Persian/Arabian Gulf area, the tectonics of the Caspian basin created structures favorable for huge accumulations of petroleum and natural gas. Some of the world's earliest major oil production came from the Baku field. In their exploitation, however, the Soviets were so negligent in protecting the environment that the entire basin became frighteningly polluted.[5]

Black Sea

The deeply foundered subplate of the Black Sea is of major importance to the littoral states that fringe its coasts. Relatively shallow near the Danube Delta in the northwest, the Black Sea depth exceeds 7,000 ft./2,135 m across much of its southern extent. The northern slopes of Turkey's Pontic Mountains plunge steeply into the Black Sea, giving deep water access to Turkey's many northern ports. Receiving a plentiful freshwater inflow from rivers in the north and several smaller rivers in the south, the Black Sea is only moderately salty. Virtually tideless, it overflows freely through the Bosporus into the Sea of Marmara and thence through the Dardanelles into the Aegean. The Black Sea is also known as the Euxine Sea, the ancient Pontus Euxinus. Commonality of certain interests has led the six Black Sea littoral states to concert their planning and actions—for example, in tackling the increasingly serious problem of the basin's pollution.

Mediterranean Sea

Of complex origin, the Mediterranean is partially a western remnant of the pre-Miocene Tethys Sea and partially a collapsed structure along the collision zone between the African and Eurasian plates. Its greatest depth (15,072 ft./4,594 m) is west of Crete, and the basin off the Levant coast is 4,787 ft./1,459 m. Except in the southeast, where Nile sediments extend seaward and have been carried eastward and northeastward by currents, most Mediterranean coasts descend sharply under the Mediterranean waters. Most ports, therefore, generally face few dredging problems, unlike virtually all Gulf ports. The extensive, deep Mediterranean waters exercise profound effects on the climate of much of the Middle East, and the sea has carried ships of many nations for thousands of years. Such maritime activity has encouraged certain interrelations among Mediterranean littoral peoples, producing a "Mediterranean" subrace, diet, agriculture, music, and history.

Middle East Lakes

Few natural freshwater lakes of any considerable size and significance occur in the Middle East outside the Tigris and Euphrates valleys, where the lakes tend to be shallow and are more similar to marshes than to lakes. However, five are noteworthy here, and these and others are discussed in more detail in the relevant country chapters. Although not large, the Sea of Galilee in Israel (also called Lake Tiberias and Lake Kinneret) has both religious-historical significance and crucial contemporary economic and political importance. Covering 64 miles²/165 km², the lake's surface varies between 685 and 710 ft./209 and 214 m below sea level, and its maximum depth is 138 ft./42 m. The lake occupies one of the enlarged basins in the Levant Rift System (see Fig. 3-1) and is now regulated as the control basin for Israel's national water system. Its generally fresh water is locally briny owing to underwater salt springs, especially near Tiberias on its west coast.

Farther south in the Levant Rift lies the Middle East's most famous salt lake, the Dead Sea. Its surface is more than 1,310 ft./400 m below sea level (lowest water body on earth), and its maximum depth is an additional 1,300 ft./396 m lower. Like other inland lakes with no outlet, the Dead Sea has become increasingly saline because of the evaporation from its surface—roughly 96.8 million ft.³/2.74 million m³ per day—and because of the addition of salt from surrounding springs. Its water shows the highest salinity of all the world's water bodies, 35 percent, ten times that of average seawater. As a result, fish cannot survive in the water (hence the name of the lake), and buoyancy of the water is so great that people cannot sink while swimming in the Dead Sea.

Another result is that dissolved salts are present in such quantities that they are precipitated naturally or can be precipitated in evaporation pans, so that they are "mined" on a large scale in Israel and Jordan. This evaporation and a rapidly diminishing inflow of water from the Jordan River in the north—the lake's main supply of fresh water—owing to an increasing use of the river basin's water for irrigation mean that the lake's surface is steadily dropping. At present the southern basin has shrunk to half its former size and, now separated from the larger and deeper northern basin by the sill extending from the Lisan Peninsula, is only a few feet deep.[6]

Numerous large saltwater lakes occupy closed tectonic basins in northwestern Iran and on the Anatolian Plateau. The two largest are Lake Urmia and Lake Van, the two lying on either side of the Iranian-Turkish boundary. Relatively shallow, not more than 66 ft./20 m deep, the very salty Lake Urmia expands in size by one-third with the spring runoff to cover 2,317 miles²/6,000 km². Nestled in the rugged eastern Anatolian highlands, the much deeper Lake Van, whose water is bitter because of several salts, has a surface elevation of 5,400 ft./1,646 m and

covers 1,434 miles^2/3,714 km^2. The structurally
and topographically complex southwestern part
of Anatolia cradles a dozen salt lakes between
Konya on the east and Denizli on the west. In
northwestern Anatolia, lakes also occupy inland
extensions of grabens east and south of the Sea
of Marmara. Tuz Gölü is a shallow evaporation
pan in the central Anatolian sump that expands
and contracts markedly according to seasonal
precipitation.

Major River Systems

Aridity in the southern and eastern sectors of
the Middle East precludes any large-scale, local
perennial runoff, and the river systems in these
regions rise in nearby areas of significant water
surplus. Structural conditions in some of the
more humid sectors interrupt drainage lines to
divert a considerable percentage of the interior
runoff into closed basins. Thus, the major river
systems in the Middle East are limited both
qualitatively and quantitatively. The two largest
stream systems are the Nile in the southwest
and the Tigris-Euphrates in the center, with all
three rivers crossing deserts but originating in
highlands with a water surplus. Escalating disputes between the countries controlling the
sources of the three streams and the downstream consuming countries are among the
potentially serious confrontations faced by the
Middle East in the 1990s and the new century
(see Chap. 11). Not one perennial stream drains
any part of the Arabian Peninsula, which serves
as compelling confirmation of the stark aridity
of this vast realm.

With the major exception of the Nile, virtually all Middle East rivers have a maximum
runoff in late spring and a minimum flow in
early fall. Most rivers at flood time are fed by
snowmelt, which comes later than the actual
precipitation maximum (November through
February); and their minimum flow after the
hot, dry summer is supplied primarily by
springs and other ground-water discharge. The
Nile regime is precisely the reverse, as it floods
in late summer and early fall after the heavy
summer monsoon rains in the river's source
highlands and is at its minimum in the spring.

Tigris and Euphrates Rivers

Although the Tigris (Arabic, Dijlah; Turkish,
Dicle) and Euphrates (Arabic, al-Furat, Turkish,
Firat) rivers enter the Gulf through a common
100-mile/160-km channel (the Shatt al-Arab),
each is otherwise a separate stream. Both rise in
the eastern Anatolian highlands hydrographic
center of Turkey, their headwaters only a few
miles from each other (Map 3-1). In the highlands, additional tributaries augment their flow,
but downstream as they course across the flat
desert they lose water through evaporation and
diversion for irrigation purposes. With diminished flow, they lose carrying capacity, drop
some of their loads of silt, and continue to build
up a common vast deltaic plain, with each channel also building natural levees.[7]

The longer of the two and the one with the
greater drainage basin, the Euphrates proper
begins at the confluence of the Kara and Murat
rivers near Keban, northeast of Malatya in eastern Turkey, and ends with its junction with the
Tigris at Qurnah, at the head of the Shatt al-
Arab. This river, 1,700 miles/2,700 km long,
drains a basin of 171,430 miles^2/444,000 km^2.
About 28 percent of the basin is in Turkey, 17
percent in Syria, 40 percent in Iraq, and 15 percent in Saudi Arabia. However, more than 90
percent of the actual water flow is from runoff
in Turkey. The Balikh and Khabur left-bank
tributaries, rising in the Anti-Taurus foothills,
join the Euphrates as it flows across Syria, and
no tributaries enter it in Iraq. Mean annual
flow at Hit, in central Iraq, was formerly 31,820
million cubic meters (m^3) per year; however,
damming of the Euphrates at four places in
Turkey and at Tabaqah (renamed al-Thawrah)
in Syria has greatly diminished the river's mean
flow and will reduce it much more from the
mid-1990s onward.

Although shorter than the Euphrates, the
Tigris (1,150 miles/1,850 km) formerly carried

an average 42,230 million m³ of water per year, 25 percent more than did the Euphrates; and since the Turkish and Syrian diversions of the Euphrates, the differential is even greater. To compensate for the dwindling lower Euphrates, water can be diverted by the Samarra barrage from the Tigris to the Euphrates by way of Lake Tharthar, a flood control facility occupying a depression between the two rivers. Other aspects of water management have been enhanced with the completion in late 1992 of Iraq's so-called third river, a 350-mile/563-km canal that extends from Baghdad to Basrah. Draining an area of more than 43,110 miles²/ 111,655 km² above Samarra, the Tigris, unlike the Euphrates, receives significant contributions from tributaries in Iraq. Bringing snowmelt and rainwater from the high Zagros in northeastern Iraq, all the tributaries enter along the left bank and include, from north to south, Great Zab, Little Zab, Udhaym, and Diyala. The Karkheh joins the Tigris at Amarah, upstream from Qurnah. More than the upper Tigris, the lower Tigris is subject to sudden flooding, especially when the Zab rivers flood simultaneously. However, flood control measures, such as the Tharthar Project, have done much to alleviate the impact of floods. Neither river is satisfactory for regular navigation, although the Tigris carried shallow-draft boats earlier in the century.

The building of the Tigris-Euphrates Delta has long been a subject of debate among geomorphologists. The enormous load of silt carried by the Tigris (about 40 million m³ annually past Baghdad) and formerly by the Euphrates (whose silt now largely settles in Turkish and Syrian reservoirs and in flood control basins between Ramadi and Karbala in Iraq) has built a huge delta beyond Hit on the Euphrates and beyond Samarra on the Tigris. The rivers could logically be expected to continue rapid construction of a contemporary common delta; however, building from the east, the much more rapidly advancing combined fan and delta of the Karun River has, in effect, dammed the outlet of the Tigris-Euphrates system into the Gulf.

The Karun fan-delta barrier causes the Tigris-Euphrates streams to slow down and drop their silt load prior to overflowing the barrier. The process created a maze of marshes and channels northwest of Basrah, although, after existing for thousands of years, most of the marshes have now been drained by the Iraqi government (map in Chap. 16). Thus, the shoreline of the head of the Gulf during Sumerian times, for example, is uncertain. Whereas Ur seems to have been a port during its heyday, 3000 BC, it may have been a river port, like modern Basrah. Problems regarding delta building and early coastlines at the head of the Gulf require further investigation.

Nile River

With a length of 4,145 miles/6,669 km, the Nile is the world's longest river. Its drainage basin of 1.15 million miles²/2.98 million km² is almost one-tenth the land area of Africa, although the Amazon, Mississippi, and Congo rivers have still larger watersheds. Seen anywhere along its lower course, the Nile, with an average annual flow at Aswan of 83,570 million m³ per year, is an amazingly large stream to have traversed the full width of the eastern Sahara, yet 32 other major rivers carry more water than does the Nile during an average year.

The Nile's main tributary, the White Nile, is born in the lake district of East Africa and channels the overflow from Lake Victoria. From this lake, whence the river's alternate name of Victoria Nile, the White Nile descends into the Sudd, the world's largest freshwater swamp, in southern Sudan. After dropping its silt load in and being regulated by the Sudd, the river flows northward and crosses progressively more desertic terrain to join the Blue Nile at Khartoum.

The Blue Nile is fed by heavy summer monsoon rains on the high Ethiopian Plateau and has a slightly different regime from that of the more uniform White Nile. It was primarily the Blue Nile floods that, prior to the two Aswan dams, caused the annual Nile flood in Egypt. From Khartoum, the Nile flows over a series of six cataracts, numbered upstream from the first cataract at Aswan, and 200 miles/322 km below the Khartoum confluence (still in the Sudan), it receives the intermittent Atbara, the river's last tributary. Debouching into the Mediterranean 1,680 miles/2,705 km below the Atbara confluence, the Nile has dropped a great silt load for thousands of years to build up the extensive delta that is an integral part of the country. However, the Aswan High Dam has changed the river regime, and the Nile no longer adds significantly to its delta (Chap. 20). Political problems concerning the Nile are discussed in Chap. 11.

Fold Belt Rivers

Asia Minor and the western Iranian highlands have many perennial streams, a limited number of which carry sufficient volume to be noteworthy. Clockwise, they include the Büyük Menderes in southwestern Anatolia; Gediz, debouching just north of Izmir; Sakarya, draining the highlands between Ankara and Istanbul and reaching the Black Sea west of Zonguldak; Kızıl, or Kızılırmak (Turkish *ırmak* = "river"), the ancient Halys, with its basin comprising much of north-central Anatolia, making a broad loop before reaching its appreciable delta between Sinop and Samsun; and Yeşil, debouching across its delta east of Samsun. Most of these Anatolian rivers have been dammed for power generation.

Farther east is the Aras, which forms the Turkish-Armenian and Iranian-Azerbaijanian borders and empties into the Caspian Sea over the combined Kura-Aras delta south of Baku. In Iran, the Qezel Owzan-Safid drains a considerable area between Tehran and Tabriz and then cuts through a steep-sided gorge in the western Elburz (where it has been dammed) to empty into the southwestern Caspian over an appreciable delta; the Zayandeh, or Zayandeh Rud (Persian *rud* = "river"), has an importance beyond its physical volume as it irrigates a considerable area around Esfahan before losing itself in a sump southeast of the city; and the

Karun carries the largest volume of all Iranian rivers across a huge delta built jointly with its tributary, the Dez, and the nearby Karkheh. In Turkey, the two parallel Ceyhan and Seyhan rivers drain into the northeastern corner of the Mediterranean across the extensive Çukurova (Turkish *ova* = "plain"), the combined deltaic plain built by the two rivers.

Three Levant Rivers

Three modest rivers in the Levant have economic and political significance far beyond their physical dimensions. The Jordan River (al-Urdunn) has several headwaters draining southeastern Lebanon, southwestern Syria, and northern Israel; and its major tributary, the Yarmuk, enters on the east bank just south of the Sea of Galilee. The Zarqa enters from the plateau south of the Yarmuk. Meandering along the rift valley floor, the Jordan cuts through old lake bed deposits laid down in the late Pleistocene pluvial periods when the ancestral Dead Sea was as much as 655 ft./200 m higher than at present (Fig. 3-4). Increased diversion of the Jordan and its tributary waters for irrigation purposes by Israel and the Kingdom of Jordan utilizes most of the river's water, except at flood time, before it reaches the Dead Sea. Thus, both the Jordan River and the Dead Sea are shrinking.

The two other Levant rivers of note arise within a few hundred meters of each other in the northern Bekaa of Lebanon, both fed by springs. The Litani flows southward, and below the Qirawn Dam it enters a rapidly deepening gorge before turning westward to the Mediterranean. Israeli water planners have long sought methods by which to divert some of the Litani's water from Lebanon into the upper Jordan basin to increase irrigation supplies for Israel. North of Baalbak, the Orontes River (Arabic, Asi) flows northward along the bend in the Levant Rift and enters the reclaimed Ghab Marshes, a graben at the north end of the rift valley. The lower Orontes flows through Antakya (Antioch) and then debouches into the Mediterranean.

Groundwater

In addition to surface water, underground water is of vital significance in the Middle East and has been for thousands of years. Some groundwater comes to the surface in natural springs—artesian springs (*ayns* in the Arab lands), or contact springs—or by emerging from caverns dissolved in limestone. Other water is tapped by hand-dug wells, many 50–100 ft./15–30 m deep. Wells in desert areas, especially those sunk by nomads, may be only a few feet deep, dug into the sand and gravel of a broad wadi or an alluvial fan. Especially in Iran, but also in other Middle Eastern areas, water in alluvial fans is tapped by a remarkable *qanat* system (also called *foggara, falaj, karez*), underground tunnels with spaced access wells reaching the surface(see Chap. 7). Thus, oases in the desert may be supplied by river water (Nile, Tigris, Euphrates), natural springs (in Egypt's Western Desert and in Saudi Arabia's Hofuf and Qatif oases), or dug wells (many in Iran and Saudi Arabia's Najd).

Greatly increased supplies of capital, rapidly growing populations, and increased exploitation of the environment in the Middle East have focused regional and national attention on water resources in general. Vast areas have no dependable surface runoff, but despite their desert character, modern hydrogeological studies have discovered that they have surprisingly large underground water supplies. Since World War I, and especially since World War II, technology has been applied to the search for and exploitation of underground water, with the result that supplies beyond any earlier expectations have been found and are being pumped by electric or internal combustion engines from deep wells. It is now known that some of this water, usually in the deeper aquifers, is fossil water that was accumulated thousands of years ago, especially during the pluvial periods of the Pleistocene. Other aquifers are inexplicably recharged in the short term, even in areas that receive only minimum amounts of precipitation. The problem is that modern technology might permit such an overuse of these limited water supplies that critical shortages will develop within two or three decades.

In the central Arabian Peninsula, outcropping sedimentary strata of the Arabian Shelf contain aquifers that are recharged by the low annual rainfall in Najd and that carry the water at increasing depths underground very slowly toward the Gulf coast. Some of this water emerges in artesian springs in Hofuf, Qatif, and Bahrain; some is tapped by wells. Some is pumped in the recharge area itself, and enormous amounts of fossil water in the Cretaceous Wasia and Biyadh aquifers are being heavily exploited in central Saudi Arabia. In the Western Desert of Egypt, the widespread Nubian sandstone, which overlies the Nubian Shield, also contains huge amounts of fossil water that is being increasingly exploited. Some of this water emerges in the five oases of the area. Groundwater plays a major role in the water supplies of the coastal plain of Israel, Mount Lebanon, western Jordan, and, indeed, every country of the Middle East.

Thus, the significance of the patterns of physical features goes beyond that of the landforms as such. Great concern focuses on the features' influence on and interaction with other patterns, cultural and biophysical. Topography has always influenced and will always influence where people cultivate their fields, build their settlements, align their transportation routes, construct their ports, fight their battles, and conduct their other activities. Similarly, landforms have interacted with climate, soils, and vegetation to create the natural environment. Above all, the utilization of water has been and is the single most critical aspect of the human experience in the Middle East. Economic and political aspects of the water problem are discussed further in Chapter 11.

Notes

1. Technical terms not explained in the text are defined in the Glossary. See also the simplified geological time chart at the end of the book.

2. The theory of plate tectonics has been a major focus of earth science since the late 1950s. Simplified presentations are given in most leading atlases, and evolving aspects are discussed regularly in many journals, e.g., *Scientific American.* See the National Geographic Society 1983 and 1999. No single work in English covers the geomorphology of the Middle East, but see several studies listed in the Bibliography (Brown and Coleman 1972; U.S. Geological Survey 1966–1967, 1975, and 1989; Said 1962; and the very technical Dixon and Robertson 1984). Vita-Finzi 1986 is scientific yet readable and uses many examples and illustrations from the Middle East and North Africa.

3. El-Baz 1992, 74.

4. The term "Horn of Arabia" was used for the first time of which I am aware by Erhard F. Gabriel in Gabriel 1988, 233.

5. Cullen 1999, which includes a very useful National Geographic map supplement.

6. Kreiger 1988 is a readable account of several aspects of the Dead Sea and includes a very a useful bibliography.

7. Both rivers are examined in detail in Kolars and Mitchell 1991. See also Rogers and Lydon 1994 (with good bibliography), Ventner 1998, Soffer 1999, and Biswas et al. 1997.

4
The Skies and the Winds: Climate

Middle East Climate Factors

Climate has as much direct and indirect impact on people and their activities as any other geographic factor. It affects the clothes people wear, the design of their houses, the vigor of their outdoor labor, the need for energy to cool or heat their homes, and virtually all of their daily activities. In its interaction with other biophysical elements, the role of climate in a given environment is of pervasive significance. Temperature, precipitation, and winds, for example, influence other natural elements in the landscape—vegetation especially but also soils, landforms, and animal life.

Whereas weather is the sum of day-to-day conditions of the atmosphere, climate is the long-term average of those conditions. Thus, climate may be thought of as "statistical weather." Six basic factors of climate in the Middle East, as elsewhere, control climates in general, although they have their own regional characteristics and balance. These six factors are latitude, seasonal pressure belts, passing pressure systems, land-water relationships, ocean currents, and landforms.[1] All of these except ocean currents, which are not of major importance in this area, are examined in their Middle East context.

Latitude

The latitudinal location of a place has two critical direct influences that in turn exercise major indirect influences. First, the latitude determines the angle at which the rays of the sun strike the earth and, thus, basically determines the amount of insolation, or solar radiation, a place receives. Second, as the vertical rays of the sun at noon shift latitudinally with the seasons, belts of atmospheric pressure and winds shift accordingly. Located between 13° and 42° N Lat, the Middle East lies in the lower to middle latitudes. For comparison purposes, all of the United States lies north of 25° N Lat.

Seasonal Pressure Belts

Atmospheric pressure, whether in a belt or in a "cell," influences both horizontal airflow (winds) and whether air in a given belt is descending or rising. Most of the arid southern two-thirds of the Middle East lies much of the year under a subtropical high-pressure belt, a discontinuous east-west zone in which descending dry air heats adiabatically and desiccates by compression. The belt itself is marked by calms; however, once the subsiding air reaches the surface, it pours outward both northward and southward. The airflow toward the equator becomes the northeast trade winds, and the flow toward the pole joins the westerlies. The dry high pressure and the dry trade winds result in desert belts that extend from the Atlantic Ocean eastward across North Africa, such as the great Sahara (Arabic *sahra* = "desert"), then across Arabia and Iran to merge with the interior, midlatitude deserts of central Asia (Fig. 4-1).

The more humid northern third of the Middle East, extending from the Aegean and Mediterranean seas to central Iran, is primarily a zone of transition between pressure belts and generally has a typical Mediterranean climate. In this climate type, conditions alternate between hot, dry summers and cool or cold,

FIGURE 4-1 Giant sand dunes in vast dune field of al-Liwa in southwestern Abu Dhabi, UAE, indicating the extreme desert conditions of the lower Gulf region. Although surficially useless even for nomadic herding, the area has subsurface structures that contain huge petroleum and natural gas reservoirs.

relatively moist, winters. In summer, this zone lies under dry continental trade winds or descending hot, dry air, a seasonal extension of the full desert conditions farther south. In winter, this same zone lies under a belt of stormy westerlies and passing atmospheric depressions that migrate southward during the low-sun season. An added contrast between winter and summer conditions in the southernmost Middle East results from the seasonal reversal of the great Asian pressure systems. It is this reversal, from prevailing high pressure in winter to low pressure in summer, that produces the conditions known as the monsoons ("seasons," from the Arabic *mawsim*).

When the Asian atmospheric conditions reverse in spring with the northward migration of the vertical rays of the sun, the shift in pressure and winds brings with it an equatorial low-pressure belt, or doldrums, technically the Intertropical Convergence Zone (ITCZ).

Extending across the extreme southern Arabian Peninsula, the ITCZ breeds critical late spring and early fall precipitation in Asir and Yemen in the southwestern part of the peninsula and in Dhufar in southern Oman in the southeast.

Passing Pressure Systems

Passing low-pressure systems—depressions or cyclones—are the winter weather makers for the northern and central parts of the Middle East. In autumn, as the vertical rays of the sun at noon shift southward, the belt of the stormy westerlies and the mean position of the polar front also shift southward over the northern half of the region. Within that belt, in response to positioning of the jet stream, cyclonic depressions move periodically from west to east, following several regular tracks through the eastern Mediterranean.

The main paths meet near Cyprus and continue across Lebanon, Syria, and Iraq into Iran, although one track goes north of Asia Minor through the Black Sea. Because of the barrier effect of the north-south mountain ranges in the Levant, plus the frictional effect of the island of Cyprus, the lows tend to pause near that island. This delay gives rise to an average low-pressure center over the eastern Mediterranean during winter months, the Cyprus low, which produces the normally considerable precipitation in the area. Less frequently, depressions cross Israel and Jordan and veer southeastward into the Arabian Peninsula. In most of the region, these weather makers bring the winter precipitation, much of it in the form of snow in the highland areas, that is characteristic of the Mediterranean climate.

Land-Water Relationships

Land-water patterns in the Middle East are major influences on climatic conditions in the region. Since the sea is the ultimate source of all moisture, the presence of water bodies, especially on the windward side, increases the potential for precipitation and humidity. Because of the high specific heat of water, large bodies of water also moderate the temperature of the air above them, warming onshore winds in winter and cooling them in summer in a heat exchange. This phenomenon especially affects the more northern areas, along the Black Sea and Caspian coasts, and along the eastern Mediterranean shores.

Landforms

Topography influences every aspect of climate. Highland areas have lower temperatures; mountain barriers intercept winds and wring moisture from them; mountain masses shunt storms to one side or the other; and open plains give full play to prevailing winds. Highland masses such as the Anatolian Plateau divert passing storms to the north or south, influencing the storm tracks and other climatic elements. Since, in the normal lapse rate, temperature decreases 3.3°F/

1.9°C for each 1,000 ft./305 m of elevation, highland areas enjoy temperatures lower than those of adjacent plains. Many favored mountain areas in the Middle East become resort centers during the hot summers.

Highlands may also produce orographic (mountain-induced) precipitation from moisture-laden winds. Mount Lebanon is a classic example: Moist winds from the Mediterranean blow against the western slopes of the mountains behind Tripoli, Beirut, and Sidon. As the winds move upslope they are rapidly cooled adiabatically at 5.5°F/3.1°C for each 1,000 ft./305 m, reach cloud stage and then dew point, and precipitate rain at middle elevations and snow on the upper slopes (Fig. 4-2). Similar orographic influences operate on the slopes north and south of Mount Lebanon, as well as in the Anatolian, Zagros, Elburz, and Yemen mountains. Areas on the leeward side of mountain chains, by contrast, tend to be drier, or even arid.

Elements of Middle East Climate

The climate factors just reviewed combine to produce various climate characteristics: temperature, winds, precipitation, humidity, and evaporation. Each of these elements is examined for the region as a whole, and the next section looks at how they combine in specific areas to produce certain climate types: deserts, steppes, and humid temperate climates. Temperature and precipitation patterns are shown in two maps, and data for those same elements at selected stations are given in the table at the end of the chapter. The table also gives elevation, latitude and longitude, and climate type for each of the stations, and the patterns of the climate types are given in a third map.

Temperature

Markedly high temperatures prevail more than half of the year in most of the lowland areas of the Middle East. Although July and August are

FIGURE 4-2   The Dahr al-Baydar Pass in central Mount Lebanon with its typical heavy winter snow cover. Moist winds blowing off the Mediterranean ascend the steep slopes and during January to March drop several feet of snow at upper elevations. Apple orchards are on the terraces in foreground. Jabal Baruk is in distance, with one of the remaining groves of Cedars of Lebanon.

the hottest months, the period from April through October is warm to hot in most of the region. Afternoon temperatures of 100°F/38°C are registered in the middle Nile Valley and in the interior of Arabia by early March, and such temperatures may continue well into November.

Lowland desert areas that are located in the interior or are subject to airflow from the interior have the highest average summer temperatures (Map 4-1A). Means of more than 90°F/32°C for the hottest months are common for extensive areas in Iraq, Iran, and especially the Arabian Peninsula. The cloudless summer skies, typical of desert and Mediterranean climate conditions, add to elevated daytime temperatures.

At one desert station—Abqaiq, an oil-production center in eastern Saudi Arabia 27 miles/43 km from the Gulf coast—the averages mask the extremes of temperature. The mean daily temperature for July and

August at Abqaiq is a broiling 98°F/37°C— compared, for example, with 91°F/33°C for Yuma, Arizona, in July, one of the highest monthly means in the United States. However, even more revealing is the average of Abqaiq's daily *maximum* temperatures (afternoon highs) for July, August, and October— 112°F/44°C, 113°F/45°C, and 114°F/45.5°C, respectively. An absolute maximum of 125°F/52°C has been recorded, in July, at Abqaiq, and in many years, fifteen or twenty consecutive weeks will pass during which after-noon highs are never less than 100°F/38°C.

Before the installation of evaporative coolers and then full air conditioning, many older homes in the Middle East included an under-ground room (known as a *sirdab* in Iraq) in which the family sought relief from the summer heat. In the hotter areas, especially along the humid coasts, summer nights bring little respite from the heat of day, either because of a small diurnal range of temperature (difference between day and night) or because of high humidity, or both. In low-income neighborhoods of crowded cities such as Cairo, Baghdad, Abadan, and Aden, and in many villages, families often sleep on the flat roof of the home. By contrast, in open deserts or at considerable elevations, summer nights can be cool or even chilly.

Despite the prevalence of high summer temperatures in the Middle East, the temperature of some interior locations is moderated by elevation. Midsummer afternoon readings exceed 100°F/38°C in Damascus, Tehran, and Amman; but the mean of the warmest month, which includes the lowest daily temperature, is moderate. At these interior locations and elevations, the heat accumulated during the day radiates back into the cloudless sky and dry air, dropping the predawn minimum temperatures to levels 35–40°F/20–22°C below the afternoon maxima. This appreciable diurnal range provides a respite from the enervating, dehydrating heat of the day. Coastal localities generally experience smaller diurnal and seasonal ranges, especially in the eastern Mediterranean.

Several mountain areas have become prosperous summer resorts not only for local lowlanders but also for visitors from the Gulf states, Saudi Arabia, and elsewhere. Resorts in the mountains behind Beirut were crowded with summer residents prior to the outbreak of internal warfare of the mid-1970s, and similar climate areas in the mountains of Syria, Turkey, and Iran offer temperature relief, especially in the evenings. Hamadan, at 5,822 ft./1,775 m in western Iran, served as a summer capital for early Persian kings; and Taif, at about the same elevation in the Hijaz, serves as the Saudi summer capital and resort area.

Cities on the Anatolian and Iranian plateaus combine characteristics of dry highland summers, and thus clear nights, with the effects of lying at a more northerly latitude. For example, the highest mean at Ankara is 25°F/14°C cooler than that at Dhahran near sea level in Saudi

MAP 4-1 Temperatures for warmest and coolest months.

Arabia. At Mashhad, in northeastern Iran (3,232 ft./985 m and 36° N Lat), the July mean is 79°F/26°C.

The degree of contrast between summer and winter temperatures depends primarily on latitude, interior location, and elevation. Samsun, on Turkey's northern coast, and Ankara, 115 miles/185 km inland, have the same August mean temperature; but Samsun's January mean is 12°F/7°C higher than Ankara's because of the warming effect of the Black Sea. The uplands of Anatolia and Iran, with higher elevations and more northerly and continental influences, register the coldest winters of the Middle East. These cold conditions are reflected in the data for Erzurum in eastern Anatolia and for Tabriz in northwestern Iran (see Table 4-1).

TABLE 4-1 SELECTED MIDDLE EAST TEMPERATURES AND PRECIPITATION (°C and mm).

CLIMATE STATION		JAN	FEB	MAR	APR	MAY	JNE	JLY	AUG	SPT	OCT	NOV	DEC	ANNUAL
Istanbul, Turkey	40 m	5	4	5	10	15	20	22	22	18	14	10	7	13°C
40°58'N/29°05'E	Csa	88	80	61	37	32	28	27	22	49	62	87	96	669 mm
Izmir, Turkey	25 m	9	9	11	15	20	25	28	27	23	18	14	10	17°C
38°26'N/27°10'E	Csa	141	100	72	43	39	8	3	3	11	41	93	141	695 mm
Ankara, Turkey	894 m	0	1	5	11	16	20	23	23	18	13	7	2	12°C
30°57'N/32°53'E	Csa	37	36	36	37	49	30	14	9	17	24	30	43	362 mm
Rize, Turkey	4 m	7	7	8	11	16	20	22	23	20	16	12	9	14°C
41°02'N/40°30'E	Cfa	259	215	187	97	97	131	150	211	270	299	278	246	2440 mm
Erzurum, Turkey	1863 m	-9	-7	-3	5	11	15	19	20	15	9	2	-6	6°C
39°55'N/41°16'E	Dfb	29	32	41	53	78	55	31	19	27	49	38	25	476 mm
Anzali, Iran	-15 m	8	8	9	13	19	22	26	25	23	18	14	10	16°C
37°28'N/49°28'E	Cfa	133	125	111	75	56	57	45	131	298	326	227	173	1757 mm
Tabriz, Iran	1362 m	1	1	5	11	16	21	24	25	21	14	6	0	12°C
38°08'N/46°15'E	BSh	15	32	45	47	43	23	11	1	9	14	29	16	285 mm
Esfahan, Iran	1598 m	4	6	10	16	20	25	28	26	23	16	9	4	16°C
32°37'N/51°40'E	BWh	19	16	18	16	8	1	5	1	0	3	19	20	126 mm
Tehran, Iran	1519 m	4	5	10	15	21	26	30	28	25	18	11	5	16°C
35°37'N/51°40'E	BSh	37	23	36	31	14	2	1	1	1	5	29	27	207 mm
Zahedan, Iran	1370 m	6	12	15	19	23	27	28	26	22	18	12	7	18°C
29°28'N/60°53'E	BWh	30	24	14	16	7	0	0	0	0	0	13	9	113 mm
Nicosia, Cyprus	217 m	11	11	12	17	21	26	28	28	25	21	16	12	19°C
35°09'N/33°17'E	Csa	74	43	37	17	21	9	1	2	7	21	32	75	339 mm
Aleppo, Syria	392 m	6	7	10	16	21	25	28	29	24	19	12	8	17°C
36°11'N/37°13'E	Csa	63	46	36	35	14	4	0	2	0	18	27	74	319 mm
Damascus, Syria	729 m	8	9	12	17	21	25	27	28	24	21	14	9	18°C
33°29'N/36°14'E	Csa	54	39	29	15	6	0	0	0	0	5	26	60	234 mm
Dayr al-Zawr, Sy	203 m	8	10	13	19	24	30	32	32	28	21	14	8	20°C
35°20'N/40°09'E	BSh	35	33	32	20	7	2	0	0	0	3	12	33	177 mm
Beirut, Lebanon	16 m	14	14	15	18	21	24	26	27	26	23	19	16	20°C
33°47'N/35°29'E	Csa	113	80	77	26	10	1	0	0	7	20	78	105	517 mm
Bhamdun, Leb	1130 m	7	7	9	13	17	20	22	22	19	17	13	9	15°C
33°46'N/35°39'E	Csa	302	262	194	95	40	1	1	1	3	54	132	239	1324 mm
Jerusalem, Israel	810 m	9	10	12	16	20	22	23	24	22	20	15	11	17°C
31°47'N/35°13'E	Csa	128	106	85	17	4	0	0	0	1	8	61	76	486 mm

CLIMATE STATION		JAN	FEB	MAR	APR	MAY	JNE	JLY	AUG	SPT	OCT	NOV	DEC	ANNUAL
Elat, Israel	11 m	16	18	20	24	29	32	34	34	31	27	22	17	25°C
29°33′N/34°57′E	BWh	2	5	5	3	0	0	0	0	0	0	2	9	26 mm
Amman, Jordan	771 m	8	9	12	16	21	24	25	26	23	21	15	10	18°C
31°57′N/35°57′E	Csa	68	59	44	13	5	0	0	0	1	4	31	48	273 mm
Mosul, Iraq	222 m	6	9	12	17	24	30	34	33	30	20	13	8	20°C
36°19′N/43°09′E	Csa	70	67	65	55	20	1	0	0	0	7	43	62	390 mm
Baghdad, Iraq	34 m	10	12	16	22	28	33	35	34	31	25	17	11	23°C
33°20′N/44°24′E	BWh	25	25	29	16	7	0	0	0	0	3	22	26	153 mm
Basrah, Iraq	2 m	12	14	18	24	29	32	34	33	31	26	19	14	24°C
30°34′N/47°47′E	BWh	26	17	25	22	7	0	0	0	0	1	28	38	164 mm
Kuwait, Kuwait	11 m	14	16	20	26	31	35	37	37	33	27	21	15	26°C
29°20′N/47°57′E	BWh	15	7	8	11	3	0	0	0	0	0	25	41	110 mm
Hayil, Saudi Arabia	914 m	12	13	17	20	25	29	30	31	28	23	19	12	22°C
27°31′N/41°44′E	BWh	9	8	6	11	7	0	0	0	0	11	22	3	77 mm
Dhahran, Saudi Ar	25 m	17	17	22	27	32	35	36	37	34	29	24	18	27°C
26°16′N/50°10′E	BWh	26	15	12	2	3	0	0	0	0	0	4	24	86 mm
Riyadh, Saudi Arab	609 m	16	16	21	26	30	34	40	36	32	25	20	16	26°C
24°42′N/46°43′E	BWh	24	6	6	11	15	0	0	2	0	0	11	7	82 mm
Jiddah, Saudi Arab	12 m	23	23	24	27	30	31	32	31	30	29	27	26	28°C
21°30′N/39°12′E	BWh	17	2	13	11	13	1	0	2	0	0	6	12	77 mm
Sharjah, UAE	2 m	18	18	22	25	28	30	33	34	31	28	24	20	26°C
25°21′N/55°23′E	BWh	34	13	9	18	1	0	2	0	0	0	18	21	116 mm
Muscat, Oman	5 m	22	22	25	29	33	34	33	31	31	30	26	23	28°C
22°37′N/58°35′E	BWh	28	13	10	10	1	3	1	1	1	3	10	18	99 mm
Aden, Yemen	3 m	26	26	27	29	31	33	32	32	32	29	27	26	29°C
12°50′N/45°02′E	BWh	7	3	6	0	1	0	3	2	7	1	3	6	39 mm
Sana, Yemen	2350 m	12	15	16	18	19	20	20	20	18	14	12	11	16°C
15°23′N/44°11′E	BWh	0	4	21	46	46	0	20	102	3	9	0	0	251 mm
Alexandria, Egypt	7 m	15	15	17	19	20	24	26	27	26	24	21	17	21°C
31°12′N/29°57′E	BSh	44	25	11	3	2	0	0	1	1	7	30	48	172 mm
Cairo, Egypt	74 m	14	15	18	21	25	28	29	29	26	24	20	16	22°C
30°08′N/31°34′E	BWh	4	4	3	1	1	0	0	0	0	1	1	7	22 mm
Luxor, Egypt	89 m	14	16	20	25	30	32	32	32	30	27	21	16	25°C
25°40′N/32°42′E	BWh	0	0	0	0	0	0	0	0	0	0	0	0	0 mm

Table includes station latitude and longitude, elevation in meters, and Koeppen classification. See text for explanation of Koeppen symbols. Source: Willy Rudloff. *World Climates*. Stuttgart: Wissenschaftliche Verlagsgesellschaft mbH, 1981 (except Bhambdun and Hayil). (With permission)

Winds

Wind is both a factor and an element in climate. As it transfers large amounts of air from one place to another, wind influences temperature, humidity and precipitation, evaporation, and bodily responses in both people and animals. Higher-velocity winds create or reduce sand dunes by shifting large amounts of sand, and, using sand and other rock particles as tools, they are major agents in desert erosion. On Middle Eastern waterways, mariners have depended upon the steady winds for centuries. The influence of wind on precipitation is of particular significance. Therefore, it is necessary to examine several aspects of winds in the Middle East, especially their role in influencing precipitation, and to discuss the more significant specific winds.

The ITCZ equatorial low-pressure belt, displaced and intensified in its May–August persistence over the Indian subcontinent, controls winds over the entire Middle East for more than four months during the summer monsoon. Whereas wind direction in the Arabian Sea area is prevailingly northeasterly in winter (the northeast monsoon), the summer flow of air is the opposite and is referred to as the southwest monsoon. When the Indus Valley low is deepest in July, the monsoon winds reach gale force over the sea. These winds are so strong that they pull the surface waters away from the south shore of the Arabian Peninsula, causing an upwelling of cool water from the deeps next to the coast and enhancing fishing conditions. Sailors have traditionally followed the summer winds eastward to the Indian subcontinent.

North of the low-pressure belt, air circulation pulls in the northeast trade winds toward the ITCZ. Blowing on clear, cloudless summer days, these strong northerly winds in the Aegean and the Mediterranean are called *etesian* ("annual") winds by the Greeks and *meltimi* by the Turks. Useful to sailors when moderate, the *meltimi* become hazardous when their velocity is higher.

These prevailing winds continue over the low relief of Egypt as normal northeast trade winds, and they blow steadily through the Nile Valley for most of the year. They are of considerable economic value to Egypt, since they fill the sails of hundreds of Nile River boats, *faluqas* (feluccas), as they sail upstream against the Nile current. The *faluqas* then furl their sails for the return trip and drift downstream. On the other side of the Arabian Peninsula, blowing down the Mesopotamian trough and the Gulf basin, is the early summer *shamal* (Arabic for "north"). This dry wind blows at 25–30 mph/40–50 kph in June and early July, bringing frequent dust storms from Mesopotamia before moderating to 15–20 mph/25–32 kph in late summer. At its higher velocities, the *shamal* poses hazards to small sailing dhows and even to terminal loading operations of the huge oil tankers in the Gulf. One of the factors that prompted coalition commanders to decide on the starting date of Desert Storm operations in January 1991 was the intention to expel Iraqi forces from Kuwait before the onset of *shamal*-season sandstorms. If goals were achieved rapidly, such a starting date would also allow completion of the campaign before the winter rains and the ensuing spring and summer heat. Windborne dust is common in all seasons, primarily in the most barren desert areas, which have a minimal vegetative cover to hold the loose soil.

In various other parts of the Middle East where the strong flow of air during the summer monsoon is especially constant, the wind has many local names. For example, in the eastern Iranian province of Sistan, just west of the seasonal low-pressure center, it is called *bad-e sad-o-bist* ("the wind of 120 days"). The prevailing winds are often put to practical use by people. In southern Iran and along the Gulf coasts a traditional and practical architectural feature of many homes is the *badgir*, the so-called Persian wind tower, which uses vertical ducts on a square tower to direct the air downward into rooms below. These wind towers are disappearing, however, as older homes are razed for newer structures and as artificial air-conditioning becomes commonplace (Fig. 4-3).

Cool-season conditions originate in a standard set of meteorological occurrences. As a depression, with its counterclockwise circulation, approaches the eastern Mediterranean from the

FIGURE 4-3   Persian wind towers *(badgirs)*, center, in a historic preservation area of Dubai City surrounded by modern structures. With air conditioning now virtually universal in this cheap-energy region, only a few preserved *badgirs* remain of the thousands formerly common around the Gulf.

west, winds are southerly or southeasterly on the front of the low and will pull warm or even hot air out of the Sahara into the Mediterranean coastal areas. The southerly winds in the southeastern quadrant of the low are often dry and dusty as well as warm. Such conditions are especially likely in spring and autumn.

Through much of the Mediterranean Basin, the hot, dry wind on the front of a passing low is called a *sirocco,* originally an Italian word derived from the Arabic *sharq* ("east"). Siroccotype winds, similar to the Santa Anas in California, desiccate the landscape, wither leaves and fruit on trees, render the brush vegetation susceptible to fires, and cause respiratory difficulties for people. As the depression tracks eastward, the winds have local names in the areas through which the system moves: *Jibli* ("south" or "southeast") in Libya, *khamsin* (Arabic for "fifty," probably suggesting the average number of days it might blow) in Egypt, *shlur shluq* in Lebanon and Syria, *sharqi* in Iraq, *kaws* ("the archer") in the Gulf, and *simoon* ("poison") in parts of the Gulf area are examples. In the Gulf,

strong southwestern winds known locally as *swahili* ("coastal") replace the *kaws.*

Some winds can start out quite cold in winter when the air is pulled out of the elevated northern plateaus, but they warm by compression in descending from the plateaus and can raise temperatures rapidly at the foot of the slope. Such winds are known as foehn winds in the Alps and as chinook winds on the eastern slopes of the Rocky Mountains in North America. Strong foehn-like winds known as *raghiehs* blow along the coasts of Turkey and Syria in the northeastern Mediterranean, originating from the plateau north of the Taurus Mountains. *Nashi,* northeasterly winds along the southern coast of Iran, likewise come from the plateau behind the coast and have a foehn effect.

Precipitation

Climate is the single most influential factor among Middle East biophysical patterns, and of the various climatic elements, the significance of precipitation must be emphasized. One clear indication of its significance is the immediately apparent evidence of the correlation between the areas of heavier precipitation (or runoff from heavy precipitation) and the areas of concentrations of population in the Middle East. Water plays a vital role even in those regions of the world in which it is plentiful, but its role in the Middle East, where water supplies are marginal in so much of the region, is critical. Water is life.

High seasonal temperatures in much of the Middle East typically accompany low seasonal precipitation. Thus, dryness is the key word for the climate in most of this region. At the extreme, the interior of the southern half of the Arabian Peninsula, the Rub al-Khali, is probably as dry as any area of comparable size on earth.

In the remaining interior of the peninsula, called Arabia Deserta (although the Roman term actually was applied to far northern Arabia), as well as in northern Egypt and in the Syrian Desert, vast areas have only 1–5 in./25–125 mm of precipitation annually (Map 4-2). This zone of aridity is too far south to benefit from the invasion of the westerlies in winter and too far north to receive rain from the ITCZ in summer. Map 4-2 also shows, however, that much of the northern quarter of the Middle East receives 15–40 in./380–1,015 mm of precipitation. Obviously, a rather sharp contrast exists in rainfall amounts, and thus in vegetation and agriculture, between the northern one-fourth and the southern three-fourths of the region. Except in the southern Arabian Peninsula and in limited areas in the north, by far the most of the Middle East's precipitation falls during the months October–April, which is typical of the Mediterranean climate (cf. Beirut, Jerusalem, and Mosul in Table 4-1).

Precipitation at desert stations varies greatly from year to year, so that the percentage variation can be high because of the limited amounts involved. By its very nature, desert rainfall tends to be sporadic, often coming in sudden, brief downpours that are sharply restricted in area; however, broad frontal rains do sometimes occur and are also important. The sudden rains penetrate quickly into the porous ground in a sand desert area to produce a prompt growth of grass and flowers, which soon attract Bedouin herdsmen with their camels, sheep, or goats. In a rocky area with only a limited sand sponge and with no vegetation to absorb the rain, the runoff quickly concentrates into the local wadis—dry drainage channels, sometimes so broad and flat that they are hardly perceptible as drainage lines—and causes flash floods.

Typical desert precipitation conditions exist at Dhahran, the oil center in eastern Saudi Arabia and a station with good climate records. With an average annual rainfall of 3.4 in./86 mm (slightly less than that of Yuma, Arizona), the station had a 93 percent negative departure from "normal" in 1970 when only 0.24 in./6 mm of rain fell during the entire year. Similarly, it had a 322 percent positive variation in 1976 when 10.9 in./277 mm fell. In 1974 nearly 5 in./118 mm fell at Dhahran in the month of December.

North of the zone of maximum aridity in the Egyptian and Arabian deserts, precipitation nearly everywhere is concentrated in the winter season, and annual totals generally increase with increasing latitude, elevation, and western exposure. The effect of latitude is exemplified by the south-to-north increase in rainfall shown by the data for Luxor, Cairo, Alexandria, Gaza, Tel Aviv, Haifa, and Beirut.

Rarely is there measurable rainfall in the central third of the Middle East between May and September. In Dhahran, no rain has been recorded between late May and early November since the station opened in the late 1930s—although there was one freak heavy summer rain in Abqaiq. Thus, the hottest time of the year is rainless, with all that implies for people and vegetation, including crops.

The mountains in the southwestern corner of Turkey are an example of the orographic influence of west-facing slopes as they receive more than 60 in./1,525 mm of precipitation during the winter. The mountains of northern Lebanon also receive about the same amount, much of it as heavy snows, the basis for several ski resorts such as the Cedars. Depressions

MAP 4-2 Middle East precipitation. Note heavy orographic precipitation on mountains rimming Asia Minor and on other mountain ranges—Elburz, Zagros, Lebanon, Asir, and Oman.

reaching the southeastern corner of the Black Sea rise up mountain slopes and yield more than 90 in./2,285 mm at Rize, probably the highest total precipitation in the Middle East. Inland, 25–40 in./635–1,015 mm of precipitation, much of it as snow, falls on the upper ridges of the Zagros Mountains and the higher slopes of the eastern Anatolian mountains. The slow melting of the deep snows in the eastern Anatolian hydrographic center during the spring and early summer supplies the runoff for the Tigris and Euphrates rivers and other streams that have their headwaters in these highlands.

Snow falls every winter in the uplands of the Middle East north of about 33° N Lat. Once or twice in most winters it also falls as far south as the Jerusalem hill country (which received 3 ft./ 0.9 m of snow in 1920) and the southern highlands of Jordan. In early 1992, heavy snow— from 12 to 20 in./350 to 508 mm—fell in Damascus, Jerusalem, and Amman in January and again in February. After the dry late 1990s, heavy snows blanketed the Levant in late January 2000—15 to 24 in./381 to 610 mm in Jerusalem and Amman and even 6 in./152 mm in the Negev. The Syrian and Mesopotamian deserts receive occasional snowfalls, and it has snowed in Riyadh and even—in 1987, for the first time in memory or records—in the Buraymi Oasis on the United Arab Emirates-Oman border.

In the southwestern corner of the Arabian Peninsula, the Yemen Mountains and their extension northward into the Asir of Saudi Arabia intercept moisture-laden southwest monsoon winds between April and September, producing 20–40 in./500–1,000 mm of orographic rain on the west-facing slopes. Because of this relatively abundant rainfall, the area earned the ancient designation Arabia Felix (Fortunate Arabia). Lying between 13° and 17° N Lat, the Yemen Mountains receive monsoon rains in two periods during the shifting of the vertical rays of the sun, northward in late April—early May, southward in August. Thus, the area has a double-maximum precipitation regime, with rain in spring and again, more plentifully, in late summer with a dry early summer in between. Such a regime reveals the role of the migrating equatorial low pressure zone, the ITCZ (see Sana, Table 4-1). Similarly, the lingering ITCZ creates a local cool, cloudy, misty summer in Dhufar, southern Oman.

Averages of precipitation obscure the important variability of amounts received from year to year in even the more humid areas as well as in the deserts. The recent effects of El Niño and La Niña on global weather patterns are indicative of the differences in precipitation patterns that have been typical of the Middle East for millennia. A low-rainfall year in the Levant, for example, not only radically reduces the yield of wheat and other major crops, but also reduces the recharge water for aquifers, springs, and wells furnishing basic supplies of water for irrigation and domestic use. The dry year of 1998–1999 in the Levant reduced lakes and reservoirs to a critical level, whereas the wet winter of 1999–2000 brought floods and rising water levels. Details are given in Chapters 14 and 15.

Humidity

Three generalizations can be made about humidity in the Middle East. First, generally low humidity characterizes deserts and higher elevations—the year-round low humidity in Egypt has preserved human and animal mummies and delicate inlaid wood for more than 5,000 years. At stations in the interior deserts, the average relative humidity for the three summer months varies between 12 and 18 percent, with minima falling to 5 percent and occasionally even to an extreme 3 percent. With temperatures of 100°–120°F/38°–50°C and winds of 10–20 mph/16–32 kph, such low humidity parches the skin, causes nosebleeds, and scorches vegetation.

Second, the humidity along the coasts, even in arid areas, tends to be quite high, causing an uncomfortable combination of heat and humidity in summer. Such coastal cities as Beirut, Tel Aviv, and Alexandria on the Mediterranean; Ramsar on the southwestern Caspian coast; Jiddah on the Red Sea; and Kuwait, Manama, Dammam, and Abu Dhabi on the Gulf are very humid (70–75 percent average relative humidity) during August and early September. In comparison, Riyadh, in the interior of Saudi Arabia, has humidities of 49 percent in January and 15 percent in August. As one consequence of the high coastal humidity, heavy dew accompanies the predawn drop in temperature resulting from nighttime heat radiation into the clear air. Along the Mediterranean coast near Tel Aviv, dew falls an average of 200 nights each year, reaching a cumulative total equal to 1.2 in./30 mm of rain.

The third generalization is that humidity is moderate and exercises no remarkable effects in much of Asia Minor. Ankara, Sivas, and Erzurum all have percentages within a moderate range.

Evaporation

Evaporation plays a key role in determining aridity, but unlike temperature and precipitation, it is difficult to measure precisely, and no universally practiced system has been adopted to record it. If the mean water loss exceeds the mean precipitation annually, conditions tend toward aridity. Measurements of evaporation in central Saudi Arabia show rates ranging from 35 to 100 times the local mean annual rainfall. Actual evaporation in al-Sulayyil, in the southern Najd, for example, averages 207 in./5,250 mm annually,[2] more than 100 times the mean annual rainfall. Similar conditions exist in southern Egypt—where evaporation from Lake Nasser is a major problem—and southern Iran. However, other influences—season of precipitation, temperature, soil conditions—can be of major importance and can affect the ecology. Other factors being equal, natural vegetation is indicative of aridity and indirectly of evaporation.

Climate Regions

The preceding analysis of factors and elements in the climate of the Middle East and description of sample areas permit a synthesis of the elements into specific regional climate types. Such a synthesis requires both a system to determine the climate types and also the drawing of approximate boundaries between the regional types. The widely used classification developed by W. Koeppen and R. Geiger can be meaningfully applied to the Middle East (Map 4-3).[3] Each of the stations listed in Table 4-1 is assigned its Koeppen climate classification, and it is instructive to see how individual stations (shown on Map 4-3 by initials) fit into the patterns of climate types.

More than 85 percent of the Middle East is dominated by dry or summer-dry climates. In Koeppen's year-round dry (B) climates, evaporation exceeds precipitation; but degrees of dryness separate B climates into arid (BW) and semiarid or steppe (BS), which is characteristic of a short grassland vegetation area. Nearly half the Middle East is actual desert, BW; another 18–20 percent is steppe, BS. The division is economically important, since nomadic herding predominates on the dry side of the steppe, whereas barley and even wheat can be grown in most years on the moist side of the steppe. Most of the BW/BS climates are hot in summer and either warm or mild in winter, thus falling into

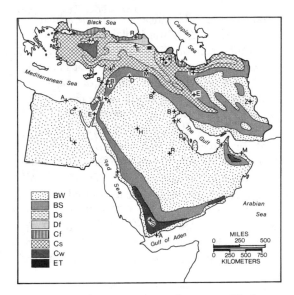

MAP 4-3   Climate types according to modified Koeppen system. BW = desert, BS = steppe. Initials indicate climate stations listed in Table 4-1. See text for explanation of other symbols.

the Koeppen category of BWh or BSh ("h" signifies hot or warm). The dry climates in areas of high elevation fall below the boundary between hot and cold and are therefore BWk or BSk.

Still another third of the region receives sufficient precipitation to balance or outweigh evaporation, although nearly all of it falls during the cool months, November–April. This cool-season precipitation evaporates less than summer moisture and is therefore more effective. These areas of Mediterranean-type climate are designated Cs by Koeppen ("C" indicates a mesothermal, temperate climate; "s" indicates summer dry). The warmer areas of Cs climate are classed as Csa, the cooler areas Csb. The Csa climate is the typical Mediterranean climate, continuous along the shores of the Levant and western and southern Asia Minor. An upland Cs extends along the highland Fertile Crescent, along the Zagros, and into northeastern Iran.

The climate of a small area in Yemen is similar to the Csa except that its rain comes mostly in summer, during the summer monsoon, a condition identified by Koeppen as Cwa ("w" indicates winter dry), a cooler version of the savanna climate. If sufficient data were available, a small area of Cwa might also be identified in the Dhufar area of southern Oman. Tundra climate occurs on a few high mountaintops in eastern Anatolia and northern Iran (ET on Map 4-3).

Adding to the complexity of the climates of the Anatolian and Iranian plateaus are four limited areas with conditions unusual for the Middle East. Two areas along the southern coast of the Black Sea and two along the southern coast of the Caspian receive sufficient precipitation in summer as well as in winter to be recognized as year-round moist climate areas, Cfa ("f" indicates moist all year). Also unusual for the Middle East are several interior mountain areas in Turkey and Iran with sufficiently cold winters to place them

in the Koeppen D category (microthermal, continental climates). Whereas these types of climate cover two-thirds of North America, they are relatively limited in the Middle East.

Notes

1. Factors and elements of Middle East climate are examined in Taha et al. 1981 and Rudloff 1981. Interesting data are in the Arabian American Oil Company n.d. (ca. 1978), which is unfortunately hard to find. Additional climate maps and diagrams are included in most good world atlases.

2. Mandaville 1990, quoting Saudi Arabia's Ministry of Agriculture and Water data.

3. Several sources describe the system, including Goode's World Atlas 1999.

5
Soils, Vegetation, and Animal Life

Ecological Relationships and Soils

Elements of the environment exert complex reciprocal effects—between topography and climate, between climate and vegetation, between vegetation and soils, between climate and soils—and the human element adds still other types and degrees of reciprocal influences. These ecological interactions constitute a fundamental dynamic in the geographic system, and it follows that a change in any one element in the ecosystem generates a change in the system as a whole.

A soil is the product of several environmental factors: climate, parent material, vegetation, fauna (especially including man), relief, and time. A comparison of Maps 3-1, 4-2, 4-3, and the second map in this chapter suggests a pattern among the factors that influence the general character of soils in the Middle East.

For example, predominant aridity and heat are two of the strongest general influences on the soils of the vast area from western Egypt to eastern Iran, excluding Asia Minor and the Levant. Limited vegetation cover in this same general area, also largely a consequence of aridity, deprives soils of humus. Extensive limestone and sandstone outcroppings, as well as loose sand, also profoundly affect soil characteristics. Mountain soils are especially influenced by relief, specifically the slope on which they develop. Proper management is important for all soils, and one characteristic that is amenable to management is soil salinity, a serious problem especially in southern Mesopotamia but also in most desert areas where crops are irrigated on poorly drained land.

Middle East soils are as varied as other aspects of the regional environment. Not only do soils of the Turkish forests differ markedly from those of the Syrian steppes, but the prevailing types of desert soils over extensive desert areas also exhibit subtle but important variations. Moreover, large desert areas are totally lacking in true soils—widespread expanses of sand and virtually bare rock are obvious examples. The surface materials in much of the Middle East have not developed a soil "profile," a cross section that reveals identifying horizons (the vertical sequence of colors and textures that differentiate soils).

Lack of a mature soil profile results from several ecological conditions, including extreme aridity. In arid areas, there is no soil water to move downward and leach chemicals and other materials into the lower horizons of the soil profile. Also, where a vegetation cover is limited, sudden heavy but infrequent rains and frequent strong winds cause surface materials to erode rapidly, thus preventing profile development.

With little or no organic matter on the surface or in the upper horizon of soils, especially those of desert areas, soils of light color predominate in the region. Light color likewise prevails in soils that have an accumulation of salt near the surface. Around the desert margins, in semiarid and subhumid environments, most of the soils have an elevated calcium content, often from the underlying limestone that is frequently the parent

MAP 5-1   Middle East soils. (Adapted from several sources, especially the UNESCO world soils map and Clawson et al. 1971)

material. However, soil calcium also builds up
in moisture-deficient areas because soluble
products of weathering accumulate within
the upper horizons of the soil to form calcium carbonate and soluble salts. In moderate
amounts, both salt and gypsum reduce soil
productivity, and in large quantities they render soils unfit for cultivation.

Thus, agriculture in desert areas is limited
not only directly by aridity but also indirectly
by the effects of aridity on soil development.
There are, nevertheless, exceptionally productive soils in certain desert areas—in numerous oases, the Nile Valley and Delta, and the

floodplains of the Tigris and Euphrates rivers,
for example (Map 5-1).

However, it is in the coastal plains, plateaus,
and rolling lands of the northern and northwestern areas of the Middle East that soils have
reached mature development because of humid,
temperate conditions. In Asia Minor, western
Iran, and the Fertile Crescent, where annual precipitation exceeds 10 in./255 mm and averages
perhaps 25 in./635 mm, there are extensive areas
of well-developed and productive soils (Map 5-1).
These regions exhibit greater varieties of soil
groups as well as greater variations within the
groups.

Middle East Soil Patterns

Soil taxonomy—the systematic classification and nomenclature of soils—has been a problem ever since the burgeoning of soil science. Unlike flora, fauna, rocks, and similar landscape elements, soils were often classified and named by different soil scientists according to different characteristics and genetic factors. A general ecological-genetic system developed by the Russians was widely used—but also widely debated—for several decades before the 1970s. Of several national systems that have emerged, the U.S. "Seventh Approximation," published by the Department of Agriculture in 1975 in its *Soil Taxonomy,* has been the most influential. Based on inherent soil characteristics, the classification is highly scientific and precise. However, since its precision introduces technical detail that is confusing to the nonspecialist, the following discussion utilizes a simpler taxonomy based on the traditional ecological-genetic concept.

Barren Sands and Rock and Other Non-Soils

Generally speaking, the area of barren land and desert soils in the Middle East extends southward, southeastward, and eastward from the 10-in./ 250-mm rainfall line (compare Map 4-2). Approximately half of the surface of the roughly 2 million miles^2/5.2 million km^2 extending from western Egypt across the Arabian Peninsula and the Syrian Desert to eastern Iran is so barren that it lacks either true soil or appreciable vegetation cover. Much of the barren area is gravel and loose sand, including dune sand (see Figs. 1-1 and 5-1a); much of the rest is virtually bare rock. Prominent sand areas include western Egypt and, on the Arabian Peninsula, the Great Nafud in the north and the enormous Rub al-Khali in the south, with the arc of Dahna sands connecting the two. Huge gravel plains lacking true soils extend across the north of the Arabian Peninsula and appear in extensive patches in the eastern third of the peninsula.

Large areas of Lithosols (rock soils) extend along the east side of the Levant Rift System-Red Sea rift on the basaltic lava outpourings. A particularly common type of landscape in this area is the *hamadah,* typically an extensive plain with barren rock or a surface cover of stones and pebbles (Fig. 3-2). Actual soil development is limited, and vegetal cover is generally lacking. Even larger areas of Lithosols extend over the limestones of eastern Syria and Jordan, of Iraq west of the Euphrates, and along the axis of the north-south escarpments in central Arabia shown in Chapter 17. Soils of the Lithosol group are also intermixed with varied Mountain soils in all the mountainous areas of the Middle East, especially those in the southern and southwestern sectors. These soils are grouped with Undifferentiated Mountain soils on Map 5-1.

True Soils of the Desert

The other half of the desert areas referred to above contains true soils, with developed profiles and vegetation cover: Desert soils, Red Desert soils, Sierozem soils, and Solonchak (salty) soils. All except Solonchaks are grouped as Undifferentiated Desert soils on Map 5-1. Some profiles are weakly developed, and some of the vegetation is thin and scattered; but the landscape is less barren than the desert areas of Egypt, the Nafud, and the Rub al-Khali.

Desert soils are light gray or light brownish-gray, are low in organic matter, and closely overlie calcareous (calcium-containing) material, typically limestone. They normally support scattered shrubby desert plants but can be quite productive when irrigated. Much the same may be said of the Red Desert soils, although they are reddish in the upper part of the profile, as the name suggests, and they tend to develop in the hotter parts of the deserts. Sierozems are more widely scattered but are found in two large areas: on the floor of the great central basin of Turkey, around Tuz Gölü, and in much of northern Syria, where they support scattered short grass and brush as well as desert shrubs.

FIGURE 5-1   Eastern Arabia vegetation and soils: *Adhir* and *rimth* bushes on compact sandy soils southwest of Dhahran *(top)*, with tracks indicating grazing of the vegetation by animals; and Sabkhat Matti, a typical *sabkhah* (tidal salt flat) *(bottom)*. With a white crust of silty salt, such flats are inviting to vehicles and aircraft, but using them can be risky, especially after a rain. The soil on the *sabkhah* is a Solonchak, as the salt crust suggests.

Solonchak soils are especially found in large interior undrained basins and low-lying areas: the Dasht-e Lut and the even saltier Dasht-e Kavir (Salt Desert) on the Iranian Plateau; the Qattara Depression in northwestern Egypt; southern Mesopotamia back from the river floodplains; in the tidal flats (*sabkhahs*) along low coastlines on both sides of the Arabian Peninsula; and over the inland coastal plain of the Gulf (Fig. 5-1b and Map 5-1). Either because of interior drainage or periodic tides, all these areas have high saltwater tables that supply salty water to the surface, evaporation of which forms the typical salt crust of Solonchaks. Most Solonchaks are useless for agriculture, but some can be made reasonably productive by artificially flushing the salt with fresh water and then applying proper fertilization. The area suffering most seriously from salt accumulation in otherwise irrigable and cultivable soils is southern Iraq.

Alluvial Soils

Alluvial soils—or, more properly, soils on alluvium as a parent material—appear in only relatively limited areas in the extensive desert lands of the area. However, these limited alluvial soil areas are among the most intensively cultivated and productive in the world, certainly in the Middle East. They include the rich soils of the Nile Valley and Delta, floodplains of the Tigris and Euphrates rivers, valleys of west-central Iran, and small scattered oases and larger wadi bottoms of the Arabian Peninsula (see Map 5-1). They possess young profiles, are usually of good texture and tillability, and display most of the other characteristics of an ideal agricultural soil. Moreover, water for irrigating the soils is typically nearby.

Soils of the Humid Areas

Except for the irrigated alluvial soils, most of the cultivated and agriculturally productive soils of the Middle East are those of Asia Minor, the Fertile Crescent proper, and western Iran. On the inner, less humid side of the curve of the Fertile Crescent, there is an irregular belt of grassland soils that have developed in a zone receiving 6-10 in./150-250 mm of annual precipitation. They belong, in groups of decreasing aridity, to the traditional Reddish-Brown, Chestnut, and Reddish-Chestnut groups (grouped as steppe soils on Map 5-1; see Fig. 5-2). Such soils vary from well-developed and deep to poorly developed and thin on hillsides. Most are calcareous, especially since many overlie the widespread limestones of Jordan, Syria, southeastern Turkey, and Iraq. They receive sufficient precipitation to permit grain farming without irrigation.

In a major portion of the Mediterranean climate areas, a particular group of soils develops because of the regime of cool, wet winters and hot, dry summers. Usually called Mediterranean soils (as on Map 5-1), they are of a reddish-brown color, because of their iron content, and are referred to as *terra rossa* ("red earth"). In recent years, *terra rossa* has received increasing consideration as more of a red clay parent material for the true soil. Especially in early spring, this soil contrasts dramatically with the white limestone hills that surround pockets of the soil in southern Turkey and the Levant. Although this soil has eroded badly on the limestone slopes in many areas, it has been productive for thousands of years throughout the Mediterranean Basin.

Rendzina soil is also derived from limestones, usually the softer types such as marls, and it is often associated with *terra rossa.* Usually gray or black, in contrast to the rust of the *terra rossa,* it is also calcareous, clayey, and productive. It alternates with *terra rossa* in the uplands inland from the Levant coast from northwestern Syria south to Beer Sheva in Israel (its occurrences are too limited to show on Map 5-1).

Most of the remaining soil pattern is a complex one, forming a mosaic of Noncalcic Brown soils, Brown Forest soils, and Lithosols and other Mountain soils of Anatolia, northwestern Iran, and the mountains behind the eastern Mediterranean coast. These soil associations produce a great variety of foods, fodder, and industrial crops, including timber forests and tree crops of nuts or fruits, on moderate slopes in the better climate areas.

FIGURE 5-2   Cultivated Reddish-Chestnut steppe soils in the western Fertile Crescent south of Aleppo, Syria. This is productive wheat country. Archaeological excavations in foreground are of ancient Ebla.

Vegetation

As an effective product of interacting influences on landscape, the natural vegetation of an area is often indicative of the general character of the local precipitation, temperature, soil, animal life, pressure of human population, and other aspects. Like the region's topography and soils, Middle East vegetation has also undergone natural changes during recent geological times. Certain plants are survivals from earlier periods; other plants from those periods have completely disappeared, from either natural or human causes, and their former presence is indicated only by seeds, spores, fruits, or leaves in old lake beds or in archaeological mounds (tells).

Human activities, including agricultural exploitation, have decisively altered vegetation, soil, drainage, and other aspects of the environment in the millennia since the Agricultural Revolution and the first Neolithic settlements.

Unfortunately, the human impact on natural vegetation in the Middle East has been one of destruction as well as change. People have cleared forests not only to gain land for agricultural purposes but also to obtain timber and fuel. Cedars of Lebanon and other trees of the Levant supplied timbers for Egyptian and Phoenician ships, as did trees from Anatolia for ships of the Greeks, Romans, Byzantines, and Ottomans. Wood has also been employed in the Middle East for making charcoal, long used in heating and cooking and in lime and pottery kilns. Not only trees but also grasses, shrubs, and other low vegetation have been degraded or destroyed because of human activity and because of overgrazing by sheep and goats.

Humans have also changed vegetation without destroying it, as, for example, by exploiting a particular tree or plant and/or altering the floristic composition or geographical range of a species. Only in the remotest areas of the Middle

MAP 5-2 Middle East natural vegetation. Both "Grassland" and "Semi-desert" may be roughly equivalent to steppe.

East does the original type of vegetation remain; and, except in cultivated areas, the change has primarily been one of vegetal degradation.

Middle East Vegetation Patterns

Varied vegetation types extend from the dense high forests inland from the Black Sea and Caspian coasts to the scattered desert shrub of the Arabian Peninsula and the barren, salty *kavirs* of the interior Iranian Plateau (Map 5-2). Notwithstanding extensive forests in several northern mountain areas, the vegetal formations occupying the greatest expanses of the region are annual grasses and broadleaf annuals and shrubs of the steppes and deserts.

Rather specialized scrub forms, known by their French names *maquis* and *garigue,* are typical of the Mediterranean areas with their cool, wet winters and hot, rainless summers (Fig. 5-3).

The phytogeographical (phyto = "plant") patterns examined in this section are primarily the plant associations, inferred from existing vegetation in noncultivated areas, that would exist without human interference.[1]

Desert Shrub

The desert is the product of aridity, and its xerophytic (dry plant) vegetation gives the desert its true expression. The desert environment supplies plants with favorable warmth and light but then imposes unfavorable moisture

FIGURE 5-3 Typical Mediterranean flora on south-facing slopes of the Taurus Mountains of southern Turkey. Growing in limestone-derived soil in this summer-dry climate, the taller vegetative association is maquis, the lower is garigue. The road in lower left fringes the Mediterranean shore.

conditions. Some desert plants tolerate drought, some resist it, and some avoid it. When water occasionally does become available, plants respond immediately and profusely.

Areas that are barren of vegetation are generally coextensive with the areas of barren sands, rock, and salt surfaces on the soil map (Map 5-1), as well as with the areas that receive less than 1 in./25 mm of annual rainfall—even so, the Rub al-Khali has areas that have a surprisingly well-developed vegetation. Deserts that are truly barren of vegetation are less common than is often supposed, and the typical desert exhibits at least a scattering of especially equipped dry bush or shrub (see Fig. 5-1a).

Beginning with its small size—3–5 ft./ 1–1.5 m—and the wide spacing among individual plants to accommodate the limited supply of moisture, xerophytic vegetation has an impressive array of survival devices. With low shoot-to-root ratios, some shrubs have root systems that extend to depths of 30–50 ft./ 9–15 m. Their leaves are small, are often coated against excess transpiration (moisture loss), and in some species curl or even drop

during unusually dry periods. Tough stems resist drought, and the shrubs often have thorns for protection against grazing animals. Some of the lower bushes, 6–18 in./15–46 cm high, have woody or wiry stems and tiny leaves but a deep root system. By contrast, other desert plants, such as *Euphorbia,* store water in expandable succulent parts.

Scattered among the perennial and often long-lived shrubby plants are other low vegetal forms (4–12 in./10–30 cm) that sometimes constitute more than two-thirds of the typical desert plant community, including some species of grasses and many herbaceous forms. Some of these small plants are perennial, some are annual, and a few are both, depending upon their ecology. Most of the herbaceous annuals have an ephemeral life cycle of six to ten weeks, after which they lie dormant as seeds that burst into sprouts with the next rain, sometimes several years later. Along with a few of the xeromorphic perennial shrubs, they "avoid" the dry season instead of trying to endure it.

Shrubs in extensive fields of eolian (wind-blown) sand may be passive sand dwellers or sand binders; the latter hold the sand around extensive root systems and thus build prominent phytogenic (plant-created) mounds or hillocks. The resulting landscape, usually called *dikakah* or *marbakh* in Arabia, makes cross-country travel difficult. Some salty soils support halophytic (salt plant) vegetation. Over much of the eastern Arabian Peninsula, a common saltbush, popularly called *rimth*—useful for fodder and dietary salt for camels and other animals—is usually associated with at least slightly salty groundwater in poorly drained areas. However, on the true *sabkhahs* along the eastern Arabian Peninsula coast and on the *kavirs* of interior Iran, with their salt crust and briny subsurface, not even the most salt-tolerant plants can survive (see Fig. 5-1b).[2]

The acacia, one of the largest desert shrubs, grades into a modest tree—up to 20 ft.—in moister soils. With its characteristic umbrella crown, it is a prominent and readily identifiable vegetative form in the silts, sands, and gravels in drainage channels or sheets from the central to the southern Arabian Peninsula. Where no other shade is available, it offers shade to animal and man in the broiling sun.

Grasslands (Steppes)

The change from desert to grassland is actually a zone of transition, and the exact boundary between the two is difficult to delineate because many of the desert species carry over into the adjoining grasslands. As moisture increases away from the desert, the more xerophytic species increasingly yield to plants adapted to the greater precipitation and better developed soils. More important, plant population density increases until the grasses form a virtually continuous vegetal cover.

The steppes constitute a discontinuous belt extending from the Sinai Peninsula northward through western Jordan and Syria, across southeastern Turkey and northern Syria, in an arc around northern Iraq, and along the Zagros piedmont. There are also some of the region's most extensive steppes in central Anatolia and smaller areas in scattered locations in west-central Iran. (Steppe and semidesert are

much the same in many areas, as is noted in the caption for Map 5-2.) With their short-grass vegetation, the steppelands are thus the core of the Fertile Crescent, with all that fact implies historically and agriculturally.

Mediterranean Zone

Whereas desert and steppe plants are especially equipped to survive a drought that lasts even many years, Mediterranean flora survive the characteristic summer drought of two to six months and then take advantage of the winter rain. Such flora appears as a low evergreen forest with scattered small trees and more closely spaced bushes and scrub. The height of the plants and the density of their growth increase from the dry side (approximately along the 15-in./380-mm isohyet) to the more humid part of the habitat, where the summer drought is also shorter (Fig. 5-3). On the dry side, the Mediterranean vegetation zone is similar to the wooded steppe. On the humid side, the zone grades into the full forest of the highlands across the northern sector of the Middle East.

In between is the typical Mediterranean flora that may be divided into two main groups: garigue, the lower and more degraded of the flora, and maquis, the taller and better developed association. Some plant geographers also distinguish a third category of Mediterranean vegetation, *batha*, a kind of subgarigue. Both maquis and garigue are found in Mediterranean climate areas across southern Europe and elsewhere. In southern California, for example, similar vegetation is called "chaparral."

Garigue includes primarily a sclerophyllous (hard-leafed) scrub about 3 ft./1 m in height and also smaller shrubs, grass, and in spring, many colorful flowers—anemone, ranunculus, crocus, iris, and others. Commonly found on steeper, uncultivated hillsides in the Levant and in western and southern Asia Minor, garigue is a last safeguard against soil erosion. Maquis, which is typical of more favorable habitats than is garigue, forms a woodland dominated by low sclerophyllous evergreen trees and shrubs up to about 12 ft./3.7 m in height. In better stands of maquis, one finds trees—oaks, pistachios, and pines, especially the widespread Aleppo pine. Culinary herbs, such as thyme, marjoram, and laurel, and flowering bushes, such as oleanders, are associated with both garigue and maquis.

Forests

Few areas in the Middle East now have woodlands as well developed as those in Europe and North America, but historical evidence indicates that 2,500–3,000 years ago, forests clothed slopes that are now almost bare or are ragged—forests such as the Cedars of Lebanon or the forests of Asia Minor. Current reforestation and afforestation programs in several Middle East states are demonstrating that many previously treeless habitats can, given proper care, produce impressive forests of selected species.

The region's most extensive high forests extend along the Pontic Mountains from Istanbul eastward to the Iranian border and include impressive stands of beech, mixed with areas of spruce (especially *Picea orientalis*) in the east. On the southern, inner slopes of the Pontic Mountains, and especially in the western highlands, there are extensive areas of oak and pine (*Pinus nigra* and *P. silvestris* in the north and *P. brutia* in the west). *P. nigra* and *P. brutia* dominate the forests of the Taurus Mountains across southern Anatolia, and oaks predominate in the southeastern mountains west and south of Lake Van.

The great Euxinian Forest of northern Anatolia extends, with some discontinuity, into northern Iran to link up with the Hyrcanian or Caspian Forest in the Elburz Mountains. This humid forest facing the Caspian Sea is almost tropical in its luxuriance, with a rich variety of undergrowth as well as tall trees: linden, ash, oak, beech, elm, hornbeam, walnut, maple, and evergreens. Beech, dominant on the lower open slopes, is gradually replaced higher up, so that at 6,000–8,000 ft./1,830–2,440 m one finds the most magnificent trees in the Middle East—primarily oaks (*Quercus macranthera* and others) but also elm, ash, hornbeam, and maple.

In the higher elevations of the Zagros chains there is a somewhat dry, deciduous forest in which oaks dominate. With smaller and more widely spaced trees, and with a limited number of species, this Zagrosian Forest differs appreciably from the humid Euxinian and Hyrcanian forests.

In the west, scattered woodlands survive in areas of former extensive forests in the Levant highlands—in Israel, Jordan, Lebanon, Syria—and on the island of Cyprus (Fig. 5-4). Most of these forests are either small remnants of great expanses of trees in the past, the Cedars of Lebanon, for example, or are woodlands planted in recent decades through government programs of reforestation or afforestation.

The endemic Aleppo pine, *Pinus halepensis*, is the tree most frequently planted in these programs. Sometimes called the "umbrella pine," it has come to be identified with the Levant highlands. Efforts to regenerate forests of Cedars of Lebanon (*Cedrus libani*) have encountered many problems, especially slow growth. The broad-leaved tree most often used in plantation programs is a rapidly growing oak, *Quercus ithaburensis*. In drier areas, the pistachio serves well in planted woodlands; in still more arid areas, the tamarisk is utilized. *Tamarix aphylla* is used in group plantings and *T. gallica* as windbreaks.

Animal Life

Historical Changes

The variety of Middle East environments supports a rich variety of fauna; Iran alone has approximately the same number of species of mammals as all of Europe west of the pre-1991 Soviet border. Unfortunately, to judge by biblical and other early writings, many larger species have become extinct in the Middle East. Still others have been reduced to a fraction of their former count, are nearing extinction, or now occupy only a remnant of their original range. The residual effects on fauna of the area from the heavy fighting during the two wars between 1980 and 1991 are still not clear, but they were not as catastrophic as was originally feared.

FIGURE 5-4 Mediterranean forests in the Troodos Mountains of Cyprus: Wild pine *(Pinus brutia)* and Troodos pine *(P. nigra)* clothe the upper slopes *(foreground),* with mixed maquis and garigue scrub forest on the slopes in distance. Summer homes are scattered in the fragrant pine forests.

Appreciably different environmental conditions in the Middle East during the Tertiary period and the Pleistocene epoch supported animal groups unlike those of modern times. For example, although the ancestor of *Bos taurus,* wild and domesticated cattle, came from the Taurus Mountains of southern Anatolia, there is fossil evidence of *Bos* in the Rub al-Khali during pre-Pleistocene times. Some gazelle were numerous in the steppes and more vegetated deserts, and several species of deer grazed the wooded steppe and open forests. Wild sheep and goats kept to the heights. Lions, tigers, leopards, cheetahs, and other felines were formerly common in parts of the Fertile Crescent and Iran, and other carnivores, such as the wolf, fox, jackal, and hyena, roamed much of the same area.

All of these larger mammals have been decimated by nature and people, and the lion and tiger have virtually disappeared from the region. The crocodile disappeared about 1900, the ostrich in the early 1930s. The ruggedness of the north and the aridity of the south have given refuge to individual survivors and to small groups of gazelle, deer, mountain sheep and goats (including ibex), wild boar, and similar mammals, along with an occasional leopard, wolf, jackal, hyena, and fox. A considerable baboon population is found in the woodlands of Asir in southwestern Arabia. Hundreds of hamadryas baboons scurry through the brush among the granite knobs of the national park along the escarpment west of Abha; they are heedless of park visitors but nimbly steal any food left unattended. The gazelle population of the Syrian and Arabian deserts has declined precipitously, primarily as a result of hunting with rifles from cross-country vehicles. As endangered species, gazelle and oryx (a type of antelope) are now protected. In small numbers oryx, who require no water except moisture in leaves they eat or the dew they take in with the leaves in early morning, can survive in the arid Rub al-Khali. During the 1990s, some governments in the eastern Arabian Peninsula initiated programs for the preservation, scientific breeding, and restoration of the gazelle and oryx.

The numerous domesticated animals of the Middle East—sheep, camels, goats, donkeys, cattle—are of great economic significance and are discussed in connection with land use in Chapter 7.

Some Common Types

The smaller mammals are much more numerous than the larger animals in both species and population, including hare, squirrel, hedgehog, honey badger, mongoose, and many species of rodents (jerboa, gerbil, hamster, field mouse, sand rat). The many species of reptiles include few harmful types, but there are a few vipers, cobras, and adders.

Lizards, represented by dozens of species, are common in all parts of the Middle East. One common lizard of the Arabian Desert is the burrowing *dabb,* or spiney-tailed lizard, a heavy-bodied herbivorous species that grows to 18–20 in./ 45–50 cm and is eaten by the Bedouins. The longer but slimmer *waral,* or desert monitor, is carnivorous and more aggressive; unlike the *dabb,* it is not considered edible. The small *tuhayhi,* an agamid lizard, seeks protection by vibrating its body and sinking into loose sand. The sand-swimming skink and other lizards also use submergence in sand as a temperature-regulating device, since lizards—and many other animals—must maintain body temperature within a fairly narrow range. Stinging scorpions are especially numerous in the more arid areas. Since they are nocturnal, they can generally be avoided by the exercise of reasonable care.

Birds

The Middle East has traditionally been rich in bird life and is estimated to have at least 500 species. During spring and fall, the great eastern Mediterranean flyway is used by many flocks of migrating birds. The narrowness of the corridor affords an exceptional opportunity for bird observation but also adds to the vulnerability of the migrating birds to hunters. Marshes along the many coasts attract thousands of waterfowl, and many game birds are present, although now in reduced numbers. Among the common birds of prey are the falcons, traditionally used by Bedouins for hunting. The sport of hunting with falcons has increasingly become a popular pastime in the Arabian Peninsula and the drier areas of the Fertile Crescent. Field birds are especially numerous along the Nile Valley, and cotes for pigeons and doves are a common sight around villages. Doves, which are rarely hunted, are seen everywhere outside the cities in Israel. A variety of songbirds frequents the forests of the Pontic Mountains of northern Turkey.

Insects

Some insects in the region are major pests. There were formerly plagues of locusts, sometimes catastrophic, but concerted action has reduced the locust danger to a minimum. Malaria-spreading mosquitoes remain a serious problem despite pesticide programs. Flies *(Diptera)* are a widespread nuisance and also serious threat because they spread eye diseases as well as gastrointestinal disorders. Incredibly, passengers in a vehicle traveling the open desert far from any settlement who stop for a picnic will almost immediately find themselves besieged by dozens of persistent flies.

Notes

1. See Zohary 1962 and others of his many studies. Hills 1966 has general coverage of vegetation in arid lands. The interrelationships between plants and soils are also examined in Hills, and soils from an agricultural viewpoint are studied in Clawson, Landsberg, and Alexander 1971. Two sheets of the UNESCO "Soil Map of the World" (1:5 mill.) cover the Middle East: VII-1 and V-2. A major recent contribution to the flora of eastern Arabia is Mandaville 1990.

2. See Mandaville 1990, 16; Schulz and Whitney 1986; and Mandaville n.d.

6

Patterns of Peoples and Cultures

The exceedingly complex patterns of distribution of population and peoples in the Middle East are shaped by many interacting biophysical, cultural, and historical influences. As has already been noted, the correlation between the pattern of population concentration and the pattern of precipitation and available water is especially high, and complex ethnic patterns often suggest alternating mountains and valleys that give refuge to or compartmentalize different groups of peoples.

Enumerating populations is difficult in most Middle East countries, and quantifying religions and linguistic groups is even more of a problem because such quantification often confronts very sensitive issues. Governments often attempt to obscure the number—and therefore the influence—of minority ethnic groups, such as Kurds in Turkey (and other countries involved in "Kurdistan") or Druzes in Lebanon. Similarly, official enumerators sometimes manipulate data concerning religious minorities, as has occurred in Egypt regarding the Copts and in Iran regarding Armenians and Zoroastrians. Therefore, figures vary widely, even in the best reports, and the following discussion and related tables represent a careful compromise among several authoritative sources. Data in the text are usually kept consistent with those in the tables and the country summaries, although more recent figures are occasionally introduced.

Census taking in some Middle East countries may face these various problems: Nomads may be difficult to locate; technical difficulties may interfere with accuracy, and the perceived sensitivity of data may cause

some results to be suppressed. Although advanced in many ways, Lebanon, with its multiplicity of antagonistic religious communities and associated political factions, has surprisingly avoided a census since the count in 1932 under the French mandate. It is the only Middle East state not to have conducted a census since 1945. Saudi Arabia conducted only basic demographic sampling until its 1974 partial census, and it is reticent about data on the high percentage of foreign resident workers collected in its 1992 census.

Rapid growth in such oil states as Kuwait, the United Arab Emirates, and Saudi Arabia rendered statistics obsolete even before they were published during the 1970s and early 1980s. The physical destruction and human misery inflicted on Kuwait by the Iraqi invasion in August 1990 prompted the exodus of hundreds of thousands of the amirate's inhabitants, and the population had still not stabilized for the 1995 census. Qatar took its first census in 1986 and Oman in 1993. Even the statistics-conscious State of Israel experienced difficulty in maintaining reliable data during the influx of immigrants from the former Soviet Union areas beginning in 1989. Although it has quietly manipulated data on emigration, Israel maintains an excellent Central Bureau of Statistics. Bahrain, Cyprus, and Turkey also regularly collect and publish good country statistics. All Middle East governments have made enormous and admirable improvement since the 1960s and 1970s in gathering statistical data and making at least most of these data available to the public. Lebanon continues to lag in this regard. In view of the foregoing, it is obvious that extensive and intensive quantitative analyses of the region are impossible and that there is appreciable statistical unevenness among the different areas of the Middle East.

The sixteen countries of the Middle East had an estimated 1999 population total of 289.5 million, about 4.9 percent of the estimated world population of 5.9 billion. The 1999 total was more than 3.6 times the 1950 total of 79.7 million, prior to explosive population growth accompanying the oil boom. During the nearly 50-year period after 1950, population increased by 13 times in Kuwait and by more than 40 times in the United Arab Emirates, and the population in most of the other states increased at least three or four times.

Two comparisons regarding Muslim and Arab populations may be noted. First, of approximately 1.25 billion Muslims in the world, about one-fourth are in the Middle East. Second, of the estimated 1999 total population of all 22 Arab League states (including the Palestinian entity) of 273.8 million, 156.8 million are in the 12 Middle East member states. For these and other geographical and historical reasons, the Middle East constitutes the center of Islamic and Arab identity.

The following discussion of patterns of Middle Eastern peoples reveals the richness and complexity of the region's cultural patterns and gives some insight into the human dynamics behind major trends and events in the area: the fundamental political patterns, historical and contemporary conflicts, traditional group hostilities, changing cultural patterns, migrations of ethnic and religious groups, and certain irredentist claims.

Patterns: Population

Distribution

The pattern of distribution of population in the Middle East (see Maps 6-1, 6-2, and the second map in Chap. 10) is not only of great significance in itself; it also indicates the locations of more favorable environments and greater economic opportunities—twin magnets that

attract people. The degree of urbanization indicated on Map 6-1 reflects both the historical role of the city in the Middle East and the rapid urbanization after 1950. The Middle East is more urbanized than is often assumed. At least 190 cities in the region have populations that exceed 100,000, and 22 cities exceed 1 million. Cities with populations between 100,000 and 500,000 have become relatively numerous during the second half of the twentieth century and are found in almost all Middle East countries. Nevertheless, despite the trend of increasing urbanization, most of the people of the Middle East still live in villages.

Some of the scattered dots on Map 6-2 represent groups of nomadic pastoralists, whose numbers can only be estimated. The high mobility of nomads makes them difficult to count, but the numbers of all types of nonsedentary peoples have been steadily decreasing. Several hundred thousand Bedouins of the Arabian Peninsula deserts are known to have settled between 1960 and 2000, and Bedouins elsewhere are becoming more settled, partly because of government pressures and incentives. Rough estimates of the numbers of nonsedentary peoples in the Middle East are 700,000 Bedouins, 1,800,000 other nomads, and 2,750,000 who move their livestock between mountain and lowland pastures with the seasons— transhumance, or vertical nomadism (Fig. 6-1).

Populations of the sixteen Middle East states vary greatly, as Table 6-1 and Graph 6-1 indicate. As is true in any region, population variations among states can be traced to six major factors: quality of the basic geographical environment, range and quality of natural resources, effectiveness of the national economy (and outside aid)—including food supply and health care—social and political pressures for or against population increase, incidental or planned (and even forced) immigration and emigration, and size of the state territory. In Part 2 these factors are explored within each Middle East country, but some quantitative comparisons can be made here.

The three largest populations are each approaching the 65 million total and have

MAP 6-1   Middle East demography. Dominance of population size in the "big three"—Turkey, Egypt, and Iran—is obvious. Thickness of outer rings of circles indicates growth of population during the last half-century.

evolved in three of the four largest countries: Turkey, Iran, and Egypt (Graph 6-1), which also occupy three of the four major power cores (Map 2-6). Similarly, the fourth-largest population, that in Iraq, is found in the fourth major power core. The fifth-largest population inhabits the largest state in the region—Saudi Arabia. Syria and Yemen have comparable populations of 15.5–16.5 million people and exhibit moderately large populations for their partly rugged and partly arid environments. Israel's population growth is highly dependent on periodically explosive immigration and capital transfers. Of the remaining countries, Jordan, Oman, and the UAE have relatively small populations for their size because they include extensive barren areas with minimal numbers of nomadic occupants.

Kuwait, Qatar, Cyprus, and Bahrain are smaller states with smaller but prosperous populations.

Density

In addition to the basic patterns of distribution of population, patterns of density of population—the number of persons per unit of area—are also of significance. The density figures for most Middle East countries are not, however, comparable to similar data for countries in Western Europe, where few areas are actually uninhabited. As the dots in Map 6-2 show, population in the Middle East congregates in favorable areas, and there are extensive intervening areas that are uninhabited or dotted by a few nomads or widely scattered villages. Thus,

---

MAP 6-2 Dot map of distribution of rural population. The proverbial density of population in the Nile Valley and Delta is clearly shown. Scattered smaller villages are underrepresented.

except in relatively favored areas like Asia Minor and the Levant, people concentrate in "islands" of better environments.

Some small oases may be widely scattered, with only a few families occupying each, as in the Jiwa (Liwa) Oases in western Abu Dhabi; by contrast, millions of people may be crowded into a narrow, intensively cultivated valley, as along the Nile River. In both cases, only a small percentage of the country's total area is actually occupied. In Egypt, for example, 63.3 million people have an overall density of 164 per mile²/63 per km². However, population density based on the area actually

inhabited and cultivated, about 3.5 percent of Egypt's total area, soars to more than 4,962 per mile²/1,917 per km². The overall density on the small island of Bahrain is extremely high, and it is two to three times higher in the areas actually occupied. The anomalous density in the Gaza Strip reflects the appalling crowding of refugees in this artificial territory.

Rates of Birth, Death, and Increase

Statistics reveal a sharp decline in crude death rates (deaths per 1,000 population) in the

FIGURE 6-1   Bedouins in Saudi Arabia, watering their camels at wells in the broad Wadi Sahba, west of Haradh, enjoy a joke with the author.

Developing Countries in the twentieth century. Better hygiene, health education, and health care facilities have increased live births, lowered the infant death rate, and lengthened the average human life. An increase in the birthrate (births per 1,000 population), certainly in the live birthrate, has accompanied the decrease in the death rate in many countries. The result has been a marked rise in the net population increase.

As shown in Table 6-1, the growth rates of the sixteen countries, plus the West Bank and Gaza, in the Middle East follow this trend in population increase, both because of high birthrates and because of high immigration. The crude birthrates of Syria, Oman, and Yemen all exceed 40 per 1,000 and are similar to rates in many African countries; however, most Middle East crude birth rates have decreased during the 1990s. Some countries, particularly Egypt, Turkey, and prior to 1979, Iran, have adopted systematic programs to inhibit the high rate of population increase by discouraging large families, but some groups resist family planning programs because their traditional customs encourage large families. In Israel, where as a group Jews have one of the lowest birthrates in the Middle East, the government encourages Jewish families to have more children, with the aim of matching the higher Arab birthrate. For the most part, however, family size in the Middle East is tending to decrease.

Birthrates vary both from country to country (see Graph 6-2) and from group to group. For example, they differ among religious groups and ethnic groups (sometimes equivalent to economic classes) in all Middle East countries. The birthrate is substantially lower among Coptic Christians than among Muslims in Egypt, lower among Maronites than among Shiis in Lebanon, lower among secular Jews than among ultra-Orthodox and Oriental Jews in Israel, and lower among Greek Cypriots than among Turkish Cypriots in Cyprus. Birthrate differentials accentuate political antagonisms because they might lead to a change in the balance of power.

TABLE 6-1   AREA AND DEMOGRAPHY, 1999

COUNTRY	1 AREA IN SQ MI	2 AREA IN SQ KM	3 POP IN OOOS	4 DENSITY PER SQ MI	5 DENSITY PER SQ KM	6 % POP URBAN	7 % ANNUAL
Bahrain	268	694	633	2,361.9	893.4	88.4	3.3
Cyprus[a]	3,572	9,251	861	241.0	93.1	67.7	1.4
Egypt	385,229	997,739	63,261	164.2	63.4	44.6	2.1
Iran	635,238	1,645,258	61,531	96.9	37.4	57.3	1.4
Iraq	167,975	435,052	21,722	129.3	49.9	74.5	3.3
Israel	7,846[b]	20,320	5,740[c]	731.6	282.5	91.0	2.2
Jordan[d]	34,489	89,326	4,682	135.8	52.4	78.6	3.6
Kuwait	6,880	17,818	1,866	271.2	104.7	97.0	5.0
Lebanon	4,016	10,400	3,506	873.0	331.7	60.1	1.5
Oman	119,500	309,500	2,364	19.8	7.6	71.7	3.5
Qatar	4,416	11,437	579	131.1	50.6	88.0	1.9
Saudi Arabia	868,000	2,248,000	20,786	23.9	9.2	77.3	3.6
Syria	71,498	185,180	15,335	214.5	82.8	52.2	2.7
Turkey	300,948	779,452	64,567	214.5	82.8	59.0	1.7
U. A. E.	32,280	83,600	2,744	85.0	32.8	84.0	5.7
Yemen	214,300	555,000	16,388	76.5	29.5	23.5	3.4
Gaza	140	363	1,082	7,728.6	2,980.7	—	8.0
West Bank	2,270	5,900	1,881	828.6	318.8	—	9.9
TOTAL/AVG.	2,858,865	7,404,290	289,528	101.3	39.1	69.4	3.6
United Kingdom	94,251	244,110	59,126	627.3	242.3	89.1	0.3
Spain	195,364	505,990	39,371	201.5	77.8	75.3	0.1

Area includes internal waters. Population data are estimates for mid-1998. Percentage of annual growth rate (Column 7) is average for period 1992-97. [a]Data are for the entire island. [b]Excludes West Bank, East Jerusalem, Gaza Strip, and Golan Heights. [c]Includes Golan Heights and East Jerusalem, and excludes Israelis in the West Bank and Gaza Strip. [d]Excludes West Bank, formerly under Jordanian administration. Source: *Britannica World Data 1999*. (With permission)

Migration

All three basic aspects of migration—immigration, emigration, and internal migration—play a significant role in defining the contemporary pattern of peoples in the Middle East. For example, immigration into the region (by Jews, Indians, and Pakistanis, for example) and migration within the region (by Palestinians, Jordanians, Egyptians, Jews, Lebanese, Kurds, and others) have dramatically increased some populations and profoundly altered the ethnic composition of some states. The extraordinary influx of Jews into Israel between 1945 and 1951 and of Jews from the former Soviet Union after 1989 completely reconstituted the population, character, and political orientation of the Palestine realm.

As a general rule, people have not emigrated from the region in large numbers in modern times. However, since the middle of the twentieth century, tens of thousands of emigrants have fled conflict and limited economic opportunity in the Levant, emigrating to the United States, Canada, Western Europe, and Australia. This emigration has included many Palestinian Arab refugees, Christian Lebanese, some Syrians and Jordanians, and by the late 1970s, many thousands of Israelis.

Patterns: Peoples

It is the cultural differentiation among peoples—variations in language, religion, common memories of a shared historical past, shared

87

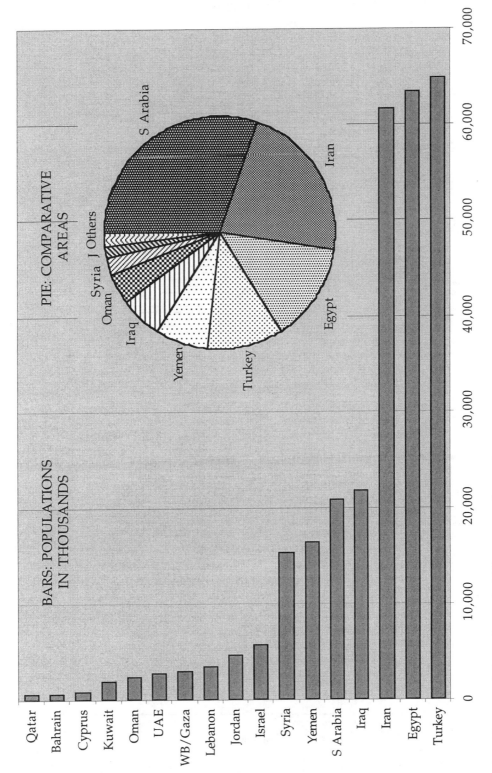

GRAPH 6-1 Population and area of Middle East countries.

88

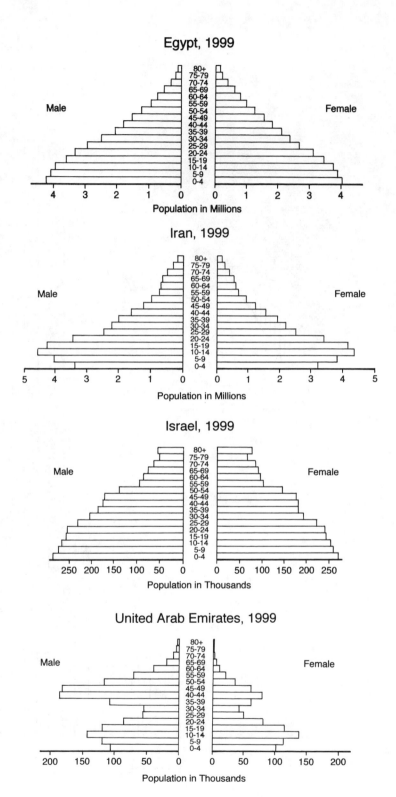

GRAPH 6-2 Contrasting population pyramids of four Middle East countries.

customs and dress, consensus of values—that creates separate group identities and nations. Thus, examination of the mosaic of peoples, or ethnic groups, is a major component of this analysis of Middle East patterns. Cultural patterns are, in effect, shuffled three times. The two dominant cultural patterns, language and religion, deserve individual attention, and sections on those patterns are then followed by a survey of ethnic groups. Two salient points to be noted in the following discussion are the fact that half of the population of the region is non-Arab, although twelve of sixteen countries are Arab states, and the fact that within its essential unity, Islam carries ethnic and political imprints and also has a number of sectarian variations. Thus, within its regional unity, the Middle East possesses great cultural diversity.[1]

Patterns: Languages

Language is the principal criterion for defining ethnic groups, particularly if the distinction is an ethnolinguistic one. Thus, Map 6-3 summarizes one of the most revealing patterns in the cultural geography of the Middle East. The depiction of only six main linguistic groupings—Arabic, Turkic, Farsi (Persian), Kurdish, Hebrew, and Greek—should not obscure the presence of approximately 25 other language groups in less accessible basins, valleys, and plateaus. Some of these other languages appear on Map 6-3, but many others are covered in the listing of ethnic groups later in the chapter, and some of them are discussed in this section. The principal languages of the region are, in order of the number of speakers, Arabic, Turkish, Farsi, Kurdish, Azeri, and Hebrew.

Semitic and Berber

The Semitic language group includes Arabic, the numerically predominant regional language; Hebrew, spoken in Israel; and vestiges of Aramaic, formerly spoken widely throughout the Middle East for more than 2,000 years. The

North African Berber and Coptic languages are grouped here with the Semitic languages, although they belong to different subfamilies.

Arabic. Arabic is the national language of twelve of the sixteen countries of the region and is spoken by approximately 148 million Middle Easterners, nearly half the total population. Three levels of usage have emerged: (1) colloquial, informal spoken Arabic; (2) modern standard Arabic, or "newspaper Arabic," the more formal Arabic used in books and lectures; and (3) classical Arabic, the formal and highly conventionalized style based on the language of pre-Islamic poetry, the Quran, and the writings of the first few centuries of the Islamic era. Educated Arabs understand all three, but uneducated Arabs have difficulty understanding the two more formal usages. In addition, four major dialects of Middle East Arabic are generally distinguished: those of Egypt, Syria (western Arabic), Iraq (eastern Arabic), and the Arabian Peninsula. Significant differences of vocabulary and pronunciation exist among and even within these four dialects. One major example is the pronunciation in Egypt of the Arabic "j" (*jiim*) as a hard "g." Thus, *jabal* ("mountain") is pronounced *gabal* in Egypt, which creates problems with the transliteration of place-names.

Speaking Arabic as a mother tongue is the hallmark of being an Arab. Since it is the language of the Quran, the holy book of the Muslims, Arabic has a mystical quality for many Arabs. It has additional emotional overtones as the language in which speeches and documents on Arab nationalism are prepared. The written language even plays a central role in Middle East art, since it is used in traditional decorative motifs in lieu of the sometimes proscribed human, animal, and vegetal motifs. Calligraphy is one of the highest forms of the fine arts in Islam. (See the excellent example opposite the title page of this book.)

Hebrew. Compared with Arabic, Hebrew is spoken in a relatively limited area by a comparatively small number of people, approximately 3.8 million. It should be noted that not all Jews

MAP 6-3   Middle East languages, indicating ethnolinguistic groups. This pattern is the basis for political patterns and for numerous regional conflicts. Note that the complexity of the pattern of languages is greatest in mountain areas, especially in Iran.

in the region—not even all Israeli Jews—speak Hebrew. An ancient language, it was a major vernacular for more than 1,000 years in the traditional Old Testament area of Israel. It ceased to be used as a working language centuries ago, but it was studied by biblical scholars and was used in Jewish communities as a ritual language, much as Latin, Greek, and Syriac are used in Christian church liturgies. It is also a scriptural language and has a mystical quality for religious Jews similar to that Arabic has for devout Muslims. Ultrareligious Jews consider Hebrew so sacred that they reserve it for ritual use only and refuse to use it as a vernacular, employing Yiddish or other languages for everyday use.

Hebrew was revived in the late nineteenth century under the stimulus of Jewish nationalism, the Zionist movement, and because of the need for a unifying national language for the new Jewish immigrants to Israel in the twentieth century. Contemporary usage has required adaptation of old terms and the coinage of new scientific terms. Because the large number of Israeli scholarly and scientific writings would have such a limited readership in Hebrew, many are published in English.

Aramaic.   Now primarily of historical interest, Aramaic (not to be confused with Armenian) served for more than 1,500 years as the lingua franca of the Fertile Crescent and was the language of Palestine by the time of Christ. Like Latin to the west, Aramaic was used for translations of the Bible. The Syriac form of Aramaic is used in the scriptures and liturgies of several Oriental Christian churches—Maronite, Nestorian, Chaldean—and by such sects as the Mandaeans and Samaritans. It is also still spoken by a few hundred Christians in three mountain villages northwest of Damascus.

Berber.   A subfamily language in the Afro-Asiatic language family, Berber is spoken by many millions of North Africans. It is spoken in the Middle East by only a few thousand Berbers who live in oases in northwestern Egypt.

Coptic.   With its name derived from *Qibt,* a corruption of the Greek word *Aigyptos* (Egypt), Coptic was the latest form of the ancient Egyptian language. With the addition of some Greek during the Hellenistic period, Coptic served as a vernacular in Egypt until over the centuries it was gradually supplanted by Arabic after the Muslim conquest. The discovery that many Coptic words were taken directly from the ancient Egyptian aided in the deciphering of Egyptian hieroglyphics. By the sixteenth century, Coptic was used primarily in the liturgy of the Coptic Christian church in Egypt.

Altaic Turkic Languages

The Altaic family includes a large number of languages spoken in the former Soviet Union and in China, as well as Magyar (Hungarian) and Finnish in Europe and more than a score of Turkic languages spoken in central Asia and the Middle East.

Turkish.   The best known of the Turkic languages, Turkish is spoken by the largest number of Turkic language speakers. The national language of the Republic of Turkey, it was brought into the Middle East by Turkish tribes migrating from central Asia in the tenth to thirteenth centuries. As Turkish speakers adopted Islam and settled Asia Minor, the language absorbed

loanwords from Arabic, the language of the Quran, and also from literary Persian.

Lacking a standard alphabet of its own, for 800–900 years Turkish was written in the Arabic alphabet of the Quran. In 1928, the Latin alphabet, with a number of diacritical marks borrowed from German and French, officially replaced the Arabic alphabet, and the language was "purified" of Arabic and Persian terms. In the Middle East, it is spoken throughout the Republic of Turkey and by the 188,000 Turkish Cypriots in northern Cyprus; otherwise, it is spoken by only small, scattered family-size groups in the Fertile Crescent area.

Azeri.   Azeri (or Azerbaijani) is the second major Turkic language spoken in the Middle East, centered in northwestern Iran and adjacent areas in Iraq and the Republic of Azerbaijan. Regional variations of Azeri appear in the western Elburz and the southern Caspian littoral among the Afshar, Shahsavan (now called Ilsavan), and Qajar ethnic groups. Like Turkish, Azeri was carried by migrating Turkic tribes during the Abbasid Empire.

Other Turkic languages spoken by several hundred thousand people each in Iran and Turkey include Qashqai (spoken by Turkic tribes in the southern Zagros Mountains of Iran) and various Turkmen dialects spoken by scattered peoples in the Anatolian-Iranian mountains and basins and in small areas in northeastern Iraq.

Indo-European Languages

The Indo-European languages of the Middle East include more than a score of Indo-Iranian tongues, the main ones being Farsi (Persian), Kurdish, Baluchi, and Luri with its related dialect of Bakhtiari. Armenian and Greek are other languages in the main Indo-European family that are spoken in the region by several hundred thousand people each.

Farsi (Persian).   The primary Indo-Iranian language of the Middle East is Farsi, a name taken from the ancient Iranian province of

Fars. After Arabic and Turkish, Farsi is spoken by the third-largest language group in the region. The Persian languages were brought to the Iranian Plateau more than 1,500 years before Turkic languages were heard in the area. After the Muslim conquest of Iran in the seventh century, Persian, like Turkish, incorporated hundreds of Arabic loanwords and adopted a slightly modified Arabic script.

Farsi is the primary language of Iran, although nearly half of the Iranians speak a mother tongue other than Persian—Azeri, Kurdish, Gilaki, Luri, Baluchi, Arabic, and others. However, as the official language and the language used by the mass media, government, educational institutions, and most Iranian writers, Farsi is increasingly used as a second language by minority groups. Persian literature has a rich history dating from the Zoroastrian scriptures, the Avesta, written before 500 BC.

Kurdish. The Indo-Iranian language spoken by the second-largest number of people in the Middle East, Kurdish is used across a geographical range from the streets of Beirut eastward through its main concentration in the mountains of Kurdistan and into the remote valleys of Afghanistan. It is grammatically and lexically distinct from Persian. Reflecting the extension of Kurdistan into several hegemonies, Kurdish is written with the Arabic alphabet in Iraq, the adapted Arabic alphabet in Iran, and the Latin alphabet in Turkey.

Other Indo-Iranian Languages. Baluchi is spoken by the Baluch of Baluchistan in southeastern and eastern Iran but even more so outside the Middle East proper in Pakistan and Afghanistan. It is also spoken by several thousand Baluch who have migrated across the Gulf to the United Arab Emirates and to Oman. Luri, a dialect of Persian, is spoken by nomadic tribes in the central Zagros, both by the Lur themselves and also, as a slightly different dialect, by their Bakhtiari neighbors. Sometimes called "Caspian" languages, a half-dozen Indo-Iranian dialects, mixed with one or two Turkic tongues, are spoken along the

southern coast of the Caspian Sea and on the northern slopes of the Elburz Mountains back of the Caspian coast.

Armenian and Greek. Armenian and Greek, two Indo-European languages, were formerly spoken over more extensive areas in the Middle East than they are at present. Armenian was the dominant language for more than 2,000 years in the area still referred to by the regional name Armenia, the highlands at the junction of Turkey, Iran, and the new Republic of Armenia. However, the decimation of Armenian speakers and their migration from Turkey have reduced the area of the language's use to Istanbul and scattered pockets in Anatolia and urban centers such as Aleppo, Beirut, Damascus, Tehran, and Cairo.

Similarly, Greek had been a major language in western Asia Minor 2,000 years before Turks arrived in significant numbers, and early Greeks also settled several Mediterranean islands, including Cyprus. As the urban and intellectual language of the Levant for more than two centuries after Alexander the Great, Greek was used by some of the Christian missionaries and writers of books of the New Testament. By the mid-1920s, however, only a few thousand Greek speakers remained in Asia Minor, primarily in Istanbul and coastal cities of the Mediterranean and Aegean. The main concentration of Greek speakers in the Middle East is now found in southern Cyprus, with small family-size pockets in cities in the Levant.

Patterns: Religions
Complexity of Patterns of Religion

At first glance, the pattern of religions appears simple: Islam embraces all but about 8 percent of the people of the Middle East. This pattern, however, is complicated by basic divisions within Islam between Sunni and Shii Muslims and also by the splintering of Shii sects.

Divisions within the general Christian religion, which developed its early structure in the Middle East, are even more numerous. Differing theological interpretations resulted in major schisms, which were later only partly mended by the church in Rome, until more than a dozen sects claimed sole possession of Christian truth.

Several million Jews are now concentrated in Israel, where ethnic and sectarian subdivisions periodically dispute over such issues as conversion and observation of the Sabbath. Ancient or syncretic religions—Zoroastrian, Yazidi, Mandaean, Bahai—constitute small Middle Eastern minorities.

Religious divisions have long played, and at the present time increasingly play, significant cultural-political-geographical roles in the Middle East. In recent decades political instability and social violence have increasingly devolved from intensification of religious and ethnic consciousness. In turn, political polarization resulting from religious fervor has inflamed communal feelings and weakened national bonds. Of growing apprehension since the 1970s is the increasing cross-linking between politics and religions, which is explored in Chapter 11.

The pattern of religions has been strongly influenced by two historical factors in modern times. First, at the time of the Muslim conquest of the area from the Nile River to the Iranian Plateau in the seventh century, there were millions of Christians and Zoroastrians, scores of thousands of Jews, thousands of Mandaeans, and other smaller groups. In general, the Muslim invaders proselyted these conquered peoples. However, those who practiced Judaism and Christianity were considered *ahl al-kitab* ("people of the book") and were permitted to maintain their own religions and communities under certain conditions. Later, Mandaeans, Zoroastrians, and even Berbers were accepted as people of the book. Therefore, religious groups possessed a strong group identity linked with their courts, areas of residence, occupations, and usually language as well as religion. This early religious group identity still persists, and it continues to affect regional relationships and the internal politics of Middle East states.

In a second historical development, the Islamic concept of people of the book was codified by the Ottoman Empire into the *millet* system (from

millah, "religion" or "religious community"), and *millets* further imprinted group consciousness on the non-Muslims of the Middle East. Religious affiliation assumed great cultural-political significance, and identity cards in Lebanon, Israel, and other states still indicate—indirectly in Lebanon—the individual's religion.

Three Monotheistic World Religions

A familiar and significant aspect of the Middle East is that it is the birthplace of the world's three major monotheistic religions: Judaism, Christianity, and Islam (Map 6-4; Fig. 6-2). Judaism and Christianity both originated in the hill area between the Mediterranean coastal plain and the Jordan Valley, and Islam originated 700 miles/1,125 km to the southeast in hills that lie inland from the Red Sea coast. As Judaism borrowed from Mesopotamian and Canaanite traditions, so Christianity evolved from Judaic traditions and others of the region, and Islam borrowed heavily from Judaism, Christianity, and local traditions in the Hijaz. In the Middle East in 1999, Muslims numbered about 268 million, more than 92 percent of the population of the region. Christianity was the second-largest religion, with approximately 12 million adherents, and Judaism third with approximately 4.8 million.

The following discussion focuses on spatial relations rather than historical evolution or theology. Islam is examined in somewhat more detail because of its greater geographical and quantitative importance in the region and because it is less well known or understood outside the Muslim world.

Islam

The name *Islam* is Arabic for "submission," that is, submission to God's will, and a *Muslim* is "one who submits." The term *Muhammadan* is sometimes used instead of Muslim; however, the usage may be misleading, since it may suggest a parallel with "Christian" in the sense of worship of Christ, whereas Muslims do not worship Muhammad. They do revere his teachings and

MAP 6-4   Middle East religions. Note the overwhelming dominance of Islam and the extension of Shiism into southern Iraq.

consider him the last and greatest of the prophets, the Seal of the Prophets.

The origins of Islam reflect a regional character. Mecca, the Arabian town in which Islam first evolved, was an important midway caravan post between Yemen and Syria. The importance of Mecca was enhanced by the presence of the Well of Zamzam, since water was scarce along Tihamah, the barren Red Sea coastal plain followed by the caravans. The town was also the site of an ancient shrine, the Kaabah, which contained an array of idols and also housed the revered Black Stone of Mecca, a meteorite. Mecca's rapid development in the sixth century

stimulated intellectual exchange, as townspeople and Bedouins from the Hijaz mingled with the caravan travelers from Syria, Yemen, and other trade areas.

One Mecca merchant who was inspired by the ideas being discussed was Muhammad ibn Abdullah, a member of the Hashim clan of the Quraysh tribe. While meditating in a cave near Mecca, he received what he later explained were dictations from the Angel Gabriel of the Holy Word of the one God. Preaching his revelations, Muhammad denounced the idols in the Kaabah shrine and thereby reduced Mecca's tourist trade. Harassed by Mecca merchants,

FIGURE 6-2   Mosque of St. Sophia (Greek, Haghia Sophia; Turkish, Aya Sofya—Divine Wisdom) in Istanbul. Originally a Byzantine church, it was converted into a mosque when Constantinople was captured by the Ottomans in 1453. Deconsecrated in the 1930s, it is now a museum open to the public.

Muhammad and his followers, the original Muslims, emigrated to Yathrib, 210 miles/340 km north of Mecca. Yathrib later became known as *al-Madinat al-Nabi* (the City of the Prophet), or simply *al-Madina* (the City) and is known commonly as Medina. The year AD 622, when the migration to Medina occurred, became the first year of the Islamic calendar. Muslim years, reckoned on the lunar system (which makes them eleven days shorter than Gregorian calendar years), are designated as *anno Hegirae* (AH), year of the Hegira (Arabic, *hijrah*, "flight").

In Medina, dictations from the Angel Gabriel were recited by the Prophet to his followers until his death in AD 632. These recitations were assembled in 651 into the Muslim scriptures, the Quran (Koran), meaning "recitation," which plays a central role in Islam. Accepted by Muslims as the precise Word of God, the Quran links God and man, and its poetic language echoes the Hijaz desert area and village and Bedouin traditions, as the Old and New Testaments refer to the desert and nomadic traditions of Sinai and the Syro-Palestinian area.

Translation of the Quran from Arabic was long forbidden, since that would mean altering the direct Word of God, and converts to Islam perforce learned the Arabic language in order to understand the Quran. As Islam spread throughout the Middle East and North Africa to Spain and into central Asia (Map 6-5), the Arabic language also spread, with crucial historical and political-geographical consequences. The Muslim place of worship is the mosque (a corruption of the Arabic *masjid*, "place of worship"), with its intrinsic exterior minaret and its interior *mihrab*, which shows worshipers where to face—the direction of Mecca—during prayer. Fig. 6-3 pictures one type of mosque. Over the centuries, thousands of Muslim shrines have also been built by local groups; they are interesting and moving features in many otherwise barren landscapes (Fig. 6-4).

Although, like all religions, Islam has been elaborated into a complex and subtle body of

MAP 6-5   Present extent of Islam, with major medieval caravan and sea routes that contributed to the spread and persistence of Islam.

theology, both its essential message and practice are simple and straightforward. Its one basic essential is that a new convert express and believe the *shahadah,* or profession of faith: "There is no god but God; Muhammad is the messenger of God," a translation of the euphonious Arabic *La ilaha illa Allah; Muhammadun rasulu Allah.* The *shahadah* and four additional primary obligations constitute the five pillars of Islam, which have profoundly affected regional character in the Islamic world: *salah,* devotional worship or prayer five times a day while facing toward the Kaabah, the House of God, in Mecca; *zakah,* religious tax (and *sadaqah,* voluntary almsgiving, as additionally meritorious); *sawm,* fasting during the holy month of Ramadan, ninth month of the Muslim year; and the *hajj,* the pilgrimage to Mecca.

The Quran also underlies the Shariah, the sacred law of Islam, which covers all aspects of the lives of Muslims—not only religious and private but also political and public, social and economic. Shariah still plays an important role in the law of several Middle East countries

(Saudi Arabia, Qatar, Iran) and complements the more westernized legal codes of countries such as Egypt, Syria, and Iraq. Resurgent Islamic fundamentalism has brought a renewed interest in Shariah law, which has at various times been in conflict with modern secular trends in the region.

Islam was for many centuries both religion and government, and when the Shariah was compiled, it combined religious and civil matters. The caliph (Arabic, *khalifah,* "successor") thus led both the community of believers (the *ummah*) and the Islamic state. Subsequent schisms within Islam have placed severe strains on this unity of religion and state.

The most momentous schismatic dispute within Islam occurred with the seventh-century division between Sunni and Shii. This split has precipitated wars, assassinations, civil conflict, and rancor in the Middle East and North Africa for more than 1,300 years and still has grave repercussions in the area today. Part of the bitterness between Iran and Iraq during their 1980s war may be traced to the Sunni-Shii

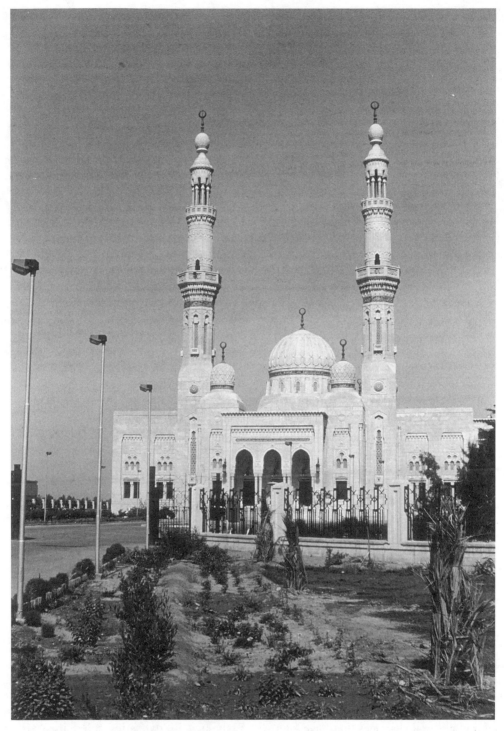

FIGURE 6-3   Martyrs' Mosque, Baghdad. An unusual style, incorporating certain Persian influences from the east and Umayyad influences from the west.

FIGURE 6-4 Muslim shrine and tomb of Shaykh Ahmad bin Isa in the Wadi Hadramawt, eastern Yemen. A visit to the tomb is an especially moving experience, but many such shrines are found throughout the Middle East.

differences. The Sunnis (or Sunnites)—*ahl al-sunnah wa-l-jamaah,* "the people of custom and community"—consider themselves the original, Orthodox Muslims and have always been in the overwhelming majority. They believe that caliphs could be chosen by leaders of the *ummah* and were secular leaders only. The Shiis (or Shiites or Shiah)—*shiat Ali,* "partisans of Ali"—evolved as a separate sect beginning in AD 657 because they believe that only descendants of Muhammad's daughter Fatima and his son-in-law Ali were legitimate successors to Muhammad. To Shiis, these successors are divinely guided, sinless, infallible religious leaders (imams) with authority to interpret the Prophet's spiritual knowledge. This fundamental theological schism has accentuated the political and cultural cleavages that have long divided Arabs and Persians, especially since Safavid shahs adopted dormant Shiism as the imperial religion in the early 1500s.

After the initial split from Sunni Islam, Shiis experienced further divisions over the issue of succession (Table 6-2).

1. The predominant Shii group accepted Ali and eleven of his descendants as the true imams and became known as Twelvers (also Ithna Ashari, Imamis, and Jafaris). They are concentrated in Iran and Iraq, but considerable numbers are found in every Middle East country, including Lebanon.

2. A smaller group preferred a different seventh imam, Ismail, and became known as Seveners (also Ismailis). Greatly reduced in numbers, most are now divided into heretical sects such as the Druze and the Alawi. The Ismailis developed their political power between the tenth and thirteenth centuries. Early Ismaili dynasties ruled in Syria and Bahrain, and the Ismaili Fatimids, named for Muhammad's daughter, achieved an Egyptian renaissance in Cairo during the tenth to

TABLE 6-2 RELIGIONS OF THE MIDDLE EAST.

RELIGION, CHURCH, SECT (INCLUDING ALTERNATE NAMES)	MAIN CENTER OR PAT. SEAT	LITURGICAL LANGUAGE	MAIN AREAS IN WHICH FOUND IN MIDEAST
──────── ISLAM ────────			
Sunni Islam (largest sect by far)	None (Mecca)	>Ar; Turk, Farsi	Most of Mideast
Shii Islam (second-largest sect by far)	None (Mecca, Karbala)	Farsi, Arabic	Iran, Southern Iraq, South Lebanon
Imamis (Jafaris, "Twelvers," Ithna Ashari)	—	Farsi, Arabic	Iran, Iraq
Ismailis ("Seveners")	----	Arabic	Levant
Zaydis ("Fivers")	----	Arabic	Yemen
Alawis/Alevis (Alawites, Nusayris, Ansaris)	None	Arabic, Turkish	W Syria, Turkey
Druzes (Muwahhidun ["Unitarians"])	None	Arabic	S Syr, C Leb, N Isr
Ibadhis	Nazwa, Oman	Arabic	Inner Oman, <Iran
──────── CHRISTIANITY ────────			
Churches with no outside affiliation			
Coptic Orthodox Church (C O C, Alexandria)	Cairo	Coptic, Arabic	C and N Egypt
Armenian Orthodox Ch. (Arm. Georgian Church)	Antilyas, Leb	Armenian	C Middle East
Syrian Orth. Ch. (Jacobite Ch., W Syr. Church)	Damascus	Syriac, Arabic	Syria, Iraq
Ethiopian Orthodox Church (Ethiopian Church)	Addis Ababa	Geez	Egypt
Church of the East (Nestorian Church, East Syrian Church, Assyrian Church)	Baghdad (official)	Syriac	Syria, Iraq
Churches affiliated with the Patriarchate of Constantinople			
Orthodox Patriarchate of Constantinople (Greek Orthodox Church of Const., The Great Church)	Istanbul	Greek	Levant
Greek Orth. Church of Antioch (Rum Orth., etc.)	Damascus	Arabic	Levant
Greek Orth. Church of Alexandria (Ch. of Alex.)	Alexandria	Greek, Arabic	Egypt
Greek Orth. Church of Jerusalem (Ch. of Jerus.)	Jerusalem	Arabic, Greek	Levant
Greek Orthodox (Several other names)	(Several)	(Several)	Levant
Uniate Churches: Churches united with the Roman Catholic Church			
Coptic Catholic Church (Coptic Cath. Ch. of Alex.)	Cairo	Coptic, Arabic	Egypt
Maronite Church (Maronite Church of Antioch)	Bkirke, Leb	Syriac, Arabic	Central Lebanon
Syrian Catholic Ch. (Patriarchate of Antioch)	Beirut, Leb	Syriac, Arabic	Levant
Armenian Cath. Church (Arm. Cath. Ch. Cilicia)	Bzummar, Leb	Armenian	Levant
Chaldean Catholic Church (Chaldean Church)	Baghdad	Syriac, Arabic	Iraq
Melkite Church (Rum Catholic Church, Greek Catholic Church of Antioch)	Damascus	Arabic	Syria
Western Churches			
Roman Catholic Church	Rome	(Various)	Mideast exc Arabia
Protestant Churches (Presbyterians, Methodists, Baptists, Anglicans, several others)	----	English, others	Mideast exc Arabia
──────── JUDAISM ────────			
Orthodox Judaism	(Jerusalem)	Hebrew	Israel, <other ME
Hasidic Judaism [ultra-Orthodox Judaism]	(Jerusalem)	Hebrew	Israel
(Samaritanism [offshoot of Judaism])	Nabulus (PA)	Aramaic	Pal Auth, Israel
──────── OTHERS ────────			
Yazidism (erroneously: "Devil Worship")	None	Kurdish, Ar	NW Iraq, NE Syria
Mandaeism (Sabianism, Mendaism)	None	Aramaic dial.	Baghdad, S Iraq
Bahaism	Haifa	(Several)	Iran, Levant
Zoroastrianism	None	Farsi	Central Iran

"Pat." = Patriarchal. "PA" = Palestinian Authority. Some liturgies use local languages (Arabic, Turkish, Farsi [Persian]) in addition to the traditional languages. Syriac is a form of Aramaic. Memberships vary widely, from more than 268 million Muslims to about 611 Samaritans. (From various sources, including Joseph 1983, *Britannica World Data 1999*, and author's field research.)

twelfth centuries. Ismaili "assassins" engaged in political sabotage and murder, primarily in northern Iran, until they were decimated in the thirteenth century, but contemporary Ismailis are a mild sect found in India, Syria, the Gulf area, and along the coast of eastern Africa.

Two offshoots of the Ismailis mentioned above deserve attention. The larger sect, the Druze, originated in 1017 in Cairo with followers of the Fatimid caliph al-Hakim. Although they called themselves Muwahhidun (Unitarists), outsiders called them Druzes after the name of an early missionary. The Druzes won especially large numbers of converts among isolated mountain peoples in southern Lebanon and adjacent areas, where the Druzes, an esoteric and non-proselyting sect, are still concentrated.

The second offshoot sect, the Alawis (or Alawites, also known as Nusayris and sometimes Ansariyahs) are concentrated in northwestern Syria. Although the name "Alawi" indicates "followers of Ali," the rituals of their esoteric religion are known to include pre-Christian, Christian, and Sabian elements as well as Shii Islamic practices. Using neither mosques nor churches, Alawis conduct rites around shrines near revered tombs and sacred groves. A much larger group in Turkey is called *Alevi,* the Turkish version of the same name, and holds many similar beliefs; however, the Alevis include Arabs, Turks, and Kurds, who often conceal their religion.

3. A third group of Shiis chose a different fifth imam, Zayd, and became known as Fivers (also Zaydis). They are concentrated in Yemen, where a broken line of Zaydi secular imams held power until the overthrow of Imam al-Badr in the mid-1960s. Yemeni links with the Shiis originated in the support given Ali by Yemeni tribesmen who, settling in southern Mesopotamia after the Arab Muslim conquest of the area, allied themselves with the supporters of Ali.

An isolated, little-known group of Muslims, the Ibadhis, live in Inner Oman, where they were banished from southern Iraq in the seventh century. They are descendants of the Kharijites ("seceders"), who assassinated Ali and withdrew from the belief systems of both the Sunnis and the other Shiis regarding the right of caliphal succession. The Ibadhis intermittently maintained their own imamate in Inner Oman and periodically fought for control of Muscat and all of Oman into the mid-twentieth century. With Nazwa as their main center, they are now a conservative, dignified group and are joining in the development of modern Oman (see Fig. 6-5).

Christianity

Middle East Christianity embraces more than a dozen sects centered on the spiritual and ethical teachings of Jesus of Nazareth, who is believed to have lived and taught in Palestine 2,000 years ago. In the Occidental world, calendar years are designated, with an inadvertent error of about four years, as *anno Domini* (AD), indicating years that have lapsed since the birth of Jesus.

Although other religions believe in the messianic concept, the Christian religion preaches, as a central belief, that Jesus was the long-awaited Messiah (Greek, *Christos,* "the anointed," anglicized to Christ). The early apostles compiled his teachings in the Gospels ("good tidings") and added their own preachings and letters. Assembled, these writings form the New Testament (New Covenant), the main scriptures of the Christian religion, which is coupled with the Old Testament to constitute the Holy Bible of Christianity. Even in its early years, Christianity incorporated influences from the region's several cultures—Jewish, Greek (Hellenistic), Roman, and Aramaic.

By New Testament accounts, Jesus was acclaimed during his three-year ministry in the area of Judea, Galilee, and neighboring places. However, only a few of his followers, mainly converted Jews, remained faithful after his crucifixion by the Roman authorities. In AD 66, when the Christian Jews of Jerusalem refused to support the Jewish revolt, Jewish leaders rejected the Christians and their concepts.

After this breach between Christians and Jews, the apostle-missionaries decided to preach to the Gentiles (Greeks) in Asia Minor and Syria. Antioch became the first Christian center, soon followed by Edessa (modern Urfa) farther east. Suppressed for 200 years by Roman authorities as inimical to their own religion and positions, Christianity was officially permitted by the Edict of Milan (313), was accepted by Emperor Constantine after he moved his imperial capital from Rome to Constantinople in 330, and was made the state religion of the Roman Empire in 380. A series of ecumenical councils, convened in or near the eastern imperial capital of Constantinople, debated heresies and sought unity but engendered fragmentation. Christianity was the dominant religion of the Middle East outside

FIGURE 6-5   Young shoppers at an outdoor *suq* in Nazwa, famous ancient town in Inner Oman. Note the handsomely embroidered, typically Omani headwear of the young men.

Iran and the Arabian Peninsula between the fourth and the sixth centuries, but today it is a minority faith in an overwhelmingly Muslim area (Fig. 6-6).

The approximately 12 million Christians in the Middle East are divided among more than a dozen Orthodox and Catholic sects, with a minority divided among a number of Protestant churches (see Table 6-2). The largest group, the Coptic Christians, live in Egypt. The second-largest group, the Maronites, are concentrated in Lebanon, where a variety of Christian groups constitute about one-third of the population. The third-largest number are in Syria, where they constitute about 10 percent of the population. The fourth-largest number of Christians are found among a variety of sects in northern and northeastern Iraq, where mountains shelter numerous relict groups—non-Christian as well as Christian. The fifth-largest number of Christians, and the greatest concentration of Greek

Orthodox in the region, are in Cyprus, where they constitute about three-fourths of the island's population and nearly 100 percent of the population in south Cyprus. Finally, Turkey, Iran, and Jordan each have Christian minorities that number more than 400,000 in Turkey and Iran and 200,000 in Jordan.

Judaism

Oldest of the three great monotheistic religions, Judaism evolved over a period of more than 1,500 years, a development that is the theme of the Old Testament. It takes its name from Judah, the southern kingdom associated with the northern kingdom of Israel, from which the term Jew is also derived. The patriarch Jacob, through his religious name, Israel, became the traditional eponymous ancestor of the Bnai Yisrael, Children (literally, Sons) of Israel.

FIGURE 6-6   The famous St. Katherine's Monastery, Orthodox monastery of the sixth century, nestled at the foot of Mt. Sinai (Jabal Musa) in the southern Sinai Peninsula.

Judaism's roots lie in traditions of a seminomadic Aramaean tribe that is personified in the patriarch Abraham. In the Old Testament account, the original group migrated from southern Mesopotamia, Ur of the Chaldees, up the Euphrates Valley to the Harran and then, probably about 1700 BC, southwestward to the southern hills of Canaan. Out of the tribal growth and development of the Bnai Yisrael evolved the elements of the monotheistic religion that came to be known as Judaism. It revolved around the one God (Yahweh), the covenant between God and the people of Israel, the comprehensive law, and for many Jews, the land.

Missionary activity among the Hebrews (called Jews after the 50-year Babylonian Exile) following the return of many exiles in 538 BC reflected the belief in Israel's election by God to mediate divine blessings to all nations. By the time of the birth of Jesus, Judaism was winning many converts in the Roman Empire. However,

after the Romans destroyed the temple in Jerusalem in AD 70 and dispersed the Jews from Palestine, missionary activity by Jews almost ceased. Particularism and separatism, as opposed to universalism, increasingly characterized Judaism, which became a token religion in its original territory for more than eighteen centuries.

Different interpretations of the Torah (the Law, the first five books of the Old Testament, also called the Pentateuch) and the Talmud (a body of commentary and guidance) have led to various groupings within Judaism. In modern times, Judaism embraces such groups as the ultra-Orthodox Hasidim ("those who are pious"), the Orthodox, the Conservative, the Reform, and the Reconstructionists. Neither Reform Judaism, which seeks to liberalize orthodoxy and bring Judaism into modern Western life, nor Conservative Judaism, seeking a middle position, achieved recognition in Israel until the

1970s. Bitter debate continued in 2000, both in Israel and between Israeli religious authorities and American Jewish leaders, regarding the status of Conservative and Reform Jews. The debate is especially relevant to the "right of return" of liberal Jews and of Jews converted by liberal rabbis. Nevertheless, Judaism has not experienced the degree of institutionalized sectarian fragmentation suffered by Christianity and Islam. Reimplanted in its native locale in the mid-twentieth century, Judaism has become for many of its adherents a belief system that is quite different from its original theology. Surveys have shown that only a minority of Israeli Jews actually practice Judaism, and distinctions must be drawn among Jews, practitioners of Judaism, Zionists, and Israelis. The cleavage between ultra-Orthodox and secular Jews in Israel is discussed in Chapter 15.

Other Religions

The primarily Kurdish Yazidis (or Yezidis), who are scattered across northern Syria and northern Iraq and in adjacent areas of Turkey and Iran, call themselves Dawasin, and are called Dasnayis by the Syrians; they are strictly self-segregated and endogamous. Their highly syncretic religion borrows heavily from Zoroastrianism, Judaism, Nestorian Christianity, Islam, and other religions; their major divine figure is a repentant and pardoned Satan, the Peacock King, who is the chief angel of six other angels. The Yazidi practice of "prudent propitiation" of the Peacock King has been mistakenly interpreted as worship of the devil.

Zoroastrianism is named after its traditional founder, Zoroaster (or Zarathustra), who is believed to have lived in the sixth century BC. It was widespread in the Iranian-Mesopotamian realm and was the major religion of the Achaemenid Empire and then the Sassanian Empire. Essentially monotheistic in its worship of Ahura Mazda ("Lord Wisdom"), it exercised significant influence on Judaism and on Christianity. Taught by magi (magians) as priests, Zoroastrianism emphasizes the eternal cosmic contest between good and evil, falsehood and truth, darkness and light. Traditional Zoroastrian practices include fire worship and exposure of the dead to vultures on "towers of silence" (*dakhmes* or *qala-e khamushan*), many ruins of which remain in central Iran. The Zoroastrian scripture is the Avesta, which has been supplemented by the commentary Zend-Avesta. Disfavored during the seventh-century Muslim invasion, many Zoroastrians converted to Islam. Zoroastrianism is also opposed by the current Islamic fundamentalist government in Iran but does survive primarily in the Yazd and Kerman areas of central Iran as well as among the Parsees in India, especially in Bombay.

A minor religious group concentrated in Iraq is the Mandaeans (from Aramaic *manda*, "knowledge"), also called Sabians ("baptizers") and John the Baptist Christians—although they are not Christians. John the Baptist is a central figure in this highly syncretic religion, which includes Jewish, Iranian, Babylonian, Gnostic, and Christian elements. Because Mandaeans stress the importance of immersion and regular absolutions, they live near running water, mostly along the lower Tigris River. Their scriptures and liturgy are in Syriac.

A fairly recent, eclectic faith, Bahaism evolved in Iran in the 1840s as an offshoot of Shii Islam. Babist mysticism spread rapidly after a Shii religious leader was acclaimed the *bab* ("gate") between the worldly and the spiritual. Advocating a universalistic faith synthesizing Islam, Judaism, and Christianity, Bahaism has spread widely in Europe and North America. The Bahai world center is on Mt. Carmel, in Haifa, Israel, and its members number tens of thousands in the Middle East, chiefly in central Iran, where they have been persecuted since the revolution of 1978–1979.

Patterns: Ethnic Groups

Aspects of Middle East language and religion patterns may now be merged in a survey of ethnic groups of the region (Table 6-3). This survey of peoples examines four major ethnic aggregates—Arabs, Turks, Persians, and Jews—

TABLE 6-3 ETHNIC GROUPS OF THE MIDDLE EAST (WITH ETHNOLINGUISTIC GROUPING).

ETHNIC GROUP (AND ALT. NAMES)	MAIN LANG.	MAIN RELIGION	NO., OOOS	MAIN AREAS/COMMENTS
————AFRO-ASIATIC: Semitic and Berber————				
ALAWIS (Alawites, Nusayris)	Arabic	Alawi	1,850	W Syria, N Lebanon
ARABS	Arabic	Islam (>Sunni)	148,000	Mid East, N Africa
ASSYRIANS (Aissores)	Syriac, Arabic	Christn (Nestorian)	? 175	NE Syria, N Iraq
CHALDEANS ("Assyrians")	Arabic, Syriac	Christn (Chaldean)	? 130	N Iraq, B'dad, E Syria
COPTS	Arabic	Christn (Coptic)	5,500	C and N Egypt
DRUZES (Muwahhidun)	Arabic	Druze	900	S Syr, C Leb, N Israel
JEWS (Yahudis)	Hebrew, Ar.	Judaism	5,000	Israel, Iran, Turkey
MANDAEANS (Sabians, Mendai)	Ar., Aramaic	Mandaean	25	Baghdad, S Iraq, Iran
MARONITES	Ar., French	Christn (Maronite)	675	NC and C Lebanon
(MUTAWALIS) (Metouali)	(Arabic)	(Shii Islam)	1,000	(C and S Lebanon)
SAMARITANS	Ar. , Aram. di.	Samaritan	<1	611 in Nablus, Holon
BERBERS	Berber	Sunni Islam	8	NW Egypt (mils. to W)
————URAL-ALTAIC: Turkic————				
AFSHAR (include several groups)	Azeri	Shii Islam	700	NW Iran, SC Iran
AZERIS (Azerbaijanis)	Azeri	Shii Islam	11,000	NW Iran
QAJARS (include several groups)	Azeri	Shii Islam	? 200	SE Caspian Coast
QASHQAI	Qashqai	Shii Islam	800	Iran: C Zagros Mts.
ILSAVAN/SHAHSAVAN (sev.)	Azeri	Shii Islam	375	NW Iran, other Iran
TATARS ("Tartars")	Tatar Turkic	Sunni Islam	? 90	E Turkey, N Iran
TURKS	Turkish	Sunni Islam	55,000	Turkey; few scattered
TURKMEN (Turcomans)	Turkmen	Sunni Islam	1,500	N Iran, NE Iraq, Trky
YORUK	Turkish	Sunni Islam	390	W and SE Turkey
————INDO-EUROPEAN: Indo-Iranian, Armenian, and Greek————				
BAKHTIARI	Luri	Shii Islam	1,000	Iran: C Zagros Mts.
BALUCH (Baluchis)	Baluchi	Sunni Islam	1,300	SE Iran (& Pak & Afgh)
GILANI (include several groups)	Gilaki	Shii Islam	? 3,250	SW Caspian Coast
HAZARAS (Berberis)	Hazaragi	Shii Islam	300	E Iran; >in Afgh, Pak
KURDS	Kurdish	Sunni Islam	22,500	Iran, Iraq, Syria, Trky
LUR (include several groups)	Luri	Shii Islam	3,000	C Zagros Mts., E Iraq
MAZANDARANI (incl. sev. grps)	Mazandarani	Shii Islam	? 3,300	SW Caspian Coast
PERSIANS	Farsi (Persian)	Shii Islam	31,000	C & N Iran; <Iraq, UAE
PUSHTUN (Pukhtun, Pathans)	Pashto	Sunni Islam	110	E Iran (mils. to E)
YAZIDIS (Dasnayi, Asdais)	Kurdish	Yazidi	? 100	N Iraq, NW Syria
ZOROASTRIANS (Parsis,Gabres, Zardoshti)	Farsi (Persian)	Zoroastrian	100	SC Iran (Yazd), Tehran (also many in India)
ARMENIANS (Hai)	Armenian	Christn (>Arm Orth)	900	Leb, Syria, Iran, Trky
GREEKS (Elleniki)	Greek	Christn (Orthodox)	660	Cyprus, Istanbul, Egypt
————CAUCASIC————				
CIRCASSIANS (Adyghe,Cherkes)	Circassian	>Sunni Islam	150	Trky, Syria, Jrdn, Israel
GEORGIANS	Georgian	>Sunni	? 65	N Turkey, WC Iran
LAZE (Laz, Chan)	Laz, Turkish	Sunni Islam	100	SE Black Sea Coast
————MISCELLANEOUS————				
BEJA	Beja	Sunni Islam	<20	<SE Egypt (>NE Sudn)
GYPSIES (Rom, many others)	Romany, etc.	Various	?>1,000	Scattered
NUBIANS	Nubian, Ar.	Sunni Islam	150	<S Eqypt (>N Sudan)

Groups may overlap and are, therefore, not necessarily mutually exclusive (e.g., Druzes and Alawis are Arabs). Mutawali are Lebanese Shii Muslims; the name is from the nineteenth century. Numbers can be only rough estimates in some cases. See text regarding Armenians, Azeris, and Georgians. (Data from *Britannica World Data 1999; World Factbook 1999; Ethnologue 1996;* Weekes 1984; and author's field research.)

and briefly discusses related smaller groups associated with each major group. The relationship between primary group and associated groups may involve language, religion, cultural affinity, or geographical proximity, including shared nationality. For example, the

Lur and the Bakhtiari are considered with the Persian group, since all three live in Iran, speak Indo-Iranian languages, and belong to the Shii sect of Islam. Similarly, the Maronites and Druzes are considered with the Arabs, since both groups are associated with Lebanon and speak Arabic, even though the Maronites are Christians and the Druzes are a heretical sect of Shii Islam. Because of cultural and historical complexities, the categories used are not always exclusive. The significance of minority ethnic groups in the region's various bodies politic is directly addressed in Chapter 11.

Arabs and Related Groups

Arabs.   Even with the diversity of traits and the distribution over vast distances of this largest Middle East group, the ethnic identity of the Arabs is one of the basic realities of the pattern of peoples in the region. Numbering about 148 million, not only are Arabs the overwhelmingly dominant ethnolinguistic group in twelve of the sixteen countries, they also include at least one million nationals in each of three more of the countries—Israel, Turkey, and Iran—and are numerically negligible only in Cyprus.

All Arabs share two cultural elements, and most share a third. First, the Arabic language provides an element common to all Arabs, despite variations in dialect. As the language of the Quran, it has deep religious and cultural significance for most Arabs. Second, the Islamic cultural heritage embodied in architecture, design, calligraphy, and art provides a common history for Arabs—Muslim and Christian, orthodox and heretic, Bedouin and city dweller, Syrian and Qatari. The region's Islamic heritage underlies modern Arab political identity, a relevant factor in many modern problems and conflicts (Chap. 11). Third, since more than 92 percent of Middle East Arabs are Muslim, Islam as a religion unites the majority of them.

Copts.   Coptic ethnic identity derives primarily from the Coptic religion. Numbering about 8–10 percent of the population of Egypt, Copts are the largest non-Muslim ethnic group in the Middle East, a remnant of the ancient Hamitic Egyptians who converted to Christianity. Practicing endogamy and segregation from other Egyptians and from invaders, they have preserved their Monophysite Christianity as well

as a genetic physical kinship with the early Egyptians. The Coptic language survived as the vernacular until supplanted by Arabic 1,000 years after the Islamic conquest. Outside the urban centers of Cairo and Alexandria, the Copts are concentrated in Upper Egypt, in Asyut and Luxor. Friction with the majority Muslims in Egypt is discussed in Chapter 20.

Maronites.   Like the Copts, Maronites are differentiated primarily on the basis of their religion. However, their geographical isolation in the Lebanon Mountains has encouraged independence and endogamy, and has produced a cultural differentiation and substantial political autonomy. Arabic supplanted Syriac during the eighteenth century as a working language, and ties with the French (Franks) during the Crusades and the mandate years (1920–1943) promoted the use of French as a second language. The determined separatism of the Maronites has been a compelling dynamic in Lebanese political-geographical events (see Chap. 13).

Oppressed for their adherence to a Christian heresy, the Maronites left Syria in the tenth century and concentrated in the Lebanon Mountains around Qadisha Gorge. Their cooperation with the Crusader invaders alienated them from the Muslim population, and a small group of Maronites left with the retreating Crusaders to settle in Cyprus, where a small community remains. Thousands of Maronites emigrated from Mount Lebanon around 1900, and emigration increased after the 1950s because of the civil conflict in Lebanon. An estimated 675,000 Maronites—many claiming Phoenician descent—remain in the Levant, the overwhelming majority of them in Lebanon but a few in Cyprus and in Syria.

Druzes.   Druze identity also originated in religion, with cultural and physical differentiations developing over the centuries. Although originating in Egypt, the Druzes won adherents in the Mount Hermon area, where they are still centered. Additional contemporary concentrations are in the Shuf area in central Mount

Lebanon and in the Jabal al-Druze (officially now Jabal al-Arab) of southern Syria.

As heretics, the Druzes were alienated from other Shii Muslims, as well as from their Sunni Muslim neighbors, and clashed with the Maronite Christians as both groups migrated into central Mount Lebanon 1,000 years ago. Rejected by their neighbors, the Druzes separated themselves through endogamy. The Druze sense of independence and separatism contributed to their military orientation, which has been exhibited against the Crusaders, against the Maronites in the 1840s–1850s and 1958, and in the 1975–1991 civil conflict in Lebanon.[2] On the other hand, Druzes in Israel generally accepted the new Jewish government in 1948–1949 and have been the only Arabs permitted to serve in the Israeli army. However, Druze-Israeli relations deteriorated as a result of Israel's annexation of the Golan Heights in 1981 and the Israeli army's occupation of southern Lebanon.

Alawis.   The Alawis are also primarily distinguished by their religion, and they too have developed distinct cultural attributes through segregation and endogamy. They are concentrated in and around the Jabal al-Sahaliyah in northwestern Syria and constitute about 12 percent of the population of that country.

The Alawis have preserved no ancient language and use Arabic regularly. Although criticized by other Syrians for their cooperation with French mandate authorities between the two world wars, after World War II the Alawis were trusted in the army and in government because of their minority status. A climax of their group's role came in 1969, when Syrian Air Force General Hafiz al-Asad, an Alawi, seized power in Damascus and retained the presidency from 1971 until his death in June 2000. In religion, but not necessarily in other characteristics, the Alawis are similar to the Alevis in Turkey (Chap. 21).

Chaldeans.   The Chaldeans are differentiated primarily on the basis of religion, forming an Arabic-speaking Christian collectivity within a dominantly Sunni Muslim area of Iraq. Named after (but not descended from) the ancient Chaldeans of southern Iraq, the Chaldeans are the largest Christian group in Iraq and are centered in the northeastern part of the country and in Baghdad. Many emigrated to the United States after World War II.

Assyrians.   The Assyrians are not descendants of the ancient imperial Assyrians, as many of them claim. Syriac remained their vernacular until recent times, and older Assyrians retain some fluency in the traditional language, but Arabic is the modern vernacular of the group. Dating only from the dispersion of the Assyrians in 1932, their present pattern of distribution has three concentrations: in approximately a score of villages on the upper Khabur River in northeastern Syria; in Baghdad, Kirkuk, and the hills north of Mosul in Iraq, where they were pushed by Mongols in the Middle Ages; and in extreme northwestern Iran, west of Lake Urmia. By the early 1980s more Assyrians probably lived in North America than in the Middle East.

Circassians.   Half a million Circassians migrated into the Middle East from the Caucasus Mountains when czarist Russia took over their homeland after the Congress of Berlin in 1878. The Ottoman sultan permitted them to settle along the axis from Damascus southward to Amman and beyond, as well as in Asia Minor and in the mountains of Kurdistan. They still live in these areas and play modest roles in Syria, Jordan, and northern Israel. Prior to its destruction by the Israelis, Qunaytirah, in the Golan Heights, was a center of Circassian settlement.

Yazidis.   The Yazidis have Kurdish ethnic roots. They are settled farmers concentrated in the Jabal Sinjar west of Mosul and in the hills northwest of Aleppo, with scattered groups in adjacent states. Yazidis do not interact with neighboring tribes; they practice endogamy and prohibit conversion into the group—membership is only by birth.

Nubians.   Nubians lived in the area between Aswan, Egypt, and the Dongola region of

Sudan for perhaps 3,000 years before the construction of the Aswan High Dam. More African in appearance than the Egyptians farther down the Nile, the Nubians converted to Christianity in the sixth century AD and resisted Islam until 1366. Nearly all speak the Nubian language, but most of them also speak Arabic. Of the total Nubian population in Egypt and the Sudan, about one-third live in Egypt and are Sunni Muslims. (See more about them in Chap. 20).

Others. Smaller ethnic groups interrelate with the dominant Arab group because of geographical proximity. Some are differentiated by language, some by religion, and some by both.

The Beja are nomadic pastoralists who migrate seasonally into the southeastern corner of Egypt from northeastern Sudan. The Berbers are a major ethnic group in North Africa and in the Arab World, numbering more than 11 million from Egypt westward to the Atlantic. However, only a few thousand live in the Middle East as defined in this study, primarily in the Siwa Oasis of northwestern Egypt. Their name comes from *barbari* ("barbarians"), as they were called by the Romans. The Mandaeans are a dwindling relict group in Iraq, and its members live in al-Amarah, Suq al-Shuyukh, and Baghdad. The Shabak form another small group in the "ethnic shatter zone" of northern Iraq. Originally Sufi mystics in the fourteenth and fifteenth centuries, they became secretive and heretical, practiced endogamy, and became a closed and isolated community.

The Sulaba (or Sulayb) are a gypsylike people in the Arabian Peninsula who, in small groups, follow Bedouin tribes in their nomadic migrations and serve as tinkers, musicians, and entertainers for the Bedouins and villagers. They are not considered Arabs, and they are so ostracized that their group origins and traditions are little known. Gypsies wander by the thousands in many parts of the Middle East as traditional migrants. Many claim to be Muslims, but others engage in varied religious practices. Like all true gypsies, they originated in northwestern India and speak dialects of Romany, an Indic branch of Indo-Iranian. They often also speak local languages.

Chechens migrated into the Middle East from the northern Caucasus in the mid-nineteenth century. In 1865, 40,000 arrived in Turkey, where most have been assimilated. Later, other small groups of Chechens settled farther south in the Ottoman Empire; and more than 2,000, sometimes called Shishanis, still live in west-central Jordan alongside their fellow Caucasians, the Circassians.

Turks and Related Groups

Turks. The second-largest ethnolinguistic group in the Middle East (after the Arabs), ethnic Turks number about 55 million, somewhat more than one-third of the total number of Turkic-speaking peoples of the world. Generally, Turks speak Turkish as a primary language, are Muslims (90 percent are Sunni), claim a Turkish heritage, and are patriotic about the Republic of Turkey. Culturally, the Turks combined Persian, Arab, Byzantine, and Anatolian cultural elements with their former nomadic central Asian culture. Turks, Tatars, and Turkmen are difficult to differentiate, despite distinctive characteristics, partly because of intermarriage and cultural assimilation.

Four groups of Turks in the Middle East can be identified on the basis of cultural and geographical differentiations. First, the Anatolian Turks in Asia Minor are a thorough biological mixture of earlier Anatolian peoples. Second, the Rumelian Turks (from Rum, meaning Roman or European), are European Turks who remained in Europe after Ottoman days and who later returned to Turkey. More than 400,000 were expelled from Greece in exchange for a similar number of Greeks expelled from Turkey after World War I, and many other scores of thousands later arrived in Turkey from Bulgaria, Romania, and Yugoslavia. Along with ethnic Turks from Bulgaria came about 150,000 Pomaks, most of whom were Bulgars who converted to Islam during Ottoman control of the Balkans. Now highly Turkified, they live in western Anatolia.

The third group is made up of descendants of the Ottoman Turks who stayed in areas of the Middle East when they were detached from the Ottoman Empire after World War I. They live in small groups in Syria, Lebanon, Egypt, Jordan, and Iraq but are steadily becoming Arabized. Similar to this group is the fourth, the 188,000 Cypriot Turks, who live in the northern third of Cyprus and most of whom are descendants of Ottoman Turks who moved to the island after the Ottoman conquest in the early sixteenth century. Cypriot Turks have been joined by Turks from Turkey since 1974, augmenting their numbers appreciably.

Azeris. The Azeris form the second-largest Turkic group (after the Turks themselves) and the fifth-largest ethnolinguistic group in the Middle East. They live to the north and east of the more numerous Kurds, and some related Turkic groups—including the Ilsavan/Shahsavan, Afshar, and Qajars—live to the east of the main group. Some Azeris also live in Turkey. They are the dominant group in the Azerbaijan region of northwestern Iran, where they live primarily as settled farmers and herders. Another several million live in the Azerbaijan Republic, adjacent to northwestern Iran. Like the Persians, and unlike most Turks, the Azeris are Shii Muslims. Tabriz serves as an Azeri center, although its population is ethnically complex.

Turkmen. Despite a common Turkic language, Turkmen are distinct from true Turks and from Tatars. Most of them remain in Turkistan, primarily in the Republic of Turkemistan, adjacent to Iran and east of the Caspian. They are highly tribalized, and their tribal names serve as familiar designations for their traditional hand-knotted rugs. Although they are one of the most widely scattered ethnic groups in the region, main concentrations appear in central Anatolia, eastern Anatolia, northeastern Iraq in the foothills near Mosul and Kirkuk, and across northern Iran, particularly in the northeastern mountains of Khorasan. They tend to live in mountainous areas and to preserve their nomadism for both economic and defensive reasons; however, as with most nomadic groups, the Turkmen are becoming settled and are integrating into the sedentary economy and society. They are all Muslims, about two-thirds Sunni and one-third Shii.

Yoruk. The Yoruk are apparently descendants of some of the earliest Turkish tribes to enter Asia Minor. As one evidence, their Turkish language has been less influenced by Arabic and Persian than has the national Turkish language. Nominally Muslim, their Islam is unorthodox, with neither clergy nor mosques. Rug knotting is a traditional skill among the Yoruk.

The changes in Yoruk areas and life-style are indicative of development in the Middle East. Under the Ottomans the Yoruk maintained a nomadic existence in western Anatolia in the uplands between Konya and Bursa. Intensive government projects during the 1920s and 1930s to develop pastures and to improve agricultural practices in western Asia Minor interfered with their seasonal migrations, producing gradual sedentarization. The changing agricultural economy diminished the Yoruk livelihood, and in the mid-twentieth century, several thousand migrated to southeastern Turkey, where they resumed nomadic pastoralism. Many Yoruk now migrate by truck rather than by camel or on foot.

Ilsavan/Shahsavan. The name Shahsavan ("shah lovers") was impolitic after the 1979 overthrow of the shah of Iran, and the designation was changed to Ilsavan ("tribe lovers"). The Ilsavan are a large nomadic group who are closely related to the Azeris and Afshars, traditionally sharing territory and nomadic migrations to some extent. Like those groups, the Ilsavan are also Shii Muslim. They were given special tribal status in the seventeenth century because they were loyal to the shah, and they traditionally supported the ruling dynasty; however, they seem to have accepted the revolutionary republican government.

Qashqai. The Qashqai are descendants of Turkic tribes who left central Asia in the eleventh century and moved into the Zagros

Mountains in the fifteenth century. Like the great majority of ethnic groups in Iran, the Qashqai are Shii Muslim. The persistence of their nomadism, both horizontal and vertical (transhumance), is legendary. Herding large flocks of sheep, they make an arduous seasonal migration, sometimes over distances of as much as 350 miles/560 km, between their summer and winter pastures. Herding is supplemented by making knotted rugs, kilims (woven rugs), and bags in traditional Qashqai patterns.

Afshars. The Afshars are another Turkic group who are assumed to have migrated onto the Iranian Plateau from Turkistan during the Middle Ages. Like the Ilsavan (with whom they at times migrate), they are sometimes considered a subdivision of the Azeris: All three groups speak related Turkic dialects, practice Shii Islam, and engage to some extent in nomadism. The Afshars are widely distributed in the northern Zagros Mountains from north of Tabriz to Hamadan, and there are two other concentrations, one in Iran in the mountains south of Kerman and the other in Turkey east of Kayseri.

Qajars. The Turkic-speaking Qajars are one of several interlocked ethnic groups in northwestern Iran and the southern Caspian coast area, with some of the related groups belonging to the Turkic family and others the Iranian language family. The Qajars supplied a dynasty that ruled Persia for 131 years (1794–1925). Mostly settled farmers, with small groups of seasonal nomads, the Qajars form a small enclave among the more numerous Mazandarani along the southeastern Caspian coast.

Tatars. Sometimes incorrectly called "Tartars," the Tatars ("archers") were named after (but not directly descended from) the Ta-Ta Mongols who invaded the Middle East along with other Mongols in the thirteenth century. In succeeding centuries, Turks and Tatars intermarried, creating a widespread Turko-Tatar group. Turks, Turkmen, Tatars, Turko-Tatars, and Mongols are often confused in historical writings. The Tatars north of the Black and Caspian seas are far more numerous than in the Middle East and number in the millions. Although scores of thousands of Tatars emigrated from Russia into Turkey during the nineteenth century, they have since become assimilated. Tatars speak a Turkic Kipchak language rather than a Mongolic tongue, and virtually all are Muslim, most of them Sunni.

Persians and Related Groups

Persians are numerically the third-largest ethnolinguistic group in the Middle East, after the Arabs and Turks. Indo-Iranians immigrated into the mountains and basins south and southwest of the Caspian Sea during the second millennium BC. One branch migrated southeastward into the Indus Valley and evolved into the Hindus, and other groups halted in the rugged folds of the Zagros Mountains and settled in western Iran. Those south of the Caspian evolved as Medes (or Medians), and those in the southern Zagros became Persians. They called themselves Aryans ("nobles") and named their new mountain and basin homeland after themselves—Iran.

Persians. Evolving for a thousand years in the folds of the Zagros, the Persians emerged as a unified sedentary people in the sixth century BC and built an unprecedented empire (see Chap. 2). Although they were later defeated by Alexander the Great and were overwhelmed by Arab Muslims in the seventh century, the Persians repeatedly restored a power base on the intermontane Iranian Plateau. Since World War I, the Persians have become the leading ethnic group in the Iranian nation and fill most government, industrial, professional, and cultural positions. By the 1970s most educated Persians spoke French or English in addition to Farsi, and many have been educated in the United States or France; however, after the Islamic Revolution, the authorities discouraged Westernization and forced a return to Islamic fundamentalism.

More than 95 percent of Persians adhere to the Twelver, or Jafari, sect of Shii Islam, for nationalistic as much as for theological reasons. A small but significant number of Persians are Zoroastrians and Bahais. Although Persians live throughout Iran, by far the majority of the population in the foothills, valleys, basins, and plateaus in the area from Hamadan to Qom to Tehran to Shiraz to Kerman is true Persian, and Persians also predominate in those cities.

In addition to the approximately 30 million Persians in Iran (nearly half the population of the country), another million live on the west side of the Gulf and, as Arabized Persians, in the Qatif and al-Hasa oases in the Eastern Province of Saudi Arabia, as well as around the Shii shrines in Iraq. Pro-Iranian sentiments among some of these Persians outside Iran have been a matter of concern to their host countries since the early 1980s. Wherever they live, but especially in Iran itself, Persians proudly differentiate themselves by their language, Shii religion, history, 2,000 years of literature, and distinctive arts. The cleavage between Persians and Arabs along the Zagros piedmont has repeatedly been reignited over the centuries, most recently in 1974–1975, 1979, and then in the bloody 1980–1988 Iran-Iraq war.

Kurds. The fourth-largest ethnolinguistic group in the Middle East, the Kurds occupy a centuries-old mountain homeland, the politically fragmented Kurdistan, which embraces an irregular area at the junction of Turkey, Iraq, and Iran (see Map 6-3). The Kurds not only predominate in Kurdistan but also intermingle with neighboring Azeris and Armenians and with Turks, Turkmen, Arabs, and others. Both the total Kurdish population and its distribution among the three countries that share most of Kurdistan can only be estimated and are debatable. Kurdish leaders claim much higher numbers than are accepted by officials and scholars. Reasonable figures as of late 1992 suggest a total of 20 million Kurds in "Kurdistan"— 10 million in Turkey, 4.5 million in Iraq, and 5.5 million in Iran. In addition, perhaps another 1–2 million Kurds live in northern Syria, central Anatolia, Lebanon, the central Zagros Mountains, and the Elburz and Kopet mountains.

Language and heritage define Kurdishness rather than physical derivation; many Kurds consider themselves descendants of the Medes, while others believe they were formerly part of the Lur. Most Kurds are Sunni Muslims, which separates them from the Shii Persians, but some Kurds in Iran and parts of Iraq have become Shii. Retaining a tribal structure, the Kurds are settled farmers, herdsmen, and townsmen. Formerly nomadic, Kurds are becoming settled and even urbanized. Especially in their core mountain home area, the Kurds resist outside authority. Although Kurdish nationalism evolved with Arab, Turkish, and Persian nationalism in the late nineteenth century, the Kurds have failed to achieve political independence.[3]

Both the historical and contemporary plights of the Kurds became the focus of intensive media coverage after the Gulf war of 1990–1991. Further details on the situation of the Kurds in the respective countries that share Kurdistan are given in the chapters on Iraq, Turkey, and Iran, and the general Kurdish problem is discussed in Chapter 11.

Baluch. Like the Kurds, the Baluch are primarily Sunni Muslims, speak an Indo-Iranian language, live in an isolated mountain environment, and have a traditional homeland— Baluchistan—at the junction of three countries—Iran, Pakistan, and Afghanistan. However, Baluchistan is an arid realm, and the Baluch are much more nomadic or seminomadic, with only a few settling in the impoverished villages of the area. Although tribal organization does remain strong among the Baluch, the various tribes are not closely integrated. Isolated in their spare desert and mountain environment, the Baluch are the poorest and most neglected major group in Iran. Probably a mixture of Dravidians of the Indian Peninsula and seventh-century Arab invaders, the Baluch are culturally more closely related to the Pakistanis and the Pushtun of Afghanistan than to the Persians.

Emigrants from Baluchistan have crossed the Gulf of Oman to both Oman and the present United Arab Emirates, where their round tents have provided a contrast to the rectangular Arab tents. The Baluch serve in large numbers in the various military forces of the southeastern Arabian Peninsula.

Lur. Of uncertain origin, the Lur speak a dialect of Persian and are linguistically and culturally related to the Persians and to the nearby Bakhtiari. They occupy Lorestan, a homeland in the central Zagros Mountains between Bakhtaran (Kermanshah) and Shiraz, and are racially mixed.

The basic social organizational unit among the Lur is the tribe (*il*). Some nomadic tribes migrate to the high mountains in the summer, but other Lur tribes have become sedentary or semisedentary, especially in the eastern valleys. The sedentary tribes have adopted Persian (Farsi) as a second language. Tribal structure has gradually become less rigid as the power of the tribal chiefs (khans) has been undermined by the central government. Most Lur are Shii Muslims but hold some beliefs that are inconsistent with Persian and Bakhtiari Shiism. Of the Lur who have spilled over into Iraq, a few roam the Zagros piedmont in the Mandali area east of Baghdad while others work in towns along the Tigris. Estimates of the number of Lur vary greatly.

Bakhtiari. Tribes in the Il-e Bakhtiari confederation relate geographically and culturally not only to the nearby Lur but also to the Turkic Qashqai. Like the Qashqai, the Bakhtiari are tribally organized, disciplined, and still largely nomadic. Traditionally playing a powerful role in Iranian politics, Bakhtiari leaders periodically held high government positions until the 1920s. Bakhtiari tribesmen have served in the Iranian army for centuries, but the political influence of the khans was restricted by the central government after World War I. Like many Iranian tribes, the Bakhtiari produce handmade rugs with distinctive design. Their ethnic costumes evoke statues and bas reliefs of Parthians of 2,000 years ago.

Zoroastrians. Zoroastrians are probably the least physically mixed ethnic Persians in Iran, comparable to the Copts in Egypt, and they are so sharply distinguished by their religion that they constitute an ethnic group as distinct as the Maronites or Druzes in the Levant. By adhering to a definite geographical area, practicing endogamy, and exercising group determination, Zoroastrians have survived and preserved their identity despite persecution. The several thousand who fled to western India during the Arab invasion of the 630s became known as Parsees, who are now concentrated in Bombay and make up some of the major industrialist families of southern Asia.

Others. Another score of ethnic groups related to the Persians are found in pockets on the Iranian Plateau, further illustrating the complexity of the ethnic pattern in the eastern Middle East. Two such groups, neither sharply differentiated from their neighbors, live as farmers and fishermen along the shores of the Caspian Sea—the Gilani along the southwestern shore around Rasht and the Mazandarani in the coastal lowlands and adjacent mountains southeast of the Caspian. Two other Persian ethnic groups are listed in Table 6-3; the others are too small to be distinguished.

Jews and Samaritans

Jews. After an early history chronicled in the Old Testament, Jews were deported in the first century AD from most of Palestine by the Romans. In this second phase of the Jewish Diaspora (the first was the Babylonian Exile), Jews settled around the shore of the Mediterranean Basin, and sizable communities developed in several major Mediterranean coastal cities, including Alexandria, Egypt, which had a major Jewish community for more than 2,000 years until after World War II. Under the Ottoman Empire, Jews (like Christians) constituted a *millet,* and Jewish minority rights were sufficiently protected so that after 1492, tens of thousands of Sephardic (Spanish) Jews who fled the Spanish Inquisition settled in the Ottoman Empire. They thus became citizens of successor Arab states after 1918 and continued to receive the rights of *ahl al-kitab.*

Ashkenazi (German) Jews from central and eastern Europe have migrated to the Middle East comparatively recently, in the late nineteenth and twentieth centuries, especially in waves of immigration (aliyah) after World War II. After the establishment of Israel in 1948, most of the Jews in Middle East Arab countries emigrated to Israel, and an estimated 300,000 Jews had left Egypt, Lebanon, Syria, Iraq, and Yemen by the early 1990s.

In spite of generally endogamous traditions, Jews arriving in Israel have exhibited physical differences related to their countries of origin in addition to variations in linguistic, political-geographical (or national); and ideological backgrounds. Subethnic divisions have emerged between Ashkenazi Jews and Oriental or Eastern Jews, including Sephardim, with the Sabras, or native-born Israelis, forming another subgroup. The continuing question, Who is a Jew? and the distinctions among observant Jews, nonobservant (or nonpracticing) Jews, halakic Jews (strictly adherent to religious law), assimilated Jews, and even Christian Jews complicate problems of Israeli citizenship, especially in connection with the Israeli Law of Return. Of a world total of about 13.5 million Jews, about 4.8 million lived in Israel, and about 60,000 of an original 1 million in the rest of the Middle East, mainly in Iran and Turkey, in 1999.[4]

Samaritans. The Samaritans, mentioned in the New Testament, are a very small but particularly interesting group that originated among Israelites who remained in Samaria during the Babylonian Exile and, through intermarriage with other groups, emerged as a new people. They found themselves irreconcilably estranged from the Jews who returned from Babylon, and the two groups remain theologically incompatible even today. Decimated in battles with the Romans and Byzantines, the Samaritans numbered only 611 in early 1998, about half in Nabulus, north of Jerusalem, and the other half in Holon, near Tel Aviv.[5] This relict group scarcely reproduces itself but rejects contacts with outsiders.

Armenians, Greeks, and Others

Armenians. The Armenian people date back more than 3,000 years, to about the time the Hittites disappeared from Anatolia. Prior to World War I, they were centered in the Lake Van area and surrounding eastern Anatolian mountains, long referred to as Armenia. The ancient kingdom of Armenia, located in the same area, was the first state to adopt Christianity as its official religion.

Although Armenians constituted an influential *millet* during the Ottoman Empire, relations between Armenians and Turks became hostile after 1878, and there were battles in 1895–1896, 1909, 1915–1917, and 1920–1921. In a confused, complex, and disputed series of circumstances involving local relationships (including Kurdish-Armenian-Turkish-Russian relations), reciprocal attacks, Russian interference, and European entanglements, hundreds of thousands of Armenians in central and eastern Asia Minor were persecuted, massacred, and deported; thousands more fled into adjacent lands for safety. A post-World War I Armenian republic was proposed by the Allies at the Paris Peace Conference, but it never materialized.

Although the Armenians, who call themselves Hai, lost their traditional homeland in the early 1920s, they maintain a strong ethnic identity, language, and religion, partly through a tradition of endogamy. Armenian communities in the Middle East and elsewhere center on the church (usually Armenian Orthodox), school, newspaper, and businesses and have a cultural emphasis on education and achievement. Armenians in the Middle East total about 900,000 and are distributed among Syria (more than 2 percent of the population, and found especially in Aleppo and Damascus), Lebanon, Iran, Turkey, and Iraq. The new Armenian Republic, successor to the former Soviet Armenian SSR, has a population of more than 3.8 million, and thousands of Middle East Armenians have emigrated there as well as to the West since World War II.

Greeks.   Greeks occupied the Aegean Sea fringe of western Asia Minor from 1000 BC until they fled, were expelled, or were exchanged for Turks in Greece in the mid-1920s following the failure of a Greek military expedition against the new Turkish Republic in 1922, which was another in a centuries-long series of hostilities between Greeks and Turks. From about 2 million Greeks in Asia Minor before World War I, only a few score thousand remain in Turkey—mostly in Istanbul. Groups of Greeks remained in Egypt and Syria-Palestine after the time of Greek (Hellenistic) control, although many of Alexandria's thousands of Greeks finally left because of Egyptian nationalist pressure during the 1950s and 1960s. Jerusalem maintains a small Greek colony, considerably Arabized. The largest concentration of Greeks in the Middle East today, about 660,000, lives on the island of Cyprus and constitutes the sole national group in the Republic of Cyprus. Greek Cypriots maintain their strong identity not only through continued use of the Greek language but also through close ties with Greece, with which many Greek Cypriots sought *enosis* ("union") during the civil war of the 1950s.

Georgians.   Originally a Christian group in the southern Caucasus Mountains, the Georgians were dispersed over Asia Minor and Iran during the seventeenth century and later, when many of them became Muslims. Like the Armenians and Azeris, the Georgians had their own soviet socialist republic in the former USSR and also converted it into an independent republic in 1991. The small group of Georgians in the Middle East live mostly in Turkey and are being gradually assimilated.

Laze.   Many Laze left the southern Caucasus following Russia's seizure of the area after 1878 and settled just across the border in northeastern Turkey. Traditionally seafarers and fishermen living on or near the Black Sea coast, where Rize is a Laze center, the Laze often serve on Black Sea ships or on Turkish naval vessels. They speak their own language, Laz, which is akin to Georgian.

Notes

1. Of many useful studies of peoples, religions, and languages of the Middle East, a particularly helpful one is Weekes 1984, which has a bibliography for each people. Non-Muslims are included in Bates and Rassam 1983, Eickelman 1981, Gulick 1983, and Bengio and Ben-Dor 1999. Relatively up-to-date statistics of peoples within individual countries are given in the annual *Britannica World Data.* For languages especially, see the excellent Grimes et al. 1996, also at URL <http://www.sil.org/ethnologue>.

2. Betts 1988 is a concise and useful study of the Druzes. For more details see Abu-Izzedin 1984.

3. See McDowall 1999. For a popular account see Hitchens 1992.

4. See *New York Times,* July 25, 1999, for an in-depth study of the subject.

5. *Christian Science Monitor,* Jan. 16, 1998.

7

The Desert and the Sown: Land Use

Agricultural conditions, systems, and products differ strikingly from one area of the Middle East to another. Agricultural landscapes vary from the irrigated gardens of the Nile Valley to the Mediterranean croplands and fruit orchards of the Levant and from the extensive wheat fields of interior Anatolia to the desert rangelands of the wandering herdsmen. Valleys and slopes of the mountains of northern Anatolia and Iran are reminiscent of the European Alps. By contrast, vast arid expanses appear to be barren wasteland. Although some desert areas, such as the Rub al-Khali, have little to offer agriculturally, other large desert stretches are effectively utilized by nomadic herders.

Agricultural lands in the Middle East fall into three broad types—not all mutually exclusive—according to the availability of moisture: (1) subhumid and humid areas suitable for rainfed crops, from wheat and barley on the drier margin to maize and tea on the high rainfall margin; (2) irrigated areas located primarily in deserts and semideserts but also increasingly as enclaves in the more humid areas; (3) arid and semiarid lands used by pastoralists for grazing their animals. This chapter surveys these patterns of land use (see Table 7-1), forestry and fishing, and land tenure and reform from a regional perspective.

Agriculture

Before the boom in oil production after the mid-1950s, the Middle East was by every criterion overwhelmingly an agricultural area. The manufacturing and services sectors were only minimally developed or were lacking. Even with only modest agricultural yields, the region was a net exporter of food. By the early 1990s, however, the sixteen Middle East states were importing more than 50 percent of their food requirements; and this percentage continues to rise as the population maintains its growth curve, acquires greater purchasing power, and shifts increasingly from agricultural employment to more varied economic activity.

The relative decline in agricultural employment has been especially marked in the petroleum-producing areas, most significantly in the areas around the Gulf. Several Gulf coastal city-states with fishing economies prior to World War II still engage in fishing, but the percentage contribution of that activity to the national economy is now negligible, as is the percentage of the work force employed in fishing. (The percentage of workers in the various economic sectors of the sixteen states is shown in a table in Chapter 9, which indicates the relative importance of agriculture statistically in each country.)

Even in those countries in which a relatively high percentage of the economically active population is still engaged in agriculture, such activity may contribute only a small percentage of the gross domestic product (GDP). For example, in Egypt, with 30 percent of the work force engaged in agriculture, only about 15 percent of the GDP comes from this source. In Yemen, where the 71 percent of the work force engaged in agriculture contributes 18 percent of the GDP, the 4.3 percent engaged in manufacturing and mining contributes 23 percent of the GDP. Moreover, manufacturing now

TABLE 7-1 LAND USE, GENERAL.

COUNTRY	1 TOTAL AREA ARABLE AND PERM. CROPS	2 AREA UNDER IRRIGATION TOTAL	3 % OF CULT. AREA	4 PERCENTAGE CULTIVA-TION	5 OF TOTAL PERM. PASTURE	6 AREA UNDER: FOREST, WOODLAND	7 WASTE, OTHER
Bahrain	2	2	100	3	6	<1	91
Cyprus	142	40	28	17	<1	13	69
Egypt	3,283	3,283	100	3	—	<1	97
Iran	18,500	7,264	39	11	27	7	55
Iraq	5,750	3,525	61	13	9	4	74
Israel	435	195	45	21	7	5	65
Jordan	410	75	18	5	9	<1	86
Kuwait	5	5	100	<1	8	<1	92
Lebanon	307	88	30	30	1	8	61
Oman	63	62	98	<1	5	<1	95
Qatar	8	13	100	<1	5	<1	95
Saudi Arabia	3,830	1,478	39	2	60	<1	42
Syria	5,971	1,082	18	30	45	3	22
Turkey	27,115	4,186	15	36	16	26	22
UAE	74	68	92	<1	2	<1	97
Yemen	1,550	485	31	3	30	4	63
Gaza	—	—	—	—	—	—	—
West Bank	—	—	—	—	—	—	—
TOTAL/AVG.	67,445	21,851	57	<10	14	3	70

Several figures are Food and Agriculture Organization (FAO) estimates. Data in Columns 1 and 2 are in thousands of hectares (1996). Percentages in Column 3 calculated from FAO data. Data in Columns 4-7 are from the early 1990s and are no longer collected by FAO because of non-uniformity of criteria. Sources: 1 and 2: UN FAO *Production Yearbook 1997*; 4-7: same, 1995.

surpasses agriculture as the leading employer in some formerly agricultural countries.

The relative decrease in the percentage share of agriculture may obscure government efforts to develop a nation's agricultural potential. Agriculture is such a vital element in the national economies that all Middle East states are conducting systematic, wide-ranging agricultural development programs. Oil income in the Gulf oil states will cease in a few decades, but meanwhile it can be invested in agricultural projects that will have a long-range benefit.

Some General Aspects

By its very nature, agriculture is highly interactive with ecological factors and cultural traditions, so it differs from one area to another as well as within an area. For example, mixed farming as practiced in the United States and Western Europe is not well developed in the Middle East; a system in which the farmer

grows feed grains and then feeds them to animals is in any case poorly adapted to an environment with more grazing land than grain surpluses. Income from livestock, including that from milk and egg production as well as that from meat and meat by-products, accounts for less than one-third of the agricultural income in the Middle East. Nevertheless, domestic animals play a significant role in the agricultural cycle, since they provide farm income between harvests. Traditional herding of livestock by nomadic pastoralists, however, is steadily declining not only in the deserts of the oil states but also in the mountains of Iran and Turkey.

Wheat is found throughout the region and leads all crops in terms of area sown (Fig. 7-1a). Highly specialized crops are produced in scattered small areas: coffee and the mildly narcotic *qat* in Yemen, frankincense in southern Oman and Yemen, tea in northeastern Turkey and northwestern Iran, dates around the Gulf,

FIGURE 7-1   Two views of agricultural development in the Syrian Jazirah, east of the Euphrates River: harvesting a bumper wheat crop by hand *(top)* (note sickle in the woman's right hand); elevated precast concrete irrigation canal *(bottom)* in a recently irrigated area, part of the major Jazirah development scheme.

licorice in southern Iraq, and pine nuts in Lebanon.

Food crops occupy most of the cultivated area in the Middle East, but industrial crops (cotton, tobacco, sugarcane, sugar beets, linseed, sesame) have also been locally important for more than a century. Cotton and flax have been major crops in Egypt since pharaonic times. Where ecological conditions are especially favorable, industrial crops have been promoted by government agencies since the 1950s—for example, sugar beets in Syria and Turkey and cotton in Israel and Turkey.

With the exceptions of the intensively irrigated lands, parts of Israel, and a few other scattered areas, low crop yields still typify regional agriculture, although yields have increased notably since the 1950s. For example, the new high-yield wheats are markedly increasing outputs in places, but wheat is usually grown on marginal lands with highly variable precipitation. Until the 1960s, mechanization was uncommon, but coordinated programs are increasing the number of machines, especially tractors (see Table 7-2, col. 7). Farming in Israel is highly mechanized.

Small farms that are primarily tenant operated characterize the region, one reason mechanization has been limited. Along with efforts to improve yields, farmers and governments have made systematic attempts to improve the quality of crops, the quality of the produce that reaches the consumer, conservation, efficiency, and other agricultural practices. Such programs produce a region-wide dynamic of change, with uneven but sometimes excellent results.

Physical Factors

1. Climate. Moisture supply is the main agricultural problem in much of the region, and except in parts of Turkey and in some mountain areas it is inadequate, seasonally concentrated, and unreliable. In areas with a widespread marginal climate, drought years are frequent and severe, and such areas experience wide swings in grain production. For example, in the locally dry year of 1984, Jordan produced only 15,000 mt (metric tons) of wheat; in 1980, which was unusually wet, Jordan's wheat crop was 134,000 mt—893 percent greater.

Only 7 percent of the region can regularly support rainfed (unirrigated) agriculture (note isohyets on Map 4-2 and see Table 4-1). Approximate precipitation parameters for agriculture in the region are the 5-in./125-mm isohyet as the minimum for regular grain production and the 12-in./300-mm isohyet as the lower limit for other crops. Irrigation can extend the cultivated area, but only to a limited extent, and it must be developed at great expense and effort for the most intensive and effective methods of water use. Available water is finite, and irrigable land is limited. Despite the problem of aridity, crops benefit from the long growing season, prevailingly clear skies, and favorable light for plant growth.

2. Soils. Because the area with naturally productive soils is limited, higher crop yields require good farm management, including intensive fertilization, good drainage, improved fallowing in lieu of the traditional procedures, and good crop rotation. Salinity buildup is an ever-present problem in drier areas.

3. Relief. The wide distribution of mountainous areas and rough terrain reduces the amount of land that is naturally suitable for cultivation. Although valuable for their cooler climate and as major sources of runoff for irrigation water, mountains can be adapted to only limited agricultural production (see Fig. 3-5). However, in places, laborious terracing and other techniques have made a moderate production of specialty crops possible. Nevertheless, population pressure on the land long ago induced cultivators to plow highland slopes; the resulting loss of shrubs and trees that slowed runoff and protected the soil seriously escalated soil erosion. For their part, most of the low-lying plains and plateaus, which do have a relief that is appropriate for cultivation, are the areas of inadequate moisture and less productive soils.

TABLE 7-2 LAND USE: MAJOR GROUND CROPS AND NUMBER OF TRACTORS.

COUNTRY	1 WHEAT AREA	2 WHEAT PROD.	3 ALL VEGE-TABLES	4 TOMA-TOES	5 COTTON LINT	6 GRAPES	7 TRACTORS
Bahrain	—	—	12	5	—	—	—
Cyprus	6	13	132	40	—	97	17,000
Egypt	1,045	5,849	11,505	5,950	315	850	90,000
Iran	6,600	11,500	10,250	3,500	156	1,915	235,000
Iraq	1,405	1,063	2,948	850	9	300	37,000
Israel	70	140	1,798	440	47	90	25,700
Jordan	50	54	1,186	641	—	61	6,000
Kuwait	—	—	86	21	—	—	100
Lebanon	24	45	967	240	—	350	4,000
Oman	1	1	167	33	—	—	150
Qatar	—	—	43	10	—	—	69
Saudi Arabia	336	1,500	2,395	500	—	135	9,500
Syria	1,761	3,031	1,725	405	327	452	86,652
Turkey	9,500	18,650	21,026	6,600	755	3,650	807,303
UAE	1	1	835	545	—	—	283
Yemen	104	129	526	225	5	153	5,945
Gaza	1	1	158	48	—	2	750
West Bank	—	—	—	—	—	—	—
TOTAL	20,904	41,977	55,759	20,053	1,614	8,055	1,325,452

Many of the data are Food and Agriculture Organization (FAO) estimates or are unofficial figures. Wheat area, column 1, is in thousands of hectares. Crop production, columns 2-6, is in thousands of metric tons. Tractors are in units. Source: UN FAO *Production Yearbook 1997*.

Traditions, Techniques, and Technology

Improvement in agriculture has been hindered by the persistence of traditional practices that are inimical to better farming and marketing. Until recently, the cost of farm inputs (fertilizer, pesticides, machinery) was only 25 percent of the gross value of output, in contrast to 70 percent in the United States. Thus, the value added per agricultural worker has been generally low, and total farm production has also been low as a result, but the situation is improving markedly. The rapidly increasing production of horticultural crops in plastic greenhouses impresses even the casual observer, not only in the Fertile Crescent but also in Egypt, Saudi Arabia, and the Gulf amirates. Although more expensive, greenhouse or hothouse production of tomatoes, beans, peppers, egg-plant, strawberries, and similar crops permits earlier marketing, much higher yield, more attractive produce, and higher pricing.

Ironically, the countries that have the wealth to supply the highest capital inputs to agriculture have, with one or two exceptions, the lowest agricultural potential: Oman, Saudi Arabia, and the smaller Gulf states. Iraq and Iran have both oil income and agricultural potential but have spread their income thinly, especially during the wars of the 1980s and 1990–1991. Iraq particularly squandered enormous capital resources on armament production and purchases; this engendered severe broad-scale economic problems under United Nations sanctions still in effect in early 2000 after nearly a decade. However, every Middle Eastern government has an active, if not uniformly effective, national program for upgrading agriculture, and oil-producing Arab states with a limited agricultural potential have given financial assistance to their less wealthy Arab neighbors who have a greater crop potential. Such aid is mutually beneficial, as it produces a multiplier effect, and regional agricultural progress has been appreciably stimulated.

Mechanization on any perceptible scale has come late and slowly, and because mechanization requires a systems approach that has been neglected, the mere adoption of machines has not achieved an optimum benefit. Even the greatly increased use of the internal combustion engine, which is common even in remote areas for pumping irrigation water, is a mixed blessing because of overpumping in some areas. The use of tractors is steadily increasing; their number quadrupled between 1970 and 1984. That increase is mainly attributable to the quintupling of the number of tractors in Turkey, which has 61 percent of the tractors in the Middle East. Iran is second, with 18 percent (Table 7-2). More sophisticated and expensive machines are still relatively unusual—cotton pickers, corn (maize) pickers, and wheat combines. Milking machines were rare, until the 1990s, except in Israel, but their numbers increased from 1,000 to 44,000 in Turkey from 1989 to 1997.

With financial aid from the United States and from international Jewish agencies, Israel devotes even higher capital inputs per unit area to land reclamation and improvement than do the Gulf states. In proportion to its size, Israel has executed the most intensive land improvement programs in the region, and one of its major land reclamation projects, the drainage and cultivation of the Huleh Marshes in extreme northern Israel, was undertaken as early as the 1950s. Whereas "making the desert bloom" has been accomplished only in limited "oasis" areas in the dry Negev of Israel, scores of projects have improved cropland or rangeland, irrigated cultivated areas, drained marshes, and installed systems for drip irrigation.

Some areas, especially in Turkey, give good rainfed yields in an average year; but in most parts of the Middle East, irrigation is either essential, as in Egypt, or highly beneficial, as on the Levant coastal plains. Thus, for most of the region the critical resource is water. Accordingly, states have undertaken engineering projects to harness more of their water resources, to distribute that water to improved cultivable areas, and to utilize more efficient irrigation techniques. Some of the world's major irrigation projects, involving construction of world-class dams, were undertaken in the Middle East

during the 1970s and the 1980s: the Southeast Anatolia Project in Turkey, the Jazirah Project in Syria, and the Aswan High Dam Project in Egypt. Some political problems ensuing from these projects are examined in Chapter 11.

Landholdings and Land Reform

Land Tenure

Land tenure is an essential socioeconomic aspect of agricultural patterns and is extraordinarily complex in the Middle East. The complexity arises partly from the number of national systems in the region and partly from the varied legal systems introduced into much of the area by earlier regional governments. The prevailing land tenure system developed in an Islamic context after the Muslim conquests of the seventh century and was modified over four centuries under the Ottoman Empire (which excluded Iran). With many land regulations rooted in Islamic law, some relationships with land are traditionally revered as religious in nature.

Highly simplified, landholdings everywhere, except in Cyprus and parts of Israel, fall into three major categories: (1) state-owned land, the most common type, with strong usufruct rights vested in the occupant (*miri* lands, called *khaliseh* in Iran); (2) freehold land or land under private ownership (*mulk*); and (3) land in a religious trust (*waqf*), a unique Islamic form of trusteeship for the endowment of some religious or other social purpose, such as a mosque or school. The amount of *waqf* land is steadily decreasing, with the trusts being discouraged by governments because they are difficult for the state to control or tax. Thus, despite traditional reverence for the institution, *waqf* land has been widely expropriated under recent land reform programs.

Two communal subcategories of land tenure play important roles in Middle East agriculture. The nomadic tribal grazing range (*dirah*) is based on the concept of land as territory rather than land as property. However, a major tribe considers that it has priority rights in its *dirah* as its communal range, along with tribal water sources. Hundreds of thousands of square miles are included in nomadic tribal ranges in the Middle East as a whole. A second subcategory, the communal village—*musha* in the Syria-Palestine realm—permits villagers in marginal environments to shift between sedentarism and nomadism as circumstances dictate.[1]

Some large state landholdings quietly passed into private control during the post-World War I confusion that accompanied the transfer of former Ottoman territories. Under many different designations, some trustees gradually assumed private ownership of tracts of *miri* land, especially tribal leaders who might have been registered as "owners" of extensive communal areas.

Traditional land tenure systems changed sharply in Palestine after World War I as land acquired by the Jewish National Fund (JNF) from Arab owners was occupied by Zionist immigrants. Under a new Jewish system, suggestive of combined aspects of the Islamic *miri* and *waqf* systems, the JNF took over the land "in the name of the Jewish people" and leased it for nominal sums to the colonists. More significantly, during the fighting in 1948 and 1949, Israeli agencies expropriated approximately 1,112,000 acres/450,000 ha of cultivated land from Palestinian Arab owners who became refugees. Such lands were absorbed by the new state or by the quasi-official JNF and similar agencies, then were leased to new Jewish settlers. As the occupying power, the Israeli government has expropriated scores of plots of lands in the West Bank, primarily for installation of Jewish settlements, state lands, and strategic roads.

Holdings and Reform

The size of landholdings is another significant aspect of land tenure and of agricultural patterns and has also had major impacts on the social and political stability of several countries in the region. Since World War II, reform-minded governments have conducted land reform programs to break up landholdings that were considered to be excessively large and to lessen the influence of powerful landlords.

Even before land reform, small holdings were typical in the Middle East, especially in irrigated areas where land is scarce, highly desirable, and expensive because of its improvements. In Egypt, for example, where all cultivated land must be irrigated, farms of less than 2.5 acres/1 ha embrace 96 percent of all agricultural land. Such small holdings occupy only 15 percent of the nonirrigated areas in Syria.

Prior to land reform programs that began in the mid-1950s, small numbers of wealthy landlords possessed huge holdings in Egypt, Syria, Iraq, and Iran. In Iraq, for example, a study by the UN's Food and Agriculture Organization (FAO) revealed that 2 percent of the landowners held 66 percent of the land in the mid-1950s; in Iran, large owners and tribal leaders controlled 50 percent of the land. Following the model of revolutionary republican Egypt under Gamal Abd al-Nasser, Syria and Iraq conducted land reform programs during the late 1950s and early 1960s. As one result of these land redistribution programs, the number of great landlords in the Middle East has declined sharply. The same reforms changed landowning patterns: Individual ownership has replaced many of the tribal rights to planting and pasture, and land consolidation programs have reduced fragmented, scattered holdings.

Rainfed Crop Farming
Extensive Grain Farming

As the mean annual rainfall increases to about 5 in./125 mm along the inner margin of the Fertile Crescent, desert and semiarid grasslands give way to subhumid cropland (Map 7-1). The cereal grains grown in this subhumid belt—wheat, barley, and millet—are in fact highly bred grasses. Here, despite frequent negative deviations from the average annual precipitation, grains grown without irrigation yield moderately good crops in occasional wet years, as in 1991–1992, and at least minimum crops in the frequent drought years. Wheat yields might range between 15 and 2.5 bu. per acre/1,000 and 165 kg per ha, and barley does as well or

MAP 7-1   Middle East land use. Note great extent of area virtually unused or useful only for nomadic herding.

better. Both the production and yields of wheat are increasing significantly in the Middle East as the new dwarf wheats are planted.

Crop failures in the marginal lands are frequent. The more drought-prone areas could be better utilized for growing high-quality forage grasses in a comprehensive range management program to increase meat production, but changing from grains to grass might be difficult, since some nomadic groups on the margins of grain-farming areas operate as both wandering herdsmen and part-time grain farmers. In a wet cycle, they tend to settle down, only to shift back to nomadic herding in a dry cycle, as in the *musha* village. Yet in each cycle, a few families tend to remain sedentary, so that the nomads gradually suffer a net loss, for this as well as for other reasons.

Whether on the dry margins or in the more humid areas, all wheat grown in the Middle East is winter wheat, planted in the autumn to take advantage of the cool-season rainfall and then harvested in the early days of the warm, dry summer.

Mediterranean Agriculture

Wheat and Other Cereals. In the rainfed agriculture of the more humid Mediterranean

climate areas, wheat is still the dominant crop in area planted, but Mediterranean agriculture is typically varied and includes specialized arboriculture (tree crops), viticulture (grape cultivation), and a great range of irrigated crops. Wheat is more intensively cultivated in this wetter area where yields are higher and more reliable than in the steppes (14–17 bu. per acre/940–1,145 kg per ha as a representative range). Millet and barley are also common in the area.

Vegetables and Fruits. Mediterranean-type agricultural conditions are ecologically suitable, particularly with supplementary irrigation, for a variety of vegetables and fruits, many of which evolved in the area (Table 7-3). Coastal plains fringing the eastern Mediterranean, from western Turkey to southern Israel and around Cyprus, are veritable vegetable gardens and fruit orchards. Irrigation helps support citrus groves, especially oranges, in favorable segments all along this coastal belt, and bananas are grown in southern Turkey, Lebanon, and Israel. Oranges from Lebanon, Israel (the Jaffa orange), and Gaza are prime products, although Iran, Egypt, and Turkey greatly exceed the Levant in quantity of production (Table 7-3 and Fig. 7-2a). Many soft fruits—peaches, apricots, plums, pears, and cherries—and vines are grown higher up, at cooler and more humid elevations. Two especially important perennial crops, olives and grapes, occupy 40 percent of the fruit area of the region. Less favorable lower hillsides are clothed with olive groves well into the interior, even east of the Jordan Valley. On dry, stony slopes in much of the eastern Mediterranean, as well as on slopes of the Zagros in Iran, tree nuts such as almonds, walnuts, and pistachios thrive, despite the hot, dry summers. The fig appears frequently where irrigation permits its survival. Smyrna (Izmir) figs, rich and purple and large as lemons, are world renowned.

Fruits, vegetables, and nuts are also specialties of favorable areas well away from the coasts and far into the interior of Anatolia, Syria, and Iran. The Bekaa-Galilee-Jordan trench shelters fruit orchards, including those for bananas in Israel and Jordan. The Damascus oasis, the

TABLE 7-3 LAND USE: TREE CROPS, TIMBER (ROUNDWOOD), AND FISH.

COUNTRY	1 ALL FRUITS	2 ORANGES	3 TREE NUTS	4 OLIVES	5 DATES	6 TIMBER	7 FISH
Bahrain	22	—	—	—	17	—	7.6
Cyprus	272	45	1	10	—	54	3.1
Egypt	5,781	1,370	6	210	710	2,698	305.7
Iran	10,001	1,600	292	25	860	7,463	314.3
Iraq	1,550	310	5	13	630	161	22.0
Israel	1,584	400	5	40	13	113	20.4
Jordan	393	29	2	82	?	11	0.1
Kuwait	2	—	—	—	1	—	7.8
Lebanon	1,244	185	20	85	—	515	2.4
Oman	202	—	—	—	133	—	118.6
Qatar	16	—	—	—	15	—	5.1
Saudi Arabia	1,041	—	—	—	597	—	58.0
Syria	1,626	236	74	403	—	55	7.3
Turkey	9,572	745	688	450	9	19,279	604.1
UAE	304	—	—	—	245	—	108.0
Yemen	471	85	—	—	26	324	82.8
Gaza	137	105	2	3	3	—	—
West Bank	—	—	—	—	—	—	—
TOTAL	34,218	5,110	1,095	1,321	3,261	30,673	1,667.3

Many of the data are Food and Agriculture Organization (FAO) estimates or are unofficial figures. All crops are for 1997, fish for 1994, and both are in thousands of metric tons; roundwood is for 1995 and is in thousands of cubic meters. Column 1 excludes melons. Sources: Crops from UN FAO *Production Yearbook 1997*. Roundwood timber and fish from *Britannica World Data 1999*. (With permission)

Ghutah, is a fabled garden, and well-tended orchards flourish in protected basins and valleys in Turkey and Iran, where harvested fruits are spread on rooftops and roadsides to dry under the summer sun. Dried apricots and a variety of pistachios from Iran are widely marketed. Oil-seeds, including sunflower, sesame, and safflower, are more commonly grown in large fields in the all-season rain areas of northwestern Turkey.

Industrial Crops. To compensate for the dry conditions in summer, farmers in Mediterranean climate areas of the region use supplementary irrigation where feasible to produce substantial quantities of industrial crops— cotton, tobacco, sugar beets, sugarcane (more common in warmer, irrigated Upper Egypt), linseed, and hemp. Egyptian long-staple cotton, an improved variety of a crop cultivated in Egypt for thousands of years, is in wide demand on world markets. Cotton production continues to be greatly expanded in Turkey, Syria, and Israel along with sugar beet production in Turkey and Syria.

The Olive: A Special Note. The most widespread tree crop in the Mediterranean climate lands is the olive, the hallmark of true Mediterranean conditions (Fig. 7-3). With a very long taproot, as deep as 30 ft./9 m, and a small, waxy leaf, the olive tree is well adapted to the cool, wet winters and the warm, rainless summers. Likewise adapted to the chemical and physical characteristics of the Mediterranean soils, the olive requires no irrigation and only modest attention to produce plentiful crops for 200–300 years and more. The olive yield varies according to soil moisture, but appreciable amounts of fruit are grown even in dry years. One result is that people of the Mediterranean Basin have depended upon the olive for both food and oil: Olive oil is the basic oil for cooking, soap, even greasing wagon wheels.

FIGURE 7-2 Contrasting types of agriculture: a citrus grove in the Egyptian Delta north of Cairo *(top)*, with fellahin sorting tangerines, and extensive date groves inland from Suhar, Oman *(bottom)*, seen from a tower of the old fort.

FIGURE 7-3   New olive groves on west-facing slopes of Jabal al-Zawiyah, near the northern end of the Ghab Depression in northwestern Syria. Syria is conducting a major campaign of increasing olive production in its agricultural development.

Carob, or "locust trees," grow on dry, uncultivated hillsides. A major crop in southern Cyprus, carob beans are exported for use as cattle feed, varnish base, and a health food substitute for chocolate. Smaller numbers of the trees also grow along the southern coast of Turkey and in the Levant.

Agriculture in Year-Round Rain Areas

Compared with the steppe and Mediterranean areas, a different crop ecology characterizes northern Turkey and northwestern Iran where appreciable amounts of summer rain complement the Mediterranean winter rain. The agricultural landscape exhibits fields of corn (maize) in Turkey (Fig. 1-2), tea plantations in both Turkey (along the southeastern Black Sea coast) and Iran (south of the Caspian Sea), rice (sometimes with supplementary irrigation) in those same areas, and the world's greatest hazelnut (filbert) groves on the seaward-facing slopes around Trabzon in Turkey. The famous Turkish tobacco predominates farther west along the Black Sea coast, and still farther west are extensive fields of sunflowers, grown for their oilseeds.

The High Yemen also benefits from summer precipitation, as does the Asir to the north. Taking advantage of the monsoonal rains to grow grain sorghum (milo maize), a summer crop, Yemen is the Middle East's leading producer of sorghum. The highlands also produce small amounts of the famous Yemen coffee, which, however, is yielding place to *qat*, another specialty crop of the steep Yemen terraces (Fig. 7-4). Two other specialty crops of the Middle East are narcotic—opium poppies in western Turkey and Iran, grown under government control, and hashish grown illegally in Lebanon and Iran. Opium poppies and hashish were, unhappily, important cash crops for farmers of the Bekaa of eastern Lebanon, especially during the civil warfare of the period 1975–1990.

FIGURE 7-4 Typical terraced agriculture on steep slopes west of Sana, Yemen. The main crops are *qat* (discussed in Chapter 19) and coffee. Agricultural villages are perched on narrow mountain ridges.

Water in the Desert: Irrigation

As it has for more than 8,000 years, irrigation plays a vital role in the life of the Middle East, where aridity and semiaridity prevail in more than 80 percent of the land area. Irrigation helps remedy the deficiency, seasonality, and variability of rainfall, so that agriculture can gain the greatest advantage from a long, frost-free growing season. Much of the irrigation is supplementary rather than the sole source of water, and rainfed and irrigated cultivation intermingle in many sectors of the region. Where primary irrigation is possible year-round in an area with a long growing season, two and even three crops a year are grown, as in parts of Egypt.

Sources of Water

Life from the Rivers. Most of the water for irrigation in the Middle East comes from rivers

(see Chap. 3). The Nile, Tigris, and Euphrates are the three main sources of river irrigation water, but scores of smaller rivers and hundreds of streamlets also supply water for irrigation. Fed by run-off from rains and snows on highlands adjacent to the desert valleys, the flow of these rivers depends on the timing of the rainfall and snowmelt. Some river water is tapped indirectly—from dammed reservoirs, shallow wells in alluvium adjacent to the riverbanks, underground tunnels, or canals carrying diverted water—but the river remains the primary source.

Groundwater. The second most important source of irrigation water in most of the area is groundwater from underground aquifers tapped primarily by wells. Some wells are only a few feet deep, some ancient hand-dug wells reach 300–400 ft./90–120 m, and thousands of modern drilled wells reach 2,000–3,000 ft./ 610–915 m. In many instances, underground aquifers have been discovered through petroleum exploration, as was the great Wasia aquifer in central Saudi Arabia. Elsewhere, modern hydrogeological technology has found moderately productive aquifers in areas long considered hopelessly waterless—the Western Desert of Egypt, western and eastern Arabia, and Inner Oman.

Springs.　Naturally flowing springs are a third source of water for irrigation. Such springs usually occur where the water table intersects the ground surface, often in a series along a stratum outcrop or fault line. Nearly every Middle East state has at least some springs, thousands of which are used to irrigate plots ranging in size from a few square feet to a score or more acres. Some springs issue from horizontal solution channels, as in Mount Lebanon, others from vertical solution shafts in limestone karst regions, as in eastern Arabia. Artesian springs bring groundwater up the solution pits from appreciable depths to support several extensive oases. Saudi Arabia's three largest oases—Hofuf, Qatif, and al-Kharj—are irrigated in this way, as are large oases on Bahrain.

Methods of irrigation depend on the water source as well as on the technology available. Since World War II, huge dams, elevated concrete water chutes (Fig. 7-1b), drilled wells, mechanical pumps, and other modern equipment have rapidly been replacing traditional techniques, yet the old methods survive in many areas. Gravity-flow canals, hand-bucket transfer of water, counterpoised buckets (called *shadufs* in Egypt), Archimedes screws, and water wheels (the picturesque *noriahs* of Hamah, Syria, on the Orontes) are all traditional methods.

A more complicated traditional method for transporting irrigation water under certain conditions is the *qanat* system (shown in Fig. 22-3), which taps water at an upslope source and conducts it downslope through an underground tunnel. The ideal environment for a *qanat* is a large alluvial fan, the cone of gravel deposited by a stream emerging from a constricted valley onto a piedmont. Originating in Persia centuries before the Christian era,

the *qanat* concept spread eastward to central Asia and westward through Arabia and North Africa to Morocco—and, indeed, eventually was applied by Spanish colonists on a small scale in the Western Hemisphere. It has been given different names in different places—*karez, falaj, foggara.*

Excavation of a *qanat* involves both horizontal and vertical digging: carefully controlled burrowing of a gently sloping tunnel to carry the water and also opening a series of regularly spaced vertical shafts from the surface to the tunnel. A *qanat* can thus be identified on the surface by a telltale alignment of holes, each surrounded by a circular spoil ridge. Scores of thousands of *qanats* tunnel through alluvial fans at the foot of mountains in Iran and surrounding countries, especially Oman. Although many still supply water to towns, villages, and fields, increasing numbers are abandoned each year for cheaper and more convenient pipelines.

Modern irrigation technology has introduced more efficient methods of applying water directly to crops, including overhead sprinkler systems and, more recently, drip irrigation. The latter system, also known as trickle irrigation, supplies moisture—sometimes mixed with fertilizer—to each individual plant through appropriately spaced openings. Although expensive initially, this system makes more efficient use of water, fertilizer, and labor, and it is certain to be utilized on an increasing scale. Overhead sprinklers, more efficient than basin and furrow methods, nevertheless waste some water through evaporation both in the air and on the surface. They require appreciable investment, but both movable impulse sprinklers and self-propelled center-pivot circular sprinklers are nevertheless widely used, with the latter formerly utilized on a grand scale in the wheat fields of central Saudi Arabia.

Irrigated Lands

In 1980, irrigated cropland covered 55,360 miles^2/143,380 km^2, which was 1.9 percent of

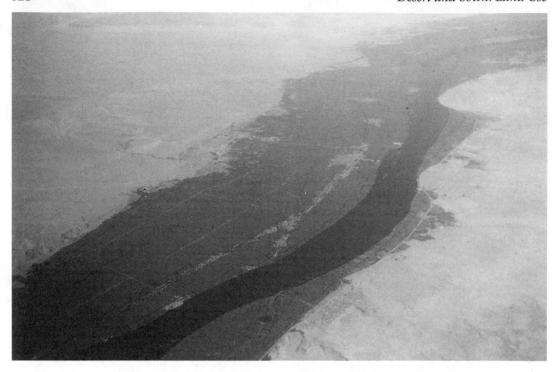

FIGURE 7-5   Air view of irrigated agriculture in the Nile Valley, central Egypt. The dividing line between verdant irrigated crops and barren desert is knife-sharp. An excellent illustration of Kipling's comment on Egypt as "that damp trickle of life."

all the land and 20 percent of the agricultural land in the sixteen states of the Middle East. Four years later, irrigated area had *decreased* to 53,734 miles^2/139,170 km^2, despite efforts in all states to increase irrigation. With the opening of extensive new water projects in Iraq, Egypt, Turkey, and Saudi Arabia, by 1988 irrigated area increased to 57,540 miles^2/149,030 km^2. Eight years later, irrigated area in every Middle East state had dramatically increased to a total of 84,367 miles^2/218,510 km^2, a 47 percent growth. Such an expansion is a significant indicator of the region-wide efforts being exerted to intensify agriculture. The value of crops raised by artificial watering constitutes a disproportionate percentage of the value of total crop production, perhaps as much as three-fourths. One explanation is that all cultivated land is irrigated in Egypt (note Fig. 7-5), agriculturally the second-most overall productive country in the Middle East (Turkey is first). From a half to a quarter of the cultivated land in most other major agricultural countries in

the region is irrigated (see Table 7-1), and even in Turkey, with 15 percent, and Syria, with 18 percent, of the cultivated land under irrigation, irrigated crops amount to more than 32 and 58 percent of production, respectively.

Although expansion of irrigation is an obvious step toward increasing crop production, such expansion encounters four serious obstacles: decreasing availability of water; increasing expense in terms of cost-effectiveness; competition for land availability; and conflicts over riparian rights. Although high expenditures per unit area in Israel, Saudi Arabia, and some of the Gulf states have produced excellent returns, such levels of expenditure are of questionable cost-effectiveness in realistic terms, and they are not practicable in most other parts of the region. In such areas as southern Iraq, expanding irrigation presents its own problems, including salination. Drainage, both surface and underground tile, may offer more benefit than irrigation in some areas.

TABLE 7-4 DOMESTIC ANIMALS (000s of head).

COUNTRY	1 CAMELS	2 CATTLE	3 SHEEP	4 HOGS	5 CHICKENS	6 GOATS	7 BUFFALOES
Bahrain	1	12	18	—	1,000	17	—
Cyprus	—	69	250	379	3,000	220	—
Egypt	136	3,000	4,300	28	85,000	3,200	3,150
Iran	143	8,600	50,000	—	210,000	26,000	465
Iraq	14	1,000	5,000	—	48,000	350	75
Israel	5	410	340	105	23,000	94	—
Jordan	18	43	2,100	—	78,000	555	—
Kuwait	9	22	320	—	22,000	75	—
Lebanon	1	80	246	55	29,000	425	—
Oman	94	142	148	—	3,000	735	—
Qatar	47	14	200	—	4,000	172	—
Saudi Arabia	422	200	7,800	—	95,000	4,400	—
Syria	7	857	13,829	1	19,000	1,098	2
Turkey	2	11,789	33,072	5	129,000	8,951	255
UAE	170	75	385	—	11,000	990	—
Yemen	180	1,201	4,267	—	25,000	3,881	—
Gaza	1	3	24	—	4,000	16	—
West Bank	—	—	—	—	—	—	—
TOTAL	1,250	27,517	122,299	573	789,000	51,179	3,947

Most of the data are Food and Agriculture Organization estimates; a few are unofficial figures.
Source: UN FAO *Production Yearbook 1997.*

Role of Animals

Livestock raising, practiced in the Middle East as early as 8000 BC, is common in all three types of land, although it differs from one environmental area to another; and nomadic herding on the desert or in the Zagros Mountains is quite different from raising animals on farms, especially on irrigated farms. Since agricultural statistics for the Middle East do not distinguish between farm animals and those herded by nomads, data in the following discussion pertain to all types of live-stock.

Commercial animal raising is at its most intensive in specialized agricultural settlements in Israel. In addition, systematic commercial raising of small animals has made rapid strides in several countries since 1950. Chicken raising, for example, increased sharply during the 1970s and has continued to mount in every country, especially in Iran, Turkey, Saudi Arabia, and Egypt. With no religious or social taboos against them, chickens have increased in Turkey, for example, from 73 million in 1990 to 153 million in 1997. Although no figures are available on the subject, pigeons are raised in large numbers by individuals in towns and villages as well as by farmers in many areas of the Middle East, especially in Egypt. Fish farming is an important aspect of land use in the Huleh Basin of Israel and is beginning on an experimental basis in Saudi Arabia and other Gulf countries.

Meat animals are produced in large numbers (Table 7-4). Chickens, sheep, goats, and cattle (*Bos taurus*) are the most numerous (Fig. 7-6a). Hogs are raised in Cyprus, Israel, Egypt, Turkey, and Lebanon, although they cannot be marketed in conservative Muslim or Jewish areas where the animal is ritually prohibited. Sheep have been relatively numerous for millennia and are an important source, not only of a favorite meat, wool, and skins, but also of milk and cheese. Of the total number of sheep, Turkey and Iran together have almost 68 percent.

Goats are 42 percent as numerous as sheep. Despite its reputation for destroying vegetation, the goat, properly managed, is hardly more damaging to forage than the sheep or

FIGURE 7-6   Two types of animal raising in the Middle East: Anatolian shepherd with sheep and goats east of Ankara *(top);* some of the goats are of the famous Angora breed. Camels watering at Todahiyah, near Harad, Saudi Arabia *(bottom).*

cow, and it is a uniquely valuable animal for grazing the poorer types of forage. Vegetation can best be protected through progressive exclusion of goats from designated areas, and goat exclusion laws have been very successful in Cyprus, Israel, and Turkey. The Angora goats of Turkey are especially valuable for their unique hair, used in making mohair.

The number of camels was slowly declining, falling from more than 1 million in 1969–1971 to 763,000 in 1985; however, it rose to 1.3 million in 1996 as interest in camels revived—for the sport of camel racing, for example. The traditional significance of the camel, including its use for religious feasts, suggests that it will continue to play an important, if diminished, role well into the twenty-first century.

The number of cattle in the Middle East, along with the population and standard of living, increased steadily from the early 1960s into the mid-1980s. In the late 1980s, however, cattle decreased dramatically in Turkey and sharply in Egypt as farmers turned more to raising crops and concentrating on smaller animals. Thus, the number of cattle stabilized during the late 1990s. The quality of cattle has improved as farmers have turned to better breeds; especially in the case of dairy cattle, better breeds have greatly improved the milk yield. A growing awareness of the nutritional benefits of milk has encouraged dairying in many areas, and Ras al-Khaymah, one of the United Arab Emirates, now produces cow's milk for the UAE urban areas. Israel has imported and bred some of the best dairy cattle in the world, and it leads the Middle East in milk production per animal by a wide margin. Egyptian farms, with plenty of water in which buffalo can submerge themselves, have three-fourths of the region's buffalo (*Babalus babulis*, or water buffalo, quite different from the American bison) and have more buffalo than cattle or goats. Water buffalo are also common in the marsh area of southern Iraq.

Horse populations have declined sharply in every Middle East state, with the special exceptions of Saudi Arabia and Qatar, as the work horse is displaced by the tractor and the automobile. Fine Arabian show horses constitute only a small percentage of the regional equine population; after becoming rare in the Middle East in the mid-twentieth century, they are again being bred by a few wealthy Saudis and other Arabs.

Nomadic Pastoralism

Nomadic pastoralism is an essential aspect of the Middle East in the popular perception and also in fact. Animal herding by nomads involves a wide range of periodic horizontal and vertical migrations by tribal groups and their animals in search of grass and water. It is these periodic movements, both across country and vertically to higher or lower elevations, that have led to the interrelated triad of nonsedentary herding—nomadism, pastoralism, and tribalism. Nomadic pastoralism extends over a larger area than any other type of agricultural activity—more, in fact, than all other types combined. It dominates the dry area from the Western Desert of Egypt across the Arabian Peninsula and interior Iran to Baluchistan and also is practiced in extensive mountainous areas in west-central Iran. Major nomadic pastoral groups include the Bedouins of the deserts and steppes except in Iran (see Fig. 6-1), Qashqai and Bakhtiari of the High Zagros, Turkmen of the Kopet ranges, Baluch of southeastern Iran, and other smaller groups. Although the number of people engaged in nomadic herding is steadily decreasing, it remains a significant aspect of tradition, culture, and economic life, especially in the Arabian Peninsula and Syrian Desert.

Using marginal resources and very basic technology, Bedouins are well adjusted to their desert environment, primarily through a symbiotic relationship with their animals. Alone on the open desert in summer, a Bedouin family could survive only a day or two as there would be no water, no food, no shelter. But the family's camels, which feed on salty shrubs, supply milk for consumption as liquid, yogurt, or cheese; supply hair for certain weaving; supply hides and leather; serve as transportation, including transport to a water supply; supply

dung for fuel; and in dire emergency, provide
meat when slaughtered.

Most contemporary Bedouins also herd
sheep and goats for wool, milk, hides, and
meat. The essential characteristic of the
Bedouins is their geographically cyclic movements to find grass for their herds and flocks.
Other nomads follow similar cycles that may
vary in frequency of migration, types of animals herded, and other details.

The Remarkable Camel

The domesticated camel appeared about 2000
BC. Although the Bactrian camel (*Camelus
bactrianus*), with two humps, is common in
parts of Anatolia and in northern and northeastern Iran, the Arabian camel, or
dromedary (*C. dromedarius*), with one hump,
has long been herded in the Arabian Peninsula, North Africa, and adjacent lands.
Nomads in the Syrian Desert, Mesopotamia,
Anatolia, and Iran, on the other hand, herd
sheep and goats and raise fewer camels—
indeed, none at all in mountainous areas.

The camel adapts especially well to life in
the desert environment, as it has a remarkable
ability to conserve water in hot weather and
has a low requirement for water in winter
(Fig. 7-6b). Its long neck allows the camel to
graze both surface vegetation and tree leaves.
Its soft, padded feet operate like snowshoes
and enable it to walk over drift sand without
sinking and over hot surfaces without pain.

Traversing terrain that other beasts cannot,
the "ship of the desert" can carry heavier
loads through greater heat and aridity for a
longer working life than oxen, horses, or donkeys. Using camel caravans, the early Arabs
monopolized ancient trade routes and laid
the bases for mercantile cities over a wide
area. The use of the camel actually delayed the
evolution of desert roads, since wagons and
carts drawn by oxen or horses were less efficient than camels. However, after the mid-
twentieth century, motor vehicles, aircraft,
and railroads displaced the camel as transport, certainly for long distances, and some

modern Bedouins even transport their camels
and other animals by pickup truck.[2]

Forest Products

Forestry plays a minor role in Middle East
agriculture, as is suggested by the sparse forest
vegetation (see Map 5-2). Only Turkey and
Iran have noteworthy forest industries, and
extensive, systematic timber exploitation is
practiced only in Turkey. Timber production
in the high Pontus in the north, the high Taurus in the south, and the highlands between
Istanbul and Ankara yields 681.6 million ft.³/
19.3 million m³ of roundwood a year, 63 percent of Middle East production (see Table 7-3).
Iran's production is 265 ft.³/7.5 million m³,
and Egypt's 95.3 million ft.³/2.7 million m³.
No other country in the region produces even
0.6 million m³.

Fishing

Surrounded and deeply penetrated by seas, and
with a total length of coastline exceeding
14,585 miles/23,470 km, the Middle East countries have an appreciable potential for a fishing
industry. However, other factors inhibit
progress toward reaching that potential, including overfishing and pollution.

With its long coastlines on three seas and
its vigorous maritime activity, Turkey leads
the sixteen Middle East countries in fish
landed. Its total of 604,000 mt is almost as
much as those of its next two competitors,
Iran and Egypt combined (see Table 7-3).
Access to rich fisheries associated with the
upwelling waters along the southern coast of
the Arabian Peninsula provides Oman and
neighboring Yemen with their considerable
catches. Iran exploits its long coastline on the
Gulf, as well as its coastline on the Gulf of
Oman and the Caspian Sea, for fishing. From
all three it takes more than 314,300 mt, and it
reaps a notably valuable harvest of caviar
(fish roe) from the Caspian. All the leading

fishing states sharply increased their landings during the late 1990s.

Notes

1. J. D. Held 1979. Studies of Middle East land use that are more general include Clawson, Landsberg, and Alexander 1971, Askari and Cummings 1976, and Beaumont and McLachlan 1985. The crucial role of water is studied in Rogers and Lydon 1994, Ventner 1998, Soffer 1999, and Biswas et al. 1997. *Britannica World Data* is very useful for production figures, and the UN's FAO *Production Yearbook,* published annually, is indispensable for production data.

2. For interesting discussions of Bedouins and camels see Dickson 1949, Jabbur 1995, *Saudi Aramco* 1995, Bulliet 1975, and Hills 1966.

8

Riches Beneath
the Earth

Underground Resources

In its enormous wealth in petroleum and natural gas resources, the Middle East is without equal and perforce has a unique role on the world scene. Moreover, the region's percentage of the world's oil reserves, as well as its percentage of the world's production, is certain to increase, since the relatively smaller reserves elsewhere are being more rapidly depleted by intensive exploitation. In income benefits, never before in history has a region achieved such explosive large-scale economic development in such a short time as the Gulf oil-producing area of the Middle East did during the four decades following the end of World War II. Western cognizance of the vital importance of Middle East oil was manifest in 1990 when U. S. and European forces responded immediately to the threat to control of Kuwaiti and Saudi oil fields. Now that the more dramatic aspects of the Gulf "oil boom" have subsided and large production is again routine, the region is often taken for granted and even disparaged. U. S. attention is more focused on the emerging (and reemerging) Caspian oil province, partly to offset the importance of the Middle East.

The importance of the Middle East's petroleum reserves notwithstanding, it should not obscure other significant aspects of the region. The Middle East also possesses historical, geopolitical, political, human, geographical, and other nonenergy economic significance. The importance of these other aspects is often overlooked or is subordinated to petroleum and more limited regional interests. Although this chapter focuses on oil, one major aim of this book as a whole is to weight the various phases of the region in order to achieve a more balanced perspective.

Petroleum and petroleum products are the sole item produced and exported on any scale by several Middle East countries. At the average rate of production during the 3 years 1996–1998, Middle East petroleum resources will last for about 88 years if no additional resources are found. Unlikely as the lack of new discoveries may be, the oil-producing countries themselves are alert to the singularity of the basis of their wealth and to its eventual depletion. They are also aware of the external forces that influence the production, transportation, and marketing of their most important exchangeable product. In view of the relatively rapid exhaustibility of this singular resource, and with the lessons of numerous boom-and-bust producing areas to guide them, Middle East oil producers have sought ways to control their own destinies—through the Organization of Petroleum Exporting Countries (OPEC), for example. In an effort to maintain economic viability for a longer period, they are also conducting intensive programs of economic diversification, including agricultural development, as was shown in Chapter 7.

With certain exceptions, the overall percentage of the world's supply of underground resources other than petroleum in the Middle East is relatively minor. Nevertheless, the exploitation of nonenergy minerals is a major item in the economies of several countries with limited oil output. Nonoil mineral industries are or have been of noteworthy importance in Turkey, Iran, Jordan, Cyprus, Egypt, Syria, and Israel.

Petroleum: Historical Development

Asphalt, gas, and oil seeps from underground hydrocarbon deposits have been known for millennia at numerous sites in the Middle East—in northern Mesopotamia, near Hit on the Euphrates, on both sides of the head of the Persian/Arabian Gulf, under the Dead Sea, at the northern end of the Gulf of Suez, and in a dozen other places in the region.[1] Bitumen (asphalt, pitch, tar) is mentioned several times in the Old Testament: Noah used pitch in constructing the ark, and Moses' mother used bitumen and pitch to line the basket in which she floated the baby Moses on the Nile. Bitumen was used as mortar in the construction of brick walls, ziggurats, and other buildings in Sumerian and Babylonian times and can still be identified in many ruins in Iraq and western Iran.

The Old Testament "fiery furnace" of Shadrach, Meshach, and Abednego was likely the still-burning gas seepage known as the "eternal fires" near Kirkuk in northern Iraq. Flaming gas seepages were the focal points of fire-worshiping religions of ancient Persia, and fire temples became numerous there. Oil from seeps and oozes was collected for lamps, and it was used in warfare long before the Christian era. Thus, twentieth-century oil explorers had certain indicators for siting their early wildcat wells.

William Knox D'Arcy, a British subject, obtained a concession in 1901 to drill for oil in western Iran. Financed by a British syndicate, his crew made the first major oil strike in the Middle East in 1908. The initial discovery was in the Masjed-e Soleyman field, the first of many fabulous Middle East reservoirs (Map 8-1). The next year the D'Arcy group formed the Anglo-Persian Oil Company (APOC), which became Anglo-Iranian Oil Company (AIOC) in 1935 and British Petroleum in 1951. The first shipment of oil from the Middle East was made by APOC in 1912 from Abadan, on the Shatt al-Arab, still a major oil center. Further development was limited until World War I, when events proved the superiority of fuel oil over coal for firing boilers on naval vessels and commercial steamers. The demand for oil spiraled upward and has never ceased.

Other European entrepreneurs sought exploration rights across the border in Mesopotamia as soon as oil was found in Iran. The Turkish Petroleum Company, formed before World War I by British, French, and Dutch interests, found oil in 1927 by drilling only a few hundred meters from the "eternal fires." The discovery near Kirkuk opened one of the major oil fields of the world. In 1928, the United States made its first entry into the Middle East oil race when the Near East Development Corporation (NEDC) obtained an equity interest in Turkish Petroleum, renamed Iraq Petroleum Company (IPC) in 1929. NEDC originally comprised five companies but later was equally divided between Standard of New Jersey (now Exxon) and Socony Vacuum (later Mobil, which merged with Exxon in 1999).

From the early years of oil exploration in the Middle East, agreements among countries and companies divided up areas of operations and marketing. One accord was the Red Line Agreement, reached in 1928, which covered former Ottoman Empire possessions, excluding Kuwait and Egypt. It provided that any oil deals involving areas within the Red Line must be unanimously approved by all companies operating inside that line. Although later rescinded, this agreement regulated patterns of concessions in much of the Middle East for several critical years.

Neither the worldwide depression nor discoveries of other large supplies of oil, as in the East Texas field, slowed intensive exploration in the Middle East during the 1930s. By World War II, exploration had revealed the presence of oil in huge quantities beyond southern Iraq in the Mesopotamian-Gulf trough (Map 8-2).

The modest but important Bahrain field, found in 1932, was the first field discovered in the Gulf area proper, outside Iran and Iraq. Bahrain Island was also the scene of the first all-American oil venture in the Middle East. First a subsidiary of Standard Oil of California (Socal) and later jointly owned by Socal and Texaco, the Bahrain Petroleum Company (Bapco) was, however, chartered in Canada in order to fulfill a requirement that oil concessions in British territories be

MAP 8-1   Middle East major petroleum and natural gas fields and pipelines, 2000. Gulf fields are detailed in Map 8-2. (Adapted from several sources)

granted to "British companies." From the hills on the upturned strata of the geologic dome on Bahrain, U.S. geologists using binoculars studied Dammam Dome on the Arabian mainland 20 miles/32 km away and became convinced that a likely oil structure lay under it.

Urged by the geologists on Bahrain, Socal obtained a concession in 1933 for the eastern part of the Kingdom of Saudi Arabia and assigned the concession to California Arabian Standard Oil Company (Casoc). Casoc found oil in 1938 in Dammam Dome, as predicted. The company changed its name in 1944 to the more appropriate Arabian American Oil Company

and became widely known by the acronym Aramco. Even after it became a national oil company and was quietly renamed Saudi Arabian Oil Company, it continued to use the famous short form in the designation "Saudi Aramco." During approximately the same 1930s period, the Kuwait Oil Company—formed by APOC (BP) and Gulf (later merged with Chevron)—discovered and developed the rich Burgan reservoir in Kuwait.

Growing realization of the region's oil potential accelerated exploration in the lower Gulf, and after the war, more than a score of new enterprises received concessions to explore various

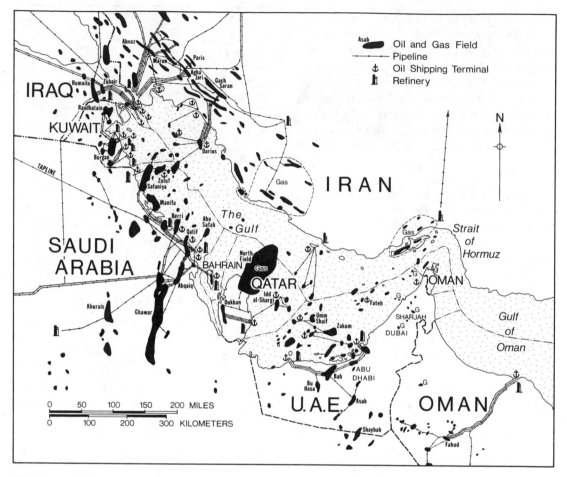

MAP 8-2 Gulf region petroleum and natural gas fields, pipelines, oil export terminals, and refineries. Ghawar in Saudi Arabia is the world's richest known oil field. (Adapted from several sources)

areas both on land and offshore. Whereas British, Dutch, French, and American "majors" had dominated the Gulf industry for four decades, they were now joined by national and private companies from Italy, Germany, Spain, Japan, Brazil, India, and elsewhere. Still later, producing countries formed their own national companies and gradually took over most or all of the controlling interest in the oil operations in their respective countries.

The Dukhan field in western Qatar was discovered in 1940 by an Iraq Petroleum Company subsidiary that later became the Qatar Petroleum Company, but production was delayed until 1949. Companies with multiple and international ownerships were given concessions

in offshore areas of Abu Dhabi; others received onshore concessions. The huge Abu Dhabi oil and gas resources are now generally under Abu Dhabi National Oil Company (ADNOC). The offshore Umm Shaif field, in Abu Dhabi territorial waters, was the first of many major offshore discoveries to complement the onshore fields in the lower Gulf. The Umm Shaif field was found in 1958, but it did not produce until 1962 because of the difficulties of producing, transporting, and storing offshore oil in the area at that time. Abu Dhabi's large onshore Bab field began production in 1963, and other amirates and larger states began production several years later, primarily with the help of smaller companies (Fig. 8-1). In Oman, after

FIGURE 8-1   FSO Safir, Floating Storage and Offloading facility of the Yemen Hunt Oil Company, permanently anchored near Salif off the north Yemen coast. The tanker is 1,200 ft./366 m long and holds 3.3 million
bbl. It receives about 150,000 bpd by pipeline from eastern Yemen. It has served its purpose since 1988.

successive concession companies had disappointing results, Petroleum Development
(Oman), or PDO, made the first discoveries in
the sultanate in 1963 and 1964, and production
began in 1967. PDO is now 60 percent government owned, with Shell holding 34 percent. A
score of other international companies operate
on a limited scale in Oman.

In the western areas of the Middle East,
exploration—which began early in Egypt—
indicates that petroleum resources are comparatively modest. Oil seepages near the
mouth of the Gulf of Suez, known as early as
Roman times, attracted exploration attention
soon after the opening of the petroleum age,
and indeed, the first well drilled in Egypt
(1886) was the earliest in the Middle East.
However, commercial production did not
begin until 1913, a year after the first oil shipment from Iran, and major output levels were
not achieved until the 1960s. Major natural gas
finds are now dominating the Egyptian energy
scene. In addition to the public-sector Egyptian General Petroleum Company, more than a
score of international companies operate in
Egypt, including BP-Amoco, Shell, Agip, and
British Gas.

In adjoining Israel, hydrocarbon indications
in and around the Dead Sea attracted surveys,
but only minor resources have been found. Gas
reservoirs in deep water offshore from southern
Israel and Gaza were being examined in 1999.
Exploration in Lebanon, including a test well in
1947–1948, showed no likely prospects, and no
development has been undertaken in that
country. Syria finally found a small field in
1956 and commercial quantities in 1959, both
in the extreme northeast in segments of the
fold belt in which the Kirkuk field had been
found in Iraq; but production was delayed for
several years until pipeline outlets could be
laid. After new finds in the mid-1980s, Syria
undertook an intensive and successful search
for new oil and gas fields, especially in the east

around Dayr al-Zawr. To the south, exploratory drilling in Jordan in the mid-1950s found nothing in either the West Bank or the East Bank. Limited finds in the 1980s raised some hopes that had not, however, been realized by late 1999.

The latest discoveries in new areas were made in the Yemens in 1984 and 1985 before their merger in 1990. Earlier tests in the west of the then Yemen Arab Republic (YAR) by U.S. interests had been negative, but another U.S. company (Hunt) made a major oil strike in 1984 in the Marib Basin area in eastern Yemen. Production and export began in late 1987. The Marib success encouraged the People's Democratic Republic of Yemen (PDRY) to drill an extension of the structure south of the border, and tests found oil in appreciable quantities that by the early 1990s far exceeded the reserves found in the original strikes to the north.

Turkey found oil in 1940, and development there achieved a steady pace in the 1960s and is continuing, but with only limited results, since the extreme folding and faulting typical of this area fragment the reservoirs and cause the individual fields to be small and scattered. Shell and Mobil have each joined efforts with the Turkish national oil company, as have other smaller companies. Finally, exploration on Cyprus during the 1940s and 1950s found no promising structures on the island and indicated that Cyprus, like Lebanon, is unlikely to have oil resources.

Patterns of Reserves

As of 1999, 677.5 billion barrels of oil—65 percent of the world's proved reserves of petroleum—lay under the Middle East, most of it around and under the Gulf and under the Gulf of Suez in Egypt (Maps 8-1 and 8-3). Despite the fact that exploration in past decades has been reasonably intensive, new discoveries during just the years 1987–1991 augmented the already huge Middle East petroleum reserves by nearly 40 percent. However, between 1993 and 1999, new discoveries

tapered off, and reserves increased by a relatively modest 9 billion bbl, less than 2 percent. One reason for the decrease in new discoveries was the reduced exploration effort because of the already plentiful supply and the falling price of oil during the period.

By far the largest in both the Middle East and the world, the Saudi reserves equal those of all the rest of the world outside the Middle East, except for the former Soviet Union and Europe, combined. After Saudi Arabia, the second through fifth greatest known reserves in the Middle East and the world are, in order, considered to be those of Iraq, UAE, Kuwait, and Iran (Table 8-1 and Graph 8-1). In fact, these four producers shift in rank among themselves periodically. These five countries are followed in rank by four non-Middle East states: Venezuela, 72.6 billion barrels of proved reserves; successor states of the former Soviet Union, 57 billion; Mexico, 48 billion; and the United States, 22.5 billion. Probable reserves add billions of additional potential.[2]

Of the region's petroleum, eastern Saudi Arabia contains nearly half, distributed over 50 fields, onshore and offshore, extending from Kuwait south to the Abu Dhabi border (Map 8-2). Prominent is the large, linear Ghawar field, the world's greatest single oil reservoir. The gently folded and domed structures of northeastern Arabia continue northward into Kuwait, with which Saudi Arabia shares the world's greatest offshore field, Safaniya-Khafji.

The Arabian-Kuwait structures extend across the Kuwait-Iraq border and join the northwest-southeast trend of the Zagros fold reservoirs in southern Iraq. One particular field, the Rumaila, straddles the Kuwait-Iraq border and became a matter of conflict in the Iraqi invasion of Kuwait in August 1990 and in discussions of boundary revisions in 1992. In Iraq, which is credited with 112 billion barrels of reserves—second-largest in the region and in the world—oil reservoirs have been found in subsurface folds from Ain Zalah in the extreme north through the Kirkuk and Baghdad reservoirs to Rumaila and Zubair in the extreme south. The next-largest reserves lie offshore and

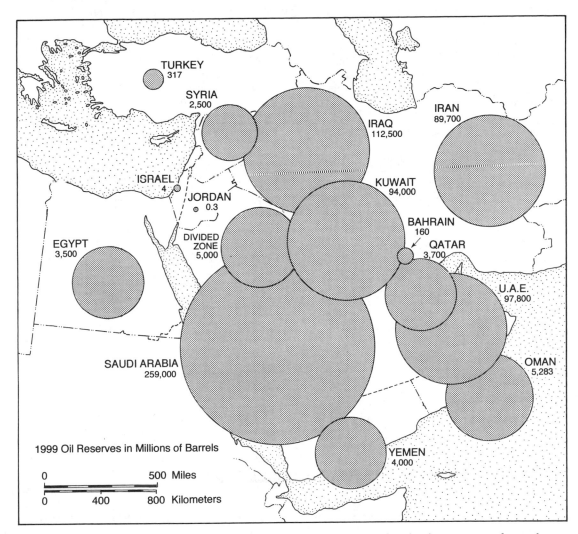

MAP 8-3   Middle East proved petroleum reserves, by country. Proportional circles show amount of proved reserves in 1999 in millions of barrels.

onshore in the southernmost Gulf area (Fig. 8-2). Most of the major fields lie in Abu Dhabi, largest and westernmost of the seven component shaykhdoms of the United Arab Emirates (UAE). By the late 1990s Abu Dhabi alone had more than four times the oil reserves of the United States. Onshore, Kuwait possesses the fabulous Burgan field, with more oil per unit of surface area than any other field known. With Saudi Arabia and Kuwait holding undivided half shares in the oil of the Divided Zone (the former Neutral Zone), Kuwait's 94 billion barrels of reserves accord it fourth rank in reserves

in the Middle East and the world. Iran possesses the fifth-largest reserves in the Middle East and the world, even after having produced 48.4 billion barrels since oil was first discovered in Iran in 1908. Virtually all of Iran's 41 oil fields follow the trend of folds in the Zagros Mountains in western Iran from Kermanshah in the northwest to Bandar-e Abbas in the southeast at the Strait of Hormuz. Lying in the southeastern part of the sedimentary basin, opposite the Qatar Peninsula and east toward the Strait of Hormuz, are more than a dozen rich gas fields. Like Saudi Arabia and Kuwait,

TABLE 8-1   PETROLEUM: RESERVES, RECENT PRODUCTION, WELLS, AND FIELDS.

COUNTRY	1 OIL RESRVS 2000 000s BBL	2 GAS RESRVS 2000 BILLS FT.^{3}	3 PRODUCTN 1999 000s BPD	4 AV. PROD. 1996-98 000s BPD	5 NO. PROD. OIL WELLS 1999	6 NUMBER OF FIELDS 1998
Bahrain	148,110	3,875	101.8	103.9	392	1
Cyprus	0	0	0.0	0.0	0	0
(Divided Zone)[a]	5,000,000	1,000	500.0	521.0	468	5
Egypt	2,947,560	35,180	850.8	852.4	1,258	135
Iran	89,700,000	812,300	3,461.7	3,632.6	1,120	41
Iraq[b]	112,500,000	109,800	2,653.3	1,297.0	1,685	20
Israel	3,900	10	0.1	0.2	10	6
Jordan	900	240	0.0	0.0	4	1
Kuwait	94,000,000	52,200	1,632.9	1,813.1	790	8
Lebanon	0	0	0.0	0.0	0	0
Oman	5,283,000	28,416	895.0	894.7	2,298	106
Qatar	3,700,000	300,000	632.5	591.3	286	6
Saudi Arabia	261,000,000	204,000	7,449.6	7,993.0	1,400	50
Syria	2,500,000	8,500	536.7	567.3	964	17
Turkey	298,650	314	68.0	65.8	793	68
UAE	97,800,000	212,000	2,060.0	2,274.9	1,458	22
Yemen	4,000,000	16,900	405.8	372.2	299	26
TOTAL/AVG.	678,882,120	1,784,735	21,248.2	20,979.4	13,225	512
Abu Dhabi	92,200,000	196,100	1,689.0	1,906.7	1,200	13
Dubai	4,000,000	4,100	300.5	297.7	200	5
Ras al-Khaymah	100,000	1,100	0.5	0.5	7	1
Sharjah	1,500,000	10,700	70.0	70.0	51	3

[a]Divided Zone production is normally divided between Kuwait and Saudi Arabia. [b]Iraq production was below normal because of UN restrictions on exports from Iraq. Note that petroleum reserves are in thousands of barrels (bbl). Natural gas reserves are in billions of cubic feet. Production figures are in thousands of barrels per day (bpd). The last four rows give data on the four amirates of the UAE that produce petroleum. Source: *Oil and Gas Journal,* Dec. 20, 1999, and *International Petroleum Encyclopedia 1999.*

Iran also possesses offshore fields with impressive reserves and production.

Qatar's reserves in its onshore Dukhan field and its three offshore fields give it proved petroleum reserves approximately equal to those of Egypt and Yemen. However, Qatar's relatively modest oil reserves are richly supplemented by the supergiant gas reservoir in the North Field, the world's largest, which alone gives Qatar the third-greatest gas reserves in the world after those of Russia and Iran (Table 8-1).

The Sultanate of Oman is the latest of the Gulf area states to achieve significant levels of petroleum production. The original discoveries in 1963 and 1964 were followed by more than 100 other scattered, modest field discoveries by 1999. Although none are as rich as the fields in

less intensively folded and faulted structures farther northwest up the great Gulf trough, Oman is now credited with 5 billion barrels of proved reserves.

Bahrain, although the earliest of the actual Gulf producers, has proved to possess the smallest reserves. However, during deep-test drilling for additional oil resources in 1949, the Bahrain Petroleum Company discovered the gas reservoir in the Khuff formation (Permian age), which has since been found to have enormous reserves in Gulf offshore fields, in several Iranian fields, and in other neighboring fields. Commercial development of Bahrain's Khuff deep gas began in 1969.

Turkey's numerous small fields lie at the upper end of the great series of structures

WORLD REGIONS PETROLEUM RESERVES, 1999

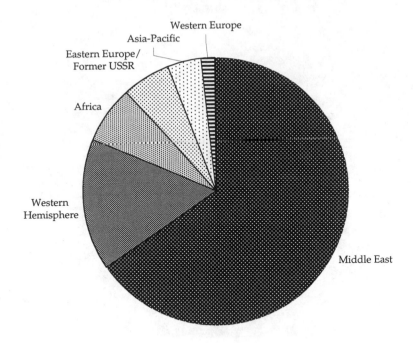

MIDDLE EAST PETROLEUM RESERVES, 1999

GRAPH 8-1 Petroleum reserves

FIGURE 8-2   Some of the surface facilities of Dubai's offshore Fateh field, 56 miles/90 km from the coast. Resting on the seabed are huge bell-shaped tanks that store oil from surrounding wells until it can be loaded on tankers such as the one shown.

reaching northwestward from Oman up the Gulf trough and through the Mesopotamian depression. In about 70 minor fields that have been discovered on the upper Tigris and, more recently, on the upper Euphrates, total reserves are only 317 million barrels.

Although petroleum reserves on the western side of the region are only a minor segment of the Middle East total, sizable fields have been found and are yielding roughly 1.8 million bpd. Production is primarily from Egypt, Syria, and Yemen, with limited output from Turkey. Israel's reserves are almost depleted, and Jordan's known reserves are negligible.

Egypt ranks eighth in reserves, just after Qatar, among the Middle East oil states (but see Chap. 20). Petroleum and gas are found in more than 135 fields in and on both sides of the Gulf of Suez, in small fields in the Western Desert, and, particularly nonassociated gas, in recently discovered promising fields in the

northern Delta and offshore of the Delta. These Egyptian reservoirs are in completely separate basins from those of the Gulf region.

Syria's older fields lie in the extreme northeastern corner of the country, just west of the Tigris River, and are an integral part of the structures containing the Batman fields of southeastern Turkey and the fields of northern Iraq. A significant discovery in late 1984 near Dayr al-Zawr initiated a modest "oil boom" in eastern Syria that spread to the center of the country and opened a dozen small new fields, for a country total of 17.

Jordan's recently found Hamzah field, near al-Azraq, has shown only limited potential. By contrast, reserves in new fields in the Republic of Yemen already exceed 4 billion barrels, ranking Yemen above Egypt and Qatar. This poorest corner of the Middle East desperately needs oil income, and the future of the Yemen oil industry is moderately promising.

Petroleum Production

Some Influences on Production

Whereas reserves reveal the production potential of individual fields and countries, the trend of actual production reflects the combination of a variety of complex factors. Production may trend steadily upward as new reserves are exploited, as in Saudi Arabia for 35 virtually unbroken years after World War II. Conversely, production may drop steadily as reserves are depleted, which happened in Bahrain after 1970. Production may drop in a country because of wartime conditions, as happened in Iran and Iraq in the early 1980s and in Iraq and Kuwait in the early 1990s. Iraq's output dropped to a fraction of its normal level in 1991–1992 because of UN-imposed sanctions. It was still under UN controls in early 2000 and continued below its 1989 "normal" level. In Kuwait after 1972, daily production was deliberately reduced by government fiat to extend the life of the reserves.

However, along with the status of reserves, market demand is obviously a crucial factor influencing level of production. (See section on marketing later in this chapter.) Middle East production curves became erratic in the early 1970s, after more than 25 years of steadily and even dramatically increasing production during the unparalleled industrial development in much of the world after World War II. Noteworthy influences on the region's production included the impact of the 1973 Arab-Israeli war and the Arab oil boycott; the sharp rise in the price of oil as the OPEC nations increasingly assumed control of the production and marketing of their own resources; the growing realization among industrialized oil-consuming nations that they must both conserve and substitute for petroleum and natural gas; the slightly shifting pattern of producing areas as North Sea production sharply increased and as increasing Soviet production had its effect on world markets; and, partly as a consequence, the decision by OPEC nations to cut production in an effort to sustain the OPEC price. The production cut halved the output of Middle East OPEC members from 21 million bpd in 1979 to 10.7 million bpd in 1986. The marketing strategy succeeded temporarily then failed when OPEC members pushed their output to more than 22 million bpd in late 1988; and they continued to escalate production despite falling prices, reaching 24 million bpd in mid-1990 even after prices dropped to less than $15/barrel. The former OPEC goal of $21/barrel was elusive except during the 1990–1991 Gulf war, when the price shot up to $35 and $40/barrel for several weeks in late 1990.

Also noteworthy is the fact that an oil or gas field has a certain optimum level of production that theoretically permits the maximum production over the maximum number of years. This reservoir optimum can be more readily determined and followed in the Middle East than in the United States. In virtually all Middle East fields, exploration and production are controlled by one operator, whereas U.S. fields are developed by multiple companies that compete for the oil underlying the checkerboard of leases. A statistical comparison shows the significant consequence: Producing countries in the Middle East averaged 21.9 million bpd from 13,189 wells in 1998 for an average of 1,660 bpd per well, while the United States produced 6.4 million bpd from 573,962 wells for an average of 11 bpd per well. U.S. production costs are thus appreciably higher, and percentage recovery of oil in the U.S. reservoirs is lower without expensive secondary recovery procedures.

Natural Gas

Natural gas reserves include both "associated" and "nonassociated" gas. The former is found with petroleum and reaches the surface along with the oil in which it is dissolved. Nonassociated gas occurs separately in underground reservoirs and is produced only as gas. The distinction is significant in several ways, including the availability to consumers of one kind of gas or the other.

Associated gas must be separated from crude oil as soon as the mixture reaches the surface. In the early years of Middle East production, the demand was for oil, and since associated gas had no market, it was separated and immediately burned off ("flared"). Gradually, as increased population and economic development created a major market demand for gas, flaring diminished, and separated gas was piped to nearby consumers. In time, rapidly increasing oil production made available enormous amounts of associated gas after separation from the primary product, oil. These seemingly inexhaustible gas supplies came to be taken for granted by consumers—power companies, fertilizer companies, water desalination plants, aluminum smelters, and residential consumers. Also, the gas was utilized in more sophisticated ways, for example, after being broken down into its major components of methane, ethane, propane, butane, and heavier hydrocarbons.

Therefore, when oil prices and production decreased sharply in the early 1980s, not only did the producing areas suffer from reduced oil-sale income, they also suddenly had insufficient supplies of the natural gas that had become a fringe benefit of the high level of oil production. The main recourse was to increase the search for and production of nonassociated gas, which could be exploited without reference to the demand for oil.

When Bahrain found a major gas reservoir in the deep Khuff formation in 1949, its neighbors also drilled into the Khuff and likewise found enormous nonassociated gas reservoirs. In addition to Qatar's huge North Field reservoir of nonassociated gas in the Khuff zone, all Gulf states are finding large reserves of gas both in the Khuff and in other deep reservoirs. When added to the country's nonassociated gas reserves, the large gas fields found in southwestern Iran in the late 1970s and early 1980s, many of them in the Khuff zone, give Iran 812.3 trillion ft.^{3} (tcf), by far the largest gas reserves outside Russia. Iran is fortunate to have a share in Quatar's offshore North Field, the world's greatest gas field, which extends some distance beyond the Gulf median line. In 1999, total Middle East gas reserves constituted more than one-third of all known world gas reserves. Thus, as it is in other areas, gas is assuming an increasingly significant role in the regional energy pattern. Middle East gas, as much as its oil, may well power much of the world's industry in the twenty-first century and beyond.

Production Comparisons

Map 8-4 presents a graphic comparison of petroleum production by Middle East countries in thousands of barrels per day in 1998. Saudi Arabia has ranked second or third in world production since the mid-1970s (the then Soviet Union and the United States were usually first and second), peaking at 9.64 million bpd in 1980, falling to 3.3 million bpd in 1985, then rebounding to 8.1 million bpd in 1991. The kingdom continued to produce about 8 million bpd for the rest of the 1990s, when it was by far the world's leading producer. Iran reached peaks of more than 6 million bpd in 1974 and 5.9 million bpd in 1976 before tumbling to 1.37 million bpd in the war year of 1981. Under stable conditions, Iran, which hovered around 3.6 million bpd in the late 1990s, could sustain an average daily production of 5 million barrels for many years.

Iraq ranked fourth in Middle East production until 1975, when it replaced Kuwait in third place; and it exceeded 1 million bpd from 1960 to the early 1980s, with a peak of 3.4 million bpd in 1979. Its production dropped periodically during the early 1970s, when confrontations with Syria interrupted Iraq's oil throughput to terminals on the Mediterranean coast via pipelines crossing Syria. During the Iran-Iraq war, Iraq's production again suffered during the early 1980s, dropping below 1 million bpd in 1981–1983. Output was poised at the 3 million bpd level in mid-1990, when Iraq expressed sharp rancor toward its OPEC comembers about quotas and over-quota production. Friction on this point and other oil issues was part of Iraq's stated rationale for invading Kuwait. After the coalition responded to its incursion, Iraq suffered heavy damage from coalition

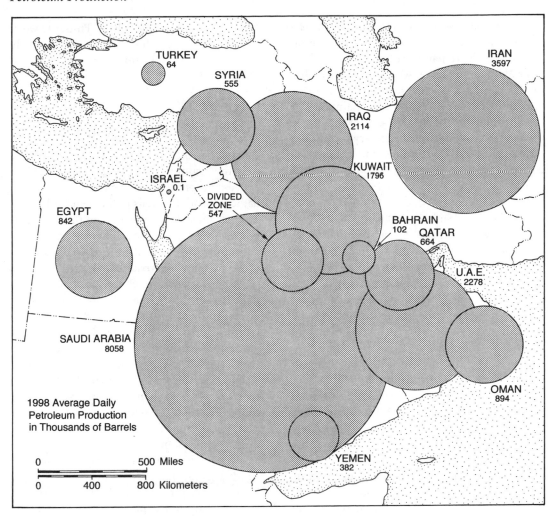

MAP 8-4   Middle East petroleum production, by country. Proportional circles show average amount of production for 1998 in thousands of barrels per day.

bombing and was temporarily forced to shut down all exports. It was still producing under UN controls for the rest of the 1990s, although it was allowed to produce 2.8 million bpd in mid-1999.

The next-largest producer in the Gulf and in the Middle East is the United Arab Emirates, whose production rose from a negligible amount in 1963 to 2 million bpd in 1977 before joining the regional downward trend. Prior to the independence of the UAE in 1971, oil was produced only in Abu Dhabi, which has continued to be by far the federation's major producer. Modest production from Dubai's offshore Fateh field has contributed an increasingly greater share of the UAE total. Regularly accused of exceeding its OPEC quota, the UAE production during the late 1990s averaged 2.2 million bpd, with 1999 output within the OPEC quota.

Kuwait led in Middle East production from 1954 to 1966; its production peaked in 1972 at 3 million bpd, was intentionally reduced for several years for conservation purposes (dropping Kuwait to fourth or fifth place), fell to 675,000 bpd in 1982 as a result of the oil crisis, and rebounded to well over 1.5 million bpd in 1989. Production, of course, dropped sharply after the Iraqi invasion in August 1990 (see Chap. 18) but recovered to average 1.8 million bpd during the remainder of the 1990s.

Production in Oman, which is not a member of OPEC, quickly reached stride in the late 1960s and, after faltering briefly, then maintained a steady production of 300,000–400,000 bpd. New discoveries and improved recovery techniques have recently led to a sustained curve of increasing production, from 283,000 bpd in 1980 to nearly 900,000 during the late 1990s.

Egypt, also not constrained by OPEC quotas, has varied between 800,000 and 900,000 bpd most years since 1984. Syria's production of very heavy crude varied from 160,000 to 175,000 bpd in the late 1970s and early 1980s, but the discovery in eastern Syria of a light sweet crude oil in the mid-1980s afforded a basis for nearly tripling output from 161,000 bpd in 1985 to more than 567,000 bpd 1996–1998. Syria can now export one-third of its production but needs further experience to determine if such output can be maintained. Far to the south, production in Yemen's several fields averaged 375,000 bpd in the late 1990s and may, like Syria's, increase within a few years. Israel's negligible production is by far the smallest of all Middle East producers.

In an assessment of the long-range significance of Middle East oil, two production ratios are important: the ratio of an area's annual production to its reserves and the ratio of its percentage of world production to its percentage of world reserves. It is noteworthy that Middle East production in 1998, for example, was 1 percent of the region's reserves, the corresponding ratio for the United States was 10.3 percent, and that for Mexico was 2.3 percent. In the same year, Middle East production amounted to 33 percent of the world total, with 65 percent of the world's petroleum reserves at that time; Western Hemisphere production was 27 percent of the world total, with only 16 percent of the world's reserves; and corresponding figures for other areas showed the same high ratio of production to reserves. The vital lesson is that intensive exploitation of oil will exhaust reserves more rapidly in areas outside the Middle East. Thus, the world will be even more highly dependent on the Middle East for oil by mid-century than it is at the present.

Major Oil Facilities

Raising petroleum and gas to the wellhead is only the beginning of a complex handling and processing procedure. The crude oil must be gathered from the wells in the field, and associated gas must be separated from the petroleum and either flared in the field or else piped to a consuming or processing facility. The degassed crude oil may then require "sweetening" before it is transported by pipeline to an export terminal or to a nearby refinery. Refining "cracks" the crude into a series of hydrocarbons from the lightest fractions at one end (naphtha and gasoline) through the middle distillates (kerosene and aviation jet fuel) to such heavy fractions as fuel oil and asphalt. Each product requires separate handling and has its own market. A salient development in the regional petroleum industry during the 1990s was the marked expansion of the petrochemical sector, especially in the major producing countries. Saudi Arabia, Iran, UAE, and—because of its huge gas resources—Qatar, are constructing large plants and expanding existing plants. Petrochemical facilities utilize a plentiful raw material, add greatly to its value, and supply a profitable export. Moreover, the oil production processed in the plants is not included in the OPEC quota (discussed later in this chapter).[3]

In the early years, most of the Middle East degassed crude petroleum was directly exported by tanker ships to overseas consumers. Most Middle East production is still exported in the same way. However, over the years, increasing amounts of petroleum have been refined in the producing countries and the products either consumed locally by the larger and more affluent populations or else exported in a more valuable refined form. Refineries were built in Iran, Bahrain, and Saudi Arabia soon after production began in each country, and oil refining is now a significant industry in every Middle East state.

A fairly high correlation exists between the pattern of producing fields and the pattern of handling and processing facilities—particularly with regard to pipelines and export terminals, but not necessarily refineries and petrochemical industries. Crude feedstock can be transported hundreds of miles by pipeline to refineries far distant from an oil field; more frequently it is transported by tanker ship to coastal refineries in more heavily populated industrial states. Pipelines, export terminals, and refineries are shown on Maps 8-1 and 8-2.

Pipelines

Pipelines are the arteries of the petroleum industry. Indeed, they are a unique land transportation system for oil and related products from the time the oil approaches the surface of the ground until it arrives at the interconnected refinery or shipping terminal. Since oil is of little value until it is moved from the well to an export or processing facility, pipelines are integral and vital links in the oil industry.

Environmental factors greatly influence the routes and costs of long-distance pipelines in the Middle East: topography, surface rock, density of population, environmental sensitivities, and others. Equally important is security of the pipelines and of the oil passing through them, the attitude of authorities concerned, and the political stability of the areas traversed. International pipelines have been particularly susceptible to shutdowns because of disputes among states along the routes, as well as subject to sabotage by dissident groups.

More than 9,000 miles/12,875 km of large-diameter pipelines transport crude petroleum from major fields in the Middle East to regional shipping terminals and refineries. Three systems merit attention because of the leading roles they play or have played and because they exemplify the problems faced by pipelines as a result of the regional crosscurrents.

The successive pipeline systems used by Iraq to export its oil illustrate the problems of an interior location and the importance of relations with neighboring states. For more than 40 years, Iraq exported its crude production through Iraq Petroleum Company (IPC) lines from Kirkuk across Syria to the Mediterranean coast. The first lines, opened in 1934, ran parallel from Kirkuk to Hadithah on the Euphrates, where they divided. One line terminated at Haifa, in the British mandate of Palestine, and the other at Tripoli, in the French mandate of Lebanon.

After World War II, new Middle East political patterns forced abandonment of the Haifa line, and the IPC built new lines to Baniyas in Syria. A series of disputes between Iraq and Syria forced indefinite closure of the system in April 1982, but not before Iraq had initiated projects to lessen its dependence on the export system through Syria.

In the mid-1970s, Iraq undertook construction of two new pipeline outlets. In 1975, it opened a strategic internal line to its own terminals at the head of the Gulf, where the export facilities were highly concentrated at the narrow outlet of Iraq's corridor to the coast. This arrangement was soon disrupted when the terminals were destroyed in 1980–1981, early in the war with Iran. However, Iraq had already supplemented its Gulf export capacity with a new 40-in./102 cm pipeline from Kirkuk through Turkey to Yumurtalık on the Mediterranean coast near Iskenderun, which opened in 1977. The capacity of this line was increased in 1984, and a parallel 46-in./117-cm line was opened in 1987, giving the system through Turkey a capacity of 1.6 million bpd.

Still concerned about its total dependence on one neighboring country for the export of its one major product, Iraq discussed with both Jordan and Saudi Arabia the possibility of extending pipelines through their territories to export terminals at Aqabah and Yanbu, respectively. Iraq eventually rejected the proposal for an export line to Aqabah, just across the border from Elat, Israel, since the system would be an easy target for Israeli artillery or air strikes; but by September 1985, contractors had completed construction of a 500,000-bpd 48-in./122-cm pipeline (IPSA-I) across northern Saudi Arabia to connect with Petroline, the huge Saudi crude oil line. Thus, balked at exporting through Syria and through its own terminals at the head of the Gulf, Iraq could export oil through Turkey and Saudi Arabia for the remaining years of its war with Iran. Later, the line from Iraq was continued as a separate 48-in./122-cm line, IPSA-II, parallel to the Saudi lines across the peninsula to a separate Red Sea export terminal, Muajjil, 30 miles/48 km south of Yanbu. The line was officially opened January 9, 1990, with a capacity of 1.65 million bpd.

Thus, Iraq had an export capacity of 3.15 million bpd through Turkey and Saudi Arabia, plus 800,000 bpd through its Gulf terminals when they were in operation, plus another potential 1.25 million bpd across Syria through the old IPC lines. However, Iraq's dependence on the goodwill of its neighbors in order to export its oil became dramatically evident once again in 1990 when Iraq inexplicably disdained all its favorable neighborly ties and invaded Kuwait. Complying with UN sanctions against Iraq, both Turkey and Saudi Arabia closed the lines crossing their territories and vowed to keep them shut in as long as the UN sanctions required it. Thus, Iraq had no lines through which to export its production—which is the price of its being virtually landlocked and of failing to maintain friendly relations with neighbors on which it is highly dependent. By the mid-1990s, UN controls were modified so that Iraq could export oil through the Turkey lines, but by early 2000 Saudi Arabia had not relented on its line closure.

A second international petroleum pipeline of major significance was the Trans-Arabian Pipe Line (Tapline), which extended 1,068 miles/ 1,718 km from the east coast of Saudi Arabia to the Mediterranean coast in southern Lebanon. Although throughput to the Mediterranean terminal was shut in by the early 1980s, Tapline had played a noteworthy role in Middle East oil developments for three decades, and it is an excellent case study in geographic petroleum economics.

Plans considered during World War II and completed by 1946 for a Gulf-to-Mediterranean pipeline envisioned a shortcut for oil from eastern Arabia to the eastern Mediterranean to avoid the long, slow voyage around the Arabian Peninsula and through the Suez Canal. Compared with the route of the original IPC lines across the Syrian Desert, the proposed route for Tapline was much longer and its environment much more barren, virtually uninhabited except for small numbers of Bedouins, and almost unknown. Tapline's diameter of 30–31 in./ 76–79 cm was also much larger than that of any of its predecessors.

When the line was opened in December 1950, it crossed Saudi Arabia, Jordan, Syria, and Lebanon (see Map 8-1). Five main pump stations were needed to move the eventual capacity of 500,000 bpd: Qaysumah, Rafha, Badanah, and Turayf in Saudi Arabia and Qaryatayn in Jordan. A given barrel of oil required eleven days to transit the line from eastern Arabia to the Zahrani loading terminal near Sidon. Although most of the oil was exported, the line also supplied crude feed-stock to a refinery in Zarqa, Jordan, and to a smaller refinery at Sidon in Lebanon. The line operated with signal success for many years, but problems mounted during and after the Arab-Israeli war in June 1967, when a segment of the line across the Golan Heights passed to Israeli control. Problems ranged from sabotage to disputes over royalties and were exacerbated after the 1973 Arab-Israeli war.

Another difficulty was that closure of the Suez Canal after the 1967 war stimulated the construction and use of increasingly large oil tankers. Very Large Crude Carriers (VLCCs) could transport crude from the Gulf around southern Africa to Western Europe and North America even more cheaply than could the smaller tankers that had formerly followed the Red Sea-Suez Canal-Mediterranean route. More important for Tapline, VLCC per-barrel costs were even cheaper than those of the smaller tankers lifting crude from Tapline's Zahrani terminal. With mounting operational problems and expenses, Tapline finally ceased supplying the Zahrani terminal in February 1975, when oil lifted at Ras Tanura (Fig. 8-3) could be landed at English Channel ports by VLCCs more than $2.00 per barrel cheaper than oil lifted from Zahrani. Thus, technology, economics, politics, and geography combined to render Tapline obsolete after 25 years of operation. Tapline did continue for several years to pump less than 100,000 bpd to supply the Jordanian refinery at Zarqa, in accordance with the Saudi government's goodwill efforts to maintain shipments to Jordan into the late 1980s, using only a small fraction of the pipeline's capacity. Saudi goodwill shipments gradually lessened, partly because of nonpayment for the oil, and they stopped entirely in August 1990 when Jordanians expressed opposition to the UN actions against Iraq. After 1990, Tapline was virtually unused, and some legendary pump stations were closed.

A third noteworthy line began as an internal facility but gained international connections. In 1981, the Saudis opened the largest-diameter long-distance crude oil line in the Middle East, a 48-in./122-cm line that extends from the oil fields of the Eastern Province to Yanbu on the Red Sea coast, with a new export facility, refinery, and industrial center. The original capacity of 1.85 million bpd was raised to 3.3 million bpd with the opening of a 56-in./142-cm parallel interconnected (looped) line in 1987. Originally called Petroline, this East-West crude oil pipeline system was up-graded during the early 1990s to a capacity of 4.8 million bpd, primarily to ensure a protected export outlet during crisis periods in the Gulf. The amount it normally carries is only a fraction of its capacity but is sufficient to feed refineries and petrochemical plants in Yanbu and have small amounts for exports. During crises, the East-West line would deliver nearly 5 million bpd of crude to the Red Sea for export via tanker, northward either through the Suez Canal or to the Gulf of Suez for delivery to the Egyptian "Sumed" lines, or southward through the Bab el-Mandeb.

During the late 1990s, controversy arose over the routing of a possible large-capacity pipeline, the Main Export Pipeline (MEP), from the Caspian oil fields to Middle East shipping terminals. As a temporary outlet during the delay, a new limited capacity line (which began operation in April 1999) connects the Baku fields with Supsa, a Georgian Black Sea port. Tankers can deliver oil from Supsa to other Black Sea ports or they can enter the Mediterranean through the Turkish Straits. As one route for the MEP, the new Baku-Supsa line could be paralleled by a large-capacity line, but Turkey strongly objects to that plan for two reasons: first, the environmental threat created by the already heavy tanker traffic through the Bosporus, and second, Turkey's desire for the MEP to transit its own land area, from Baku west through Georgia and then through eastern Anatolia to a port near Ceyhan on the Gulf of Iskenderun.

The U.S. government has given high priority to the Baku-Ceyhan route and, because that route would cross countries friendly to the United States and avoid Iran and Russia (see Map 8-1), has put determined pressure on the players concerned. Under its growing friendship with Turkey, Israel is a key supporter for the Ceyhan area outlet, which would not only benefit Turkey but also be convenient to Israeli import facilities. However, these three advocates have not indicated a willingness to help defray the cost, $5 billion or more, of constructing the line to Ceyhan. Factors involved are extraordinarily complex and include not only the costs and problems of construction but also the security of the route from sabotage, future Caspian production, oil pricing, future markets, and political relationships among the countries transited.[4]

Another important aspect of Middle East pipelines is the large—and steadily growing—number of natural gas lines in the region. Most are internal, but plans are well along for construction of several major gas pipelines across international borders. Gas from Qatar's supergiant North Field will inevitably be exported in great quantities. Europe, Turkey, the Levant, the UAE, Oman, Pakistan, and India have been suggested as potential markets. A UAE group has evolved the Dolphin initiative for an $8–$10 billion project for piping Qatar gas to Abu Dhabi, Dubai, Suhar (Oman), and later on to

FIGURE 8-3   One of the world's largest tank farms, on a sand spit at Saudi Aramco's Ras
Tanura export terminal on the Gulf coast. The terminal is one of the world's largest.

Pakistan.[5] Preliminary plans have been discussed for supplying Egyptian gas to Israel and
perhaps Jordan and other Levant states. Other
plans envision exporting Iranian gas to Turkey,
but these plans were put on hold in early 2000.

Other Pipelines, Terminals, and Refineries

In addition to the major long lines just
described, several internal pipelines are of
major regional importance and have a significant impact on international movements of
Middle East petroleum. Both Egypt and Israel
have pipelines that permit transportation of oil
from the Red Sea to the Mediterranean, and
these lines serve tankers that are too large for
the Suez Canal or that prefer to avoid the canal.
Egypt's Suez-Mediterranean system (Sumed)
consists of twin parallel 42-in./107-cm lines that
transfer oil from the northern end of the Gulf of
Suez to the Mediterranean Sea coast just west of
Alexandria. Israel's 42-in./107-cm Trans-Israel
Pipeline (Tipline) runs from Elat to a terminal
at Ashqelon. Details on the more important oil
export terminals and refineries are given in the
individual country chapters. However, Table 8-2
gives comparative data on refineries.

Markets and Marketing

Early commercial developers of Middle East
petroleum fields envisaged exploiting the
resources for export to their respective home
countries or for fuel for naval ships. Local consumption was limited. However, as the pace of
regional economic development increased,
demand for the petroleum products mounted
in the Middle East as elsewhere, and governments in successive oil-exporting countries
achieved control over the exploitation and
marketing of their highly valuable and sometimes sole resource and then contracted for
local basic oil-processing facilities.

Marketing of large amounts of petroleum
has traditionally been on long-term contracts.
Concessionary companies operating in a producing country were often the direct sellers,
disposing of their share of the product within
a stable if highly complex world-marketing
system. For several decades, the system was
virtually controlled by a small number of major
oil companies, primarily the "Seven Sisters":
Jersey Standard (Exxon), British Petroleum,
Royal Dutch/Shell, Texaco, Standard of California (Chevron), Socony-Vacuum (Mobil), and
Gulf (which merged with Chevron in 1984).

TABLE 8-2 PETROLEUM: REFINERIES AND REFINING ACTIVITY, 2000.

COUNTRY	1 NO. OF REFIN-ERIES	2 TOTAL REF. CAPACITY (BPD)	3 LARGEST REFINERY IN RESPECTIVE COUNTRY	4 MAIN REF. CAPACITY (BPD)
Bahrain	1	248,900	Sitra	248,900
Cyprus	1	27,000	Larnaca	27,000
(Divided Zone)[a]	0	0	—	0
Egypt	8	577,760	Mostorod	145,000
Iran	9	1,474,000	Abadan	400,000
Iraq	8	347,500	Baiji	150,000
Israel	2	220,000	Haifa	130,000
Jordan	1	90,400	Zarqa	90,400
Kuwait	3	864,500	Mina al-Ahmadi	427,500
Lebanon	2	37,500	Tripoli	20,000
Oman	1	85,000	Mina al-Fahal	85,000
Qatar	1	57,500	Musayid	57,500
Saudi Arabia	8	1,710,000	Yanbu	366,000
Syria	2	242,140	Banyas	135,000
Turkey	6	690,915	Izmit	226,440
UAE	4	428,500	Ruways	145,000
Yemen	2	120,000	Little Aden	110,000
TOTAL	59	7,221,615	—	2,763,740

[a]Divided Zone refinery data divided between Kuwait and Saudi Arabia. Source: *Oil and Gas Journal*, Dec. 20, 1999, and *International Petroleum Encyclopedia 1999*.

National oil companies of Italy, Spain, and Brazil, as well as Japanese companies, joined in the programs to explore for, produce, and market Middle East oil. They thereby gained international marketing influence.

Until 1970, the main importers of Middle East crude were industrial countries that required supplies beyond their own production capacity and included those countries that held major concessions in Middle East producing countries. Some of the importers had only limited or even no known petroleum resources of their own. Virtually every major oil exporter in the Middle East during the 1960s and 1970s counted the same half-dozen leading purchasers among its top ten customers: Great Britain, France, West Germany, Japan, the Netherlands, and the United States. Main secondary buyers included Italy, Spain, Canada, and Brazil; and such countries as Australia, India, Sweden, and Switzerland also regularly made noteworthy purchases of Middle East crude.

After 1970, steadily increasing production from new and developing offshore fields on the continental shelves of Great Britain and other North Sea littoral countries afforded northwestern Europe a large supply of local oil and gas. As one result, the demand for Middle East crude by North Sea countries dropped by more than 3 million bpd as both Great Britain and Norway became net exporters, completely redirecting the world oil industry. Another significant impact developed during the middle and late 1990s with the opening of the Caspian Basin oil resources, with particular impetus from the United States, to commercial exploration and exploitation. After the early 1970s, the trend of oil exports from the Middle East from year to year has been markedly more variable than that during the 1950s and 1960s. The import pattern of the United States also changed: In 1977 the United States imported 46 percent of its oil needs, about 18 percent from the Middle East; in 1983 it imported only 28 percent of its oil requirements, just 4 percent from the Middle East; in 1988 it imported about 41 percent of its oil consumption, about 11 percent from the Middle East; and in 1999 it imported 55 percent of its needs, about 20 percent from the Middle East.

In addition to an increased local use of petroleum, consumption of natural gas in the Middle East has also grown dramatically. Whereas in 1972 more than two-thirds of the gas produced in association with Middle East oil was either flared or reinjected (pumped back into the oil reservoir), by 1982 only half of the gas was being flared, and utilization had increased by 38 percent. Industry forecasts suggest that flaring will drop to less than 8 percent of gross production in the early 2000s.

OPEC: Pricing and Participation

In the 1940s and 1950s, companies operating concessions in the Middle East generally determined production and price levels, taking into account Middle East costs of production and the world demand for petroleum. Posted prices were periodically set and publicly stated by oil companies as the "list" prices at which various grades of crude would be sold at Gulf terminals. Highly complex arrangements, royalties, taxes, deductions, and discounts affected government revenue levels and company profits.

When various factors combined to precipitate a reduction in posted prices in 1960, the governments of major producing countries, in a continuing effort to gain greater control over the pricing system, met in Baghdad in September 1960 and created the Organization of Petroleum Exporting Countries (OPEC). Charter members were Saudi Arabia, Iran, Iraq, Kuwait, and Venezuela; and by 1975, membership had expanded to include Qatar, Indonesia, Libya, Abu Dhabi (later the United Arab Emirates), Algeria, Nigeria, Ecuador (withdrew in 1992), and Gabon (withdrew in 1995). Of the 11 current members, 6 are in the Middle East, and 5 of these are Arab countries (2 additional Arab members are in North Africa). Bahrain, Oman, Egypt, and Syria are not OPEC members. Eight

years after the formation of OPEC, Arab oil exporters, partly as a result of the impact of the 1967 Arab-Israeli war, formed a parallel group, the Organization of Arab Petroleum Exporting Countries (OAPEC), which included all Arab members of OPEC and also Bahrain, Egypt, and Syria. Oman has not joined either organization. OAPEC has failed to achieve a consistent major role in the regional oil industry.

With prices of virtually all other commodities and services having risen steadily since the late 1940s, petroleum was increasingly underpriced into the early 1970s. Not until late in 1973 was the FOB price of the benchmark Arabian Light crude at Ras Tanura to surge decisively above $3.00 per barrel (all prices and sales were, and still are, in U.S. dollars). Mounting determination by OPEC members to strengthen their hold on the pricing and handling of their petroleum was sharpened, especially for members of OAPEC, by the impact of the 1973 Arab-Israeli war, and OAPEC members embargoed oil shipments to the United States and the Netherlands in retaliation for actions or policies considered supportive of Israel in that war. Late 1973 was the turning point in company-government relations in the region, as company-set posted prices were abandoned in favor of the OPEC-announced price levels. The Gulf posted price had been increased from the long-set $1.80/bbl in 1970 to $2.18 in 1971, then in three raises in six months to $2.90 in mid-1973, to $5.12 in October, and in one historic jump to $11.65 in December. OPEC had arrived.[6] The price then rose through a series of gradual increases to $13.34 at the beginning of 1979, doubled in one year to $26.00, and peaked at $34.00 a barrel in October 1981 as a consequence of Iran-Iraq war jitters. Unified pricing, however, was often disregarded by some OPEC sellers—increasingly so into the middle and late 1980s, until the price fell to about $13.00 a barrel.

The 1973–1974 escalation of oil prices (which proceeded independently of the OAPEC embargo) broke, for virtually the first time, the previously steady and often rapid growth of world petroleum consumption since 1945. Shaken by a tenfold price increase per barrel of petroleum from late 1973 to early 1981, major consuming countries attempted to minimize the shock of the increases not only by conservation and more efficient use of oil but also by utilizing alternate forms of energy. In addition, the price increases stimulated a greater development of oil resources and higher production in non-OPEC countries, depressing demand for OPEC oil. The changing balance dropped the OPEC share of world production from 56 percent in 1973 to 29 percent in 1985. However, its share rebounded and averaged about 40 percent between 1993 and 1996. The seemingly insatiable demand for oil into the late 1970s, despite escalating prices, created a surplus productive capacity, which, in turn, exerted a downward pressure on market prices and caused financial stress in several OPEC states.

In the early 1990s, OPEC continued to struggle with the delicate problem of the fair apportionment of production quotas among its members and hence with the problem of price maintenance. As in any such arrangement, members sought high prices, but some were unwilling to adhere to the assigned production quota limit—the sine qua non for achieving higher prices. OPEC achieved mixed results during the 1990s, but prices trended downward until they reached less than $10/bbl in early 1999, an all-time low in adjusted real prices. However, OPEC policies set at its March 1999 meeting stimulated lower, more realistic output by its members and by several non-OPEC producers interested in higher price levels. As late as January 2000 the OPEC basket price was well above $25.00 per barrel.

Thus, during the late 1990s, the balance of market forces made clear the dilemma faced by oil companies and oil-producing countries. If meaningful controls can be exercised, artificially reduced production has a push-pull effect: It extends field life, and it supports higher prices; but it also reduces consumption (especially in poorer countries) drives conservation efforts, encourages the search for alternative sources of energy, and lowers the threshold for such economic exploitation of unconventional oil resources as heavy oil, tar sands, and oil shale.

Moreover, in accordance with standard cartel theory, artificially reduced production inevitably leads to greater centrifugal forces within OPEC and cheating on assigned quotas; this soon induces a breakdown in the production and pricing structure, and the cycle starts all over again. When the price falls below a certain optimum (not just a certain minimum), the income squeeze on producing countries and oil companies seriously impacts the entire world economy. Similarly, an excessively high price—for example, $28/bbl or more—depletes the budgets of the poorer nonproducing states and creates resistance from main consumers. One repercussion of an excessively low price during late 1998 and early 1999 was the series of mergers of western oil companies—even majors like BP and Amoco (which then took over Atlantic Richfield Company, ARCO); Total (France) and PetroFina (Belgium); and Exxon and Mobil with Chevron and Texaco having unsuccessfully flirted with merging. In addition, the new TotalFina combine absorbed the French major, Elf Aquitaine, in September 1999.

For more than two decades after World War II, much of the industrial world had enjoyed rapidly expanding economic growth while relying heavily on a steadily increasing and seemingly inexhaustible supply of incredibly cheap energy from beneath the sands and seas of the Middle East. Continuation of such an incongruous economic arrangement should not have been expected, and OPEC became the channel for an inevitable reversal of the economic trend. Realizing that their petroleum supplies are a nonrenewable resource serving as a crucial energy source worldwide, the Middle East producers naturally insist on receiving a maximum return on their sole export and thereby conserving their supplies.

While Middle East producers were pooling the marketing prices of their output in OPEC in the 1960s and 1970s, each individual government steadily increased its "participation" in the private companies holding concessions in its country. By 1980, most OPEC countries had raised their share of ownership of local producing operations to 100 percent and had

MAP 8-5   Distribution of more important deposits of solid minerals in the Middle East. Note the richness of mineral occurrences in the zones of tectonic plate contacts in Turkey, Iran, and Cyprus. (Adapted from several maps in U.S. Geological Survey, Minerals Information, 1996)

turned their interests over to national oil companies. By the late 1980s, the national oil companies were increasing their downstream operations (refining, distributing, retailing) both domestically and in customer countries, thus expanding a healthy interdependence.

Other Minerals

The production and utilization of petroleum and natural gas have been the focal point of economic mineral activity in the Middle East

for several decades. However, several areas are highly mineralized, have produced limited to modest quantities of ores for many centuries, and are now the focus of intensified mineral exploration activities (Map 8-5). The oil-producing countries have joined their neighbors in intensively searching for commercially useful ores and rocks.

Even limited production can bring significant benefit to a local area, especially one lacking petroleum resources; and the processing of ores in areas such as western Iran and northern Oman can be relatively economical because of the availability of large amounts of local natural gas. Thus, income from mining and quarrying industries is expected to increase significantly in the near future.

Turkey and Iran, which occupy extensive segments of the mineralized Fold Belt, have long produced the greatest amounts and variety of solid minerals. Cyprus also is part of the mineralized belt and has been a considerable mineral producer historically, but it faces approaching depletion of its formerly appreciable resources of copper, iron pyrites, and chromite. Jordan, Syria, Israel, Egypt, and Iraq have achieved significant production of phosphate rock, and Israel and Jordan produce noteworthy amounts of potash from the Dead Sea. Both Saudi Arabia and Egypt hope to revive and expand mining in the crystalline shield areas in their respective territories.[7]

Solid Fuels

Although a deficiency in coal resources contributed to the retardation of industrial development in the Middle East during the nineteenth century, the effects of this deficiency have diminished since World War II. Only Turkey, Iran, and—to a minor extent—Egypt have noteworthy coal reserves, and only Turkey's production is significant, with Iran's gradually increasing.

Turkey compensates for its small petroleum output by intensively exploiting its considerable resources of coal (1.4 billion mt) and lignite (8 billion mt). Solid fuels production by the early 1990s exceeded 55 million mt per year. Although Iran possesses modest coal reserves in some of the same structures that contain coal beds in Turkey, it has allowed production to lag at about 1.5 million mt/year, because it possesses enormous reserves of petroleum and natural gas. Egypt's modest coal production is useful locally, and production is increasing in newly opened mines in northern Sinai.

Metals

Most (although not all) metallic ores occur in mineralized igneous and crystalline rocks. They cannot, therefore, be normally expected in the extensive sedimentary areas of the Fertile Crescent countries or the Arabian Peninsula. Certain metals may be found in either class of rocks, and, indeed, some limited deposits of iron, lead, and zinc are found in the sedimentary strata just mentioned. Therefore, it is primarily in (1) the complex rocks of the Anatolian and Iranian plateaus, (2) the shield blocks on either side of the Red Sea, and (3) the unusual Oman Mountains that concentrated mineralization has been found and is exploited.

As is the case for solid minerals in general, Turkey possesses by far the greatest variety and greatest quantity of metal ores, and Iran is second. Several metallic ores in Turkey are minable by large-scale methods: bauxite, chromite, copper, zinc, gold, iron, and silver. Only its chromite production ranks on a world scale—a comfortable second. More significant, though, are several industrial minerals: barite, boron, kaolin and other clays, magnesite, pumice, and strontium. Turkey is world leader in the output of boron and magnesium, second in pumice, and seventh in barite. Its minerals industries exports, including cement, regularly exceed $600 million annually. Iran, with its great emphasis on its oil and gas resources, has not given commensurate effort to its solid mineral production. However, it has developed some major deposits and is a significant producer of copper, chromium, iron ore, lead and zinc, and molybdenum. Iran, Turkey, and Egypt, the same states that lead in iron ore resources, also share leadership in the production of pig iron and steel. Iron was exploited in Anatolia before 1800 BC by the Hittites, who maintained a near-monopoly on ironworking for several centuries. Iran's iron reserves are twice those of Turkey and Egypt combined, but its production is appreciably less than Turkey's.

Nonferrous metals regularly produced in noteworthy quantities in the region include notably copper but also lead, zinc, mercury, and bauxite (aluminum ore). Although Turkey, Cyprus, and Iran have traditionally been the leading copper producers, Iran became the distinct leader in 1982 after more than a decade of developing its copper resources. Oman appeared as a copper producer for the first time in 1983 and ranks third, after Turkey, in output, although its quite limited reserves are nearly exhausted. Production from Cyprus's ancient mines varies and in some years ceases to be commercially worthwhile.

Iran normally leads in the output of lead and zinc, with Turkey in second place. Turkey is the region's only producer of bauxite and mercury worth noting, and it has significant reserves of uranium, unexploited at the present time. Israel, however, produces small amounts of uranium from its Negev phosphate deposits for supplementary use in the nearby Dimona reactor.

Nonmetals

Certain types of nonmetallic minerals may be found in several different rock environments, others are found only in sedimentary rocks, and still others occur only in igneous rocks. Thus, the Middle East's nonmetallic ores are more widely distributed over the region than are its metallic resources and may even be processed from sea or lake water.

The most widely produced solid mineral is salt, produced in virtually every country in the region but in especially large quantities in Turkey, Egypt, and Iran. Lebanon, Yemen, Egypt, and Iraq produce salt by evaporating seawater in small ponds or evaporation pans along the shore. Other producers evaporate surface or underground brines, and Iran and Yemen mine rock salt from underground salt plugs that have pushed their way toward the surface from deep subsurface strata.

The region's production of phosphate rock, valuable for making chemical fertilizers, is of considerable significance on the global scale, as the world demand for phosphate rock has mounted sharply with the growing need for soil fertilizers to increase soil productivity. Middle East resources have, therefore, been more vigorously exploited, with production steadily growing through the late 1970s and 1980s. The region's leading producer is Jordan, which also

usually ranks fifth or sixth in the world, with a 1997 output of 5.9 million mt. Four neighboring states are, in 1997 order of production, significant producers from similar rock strata: Israel, Syria (Fig. 8-4), Egypt, and Iraq.

Other nonmetallic minerals of the region may be noted, especially with regard to the unusual aspects of several of them. For example, meerschaum is found in significant commercial quantities only in Turkey. Despite its name ("sea foam" in German), it is a hydrous magnesium silicate—a fine white clayey mineral—used to make special kinds of smoking pipe bowls, many of which are elaborately carved. Potash is produced in large amounts from Dead Sea water by both Israel and Jordan, with Israel's output constituting about 4 percent of the world output. Among other minerals Israel produces from the Dead Sea, the bromine output is about one-third of the world total. Asbestos has long been a major product of the metamorphic rocks of Cyprus and is produced from related structures in Turkey and Egypt. Output has decreased sharply since revelation of asbestos fiber dangers to health.

Notes

1. Hundreds of sources cover various aspects of Middle East oil both in general and for respective producing states. For detailed early development of the Gulf oil industry, see Marlowe 1962. Peterson 1983 discusses the politics of oil. An excellent source for current data on petroleum, natural gas, and coal is *EIA* (Energy Information Administration), U.S. Dept. of Energy, also at URL <http://www.eia.doe.gov/emeu/cabs/>. PennWell's annual *International Petroleum Encyclopedia* (IPE) is very useful. (PennWell also publishes the weekly *Oil and Gas Journal*.) *Saudi Aramco* 1995 and earlier editions are authoritative and available. Exxon 1984 is a handy, concise discussion with good maps. Danielsen 1982 looks at OPEC. Peterson 1983 examines regional oil and politics. For solid minerals, refer to the Bureau of Mines *Minerals Yearbooks,* which also include some petroleum information. They are published every year or two, and the three or four latest pertinent *Minerals Yearbooks* may also be found at <http:// minerals.usgs.gov/minerals/pubs/>. For a readable best-seller account of the oil industry, see Yergin 1991.

FIGURE 8-4   Open-pit mining of phosphates near Palmyra in central Syria. Phosphate-rich beds extend through much of Syria, Jordan, Iraq, and Israel.

2. Statistics on reserves and production differ among sources, and criteria for estimating reserves vary among companies and countries. "Proved" reserves are those that engineering evidence indicates can be commercially produced with reasonable certainty with normal techniques. "Probable" reserves are those whose existence is less well known but that are expected to be commercial in the future. Some companies also include "possible" reserves. A standard and available source is the annual *International Petroleum Encyclopedia.*

Most countries report reserves (and production) in barrels (bbl) of 42 U.S. gallons, but some report in metric tons (mt), and equivalents are not always precise. One mt is equal to 7.31 bbl of average gravity crude but may vary considerably with variations in gravity. Also, some information may be kept confidential, thus skewing other information.

3. For Saudi Arabia's petrochemical industry, see *Oil and Gas Journal,* Aug. 16, 1999, 65–71. For Iran, see same issue, 20–24.

4. See *International Petroleum Encyclopedia* 30 (1997): 202–207; *Oil and Gas Journal,* Nov. 15, 1999, 23–28, with map; *EIA:* "Caspian Sea Region," Dec. 1998; and *New York Times,* Jan. 24, 1999.

5. See *Oil and Gas Journal,* July 19, 1999, 28–30.

6. See Danielson 1982; *Oil and Gas Journal,* Dec. 28, 1998, 18–23; and *EIA:* "OPEC Fact Sheet," Sept. 1999 (also on URL <http://www.eia.doe.gov/emeu/cabs/>).

7. The best source for solid minerals information is U.S. Bureau of Mines, *Minerals Yearbooks.*

9
Manufacturing and Transportation

Preliminary View

The Stimulus of Oil

The unparalleled petroleum development surveyed in the previous chapter naturally stimulated expansion in other economic sectors. The entire Middle East benefited from the ripple effect on a grand scale, but the expansion was most remarkable in the Gulf states. Rapidly developing Gulf areas soaked up surplus labor from Yemen, Egypt, Lebanon, Jordan, and Syria. At the same time, a reverse flow of cash in grants, loans, and remittances transferred a share of oil profits to nonproducing areas or smaller producers. From Baghdad to Beirut, Kuwait to Cairo, Dubai to Damascus, capital and development fever became the common denominator. Contractors, artisans, and consultants came by the hundreds to take advantage of the boom.

Along Gulf coasts tiny fishing villages such as Abu Dhabi and Doha became wealthy national capitals with some of the world's largest per capita incomes. Farther inland, splendid paved highways threaded their way across rolling deserts, replacing caravan trails and rutted tracks. By the early 1990s, the Gulf states, including Saudi Arabia, had achieved stunning material progress that was awesome to local inhabitant and outside specialist alike. The splendor and even opulence of public buildings, hotels, airport terminals, shopping centers, and universities were matched by the number and complexity of technologically advanced gas-oil separating facilities, shipping terminals, oil refineries, petrochemical plants, drydocks, aluminum smelters, and similar installations that

appear to sprout from deserts and beaches. The insatiable demand for labor in the boom economy guaranteed the indigenous population full employment, favored treatment, many free benefits, and a high standard of living.

Despite the general advancement, the Middle East still has contradictions and inequalities in its standards of living and development patterns. Several states have laid modest-to-appreciable industrial foundations and have developed several diversified producing areas. Even so, none of the Gulf oil producers is a true "industrial" state, in the Western sense, although prerevolutionary Iran as well as Iraq sought high levels of industrialization. Development of modern manufacturing started earlier in the eastern Mediterranean, especially in Egypt, where it began in the early 1800s under Muhammad Ali, and in Turkey, where it originated under the nineteenth-century Ottoman new order. Economic evolution during the regional oil boom and the emergence of Israel contributed to the pattern of manufacturing discussed later in this chapter, which reveals the importance of manufacturing in the older areas of Turkey, Iran, and Egypt, as well as the later belts in Syria, Israel, and Iraq. On a smaller scale are Cyprus and, in normal times, Lebanon, which was one of the most intensively developed areas in the Middle East in the early 1970s.

Exact quantification of the industrialization of states in the region is difficult to impossible because of the lack of meaningful and comparable statistics. Determining the values of the usual criteria used to analyze the degree of industrialization—percentage of the gross national product (GNP) derived from manufacturing and other industrial output, percent of the work force employed in manufacturing and other industry, and per capita energy consumption, steel output, and other indicators—is thus problematic. Moreover, the Middle East is unique because it has a high output of electrical energy regardless of industrial output. In another connection, much of its industry is capital intensive, highly automated, and labor extensive: A refinery, for example, is a huge facility with high output, but it employs few workers.

Since the overwhelming emphasis is on petroleum exploitation in the Gulf region, that area's recently evolved economic patterns and activities differ from those of neighboring non-oil areas. There are considerable gaps in the gross domestic product (GDP) and in per capita income between the Gulf and the eastern Mediterranean, but the ripple effect of oil income in part of the region has been noteworthy in other parts. Development in Cyprus, Jordan, and—before 1975—Lebanon has been impressive because of the ripple effect. The dramatic development in Israel has been largely independent of the regional oil boom but has been heavily financed by capital transfers of aid, especially from the United States and Germany. Capital availability from oil income has set the pace for all Middle East countries, even though development has been uneven among the several states and among sectors of the economy. In any given year during the 1980s, Saudi Arabia expended $250–$275 billion for development in a large area with a relatively small population, whereas Egypt spent one-tenth that amount on a small inhabited area with a population four times that of the Saudi kingdom.

Historical Perspective

During the golden age of Islam, in the ninth and tenth centuries, the Middle East boasted the world's best-developed economy and flourishing trade. High-quality textiles were a specialty— linens from Egypt, damask from Damascus, silks from Kufah, brocades from Shiraz, and muslin from Mosul, as well as carpets from Iran, Bukhara, and other centers. Colored glass from Syria, decorated ceramic tiles from several areas, pottery, porcelain, inlaid and decorated wood, paper, engraved and inlaid brass and copper (damascene), engraved gold and silver jewelry, leather wares, and fine soaps and perfumes were produced in the small workshops of the *suqs* or bazaars. Products moved between Spain on the west and Samarkand on the east as well as into Scandinavia, India, and China.

Some goods moved by sea, and Basrah became a preeminent port of the time. However, much of the traffic was overland, and great dromedary caravans often moved eastward from Baghdad through Hamadan, Rey, and Merv (Mary) to Samarkand, where loads were transferred to the Bactrian camels of the Mongols and Chinese (see Map 6-5). Towns favorably located as trade centers thrived during the period, and some of them have maintained their prosperity into the present.

But with the age of discovery, Western European ships sailed around southern Africa and gained control of the trade routes between their home countries and southern and eastern Asia. Middle East arts and crafts declined, and, their markets lost, continued only at a survival level. By the seventeenth century, the great caravans between the Islamic world and China were only a memory.

Renewed European interest in the Middle East in the nineteenth century revived some aspects of the region's economic activity— carpet making, metalworking, and woodworking. Steamships transported far greater loads than had the earlier small sailing vessels, and European investors built railways from ports into interiors under concessionary terms.

Cooperation and Aid
Arab Economic Coordination

The concept of Arab unity has always had an economic component, but economic coordination has been inhibited by recurrent political conflict. Numerous successive economic agreements and institutions have been arranged, only to become ineffective in reality. As early as 1950, the Arab League sponsored the signing of the Arab Joint Defense and Economic Cooperation Agreement, but the agreement quietly expired after three or four years. Motivated by desire for pan-Arab cooperation, an Arab Common Market agreement was signed in 1964 among Egypt, Iraq, Jordan, and Syria. Kuwait decided not to join, and with no new members, the effort was officially abandoned in 1971.[1] The fate of these examples is typical of that of later efforts among Arab states, usually the result of regional tensions. Similar friction has precluded region-wide cooperation, and Israel, Iran, and Turkey are generally excluded from Arab groupings.

A subregional effort among Gulf states has achieved admirable success: the Cooperation Council of the Arab States of the Gulf, better known as the Gulf Cooperation Council (GCC), created in 1981. The GCC is more than an economic agency, although it has an effective economic component. A broader, business-oriented grouping that links virtually all Middle East states, including Israel, with scores of other countries is the Middle East/North Africa (MENA) Economic Conference, formed in 1994. Both of these agencies are discussed in Chapter 11.

Economic Aid

A further influence on Middle East economic patterns is that of direct transfers of capital into and within the region. Huge amounts of petrodollars flowed to the OPEC states for oil payments after 1972 and were used for development projects in the oil states as well as for aid to non-oil states.

From the 1950s to the present, industrialized states have made large grants and loans to many governments and agencies in the Middle East. The United States has extended the largest amounts, primarily to Israel, Turkey, Egypt, and Jordan, although virtually every country in the region—other than the Gulf amirates—received substantial U.S. aid at some point between 1940 and 1989, including Iran, Iraq,

and Saudi Arabia. Israel received by far the largest amounts, about one-third of all U.S. foreign aid, along with indirect grants and loans of many types. Most Western European countries—especially Great Britain, Germany, and France but also some of the smaller states—have also granted and lent large amounts to Middle East countries. The former Soviet Union gave its client states assistance, primarily military but also economic, for dams and related projects in Egypt and Syria. Japan is the leading Asian donor, although the People's Republic of China has built major highways and a textile mill in Yemen.

In addition to these bilateral amounts, technical and development aid has also been given to all non-oil Middle East states through the United Nations, and the United Nations Relief and Works Agency (UNRWA) has funneled large amounts of aid to Palestinian refugees from 1949 to the present. Technical assistance has also been given to the oil states on a reimbursable basis.

Intraregional aid after the 1960s became a wealth-sharing process. In 1961, Kuwait created the Kuwait Fund for Arab Economic Development (KFAED), which has given hundreds of millions of dollars in loans and grants for economic development not only in the Arab world but also in African countries. Similar funds were created later by other oil states—the Abu Dhabi Fund for Arab Economic Development, the Iraqi Fund for External Development, and the Saudi Fund for Development. Large grants are regularly made by oil states to non-oil states outside the channels of the funds, especially on an emergency basis. Financial aid to countries that assist in the military defense of Gulf producers is especially substantial. After the 1973 Arab-Israeli war, for example, Arab oil producers transferred $3 billion to Egypt, $1 billion to Syria, and $125 million to Jordan.

During Iraq's war with Iran in 1980–1988, Kuwait, Saudi Arabia, Qatar, and the UAE contributed more than $55 billion to Iraq's wartime expenses. When Iraq invaded Kuwait in 1990, Kuwait, Saudi Arabia, and the UAE helped defray the costs of the coalition's rollback of the

Iraqis with cash reimbursements over several months that totaled $84 billion and with material support worth another $51 billion. They also contributed several billion dollars toward losses and costs incurred by Turkey, Jordan, and Egypt because of the UN sanctions and coalition actions.[2]

Regional Development Problems

Remarkable though it has been, regional development in the Middle East has been hindered by several fundamental problems in addition to the lack of effective regional coordination and the original inadequate infrastructure. The initial shortage of skilled labor required the importation of scores of thousands of technicians and ordinary workers, then necessitated time for the training of indigenous workers and managers to replace expatriate workers. The original dependence of the Gulf oil states on northwestern Europeans and Americans for exploration and development of oil resources evolved into a mutual relationship involving oil supplies, dollar payments, technological needs, and petrodollar recycling. Nearly everywhere, the shortage of water—and in places, the actual lack of water—has had a serious negative impact on the pattern of economic development.

Therefore, despite its energy resources, the Middle East faced serious problems in the first 20–25 years of moving toward economic development and achieved admirable results. Nevertheless, it still faces difficulties in trying to bring about comprehensive economic development. Progress in certain sectors has been dramatic, but the achievement of long-term self-sufficiency in a balanced economy will be more challenging

Labor and Skills

The lack of a sufficient and trained work force was the most serious single deterrent to initial development in most of the Middle East,

especially in the Gulf oil states, and the various steps taken to meet the labor demand have had profound spatial implications. During the 35 years before 1992, there was a sharp contrast in the labor available between the northwestern part of the Middle East and the southeastern part. The northwest had a labor surplus and a small supply of technical and managerial people. By contrast, the Gulf area possessed a sparse and primarily pastoral/fishing population, which was inadequate in number and unequipped in skills to meet the labor demands of a booming oil economy.

The demand for labor in the Gulf states was both qualitative and quantitative. The potential supply of unskilled workers from nearby areas and southern Asia was almost unlimited, but the number of available engineers, technicians, business managers, and similar professionals was small. As the pace of development increased during the 1960s, workers at all levels came from Jordan, Egypt, and Lebanon to Saudi Arabia and the smaller Gulf states. Yemenis filled hundreds of semi-skilled jobs in Saudi Arabia, and Indians, Pakistanis, and Baluch poured into the lower Gulf to work. By the mid-1980s, nearly 8 million migrant workers in the Gulf constituted more than 70 percent of the labor force in the Gulf economies.

Cultural affiliations were important, since Arabic speakers and Muslims tended to adapt most easily in the Gulf. However, Pakistanis and Indian Muslims often adapted more readily than cosmopolitan Lebanese. In addition, managerial positions generally required fluency in English, the lingua franca of the oil industry. As a consequence, the work force was transformed in size and composition throughout the Gulf within a few years (Table 9-1). During the later 1970s and the 1980s, the greater percentage of the expatriate workers were Filipinos, Thai, Sri Lankans, and, under construction contractors in Saudi Arabia, particularly South Koreans. With its almost insatiable demand for additional labor, Saudi Arabia in 1997 included more than 5.5 million expatriate workers in its labor force.

TABLE 9-1 ECONOMICALLY ACTIVE POPULATION: TOTAL AND SECTOR DISTRIBUTION.

	1	2	3	4	5	6	7	8
	ECON ACTIVE POP		PERCENTAGE OF ECON ACTIVE POP IN SELECTED SECTORS					
COUNTRY	TOTAL NO. IN 000s	% TOTAL POP	AG, FOR, FISHING	MFG, MNG, QG	CNSTRC-TION	TRNSP, COMM	TRADE, HTL, RT	SERVS, OTHER
Bahrain (1991)	226	44.6	2.3	14.6	11.8	6.1	13.2	52.0
Cyprus (1995)[a]	303	47.0	10.1	15.9	8.7	6.2	25.4	33.6
Egypt (1994)	17,572	30.4	30.5	12.9	5.9	4.8	9.0	36.8
Iran (1991)	14,737	26.4	21.8	15.2	9.3	5.2	8.4	40.1
Iraq (1988)	4,127	24.7	11.6	10.6	11.2	6.4	6.8	53.3
Israel (1995)	2,100	37.9	2.7	20.2	6.7	5.5	15.7	49.2
Jordan (1993)	859	22.2	6.4	11.3	7.0	6.7	15.1	53.5
Kuwait (1995)	746	47.4	1.3	9.4	15.7	5.2	11.4	57.1
Lebanon (1988)	904	26.5	19.1	18.9	6.2	7.0	16.5	32.3
Oman (1993)	705	34.9	9.1	11.3	15.3	3.5	14.8	46.1
Qatar (1988)	293	53.7	1.6	7.5	22.0	4.1	11.7	53.2
S. Arabia (1988)	5,369	36.3	3.6	11.1	22.0	6.0	18.0	39.4
Syria (1991)	3,485	27.8	26.3	13.5	9.8	4.8	10.9	34.8
Turkey (1995)	22,899	37.1	45.8	14.8	6.0	3.9	12.1	17.4
UAE (1990)	690	47.0	6.3	13.6	17.3	10.4	14.7	37.7
Yemen (1988)	3,029	26.4	71.1	4.3	5.9	3.0	2.8	13.0
Gaza (1996)	173	18.0	5.2	9.8	10.3	3.3	12.0	59.3
W. Bank (1996)	357	22.7	11.6	14.5	17.0	4.4	14.8	37.7
TOTAL/AVG.	78,574	33.9	15.9	12.7	11.6	5.4	12.9	41.5
U.K. (1993)	28,271	49.4	1.8	20.4	5.9	5.8	17.8	48.3
Spain (1995)	15,625	40.2	8.6	18.3	9.4	5.1	21.1	37.5

Sectors include agriculture, forestry, fishing (3); manufacturing, mining, quarrying (4); construction (5); transportation, communications (6); trade, hotels, restaurants (7); and services and other (8). Data among countries are difficult to compare because of varying dates of data. [a]Cyprus data for Republic of Cyprus (Southern Cyprus) only. Corresponding data for United Kingdom and Spain given for comparison. Source: *Britannica World Data 1999*. (With permission)

The situation of Palestinian workers in the Gulf is a special one. The demand for skilled workers and professionals was rapidly escalating in Kuwait just when the Palestinian Arabs were forced to leave their homeland. Many moved to Kuwait, and by 1986, the number of Palestinian/ Jordanians there had climbed to more than 350,000. In Kuwait, as was true to a greater extent in Jordan, the Palestinians helped create the economy that absorbed them. However, Kuwait later became concerned about the growing political power of the Palestinians in that country and discouraged further Palestinian immigration. During the Iraqi occupation of Kuwait from August 1990 to February 1991, many Palestinians, among others, evacuated their homes and went elsewhere for the duration of the conflict. Many of the Palestinians and

other expatriate evacuees were neither invited back nor permitted to return, and some of the Palestinians who stayed were accused of collaboration with the enemy. By late 1992, the Palestinian population of Kuwait was, although not accurately known, estimated to be under 20,000, less than 6 percent of the number before August 1990. More Asians are being brought in to replace departed Arabs.

The migration of hundreds of thousands of people to the Gulf area between 1945 and 1985 exerted a profound effect on the work force in both the supplying and the receiving countries. For example, more than 20 percent of the population of then North Yemen was working in Saudi Arabia during the 1970s and early 1980s. However, about 800,000 Yemenis employed in Saudi Arabia were expelled during the Gulf crisis of 1990–1991 because of Saudi resentment over the Yemen government's having maintained an anticoalition stance.

Remittances

One measure of the magnitude of the labor migration to the Gulf oil states is the amount of money the migrant workers sent back to their home countries. For example, in 1981, Jordanians working outside their own country sent back more than $1.23 billion, which was equal to 28 percent of the kingdom's GNP, 39 percent of its imports, and 168 percent of its exports. Similarly, in 1982, Egyptians remitted $1.87 billion, which nearly tripled in 1997 to $3.4 billion. Illustrative of the increase in Pakistani workers in the Gulf is the fact that remittances to Pakistan totaled $339 million in 1974–1975 and $2 billion in 1980–1981, a sixfold increase in six years. Remittances to then North Yemen also exceeded $2 billion annually in the early 1980s. With the recession in the oil states after the mid-1980s, many of the expatriates lost their jobs and returned home, and others who remained had lower incomes and sent smaller remittances home. This reduction in income inevitably created economic difficulties for the labor-supplying countries. Even after the partial recovery in the late 1980s, the demand for labor in the Gulf did not return to its earlier levels, since the peak of the construction boom had passed. The service sector imported South and Southeast Asians to staff its large number of hotel and restaurant positions and similar jobs. Even more acute than the 1980s recession were the economic blows that struck many Gulf expatriate workers as direct and indirect results of the Iraqi invasion of Kuwait in 1990. Hundreds of thousands of workers and professionals found themselves without jobs and no longer welcome in their adopted lands and they were forced to return to depressed economic conditions in their home countries—Jordan, Lebanon, Egypt, and Yemen. However, many had gradually migrated back to the Gulf labor market by the late 1990s. Remittances have become the largest source of capital flows in the Middle East.[3]

Patterns of Industry

Factors of Industrial Location

Patterns of manufacturing in the Middle East are determined by the classic geographical factors of raw materials, labor supply, transportation, market, and power (energy) along with such intangibles as financial incentives, momentum, tradition, and technology. Concentrations of the greatest number of factors attract the largest ensembles of manufacturing.

Distribution of Centers

Despite the great economic development of the Middle East since 1950, industrial regions tend to be relatively modest on a world scale. Designed in early years to serve domestic requirements, more of the plants now export some of their output. The numerous petrochemical plants are highly export oriented. Many more textile mills (in Turkey, Egypt, and Israel), clothing factories (not only in the Levant but even in the UAE), wineries (in the Levant and Cyprus), and similar operations are catering to the export market. Israel is especially dedicated to export industries, from diamond cutting to armaments to high-tech electronics and software. Although data reporting lags behind developments to some extent, some comparisons are useful: In absolute terms, not considering per capita output, Turkey is by far the leading Middle East manufacturing country in total manufacturing value-added ($40.16 billion in 1993), followed by Israel, Saudi Arabia, UAE, Iran, and Egypt. Iraq was formerly a ranking industrial state but, after losing many of its factories in the 1991 bombings, has been unable to rebuild them under the UN sanctions and inspections. Iran surprisingly dropped from first place in the late 1980s to fourth in the mid-1990s, following even the UAE. Turkey has the largest number of industrial workers (3.3 million), followed by Iran and Egypt (2.2 million each). The number in each case is about 13 percent of the workforce. Turkey and Iran have the largest number of producing enterprises, many of

Patterns of Industry   167

them small. Manufacturing contributes 26 percent of the GDP in Egypt, 22 percent in Israel, 18 percent in Turkey, and 14 percent in Iran.

Certain types of industries—including such basic production as processed foods and beverages, construction materials, and clothing—are widespread and are found in every country and in many parts of the larger countries. Less widespread but nevertheless found in virtually every country are such manufacturing industries as textiles, leather, wood products, cement, printing, cigarettes, metalworking, ceramics, and jewelry. Less common is the production of glass, plastics, chemicals, tools, small appliances, and irrigation pipe and sprinklers. States with significant oil and gas production have evolved a typical ensemble of industries that use oil and gas as feedstock or as fuel—oil refineries, water distillation plants, electricity generating plants, fertilizer and other petrochemical plants, and in two Gulf states, such energy-dependent facilities as aluminum smelters.

Only in the most industrialized countries are there industries making or assembling motor vehicles, ships, machine tools, major appliances, electronic items, and armaments. Only in Israel, Egypt, and Turkey is there aircraft production, and only in Israel is there diamond cutting. Few countries engage in basic research and development to any noteworthy extent, and Israel, which ranks on the world scale, is far in the lead. During the mid-1990s, UN inspection teams found that Iraq had developed research programs well beyond anything that had been expected. Turkey, Egypt, Iran, Saudi Arabia, and others are steadily increasing their research efforts.

Seven general economic zones may be geographically differentiated within the area (Map 9-1). They form a rough arc following the trend of the Fertile Crescent but extending beyond and below it, and each area is examined in the various country chapters.

1. Nile Delta.
The Egyptian manufacturing sector is one of the two earliest and most diversified centers in the Middle East and comprises the area

Alexandria-Cairo-Suez-Port Said-Alexandria. Greater Cairo and Alexandria are the centers of the most important production areas in Egypt, along with the great textile towns in the central Delta. Served by a dense road and railway net and embracing one of the highest densities of population in the world, this sector is based on creative traditions of the ancient, medieval, and modern ages. In addition to prized handcraft items, the products range from processed foods and textiles, through aluminum and iron and steel, to metal products, fertilizers, refined petroleum products, motor vehicles, light armaments, and assembled helicopters.

2. Levant.
Northeast of the first zone is a grouping of five neighboring but unconnected manufacturing concentrations in the four Levant states and on the island of Cyprus.

2A. Israel.
The dense concentration of highly varied plants in Israel constitutes the most nationally balanced and systematized range of manufacturing facilities in the Middle East. One reason for the varied facilities is that the Israeli economy was until the 1990s basically isolated, with few materials moving into or out of the zone on the land side, which encouraged self-sufficiency. Moreover, Israel has an inventive and technologically advanced population, including technically trained immigrants from the former Soviet Union and other countries. With noteworthy support from the United States, Israel has built a highly technical military establishment that stimulates and feeds a large high-tech industrial complex. The complex, in turn, supports a dense population at a high standard of living. Most categories of manufacturing are represented in Israel, from food processing to the fifth- or sixth-largest armaments industry in the world, including a controversial nuclear facility at Dimona. Israel emphasized software development during the mid- and late 1990s; now software production has rocketed to a leading position in the state's manufacturing sector. The Greater Tel Aviv

MAP 9-1   Middle East manufacturing belts and centers.

coastal conurbation of Tel Aviv and Haifa (Fig. 9-1) are the main concentrations of industry, but industries have been widely dispersed for both development and security purposes. Many specialty factories—electronics plant, for example—operate in smaller settlements around the country.

2B. Jordan.

The industrial area of Jordan has only a modest range of light manufacturing facilities concentrated primarily in the Amman-Zarqa-Irbid triangle in the northwestern part of the country. However, Aqabah, Jordan's only port, is a growing center of production. Percentage

growth has been great since 1960, but Jordan started from a very low industrial base. As part of its "peace dividend" for signing a peace treaty with Israel in 1994, some modest Israeli-financed factories have opened in Jordan. Most of their output is marketed in and by Israel.

2C. Lebanon.

Traditionally, manufacturing in Lebanon has been primarily consumer oriented, often related to the retail trade. As in Egypt and Syria, handcrafted articles are produced in great variety, from inlaid wood furniture to jewelry. Other manufactured products include textiles, clothing, leather items, paints, chemicals,

FIGURE 9-1   Main Haifa industrial area, just north of the city of Haifa, Israel, seen from Mt. Carmel. The area specializes in petroleum refining and chemical production but has a broad spectrum of products.

cement, glasswares (a tradition from Phoenician times), cigarettes (a state monopoly), and raw steel and other metal products. Lebanon's open economy attracted huge amounts of investment capital between 1950 and 1975, but industrial production dropped sharply and at best limped along after the late 1970s. Even after a return to peacetime, Lebanon lacked the capital flow that prompted the industrial development of the period from the early 1950s to the early 1970s.

2D. Syria.

Damascus has been famous for more than 1,200 years for its handcrafted metals, inlaid woods, textiles, and glass; and since the 1960s, more modern factory-made goods have been produced: machine-made textiles, clothing, appliances, machinery, cement, chemicals, cigarettes, and similar items. The ancient trade center of Aleppo is likewise a modern production center. Homs and Hamah, on the Damascus-Aleppo axis; the coastal centers of Latakia, Baniyas, and Tartus; and the modest newly developing centers of Raqqah and Dayr al-Zawr in the Euphrates Valley are also worth noting.

2E. Cyprus.

The main producing areas on Cyprus are in the Nicosia area and on the south coast, especially in Limassol and Larnaca. Despite the separation of northern Cyprus after 1974, the vitality of the Republic of Cyprus has encouraged the emergence or expansion of establishments producing cigarettes, processed foodstuffs, wine, paper products, clothing, shoes, textiles, and cement. The manufacturing sector, like the rest of the economy of the island, has faced the problem of uncertainty in both the south and north, but especially in the north.

3. Turkey.

Endowed with many elements conducive to industrial development, Turkey reported a total value added by manufacturing of more than $40 billion in the mid-1990s, about that of Poland and Portugal combined. Excluding Israel, with $10.6 billion, the total value added for Turkey equals those of all the other fifteen Middle East countries combined. Food processing is by far the single most important producing activity and is on a much greater scale than that of the other states of the region. Textiles, handmade and machine-made rugs, leather goods, tobacco products, wood and paper products, ceramics, appliances, chemicals, petroleum products, electronic items, pharmaceuticals, heavy and light machinery, assembled automobiles, railway equipment, farm tractors, and small ships are some of the broad range of Turkish factory products. Manufacturing is widespread, and most of the larger cities have several factories. Major production centers are Istanbul, Izmir, Zonguldak, Ankara, Kırıkkale, Divriği, Mersin, Adana, and Erzurum, plus the other cities shown on Map 9-1.

4. Western Iran.

Like Turkey, Iran has a large population, work force, and domestic market as well as numerous raw materials and other advantages for manufacturing. Unlike Turkey, Iran also has huge oil resources, and it and Turkey lead in numbers of industrial workers and of manufacturing establishments, as noted above. It has a long and distinguished history of manufacturing, traditionally producing rugs, textiles, handcrafted metalwares, jewelry, ceramics (especially tiles), and similar items. Iran's highly diversified modern industrial products—many made in small five- to ten-employee shops—include fabricated metals (utilitarian wrought iron as well as traditional copper and brass, as shown in Fig. 9-2), jewelry, plain and art textiles and leather goods, hand-knotted rugs, petroleum products and chemicals, and a wide range of food products. Several major areas are dispersed over western Iran: Tehran, the Ahvaz-Khorramshahr-Abadan-Bandar-e Khomeyni

triangle area at the head of the Gulf, Kharg Island, Shiraz, Sar Cheshmeh, Arak, Esfahan, Tabriz, and Gorgan. By 1979, Iran had clearly demonstrated that it had achieved world rank with the moderately large industrial producers at that juncture. However, the Iran-Iraq war of 1980–1988 damaged many of Iran's plants, and the conservative Islamist government's policies retarded further industrial development.

5. Iraq.

The amount and variety of manufacturing in Iraq increased steadily and, during the late 1980s, impressively after Iraq's modest start in the mid-1950s. However, the industrial output was especially devoted to military equipment; indeed, more so than had been realized at the time. As one result, coalition bombing targeted and heavily damaged much of Iraq's industrial complex in early 1991—appreciably more so than Iranian bombing and shelling had done between 1980 and 1988. Because Iraq was still under UN sanctions during the entire decade of the 1990s, it underwent several years of UN inspections for illegal weapons manufacturing facilities; by refusing further inspections in early 1999, it chose to remain under UN sanctions. Under such conditions, Iraq could resume weapons production, a choice that also prolonged the suffering of the Iraqi people, delayed national economic recovery, and largely prevented industrial reconstruction. Thus, Iraq faces grave problems in restoring its pre-1990 factory output, much less developing to the level it sought in its economic planning in the 1989–1990 timeframe. Baghdad is the main center of the sprawling modern Mesopotamian industrial zone, which proved to be much more developed and sophisticated than expected when UN inspectors checked it in early 1991 for nuclear, chemical, and biological production. Government planning has spread facilities to Mosul, Irbil, Kirkuk, and the area of Basrah and al-Zubayr. The Basrah and al-Zubayr areas and other southern centers were the most heavily damaged in 1980–1988 and 1991, and reconstruction has proceeded only slowly in the south in comparison with the rebuilding of the capital

FIGURE 9-2   A one-man shop in the copper and brass bazaar of Esfahan, Iran. Traditional products such as these hand-hammered and hand-engraved trays are still major items of manufacture in several Iranian cities.

area. Petrochemicals and other petroleum-related products make up a considerable share of the country's industrial output, but 1980s wartime demands and the Baath party military ambitions also mandated the rapid development of a large and varied armaments industry. The considerable scale of that industry became clear during UN inspections of Iraqi military plants in 1991–1992. Many smaller establishments produce processed foods and beverages, cigarettes, textiles, clothing, shoes, furniture, and metal goods. Traditional handcrafts include silversmithing, copper and brass working, textile weaving, and rug making.

6. Gulf.

The Gulf industrial zone, including Oman—but excluding Saudi Arabia, Iraq, and Iran—might be subdivided into subzones based partly on national boundaries, as was the case with the Levant zone. However, the Gulf facilities have a substantial degree of similarity and have developed almost entirely since the 1960s, after petroleum development stimulated dramatic economic and population growth. The core economic activity in every subcenter of the Gulf zone is petroleum production and processing, and the main satellite facilities produce petroleum-related products—petrochemicals, fertilizers, liquefied natural gas derivatives, secondary sulfur, and a range of refinery products.

However, there is an impressive array of manufacturing in several parts of the area, and further diversification is under way, with emphasis on ready-made clothing (see Chap. 18). Because construction has been a major aspect of the economy since the mid-1950s, production of construction materials has been, but is decreasingly, a major industry. It includes cement, cement blocks, bricks, steel reinforcing rods, and metal frames for windows and doors. Dhow building is still carried on in traditional centers: Kuwait, Bahrain, Ajman, and Ras al-Khaymah. Most of the larger new industries are capital intensive as well as large energy users.

Major subcenters include (6A) the Kuwait Bay and Gulf coast area; (6B) northeastern Bahrain, which has locational advantages and the earliest

industrial development among the smaller Gulf states; (6C) east-central Qatar, primarily around Musayid (Umm Said) and Doha; (6D–6H) the five United Arab Emirates (UAE) main industrial developments of (6D) al-Ruways near the shipping terminal of Jabal Dhanna, (6E) Abu Dhabi Island with its light production, (6F) Dubai City with a wide range of small plants that produce consumer goods, (6G) Jabal Ali as a heavy industrial center south of Dubai, and (6H) Sharjah with modest manufacturing establishments; and finally (6I) the Batinah coast of Oman, which produced only a few handcrafted articles until the mid-1960s but which now has a group of copper-centered plants near Suhar and an impressive industrial estate at Rusayl, west of Muscat (Fig. 9-3a). An additional industrial park is planned for Salalah, where an expanding port is a core for manufacturing.

7. Saudi Triad: al-Hasa, Najd, Hijaz.

From a pre-1935 manufacturing production level below that of any other major country in the Middle East, Saudi Arabia by the early 1990s had developed a vigorous and diversified range of production. Latest available data on value added by manufacturing show Saudi Arabia ranking third in the Middle East, after Turkey and Israel. Initially, development focused almost entirely on the oil industry in the Eastern Province, but there are now diversified industries not only in the east but also in both mid-Arabia and the west. The latest developments include an industrial city and port on each side of the peninsula—Jubayl on the Gulf coast and Yanbu on the Red Sea coast. Therefore, Saudi Arabia now has three main producing centers: (7A) on the Gulf coast along the Jubayl-Dammam-al-Khobar axis, with outliers in the Hofuf-Abqaiq area; (7B) the two centers of Qasim and Riyadh in Najd; and (7C) the Jiddah-Mecca area in the Hijaz, with an outlier in Yanbu.

Transportation

Roads were of limited significance in the Middle East before World War I because of centuries of

FIGURE 9-3   Two recent economic development areas in the Middle East: the Rusayl Industrial Area on the Batinah Coast of Oman *(top)*, and the container storage area of Dubai port *(bottom)*.

preference for maritime trade whenever possible and cross-country transport via camel caravans when land movement was necessary. In early road construction in 1859–1863, a French company built a 69-mile/111-km road from Beirut port to Damascus, and an additional 258 miles/ 415 km of roads had been built in Lebanon by 1900. With the approach of the twentieth century, the French, British, Germans, and—in Iran—Russians were involved in building roads, railroads, and ports in and around the Middle East, mostly under concessionary terms. The Dutch, Portuguese, and British successively controlled the main sea lanes after the sixteenth century, and British steamships played a major role in the Gulf until World War II.

Consequently, the mandates and recently independent states of the Middle East had a basic transportation net by the late 1920s that was appreciably improved by the end of World War II. It soon exhibited its inadequacy for modern development, however, and movement around the Arabian Peninsula lacked any semblance of sufficiency. Fortunately, the huge petrodollar influx after the early 1960s permitted transformation of the regional communications network—road net, seaports and airports, pipeline network, and to a lesser extent, rail net.

Two aspects of the pattern of Middle East communications are worth noting. First, the Middle East exhibits a coarse pattern of "islands" or cores of development that are widely separated by uninhabited or sparsely populated deserts, mountain masses, or seas. Before the mid-nineteenth century, these various cores were linked by land caravans and, if coastal, by small sailing ships, with flexible schedules and capacities and minimum costs. Railway and road nets were not required, nor would they have been profitable, since there was little cargo traffic along the routes between the centers. Even today the two main rail nets, in Turkey and Iran, and two secondary nets, in Egypt and Iraq, are primarily internal, with relatively limited international movement of freight or passengers. On the other hand, the three most extensive road nets, in Turkey, Saudi Arabia, and Iran, are increasingly linked with neighboring nets, and both cargo and passengers cross frontiers along roads in steadily growing numbers. In peaceful periods, the main highway border crossings are, especially on weekends and holidays, normally crowded— between Lebanon and Syria, Syria and Jordan, Turkey and Bulgaria, Turkey and Iran, Kuwait and Iraq, and Saudi Arabia and Bahrain.

Second, airways in most of the Middle East developed to a significant level before railroads were built, and airlines serve the "island" pattern of urban centers of the region very well. Aircraft can fly over and thereby ignore both the physical-environmental hazards and the political perils— the expanses of desert, sea, and mountains when flying Istanbul-Bahrain, Beirut-Tehran, or Cairo-Muscat, and the political obstacles of a sanctioned Iraq after August 1990. And where airlines are locally unavailable or inadequate, the highway net serves most purposes. Therefore, at the present time, railways are of less regional importance than are the other available means of transportation (Map 9-2).

Highways

Prior to midcentury, most of the road systems in the Middle East were scattered webs around capitals or other primary cities in the Fertile Crescent countries or in the three large states of Egypt, Turkey, and Iran. Only a few miles of surfaced roads existed anywhere in the Arabian Peninsula. By the late 1990s, the Middle East had 614,311 miles/988,592 km of roads, of which more than two-thirds were paved highways (Fig. 9-4). Barring unexpected frontier closures, a motorist can now drive on paved roads—mostly first-class highways—from Istanbul over the Bosporus Bridge to the Pakistan border via Erzurum, Tabriz, Tehran, and Yazd; or from Istanbul to Aden via Adana, Damascus, Amman, and Jiddah; or turn east at Jiddah and reach Abu Dhabi and Muscat via Dhahran. Even the Gulf island state of Bahrain can now be reached by highway via a causeway opened in 1986 (Fig. 9-5).

The regional road network is also being linked to the Trans-European Motorway

Highways
Paved Roads
Railroads
Planned Railroads
⊕ International Airports
+ Other Main Airports
⚓ Main Ports
(Excluding Oil Terminals)

0   100 200 300 400 500 MILES

0   200   400   600   800 KILOMETERS

MAP 9-2   Middle East major transportation facilities.

(TEM), especially in Turkey. Now under construction, this special integrated, high-grade motorway will run north and south through eastern Europe, from Gdansk on Poland's Baltic coast to Istanbul, then east to Ankara and the Iranian border, about 6,215 miles/10,000 km. Spur roads in Anatolia will extend the main TEM to the borders of Syria and Iraq. Turkey will thus have 2,235 miles/3,600 km of the motorway.

Israel's very dense network of roads is isolated. Before 1967, there were no connections with the country's neighbors open to the public, although UN and diplomatic personnel could cross several borders, especially the famous Mandelbaum Gate in Jerusalem, before 1967. By 2000, there were moderately traveled cross-border connections with Egypt and Jordan.

Cyprus, where driving on the left side of the road is a British legacy, has a road net and administration that were divided between north and south in 1974. The island is integrated with the Levant road system by frequent car ferry, and other ferries that connect several eastern Mediterranean ports transport private cars and trucks among Istanbul, Izmir, and Mersin in Turkey; Latakia, Syria; Beirut and Juniyah in Lebanon; and Alexandria, Egypt. A

FIGURE 9-4 Highways old and new. When I made a consular visit into remote areas of the Trucial States in the northern Oman Mountains in 1964, the already rugged track (maximum speed, 10 mph/16 kmph) degenerated into a rocky streambed in one narrow pass (maximum speed, about 3 mph/5 kmph), as shown on the top. During field work after 1979 in the same area, I enjoyed one of the many blessings of the oil boom in the UAE: a first-class, well-built highway *(bottom)*.

FIGURE 9-5   Two views of transportation in the Middle East: a stretch of the causeway linking Saudi Arabia and Bahrain *(top)*, a 15.5-mile/25-km facility opened in 1986 at a cost of more than $1 billion, and railway station in Tanta, Egypt *(bottom)*, in the Nile Delta. Railways are heavily used in Egypt, especially by passengers.

TABLE 9-2 TRANSPORTATION: ROADS, RAILROADS, AND MERCHANT MARINE.

COUNTRY	1 ROADS: LENGTH IN KM	2 % OF ROADS PAVED	3 KM OF ROADS PER KM^2	4 NUMBER OF VEHICLES (ALL TYPES)	5 PERSONS PER VEHICLE	6 RR TRACK IN KM	7 KM OF RR PER KM^2	8 MERCHANT MARINE 000s DWT
Bahrain	2,835	75	4.08	171,485	3.4	—	—	192.5
Cyprus	10,150	57	1.10	323,601	2.6	—	—	36,198.1
Egypt	58,000^a	78^a	0.06	1,703,300	35.0	4,810	0.005	1,685.2
Iran	158,000	59	0.10	2,239,000	26.0	7,286^b	0.004	8,345.3
Iraq	46,500	86	0.11	1,040,000	20.0	2,032^c	0.005	1,578.8
Israel	14,700	100	0.72	1,394,323	3.9	610^b	0.03	723.4
Jordan	6,750	100	0.08	250,344	16.0	677^c	0.008	113.6
Kuwait	4,360	81	0.24	700,000	2.4	—	—	3,188.5
Lebanon	6,359	95	0.61	1,282,257	2.9	222	0.02	438.2
Oman	30,830	20	0.10	311,341	6.8	—	—	11.7
Qatar	1,210	90	0.11	189,500	3.0	—	—	635.6
Saudi Arabia	159,000	43	0.07	2,882,600	6.2	1,390^b	0.0006	1,361.7
Syria	39,243	71	0.21	352,900	40.0	1,766^b	0.01	210.4
Turkey	381,300	23	0.49	4,040,923	15.0	8,452^c	0.01	7,114.3
UAE	4,750	100	0.06	246,150	9.7	—	—	1,491.7
Yemen	64,605	8	0.12	511,699	31.0	—	—	13.7
Gaza	0	—	—	25,845	29.0	—	—	—
West Bank	0	—	—	89,923	13.0	—	—	—
TOTAL/AVG	988,592	—	0.13	17,755,191	12.8	27,245^b	0.0058	63,302.7
U.K.	366,999	100	1.5	23,217,000	2.5	37,849^b	0.15	4,355.0
Spain	343,197	99	0.67	17,196,397	2.3	13,280^b	0.03	5,077.3

^{a}National roads only. ^{b}Data more than five years old. ^{c}Route length (other railway lengths are for total track length). Column 3 is the ratio between the length of roads and the area of each country. Column 7 is the same for railways. Number of vehicles in Column 4 includes automobiles, buses, and trucks. Column 8 is the total of merchant marine ships in thousands of deadweight tons for the early 1990s. Otherwise, data are latest available in 1999. Source of basic data: *Britannica World Data 1999*. (With permission)

special truck ferry from Volos in Greece to Tartus in Syria enables truckers to avoid the long drive over winding mountain roads in Anatolia.

Predictably, the most densely inhabited areas, if reasonably prosperous, have the densest highway networks, as can be seen in Table 9-2 and Map 9-2. Israel, Cyprus, and Lebanon have the region's densest nets, but these countries are small and have a limited absolute length of roads. Turkey, Saudi Arabia, and Iran, in that order, have the longest total length of roads.

Some segments of the road net in the Middle East are noteworthy both for their engineering and for their scenic impact. The paved 62-mile/100-km highway from Hudaydah, on Yemen's Red Sea coast, up the steep, rugged escarpment to the capital, Sana, affords magnificent vistas as it winds past terraced fields and picturesque villages to reach the plateau, 9,000 ft./2,743 m above

sea level. Similarly, the highway from Jiddah to Taif offers spectacular views as it leaves the heat of the coastal plain and ascends into the cooler heights of Saudi Arabia's summer capital. The highway from Beirut over the mountains and across the Bekaa toward Damascus is famed for its landscapes. Less dramatic because of the lower elevations, but also interesting, is the drive from Tel Aviv and Jaffa on the Mediterranean coast to Jerusalem (2,500 ft./762 m) and down the eastern slopes to Jericho and the Jordan (1,200 ft./365 m below sea level).

The drive along the Mediterranean coast of southern Turkey has some of the scenic beauty of that along the French and Italian rivieras as well as sites of major archaeological interest. Another dramatic mountain drive is that from Tehran over the Elburz Mountains at 9,000 ft./2,745 m, to Chalus on the Caspian Sea shore,

80 ft./24 m below sea level. Spectacular scenery also characterizes two roads into northeastern Iraq, into the Rawanduz Gorge from Irbil and into the Sulaymaniyah area from Kirkuk (photograph in Chap. 16). With almost no change in elevation, the drive between Cairo and Alexandria on the Delta Road, through the villages and the green landscape of the irrigated Nile Delta, provides an interesting contrast to the other Cairo-Alexandria link, the Desert Road.

The Middle East road net is rapidly achieving maturity of pattern. All major cities and towns are now connected, and the need in the new century is to integrate more of the villages, to construct shorter routes between some major cities, to make dual highways of standard roads in some high-traffic areas, and to continue to densify the net. In Table 9-2, data on the number of all types of vehicles (col. 4) and persons per vehicle (col. 5) in each country are revealing in several ways: They may indicate aspects of a country's standard of living according to income per capita; however, because they include all types of vehicles, they may also suggest the usage level of mass transportation (number of buses) and the degree of automotive transport (number of trucks or lorries). The entire population of nine countries could be transported by available vehicles at one time. Kuwait has the smallest number of persons per vehicle (2.4), and Cyprus, Lebanon, Qatar, Bahrain, and Israel have fewer than 4. All six countries in this category have smaller areas and populations, but they are either oil states (e.g., Kuwait) or they have more advanced industrialized economies (e.g., Israel). Syria and Yemen have appreciably more trucks and buses than passenger cars, and Saudi Arabia has equal numbers of cars and heavy vehicles. Large numbers of heavy trucks are required for the huge oil industry and the kingdom's long distances.

Railways

The Middle East economic situation did not justify the construction of extensive rail nets during the heyday of railway building in other parts of the world, and the region's development from the 1960s onward took advantage of the more flexible facilities of highways and airways. As in many other areas with numerous long-distance travelers, passenger traffic in the Middle East is mostly by air, and since most cargo can be more easily shipped by truck, cargo aircraft, ships, or—in the case of petroleum and petroleum products—via pipelines and tankers, any appreciable expansion of Middle East rail nets seems unlikely in the foreseeable future.

The total length of railway lines in the Middle East is 16,930 miles/27,245 km, less than 3 percent of the total mileage of paved roads. The region's average 0.006 km of rail line per square kilometer of area compares with Australia's 0.005 km per km^2 in roughly the same amount of territory. By contrast, the United Kingdom, somewhat smaller than Oman, has a total 23,519 miles/37,849 km of rails, 28 percent more than that of the entire Middle East, and 0.15 km per km^2.

As is shown on Map 9-2, the densest rail net among the Middle East states is in Turkey, which has nearly one-third of the region's rail total. The nets of Egypt and Iran are more open than the Turkish rail net, but they are nevertheless heavily traveled (Fig. 9-5b) and are reasonably adequate in length, particularly in view of the two countries' extensive and virtually uninhabited desert areas. The entire Arabian Peninsula, with more than 1.3 million miles^2/3.17 million km^2, has only 864 miles/1,390 km^2, of railway in Saudi Arabia. None of the six peripheral states of the Arabian Peninsula has any railways, nor does the Mediterranean island state of Cyprus.

Certain rail lines in the Middle East are renowned: the Orient Express from Calais, France, which technically terminated in Istanbul but actually continued to Konya and Aleppo on a reduced scale; the line from Cairo to Luxor and then to Aswan, part of the never-completed Cape-to-Cairo railway; the line built in Palestine in 1892 to transport pilgrims from Jaffa on the Mediterranean coast to Jerusalem; the Hijaz Railway from Damascus to Medina, which was built by the Ottomans at the beginning of the twentieth century for Muslim pilgrims traveling to the holy city of Mecca but which was wrecked south of Maan by the Arab Revolt in 1916–1917; and the line through the scenic Dez River gorge through the Zagros Mountains in southwestern Iran.

Airways and Airfields

The Middle East's location, astride the land, sea, and air routes across the tricontinental hub, led to establishment of a few transit airports prior to World War II. Rapid petroleum development stimulated demand for air service and airports after the early 1950s, and by the early 1990s, the Middle East possessed an excellent pattern of airports (see Map 9-2), including not only the world's largest but some of the world's technologically best equipped. Terminals such as Jiddah, Istanbul, Cairo, Tehran, and Lod (Tel Aviv) rank (in that order) between 26th and 50th on the list of international airports outside the United States in numbers of passengers embarked and disembarked.[4] Passenger traffic at all three Saudi airports decreased sharply after 1983–1984, although Jiddah, with 8 million arrivals and departures annually, ranks high because of the flow of pilgrims to nearby Mecca. Beirut was, before 1975, a top-ranking central airport but has dropped to a second-tier category. The number of airports with regularly scheduled service varies from 27 in Saudi Arabia and in Turkey to only 1 each in Bahrain and Qatar.

Except that Bahrain, Qatar, Abu Dhabi, and Oman jointly operate one regional airline, Gulf Air, every country in the Middle East has its own national airline. Even tiny Dubai now operates Emirates Air, with a fleet of 9 Airbuses; and Oman has formed its separate airline, Oman Air, competing on some routes with Gulf Air. Saudia, the airline of Saudi Arabia, is the largest and flies more than 80 major jet aircraft. Egypt Air and Iran Air fly 54 and 50 major aircraft, respectively. Most of the other national airlines have 20–30 major aircraft each, although Cyprus Airways registers only 11 jets. All of the major airports of the Middle East dispatch regular flights to Western European capitals, but most connections are intraregional, with the exception of those involving Israel's Ben Gurion Airport at Lod.

Water Transportation and Ports

A glance at Map 9-2 will serve as a reminder that land-water relationships in the Middle East offer easy human use of the interpenetrating seas. Only the heart of the Arabian Peninsula lies more than 200 miles/322 km from a seacoast. The seas have been sailed for at least 5,000 years, and numerous ruins of ports from earlier days are found in the Gulf and the eastern Mediterranean. Sailing the region's seas reached a golden age during the Abbasid Empire, especially during the eighth to twelfth centuries. The basic seagoing craft has long been some version of the ship popularly known as the dhow, and as they have been for more than 2,000 years, dhows are still equipped with the lateen sail, a triangular fore-and-aft sail hung from a very long yard. This rigging permits the ship to keep very close to the wind.

Following tradition, many dhows still sail around the shores of the Gulf, along the coasts of Oman and Yemen, along the east African coast, and on the age-old routes to the mouths of the Indus and to the Malabar coast and Ceylon. Small modern ships are increasingly replacing the picturesque dhows; nevertheless, the latter serve a unique function and are still to be seen by the score anchored in "the Creek" in Dubai and in other Gulf ports. They are still built in small numbers in the traditional way in Kuwait, Bahrain, most of the coastal towns of the UAE, and in Oman.

Despite construction of the Suez Canal in the 1860s, the Middle East did not enter the main-stream of modern shipping until the mid-twentieth century. Turkey was most active in sailing, having regained its maritime lead after its World War I defeat; and as oil production mounted in the Gulf, the leading petroleum states entered the tanker market so as to be able to ship their own exports. Iran and Kuwait developed sizable national tanker fleets, and Egypt, Iraq, the UAE, and Saudi Arabia have a modest tonnage in tankers (see Table 9-2). Offering both a neutral flag of convenience and a long shipping tradition, Cyprus ranks first in the Middle East and fourth in the world in registered fleet tonnage.

With the notable exceptions of the Nile, Tigris, and Euphrates, inland waterways, and therefore inland water transportation, are negligible in the region. Until the last few decades, shipping on the Nile had constituted the main method of movement of persons and goods up and down the linear axis of Egypt for more than 5,000 years. Construction of modern rail lines and highways has scarcely diminished either the number of picturesque but practical *faluqas,* the typical Nile sailboat, or the tonnage of cargo they transport. More than 300 modern motor cruise ships transport hundreds of tourist passengers up and down the river daily, most of them foreign visitors.

Shallower and more irregular than the Nile, the Tigris and the Euphrates are little used for navigation, and they can accommodate only small boats with very shallow draft. The picturesque circular rafts (*balams*), which were waterproofed with bitumen and used to float small loads downstream on the Tigris, have given way to modern land and air transportation. By contrast, on the Shatt al-Arab, below the confluence of the Tigris and Euphrates, and on the Karun, which joins the Shatt al-Arab at Khorramshahr, there is normally a fair number of medium-large ships of considerable draft. Basrah, Khorramshahr, and Abadan, all fronting on the Shatt al-Arab, are normally three of the major river ports, not only of the Gulf but of the Middle East. As Iraq's only port for several decades, Basrah was wholly inadequate by the 1970s.

The Marsh Arabs (Madan) along the regularly flooded lower Euphrates have been entirely dependent upon boat transportation for centuries, and their especially designed and locally built *mushhuf* is a variety of canoe ideally suited to transporting people and goods, especially loads of the local reeds, in the shallow but ever-present water. School children of the marshes use the *mushhuf* to go back and forth to school in the same way that children in some countries use bicycles. The marshland area was almost eliminated by drainage projects in the 1990s.

Many modern Middle East coastal cities have served port functions for hundreds or even thousands of years—Istanbul (Byzantium or Constantinople), Beirut (Berytus), Jaffa, Alexandria, Aden, Muscat, and several Gulf ports. Some ports famed in antiquity now lack sufficient harborage or depth for modern shipping, such as Sidon and Tyre; other ports have silted up and now lie well inland, as is true of Miletus, Ephesus, and Ur, for example.

By virtue of the tonnage represented by the millions of barrels of oil pumped through an export terminal, large oil-shipping ports exceed even the most major dry-cargo ports in tonnage handled. (An average barrel of petroleum weighs about 300 lb./136 kg, so that only 7.35 bbl weigh 1 mt.) Petroleum shipments pushed Saudi Arabia to first rank and Iran to third rank in export tonnage among all countries of the world in 1982, before the drop in the oil export market. Thus, the relative ranking of Middle East general-cargo ports differs from the ranking of ports that include oil handling. Leading oil export terminals are Mina al-Ahmadi and Mina Abdullah, Kuwait; Juaymah and Ras Tanura in eastern Saudi Arabia, and Yanbu on the Red Sea; Kharg Island (Darius) and Bandar-e Khomeyni, Iran; Musayid (Umm Said), Qatar; Jabal Dhanna, Abu Dhabi; and Mina al-Fahal, Oman. Export terminals in Yemen, Egypt, and Syria handle smaller tonnages.

By the early 1990s, major modern ports were well distributed among the Middle East states, and in the late 1990s several dry cargo ports handled well over 5 million tons annually: Shuwaykh, Kuwait; Dubai and Khor Fakkan, UAE (Khor Fakkan is on the UAE east coast), both important for transshipment; Jiddah, the main Saudi Red Sea port; Alexandria and its auxiliary ports, Dikhaylah and Damietta, and Port Said, Egypt; and Haifa, Israel. (See port symbols on Map 9-2.)

TABLE 9-3 FOREIGN TRADE: EXPORTS AND IMPORTS (Values and selected products).

COUNTRY		1	2	3	4	5	6	7	8	9	10
		TOTAL VALUE		RAW MATERIALS (%)				MANUFCTRD GOODS (%)			
		(MILLIONS $US)		AGRIC, ETC.		FUEL/ENR		TOTAL		% MACH/TE	
		EXPORTS	IMPORTS	EXP	IMP	EXP	IMP	EXP	IMP	EXP	IMP
Bahrain	1995	4,092.1	3,624.8	2.4	13.3	60.0	38.1	37.6	48.5	1.3	16.2
Cyprus	1996	1,391.0	3,982.5	57.4	25.5	4.4	8.5	37.0	65.6	11.1	24.3
Egypt	1995	3,444.1	11,739.0	16.0	35.4	37.3	1.2	46.1	61.9	0.6	25.3
Iran	1992	19,868.0	30,712.1	7.8	11.4	80.9	1.3	9.3	87.4	0.5	50.3
Iraq	1990	6,659.0	4,833.9	0.8	31.5	96.8	0.4	2.1	68.1	0.2	30.3
Israel	1995	19,046.0	29,579.0	7.3	8.2	0.5	5.9	61.2	68.8	28.4	34.0
Jordan	1995	1,782.0	3,722.7	24.1	22.7	—	12.9	56.5	63.4	13.1	24.5
Kuwait	1995	12,944.4	7,789.8	0.3	16.6	94.7	0.5	4.7	82.4	1.4	41.2
Lebanon[a]	1994	572.7	5,990.0	19.6	21.7	10.5	13.3	69.9	65.0	11.5	27.0
Oman	1995	5,917.4	4,248.6	5.1	20.6	78.6	1.5	15.9	76.0	9.6	39.4
Qatar	1994	3,212.9	1,927.4	0.5	15.8	73.8	0.6	25.4	80.8	1.4	39.7
Saudi Arabia	1994	42,584.0	23,343.5	1.1	14.0	91.1	0.2	7.5	84.8	0.9	40.1
Syria	1995	3,969.9	4,708.8	18.6	20.0	62.5	1.1	18.2	78.4	0.8	31.6
Turkey	1995	21,598.7	35,707.5	21.0	12.6	1.3	12.9	75.6	70.7	11.1	32.2
UAE	1992	24,756.0	17,410.0	0.3	11.6	96.6	1.7	3.0	86.1	0.2	35.1
Yemen	1994	933.9	2,087.4	9.6	39.3	89.0	5.2	1.2	55.3	0.0	20.5
TOTAL/AVG.		172,772.1	191,407.0	12.0	20.0	54.9	6.6	29.5	71.5	5.8	32.0
U.K.	1990	261,950.2	287,528.6	7.8	12.2	6.5	3.8	83.1	81.1	44.1	42.1
Spain	1996	100,955.5	121,255.4	16.9	14.9	2.5	9.1	79.9	73.9	42.7	37.3

Columns 3 and 4 include animal and vegetable foods, beverages, and industrial agricultural products (tobacco, cotton, etc.). Columns 5 and 6 (Fuels and Energy materials) include mineral fuels (petroleum, natural gas, coal, lignite), lubricants, and related products. Manufactured goods include all classes of manufactured products, including machinery. "% Mach/TE" indicates the percentage of machinery and transportation equipment included in the percentage total of manufactures. [a]Data for Lebanon in columns 5 and 6 include minerals. Spread of data over six years makes comparisons difficult and risky. Source: *Britannica World Data 1999*. (With permission)

Seven Middle East ports handle from 1 to 5 million tons of general cargo annually: Dammam, the main general cargo port for the sprawling oil industry and cities of the Eastern Province of Saudi Arabia; Abu Dhabi, UAE; Muscat/Matrah, Oman; Aqabah, Jordan's only port; Ashdod, Israel; Beirut, Lebanon and Iskenderun in the northeast Mediterranean, Izmir on the Aegean, and Istanbul, Turkey.

Trade

The external trade of Middle East states has expanded exponentially since the 1960s, particularly under the impetus of enormous exports of petroleum; income from the sales of such quantities of a vital product has created a large market for imports of capital and consumer goods. Intraregional trade in the Middle East (Table 9-3) has also expanded greatly. Non-oil producers import petroleum from their oil-exporting neighbors, and several such importers exchange food products in return. However, quantitatively, only the oil-deficient industrialized countries can absorb the enormous petroleum exports of the Gulf states, and the developing petroleum-exporting countries turn to their industrialized-country customers for the advanced technology items that constitute the bulk of their nonfood imports (Table 9-4). Thus, intraregional trade is constrained by the fact that neighboring states often produce similar crops, consumer items, or energy products.

Few of the states in the region include even one other Middle East country as one of their three leading customers according to percentage

TABLE 9-4   DIRECTIONS OF FOREIGN TRADE (Export and import percentages).

COUNTRY AND YEAR OF DATA		1	2	3	4	5	6	7	8	9	10
		PERCENTAGE	OF	EXPORTS	TO		PERCENTAGE	OF	IMPORTS	FROM	
		EU	USA	JAPAN	EE	OTHER	EU	USA	JAPAN	EE	OTHER
Bahrain	1995	4.0	3.2	8.2	—	84.6	19.7	8.2	4.1	0.2	67.8
Cyprus	1996	28.4	0.7	0.1	36.3	34.5	48.6	16.8	6.0	5.5	23.1
Egypt	1995	45.8	15.2	1.3	2.7	35.0	38.9	18.8	2.7	7.1	32.5
Iran	1992	39.8	0.8	13.5	10.4	35.5	49.8	2.7	12.0	3.0	32.5
Iraq	1990	26.6	33.6	9.5	6.8	23.5	45.7	10.8	4.6	3.0	35.9
Israel	1995	32.2	30.1	6.9	3.3	27.4	52.3	18.6	3.3	1.9	23.9
Jordan	1995	8.0	3.9	1.1	1.3	85.7	33.2	9.3	3.5	4.6	49.4
Kuwait	1995	11.7	10.3	19.4	—	58.5	38.1	16.1	9.4	0.9	35.6
Lebanon	1994	17.0	3.7	0.7	4.9	73.7	49.1	9.3	4.2	4.6	32.8
Oman	1995	0.9	2.8	28.5	0.1	67.7	27.9	6.5	15.8	0.4	49.5
Qatar	1994	1.9	2.5	55.6	—	40.0	33.9	10.6	13.4	1.4	40.8
Saudi Arabia	'94	22.6	18.5	16.0	—	42.9	34.7	21.3	11.7	0.6	31.6
Syria	1995	57.0	0.9	0.2	6.1	35.8	34.4	6.8	4.4	10.8	43.7
Turkey	1995	51.3	7.0	0.8	11.8	29.1	47.2	10.4	3.9	11.4	27.0
UAE	1992	7.0	3.2	35.7	0.1	53.9	33.5	8.9	16.6	0.5	40.5
Yemen	1994	6.8	12.3	13.3	1.3	66.4	30.0	9.0	4.5	1.4	55.1

EU= member states of the European Union. USA=United States. EE=East European countries, including Russia and European republics of the former USSR. OTHER=mainly neighboring Middle East states, India, South Korea, and Singapore. Many of the figures are estimates based on data from trading partners. Source: *Britannica World Data 1999*. (With permission)

of value of commodities traded. (All rankings of countries and commodities in this discussion are based on value percentages.) By contrast, four of Jordan's and Lebanon's top five customers are Middle East states. Isolated as it has been from its neighbors, Israel had no overt trade with its neighbors until the Camp David accords, which provided that Israel could purchase its petroleum supplies from Egypt. One result was that Israel was Egypt's second-largest customer for several years, until the trade pattern shifted.

It should be noted that of the relatively limited exports from the non-oil Middle East states, the exports to neighboring states normally form a considerable percentage. For example, because Jordan produces only modest amounts of vegetables, pharmaceuticals, and clothing, its markets need to be rather close. Since the mid-1990s, Israel has been among those markets under reciprocal arrangements. Iraq was particularly important in Jordan's foreign trade, since it was Jordan's main customer and virtually its main supplier prior to August 1990. The Gulf crisis adversely affected Jordan's

trade with Iraq and Saudi Arabia, and Jordan is eager to restore trade relations with both. Natural gas exports by Egypt, Saudi Arabia, Qatar, and Iran will reorient some trade patterns when agreements and pipelines are in place. An overall significant aspect of the exports from Lebanon, Bahrain, and the UAE is that many of the exports are, in fact, reexports. Such trade has made Dubai and Sharjah major commercial centers.

From the general perspective of Middle East trade, the overwhelmingly main export of the area to the rest of the world is petroleum, with petroleum and petroleum products constituting at least 85 percent of the primary exports of all the major oil producers and normally more than 95 percent of the exports of Iraq, Kuwait, and the UAE. Petroleum even constitutes one-third of the exports of Egypt and 60 percent of those of Syria (see Table 9-3).

Among the top two or three non-oil exports of several states are, by percentage, fruits and vegetables (Cyprus, Turkey, Lebanon, Jordan, Syria, Egypt); chemicals (Israel, Saudi Arabia, Qatar, Turkey, Jordan); textiles (Turkey, Syria,

Egypt, Israel); and clothing (Cyprus, Turkey, Israel). A few of the region's specialty exports include aluminum (Bahrain, Egypt, UAE), footwear (Cyprus), and phosphates (Jordan, Israel, Syria, Egypt, and Iraq). A unique export from the region is cut diamonds from Israel, with the gems forming 29 percent of the state's exports. Armaments from Israel constitute more than 25 percent of its exports and are another unusual export item from the regional perspective.

As they are around the world, oil and petroleum products are the main imports of the non-oil states of the Middle East (see Table 9-3). They constitute about 13 percent of Turkey's and Jordan's imports but only 6 percent of Israel's. Although almost 40 percent of Bahrain's imports is crude petroleum, through a direct underwater pipeline from Saudi Arabia, that crude is refined in the island's Sitra refinery and is reexported as product.

Food ranks among the three leading imports into virtually all Middle East countries with the notable exception of Turkey. Nearly one-fifth of Egypt's imports is foodstuffs, a major shift from the early 1960s. Again with the exception of Turkey, Israel's food import percentage is the lowest among the Middle East countries. Excluding food, the region's leading three or four imports by percentage are usually machinery, motor vehicles, chemicals, and iron and steel. Until the worst years of Lebanon's civil war, that country's second leading import was gold bullion. In Israel, a leading import (14 percent by value) is rough diamonds, which are cut and reexported.[5]

Notes

1. See Roger Owen, "Inter-Arab Economic Relations during the Twentieth Century," Hudson 1999.
2. See *New York Times,* Sept. 8, 1992.
3. Nemat Shafik, "Labor Migration and Economic Integration in the Middle East," Hudson 1999.
4. See Airport Operators Council International periodic reports and UN ICAO annual reports.
5. The material covered in this chapter has been the subject of scores of studies since the late 1960s. For a historical perspective, see Issawi 1982. Sayigh 1978 explores the economies in depth. Latest data on production, transportation, and trade are in Country Commercial Guides; *Britannica World Data; World Factbook; Middle East and North Africa;* UN annuals; and *Middle East Economic Digest* and *Middle East Economic Survey.*

10

Where People Congregate

Settlers and Settlements

Variety of Patterns

The Middle East has a wide range of settlement types, forms, and functions within its great variety of environments, historical traditions, and state systems. In size, settlements range from hamlets sheltering a dozen families to one of the largest cities in the world (Cairo). Villages by the scores of thousands dot the agricultural landscape, from Turkey's bridgehead in Europe to the cultivated mountain valleys of northeastern Iran (see Figs. 10-1, 10-2, and 10-3), and more than 200 cities have passed the 100,000 population mark. In morphology, Middle East settlements have traditionally exhibited a wide variety of forms, from very compact to widely dispersed, depending on topography, water supply, and other influences.[1]

Settlements in intensively irrigated areas, such as the Nile Valley and Delta, are compact to conserve valuable farmland (Chap. 20), whereas villages on the steppes of Syria and Iran show a more dispersed pattern (Fig. 10-1a). Settlements that were—or still are—walled exhibit the usual crowding of enclosed places; but urban expansion since World War II has tended to open the settlement texture on the fringes, and newly established suburbs are more dispersed than are settlements that evolved in earlier centuries (Map 10-1). The typical Middle East urban structure has certain characteristic features, which have traditionally been designated as "Islamic," examined later.

The agricultural-settlement landscapes of the Middle East differ markedly from the rural landscapes of humid Western Europe and eastern North America. From house design and construction materials to street patterns and connecting roads, the settlements express their regional context—and are somewhat comparable to settlements in northern Mexico and the southwestern United States. The irregular patterns of fields around the agricultural villages on the Jordanian steppe contrast sharply with the geometric grid of the U.S. Corn Belt, and the pattern of wheat and barley fields on the steppes of the inner Fertile Crescent bears little resemblance to the field pattern in the intensively irrigated Nile Valley and Delta. Similarly, the agricultural villages and their surrounding fields in the basins and valleys of Iran, which are irrigated by *qanats,* contrast with villages perched on terraced mountain slopes in Lebanon and Yemen (Fig. 10-3).

Five Types of Patterns

Five settlement patterns have evolved: (1) the house and its elements (courtyard, storage facilities, adjacent garden, and perhaps even its construction materials); (2) houses and other structures within the settlement; (3) distribution of settlements and their related fields over the landscape; (4) interdependent relationships among the settlements (central places); and (5) links (roads and paths) between settlements. Although settlement patterns have become immensely more complex since the 1950s, these fundamental categories are the same.

However managed, the five settlement patterns interact and are interrelated in a regional spatial system. Nomads or scattered peasants are interdependent with nearby villages and

FIGURE 10-1   Two types of traditional agricultural villages in the Middle East: mud village in northwestern Iran *(top)*, with dung patties for fuel in foreground, and more compact mud village of Majmaah *(bottom)* in the Sudayr area of Najd, central Saudi Arabia. Majmaah has been greatly modernized since this 1965 view.

FIGURE 10-2   Kurdish village in open steppe landscape of southeastern Turkey.

FIGURE 10-3   Yemeni agricultural hamlet perched on mountain shoulder surrounded by steep terraced slopes of escarpment west of Sana. Well protected from surprise attack, settlements in these areas are small and close together, since farmers avoid long walks to their fields in such rugged topography.

MAP 10-1   Muharraq, Bahrain: Traditional street pattern in an Islamic city—unplanned, narrow, winding. On the edges of the old core are planned, right-angle streets with larger blocks of post-1960 period. Area shown is same as that in Figure 10-4. (Courtesy Survey Directorate, Bahrain)

cities, villages with their central city, cities with their hinterland villages, and so on up and down the hierarchy. Since no one element is an isolate, each can be fully understood only in its regional context.[2]

Many factors influence patterns of distribution, density, and dispersion of human groupings and their structures. Water supply is always a basic consideration, but other ecological factors are also significant: topography, vegetation, climate, soils. Cultural factors are often equally influential; transportation facilities, government support, regional function, defense, aesthetics, traditions, and industrial relationships. Such considerations condition a settlement's size, shape, morphology, function, and position within the regional hierarchy of places; and as Middle East settlements have vividly demonstrated since World War II, the historical-technological context is a compelling factor.

Obviously, then, the ways in which people group themselves and their structures are a major expression of people's management of the space in which they live. Countryside, village, and city make up a spatial system, an ensemble of interacting subsystems that combine in a dynamic whole. None is a discrete realm unto itself.[3]

Overall Settlement Pattern

The distribution of population has already been examined (see Chap. 6). Map 10-2 shows that the principal concentrations of population, and therefore settlements, are in the Nile Valley and Delta, Asia Minor, western Iran, and the Levant, with secondary concentrations along the Tigris and Euphrates rivers. Map 6-2 indicates the virtually uninhabited areas of the region and emphasizes the repelling influence of extreme aridity on permanent human settlement.

Until the mid-twentieth century, the overwhelming majority of Middle Easterners resided in villages. With the exception of nomads, whose mode of "settlement" is a special case, the isolated rural resident was rare in the Middle East and was restricted to special

environments in Asia Minor and northwestern Iran. Although cities had long been important in the socioeconomic pattern of the region, they had declined in number, size, and importance after the sixteenth century. Modernization of the region, especially in the newly wealthy petroleum-exporting states, reversed the rural-urban percentages and gave impetus to a steady urbanization of the Middle East (Map 6-1 and Table 6-1).

Urbanization

By the late 1980s, more than 50 percent of the population of the Middle East lived in cities, and a decade later the percentage was more than 70 percent. The urban trend was primarily the result of internal migrations from the villages to the cities and, in the Gulf, also of immigration from neighboring areas such as Yemen, Pakistan, and Jordan.

Unusual circumstances have created extraordinary percentages of urbanization in certain areas. Petroleum development attracted concentrations of population in virtual city-states on the western desert coastal fringe of the Gulf, areas that formerly supported only fishing hamlets on the coast and scattered nomads in the hinterland. Today, virtually the entire population along this fringe is technically urban. Kuwait, for example, exploded from approximately 50,000 people in 1940 to 2 million in 1999, nearly all of whom lived in Kuwait City and its immediate suburbs. Similar urbanization has evolved in Bahrain, Qatar, and the UAE since 1950.

For different reasons, urbanization is also high in Israel, despite the existence of scores of small settlements of several types. Even Egypt, the agricultural country par excellence, exhibits 45 percent urbanization. Surplus agricultural workers from the villages have migrated into Cairo especially, swelling the population of the Greater Cairo Region to 14–15 million. Alexandria and other cities have likewise expanded greatly. In Iran, a similar inpouring of villagers into Tehran has

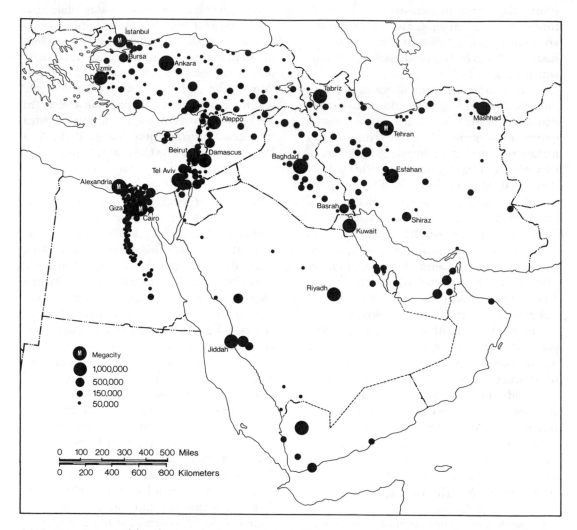

MAP 10-2   Pattern of distribution of urban populations. Note concentration of cities in the northern half of
the region, in the Levant, and especially in the Nile Valley and Delta. Istanbul, Tehran, Alexandria, and Cairo are
megacities, marked with "M," and Ankara, Baghdad, Mashhad, Giza, and Riyadh are in the multimillion population category.

prompted its population to surge to more than
8 million, with Mashhad near 2 million and
Esfahan and Tabriz more than 1 million each.
Across the Gulf, Saudi Arabia experienced
remarkable urbanization during the 1970s and
1980s. Dammam and nearby fishing villages
rocketed from a few hundred dwellers to a
conurbation of more than a million population. In the interior, Riyadh, a desert capital of
30,000 before World War II, exploded during
the kingdom's oil boom and was estimated to

have more than 3.5 million inhabitants in
1999.

Similarly, the urbanization that has characterized population movements in much of the
world since mid-century has resulted in special
permutations in the Middle East (see Chap. 6).
Not only have millions of expatriates swelled
the populations of the Gulf cities—Kuwait,
Dammam, al-Khobar, Manama, Doha, Abu
Dhabi, Dubai, Ahvaz, Bandar-e Abbas, and
others—but also hundreds of thousands of

FIGURE 10-4   Traditional pattern of houses and streets in a small Islamic city. Air view in the mid–1960s, looking southwest along old causeway connecting Muharraq *(foreground)* with Manama, capital of Bahrain. Compare patterns in this photograph with map of the area (Map 10-1).

nomads in much of the Middle East have abandoned their wandering lifestyle to become city dwellers. This process of sedentarization has been one of the major socioeconomic phenomena of the Middle East during the last several decades. However, despite increasing sedentarization and the reduction of tribal nomads to a minimum level, urbanized former nomads remarkably retain their tribal consciousness and relationships for many years, even decades.

Internal Structures of Cities

The internal morphological and structural patterns of settlements reflect interaction between urban development and historical-geographical influences. These patterns include the street pattern, placement of central squares and other open areas, location and shape of commercial activities, presence and character of ethnic concentrations, and other aspects of settlements. Identification and analysis of such characteristics aid in understanding the initial role intended for a settlement in its regional system, as well as understanding subsequent accretions to its functions, successive modifications of the urban morphology, and the interrelations between the settlement and its several neighbors.

For many centuries past, the traditional Middle East settlement, whether village or city, has had a highly irregular pattern of narrow streets, with house blocks uneven in size and "cellular" because of the usual open courtyard in each house (Figs. 10-1b and 10-4). Such an appearance identifies the older core of virtually every Middle East city that developed before 1800 and also typifies villages in the region that predate the nineteenth century. The fundamental compactness of settlements in areas of aridity and heat minimized the length of water conduits and also reduced heat from the direct sun. Streets were pathways or lanes among the houses, and since wheeled vehicles were rarely used during the periods of morphological evolution of most of the towns, the narrow lanes were sufficient for pedestrians, porters, and animals.

Urban Core Elements

Except in Israel, Cyprus, and parts of Lebanon, virtually every older town and city exhibits the traditional Islamic pattern of a core area comprising six elements: (1) a large mosque—the Friday Mosque (*Masjid al-Jami*); (2) the city's principal educational facilities, the *madrassah*, typically operated in conjunction with the mosque; (3) the main public water-based facilities—drinking fountains, latrines, and baths (*hammams*); (4) courts and other institutions of justice (*al-adl*) along with other related administrative institutions, depending upon the role of the particular city; (5) the citadel (*al-qalah*), often large and well fortified in most older cities; and (6) most extensive of all in area, the commercial district.

The last element—the very characteristic Middle Eastern *suq* (Arabic), *bazaar* (Persian), or *çarsı* (Turkish)—sometimes surrounds the other core elements and sometimes radiates along one main axis in an alignment conditioned by environmental factors. Any major *suq* includes numerous craft shops in which artisans produce such items as copper and brass wares, leather goods, textiles, jewelry, and perhaps such specialty goods as inlaid woods. Formerly, inns (caravanserais and khans), which provided housing for travelers and their animal trains, were also included in or were adjacent to the *suq* area. Offices for levying customs (*gumruk*), banking facilities—especially for currency exchange—and related financial offices were usually included in the commercial core, and some still are. A quiet stroll through any of the traditional *suqs*/bazaars (Istanbul, Cairo, Aleppo, Damascus, Baghdad, Mosul, Tehran, and Esfahan) becomes a brief education in local history,

geographical relationships, economy, customs, culture, and other aspects of the area.

Urban Quarters

Although the system is declining, the Middle East city has traditionally been divided into "quarters" (*harat, rayyat, mahallat, akhtat*). Many such quarters were closely knit and homogeneous communities in which people sought safety and protection among others of their own kind. Such group protection was the main or only recourse during many lengthy periods, and identity factors included religion, ethnicity, and village origin. There were commonly quarters, among religions, for Christians, Jews, Armenians, and Muslims; among Muslims, for Kurds, Turkmen, Persians, and Turks; among Arab Muslims, for Sunni, Shii, Druzes, or for respective villagers.

The contemporary quarters in most older Middle East cities had their genesis during the tenth century, the second or third century after the entrenchment of Islam in most of the region. It was during this time that the concept of "clients" (*mawali*) and "people of the book" (*ahl al-kitab*) became a firm tradition (see Chap. 6). There were as many as 37 quarters in medieval Cairo, 40 in Jerusalem (but only 9 major ones), 50 in Aleppo, and an impressive 70 in Damascus. Sectors for Europeans were set aside in the Galatea section of Constantinople for many centuries by both the Byzantines and the Ottomans, and similar European quarters evolved in several other cities after 1900 and especially after World War II—in Beirut, Damascus, Cairo, Baghdad, Tehran, and Gulf cities. Thus, the concept and pattern of "quarters" has become deeply ingrained in the cities of the region. Even with the less sharp definition of boundaries, the expansion of cities on a vast scale, and the growing homogeneity of population in the various *mahallat*, the designation of quarters continues as a tradition.

The expansion of diplomatic communities in burgeoning Middle East capitals added to the "foreign" quarters and in some cases created predominantly *corps diplomatique* enclaves, although the events in Beirut and Tehran during the 1980s disrupted this development. When the Saudi government permitted the shift of foreign embassies from Jiddah to Riyadh in the early 1980s, it set aside a spacious new area in Riyadh for development of a splendid, exclusive diplomatic quarter. The Omani government has likewise established a handsome diplomatic quarter in the new suburb of al-Khuwayr, west of Muscat, where both Omani government ministries and foreign embassies are concentrated.

In most cities in the region, each major urban quarter replicated the city core on a reduced scale. During the centuries that most major Middle East cities evolved, a neighborhood mosque was required every few blocks to permit the muazzin (muezzin) giving the call to prayer to be heard from the mosque minaret. A hierarchy of mosques often developed, with the main mosque in a quarter becoming the hub for reduced versions of the institutions and facilities found in the city core. Facilities necessary for a subsection's social life were a *suq*, including bakeries, fruit and vegetable sellers, spice and ghee merchants, and public kitchen and restaurant; *hammam;* and khan. Spacing among mosques increased after World War II when electronic amplifiers and loudspeaker systems greatly increased the distance over which the muazzin could be heard. Indeed, the call to prayer and Quranic readings have increasingly been tape recorded and, in many places, televised.

In several Islamic cities, as in certain well-known cities in Christendom, the nucleus is a religious monument or shrine dedicated to a religious leader or saint. The shrine attracts the usual array of ancillary facilities and institutions, particularly service facilities for the visiting pilgrims. Mecca is the prime city of pilgrimage in Islam, although it had an important shrine and served a significant commercial function prior to the time of Muhammad. Other major shrine cities are Medina, with the tomb of the Prophet Muhammad; Karbala and al-Najaf, just west of the Euphrates in Iraq, the two main Shii shrines; Mashhad and Qom in

Iran, both tomb shrines of Shii imams; and such multifunctional cities as Jerusalem, Damascus, Konya, Istanbul, and others with major shrines that attract thousands of pilgrims annually.

Significant as the mosque and related core elements may be in Middle East cities, residential sections obviously occupy most of the built-up areas. Here the texture is finer and more uniform than in the grosser pattern of the city core. The traditional house, although not necessarily the contemporary dwelling, in the Middle East city is modest in size, with walls built to the edge of the property line, an open courtyard in the center or to one side, and different living quarters for males and females. Male members of the family have more open quarters as opposed to women's quarters, which have shuttered windows and generally greater privacy. Typically, the house is one or two stories high, and the staircase to the second story, if any, is in the courtyard. The flat roof is often surrounded by a low parapet and is regularly used by the family as a sleeping area during the warm season, which is also the dry season for most of the Middle East. The overall pattern of such houses, built wall against wall in small blocks and divided by narrow zigzagging streets, is one of cellular regularity (see Fig. 10-4).

These traditional characteristics have been appreciably modified with the expansion and modernization of settlements virtually everywhere in the Middle East since 1950. New and old have come face to face. Although the traditional has yielded to the advantages of modern technology, the heritage of the past in many cities, but not in all parts and not in all cities, is often still perceptible in both architecture and city planning. Villages especially retain the character of fortified compounds and protected sites in certain areas (Fig. 10-3). Air-conditioning has become almost universal in the energy-rich Gulf amirates and Saudi Arabia; here, the ancient tradition of sleeping on the roof during the warm season has almost disappeared, although it is still common in many other areas of the region. Air-conditioning also permits flexibility in house design, especially in window arrangement, and in many

194

Where People Congregate

respects, middle-class and upper middle-class residences in many cities of the region would be acclaimed by Westerners of comparable income levels. Nevertheless, the traditional construction of walls along the property lines, preference for courtyards, and limited yard or garden area are readily identifiable. The broad green lawns of the American suburb are impractical virtually everywhere in the water-deficient Middle East, but smaller ones are seen around some mansions in Riyadh, for example, and in Jewish settlements in occupied territories.

A more striking departure from tradition is seen in the post-1960 urban street design. With very high automobile ownership per family in much of the region (see Table 9-2), especially in the Gulf area and in Cyprus and Israel, many new streets have been designed with generous widths. Newly planned cities such as Kuwait, Doha, Riyadh, Dammam, and Dubai had ample areas of desert over which to expand, and planners took advantage of the space to provide wide main boulevards and wide secondary and tertiary streets in the new quarters, in contrast to the traditional lanes in older quarters.

Blending of traditional and modern also characterizes the commercial sections of many Middle East cities. The basic principle of the *suq,* with its rows of small shops, is too deeply ingrained in Middle East tradition and has served the purpose too well and too long to be discarded entirely in preference to European or American mercantile fashions. The old vaulted underground aisles lined with shops, or the palm-frond-covered lines of shops above-ground, still exist in less affluent areas or in carefully preserved places.

However, many old *suqs* have been replaced in the most extensively modernized cities with attractive air-conditioned commercial centers that combine the best features of the traditional *suq* and the American shopping mall—itself an adaptation of the oriental *suq.* The range of goods traditionally offered for sale has also been enormously expanded since the 1950s, so that the *suqs* in Cairo, Riyadh, and Abu Dhabi;

the bazaars in Esfahan, Tabriz, and Tehran; and the *çarsıs* in Istanbul, Konya, and Ankara now also offer virtually every type of equipment, Japanese and Swiss watches, pocket calculators, and a full range of household electric appliances. Indeed, the huge Shakiyah shopping center in Riyadh, Jamjoom Center in Jiddah, Suq al-Majariah in Sharjah, and similar centers in Kuwait are crammed with electronic and photographic items, jewelry, apparel, toys, and similar items to match the desires of the most avid consumer.

Urban areas planned and constructed since 1960 display a markedly different morphology from the older sectors, and dramatic changes in structural and textural patterns designate the lines beyond which the new planning has been carried out (Map 10-1). Such changes are obvious in Damascus, Jerusalem, Ankara, and Abu Dhabi; the urban morphology of the West is especially evident in cities along the western Gulf, from Kuwait (Fig. 10-5) to Dubai, but also in Istanbul, Cairo, Beirut, and Tel Aviv. High-rise office and apartment buildings, extensive suburbs, the coalescence of cities into conurbations, divided freeways (dual carriageways), and futuristic airports became commonplace in only two decades.

Urban Problems and Prospects

In many cities where expansion was extreme, whether in Ankara, Baghdad, Amman, Abu Dhabi, or a score of other explosively growing metropolitan areas, newcomers poured into the urban fringe and erected spontaneous (squatter) settlements faster than adequate housing could be planned and constructed. Fortunately, in much of the Gulf area, central government funds from petroleum exports were available for adequate public housing to replace the squatter huts, although construction initially lagged behind the influx of new population. Lacking great oil income, Turkey, Jordan, and Egypt have found it difficult to fund housing in expanding areas. Jordan, Lebanon, and Syria faced the unique problem

FIGURE 10-5   Central Business District (CBD) of Kuwait City in 1997, entirely developed since the late 1950s.

of having both unofficial and official Palestinian refugee camps spring up around Jericho, Amman, Irbid, Sidon, Beirut, and Dara.

Official camps were given minimal support by the United Nations Relief and Works Agency (UNRWA). Improved housing for the refugees was financially and politically difficult to provide, even over a period of more than four decades. Israel is a special case in that foreign aid from both private and government sources supplied reasonably adequate amounts for housing—after some delay—the flood of immigrants in the late 1940s and the 1950s. Later *olim* (immigrants) were very well housed, and impressive homes were built—a large number in settlements in the West Bank and Gaza—for many of the hundreds of thousands of Jews who arrived from the former Soviet Union during the 1990s. Principal funding came from a controversial multibillion dollar United States-guaranteed loan in 1991–1992.

Spontaneous settlements in Turkey, *gecekondus,* were first built when surplus agricultural families began migrating into main urban centers—Istanbul, Izmir, Ankara—after World War II. These migrants erected simple huts on the urban fringes, and under Turkish law, a house built and roofed before government authorities can prohibit further construction must be allowed to stand where and as built. Most of the huts were constructed between dusk and dawn to avoid observation by authorities, hence the name *gecekondu* ("built overnight"), and the government generally did not attempt to prohibit the *gecekondu* settlements.

Under similar circumstances in Iraq, when villagers and Bedouins poured into Baghdad in search of employment and improved living standards during the 1950s, authorities were overwhelmed in their limited efforts to provide funding, planning, space, and quarters for the hundreds of thousands of migrants. The settlers themselves built the same type of mud huts that lower economic group members had built in Mesopotamia for thousands of years—solid mud walls with palm fronds and reed mats forming a pitched roof. Spaced only a few feet apart and lacking basic amenities, these *sarifah* huts multiplied into sprawling settlements until they were replaced by public housing as Iraqi oil income increased.

Despite the problems of numbers in many instances, town planning in the Middle East has been on a scale unprecedented in the region's history and perhaps unmatched anywhere else in the world. The reconstruction of war-devastated cities in Europe during the 1950s demanded extraordinary town-planning efforts, and expertise developed at that time was later applied to the unparalleled urban expansion in the Gulf area. Urban planners had to be imported by most of the rapidly expanding Middle East countries, since their own experts were few in number and were relatively inexperienced in such large-scale planning.

Most of the Gulf states turned to the British for expertise, since most of these countries had been under British tutelage prior to gaining independence in the 1960s and early 1970s. One consequence is that major Gulf cities bear the unmistakable stamp of British town-planning concepts, for example, the traffic "roundabout," known as a rotary or traffic circle in the United States, where it is rarely used. Local technicians were rapidly trained in town planning, and Middle East governments soon took over the enormous task of planning their own cities and villages. Some of the designs are striking, having been facilitated by the fact that cost of execution was often no object.

Planning in Israel after 1948 is unique in that a high degree of expertise had been developed during the mandate years and also a large number of expert planners immigrated to the Jewish state. As the new state expanded, they participated in a highly coordinated and well-financed program for planning at every level. The site of each settlement was carefully selected, whether as an adjunct to a former Arab village, a restoration of a known or supposed biblical site, or a

completely new settlement. Once the site was determined, the internal design of the settlement was drawn up, and a selection of house types was supplied by the planners. Such planning assured balanced distribution of immigrants, efficient use of water, economic activity for the new inhabitants, and a systematic security pattern in the expanding state.[4] The category of settlement for a given site was also determined by the central planners—kibbutz, moshav, *nahal*, or multifunction town (see Chap. 15).

Despite planning efforts, virtually every Middle East city—and especially those with a population of more than 500,000—has found itself faced with the same urban problems that have caused difficulties in similar cities elsewhere and particularly those in developing countries. Traffic problems are near the top of the list, as increasing affluence doubles and triples the number of automobiles crowding onto the space allotted to them, which is expanding only slowly. Crowded streets, inexperienced drivers, lack of parking facilities, lack of adequate traffic policing, narrow streets in the older sections that often house the commercial core, problems with traffic lights, and, in some cities (Cairo, as a prime example), admixtures of animals and carts—all combine to create a traffic nightmare in many of the region's larger cities. Tehran, Beirut, Cairo, and Istanbul rank high on a world traveler's list of cities with the worst traffic congestion.

Along with traffic problems, some major cities of the region also struggle with serious shortages of water, gas, electricity, sewerage facilities, telephones, and similar utilities and services. Even cities in the more humid areas—Istanbul, Beirut, Haifa—suffer water shortages during the long, dry summers because their water distribution systems are inadequate. Likewise, Cairo, with a plentiful source of water in the Nile, may have water shortages during the hot summer as a result of an incapacity to distribute supplies at a sufficient rate. For many years municipal water was supplied in Ankara for only brief periods two or three times a day.

Jiddah, in wealthy Saudi Arabia, periodically has no water in summer, and 1998 was a particularly trying season. In Beirut, apartment houses even in normal times are, by design, supplied with water through such small pipes that it must be stored during the night in roof tanks, one for each apartment. Similarly, virtually every house on the Greek Cypriot side of Nicosia has a prominent but essential water tank on its roof.

Coastal plain cities in Israel recycle their treated sewage in order to sustain a water supply, pumping the treated waste back into the aquifers under the coastal plain from which the basic water supply is obtained. Continuous recycling without plentiful recharging by natural runoff in dry years affects the taste of the drinking water in the Tel Aviv metropolitan area and worries some Israeli planners, but the procedure is basically a conservational success. Occasional wet seasons such as the winters of 1991–1992 and 1997–1998 help counteract some of the problems.

Kuwait City is unique in having originally developed with virtually no natural surface or underground water supply. During earlier centuries, the small village on Kuwait Bay brought most of its fresh water in goatskins and other similar containers by boat from the Shatt al-Arab, south of Basrah. With the beginning of its petroleum age, Kuwait took advantage of the availability of large supplies of fuel (and funds) to distill seawater in order to obtain its water supplies. In the mid-1950s, the price of a gallon of water delivered by tanker truck in Kuwait equaled the price of a gallon of gasoline. As the city's population doubled and redoubled, Kuwait installed additional and more efficient distillation facilities, along with exploiting newly discovered, limited groundwater supplies north of the bay. Distillation of seawater has been practiced on an increasing scale by other cities along the Gulf coast and on the Red Sea coast since 1970. By the late 1990s, Saudi Arabia alone had installed more than 30 large desalination plants that provide 70 percent of the supply of the country's drinking water. At least 40 such plants are scheduled to be in operation in the region by 2005.

Partly because of a failure to modernize for either financial or technical reasons, partly because of problems with distribution systems, many Middle East cities and a substantially higher percentage of towns and villages utilize water that cannot be relied upon to be safe to drink as it comes from the tap. Since many residents nevertheless drink the water, intestinal parasitic diseases are endemic. Whereas Istanbul, Nicosia, Baghdad, Cairo, Damascus, and Tel Aviv supply relatively safe potable water, Ankara, Beirut, and Amman, among other capitals, do not. Even so, bottled water is preferred, or essential, in most cities and villages in the region.

Nearly all Middle East cities have developed the capacity to supply reasonably reliable electrical power to their citizens. The electricity age has thoroughly pervaded the Middle East region and, indeed, has swept the Levant and the Gulf as much as it has most areas of Western Europe and North America. Seemingly inexhaustible supplies of energy in the Gulf have permitted the servicing of virtually every urban household with electricity, and air-conditioning, refrigeration, and a full range of household appliances have become as common as in American cities. With plentiful electricity, main city streets—and even lengthy intercity highways—are well lighted, for example, the 100-mile/161 km dual-lane highway between Abu Dhabi and al-Ayn.

The typical settlement morphology in the Middle East since the 1950s has evolved under unique conditions. Explosive development accompanying the oil boom has had profound effects on settlements in the region, especially in the Gulf area. There the impact of Western technological influences on Middle Eastern traditional cities created a certain dichotomy of urban planning and execution: A major dilemma has been how to modernize and provide the desired conveniences without destroying or detracting from the charm and historical values of a Jerusalem, Cairo, Istanbul, or similar traditional city. Charm and tradition have too often yielded to technology, economic demands, and the urge to modernize, and historic structures and quarters have been razed to make room for stark, modular high-rise office and apartment blocks.

Hardly a city has escaped an unfortunate over-use of the bulldozer blade—Jiddah, Kuwait, Baghdad, Tehran, Beirut, and Jerusalem. Sharp debate has accompanied the razing of older quarters in some of these cities, particularly in Jerusalem, a city sacred to three great world religions. Plans to rebuild the war-damaged old core of Beirut were fiercely disputed in the early 1990s before the design was adopted; reconstruction was nearing completion in early 2000.

The dilemma for urban planners in the Middle East had no simple solution: Central business districts either had to be modernized or be overwhelmed with automobile traffic. Vigorous efforts of conservationists have rather successfully preserved most of the picturesque charm of the old cores of Sana, Istanbul, Esfahan, and Damascus. The entire town of Shibam, in the Wadi Hadramawt of eastern Yemen, has been declared a world historic site by the United Nations Educational, Scientific, and Cultural Organization (UNESCO) (see Chap. 19).

Notes

1. Several works on Middle East cities have appeared since the mid–1960s, most of which have been collections of papers given at conferences and symposia; for example, Serjeant 1980, with especially stimulating and authoritative perspectives on the Islamic city at a UNESCO colloqium; Saqqaf 1987, which focuses on the ancient-modern confrontation; and Blake and Lawless 1980. Bonine 1977 contemplates the Islamic urban experience. Antoniou 1981 is another UNESCO look at the Islamic city from the aspect of conservation. English 1966 and Bonine 1979 focus on Iranian urban development, and Grill 1984 looks at Arabian Peninsula urbanization. Abu-Lughod 1971 and Rodenbeck 1998 examine Cairo. Ragette 1983 considers the reconstruction of Beirut, as does Gavin and Maluf 1996. AlSayyad 1991 looks at the genesis of Arab Muslim urbanism.

2. Christaller's classical theory of central places, the most widely applied model for the study of the hierarchy of settlements, is of limited applicability in much of the Middle East. See Christaller 1966.

3. Vance 1977 takes a stimulating philosophical look at the city, primarily the Western urban phenomenon.

4. See Soffer and Minghi 1986.

11

The Earth and the State: Geopolitics

The Middle East has functioned as a tricontinental hub for thousands of years. During that time, peoples, armies, merchants, and ideas have flowed to, from, and across the region. Political ideas and political processes included in the flow were sometimes adapted and sometimes rejected but were often influential in the evolving pattern of the present sixteen states. Beyond each state, the complex political and other relationships established among the states, with neighboring areas, and with distant lands have been profoundly influenced by the several spatial patterns already examined. The reciprocal influence between these patterns and political behavior, that is, geopolitics, is the theme of this chapter.

In this book, geopolitics pertains to the spatial interaction between geographical area and political phenomena. It is conceptually equivalent to political geography, and the terms will be used almost interchangeably. Although the focus of this chapter is on the state as a political-geographical phenomenon, it also covers internal and external geopolitical relations of the Middle East.

Hub and Heartland

Early geopolitical concepts of "Heartland" and "World-Island" emerged in Sir Halford J. Mackinder's paper of 1904[1] and his conceptual modifications in 1919 and 1943. Mackinder defined the Heartland bastion as the general area of Siberia, which he conceived of as partially ringed by an Inner Crescent extending from northwestern Europe through southern

Asia to northeastern Asia. Beyond the Inner Crescent he viewed an Outer Crescent, comprising the Americas, southern Africa, and Australia. He labeled Europe, Asia, and Africa the "World-Island" and proposed in 1919 that:

Who rules East Europe commands the Heartland;
Who rules the Heartland commands the World-Island;
Who rules the World-Island commands the World.

Although the Mackinder dictum has received its just share of criticism, the idea of a World-Island emphasizes the links among Europe, Asia, and Africa. In emphasizing those links, it coincidentally spotlights the pivotal location of the Middle East in the World-Island.

Mackinder's Heartland concept was challenged by the theory of the "Rimland" proposed by Professor Nicholas John Spykman during World War II. To Spykman, control of the Heartland is only a strong defensive position; it is control of western and southern Europe, the Middle East, southern Asia, southeastern Asia, China, and Japan that is crucial. Spykman thus gave the key significance to Mackinder's Inner Crescent, which Spykman called the Rimland. He further theorized that domination of both the Heartland and the Rimland by one superpower or power group would create an unmatched power base. On the other hand, control of the Rimland, or most of it, by one power would offset domination of the Heartland by another power.

Viewed from the Mackinder, Spykman, or other world geopolitical perspective, the Middle East location alone is of enormous global strategic importance. The region's geostrategic value thus enhances its oil wealth, human resources, and commercial role. The Middle East has repeatedly proved its significance under a variety of circumstances.

In World War I, Ottoman Turks, Germans, Russians, British, French, and even Greeks and Italians contended for Middle East territory. The British and French emerged dominant and became the main imperialist powers in the region between the wars. France held sway in Syria and Lebanon and also in part of the Horn of Africa; Britain held not only the three mandates of Palestine, Transjordan, and (until 1932) Iraq but also the Gulf shaykhdoms and Aden.

In World War II, Germany sought to control the Suez Canal and other lines of regional communications as well as the Middle East oil fields. Nazi plans called for a three-pronged attack through North Africa, the Balkans, and, as part of the assault on the Soviet Union, the Ukraine and Caucasus. British and Commonwealth forces, with U.S. assistance, resisted the attacks across North Africa, and they cooperated with the United States in transferring lend-lease war matériel through western Iran to the Soviet Union. Such supplies contributed to the USSR's strength to stop the Nazi advance at Stalingrad. Axis forces failed to gain a foothold in the Middle East, although troops from Vichy France (the French government during German occupation) held Syria and Lebanon for a brief time. Contemporary maneuvering for dominance in the area is examined later in this chapter.

The State in the Middle East

A Recent Political Mosaic

Of the sixteen contemporary Middle East states, only seven were independent states before 1943—Egypt, Turkey, Iraq, Iran, Saudi Arabia, Oman, and the Imamate of Yemen; and British influence limited the sovereignty of Oman, Iraq, and even Egypt. The area has, therefore, ancient cultures in new states—old wine in new bottles.

Much of the recent history of the Middle East emanates from the political adolescence, inexperience, and insecurity of the recently emerged states of the region. Although Kuwait gained its independence in 1961, middle and lower Gulf states achieved sovereignty only in 1971 after decades as British protectorates or protected states. Following several months of uncertain status, the crown colony of Aden and adjoining protectorate of the Hadramawt merged into an independent unity of the People's Democratic Republic of Yemen (PDRY) in 1967; and the PDRY, in turn, merged with the Yemen Arab Republic as recently as May 1990. Cyprus shed its British crown colony status and achieved independence in 1960, only to experience an invasion by Turkey in 1974 and creation of a de facto Turkish republic in the north of the island. The four Levant states emerged from mandate status and achieved independence between 1943 and 1948, with the fifth mandate (Iraq) having already realized nominal sovereignty in 1932. Even Saudi Arabia declared itself a united kingdom as late as 1932, and Egypt emerged from its British protectorate status in 1922. Both Turkey and Iran are centuries-old sovereign countries, although both declared republican status after centuries of monarchical rule only in 1923 and 1979, respectively. Egypt, Iraq, and North Yemen (YAR) also replaced their monarchies with republican governments between the early 1950s and early 1960s.

Thus, the overall political character of the Middle East is a complex of ambiguities, contradictions, and differentiation. Among Muslim states, and especially Arab states, there exist conceptual efforts toward solidarity, but practical obstacles repeatedly defeat the efforts. Because of the varied imperial/colonial influences that have affected them, most of the states have nonindigenous, artificial structures; they have not naturally evolved out of their own socio-economic-political context or their own cultural traditions.[2] Not only have most of the contemporary states emerged from an imperialist context institutionally, they also owe their general political-geographical configurations to British-French boundary delineations. Only one or two initial boundary alignments in the entire Middle East were negotiated entirely by indigenous states on

FIGURE 11-1 Topkapı Saray, palace complex of the Ottoman sultans and heart of the Ottoman Empire (see Map 11-2) for more than 550 years. The sultan's private quarters were to the right, harem in the center of the figure, and huge kitchens in lower wing. The complex is now a world-class museum, with unique collections of porcelain, timepieces, jewels, and tiles.

the two sides of a line. Boundary determinations from the outside sometimes ignored local tribal or traditional elements and in many cases created resentment against imperialist dictates. Iraqi bitterness over British definition of the boundary between Iraq and the then British protectorate of Kuwait has repeatedly manifested itself, as late as 1990. In other instances, imposition of borders from the outside has settled territorial and boundary disputes of long standing.

World War I Territorial Agreements

Among several such accords, three contradictory World War I agreements, plus others after the war, profoundly influenced future Middle East developments and contemporary political-geographical boundaries. Current patterns, crises, and conflicts can be understood only through a comprehension of these agreements.

Two incompatible agreements were made by the British in 1915 and 1916 with regard to the disposition of Ottoman territories in the Middle East after the war (Fig. 11-1). The first was reached in 1915 in an exchange of official correspondence between Sir Henry McMahon, British high commissioner in Cairo, and Sharif Husayn of Mecca, governor of the Ottoman province of the Hijaz. In the exchange, the correspondents agreed that the sharif's Arab followers would revolt against the Ottoman Turks in Arabia and Syria and that Britain, in return, would support the creation of an independent Arab state in former Ottoman lands after the end of the war.

In spite of thus having committed His Majesty's Government to supporting Arab independence in most of the Fertile Crescent, Britain signed the Sykes-Picot Agreement with France and Russia in May 1916. This second

MAP 11-1   Sykes-Picot Agreement territorial allotments that, although later disavowed, became the
basis for the post-World War I mandate system.

agreement specified areas in the Fertile Crescent to be divided between British and French
control and influence in the partition of the
Ottoman Empire after the Allied victory (Map
11-1). Much of the same area was involved in
both agreements.

A third agreement was the Balfour Declaration of November 1917, in which Britain unilaterally promised support for a Jewish
homeland in Palestine (see the section "The
Arab-Israeli Problem" later in this chapter).
This statement provided for a third disposition
of certain Fertile Crescent territory.

The Arab Revolt

In accordance with the Husayn-McMahon correspondence, and with British support, the Arab
Revolt against the Ottomans began in June 1916.
Coordinating the Arab attacks with British operations in Palestine was the legendary Lawrence
of Arabia (Col. T. E. Lawrence), who chronicled
the fighting from the Hijaz to Damascus in his
Seven Pillars of Wisdom.[3] The principal Arab
leader in the field was Amir Faysal, third son of
Sharif Husayn of Mecca.

The Arabs, having upheld their commitment
under the Husayn-McMahon correspondence,

were later dismayed to learn of the Sykes-Picot
Agreement and the Balfour Declaration, both
of which effectively negated Britain's promises
to Arab leaders. The Arabs were encouraged by
President Woodrow Wilson's Fourteen Points,
the twelfth of which specifically supported the
principle of self-determination of peoples formerly under Ottoman control. However, the
Arabs later became distrustful of Britain,
France, and the United States as the Allies
repeatedly reneged on promises to Arab
groups; by contrast, Jewish groups succeeded in
gaining support for their proposed homeland
in the Middle East.

Peace Treaties and Mandates

In the postwar peace conferences, Britain and
France dominated discussions, including the
decisions on the future of the former Ottoman
areas of the Middle East (Map 11-2). Unable to
reconcile the agreements made in 1915–1917,
they adhered generally to the Sykes-Picot
Agreement and specifically to the Balfour Declaration. At U.S. insistence, a commission of
inquiry, the King-Crane Commission, went to
the Levant from the Paris peace meetings to test
Arab opinion. However, the commission lacked
British or French support, and its report—
warning against French control in Syria and
against application of Zionist goals in Palestine—
was ignored and was not even published for
more than three years.[4]

A system of Middle East mandates under the
proposed League of Nations emerged from
talks among the Allied powers at the San Remo
Conference in April 1920. Territorially, the suggested mandates followed the outlines of the
Sykes-Picot Agreement (see Map 11-1). The
agreements divided traditional Greater Syria so
that the north passed to French control and the
south to British control, and Mesopotamia
became an additional British mandate (Iraq).
Other mandates were set up in Africa and the
western Pacific.

Mandatory controls were to be temporary, to
observe the principles of self-determination,

MAP 11-2 Ottoman Empire at its maximum, showing territorial losses by 1914 and after World War I. Losses after 1914 are of especial interest in this book.

and to lead to early independence of the polities involved. Unique among all the mandates, the Palestine mandate document included provisions that were incompatible with the purported intent of the mandate system. These provisions were the essential points of the Balfour Declaration, the basic commitment by Great Britain to support a Jewish homeland in Palestine. Their inclusion was a distinct victory for the Zionists, but it angered and alienated the indigenous Arabs of Palestine, who constituted more than 90 percent of the population of the mandate. After complex territorial trades and divisions, the mandates became official and de jure in 1923. By that time, Transjordan had been clearly excluded from the Palestine mandate, and Greater Lebanon had been constituted as a separate French mandate.

Present Basic Patterns

The State and Its Location

A major thesis of political geography is that *where* a state is located is the most important single factor in its evolution. Whether the location is a matter of latitude, coastal versus landlocked, island versus mainland, astride a mountain range as opposed to being in an intermontane basin—each aspect influences the state's geopolitical development.

Lebanon's à cheval position (literally, "on horseback") astride a linear mountain range imposes a problem of uniting people and communications on opposite sides of the mountains. Egypt's extension up the Nile Valley to just beyond the first cataract and its union of the valley and the delta is a classic case of a riverine state maintaining a linear unity, although the entire Nile Basin has never been united. Iraq, as modern heir to the Tigris-Euphrates Basin, is another classic example of a riverine state. Turkey and Iran illustrate mountain bastions holding longlasting, independent polities.

Every Middle East state possesses some seacoast, although only Oman and Yemen face the open ocean (Indian Ocean), with the UAE also having coastal outlets on the Indian Ocean. Deep indentations of seas and gulfs into the region facilitate access to the seas, and most states are well endowed with coastlines. Jordan and Iraq, however, are exceptions, as Jordan has only a 16-mile/26-km corner of the Gulf of Aqabah for its single port of Aqabah; and Iraq, with a narrow 36-mile/58-km corridor to the marshy head of the Gulf, suffered serious disadvantages from a lack of adequate harbor and port facilities as it developed its independent economy as a mandate. The lack became critical in the late 1970s and even more so during the Iran-Iraq war. Iraq alleged that the problem was one factor in its seizure of Kuwait in 1990. Saudi Arabia, Israel, Egypt, and Iran have two-sea locations, and Iran also has a 460-mile/740 km frontage on the inland Caspian Sea. Turkey has by far the longest seacoast of all states in the region, opening onto the Mediterranean, Aegean, Marmara, and Black seas.

In an area as strategic as the Middle East, the location of virtually every state involves some strategic aspect. Bahrain's situation midway in the Gulf has historically been a strategic asset and still affords the island state advantages as an entrepôt and meeting point—now enhanced by the causeway link with the mainland. Similarly, the island state of Cyprus benefits from its eastern Mediterranean situation, which permits it to serve as neutral ground for Arabs and Israelis, Lebanese factions, Europeans and Middle Easterners, and, in better times, Greeks and Turks. On land, Turkey's "bridge" location has brought advantages and disadvantages from Hittite times to the present; and Syria's central location has provided commercial advantages, now

reduced by political circumstances. These aspects are discussed in the respective country chapters in Part 2.

The State and Its Population

Both demographically and geopolitically, a state's population is of significance in terms of number, distribution, density, and composition (see Maps 6-1 and 6-2; Tables 6-1 and 6-3). Each major ethnic group has strong sentiments of nationalism.

Every Middle East state has minorities, and some states have ten or twelve sizable ethnic groups. Even the existence of minorities within a population is important, but the geopolitical significance of minorities increases with the degree of antinational sentiment or separatism manifested by such groups. Militant minorities in Lebanon and Cyprus have fractured the basic integrity of those states; Israel considers its Arab minority, increasingly militant over being transformed from a 9–1 majority in 1920, a threat; in Iraq, Turkey, and Iran, the central governments have periodically faced major rebellions by Kurdish minorities. Egypt, with the Copts; Saudi Arabia, with the Persian-descended Shii; Iran, with the Azeris, Arabs, Baluch, and a dozen other groups, have all experienced ethnic conflicts.[5]

The State and Its Institutions

Most of the polities of the Middle East entered the second half of the twentieth century with traditional societies and traditional monarchies as governments. However, those societies have been forced to adjust to the contemporary technological, economic, and political influences brought by post-World War II developments. Such adjustment has involved replacement of monarchies in Egypt, Iraq, and Yemen by republics, yet the Iranian monarchy was overthrown as a reaction against modernization and for the restoration of religious traditionalism.

Although the more leftist revolutionary pressures have declined since the 1970s, traditional regimes were for several years under pressure from neighboring revolutionary regimes and from revolutionary groups within their territories. Increasingly in the early 1990s, many of the Middle East governments were most threatened by extremist religious fundamentalist movements both from within and, partly, from without. Monarchies in Saudi Arabia and Oman, and especially in Jordan, have adapted through gradualism; the individual rulers of Kuwait, Bahrain, Qatar, and the constituent amirates of the UAE have practiced economic liberalism while maintaining political traditionalism. The Gulf states upon occasion stabilize political trends with the expulsion or threat of expulsion of troublesome noncitizens. As of 2000, nine Middle East states are republics, six are basically monarchies, and one—the UAE—is a combination.

The degree of citizen participation in government in the nine or ten republics is highly variable, and the search for legitimacy is characteristic of several republican governments in the region. Democratic processes are best represented in Israel (excluding the occupied territories), Turkey, and Cyprus, the only states in the region that generally conduct open elections with freedom for most opposition parties. Prior to its civil war, Lebanon conducted open parliamentary elections and exhibited many aspects of a laissez-faire democracy, and it has held two parliamentary elections—the latest in 1998—since the end of the fighting. Yemen has been moving haltingly toward open elections, having held parliamentary elections in 1997 as well as its first direct election for president in September 1999. Party membership or participation is limited in the other republics, so that some elections are at best of questionable authenticity. Iran has had relatively open voting since 1979, but candidates are screened for acceptability by the conservative clerics. Among the monarchies, Jordan has adopted the most progressive measures, having had probably the freest election in the Arab world when it elected its parliament in 1989. Firm pressure, although not an open revolutionary threat, moved all

other monarchies to demonstrate a more liberal stance after the Gulf crisis of 1990–1991, but meaningful progress has come slowly. In the 1960s and 1970s, advisory councils were elected by popular vote in Kuwait and Bahrain but were dismissed or threatened with dismissal by the rulers for exceeding their mandates. The ruler of Kuwait promised several broad steps toward democratization of his amirate during and soon after the Iraqi occupation in 1990–1991. Although reforms were slow and modest, the parliamentary elections scheduled for 1992 and 1996 took place on schedule and were open. No elections have ever been held in Saudi Arabia, Qatar, or Oman, although each monarch has agreed to appoint a consultative council and has made promises of greater power-sharing in the future. In the UAE, the booming and open economy and the general openness of society appear to counterbalance the lack of elections.

Such steps may appear to be small advances in the Western lexicon, but they are progress in a broader context, if they are made effective. Western democracies did not spring full-blown from their Greek model, and Middle East states similarly require time to achieve self-identity, social balance, and political maturity (see the next section). They too will periodically slip backward before they resume forward momentum. It must be noted that civil rights or human rights are denied one group or another in every country in the Middle East—including Israel, Turkey, and Cyprus.

Raison d'Être

The state idea, or its raison d'être (reason for being), is a state's basic centripetal force—the unique, distinctive idea manifested in the emergence and maintenance of a particular piece of territory and segment of humanity in a unit state.[6] As developed by Richard Hartshorne[7] the raison d'être reflects the dominance of unifying factors over divisive factors in a state, therefore the dominance of centripetal over centrifugal forces. The impact of an abstract idea on state evolution was further examined by Stephen B. Jones,[8] who traced the motivating political idea through four subsequent links: decision, movement, field, and political area (the state). Both the examination of the raison d'être and the tracing of the progress of Jones's unified field idea aid in understanding Middle East state patterns.

Many of the Middle East states were created by and delineated by outside powers in contradiction to British promises and to pre–1919 Arab aspirations and expectations in the area. These states have thus faced problems in evolving successfully within their respective contexts without an indigenous initial idea or a consensus regarding their raison d'être. Developments after 1920 brought frustrations in the mandates of Syria, Iraq, and Palestine as well as to large segments of the populations in Lebanon and Transjordan. Later independence for the mandates found them still lacking consensus on a state idea.

Formerly independent areas, on the other hand, had a traditional reason for being, which could be adapted and followed. Turkey, under Mustafa Kemal Atatürk, was clearly motivated by "Turkey for the Turks, and the Turks for Turkey!" Iran under Reza Shah had centuries of Persian culture as a core state concept. Egypt had a long history as a polity and had a rather firm sense of direction. In the south of the region, although both were ruled by benighted monarchs, Oman and Yemen also had a centuries-long sense of polity. To their north, after 1932, the tribal leader in the Arabian Peninsula, Abd al-Aziz Al Saud (Ibn Saud), developed a raison d'être for Saudi Arabia. The Middle East state with the most explicit reason for being is the region's only settler state, Israel, which extended "a national home for the Jewish people" in the Palestine mandate into an independent Jewish state. By contrast, Cyprus has not found a commonality of purpose and modality between its Greek-Cypriot majority and its Turkish-Cypriot minority. Cyprus the island consists of two de facto Cypruses as polities, although the northern "republic" has received no international recognition.

Regional Linkages

Bases for Links

A region as large and diverse as the Middle East is inevitably faced with several centrifugal forces, but it also possesses some regional centripetal forces, with Islam being the strongest unifying link. Only Israel and South Cyprus lie outside the Islamic realm (*Dar al-Islam*), with Lebanon divided. In times past, Islam has held all of the Middle East area—and more—in one Muslim empire (see Map 2-5).

Nevertheless, as in times past, localism, ethnic separatism, nationalism, religious zealotry and militancy, and the ambition of leaders disrupt unity. Turkey and Iran sharply distinguish themselves from the rest of the Muslim Middle East, but all other states also have local concerns that counterbalance regional unity. Israel does not participate in regional political institutions—indeed, it is excluded from them. Arab nationalism and Arab unity repeatedly yield to national interests and competition among state leaders, to the extent that Arab unity appears to be observed as much in the breach as in the honoring.[9]

Regional and Subregional Organizations

Nevertheless, regional cooperation, coordination, and joint action can be underestimated because of the more obvious and more publicized regional differences. Six regional agencies exemplify both the efforts to coordinate action and the difficulties in achieving effective action.

OIC.   Although it is somewhat specialized, the regional organization that embraces the largest number of Middle East states—fourteen of the sixteen, excluding only Israel and Cyprus—is the Organization of the Islamic Conference (OIC), with headquarters in Jiddah. The OIC also includes 54 other predominantly Muslim states, from Suriname in South America and Morocco and Gabon in western Africa to Brunei on Borneo, plus the Palestine Liberation Organization (PLO). Established in 1969, the

OIC has held periodic summit conferences, the latest in 1997. It is significant that this latest meeting, which signaled a lowering of the tensions between some of the Middle East Arab members and Iran, was held in Tehran. Primarily intended to promote Islamic solidarity among member states, the organization sponsors economic, cultural, and political cooperation and serves as an umbrella for several agencies serving Islamic states.

Arab League. The twelve Arab states of the sixteen countries of the region constitute the core of the total 21 members (plus the Palestinian Authority) of the League of Arab States. Although Egypt's membership was suspended when it signed the peace treaty with Israel in 1979, it was revalidated in 1990, and league headquarters were moved back to Cairo from Tunis, where they had been located for eleven years. Usually referred to as the Arab League, the organization also includes eight North African states—Mauritania, Morocco, Algeria, Tunisia, Libya, Sudan, Comoros, Somalia, and Djibouti. The Middle East Arab states initiated the league in 1945, with its center in Cairo.

The Arab League never completely succeeded in achieving the integrating role that it was designed for and that its members rhetorically claimed for it. Nevertheless, it is institutionally the most unifying of the agencies in which most Middle East countries are members, even though it includes members from well beyond the Middle East core. Despite the fact that it regularly exhibits sharp disagreement and disharmony over major issues, as it did conspicuously regarding the Gulf crisis in 1990, it is the region's best sounding board. The league maintains offices and information centers internationally and carries out many of the same activities and has many of the same difficulties as similar regional organizations. Many of the league's most important statements and actions pertain to the Arab-Israeli problem.

OPEC and OAPEC. Scores of specialized organizations deal with specific aspects of inter-Arab coordination and with Arab participation in wider organizations. Two of the best known are the Organization of Petroleum Exporting Countries (OPEC) and the Organization of Arab Petroleum Exporting Countries (OAPEC), discussed in Chapter 8. Although most of the other agencies are economic (many under the aegis of the Council of Arab Economic Unity) and deal with everything from olives to tourism, some agencies unite, for example, Arab historians, jurists, and sports activities. Other organizations have a wider membership, as does, for example, the Afro-Asian Peoples' Solidarity Organization, founded in 1957 and headquartered in Cairo.

GCC. Created in 1981, a key subregional organization is the Gulf Cooperation Council (GCC), which coordinates economic, cultural, military, and political operations among its six member states: Saudi Arabia, Kuwait, Bahrain, Qatar, the UAE, and Oman. Their main concerted interests include management of their huge oil income, common problems of development, social problems (including expatriate labor flow), Gulf trade, and—as quickly became apparent—security. Membership comprises only conservative monarchies that to some extent sought security for their regimes as well as for their respective states. The revolutionary republican neighbors of Iraq and Iran, which were at war when the GCC was formed, could be justifiably excluded; and events later—especially in 1990–1991—reinforced the policy of exclusion. A unified defense against threats from Iran and Iraq was, after all, a prime impetus for establishment of the organization. The GCC gave its members some assurance during the 1980–1988 Iran-Iraq war and played a useful role in the 1990–1991 Gulf crisis. Members established a $15 billion fund in December 1990, in the midst of the Gulf crisis, to aid friendly countries. They also agreed in April 1991 to create a lending fund of $5 billion to aid development in the private sector of Arab countries. Also known formally as the Cooperation Council for the Arab States of the Gulf, the GCC is the most successful of the regional and subregional organizations of the Middle East.

ECO. In 1964, Turkey, Iran, and Pakistan—key members in the pre–1979 Central Treaty Organization (CENTO) (see discussion in the next section)—sought common nonmilitary economic benefits in a new organization, the Regional Cooperation for Development (RCD). Financial underwriting came primarily from increasingly oil-wealthy Iran, whose shah was continuing a historic quest for Iranian hegemony in the Northern Tier and the Gulf. The RCD achieved modest success in coordinating transportation connections and practices, tourism, postal arrangements, frontier formalities, and similar affairs. It phased down after the 1979 Iranian revolution but was revived in 1985; it was renamed the Economic Cooperation Organization (ECO), and its goals were expanded. Swinging into action in 1992 to take advantage of the disintegration of the Soviet Union, it signed agreements in November incorporating the six new Muslim republics that broke away from the USSR (Azerbaijan, Kazakhstan, Kyrghyzstan, Tajikistan, Turkmenistan, and Uzbekistan) as well as Afghanistan. The ECO thus had ten members, making it the largest economic bloc after the European Economic Community (EEC).

Unions: Attempts and Failures

Although post-World War I Arab aspirations for unity in the Fertile Crescent were frustrated by Britain and France and partly by inter-Arab rivalry, Arab states attempted several subregional political mergers between the late 1950s and 1980. A major effort toward Arab unity was the United Arab Republic (UAR), in which Syria and Egypt joined in 1958 and from which Syria withdrew in 1961, although Egypt called itself the UAR for another decade. The Yemen of that time also nominally federated with the UAR in 1958 to form the short-lived United Arab States, but this alliance collapsed in 1961 after Syria withdrew.

Jordan and Iraq, ruled at the time by related Hashimite monarchs, merged briefly in the Arab Federation in 1958 to counterbalance the UAR, but this was dissolved after the overthrow of the king of Iraq the same year. The new Iraqi leader proposed a union of Iraq, Syria, and Jordan, but this plan was not accepted. Other political unity efforts have been proposed but shortly failed: the re-creation of the United Arab Republic with Egypt, Syria, and Iraq in 1963; plans for a Federation of Arab Republics with Egypt, Syria, and Libya in 1971; and a merger of Egypt and Libya in 1972. Prompted by Egyptian President Sadat's dramatic visit to Jerusalem in 1977 and the ensuing moves toward Egyptian-Israeli détente, intensive talks between Syria and Iraq during the period October 1978–June 1979 almost produced agreement for a historic union between the two Fertile Crescent states. However, the talks broke down over several points, including leadership of the resulting united state—which is often the obstacle in such negotiations.

In preparation for its withdrawal from east of Suez, Great Britain created the Federation of Arab Amirates of the South in 1959 in the Aden Protectorate, which then, with some expansion, became the Federation of South Arabia. Militant leftist actions in 1967 forced the creation of the Marxist People's Democratic Republic of Yemen, which in turn merged with North Yemen in 1990 to form the Republic of Yemen (see Chap. 19). Different though the two parts are, and despite a bloody but mercifully short civil war in 1994, the union promises to be a lasting one. It was achieved after years of love-hate deliberations, and mutual benefits are obvious. After the series of failed attempts at political union, unified Yemen became the second successful political union, at least so far, in the region.

The first successful union took place two decades earlier on the other side of the Arabian Peninsula within a quite different framework. As Britain planned its withdrawal from the Gulf, the seven Trucial States of the time discussed with Bahrain and Qatar in 1968 the formation of a Federation of Arab Amirates. However, by mid-1971, Bahrain and Qatar had each opted for independence, and the seven Trucial shaykhdoms federated in the United Arab Emirates (UAE). This extraordinary polity is the combination of seven principalities whose respective monarchs maintain their semi-sovereign realms but voluntarily join their peers in certain common political, economic, cultural, and security structures. Despite some minor frictions, the federation—instead of full union—has indeed afforded strength through cooperation and has served as a model of stability and maturity (see Chap. 18).

Alliances: Baghdad Pact

In addition to the informal alliance implied in the Arab League, regional military alliances—which sometimes involve little more than placement of military forces under one command—are formed during emergencies and then disbanded when they are over. The major impetus for such pacts has usually been a crisis between the Arab frontline states and Israel, and temporary alliances preceded the four major Arab-Israeli wars. The inclusion of some Arab states in the 1990–1991 coalition against Iraq was unusual because it mixed Arab states with outside, non-Arab states and also because it created frictions between the participating states and the rejectionist states.

The Baghdad Pact, a long-range pact involving Middle East states, was formed, with U.S.-British encouragement, in 1955 as a *cordon sanitaire* of the Northern Tier of states against Soviet expansionism. Formally termed the Middle East Treaty Organization, it initially included only Turkey and Iraq; but Britain, Pakistan, and Iran later joined. It was continually and vigorously opposed by Nasserist Egypt and its allies. Following the overthrow of the monarchy in Iraq in 1958, that country withdrew from the pact. Renamed the Central Treaty Organization, the pact was headquartered in Ankara for two decades until it disintegrated in 1979 when revolutionary Iran, and then Pakistan, withdrew.

Regional Conflicts

The Middle East has had its share of conflicts over borders, access to scarce resources, competing ideologies, leadership, and self-determination since the establishment of numerous newly independent states. Geographically, the conflicts may be across frontiers, subregional, regional, or between the region and extraregional forces.

Not all major clashes have been between sovereign governments. Some of the conflicts have been and are between nonstate organizations and states, between paramilitary forces of subnational groups, or between leaders as personalities contending for regional supremacy. Lebanon was fragmented for more than fifteen years by fighting between the PLO and Kataib, the PLO and Shiis, Druzes and Kataib, and other intergroup conflicts (see Chap. 13). The PLO also fought Jordanian forces in 1970 and has periodically battled Israeli troops and conducted guerrilla raids in Israel. Militant and extremist groups, some claiming to be acting under the banner of Islam, others from Islamist organizations, have provoked both real and exaggerated dangers. As with extremist factions everywhere, such groups constitute a tiny minority of the Muslim community and are condemned by the rational majority. During the years 1991–1997, antigovernment extremist groups in Egypt manifested their hostility by a virtual insurgency, some seeking political power, some expressing opposition to Egyptian-Israeli détente, and some demanding that the highly secular government follow their version of Islamic principles. The Muslim Brotherhood, originally an Egyptian opposition group, has been active not only in Egypt but also in Jordan and especially in Syria (see the next section). Some organizations have created internal and transnational movements, discussed later. The Baath (Arab Renaissance Party) has been influential in the Fertile Crescent states, and opposing factions of the Baath govern in Syria and Iraq. Unfortunately, before 1990, this intra-Baath dissension contributed to the failure of Syria and Iraq to take advantage of their contiguity and several common interests.

Boundary and Territorial Disputes

Most Middle East countries have disputed with at least one neighbor over territory along part of their common boundary. Usually limited to diplomatic exchanges, some disputes have provoked skirmishes, and three have provoked devastating wars.

Early Disputes. Three territorial disputes in the preindependence Fertile Crescent involved (1) inclusion of the Mosul area in the British mandate of Iraq; (2) delineation of the southern Transjordan-Arabia border; and (3) transfer of Alexandretta (Turkish, Iskenderun), located before 1938 in northwestern Syria. The first two were readily resolved, but the third echoed for several years. A 1921 accord provided that the Sanjak (subprovince) of Alexandretta, which had a large Turkish minority and port facilities desired by both Turkey and Syria, would have a special regime in France's Syrian mandate. A League of Nations compromise created a separate Republic of Hatay in 1938, and in 1939 France ceded Hatay to Turkey, in violation of mandate provisions. Syria has not entirely accepted the loss of Alexandretta, and many Syrian-made maps show both the 1936 and 1939 boundaries with Turkey.

Arabian Peninsula Boundaries. Saudi Arabia, with the largest number of immediate land neighbors in the region (seven), sought to rationalize most of its boundaries through quiet negotiations during the 1960s and 1970s, although border tensions continue with Yemen.[10] An agreement with Jordan in 1965 gave Jordan an extra 10-mile/16-km coastal strip for the expansion of its port of Aqabah in exchange for a linear inland strip of desert. Another agreement with Kuwait in 1969 divided the Arabia-Kuwait Neutral Zone—a major accord. A treaty with Iraq in 1981 divided the other Neutral Zone left from the early 1920s, the Arabian-Iraqi zone, and straightened the boundary extending westward. An agreement with Qatar in 1965, revised in 1992, defined their common boundary; and one with the UAE in 1974 defined a disputed

boundary, including a prolonged problem regarding the Buraymi Oasis. Settlement of these two boundaries was especially remarkable, since they had a long and tortured history of friction not only between the indigenous governments concerned but also between Saudi Arabia and the pre-1971 British protectors of the two amirates. Even so, final ratification of Saudi boundaries with Iraq, Qatar, and the UAE was delayed for several years, although the lines were generally accepted and were shown on the official maps of all four countries. The lines have thus been considered de facto and are so indicated on relevant maps in this book. However, because the several boundaries were registered with the UN by Saudi Arabia in 1995, they are sometimes considered to be de jure. A Saudi agreement with Oman in 1982 deferred territorial questions, but in March 1991, the two governments ratified the delimitation of their common border of more than 400 miles/ 645 km through the eastern part of the barren Rub al-Khali.

The border between Saudi Arabia and Yemen has been disputed for decades and has been particulary difficult to settle because of the multifaceted antagonism between the two governments. The 1934 Treaty of Taif succeeded in settling that relatively short segment of the boundary between Yemen and the Asir region of the Saudi kingdom, but the remaining greater part of the border continued to be disputed. The heightened hostility between the two governments after the 1990–1991 Gulf crisis further hindered agreement until talks in 1997 suggested progress. Both countries heralded the signing on June 12, 2000, of a boundary treaty covering the entire line from the coast to Oman; ratification followed in July, and demarcation of the segment not settled in 1934 is to be undertaken "in an amicable way." The improvement of general relations between Saudi Arabia and Yemen is as significant as the resolution of the boundary problem.

At least one long-standing boundary problem in Arabia Felix—over the border between the two former Yemens—was solved coincidentally with the creation of a united Yemen republic in 1990. Several other conflicts over boundaries actually involve territorial claims and are discussed in the next section.

Other Boundary and Territorial Problems. Of the four other Arabian Peninsula boundary problems that merit attention, two were resolved without great difficulty. In the south, the frontier between Oman and the former South Yemen was a venue for vicious fighting during the 1970s, but in 1992 the united Yemen readily agreed to a definitive boundary settlement, with final papers ratified in 1998. Similarly, in an announcement by Oman in 1993, the long-disputed border between Oman and the UAE was declared completely settled. In the north, Iraq and Jordan agreed in 1984 to a slight modification of their boundary to permit an exchange of small parcels of territory; this agreement is still considered to be de facto.[11] The fourth disputed boundary, that between Iraq and Kuwait, also involved Iraq's claim to the whole of Kuwait (discussed below); indeed, the Iraq-Kuwait boundary has a long and complex history. A border defined (but not marked on the ground) by an agreement between Iraq and Kuwait in 1963 was officially confirmed and meticulously demarcated by a special UN Iraq-Kuwait Boundary Demarcation Commission after Iraq was forced to withdraw from Kuwait in 1991. The commission's work and report were accepted by the UN Security Council in May 1993. Iraq first refused to accept the demarcated line, but grudgingly accepted it in November 1994; later, however, Iraq again reneged, even though the frontier is now virtually the same as the one it agreed to in 1932 and 1963.[12]

Four disputes involving irredentist territories on the Arabian Peninsula and in offshore areas became acute during the period 1961–1991.

1. Iraq bitterly denounced the British boundary delineations and territorial allotments at the head of the Gulf as soon as the political-geographical patterns were made public in 1923. The fledgling mandate had two related complaints: that its access to the Gulf was incompatibly narrow compared with the state's breadth farther north, and that the territory used to create the shaykhdom of Kuwait should have been allotted to Iraq. Iraq emphasized that this territory had officially been included in the former Ottoman province of Basrah, most of which had otherwise been allotted to the mandate of Iraq. Since former Ottoman administrative units were divided in the creation of other mandates, Iraq's claim has repeatedly been declared invalid by specialists in international law. Although Iraq declared its acceptance of the status of Kuwait when Iraq became independent in 1932, it reasserted its irredentist claims periodically, especially during the late 1930s, sometimes including threats of military action. When Kuwait became independent in 1961 and was officially no longer a British protectorate, Iraq (by then a revolutionary republic) announced plans to annex Kuwait by force; but when both Britain and the Arab League firmly resisted Iraqi claims, Iraq reiterated its acceptance of the status quo in 1963. Nevertheless, in 1973–1974, Iraq attempted once again to take a part of Kuwait, at least the two islands of Warba and Bubiyan, in order to expand its outlet to the Gulf; but, as before, it dropped its claims and withdrew its forces.[13] Therefore, Saddam Husayn's military threat to invade Kuwait in August 1990 did not at that time appear to pose the imminent grave danger that in retrospect might have seemed obvious. Relevant aspects of the Gulf war of 1990–1991 are covered later in this chapter.

2. In 1968, with the approach of Britain's withdrawal from the lower Gulf states, Iran moved to fill the impending vacuum and definitively to affirm Iranian dominance in the Gulf, reasserting its old claims to Bahrain as Iran's "fourteenth province," as well as to several small islands in the southern Gulf. However, in 1970 the shah accepted the finding of the United Nations that Bahrainis preferred

independence, and he renounced further claims to Bahrain.

3. Iranian claims in the south were successful. On November 30, 1971, the day before Britain withdrew from the Gulf, Iran occupied three islands in the lower Gulf that had long been understood to belong to Sharjah and Ras al-Khaymah, asserting that it required the islands in order to protect the Strait of Hormuz. Accords regarding one of the islands, Abu Musa—well away from the strait and appreciably closer to Sharjah than to Iran—included agreement that income from oil production on or around Abu Musa would be divided between Iran and Sharjah. In 1992, Iran tightened its control of Abu Musa by restricting access to the island, an action protested by the UAE. The other two islands, Greater Tunb and Lesser Tunb, at the Gulf end of the Strait of Hormuz, had been considered to be under Ras al-Khaymah's sovereignty before 1970, but Iran occupied them as well prior to the independence of the proposed United Arab Emirates.[14]

4. A long-festering dispute between Bahrain and Qatar also involves island territory. Because of its early connections with western Qatar, the ruling family of Bahrain claims the small island of Hawar and the Dibal and Jarada shoals off Qatar's western coast. Though seemingly minor, the dispute has had serious ramifications: Qatar took its case to the International Court of Justice in 1996, and the case was still in adjudication in late 1999.

The Gulf has also presented problems regarding maritime boundaries on the continental shelf of this semienclosed sea. As offshore oil discoveries pushed farther into the mid-Gulf from both sides, definition of maritime boundaries became essential. International discussions on the Law of the Sea at that time supplied possible solutions, and several median lines in the central Gulf, as opposed to the north and south, were agreed upon and surveyed in the late 1950s

and the 1960s. Complexities regarding the lines among Iran, Iraq, Kuwait, and the now-divided Neutral Zone have delayed final agreement in the north, as have similar problems among the amirates and Iran in the south. Considering the amounts of oil beneath the Gulf and the potential for confrontation, agreements have been reached relatively promptly, and nonagreed-upon lines have caused few difficulties.[15]

Another continental shelf dispute is under way in the northwestern corner of the Middle East, where the question concerns location of a median line in the Aegean Sea between Turkey and Greece. Since Greece exercises sovereignty over the large islands just off the western coast of Asia Minor, a basic median line would seem to belong between the islands and the mainland. However, such a division would extend Greek Exclusive Economic Zone rights over the entire Aegean Sea, including all potential offshore petroleum resources—a division that Turkey has declared it cannot accept.

The conflict over the Aegean partition is heightened by the Greek-Turkish split over Cyprus (see Chap. 13). Since both Turkey and Greece are members of the North Atlantic Treaty Organization and must otherwise be encouraged to be peaceful neighbors, the prospect of military action between them over the Aegean or Cyprus is of grave concern to the Atlantic community. Talks under UN auspices, as well as under U.S. and EU good offices, have kept passions in check; some warming of relations evolved from mutual assistance following earthquakes in both countries in 1999. The dispute has simmered for many years, however, and will not be easily resolved (Fig. 11-2).

Finally, the median line/thalweg river boundary down the Shatt al-Arab between Iraq and Iran has been a matter of dispute and then of warfare between these two riparian states, as is discussed in detail later in this chapter.

Hydro-Geopolitics

The natural resource of petroleum, a physical-geographical element, has been a major factor in the shaping of internal and external political

FIGURE 11-2   Signs of bitterness at the dividing line between north and south in Cyprus: Greek Cypriots use irony to condemn the Turkish occupation of the north *(top)* to those leaving the south to visit the north, while a few meters away Turkish Cypriots welcome visitors *(bottom)* with "Turkish Republic of Northern Cyprus FOREVER" and, in the smaller sign, "Welcome to TRNC. You are now entering the sovereign republic of North Cyprus."

relations of countries of the Middle East. Similarly, the availability, management, and sharing of the natural resource of water are, and increasingly will be, factors in the political geography of the area that are beginning to surpass petroleum in import. Petroleum is a valuable economic resource; water is essential to life itself.

With great population increases in many countries of the Middle East, maximal use of water resources has become epidemic. Rivers, because of their transnational character, automatically become subjects of international concern. Egypt, with its explosive population growth, has seen the water in the Nile—with its sources in Ethiopia and the Sudan—decrease in recent decades. Exploitation of Tigris and Euphrates water by the three riparian states has dramatically increased since the 1960s. Such exploitation has been on an especially grand scale in Turkey's Southeast Anatolia Project (GAP), including the great Atatürk Dam on the Euphrates, for generation of electric power and for planned irrigation of millions of acres of land in southeastern Turkey (see Chap. 21). This large-scale use of Euphrates and Tigris water by Turkey obviously diminishes the downstream flow in both Syria and Iraq. Syria's Jazirah Project, with its core facility of the Euphrates (al-Thawrah) Dam, calls for irrigation of hundreds of thousands of acres in the Euphrates Valley and Jazirah and has also decreased the Euphrates flow downstream for Iraq. Turkey, Iraq, and Syria met in Ankara in June 1990 to discuss arrangements for sharing Euphrates and Tigris water, but no agreements were reached. Iraq's aggressions in 1990, as well as tensions between Syria and Turkey over Kurdish activities, caused meaningful progress in the water-sharing process to be forestalled during the 1990s. In a wholly internal problem, Saudi Arabia overused ground water to achieve self-sufficiency in wheat production for several years. The water table dropped by 7 or 8 ft./2.1 or 2.4 m before irrigation was reduced.

Control over access to the Jordan, Yarmuk, and Litani rivers and to underground aquifers played a significant role in the Israeli policy of control of the Golan Heights, southern Lebanon, and the occupied West Bank and Gaza (Palestinian Authority in part of the West Bank after the mid-1990s).

Talks that began in Moscow at the end of January 1992 as part of the Arab-Israeli peace process emphasized water-sharing agreements as one of the central issues, but despite successive agreements, such water negotiations made slow progress. The nine states of the Nile Basin discussed regional cooperation in Cairo in June 1990, and the United Nations Economic Commission for Africa and the UN Development Program are providing auspices for group water projects. Thus, initial steps have been taken toward water-sharing protocols, but the real problems have yet to be addressed.

Two international conventions apply in these discussions, but they are contrary to prevailing international law. According to the Helsinki Rules of 1966 and a UN 1972 convention, water rights are to be shared according to population and need, with historical allocations to be kept in mind; however, international law acknowledges the absolute sovereignty of states over the resources they control. Unless meaningful regional and international agreements can be reached regarding fair allocations of these river waters among the riparians, the national ambitions for development and the growing demands for water by the steadily increasing populations will inevitably lead to more rancor over water use in the Middle East.[16] Details of the several national projects and the problems involved in this increasingly crucial issue are discussed in relevant country chapters in Part 2.

Religious and Ideological Conflicts

The Role of Religion. Religious movements have periodically had strong impacts on part or all of the Middle East, and they remain important in the geopolitical equation of the Middle East today. Islam originally emerged as a theocracy, and religion and politics—"church and state"—are congenitally linked in the Muslim concepts. The extreme politicization of Islam is divisive among Muslims and creates some of the sharpest cleavages in the region. As is true in many so-called religious conflicts, the real discord often arises from national political hostilities, economic competition, ethnolinguistic and cultural dissensions, territorial disputes, and outside interference, which are then exacerbated by religious cleavages.

Such merging of religious and other discords may be seen in several of the current struggles between different religious groups in the Middle East. A closer look at the conflict "between Jews and Muslims" quickly reveals the territorial, political, and cultural bases for the hostility, plus showing that the fundamental hostility is between Zionists and their opponents, including many Christians. The fifteen-year civil war in Lebanon, "between Christians and Muslims," was driven as much by dominant-group economic-cultural discrimination and competition as by religion. The religious component in the revolutionary activities of the Shiis in Lebanon and elsewhere is overridden by economic disadvantages and partly by Iranian nationalism.

Modernization in most of the Middle East since about 1960 has caused social stresses that call attention to the inadequacies of modern industrialized culture, and major groups of Middle Easterners have opted for their own religious-political framework, Islam—a choice that has had an impact on Israel and Cyprus as well as on the Islamic states. In some Arab states, organizations such as the Muslim Brotherhood (Ikhwan al-Muslimun), established in Egypt in 1929 to urge a return to conservative Islam, have received new impetus. Numerous other "fraternities" (*jamaats*) emphasizing various lines of action have appeared in Egypt and Fertile Crescent countries, and many of these organizations advocate revolutionary and antigovernment positions. In advocating the rejection of modern trends and a return to traditional Islam, most fundamentalists in Arab states also reject the Arab socialism (but not the pan-Arabism)

that was advocated by Nasser of Egypt and other Arab leaders of the 1950s and 1960s.

Called to the world's attention by the Iranian revolution of 1978–1979, the Islamic fundamentalist movement was a major regional dynamic in the late 1970s and after. Although it embodies a strong religious element, the movement is also a religion/ideology that combines expressions of the regional mood. This mood includes rejection of Western secular influences and of Western political modalities and reassertion of traditional Islamic values and religious-political relationships. Islamic fundamentalism became both cause and effect in radical political developments in the Middle East after the early 1970s. Extremists such as the late Ayatollah Khomeini have used it as banner and weapon, frightening less radical neighbors and opponents. Such rejection of Western influences is mirrored by "demonization" of Islamic influences in the West—making Islamic fundamentalism a target and a scapegoat for anti-Arab and anti-Islamic sentiment. Religious conservatism has also found expression in Israel, where religious differences within the Jewish population have become increasingly divisive. No less than radical Muslim fundamentalists have manipulated their religion, extremist Jews have exploited various aspects of Judaism to justify self-serving actions against both the Israeli government and Arabs, especially in the occupied territories (see Chap. 15).

Arabism in the Region. "Arabism" is partly an outgrowth of the regional identification of Arabism with Islam and partly a product of anticolonial nationalism and self-determination in the decades preceding World War II. Various unifying movements developing from Arabism have been the ideological dynamics that have matched those of religion. The linguistic and cultural homogeneity among the peoples of the Arab Middle East has generated strong emotional linkages among the Arab societies of the region and among Arab political systems. However, these emotional links have not translated into meaningful or sustained congruity or solidarity and certainly not into a unified polity, despite verbal expressions of Islamic and Arab unity.

Successful or not, the ties display slightly different emphases but are categorized under such names as Arabism, Arab nationalism, Arab solidarity, Arab unity, and, earlier, Arab socialism. Under some circumstances, the sense of Arab identity transcends nationalism of individual states and actuates joint stances on the basis of Arab kinship.[17] Under other circumstances, differing interpretations of Arab identity have engendered intense conflict among Arab states. Consensus is of almost mystical significance to Arabs, but in political crises consensus among Arab states is often little more than a noncommittal gesture. Even so, by the late 1990s, relations among Middle East Arab states had become more pragmatic, particularly after the Gulf crisis of 1990–1991, with national interests often being given precedence over ideology.

From outside the "Arab system," the impact of Iranian Shii fundamentalism has stimulated self-examination. Also outside the Arab system, Turkey has faced a similar sequence of developments, with internal ideological conflicts between secular and Islamic orientations. Nationalism, clashing ideological positions, and religious divisions have also caused internal conflict in Israel.

The Arab-Israeli Problem

Among the problems in global geopolitical relations of the post-World War II era, the conflict between Arabs and Israelis is exceptionally intractable. It is unique in its profound regional impact, its worldwide ramifications, its great-power involvement, and its emotional associations. It has many facets: ethnic confrontation, conflicting historical-territorial claims, religious implications, ethical dilemmas, and political and geopolitical impacts. It also has many perspectives, with the two main contenders fragmented into many subperspectives.[18] From any

MAP 11-3   Political-geographical setting of the Arab-Israeli problem, showing the territories directly involved in the conflict.

perspective, the problem and its ramifications have caused a tragic number of casualties, prolonged human suffering, extensive physical destruction, and explosive divisiveness as well as retardation of development and a waste of human and other resources in the area. This study emphasizes the essentially geographical basis of the conflict, with "geographical" including the human factor. Indeed, most similar clashes likewise have geographical bases (Map 11-3).

The modern conflict began with the increasing spirit of nationalism among many groups of the late nineteenth century, including Jews in Europe and Arabs in the Middle East. Jewish nationalism evolved especially after 1880 as Zionism, the aspiration to establish a Jewish polity in "Zion," named after a hill in Jerusalem but extended to the area of Palestine. Zionism expanded in area and influence until, with support from several sources, it achieved a Jewish state in Palestine in 1948. By contrast, Arab nationalism developed in regional isolation, focused on local problems—of which Palestine was only one—and was weakened by colonial influences that fragmented and frustrated its aims and methods. Some aspects of the background to the problem are included in Chapters 2, 6, and 15; a few highlights and twentieth-century developments are discussed in this section.

As Jews in late nineteenth-century Europe achieved equality in European society, many of them began seeking a national identity similar to that of the Germans, French, and British. They joined in common efforts to achieve self-determination and group liberation, all according to the concepts of the Enlightenment. Jewish nationalism combined with secularism to direct Jewish attention to the Land of Israel (Eretz Yisrael) as a territorial base for a revived Jewish nation. Leaders emphasized links between Jews in the Diaspora (dispersion) and the Land of Israel and also focused on the perception of Jews as a minority "in exile," not just a religious group. The leaders encouraged the revival of Hebrew, which, having served for centuries as a liturgical language, was to be the literary and colloquial medium of Jewish-Hebrew nationalism.

Evolution of Zionism

In the early 1880s, pogroms against Jews in eastern Europe engendered a movement, Hovevei Tzion (Lovers of Zion), which called for the migration of Jews to Palestine. The movement was institutionalized by Theodor Herzl, a Hungarian Jewish journalist, who came to believe, after covering the Dreyfus affair in France,[19] that Jews must achieve self-determination by having their own state. In 1896 he published *Der Judenstaat* [The Jews State], which called for an independent state for Jews; in 1897 he organized the First Zionist Congress.

At a meeting of the congress in Basel, Switzerland, Herzl founded the World Zionist Organization (WZO), which became the instrument of Jewish nationalism and is still the focal organization for support for the state of Israel. Herzl directed Jewish and world attention to

Zionism, and many other movements and organizations evolved as vehicles to support Jewish efforts and channel people to Palestine. A leading Zionist encouraged his co-workers to "make Jewish Palestine the mother country of world Jewry, with Jewish communities in the Diaspora as the colonies—and not the reverse."[20]

The WZO and subsidiary organizations attracted Jewish settlers to the Ottoman provincial area of Palestine and enlisted the support of world Jewry for Jewish nationalist aims. In Jones's "Unified Field Theory," mentioned earlier, Zionism is the idea that led through decision and movement over a world field to the Palestine area. One Zionist writer encouraged immigration for "a people without a land for a land without people"[21] in 1901—when more than 400,000 Palestinian Arabs lived in Palestine. Nevertheless, even against Ottoman opposition, the settler effort proceeded, and immigrants outnumbered the indigenous Arabs within three decades after the initiation of the serious drive for a Jewish national home. Colonists immigrated for various reasons, but the predominant objective was to establish a modern, secular, socialist state to serve as a national territorial base for Jews, not as practitioners of Judaism but as a people.

The Balfour Declaration

World War I offered opportunities for Zionist leaders to lay the practical groundwork for a Jewish state. Of the World War I British pronouncements already mentioned, the Balfour Declaration deserves a closer look because of its crucial role.

With change of territorial control in the Middle East imminent by 1917, British Zionists pressed the British government to announce official support for the establishment of a Jewish state in Palestine. Zionists emphasized that such a statement would attract the support of Jews in Germany and would rally Jews in the United States to urge that country to join the Allies against Germany. After intensive lobbying on both sides of the Atlantic, Britain issued the

MAP 11-4   The territorial evolution of Israel, from Palestinian mandate to contemporary state with occupied territories. See also Map 11-5.

one-sentence Balfour Declaration on November 2, 1917:

> His Majesty's Government view with favour the establishment in Palestine of a national home for the Jewish people, and will use their best endeavours to facilitate the achievement of this object, it being clearly understood that nothing shall be done which may prejudice the civil and religious rights of existing non-Jewish communities in Palestine, or the rights and political status enjoyed by Jews in any other country.

This sentence, with its two conflicting parts, was as internally contradictory as were Britain's several wartime pronouncements. Its first phrase changed the course of the history of the Middle East.[22]

World War I through World War II

A 1922 British White Paper significantly clarified British intentions regarding the Balfour Declaration. The paper stated that the declaration, although it was a basic factor in the establishment of the Palestine mandate (Map 11-4A), did not intend that Palestine as a whole should be converted into a Jewish national home, nor that Palestine was to become a wholly Jewish polity, nor that the declaration contemplated the "disappearance or subordination" of the indigenous Arab population or its culture. It also repeated that Britain regarded Palestine as excluded from the area of Arab independence contemplated in the Husayn-McMahon correspondence. The organization and momentum of the Zionists, inflow of Jewish settlers (especially refugees from Nazi Germany), systematic purchase of prime agricultural land by the Jewish National Fund (JNF), and increasing support of Zionism by world Jewry combined to create favorable conditions for the emergence of the Jewish state called for by Herzl in 1896 and 1897.

Assurances by the British and French in November 1918 that they would establish in Greater Syria and Mesopotamia "national governments that drew their authority from the initiative and free choice of the native populations" were ignored by the British mandate government, as were declarations in Wilson's Fourteen Points and in the Covenant of the League of Nations. The Palestinian Arabs and their neighboring Arab supporters found that Zionist influence in London and Jerusalem negated Arab influence and that only the first half of the Balfour Declaration was being applied. Arab violence followed.

As early as 1919 and 1920, Palestinian Arabs attacked Jewish settlers in attempts to forestall further Zionist colonization. Periodic Arab forays evoked Jewish counterattacks and the formation of Zionist defense forces, since settlers claimed that the protection given them by British forces and mandate police was inadequate. Whereas Jewish efforts were highly organized, Arab efforts were fragmented and disorganized, partly because the Arab leaders were divided. The cycle of violence had begun and was to recur at least until the end of the century. As successive outbreaks made clear, a given act of violence and the retaliation by any party was virtually never an isolated, singular occurrence but nearly always an eruption of accumulated frustrations, grievances, and rage.

Progressive land purchases by the Jewish National Fund not only increased Jewish land-holdings but also displaced increasing numbers of Palestinian fellahin (farmers) and their families. The worst Arab-Jewish fighting of the first fifteen mandate years occurred in August 1929, when, after ten days of mutual provocations and rioting, an Arab attack killed 59 Jews in Hebron, causing the Jews to abandon that city until 1967. General strikes and virtual rebellion by the Arabs against both British and Jews broke out in 1936. Partly in response to British consideration of the partition of Palestine and partly because of events in neighboring areas, the violence upsurged periodically until the outbreak of World War II in 1939. Zionist leaders were able to exert greater pressure against both the Arabs and the British administrators as the Jewish population increased and as the Zionists gained support because of the brutality of the Hitler regime.

Even before the end of World War II, Jewish extremists conducted terrorist campaigns to seize control of Palestine from the British mandatory authorities. At the end of the war, Zionist recruiters in war-torn Europe facilitated the movement of Jewish refugees into Palestine to become both fighters for the emergence of a Jewish state and settlers in that state. Efforts by the British mandatory officials to maintain some control over the immigration into Palestine were unsuccessful and exacerbated attacks by Jewish extremists. A climactic terrorist attack on the British on July 22, 1946, blew up government offices in the King David Hotel in Jerusalem. Conducted by the Jewish terrorist group Irgun Zvai Leumi, under the command of Menachem Begin (prime minister of Israel 1977–1983), the blast killed 91 British, Jews, and Arabs. The attack is considered by many observers as the initial use of classic terrorism in Palestine.

The Emergence of Israel

War weary and frustrated, Britain announced in 1947 that it intended to relinquish the mandate and leave the future of Palestine to the United Nations, successor to the League of Nations. Not only fatigued after their years of engagement in World War II, the British were also tired of the 30-year quandary they had been in because of their obligations to various parties in the Palestine problem. They clashed with both Jews and Arabs. Zionist pressure came from every direction, including the United States, with President Truman demanding that 100,000 Jews be admitted immediately to Palestine. Arabs demanded that the British keep their promises to the indigenous Palestinians.

As the British prepared to depart, the United Nations Special Committee on Palestine (UNSCOP) drew up a proposed plan for the partition of Palestine. The United Nations voted for the plan in November 1947, with U.S. pressure making a crucial difference in the vote. Although the plan was not put into effective operation, its provisions still have a certain juridical force and still retain importance.

The UN Partition Plan called for three entities: A Jewish state was to have 56 percent of mandate Palestine; an Arab state was to have 43 percent; and a small enclave comprising Jerusalem was to be a UN-administered, internationalized zone (Map 11-4B). It is of signal importance that Jerusalem and its environs were, therefore, to be a *corpus separatum* ("separate entity"), accessible to all faiths and peoples but belonging to neither Arabs nor Jews (Fig. 11-3). Theoretically based on ethnic distribution, the proposed political-geographical jigsaw reflected the difficulties of equitably partitioning the mandate territory. Zionists resented not receiving endorsement for a Jewish state in the whole of Palestine in accordance with their singular interpretation of the Balfour Declaration. Other critics of the plan pointed to its partiality for the suggested Jewish state, which received 56 percent of mandate Palestine although Jews made up only one-third of the population and owned only about 7 percent of the land. The proposed boundaries would have included 407,000 Arabs in the Jewish state and 10,000 Jews in the Arab state, as well as 142,000 Jews and 68,000 Arabs in the internationalized district of Jerusalem.

The Arabs, relying on the principle that a mandate territory could not legally be alienated from the indigenous population, rejected the proposed surrender of over half of their Palestinian homeland to a settler people. Besides, they felt sure that they could, by force if necessary, prevent actual establishment of the Jewish state. The Zionists accepted the territorial proposal. Not only was it generous in its award of territory to the Jews, it also implied UN recognition of legitimacy for the Zionist assumption of sovereignty over half of Palestine. Jews and Arabs engaged in preliminary fighting, sometimes sweeping British forces into the conflict.

The Zionist leadership in Palestine proclaimed the new independent state of Israel, without mention of boundaries, immediately upon British relinquishment of the mandate and withdrawal of troops on May 14, 1948. At the same time, contiguous Arab states and Iraq sent military units into Palestine to aid their fellow Arabs, the Palestinians. Only the British-trained Jordanians and Iraqis held their ground in the highlands. After several months of alternating fighting and cease-fires, other Arab troops were defeated by the better armed, motivated, and organized Israelis.

Israel then controlled not only all of the area allotted the Jewish state in the Partition Plan but also half of the territory allotted the Arab state. The Jordan Arab Legion, with Iraqi troops on its right flank, held the highlands to the north, south, and east of Jerusalem, and the Egyptians held the short, narrow strip northeast of the Sinai that came to be known as the Gaza Strip. Jerusalem was divided between Jordan and Israel, with Jordan holding the Old City and most of the holy sites along with the rest of the West Bank.

Territorial Phases

Theoretically, Israel became an independent state in May 1948 within the borders defined in the UN Partition Plan (Map 11-4B). However, more long-lasting borders resulted from the fact that the battlefronts at the end of the 1948–1949 fighting became the "cease-fire

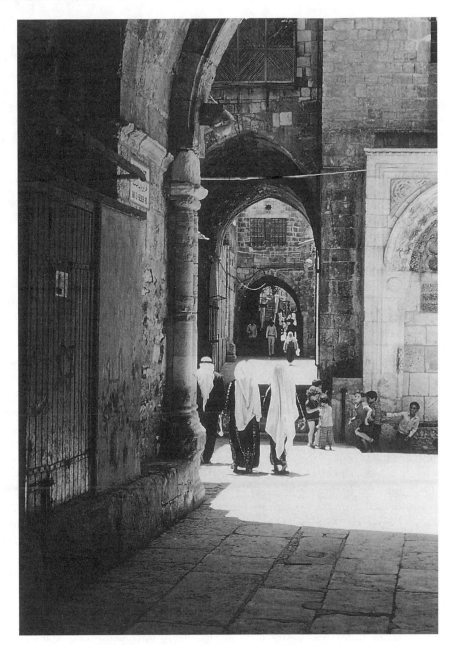

FIGURE 11-3   This view from the Haram al-Sharif, which includes the Dome of the
Rock, looks from arch to arch along the corridors of time in the heart of the Old City of
Jerusalem.

lines," negotiated by a UN mediator. These lines, which expanded Israel's original area by 50 percent, became and still are the de facto boundaries of Israel (Map 11-4C). Even with Jordan holding the eastern sector of Jerusalem, including the Old City, Israel unilaterally declared Jerusalem as its national capital in 1950. The declaration was pronounced invalid by the United Nations, on the basis that the original Partition Plan had designated

Jerusalem as a *corpus separatum* under UN administration. Israel also seized the Sinai during the Israeli-British-French assault on Suez in 1956, creating a short-lived third territorial phase. The young state occupied the Sinai for several months but later evacuated it under international pressure, especially from the United States.

The fourth phase of Israel's territorial evolution began after the Six-Day War (or June War) in 1967, which resulted in Israeli occupation of the Sinai, Gaza Strip, West Bank, and the southwestern corner of Syria, the Golan Heights (Map 11-4D). Seizure of the West Bank reunited the city of Jerusalem, a major Israeli goal, and Israel also extended the metropolitan boundaries of East Jerusalem and unilaterally annexed the entire area to the state of Israel. On the basis of a 1980 declaration by the Israeli parliament, the Knesset, Israel still insists that Jerusalem is its eternal capital, never to be surrendered or divided, but only a few small states have recognized that claim, and all major embassies are located in Tel Aviv. The U.S. Congress, urged by domestic pressure groups, has attempted to force the administration to move the American Embassy to Jerusalem; the administration has so far resisted the effort.

Israel's fourth territorial phase continued from mid-1967 until the beginning of Israel's step-by-step withdrawal from the western part of the Sinai under agreements reached through mediation by U.S. Secretary of State Henry Kissinger. The Kissinger mediation was conducted after Egypt and Syria attacked Israelis in occupied Sinai and occupied Golan in 1973, a conflict called by Israel the Yom Kippur War and by Arabs the Ramadan War. Israel's withdrawal from the Sinai continued under new accords reached in the 1978 Camp David negotiations and after the Egyptian-Israeli peace treaty of 1979. Completion of the evacuation of the Sinai, except for the Taba enclave, took place in 1982 (Map 11-4E). Taba remained in dispute between Egypt and Israel until it was awarded to Egypt in late 1988 by binding arbitration.

A debatable fifth phase began in 1981 when Israel declared its annexation of the Golan Heights, a unilateral annexation not recognized by any other country. Negotiations between the new Israeli government and Syria over Golan and normalization of relations that were under way in early 2000 were soon suspended. A possible sixth phase might be identified as a consequence of the Israeli invasion of Lebanon in 1978 and June 1982. Although most Israeli forces were withdrawn during 1983 and 1984, Israel continued to maintain heavily fortified control, begun in 1978, of a 440-mile^2/1,140-km^2 so-called "security zone" just north of its border with Lebanon. To take the brunt of the patrolling, a proxy South Lebanese Army (SLA) of 3,000 mixed Lebanese was organized, trained, armed, paid, and supplied by Israel. The zone was used to match Israel's control from the air with control of southern Lebanon from the ground and to attempt to prevent rocket attacks and infiltration of northern Israel from the area. After 22 years of loss of Israeli young men (more than 900), mounting protest at home, of criticism from abroad, and of increasingly effective and costly resistance by Hizballah and other guerrillas, Israel indicated in mid-1999 its intention unilaterally to withdraw from Lebanon a year later. It actually withdrew in May 2000.

First called by the Israelis "occupied territories," then "administered territories," then simply "territories," four areas—the West Bank, Gaza Strip, Golan Heights, and Sinai—were under Israeli military government from 1967 until the Sinai was evacuated and the Golan Heights annexed.

The West Bank and East Jerusalem remain the territorial core—but not the only territorial aspect—of the Arab-Israeli conflict, globally as well as locally. Palestinian Arabs declare their determination to remain in this area of Palestine; Israelis show their equal determination to control the land and settle it as they did on the plains of Palestine. One of the most controversial aspects of the Arab-Israeli problem has been the program of Jewish settlement and displacement of Arab inhabitants in the remaining occupied territories (see Chap. 15). Clashes occurred periodically, until young Palestinians rose up in a citizens' rebellion in Gaza and the West Bank beginning in December 1987. The *intifadah* ("uprising") involved frequent confrontations between Israeli soldiers and rock-throwing Palestinian youths demonstrating against 26 years of military occupation, humiliation, and increasing Israeli settlements. Unlike earlier ephemeral demonstrations, the *intifadah* became a sustained outlet of frustration that continued despite admittedly ruthless repression by the Israeli army. By maintaining their zeal, the resistance gained confidence and pride and achieved a greater sense of direction and organization. One outgrowth of this sense of organization was the emergence of Hamas (see glossary). Although the intensity of the *intifadah* diminished after four years, it had achieved goals where other efforts had failed. Furthermore, its demands coincided with and complemented the realization by the coalition partners in the 1990–1991 Gulf crisis that a genuine peace process must be initiated. The *intifadah* subsided after the initiation of the peace process in 1991 and ended with the Israeli-Palestinian accord in Gaza in September 1993. By that time, 1,119 Palestinians had been killed by Israeli soldiers or civilians, and more than 100,000 wounded or injured; 124 Israeli soldiers and civilians had also been killed.[23]

The Palestinians

Although Palestinians are primarily refugees, they may be grouped geographically into six categories: those who stayed in the areas taken over by Israel in 1948–1949; those who stayed in the West Bank and Gaza; those who fled the areas incorporated into Israel in 1948–1949 and became refugees in adjoining districts (West Bank and Gaza) that were later occupied by Israel; those who fled to the East Bank between 1947 and the present (Jordan conferred citizenship on them); those who fled into adjoining countries and have remained there; and those who immigrated to other countries.

Even before the outbreak of full-scale fighting on May 15, 1948, Palestinian Arabs had lost the initiative to the better organized, motivated, and equipped Zionist fighters, and thousands of Palestinians had fled from areas in which Arabs and Jews were fighting for land and military advantage. They had been especially terrified by the massacre of 254 villagers in Deir Yassin, near Jerusalem, by Jewish forces on April 9, 1948, that was widely reported in order to panic the Arabs. After mid-May, the thousands of refugees became hundreds of thousands as Israeli military units gained momentum.

By the time the 1948–1949 fighting had subsided, approximately 800,000 (official estimates vary from 720,000 to 960,000) Palestinians had fled or been expelled from their homes and lands in the areas taken over by Israeli forces. These watershed events in Middle East and world history are designated by the Arabs as *al-nakbah*, "the catastrophe." Although versions of the events surrounding the origin of the Palestinian refugee saga differ widely, the differences have been narrowed by the "New Historians." After studying newly available documentation in the mid-1980s, this group of Israeli scholars have written that inter alia the panicking and expulsion of the Palestinians was more deliberate and common than had been admitted. The New History has been widely accepted.[24] (Also discussed in Chap. 15.) The largest numbers sought refuge in the hill country of central Palestine, and many continued across the Jordan River into the Kingdom (former mandate) of Transjordan. Others crowded into the southwestern corner of Palestine that later became the Gaza Strip, and still others fled to Lebanon and Syria. About 160,000 Arabs, most of them in Galilee, refused to evacuate their lands and homes and stayed in the new Jewish state. These "Israeli Arabs" have increased to constitute about 20 percent (1.15 million) of the population in Israel at the end of the century.

The refugees assumed that they would return home in a few days or weeks when the fighting ceased. As it became clear after the 1949 cease-fire that the Israelis would not allow the Palestinians to return to their homes, the United Nations created the United Nations Relief and Works Agency (UNRWA) to administer emergency care to the refugees. UNRWA set up more than 50 camps in and around the concentrations of homeless Palestinians: Gaza, the West Bank, East Bank Jordan (especially around Amman), southern and central Lebanon (especially around Beirut), and Syria. Although UNRWA aid permitted only a marginal existence, it sustained— and continues to sustain—thousands of refugees in the 59 camps, including the ten extra ones it set up after 1967, that the agency administered in its area of operations in 2000. Not all refugees, of course, have been forced to call the camps home. Those with professional skills or sufficient funds generally neither registered with UNRWA nor resided in camps.

The status of the refugees within their host countries is varied: Only Jordan has extended full citizenship to the refugees; Syria has extended equal rights (except the right to passports) but maintained strict control; and Lebanon, while accepting the Palestinians originally, feared the impact on the country's internal balance between Christians and Muslims and after 1972 fought them militarily. The Lebanese government has officially declared its intention to refuse permanent settlement of the refugees in Lebanon. Some Arab countries received only limited numbers of Palestinians. Many refugees have rejected integration into their host country's economy and society, deliberately maintaining their refugee status as a symbol of determination to return to their homeland and regain their patrimony.

After Israel seized the Golan Heights, West Bank, Gaza Strip, and the Sinai in 1967 (Map 11-5), more than 116,000 original Palestinian refugees were again uprooted, mostly from the West Bank. As 100,000 new refugees (referred to as "displaced persons" by UNRWA) fled across the Jordan River to the East Bank, 99,000 Syrians from the Golan Heights fled deeper into Syria and 35,000 Bedouins and villagers in the Sinai fled across the Suez Canal. (As with the earlier figures, these are estimates.) Thousands of the original Palestinian refugees who had gone to southern Lebanon fled again from their camps and villages as a result of Israeli incursions into southern Lebanon after 1969, especially after the Israeli invasion of 1982.

Whereas unskilled Palestinian refugees could find only menial jobs or no employment outside the UNRWA camps, large numbers of educated Palestinians have done well in their host countries, and many were significantly involved in the development of the Gulf states. Beirut became a center of Palestinian intellectual activity, Amman a demographic center, and Kuwait a center of Palestinian commercial activity. However, the role of Palestinians in Beirut diminished as the fighting in Lebanon continued into the late 1980s; and, more notably, of the approximately 350,000 Palestinians in Kuwait before the Iraqi invasion, fewer than 30,000 remained in 2000. Partly because of changing economic conditions but also because of altered political and social environments, the geographical distribution of Palestinian populations throughout the Middle East changed appreciably after the Iraqi occupation of Kuwait.

Palestinians categorized in the seven geographical groups mentioned earlier may also be divided into four categories according to their status as refugees: (1) All Palestinians, (2) Palestinians who are registered refugees from the 1948–49 fighting (under specific UNRWA criteria), (3) "displaced persons" who first fled Palestinian territory in the 1967 war; and (4) Palestinians living in official UNRWA camps— about one-third of the registered refugees. Among these several groupings and their geographical distribution, differences in enumeration inevitably arise.[25]

Generally accepted estimates in 1999 give a world total of 7.9 million Palestinians. Of these, 2.9 million, by Palestinian Authority census, reside in the West Bank (including Jerusalem) and Gaza; 1.15 million in Israel proper; 2.3 million in Jordan; 380,000 in Syria; 375,000 in Lebanon; 400,000 in other Middle East countries (less than half the pre-1991 number); and 450,000 elsewhere.

As the years dragged on after 1949 and the Palestinians saw little evidence that they or their problems were receiving significant attention in the world councils, they sought some organized approaches to their problems. One major group, founded in 1958, was Fatah (the

MAP 11-5 Territories occupied by Israel in 1967 and, except for the Gaza Strip, still partly occupied in early 2000, although negotiations were in progress over the Golan and additional areas in the West Bank to be evacuated by Israeli forces. Jewish settlements in the West Bank are updated in Chapter 15.

name is the reverse acronym for *Harakat al-Tahrir al-Filastiniyah,* Palestinian Liberation Movement). It conducted guerrilla raids by fedayeen (literally "sacrificers") into Israel from neighboring countries. Not until 1964 did a broad-based Palestinian organization emerge that had as its goal the recovery of the Palestinian homeland.

This was the Palestine Liberation Organization (PLO), which gradually gained a major but highly controversial role in Palestinian and Middle East affairs, especially after Yasser Arafat became its chairman in 1969. After the late 1960s, the PLO evolved into an extensive and complex institution with a broad range of units that included not only guerrilla groups—some of whose earlier terrorist activities gave the PLO

its often unfavorable image—but also several welfare agencies serving Palestinian refugees. Using Jordan as its first base, it demonstrated its military buildup and assurance by creating a "state within a state." King Husayn, having shown his sympathy for Palestinians and their cause for many years, was alarmed at the growing and overt aggressiveness of the PLO; in September 1970, he fought a short but bloody war to break the PLO's hold in Jordan. The event became "Black September" to the Palestinian guerrilla movement. Seeking another base in a country bordering its enemy territory, the PLO moved its center of operations to Lebanon, which, unlike Syria and Egypt, was too disunited to resist. In 1974, Arab governments recognized the PLO as the sole official representative of the

Palestinian people, although some small opposition groups have never accepted that role for the PLO. For twelve years after 1970 the organization's periodically well-financed activities were centered in Lebanon until Israeli military pressure on the PLO forces and other activities of the organization in 1982 forced PLO military withdrawal from Beirut to several other Arab countries. A new headquarters was established in Tunis, and although it was bombed by Israeli warplanes in 1985, it was rebuilt and expanded on the same site.

In late 1988, after a year of the *intifadah,* the 480-member Palestine National Council (PNC) met in Algiers and on November 15 proclaimed an independent State of Palestine in the West Bank and Gaza, with its capital as Jerusalem. The Palestinian state was to fulfill the establishment of the Arab state envisioned, along with the Jewish state, in the United Nations General Assembly Partition Resolution in 1947 (which also gave Jerusalem the status of *corpus separatum*). More than 80 governments had recognized the projected Palestinian state within one year. Israel not only categorically rejected the PNC declaration but also bitterly opposed the PLO and refused to deal with it for several years; the United States concurred in both of these stances. By 1992, the PLO could no longer be ignored, as the new Israeli government under Yitzhak Rabin recognized.

The Peace Process

In response to Iraq's invasion of Kuwait in August 1990, U.S.-European leaders forged a broad coalition to oppose the audacious move. To gain and consolidate participation by several countries, and partly in recognition of the *intifadah,* the Western leaders solemnly pledged that after the liberation of Kuwait the basic premises of the coalition's goal in the northern Gulf would also be applied to the Palestinian-Israel problem. Thus the decade-long "peace process" was initiated. It quickly became institutionalized and proceeded step-by-step, with an occasional move backwards. The first stage was the Madrid Conference of October 1991,

sponsored and attended or observed by more than 25 countries. It made a vigorous start, mostly in airing grievances. The talks continued in Washington, then Moscow, then Washington again. Subconferences met in Brussels, Ottawa, Vienna, Lisbon, and elsewhere. Despite stalemates, walkouts, cancellations, and rancor, participants discussed all aspects of the conflict: status of occupied areas, Jewish settlements, refugee rights, Palestinian self-rule and statehood rights, water, terrorism and security, and related matters.

In a surprise move in January 1993, the Israeli Knesset lifted a 1986 ban against contacts between Israeli citizens and the PLO. The reason for the revocation was revealed in August when the Israeli government and the PLO disclosed that they had negotiated and initialed a Declaration of Principles (DOP) after eight months of secret bilateral sessions in Oslo, Norway. Israeli Prime Minister Yitzhak Rabin and PLO Chairman Yasser Arafat signed the declaration at a celebratory ceremony in Washington on September 13, 1993, when they performed their famous handshake. Critics on both sides condemned the terms, and some vigorously opposed the prospect of a peace settlement. The mutual attacks in the *intifadah* as well as violence elsewhere diminished during 1991–1993, although occasional violent acts continued for another several years.

Building on the Oslo accords, the parties by mid-1994 had agreed on Israeli troop withdrawal from Gaza and Jericho, and Chairman Arafat had triumphantly entered Gaza and then Jericho. The first steps toward a Palestinian Authority and quasi-state had been taken. In related negotiations, Jordan became the second Arab country to make peace with Israel when the two neighbors signed a peace treaty in Washington on July 25, 1994. Achieving unexpected progress, Israel and the PLO signed the "Oslo II" agreement in Washington on September 26, 1995; the agreement extended Palestinian self-rule to more areas of the West Bank—seven cities, not including Hebron.

The emotional reaction to these moves among extremist Israelis, as well as among militant Arabs, reached a climax on November 4, 1995, when a Jewish fanatic shot and killed Yitzhak Rabin in Tel Aviv. Among Palestinians, frictions mounted between the Arafat-led PLO and Hamas, which, asserting the Islamic cachet, opposed both Arafat and the peace process. Bolstered by the seething bitterness in Gaza, Hamas became increasingly involved in events. Following several acts of violence, a Hamas leader was assassinated by Israeli agents (January 1996); in retaliation, and to torpedo the peace process, Hamas suicide bombers killed 61 Israelis. In this atmosphere, Israeli peace supporters lost favor and the right-wing Binyamin Netanyahu was elected the new prime minister (May 1996). For the next three years, the peace process made only limited substantive headway and, indeed, took several steps backwards. Two advances were the Netanyahu-Arafat agreement on partial Israeli withdrawal from Hebron (January 15, 1997, in Israel) and the Wye River Memorandum (October 23, 1998, in Maryland in the United States) (Fig. 11-4). Prime Minister Netanyahu claimed that Israel's security continued in jeopardy because Chairman Arafat failed to control terrorism; hence Netanyahu's refusal to implement the Oslo accords and Wye agreement.

At a session of the Palestine National Council in Gaza on December 14, 1998, which he addressed, President Clinton observed a vote that confirmed revocation of the PLO charter's provision calling for the destruction of Israel. This confidence-building measure notwithstanding, the peace process did not resume until Ehud Barak replaced Netanyahu as prime minister in May 1999 and restructured some of the past agreements. With the dynamics of the dialogue significantly changed, progress accelerated. By September, agreements were being reached almost weekly—at Sharm al-Shaykh September 3–4 (dubbed Wye II), and on the Israel-Gaza border September 13. Israel promptly began withdrawals from West Bank territories that were to become Area A lands (under Palestine control); and arrangements were made for more Area C designations to become Area B, and more Area B designations

to become Area A. It is significant that the parties reached agreement on a "safe passage route" for Palestinians to travel between Gaza and the West Bank (shown on Maps 11-3 and 11-5), which opened October 25, 1999. Negotiators gave themselves one year to achieve final settlement—September 2000. But because fifty years of conflict over a score of emotion-charged issues are not easily resolved, the peace process made slow progress well into mid-2000. Weary of seeing deadlines come and go, Palestinian officials announced in early July 2000 that they would declare a Palestinian state in mid-September if there is no final settlement by then. About the same time, President Clinton urged Prime Minister Barak and President Arafat to join him in summit talks at Camp David beginning July 11 (see epilogue).

The Iran-Iraq War, 1980–1988

Following the Khomeini revolution in Iran in 1978–1979, the millennia-long enmity along the Zagros piedmont, between "Mesopotamians" and others to the west and "Iranians" to the east, once again flamed into open conflict. For hundreds of years, the Sunni Ottomans were the power to the west of the piedmont and the Shii Persians and other Iranians were the power in the Zagros and the Iranian plateau. Post-World War I Iraq and Iran inherited the animosity and periodically clashed along the Zagros piedmont ridges and, more acutely, along the Shatt al-Arab. The new revolutionary Islamic republic's militancy and apparent instability in 1979–1980 led Iraq to deem that the time was right to force Iran to accede to several long-standing Iraqi demands. Iraq invaded Iran across the Shatt al-Arab on September 17 and by late September held several positions inside Iran and called upon Iran to return the Tunbs and Abu Musa islands occupied in 1971. Thus began the Iran-Iraq war, which Iraq expected to last a few weeks but which dragged on for eight years.

One of the Baathist Iraqi aims was to force the reinstatement of the Iran-Iraq boundary

FIGURE 11-4   Jewish settlers in the West Bank: Armed young settlers in the heart of Hebron *(top)*, although Hebron has theoretically been turned over to the Palestinian Authority, and a new settlement near Hebron *(bottom)* in process of development: first come the mobile homes (shown here), then the permanent houses.

MAP 11-6   Iran-Iraq boundary along the Shatt al-Arab. Shift of the boundary from the east bank of the river to the deepest part of the channel (the thalweg) in 1975 was one reason for the Iran-Iraq war. (Redrawn from Tareq Y. Ismael, *Iraq and Iran: Roots of Conflict* [Syracuse, NY: Syracuse University Press, 1982], p. 23. Names as on original. Used with permission.)

along the lower Shatt al-Arab that had existed prior to 1975. Difficult to delineate equitably, the Shatt al-Arab boundary of modern times was first determined in 1847 and was slightly modified in 1913–1914. In 1937, another change ran the boundary line around Abadan to follow the *thalweg* (the deepest channel of the river). The remainder of the border continued to follow the low-water mark of the east (Iranian) bank (Map 11-6a), in accordance with the 1913–1914 agreement.

Tensions rose in 1969, when the shah of Iran abrogated the 1937 treaty. By 1975, Iran was clearly more powerful than Iraq, which had been weakened by an Iranian-backed Kurdish rebellion and was also isolated from other Arab countries; so Iraq agreed, in Algiers on March 6, 1975, to the Shatt al-Arab boundary claimed

by Iran. The new boundary followed the *thalweg* along the entire Shatt al-Arab border (Map 11-6b). In exchange, Iran stopped supporting the Kurdish rebellion, which then abated.

War operations disabled some of the major facilities in the northern Gulf, including Basrah and all of Iraq's most important ports. Air raids and missile attacks damaged major cities on both sides, and oil production decreased sharply in both countries. Casualties were tragically high, especially among young Iranians, and were reliably believed to exceed 1.2 million.[26]

All of the Gulf states incurred economic losses because of the Iran-Iraq war, estimated to have cost $200 billion directly and more than $1,000 billion indirectly. Attacks by both sides on oil tankers calling at export terminals led to the "tanker war," which intensified in late 1987.

All of the oil-producing Gulf amirates and Saudi Arabia combined to extend about $50 billion in aid to Iraq as a sister Arab country that was deflecting Iranian revolutionary danger from them. Saudi Arabia permitted construction of a "back-door" pipeline from Iraq to the Saudi East-West line. Contradictorily, the Gulf states also continued certain relations with Iraq's opponent, since they were reluctant to cut their long trade contacts with Iran. The United States continued its commitment to Gulf access by furnishing naval escorts to U.S.-registered tankers in the Gulf, most of them reflagged Kuwaiti ships. Before the convoying became regularized, the frigate USS *Stark* was mistakenly damaged by an Iraqi air-to-ship Exocet missile in a night attack on May 17, 1987, killing 37 of its crew; and the cruiser USS *Vincennes* mistakenly shot down an Iranian civilian aircraft with a ship-to-air missile on July 3, 1988, with a loss of all 290 people aboard. Both Iraq and the United States later agreed to pay damages for their errors.

Both Iran and Iraq were exhausted by mid-1988, but on July 18, Iran surprisingly accepted UN Security Council Resolution 598 calling for an immediate cease-fire between the two combatants. One reason for Iran's turnabout may have been its fear of further chemical warfare attacks by Iraq. In March 1988, Iraqi military forces killed several thousand people in the Kurdish village of Halabja, near the Iranian border, with poison gas as reprisal for the Kurds' having joined Iranian forces in a recent attack. A UN-sponsored armistice took effect on August 20.

Alignments in the Iran-Iraq war engendered some curious transnational relationships, as well as arms sales, in the Middle East. Both the People's Republic of China and the Republic of China on Taiwan supplied equipment to Iran. Syria, Iraq's Arab neighbor, refused to reopen Iraq's major pipelines across Syria to the Mediterranean and otherwise aided Iran. Despite public condemnation of Israel by the Republic of Iran, Israel regularly supplied spare parts and arms to Iran under its foreign policy principle of supporting enemies of Arab

countries. A U.S.-Israel collusion was also exposed in October 1986, the Iran-Contra scandal, revealing that the United States and Israel were secretly supplying arms to Iran for complex and contradictory reasons, including seeking freedom for U.S. hostages in Lebanon. Ironically, it was two of Iraq's chief supporters, financially and logistically—that became Iraq's main victims two years later.

The Gulf Crisis, 1990–1991

Despite its human and material losses during the 1980–1988 fighting, Iraq launched a second Gulf war less than two years after the end of the first. Emboldened by the outcome of the Iran-Iraq war, Saddam Husayn, the Baathist president of Iraq, reiterated the long-standing Iraqi claim to Kuwait in mid-1990. He also demanded that Kuwait forgive the multibillion-dollar loans made to Iraq during the Iran-Iraq war and that Kuwait cede the extension of the rich Rumaila oil field into Kuwait. Kuwait rejected these demands. While giving assurances that Iraq would not attack a sister Arab country, on August 2, 1990, President Saddam ordered the 100,000 troops that had massed on Kuwait's border in late July—which he had announced were only on maneuvers—to advance into Kuwait.[27]

Regional and world reaction to Iraq's assault on Kuwait varied in kind and degree. Since both Kuwait and Iraq were members of the Arab League, the Organization of the Islamic Conference, OPEC, OAPEC, and the UN, and Kuwait was also a member of the GCC, some members of these agencies reacted with ambivalence. Members of the GCC and the OIC condemned the action but could not confront Iraq militarily. The Arab League condemned the invasion, although with disabling internal disagreement, and discussed a military response.

Iraq sought support of the more oppressed and militant Arabs by proclaiming that it was championing Arabism, Islam, the Palestinian cause, the overthrow of wealthy monarchies, anti-imperialism, and other popular causes. One Iraqi proposal linked Iraqi withdrawal from Kuwait with Israeli withdrawal from the occupied territories and with Syrian withdrawal from Lebanon. Frustrated, embittered Palestinians—including those in Jordan, which had close economic ties with Iraq—endorsed the Iraqi declarations, and the PLO leadership expressed support for Iraq. (This was, of course, more than a year before the beginning of the peace process.) Yemen also expressed some pro-Iraq sentiments, as did the Sudan, Libya, Algeria, and Tunisia (headquarters of the PLO). Iran, after eight years of warfare with Iraq, echoed Iraq's denunciation of the United States and other Western governments, especially for sending forces to the Gulf, although it condemned Iraq's annexation of Kuwait. Iraq then ensured Iran's neutrality by informing the new government that Iraq would accept the Iranian terms of two years earlier for a peace treaty ending the Iran-Iraq war.

Coalition Response

Acting under the 1980 Carter Doctrine, the United States sought and received prompt Saudi endorsement for the dispatch of U.S. troops to northeastern Saudi Arabia within days after Iraq invaded Kuwait. Otherwise, most of the Western reaction to the invasion of Kuwait was channeled through the UN Security Council (UNSC). The dozen little-opposed UNSC resolutions focused on the one aim of freeing Kuwait and did not authorize the invasion of Iraq or the overthrow of its government. Under the UN resolutions, 28 states joined in the U.S./U.K.-led coalition and cooperated, in some form, in the liberation of Kuwait. Germany and Japan sent no troops but contributed large amounts of funding.

Although Iraq claimed that it had annexed Kuwait as its "rightful nineteenth province," Iraqi occupation forces committed executions, widespread mistreatment of hundreds of Kuwaitis, hostage-taking, and large-scale looting. The systematic looting included not only motor vehicles, technical equipment, store inventories, and other consumer goods but also museum collections and $3–4 billion in gold

bullion as well as cash in the banks. Later UN resolutions obtained the return of most of the museum collections and gold bullion.

Iraqi actions set in motion a human tide of more than 3 million refugees of many nationalities. Tens of thousands—Pakistanis, Indians, Sri Lankans, Thais, Filipinos, and others, as well as Kuwaitis, Palestinians, and other Arabs—fled Kuwait, many of them through Iraq to Jordan, which bore much of the burden of aid to the refugees. Hundreds of thousands of Egyptian laborers left Iraq. Hundreds of Europeans and Americans were held hostage in Baghdad.

The UN Security Council gave Iraq a deadline of January 15, 1991, to leave Kuwait or face a full-scale military attack in both Kuwait and Iraq. When Iraq did not withdraw, on the night of January 16–17 the most intensive target-specific air strikes in history were directed at Baghdad and other major cities in Iraq. Iraq refused to capitulate, and the coalition ground attack began on February 24, 1991, overwhelming the Iraqi forces in Kuwait and adjacent areas.

Regional biophysical and cultural elements strongly influenced the coalition timetable: scheduling of the coalition buildup, late winter rains, winter cold and summer heat, *shamal* (north winds) of late winter, and the approach of Ramadan in mid-March. This ensemble of factors pointed to mid-January as the time to launch the coalition counterattack.

Destruction and Eco-Terrorism

Details of military operations are covered in sources mentioned in Note 27. However, Iraq inflicted damage and caused casualties in two noteworthy respects in addition to its occupation of Kuwait. Thirty-two ground-to-ground Scud missiles were launched at targets in Saudi Arabia and 39 at targets in Israel. Some Scuds were destroyed by Patriot antimissile missiles, but others caused damage to buildings in both Saudi Arabia and Israel, and one caused 27 fatalities among U.S. military personnel in Dammam, Saudi Arabia.

Second, after the beginning of hostilities in mid-January, one tactic used by Iraqi forces was a quantitatively new tactic in environmental destruction, well labeled as "environmental terrorism" or "eco-terrorism"—dumping and setting fire to oil, thus making a weapon of the one commodity available in abundance. To deter the expected coalition offensive operations along the Kuwaiti coast, the Iraqis opened the valves of oil storage facilities in the amirate's export terminals and on tanker ships in the area. They thereby deliberately created the greatest oil spill in history, 4–6 million barrels (the Valdez, Alaska, spill was 258,000 barrels). The spill gradually worked its way down the coast of Saudi Arabia, destroying enormous quantities of plant and animal life.

As the Iraqis evacuated Kuwait, they blew up and set fire to most of the oil wells in the amirate. About 651 wells were set ablaze, and another 60 spewed crude petroleum under high pressure; still others were damaged in various ways. By early summer of 1991, about 5.5 million barrels of oil and enormous quantities of natural gas were lost each day—approximately twice the normal average daily production of Kuwait (also of Iraq)—with a value at that time of $75 million. Upon the liberation of Kuwait, the best oil-well fire-fighting teams in the world were immediately assembled to extinguish the blazes and cap the flowing wells, which, despite dangers and difficulties, they accomplished by early November 1991.[28]

The response to the Iraqi invasion of Kuwait involved enormous sums of money. Authoritative estimates in 1993 indicated that the war costs to Arab states totaled $676 billion, including $160 billion in damages in Kuwait and $256 billion in Iraq. U.S. officials estimated a cost to the coalition of about $61 billion, all of which was reimbursed by Saudi Arabia, Kuwait, the UAE, Japan, and Germany.

The stance of Yemen, Jordan, Sudan, and the PLO regarding Iraq's actions resulted in the loss of financial aid from Saudi Arabia and other former donors and in the expulsion of many of their citizens from Saudi Arabia and the Gulf states. More than 800,000 Yemenis were forced to return home, surrendering their jobs and depriving their families of millions of dollars annually in remittances. More than 300,000 Palestinians were forced to leave Kuwait without their property or funds, but most were largely reimbursed by the Kuwaiti government.

One positive aftermath, as was discussed earlier in this chapter, was the efficacious focusing of the attention of Western powers on the Palestinian-Israeli conflict. One negative aftermath was the failure of Iraq and the UN coalition—primarily the United States—to resolve the impasse over UN weapons inspections (and other provisions of the sanctions) for the remainder of the 1990s. As one result, U.S. aircraft engaged in almost daily exchanges with Iraqi ground units during 1999.

Strategic Straits

Five sea passages, four major and one minor, in the Middle East are of geostrategic significance: the Suez Canal, the Turkish Straits (Dardanelles and Bosporus), Strait of Hormuz, Bab el-Mandeb, and Strait of Tiran. Some are familiar historically, and all have figured prominently in the news in recent decades.

Suez Canal

The man-made Suez Canal was excavated between 1859 and 1869 through the Isthmus of Suez, which formerly linked Africa and Asia. Because it is entirely a sea-level canal, it has no locks and was designed to utilize the three natural lakes on the isthmus. It is approximately 110 miles/177 km long, including approach channels at Port Said and Suez, and has been enlarged at least nine times, the latest in the early 1990s, when it was given a navigational width of 650 ft./198 m and a depth of 58 ft./17.7 m. Current dimensions permit passage of ships of 200,000 dwt fully loaded, which would include the largest bulk carriers; however, the depth would have to be further increased to 68 ft./20.7 m to accommodate fully laden, very large crude carriers (VLCC's). Egypt has conducted feasibility and

MAP 11-7 The Turkish Straits (Bosporus and Dardanelles) and their geographic setting—a major world maritime connection and "choke point." The disastrous earthquake of August 17, 1999, was centered just south of Izmit.

cost-effectiveness studies on projects to deepen the canal. In the late 1990s, about 38 vessels transited Suez daily, down from about 49 per day a decade earlier. As a result, annual revenues decreased to $1.7 billion despite increases in transit charges.

The opening of the Suez Canal shortened the sea trip between Britain and India by 5,000 miles/8,000 km, so that during the 1870s most world shipping shifted from the route around the Cape of Good Hope, in southern Africa, to the Mediterranean-Suez-Red Sea route. Closures of the Suez Canal, for six months in 1956 and for eight years prior to June 1975, diverted traffic to other routes, and some shipping never returned to Suez. Also, the closures helped stimulate increased use of supertankers for shipment of petroleum from the Gulf exporting countries around southern Africa to Western Europe and the Americas. The canal has also faced increasing competition from Egypt's

own Sumed pipeline, which can pump crude oil from the Red Sea coast to the Mediterranean coast and thus bypass the canal.

Straits

Turkish Straits. These straits, the Dardanelles to the southwest and the Bosporus to the northeast, are linked up by the Sea of Marmara (Map 11-7) and have been of crucial importance since the Bronze Age. The legend of the Trojan War tells of fighting over the beautiful Helen, a charming romanticization of the struggle during the twelfth century BC for control of the entrance to the Black Sea and its rich coastlands. The World War I Gallipoli campaign in 1915 is the most recent clash over control of the straits. International need for access to the straits was spelled out in the Lausanne Convention of 1923 and again in the Montreux Convention of 1936, which still governs international use of the waterways.[29]

The Dardanelles (Turkish name, Çanakkale Boğazı), the ancient Hellespont, connects the Aegean Sea and the Sea of Marmara and lies between the Gallipoli Peninsula on the northwest and Asia Minor to the south. It is about 36 miles/57 km long, 4,000 ft./1,200 m wide at its narrowest and 4 miles/6.4 km at its widest, and is 150–300 ft./45–90 m deep.

The Bosporus (Greek for "ox-ford"; Turkish name, Karadeniz Boğazı) is shorter, narrower, and shallower than the Dardanelles—about 17 miles/28 km long, 2,500 ft./ 762 m at its narrowest, and 100 ft./30 m at its minimum midstream depth. Since the Sea of Marmara is as deep as, and much wider than, the two straits, any ship afloat can make the passage between the Aegean and the Black seas. Although the three water bodies separate Europe from Asia Minor, the Bosporus was bridged in 1973 and again in 1988. Final plans either for a third bridge or for a tunnel under the Bosporus were in work in 1999.

Traffic through the straits has increased enormously since World War I—international traffic by more than ten times. Shipping passing the straits in the late 1990s exceeded 51,000 vessels annually—140 per day, compared with 38 for the Suez Canal. Half of the larger ships were tankers and nearly half of all vessels flew the new flags of Russia and other successor states of the FSU, especially Ukraine and Georgia. Straits traffic is expected to increase by perhaps one-third with the further development of Caspian oil fields and the opening of the Danube-Main Rivers waterway. More than 1.7 million bpd of crude transits the straits daily, and the increase in the number of passages by tankers has raised serious concerns about environmental safety (see Chap. 8).

Strait of Hormuz.   Connecting the Gulf and the Indian Ocean, the Strait of Hormuz is squeezed between Iran on the north and an exclave of Oman at the tip of the Musandam Peninsula on the south (Fig. 11-5). It is one of the most vital channels of trade in the world,

and although it no longer carries the 90 percent of the Middle East's petroleum exports that it did before the two Gulf wars, it carries more than 13 million bpd. It has lost some of its oil traffic to the Red Sea and the Mediterranean. The number of tankers and the quantity of petroleum transiting this strait daily vary with the world petroleum market and the political climate in the Gulf, as well as the size of the tankers. In the late 1990s, in addition to about 13 million bbl of oil, several shiploads of NGL and product passed through Hormuz each day.

With a depth of 290 ft./88 m and widths of 28–59 miles/45–95 km, Hormuz is the widest of the significant straits in the Middle East. Nevertheless, it is vulnerable to several kinds of weaponry and sabotage, and its defense is vital to both the Gulf petroleum exporters and the petroleum-consuming countries. The security of the Gulf and the strait was a major aim of the Western powers and their regional allies, but that security came under serious threat from Iran and Iraq between 1980 and 1991.

Bab el-Mandeb.   At the opposite corner of the Arabian Peninsula, the Bab el-Mandeb (Gate of Lamentation) connects the Red Sea and Gulf of Aden. The strait is divided into two channels by the small but strategically located island of Perim, which belongs to Yemen. The main channel, with a width of 10 miles/16 km and a depth of 1,056 ft./322 m, is to the west of Perim on the African side, next to Djibouti. Three states are involved in the territorial waters in the straits—Yemen, Ethiopia, and Djibouti.

The role of the Bab el-Mandeb was enhanced significantly when the Suez Canal was opened in 1869, since virtually all of the ships transiting the canal also passed through the Bab el-Mandeb. With development of more Red Sea ports because of the canal traffic, the strait continued to carry heavy traffic even when the canal was closed, in order that Jiddah and other Red Sea ports normally served from the Mediterranean could be reached from the south. Development of the Saudi export port of Yanbu has enhanced the importance of both the strait and the Suez Canal. The port of Aden,

FIGURE 11-5   Strait of Hormuz, one of the world's most important economic choke points, with Iran to the left, Oman and the UAE to the right. Space view, looking southeast. (NASA photograph)

lying a few miles east of the Bab el-Mandeb, achieved much of its modern importance as a result of the rise in importance of Suez and Red Sea traffic. An average of about 80 ships a day transit the strait.

Strait of Tiran.   Connecting the Red Sea and the Gulf of Aqabah at the southeastern tip of the Sinai Peninsula, with Egypt on the west and Saudi Arabia on the east, the Strait of Tiran is of relatively minor importance in comparison with the Suez Canal and the straits already described. Nevertheless, its closure was considered as a major justification for the Israeli preemptive attack on Egypt in June 1967. The debate over the precise international principles relating to Tiran has not yet resolved the exact status of the strait.

Great-Power Rivalry

Britain and Russia long contended for spheres of influence in the zone from the Balkans to the Himalayas. Although traditional Russian pressure on the Northern Tier diminished during the 1920s and 1930s, the then Soviet Union resumed the Russian push into southwestern Asia after World War II. With Britain unable to counter the pressure as in the past, the United States joined the British as protectors of the Northern Tier states—Turkey and Iran, sometimes Iraq—against potential Russian expansion into an area of increasingly vital concern to the West. Rivalry between the United States and the USSR in the Middle East became a major dynamic in the region's relations and geopolitics for nearly 45 years. Much of this "Great Game in the Middle East" was made obsolete by the collapse of the Soviet Union in 1991 and the subsequent cooperation between the United States and former Soviet republics. However, highlights of the rivalry are worth a brief historical review.

The policy of "containment" advocated in a watershed 1947 article by "X" (Ambassador George Kennan),[30] was formalized in the Truman Doctrine in March 1947. The declaration signaled a commitment on the part of the United States to maintain the balance of power in the Middle East while Britain made its phased withdrawals from Greece, Turkey, India, and the Palestine mandate. Later, Britain lost its influence in Iran, withdrew from Suez in 1956, and withdrew from the Gulf and the periphery of the Arabian Peninsula in 1971–1972. However, the British continue to have a vital interest in the Middle East and periodically coordinate political and military operations with the United States, as they did on a major scale in 1990–1991 during the Gulf crisis and in the later 1990s actions against Iraq.

The Eisenhower administration sought to unify the region's resistance to the Soviet Union. With U.S. and British encouragement, the Baghdad Pact was formed in 1955, eventually including Turkey, Iraq, Iran, Pakistan, and Britain. The United States was a full member of the economic committee and the major source of funding for the pact. Consequent to the Suez affair of October–November 1956 (the joint Israeli-British-French invasion), the Eisenhower Doctrine was announced in January 1957, committing the United States to counter communist actions in the Middle East. This commitment, in one doctrine or another, was maintained through successive administrations, although it was applied in contradictory ways. On the one hand, the U.S. government tried to negate or minimize Soviet influence in the region until the USSR disintegrated in 1991; on the other hand, it followed regional policies that affronted key Arab countries and made some of them more receptive to Soviet influence.

The Nixon Doctrine encouraged the region's states to be responsible for their own defense and focused on the United States' reliance on Iran and, secondarily, Saudi Arabia. In the eastern Mediterranean, Turkey and Greece continued to be the southeastern flank of NATO, with the British providing support in southern Cyprus. Among states in the Fertile Crescent, Israel became increasingly involved in the so-called special relationship with the United States.

The Carter Doctrine was announced in early 1980, following the Iranian revolution, collapse of the Central Treaty Organization (CENTO—the former Baghdad Pact), and the Soviet invasion of Afghanistan in December 1979. This doctrine emphasized U.S. interest in the Gulf and in laying the groundwork for a Rapid Deployment Force, subsequently known as the Central Command. The Reagan administration exhibited its resolve to sustain U.S. power in the area by sending U.S. naval forces to the Gulf in 1987 and 1988. As we saw earlier, the dispatch of U.S. troops to Saudi Arabia in 1990–1991 by the Bush administration was based on the Carter Doctrine and was an extension of the Reagan support of Kuwait.

These successive doctrines are expressions of U.S. concern in an area in which other great powers have—and have long had—vital interests. Great Britain, France, Russia, and Japan join the United States as Great Powers with continuing interest in the Gulf area, with or without active hostilities to focus attention.

Notes

1. Mackinder 1904, which has been reprinted in several political geography studies. Sir Halford expanded and revised his thoughts in Mackinder 1919 and again in a 1943 *Foreign Affairs* article. An underrated challenge to Mackinder came in Spykman 1944. The Rimland challenge is discussed later.

2. Ayubi 1995 comprehensively examines Arab states and gives realistic insights.

3. In addition to his own personal account in his classic *Seven Pillars of Wisdom: A Triumph,* which appeared in several versions and many editions, T. E.

Lawrence and his saga were much celebrated during the 1920s and had a renaissance in the 1970s and 1980s. In the extensive literature about him, an excellent authorized biography is Wilson 1990, which places Lawrence in the context of the momentous events of the period. A recent brief article with maps is Belt 1999.

4. See Howard 1963.

5. Ethnicity and the state have been examined in many studies. For two that focus on the Middle East, see Bengio and Ben-Dor 1999 and Esman and Rabinovich 1988.

6. Middle East state development has been analyzed in numerous recent studies. For examples, see Ayubi 1995, Netton 1986, Salamé 1987, and Ben-Dor and Dewitt 1987.

7. Hartshorne 1950.

8. Jones 1954.

9. See several papers in Hudson 1999; also see Ayubi 1995 and Kemp and Hakarvy 1997. International organizations are listed in the annual *World Factbook* Appendix, which includes Middle East regional organizations.

10. Several boundaries mentioned in this paragraph are depicted and briefly accounted for in successive issues of U.S. Department of State *Geographic Notes*. A general map of Arabian Peninsula lines is in Bradford Thomas, "Gulf Boundaries," no. 13, Mar. 1, 1991, 1–5. The Saudi-Iraq boundary is shown on p 2–3 and is covered again in 2, no. 2, Summer 1992, 11–12; Saudi-Qatar and Saudi-UAE are covered in 2, no. 4, Winter 1992–1993, 1–2; and in 3, no. 4, Winter 1993–1994, 12–13; Saudi-Oman is in 3, no. 1, Spring 1993, 2–3. All Middle East boundaries are discussed in Day 1982, 178–233. A concise review of Arabian Peninsula borders is given in Schofield 1996.

11. The Oman-Yemen boundary is shown in *Geographic Notes* 3, no. 1, Spring 1993, 3–5; the Jordan-Iraq line in no. 13, Mar. 1, 1991, 2; again in 2, no. 4, Winter 1992–1993, 2–3; and again in 3, no. 4, Winter 1993–1994, 9–10. See also Schofield 1996, which mentions the Oman-UAE boundary.

12. *Geographic Notes* 3, no. 2, Summer 1993, 1–2, with more details in 4, no. 2, Summer 1994, 23–29. For exhaustive studies, see Schofield 1993 and Rahman 1997. For concise coverage see Brown 1994 and Cordesman and Hashim 1997, 184–189. I am deeply grateful to Bradford Thomas, boundary specialist formerly with the Office of the Geographer, Department of State, for his meticulous clarification of Arabian Peninsula boundary problems in personal communications during 1999.

13. The Iraq-Kuwait territorial dispute is discussed in Long 1978, Kelly 1980, Crystal 1990, Finnie 1992, and Rahman 1997.

14. Details are given in Taryam 1987, which includes a useful bibliographical essay covering good sources on the islands and on the UAE.

15. The Gulf maritime boundaries are succinctly examined in *Geographic Notes* no. 14, Oct. 1, 1991, 11–12. See also Gerald Blake, "Maritime Boundaries of the Middle East and North Africa," in Blake and Schofield 1987.

16. Many recent studies examine various aspects of Middle East hydro-geopolitics. See especially *Water for the Future* 1999, Biswas et al. 1997, Elmusa 1997, Wolf 1995, Rogers and Lydon 1994, and Berkoff 1994.

17. The subject is examined from different viewpoints in dozens of studies, for example, Curtis 1981; Mortimer 1982; Voll 1982; Korany and Dessouki et al. 1984; Salamé 1987; Esman and Rabinovich 1988; Andersen, Seibert, and Wagner 1990; and Hudson 1999.

18. Literally thousands of books and articles examine the Palestine/Israel problem from every conceivable perspective. Some are very good even when supporting one viewpoint. Many are merely polemic, and others subtly screen their bias. Students and readers must select sources with a critical eye; many polemics focus on peripheral issues (e.g., religious ambiguities) by way of pursuing an agenda. Achieving a balance in sources requires effort: Israeli and pro-Israeli books, journals, and articles in the United States outnumber pro-Palestinian ones, as do media coverages, including motion pictures; however, increasing attention is being given by Israeli writers and others to "the New History" (mentioned later), a revision of the Israeli "national myths." Many of the revisions are being included for the first time in some Israeli textbooks in 1999 (*New York Times,* Aug. 14, 1999, and *Jerusalem Post,* No. American Ed., Sept. 10, 1999). It is worth noting that some of the severest critics of some Israeli actions are Israelis. On the overall conflict, four useful studies are Shipler 1986, Smith 2000, Gerner 1994, and Tessler 1994. See also introductory note to the bibliography and the bibliography itself.

19. The Dreyfus trial is covered in numerous encyclopedias and histories of Zionism.

20. Aharon David Gordon, "Some Observations," in Hertzberg 1969. Other concepts of Zionism are discussed in Avineri 1981 and in some readings in Khalidi 1971. See also Selzer 1970 and Tekiner et al.

1988 for dissents from traditional Zionism. Pappé 1997 looks favorably on revised Zionism as conceived by the "New Historians"; it is often called "Post-Zionism," which is vigorously criticized by Wurmser 1999.

21. Zangwill 1901.

22. The Balfour Declaration has been analyzed in many books and articles. The massive and authoritative Stein 1983 (a reprint of the 1961 edition), by a man associated with WZO, is the most detailed.

23. Figures are from Palestine Human Rights Center and *Christian Science Monitor,* Mar. 19, 1993. Three useful books on the *intifadah* are Peretz 1990, Schiff and Yaari 1989, and Nassar and Heacock 1990.

24. Regarding Deir Yassin, Begin 1977 includes an account by that author, who was commander of Irgun Zvai Leumi, the terrorist group that, along with the Stern Gang, conducted the massacre. Begin was later prime minister of Israel. For a quite different version, see the report by the local Red Cross representative, Jacques de Reynier, in Khalidi 1971, 761–766. Deir Yassin (or Dayr Yasin) is discussed in any good account of events of the period. See, for example, the four sources given in Note 18 of this chapter, as well as McGowan and Ellis 1998. Some Israeli sources contest the number of villagers killed, claiming it to be nearer 150, while not minimizing the enormity of the massacre. The birth of the Palestinian refugee problem is addressed by a leading "New Historian" in Morris 1989, which is vigorously rebutted in Karsh 1997, which is re-rebutted in a review essay by Benny Morris in *Journal of Palestine Studies* 27, no. 2 (Winter 1998): 81–95.

25. Three recent articles examine the current refugee situation: *New York Times,* Apr. 23, 1998; Isabel Kershner, "Back to Haunt the Peacemakers," *Jerusalem Report,* Aug. 2, 1999, 20–26; and Rosemary Sayigh, "Dis/Solving the 'Refugee Problem,'" *Middle East Report (MER),* 207, Summer 1998, 19–23. See also <http://www.un.org/unrwa/refugees/me.html>.

26. Among several studies of the origins and ramifications of the Iran-Iraq war, an excellent one is Khadduri 1988. See also Chubin and Tripp 1988 and Karsh 1990.

27. The Gulf crisis and war were among the most intensively covered conflicts in history. A useful, full chronology is given in the *Middle East Journal* 45, nos. 1, 2, and 3 (Winter, Spring, and Summer 1991). Also, the *Middle East Journal* 45, no. 1, has four excellent articles pertaining to the Gulf crisis. Coalition news briefings and news reporting at the time were later criticized, as in Gordon and Trainor 1995. Three standard books on the war are Schwarzkopf 1992, Cordesman 1996, and Khadduri and Ghareeb 1997.

28. Much of the information on Iraq's "eco-terrorism" is covered in media reports of the period, but a useful, concise report is Williams et al. 1991, which has excellent space imagery; see also Canby 1991 and Earle 1992.

29. See Howard 1974.

30. Kennan 1987 is a reprint of the widely read 1947 article and is accompanied by comments and a retrospect by that author.

PART TWO

Regional
Geography

12

Syria:
Middle East Heartland

Regional Keystone

Ancient Role, Modern Role

Historical-geographical Syria, lying between the Mediterranean and the middle Euphrates, has often functioned as the geographical keystone in the Middle East. Not only is its situation central, but also its location near the regional heart is enhanced by patterns of landforms, climates, and travel routes. Damascus and Aleppo have played outstanding roles as commercial and cultural centers for 3,500 years, and Syria's cereal belt has served as a granary for empires during many centuries. Two major corridors cross Syria: the main one south of the Turkish mountain wall and north of the desert, a second one through the Palmyra Oasis. The routes were for thousands of years—indeed, until after World War I—the major east-west passageways through the region for the movement of people and goods. Western Syria has also long served as a segment of the north-south land route between Yemen and the northeastern Mediterranean and beyond into Asia Minor.

With such a location, Syria has for millennia experienced migrating peoples, marching armies, and political influences. Syrians have thereby at different times absorbed several ethnic and cultural groups and have sustained challenges to their capacity for unity and even survival. Periodically during its long history, the Syrian realm has served as a major power base, reaching its apogee during the Damascus-centered Umayyad Empire, 661–750. Later it was a focus of Islamic-Arab aspirations and potentially a modern political-spiritual center of the Arab world. The Syria of the early years of the new millennium, with only moderate size, moderate population, and limited resources, has a major role in the region despite the serious problems it faces and its shifting relationships with its neighbors and with the Great Powers. Some of Syria's economic difficulties may be traced to its policy planning and relations. Other more general problems arise from the country's ideologically self-imposed isolation, anachronistic restrictions, and illiberal political agenda. Still others stem partly from a mutual failure by Syria and the West to establish meaningful rapport. This chapter will examine Syria's capabilities and role.[1]

The Three Syrias

The term *Syria* as used in this chapter will usually refer to the Syrian Arab Republic, so named in 1961. The republic is generally coextensive, except for the Iskenderun (Alexandretta) area, with the League of Nations mandate to France (1923–1946). However, a "historical Syria" existed for more than 2,000 years, and it comprised the general area that is now distributed among Syria, Lebanon, Jordan, western Iraq, Israel, and Israeli-occupied parts of Palestine. References to "Syria" in some writings imply this "Greater Syria."

The Physical Challenge

Regions of Syria

Syria has six rather well-differentiated natural regions, indicated on Map 12-1 by encircled numbers. [1] The Mediterranean coastal plain extends the full length of the country's seacoast,

Syria

Long-form official name, anglicized: Syrian Arab Republic

Official name, transliterated: al-Jumhuriyah al-Arabiyah al-Suriyah

Form of government: unitary multiparty republic with one legislative house (People's Council)

Area: 71,498 miles²/185,180 km²

Population, 1999: 15,335,000. Literacy (latest): 70.8%

Ethnic composition (%): Arab 88.8, Kurdish 6.0, Armenian 2.5, Turkmen 1.7, other (including Circassian, Assyrian) 1.0

Religions (%): Sunni Muslim 74.0; Alawi, Druze, and other Muslim subsects 16.0; Christian (various sects) 8.0; other 1.1

GDP, 1998: $41.7 billion, per capita: $2,500

Petroleum reserves: 2.5 billion barrels

Main exports (% of total value, 1997): crude petroleum and petroleum products 65.0; textiles and fabrics 4.2; raw cotton 5.0; food, beverages, and tobacco 13

Main imports (% of total value, 1997): machinery and equipment 40.0; food, beverages, and tobacco 15.0; chemicals and chemical products 10.0; textiles 10.0

Capital city: Damascus (al-Dimashq, often al-Sham) 1,550,000; other cities: Aleppo (Halab) 1,591,400; Homs (Hims) 644,000; Latakia (al-Ladhiqiyah) 307,000; Hamah 229,000

widest in the north behind Latakia and in the south near Lebanon. The plain is agriculturally productive and is also the base for the main port of Latakia, for the oil-export port of Baniyas (formerly more active when it served as terminal for the Iraqi pipelines), and for the developing port and oil terminal of Tartus. [2] A succession of mountain groups lies east of the coastal plain: In the north is the continuous north-south range of the Jabal al-Sahiliyah ("Coastal Mountains"—the new official toponym, formerly the Jabal al-Nusayriyah or Jabal al-Ansariyah); in the center are the southwest-northeast Anti-Lebanon Mountains dividing Syria and Lebanon; and in the south is the complex mass of Mt. Hermon. The uplifted Jurassic and Cretaceous limestone Jabal al-Sahiliyah is bounded on the east by an impressive fault with both vertical displacement and a strike slip of more than 12 miles/20 km. The fault is also the west side of the Ghab graben, the northern end of the Levant Rift System. East

of the mountain frame is an extensive plateau divided by [3] a southwest-northeast zone of complex folding and faulting associated with the Palmyra Folds. Several local names are applied to the successive sections of the splayed mountain ridges, including Jabal al-Ruwaq northeast of Damascus, Jabal Abu Rajmayn in the center, and Jabal Bishri toward the Euphrates River.

North of the Palmyra Folds and west of the Euphrates is [4] the level to rolling steppeland that supports a north-south zone of extensive grain agriculture and a coextensive constellation of settlements, including the sequence of cities Homs, Hamah, and Aleppo. South of the Palmyra Folds the plateau has a quite different character. Toward the west are [5] extensive basaltic lava flows of several ages, accompanied by numerous aligned cinder cones. Jabal al-Druze (Jebel Druze), which the Syrian government refers to officially as Jabal al-Arab, is a huge lava dome that reaches 3,300 ft./

MAP 12-1   General map of Syria with major towns and physical features. Circled numbers indicate geographical regions of the country.

1,000 m above the plain and is flanked on the northeast by the extensive basalt plain of al-Safa and on the northwest by the thin, scabby, blistered lava flow of al-Laja. The plains area west of the Jabal al-Arab/Jabal al-Druze is the well-cultivated Hawran (Fig. 12-1), its western edge a lava plateau that overlooks the Sea of Galilee and forms the Golan Heights. Well east of the lava belt, the Syrian Desert extends into Iraq, offering little except sparse grasses and bushes for the grazing animals of the Bedouins. In northeastern Syria is [6] the Jazirah, which lies east of the entrenched Euphrates River and continues the level-to-rolling landscape that lies west of the Euphrates.

The Jazirah has been a focus of economic development since about 1970 following increased exploitation of the oil fields located there and following completion of the Euphrates Dam and its associated installations.

The Agricultural Base

Syria's share of the Fertile Crescent's climate, soil, landforms, and other beneficial characteristics endows the state with appreciable areas of relatively productive agricultural land. Making up about one-third of the country's total area, this agricultural land supplies the sustained economic base for the country. On the

FIGURE 12-1   View over Salkhad, looking generally west over the agricultural Hawran from a volcanic neck in the Jabal al-Arab (formerly Jabal al-Druze), southwestern Syria.

other hand, the problems of aridity and rough relief of the other two-thirds of the country present a major physical challenge. This challenge and the Syrian response are a major part of the saga of contemporary Syria.

By its very nature, the Fertile Crescent's inner boundary is a zone of marginal precipitation. Cyclical oscillation of the 12-in./300-mm isohyet (see Map 4-2) between wet and dry periods is a tensional element in Syrian agriculture. Consequently, it impinges on many aspects of Syrian economic and social life, including shifts between sedentarism and nomadism along the frontier. In its seasonal distribution, rainfall in this typical summer-dry Mediterranean climate area (Koeppen Csa) is concentrated in the cool months. Annual precipitation increases from 30 in./750 mm along the coast to 55 in./1,400 mm on the upper west-facing slopes of the Jabal al-Sahiliyah/Jabal al-Nusayriyah, then

decreases sharply to the east, in the rain shadow of the mountains, to 22 in./550 mm in the Ghab Depression.

East of the mountains, the north-south subhumid agricultural belt with its steppe soils extends southward from Aleppo well into Jordan, and rainfall typically averages 12–20 in./300–500 mm along this southwestern horn of the Fertile Crescent. Eastward from Aleppo, the area averages 10–12 in./250–300 mm, with double those amounts in extreme northeastern Syria. Away from the more humid Fertile Crescent, the southeastern two-thirds of the country averages less than 8 in./200 mm, with the driest area, adjacent to the Jordan panhandle, receiving less than 4 in./100 mm. In this area and along the Euphrates in extreme southeastern Syria, mean July temperatures exceed 90°F/32°C. There the Syrian Desert is in full sway.

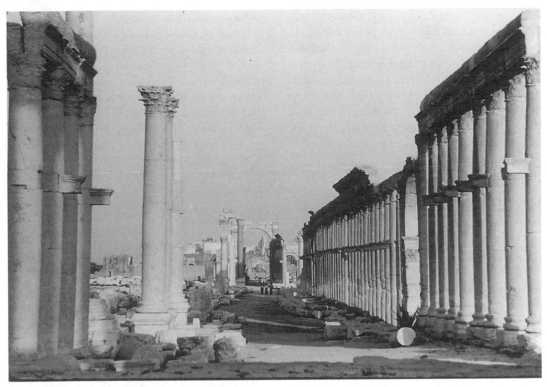

FIGURE 12-2   Ruins of the colonnade of Palmyra (modern Tadmur) in central Syria, prosperous oasis trade center under Queen Zenobia in the late third century, a key caravan station and, briefly, a military power.

The Imprint of Time

Ancient Patterns

The western and northern parts of Syria were the sites of some of the earliest villages known, settlements dating well back into the ninth millennium BC (see Chap. 2). Some of the earliest pottery ever found was discovered in Syria on the banks of the Euphrates, and Damascus contends for the title of the oldest continuously inhabited city in the world. Ugarit just north of Latakia on the Mediterranean coast, Ebla 30 miles/50 km southwest of Aleppo, and Mari on the middle Euphrates were thriving city-states or imperial capitals early in the second millennium BC (see Map 2-1), and the earliest known alphabet, with 29 characters in cuneiform script and dating from the fifteenth century BC, was found during the excavation of Ugarit. Late in the second millennium, the Syrian region became and continued to be for almost 1,000 years a marchland, an area contested among successive great empires, including the Amorite and the Aramaean (the biblical Aram), which were rooted in Syria itself.

Alexander the Great's conquest of the Persians in 334–326 BC was followed by inclusion of the Syrian realm in the Seleucid Empire for more than 200 years. After Rome supplanted the Seleucids and made Syria a Roman province in 64 BC, the evolving Greco-Roman culture in Syria became infused with Christianity. The new sect gained its first major urban foothold in Antioch and flourished under the eastern Roman Empire and the successor Byzantine Empire. Ruins of churches and of entire abandoned towns from this period—Syria's several "dead cities"—can still be visited in the northwest and south, and impressive Greco-Roman buildings and cities are important tourist sites in Palmyra (see Fig. 12-2), Apamaea, Bosra, Dura Europos, and other areas. Beginning in AD 540, the century of warfare between the Byzantines and the Persian Sassanians inflicted great destruction on the Syrian countryside and cities. Ghassanians, Christian Arabs who lived chiefly in southern Syria, were the source of many powerful families in the Syrian society of the sixth and seventh centuries.

Arab Invasions and After

When the Arab Muslim onslaught came, the war-weakened Byzantines were unable to defend their Syrian possessions. As a result, in AD 636 Syria was the first area to fall to the Muslims after their eruption from the Hijaz. Just 25 years later, Syria entered its 90-year Golden Age when the Islamic Umayyad Empire, with Damascus as its capital, was established in the realms conquered by the Muslims. Arabic, the new official language, gradually displaced Aramaic and Greek; and Islam became dominant over Christianity, although it has never entirely displaced it. As it had before and as it did later, Syria demonstrated its ability to fuse cultures and evolve something "Syrian."

When the Abbasids supplanted the Umayyads in 750 and the Muslim power center shifted to Baghdad, Syria became a contested land for the next 800 years. Egyptians, Seljuks, Crusaders, Mongols, and the Abbasids vied for control. All held Syria, or parts of it, for varying lengths of time, leaving signs of their control in aqueducts, forts, and caravansaries. Ruins of spectacular Crusader castles in western Syria attract both tourists and serious students of medieval architecture. The Ottomans conquered Syria in 1516 and controlled it for most of the following 400 years until the breakup of the Ottoman Empire after 1918.

French Mandate

When the French assumed the mandate of Syria under the League of Nations in the early 1920s, their demarcation of the mandate's borders signaled the first time in history that a

separate, quasi-independent polity of "Syria" had been formally defined. After part of the territory was detached in the creation of Lebanon, and after internal pieces were shifted as France wished, the mandate of Syria became the direct precursor of the contemporary state of Syria (see Chap. 11).

In order to inhibit Syrian nationalism and unity, French authorities divided the territory into internal "states": Aleppo, Damascus, and Alawite (called Latakia after 1930) created in 1920; Jabal al-Druze in 1921; and an autonomous Sanjak (subprovince) of Alexandretta (Turkish, Iskenderun) in 1923. In 1925, Damascus and Aleppo were united to form "Syria," and the Alawite state and Jabal al-Druze were added in 1936, re-separated in 1939, then reunited in 1942. Revolts and instability typified the years of the mandate, but finally, after World War II, Syria became formally and officially an independent state on April 17, 1946.[2] Except for a revised boundary around the Alexandretta-Antioch (Iskenderun-Antakya) area (see Chap. 11), the frontiers of post-independence Syria embrace virtually the same territory as the mandate of Syria after separation of Greater Lebanon (see Map 12-1).

The United Arab Republic

Independent Syria shared with adjoining Lebanon and Jordan the impact of insecurity and instability consequent to World War II, the sudden assumption of independence, and the trauma of the emergence of a demonstrably powerful Israel on the territory of a putative "Greater Syria." On several occasions, Syria expressed interest in uniting—perhaps as a manifestation of the Greater Syria syndrome—with one or another of its Arab neighbors. Only once did an actual merger transpire, when between 1958 and 1961, Syria and Egypt were linked in the United Arab Republic (see Chap. 11). Whereas the union with Egypt served its original purpose of forestalling a communist coup in Syria, the aggressiveness of Nasserist Egypt offended Syria, which had long considered itself the standard-bearer of Arab nationalism.

After three years of dominance by Egypt, rather than equal partnership, Syria withdrew from the UAR and has not acceded to any similar relationship since then. In 1978–1979 it did, however, discuss a possible merger with Iraq before resuming the usual confrontational stance over the question of leadership.

The Syrian Mixture
Patterns of Population

In population, Syria ranks seventh among the sixteen states in the Middle East. Its population doubled between 1963 and 1987, and its high 3.5–4 percent annual population growth rate continued to the end of the century. The rapid growth is contributing to such socioeconomic problems as high unemployment, stagnant per capita income, and shortage of housing. Families of the surplus population have even begun to move into the historically important "dead cities" of northwest Syria, which are also economically important tourist destinations. As in other Middle East countries, the raw population density figure for Syria is misleading, since the population is markedly concentrated in the more humid western area (see Map 6-2 and Table 6-1).

Syria has, from early times, had scattered cities of appreciable size and fame along the Euphrates and especially in the west. Damascus and Aleppo formerly alternated leadership in population, but since the 1960s Damascus has surpassed the northern center to become the primary city of Syria as well as its capital (Fig. 12-3). More than 50 percent of Syria's townspeople live in the two main cities.

The traditional population concentration axis along the humid steppe belt, Damascus-Homs-Hamah-Aleppo, has now expanded to include Latakia, Syria's main port. With development of the Euphrates Valley and the Jazirah east of the river, Dayr al-Zawr, Raqqah, Hasakah, and Qamishli are in the 100,000–200,000 population range and are growing rapidly. In addition, scores of villages—some of them with populations of 10,000–20,000—are evolving in the broad, flat-floored river valley and adjacent plateaus in response to government development projects in the area. Suwayda, in the Jabal al-Arab, is the largest center in the south, with nearly 60,000 people. Syria's four universities are located in the four largest cities—Damascus, Aleppo, Homs, and Latakia.

Syrian Arabs and Their Religions

Among the several separate ethnolinguistic groups in the country, the dominant group has, for more than 1,000 years, been the Syrian Arabs, and they constitute nearly 90 percent of the population. The great majority of them (nearly 86 percent of the total population) are Muslim in religion, and 64 percent are Sunni. However, other Arab subgroups, especially religious sects, deserve mention in their Syrian context. As in other developing countries, data on minorities in Syria are uncertain and variable.

Other Muslim (or quasi-Muslim) sects besides the Sunni are mainly heretical Shii groups—Alawi, Druze, and Ismaili. Largest and, since the mid-1960s, most important of these sects is the Alawis, about 11 percent of the Syrian population and more than two-thirds of the inhabitants in and around the Jabal al-Sahiliyah in northwestern Syria. Prior to the 1960s, the Alawis were primarily agricultural workers, but they served in the army in numbers beyond their percentage of the population. The Baath party coup in 1963 enhanced the Alawi role, especially in the military, and when an Alawi, Hafiz al-Asad, became president in 1971, the role of the Alawis improved decisively. When Hafiz al-Asad died in June 2000, his son, Bashar al-Asad, succeeded him and preserved Alawite control. (See also the epilogue.) It is ironic that members of this separatist minority sect with their own "state" in the French mandate, earlier isolated, deprived, and rejected by Sunni Muslims, have ascended to a role of elite position and power.

The Druzes played a major political-military role during the mandate period. The Jabal al-Druze was one of the internal states created by

FIGURE 12-3   The heart of the "new" downtown Damascus, telephoto view looking east from the top of Mount Qassiun. The multistory buildings date from the 1980s, the uniform-height buildings in the foreground from the French mandate prior to World War II. The Old City of Damascus is slightly above center, surrounding the Umayyad Mosque, whose minarets are plainly visible. The rich irrigated Ghutah is in the distance but is being encroached upon by the urban sprawl of Damascus.

France, and the periodic Druze revolts were a serious problem for the French mandatory authorities. However, the 475,000 Druzes (about 3 percent of the total population) play a subdued role in independent Syria. They are still concentrated in the rough lava dome of the Jabal al-Arab/Jabal al-Druze and in the Mount Hermon area in the south, composing more than 80 percent of the inhabitants in those areas. The Ismailis, less than half as numerous as the Druzes, are concentrated in the area of Salamiyah east of Hamah and in the mountains west of Hamah, where the Ismaili Assassins played an important role during the Crusades.[3]

Almost 9 percent of the Syrians are Christians, and except for the Armenians, a separate ethnolinguistic group, they are nearly all Arabs. Syrian Christians have a longer tradition than any other Christian group (they recall Paul's conversion near Damascus and the early role of Antioch), and their spiritual ancestors predated the Muslims in Syria by more than 500 years.

The Christians tend to congregate in the larger cities of western Syria and are splintered into a dozen identifiable sects, the largest of which are the Greek Orthodox (nearly 5 percent of the Syrian population, but with several subsects), Armenian Orthodox (Gregorians), and Syrian Orthodox (Jacobites). Greek, Latin, Arabic, and Syriac (Aramaic) are employed as liturgical languages by the various sects, and Syriac is preserved as an everyday language among some of the Greek Catholics in three mountain villages north of Damascus, including Malula and Saydnaya (Fig. 12-4).

Traditionally, Syrian Christians have affiliated with Arabism and were early leaders in Arab nationalism. Yet they have also felt an appreciable affinity with the West, having been a favored group during the Crusader occupation of the Levant and during the mandate period. The Nestorian Assyrians are some of the most recent arrivals in Syria. Having fled Iraq in 1933, they were settled in

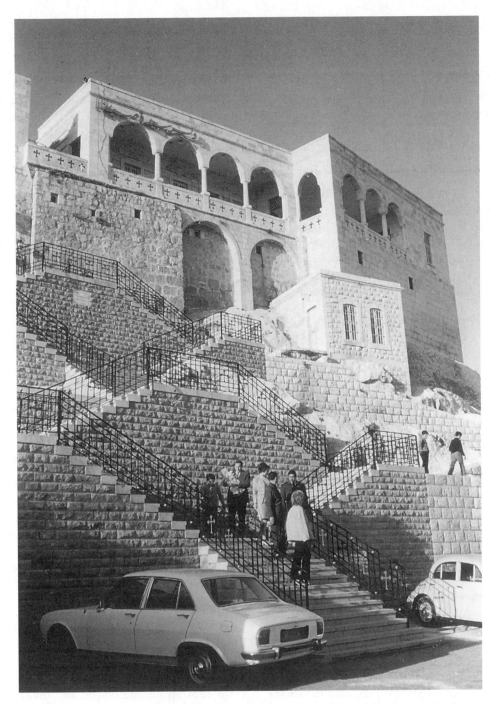

FIGURE 12-4   The Greek Orthodox convent of Saydnaya, located 12 miles/20 km north of Damascus at the foot of the Anti-Lebanon Mountains in western Syria. The shrine of the Virgin in the convent was at one time a major attraction for pilgrims and still brings scores of visitors each day.

a score of villages on the upper Khabur River, west of Hasakah.

Ethnic Minorities

The largest ethnolinguistic minority in Syria is the Kurds, perhaps 1.3 million in number—about 9 percent of the population. Speaking their own language, Kurds are primarily distributed across northern Syria, next to their ethnic homeland of Kurdistan, with concentrations in the mountains of the northwest and in the northeast. Many of them, along with Armenians in the early years, fled from Turkey in the 1920s and early 1930s following a failed insurrection against Turkish authorities in eastern Anatolia. In addition to the main Kurdish belt in the north, several thousand Kurds live in the cities, especially in the Damascus Kurdish Quarter. Although most are Sunni Muslims, some Kurds are Shii, Christian, and Yazidis.

The second-largest ethnolinguistic minority is the Armenians, who number roughly 300,000, about 2 percent of the Syrian population, and who are the least assimilated group in the country. Entirely Christian, they fled Turkish Armenia during several episodes, especially during the 1920s and 1930s. They settled particularly in Aleppo, where nearly 75 percent of the Armenians in Syria live, and also in Damascus. Educated and skilled, they work in trade, crafts (many of the jewelry artisans in Damascus are Armenians), small industry, and the professions. They emigrated in large numbers during the 1990s in search of better socioeconomic conditions elsewhere.

Smaller minorities in Syria include Turkmen, Circassians, and Jews. Nearly all of these minorities speak some Arabic, but the Turkmen and Circassians, like the Kurds and Armenians, primarily use their own language. The roughly 110,000 Turkmen, who are Sunni Muslims and Turkic speakers, are chiefly seminomadic herdsmen in the Jazirah, but some are settled agriculturalists in the Aleppo area. The especially distinct Circassians occupy the Hawran in southern Syria, with Druzes east and west of them. Only half as numerous as

the Turkmen, the Circassians play a more significant role in the Syrian economy and society. Jews numbered more than 30,000 before World War II and, like the Armenians, lived mostly in Aleppo and Damascus. Israeli-Syrian hostility after 1948 put Syrian Jews in an ambivalent position. The status of the Jews remaining in Syria periodically becomes a topic of acute friction between Syria and Israel when Israel asserts and Syria denies that Jews are mistreated in Syria. In April 1992, under U.S. pressure, Syria declared that any of the 4,000 remaining Syrian Jews who wished to emigrate were free to do so. About 400 indicated a desire to stay in Syria.[4] Bedouins have been steadily decreasing in number and by the mid-1990s probably made up only 3 percent of the Syrian population.

Evolving Economic Patterns

Mandate Syria developed modestly during its years under French economic dominance. However, like many of the states of the area, Syria faced constraints in its efforts as a new state to enter the modern industrial world. Conflict with Israel in 1948–1949 also slowed development, and it was not until well into the 1960s that there began to be a significant rate of development and growth. As has been true of several Middle East states in recent decades, growth in productive sectors has been retarded by internal and regional instability, experimentation with political-economic ideologies, and concentration on military affairs and military buildup. In Syria, rigid government control increasingly dictated prices, wages, and what could be produced, imported, and sold. As long as the economy was propped up by foreign funding, the socialist management worked. However, when grants from outside dwindled, the centralized, inefficient, and bureaucratic system could not operate the economy at a reasonable level—as had been demonstrated in Nasserist Egypt and was later revealed in Baathist Iraq and, most dramatically, in the former USSR. For that and other more inherent

MAP 12-2 Economic map of Syria. Manufacturing centers are underlined.

reasons, Syrian development has not proceeded as well as might be expected.

Syrian economic evolution after 1961 exhibited four stages, each lasting about a decade.

1. The 1960s were a time of buildup, with annual economic growth increasing from 2 and 3 percent to 6 and 7 percent later in the decade. Syria's traditional laissez-faire economy, formerly controlled by a small urban merchant-landowner class, experienced a turning point during Syria's union with socialist Egypt in the United Arab Republic, 1958–1961. Land redistribution and nationalization of private enterprises inaugurated under the UAR increased in pace into the mid-1960s and early 1970s.

By that time, more than 100 of the largest enterprises had been nationalized, along with the mineral industries, including the petroleum industry. Railways, airline, and ports also became government owned (Map 12-2).

2. The second stage, from late 1973 until 1982, saw Syria's economy take off, with growth averaging an outstanding 10 percent annually. The determinative stimulus for such growth was the huge influx of foreign funding, primarily because income from Syria's four main sources of foreign exchange—foreign grant aid, foreign lending, foreign funding for major development projects, and remittances from Syrians working abroad, primarily in the

Gulf—were at a sustained peak. Along with foreign capital came foreign technical expertise. Major donors were Gulf oil states, other OPEC countries, the USSR (which supplied funds, military equipment, military advisers, and technical support), the UN, the World Bank, West Germany, and others. The Baghdad Agreement of 1978 extended funding from the Gulf states for Syria (and Egypt) as a "confrontation" state to receive $1.8 billion annually, and although the funding later broke down, it afforded Syria an opportunity to cap a decade of expansion. The crowning achievement of the decade was completion of the Euphrates Dam, the second-largest dam (after Egypt's Aswan High Dam) in the Middle East when it was dedicated in 1973. Syria also developed expanded irrigation and land reclamation, an extended transportation system, more diversified manufacturing, and an extensive building program.

3. The third stage of economic evolution, 1982–1990, saw a marked downturn in the Syrian economy. The initial trigger was the sharp drop in oil prices, which halved the income of the Gulf states and reduced employment of Syrians in the Gulf area. Syria's oil exports earned less, even though the amount exported increased substantially. Foreign aid, including help from the then Soviet Union, steadily diminished. Soviet aid evaporated with the collapse of the USSR in 1991, and Syria found itself unable to utilize or best exploit some of its major projects. The value of Syrian currency dropped steadily during the middle and late 1980s to one-tenth its starting point in 1982; inflation reached 50, then 100 percent; lack of foreign exchange reduced imports, not only of consumer goods but even of important producer goods; and several factories were unable to continue operating. Military equipment and the occupation of parts of Lebanon by Syrian

troops still required heavy expenditures. Syria lost credibility in the West because of its occupation of Lebanon, its continued ties with the USSR, and its apparent support of certain terrorist groups. As Israel's consistently main adversary, Syria was blacklisted by the United States; Syria also offended its Arab neighbors by its curious support of Iran against Iraq during the 1980s.

In 1986, when both the European Communities and the United States applied sanctions against Syria because of its evident ties with accused terrorists, the Syrian economy flattened still more. The government seemed unable to extricate itself from either the economic morass or the political labyrinth in which it was enveloped. However, with the Soviet Union collapsing economically and no longer being able to supply and support Syria militarily, the Syrians began to seek accommodation with the West.[5]

4. During the 1990s, the economy first improved, then declined, and finally leveled. In 1990–1991, Syria's relations with both the West and its Arab neighbors improved appreciably for several years. After Iraq invaded Kuwait, Syria promptly associated itself with the allied coalition and eventually sent 19,000 troops to join coalition forces. In return, the Gulf states renewed aid to Syria under the Damascus Declaration of 1991, followed by transfer of substantial European and Japanese financial resources, and the Syrian government finally undertook economic reforms to improve its long-term situation. A realistic parallel currency exchange rate, liberalized investment codes, improved tourism structure, increased oil production, recovery of the agricultural sector, and modernized telecommunications stimulated growth in the early 1990s. GDP annual growth of more than 5 percent in 1993–1995 followed a vigorous 9 percent in 1992. A stalled peace process and low oil prices flattened the economy in the later 1990s, but in 1999 peace prospects and oil prices both

took an upturn. Slightly increased foreign investment and returning expatriate capital helped stabilize an otherwise stressed economy. The government seemed unable to loosen its control of strategic sectors, including petroleum, electricity, banking, and chemicals. Although the privatization and liberalization of some industries had demonstrated the benefits of economic rationalization, the Asad government may have feared that an increase in unemployment would have resulted had it privatized overstaffed parastatals. Continued heavy expenditures for military purposes and the 25-year-long occupation of parts of Lebanon also restrained progress. The economy at century's end was far behind its potential pace.

Agriculture

Agriculture has traditionally been a major element in the Syrian economy, and it still engages about one-fourth of the labor force. Agriculture continues to supply a major proportion of the GDP and export trade. A large share of the capital investment in economic development after the late 1960s went into land reclamation, land improvement, irrigation schemes, and agricultural programs. Agriculture and the oil industry are the government's top economic development priorities; the goal in agriculture is to achieve maximum food self-sufficiency to free limited foreign exchange for essential uses. After 1996, Syria shifted its status as a net importer of wheat and flour to that of a net exporter— 700,000 tons per year, thus not only saving hard currency but also earning it. Cotton production reached a record high in 1997 and supplied one-fourth of Syria's agricultural exports.[6]

Cyclic variations in rainfall totals and seasonal distribution are a crucial factor in the western Fertile Crescent because of the enormous swings in grain production created by the variations. Between 1947 and 1960 about every third year was dry, and Syria's wheat crop in the dry year of 1973 was only one-fourth that in the very wet year of 1972. The advantage of and

need for expanded irrigation are obvious, and despite financial, technical, and geographical problems, Syria is working toward that goal (see Table 7-1).

As is true for the Middle East as a whole, wheat and barley are by far the dominant crops in Syria, occupying more than two-thirds of the cultivated area. The more humid agricultural lands produce cotton and sugar beets, and cotton is the major crop in the expanding irrigated areas in the Jazirah. Tomatoes and lentils grow widely, as do more than a score of other seasonal vegetables. Permanent tree and vine crops grow both in irrigated areas and on rainfed slopes: citrus on the coastal plain and in the Ghutah (the extensive oasis around Damascus) and olives, figs, and grapes on many slopes in the west, where they are well adapted to the Mediterranean regime. As part of its agricultural development program, Syria is vigorously expanding olive production by one-third (Fig. 7-3) and is already the region's second producer, only slightly behind Turkey (Table 7-3). Rice is increasingly grown in the Ghab and in the Jazirah.

Ghab Project. The Ghab Project, which involved drainage, hydroelectric production, and irrigation and which was completed in 1965, reclaimed 61,780 acres/25,000 ha of former marshland in the Ghab Depression, east of and parallel to the Jabal al-Sahiliyah in northwestern Syria. Roughly 31 miles/50 km long by 9 miles/15 km wide, this northern end of the Levant Rift System was formerly flooded by the lower Orontes River. The basalt lava flow that dammed the Orontes at the Ghab Depression's northern outlet was cut through, and the marshland was made into a productive valley. Besides the marshland reclaimed, twice as much other land was improved as part of the Ghab Project, and the area now yields cotton, rice, sugar beets, wheat, and barley.

Euphrates Dam. The most important single development project in modern Syrian history is the Euphrates Dam system, which involves not only the huge dam itself but also a hydroelectric installation, a long-line electrical distribution

FIGURE 12-5   Euphrates Dam in northern Syria, key element in the Syrian plan to develop the Jazirah (area east of the Euphrates), including the broad Euphrates Valley itself. Lake Asad to left. Note eastern valley wall in distance.

net, the lake behind the dam, an extensive irrigation system, a new town, and an agricultural
development program in the Jazirah. Like the
Aswan High Dam in Egypt, the project was
made possible primarily by Soviet financial and
technical assistance. Initiated in 1961 and dedicated in 1973, the dam is 197 ft./ 60 m high and
3 miles/4.5 km long (Fig. 12-5). The resulting
reservoir, named Lake Asad in honor of Syria's
president, extends for 50 miles/ 80 km upstream,
covers 247 miles^2/ 640 km^2, and stores 12 billion
m^3 of fresh water.[7] The power station, inaugurated in 1978, has eight Soviet-made 100,000-
kilowatt turbines, which generated more than 90
percent of Syria's electrical energy for several
years; however, the percentage is decreasing as
several new thermal power plants fueled by natural gas come on stream.

A significant long-range agricultural purpose of the Euphrates Dam is the irrigation of
1.58 million acres/640,000 ha of land along the
Euphrates and its east-bank tributaries. This
undertaking will require several more years and
will, when complete, more than double the area
under irrigation in Syria (however, see next
paragraph). Tabaqah, the village at the original
damsite, expanded into a town of 50,000 and
was then renamed Madinat al-Thawrah (Revolution City). More than a dozen new villages
have also been built to accommodate the
60,000–70,000 people brought into the Jazirah
because of the new development there.

Nevertheless, several problems surround the
project.[8] A basic one is that the Euphrates
enters Syria from Turkey and leaves it for Iraq,
so that the three states involved have contended
sharply over the complex water rights (see
Chap. 11). After the completion of the
Euphrates Dam, a dispute between Syria and
Iraq over division of the river's water brought
the two states to the verge of war in 1975 before
Saudi Arabia mediated a resolution. For its

part, Turkey largely ignored Syrian complaints when it undertook a three-step damming of the Euphrates on its own territory and thus upset the Syrian timetable for irrigation projects in the Jazirah. More immediately serious was the revelation that large sections of the areas for which irrigation was planned are underlain by easily soluble gypsum. Since dissolution of the gypsum would both reduce soil quality and result in water loss, elevated concrete-trough channels must be used to carry water, and plans to irrigate large areas have had to be canceled (Fig. 7-16). Thus, the actual irrigated area will probably be less than 50–60 percent of the area initially envisioned. Figures must also take into account the 77,170 acres/31,230 ha of irrigated land (and 18,532 acres/7,500 ha of other land) drowned by Lake Asad, whose waters also displaced nearly 60 villages.

Growth of Industry

Mineral Industries. A dearth of mineral resources hindered economic progress in Syria for centuries. Only in recent decades have modern technology and management combined to facilitate discovery of two moderately large and domestically important mineral resources, petroleum and phosphates. The mineral industry sector, primarily petroleum, accounts for half of the nation's total export earnings and more than one-third of its GDP.

Petroleum. Intensive exploration led to discovery of oil in 1956 in the extreme northeastern corner of Syria, where several small, closely spaced fields show alignment with adjacent fields in Iraq and in Turkey farther north. Following Qaratshuk (Karatshuk), Syria's discovery field, Suwaydiyah was located in 1959. Major output began only in 1968 after a pipeline 404 miles/650 km long had been constructed to the Homs refinery and Tartus terminal.

Until 1986, Syria's high-sulfur heavy crude had to be blended with lighter crude, originally tapped at the Homs refinery from pipelines from Iraq. Following Syria's shutdown of those lines in the early 1980s (see Chap. 8), light crude brought

by tanker from Iran to Tartus was blended with Syria's heavy oil. However, the new Tayyim field and a cluster of small satellite fields discovered all around Dayr al-Zawr after 1984 have moderate reserves of very light, sweet crude. Production from the Tayyim-Omar cluster is pumped to refineries and export terminals in western Syria through the former Iraq Petroleum Company (IPC) pipelines. Thus, Syria is now able to meet its own blending requirements. Average daily production rose from 27,000 bpd in 1968 to a high of 605,000 bpd in 1995, surpassing Qatar's daily average for the first time in 1991. Production continued to average 560,000 bpd in the late 1990s, but output is forecast to decline steadily after 2000. Exploring for Syria's most valuable resource is also virtually cost free for the state, since several foreign companies buy concession areas and then pay the costs of exploration. A half dozen small fields south of Lake Asad and several gas fields in central Syria, near Palmyra, supply fuel for power plants and industry. A large new gas field discovered in 1997 in the Abi Rabah area, also near Palmyra, has been connected by pipeline to Aleppo and to new power plants nearby and in Damascus and Homs. In addition to expanding its own power-generating capacity, Syria is integrating its electric grid into a five-way network that will also involve Egypt, Jordan, Turkey, and, eventually, Iraq. The 1996 integration agreement has already been partly carried out, and added Lebanon in the process. By 1999, Syria possessed 2.5 billion barrels of oil reserves (see Table 8-1).

Syria's first refinery was built in Homs and originally used feedstock from Iraq Petroleum Company pipelines. It now has a throughput of 107,000 bpd, blending Syrian heavy and light crudes, as does the 135,000 bpd Baniyas refinery on the coast, built in 1980.

Phosphates. Rock strata comparable to those in which Israel, Jordan, and Iraq have enormous reserves of phosphate rock were traced into central Syria, and phosphorite production from moderate reserves rose from 600,000 mt in 1974 to 2.5 million mt in 1998 (Fig. 8-4). Reserves are great enough near Palmyra (Tadmur) that a railroad was built into the producing area in the late 1970s (see Map 12-2). Total reserves of 1 billion mt are sufficient for many years of production, but Syria's phosphates are of lower quality than those of neighboring states. Production of other mineral industries commodities—salt, gypsum, sulfur from petroleum processing, cement (especially from two larger mills at Tartus and Hamah), and steel from a plant just north of Hamah—all unexceptional, is for domestic use only. All mineral resources in Syria were nationalized in 1964.

Manufacturing

For many centuries, Damascus and other cities enjoyed fame for their damascene metalwork, damask fabrics, muslins, linens, silk brocades, tapestries, carpets, tooled leather, carved and inlaid furniture, glassware, pottery, jewelry, mosaics, and similar craft work. Fortunately for Syria and the world, all of these crafts have survived to some degree to the present time; however, they are an inadequate basis for a national manufacturing complex in the modern technological world.

Limitations that became apparent in the late 1940s typified industrial development at that time. Management lacked modern expertise, and labor lacked technical skill. The controlling merchant families were unable or unwilling to invest the amounts needed for industrial expansion, and domestic instability discouraged outside investors, who were not encouraged to participate in any case. When the Baath government nationalized all the major industries, investment capital for certain industries became available through government channels. However, in general, all of Syria's political-economic deficiencies converged to inhibit rational industrial development.

Planning and development during the 1970s gave early emphasis to infrastructure and basic industries: highways, railroads, the Euphrates Dam, cement plants, iron and steel plants, and similar industries. Little consideration could be given to production of precision goods or high-technology items. Well into the mid-1990s, heavy industry, sugar production and other food processing, cement, chemicals, textiles,

and other enterprises continued as parastatals, as did banking and oil. But with the easing of government restrictions—especially through the 1991 Investment Law No. 10—private investment moved into food processing, pharmaceuticals, textiles, ready-made clothing, and transportation. By the late 1990s, Syrian industry was progressing better than it had in past decades; but, more than other sectors of the economy, it was dropping farther and farther behind that of neighboring states. Virtually every Syrian city is benefiting from the modest industrial expansion, with Aleppo gaining tractor and other agricultural machinery plants as well as appliance factories, cement and food-processing plants; Hamah, iron and steel, textile, and cement plants; Homs, fertilizer plants, using phosphates from near Palmyra; Tartus, Syria's largest cement plant; Baniyas, a refinery larger than the older Homs facility; and smaller plants in Latakia, Dayr al-Zawr, Hasakah, and Raqqah. Although still hampered by the legacy of state intervention, Syrian industrial entrepreneurs hoped to gain momentum in the new century.

Transportation and Trade

As a keystone in the Fertile Crescent, Syria has been the focus of route junctions and crossings for millennia, and to some extent contemporary Syria still fulfills that function. From the late Neolithic onward, the Damascus-Aleppo axis has been a junction for routes from the south—the Via Maris (Sea Route) from Egypt and the King's Highway from Arabia; east—along the Fertile Crescent from Persia and Mesopotamia; and north—through the Cilician Gates from Anatolia. Even with today's technologically advanced transportation systems, primary regional highway and air routes cross Syria both north-south and east-west.

Syria in early 2000 possesses a modest road and rail network (see Table 9-2) that is adequate for current needs. The more densely settled areas naturally have the densest network of roads, and only through-routes cross the sparsely inhabited desert areas of the southeast. The transportation net has expanded and improved markedly since the 1960s. All major cities are now connected by modern paved highways, with a four-lane divided throughway now extending from the Jordanian border along the full length of the main axis Damascus-Homs-Hamah-Aleppo. New railroads have facilitated the development of the northeast, especially the Jazirah, and the center of the country. The rail line from Latakia through Aleppo, Madinat al-Thawrah, Raqqah, Dayr al-Zawr, and Hasakah to Qamishli has been a major factor in agricultural development of the northeast, in Latakia port activity, and in stimulating the growth of all of the cities through which it passes. By the late 1940s, with no adequate general-cargo ports of its own, Syria continued to use Beirut, having lost access to Iskenderun during World War II and to Haifa in 1948. However, the government meanwhile initiated a long-range development program for Latakia and, later, Tartus. Baniyas had long served as an oil export port as terminus for IPC lines from Iraq. Latakia is now a major port facility, and Tartus has undergone significant expansion since the 1980s.

Although trade in and through Syria diminished during the later decades of Ottoman rule, exchange of goods has long been a lively activity in this centrally located area. The country's vigorous retail trade has remained in the private sector, even though it suffers from complicated government restraints. The *suq* is a prominent feature of every Syrian town and city. The bustling Suq Hamidiyah in Damascus and the underground Aleppo *suq* have been famed for centuries throughout the region, with each *suq* containing hundreds of small shops selling a wide range of specialty and common items. One reminder of Syria's commercial traditions is the annual Damascus International Trade Fair, conducted in late July since 1954. Trade continues to play a major role in the Syrian economy. Foreign commerce at century's end is primarily with Western Europe, Ukraine, and Turkey. Syria is, indeed, negotiating an association with the European Union; it has also agreed with other Arab countries to a customs reduction program.[9]

Political Geography

Internal Relations

Like other Fertile Crescent states, Syria found its political and territorial aspirations redirected at the end of World War I and, as a mandate, had its potential state form imposed upon it. Thus, when Syria emerged as a newly independent state in 1946, its boundaries were prefixed, and Syrians were forced to achieve a state idea—raison d'être—within an imposed context. As one consequence, national memories of the Umayyad Empire and the long-persistent national consciousness of "Greater Syria" resurfaced in the new state. Although mandate Syria had been unable to prevent the dismemberment of Greater Syria, the independent state could express irredentist claims regarding detached territories. The most burning issue was the severance of Lebanon, which Syria considered to be amputation of an inherent piece of Syrian land. This stance was revived as a peripheral claim after 1976 when Syrian troops occupied part of Lebanon—and were still there in early 2000—originally as the main units in the Arab Deterrent Force. A secondary territorial issue was the detachment of the Sanjak of Alexandretta from mandate Syria in 1939.

With no specific historical boundaries to influence them, France and Britain delimited mandate Syria for their own ends, to accord with the rough outlines of the Sykes-Picot Agreement (see Map 11-1). Two interesting boundaries resulted: The unique northern boundary simply followed the southern rail of the Berlin-to-Baghdad railway from north of Aleppo to Nusaybin, a distance of 200 miles/322 km. The southeastern border is entirely geometrical, with one stretch from the then Jabal al-Druze to the Euphrates a straight line of 275 miles/443 km extending across the Syrian Desert. Even though Bedouins continue their seasonal migrations across the southeastern line, and although tensions have waxed along the Turkish border on several occasions, both boundaries have proved to be reasonably satisfactory.

Three sections of the western land boundary have produced problems. The northwestern segment, around the Sanjak of Alexandretta, has already been discussed (see the section in Chap. 11 on "Boundary and Territorial Disputes"). The boundary with mandate Lebanon was objected to by Syria because some of the territory awarded Lebanon was a Muslim area whose inclusion in a Christian Lebanon mandate could not be justified. The segment along the southeastern shore of the Sea of Galilee ran several hundred meters back from the water's edge, thus giving the shore to the mandate of Palestine. The 1949 Armistice Line gave the entire shore to Israel, and after 1967 Israel occupied the whole of the Golan area.

Golan

Israel's military conquest of the strategic and heavily fortified Golan Heights in the 1967 June War, occupation of the heights after the war, and announcement of the integration of the area into Israel in December 1981 added to Syria's territorial losses. Syria has not accepted detachment of the Golan from the Syrian homeland. Syria's adamant irredentist determination to recover the Golan has been manifest in every Syrian-Israeli negotiation or discussion of aspects of the peace process. Syria considers that it has a strong case: No country has recognized Israel's annexation of the Golan, and the United States has consistently rejected Israel's integration and settlement of the Golan. In late 1999 and early 2000, ongoing discussions between Israel and Syria under U.S. good offices treated the Golan and normalization of relations (see Chapters 11 and 15).

Centrifugal Forces

Not until the early 1970s could Syria achieve sufficient internal political stability to establish a national unity and a rational government structure. Prior to that time, Syria suffered coups d'état more frequently than any other Middle Eastern state. Even with political stabilization, the government has a double minority power structure. Ideologically, the party in power is the Baath (Arab Renaissance Party),

which achieved power originally in a 1963 coup; ethnically, the man who was president 1970–2000 was from the relatively small minority of the Alawis.

A major social competition that creates a centrifugal force within the country is the increasingly important conflict between conservative and liberal Islam, along with the opposition of both of these groups to the secularism represented by the Baath-Alawi combination. The best organized of the militant fundamentalist Islamic groups, the Muslim Brotherhood, instigated the two most serious challenges to President al-Asad's basically secular regime. Stimulated by Sunni opposition to the Alawis, the Muslim Brothers killed more than 60 Alawi military cadets in Aleppo in 1979. They then, as the key members of the Islamic Front, took over Hamah in February 1982, and government security forces killed several thousand of the city's inhabitants and destroyed much of Hamah in breaking the rebel hold. The Hamah assault is the blackest mark against the al-Asad regime, and the clash is indicative of a major centrifugal factor. Otherwise, the regime has not outwardly evinced massive brutal physical repression. Whereas large Palestinian refugee groups have formed a crucial centrifugal force in Lebanon and Jordan, the very large Palestinian refugee population in Syria— approximately 300,000—has been kept under strict control, although assured of Syrian sympathy for their cause.

Centripetal Forces

In the face of the potent divisive forces just reviewed, it is noteworthy that two related aspects of nationalism, Syrian nationalism and Arab nationalism, have remained sufficiently effective to offset the centrifugal forces and to bring the Syrians together into a viable national group. The regularity and frequency of coups d'état prior to 1963 seem to have been broken, and the national will to stand firm vis-à-vis Israel and against political criticism and opposition from Iraq and Western states, including the United States, has been sufficient to maintain Syrian unity into 2000. By 1990, Syria had experienced the trials of losing Soviet support, reversing aspects of its relationship with the West, and had received promises of outside aid. By the early 1990s, the Baathist regime had yielded some of its most rigid controls, but political openness and the residual internal stresses have yet to be reconciled.

Regional Relations

A leading role by Damascus in Arab nationalism was widely accepted in the Fertile Crescent at the end of World War I. The Arab leadership that backed the Arab Revolt of 1916–1917 had been centered in Damascus, and a short-lived kingdom was established in Syria under Faysal ibn Husayn in 1920. In assuming its mandate, France forced Faysal to abdicate, but Syria has never forgotten its moment of glory. However, attempts by the state of Syria to assert a leading role for itself after the early 1960s have been viewed with caution by its Arab neighbors, several of whom are competitors for regional leadership. Observing the mistakes of Nasserist Egypt, Syria has chosen to balance its support of Arab nationalism with a focus on Syrian nationalism and Syrian development rather than to enter the overcrowded arena of Arab socialism and nationalism. Having shown its support of Palestine in three wars with Israel, Syria has taken in scores of thousands of Palestinian refugees. It was a charter member of the League of Arab States (Arab League) and has played a reasonably active role in that organization. The office for the Arab boycott of Israel is located in Damascus. While Syria considers itself part of the Islamic world and has participated in several Islamic world organizations, it advocates and practices a greater degree of secularism than do the more conservative Muslim states.

Syria's relations with virtually all of its neighbors for most of the years since World War II have been marked by frictions and, in the case of Israel, by successive hostilities. Syria's relations with Lebanon are of special significance but have already been discussed in Chapter 11 and are further examined in Chapter 13. The decades-long dispute with Turkey over Alexandretta was exacerbated by frictions over Euphrates water, but Syria and its powerful northern neighbor maintained correct relations until late 1998. The immediate trigger was Syria's support of Kurdish rebels, especially the PKK and its leader, who had been fighting Turkish troops in southeast Turkey for several years. For its part, Syria still expressed irredentist resentment over Alexandretta, again denounced Turkey for interfering with the Euphrates water flow, and condemned Turkey for its recent collaboration with Israel. After Turkish threats of military action and regional mediation, Syria withdrew its support of the PKK.[10] Relations with Jordan on the south have ranged from close ties to border closures on several occasions and even to at least two brief, abortive Syrian invasions of northwestern Jordan. Syria and Jordan differed on Iraq's invasion of Kuwait, and Syria especially condemned the Jordanian-Israeli peace treaty of 1994. However, with the ascension of King Abdullah to Jordan's throne in February 1999, Jordan and Syria soon achieved their closest relations in decades.

Syria and Iraq pursued their mutual economic interests until the mid-1960s. For many years, Iraq's only petroleum outlet was through pipelines across Syria, with terminals in Baniyas and in Tripoli, Lebanon (see Chap. 8). The pipelines and terminals were vital to Iraq, and they brought Syria royalties of more than $120 million annually, plus another $120 million annually in discounts to Syria on Iraqi crude for use in the Homs refinery. Nevertheless, because of disputes between Iraqi and Syrian Baathists, as well as disagreements over oil royalties, Syria closed the pipelines sporadically in the 1970s and definitively in 1982. Syria supported Iran during the Iran-Iraq war, despite its long and vigorous advocacy of Arab unity. Therefore, despite vigorous popular opposition in the street, in 1990 the Syrian government had little hesitation about joining, along with Egypt, the coalition that forced Iraq to withdraw from Kuwait. In early 1999, Syria and Iraq gave subdued indications of mutual interest in reaching détente.

Global Relations

On the world scale, Syria developed special relations with France during France's administration of mandate Syria. Despite its resentment of that country, Syria inevitably adopted certain aspects of French culture, but Franco-Syrian relations after 1946 diminished to an ordinary commercial exchange.

As was true with Egypt after the mid-1950s and with Iraq after the late 1950s, Syria found its channels with the West increasingly constricted because of Western—especially U.S.—support of Israel, Syria's and the Arabs' main adversary. Syria therefore turned to the USSR and its East European satellites for arms, economic aid, and technical assistance, including financial aid for such projects as the Euphrates Dam. Soviet military advisers and liaison personnel served in Syria for more than three decades. However, Syria kept communism in Syria firmly under control and, like Egypt, did not permit itself to become a Soviet satellite. Disintegration of the USSR in 1991 suddenly deprived Syria of its politico-economic mainstay and compelled President al-Asad to pursue accommodation with the West. Inter alia, he has sought greater rapport with the European Union and with individual European states.

Syria's relations with the United States had an early foundation for a friendly interchange, and in 1919, the King-Crane Commission discovered a reservoir of goodwill toward the United States, partly because of the work of the Syrian Protestant College and partly because of the ideals of President Wilson's Fourteen Points. Relations cooled after publicity of the U.S. endorsement of the Balfour Declaration and after the United States supported Zionist colonization in Palestine. Relations warmed and cooled during the 1950s and early 1960s,[11] but the trend after the 1967 Arab-Israeli war was downward. Syria broke diplomatic relations with the United States after that war and agreed to restored relations only in 1974. The United States (and other Western countries) viewed Syria with suspicion after Syrian troops entered Lebanon in 1976, and the two countries came into open conflict in

late 1983 in Lebanon. A pragmatic lessening of tensions between the United States and Syria followed the phasing out of Soviet-Syrian cooperation, Syria's increasing moderation, its participation in the Gulf coalition against Iraq, and its willingness to join in the peace process. Because it continues to harbor the leaders of ten rejectionist groups, Syria remains on the U.S. list of "terrorist states," although the State Department declares that for 13 years there has been no evidence to show that Syrian officials have engaged in terrorist acts. Also, in early 2000, the Syrian government quietly expelled several of the rejectionist group leaders. Despite its own ambiguities and the external efforts to marginalize it, Syria continues to be a key historical and geopolitical player in the region.

Notes

1. Devlin 1983 is a useful, concise survey of Syria. Khoury 1987 is an excellent account of Syria as mandate. Hopwood 1988 examines independent Syria's political and cultural evolution. *Syria* Country Study 1988 is an excellent general study in an authoritative series. Pipes 1990 is a critical study. Theroux 1996 is a recent useful illustrated *National Geographic* report.

2. Syrians also celebrate May 17, the day on which the last French forces evacuated Syria.

3. See Batuta 1981, van Dam 1978, and Bengio and Ben-Dor 1999, Chap. 7.

4. *New York Times*, Dec. 15, 1992.

5. See Perthes 1992.

6. *Agricultural Situation Report: Syria,* 1998.

7. Data supplied by Syrian engineers at the Euphrates Dam during my visit on June 8, 1990.

8. See the excellent and detailed analyses in Kolars and Mitchell 1991.

9. *Country Commercial Guide: Syria,* FY 2000; *Economic Policy and Trade Practices: Syria,* 1998; "Syria," *World Factbook* 1999; and *EIA: Syria,* 1999. Steven Plaut, "The Collapsing Syrian Economy," *Middle East Quarterly* vi, no. 3 (Sept. 1999): 3–14, is particular in its invidious perspective. See also *New York Times,* Jan. 27, 2000. Bashar al-Asad, who succeeded his late father as president of Syria in June 2000, is expected to modernize and loosen the economy.

10. See the *New York Times,* Oct. 4, 1998.

11. For a partial explanation of U.S.-Syrian discord, see Little 1990. For a broader context, see Kaufman 1996. More details are given in *Syria* Country Study, 1987.

13
Lebanon and Cyprus:
A Mountain and an Island

Lebanon

The Character of Lebanon

Lebanon differs strikingly both physically and culturally from other states of the Middle East. It is dominated by the rugged and well-watered range of Mount Lebanon, green on its western slopes, facing the blue Mediterranean, and brown from the steppes and deserts at its back. It is small enough to be traversed by car in a few hours even on its long axis. Yet it displays almost as much landscape diversity as does Turkey, with an area 76 times that of Lebanon. Culturally, it has been one of the most highly developed countries in the Middle East: It is one of the most Western, modernized, literate, and education-centered, with a laissez-faire, entrepreneurial society and economy. Lebanon is also the most multisectarian state in the region, and, as the result of interconfessional tensions augmented by regional stresses, it flamed into externally fueled civil warfare in 1975. It sank steadily into anarchy to become for sixteen years the area's most devastated and endangered country. Once called the Switzerland of the Middle East—and Beirut the Paris of the Middle East—Lebanon in the 1980s was fragmented, a nation in jeopardy, and a nation in the process of collapse. Not until late in 1990 did the internecine killings finally cease under determined pressure from other Arab League states. Even a decade later, the soil of Lebanon was still the only battleground in the Arab-Israel conflict, although Israel finally withdrew from Southern Lebanon in May 2000. However, despite periodic setbacks, Lebanon was making steady progress along the road to recovery, and the ongoing peace process promised some hope for stability.

Rich Past, Complex Evolution

The advantages and resources of Lebanon attracted humanoids to the land more than 800,000 years ago, during the Mindel glaciation, as is revealed by artifact finds near Sidon and in the high intermontane Bekaa. Byblos and numerous other sites show evidence of occupancy before and during the Neolithic period, from the ninth to the fourth millennium BC. "Phoenicia," the name applied to the area after about 1200 BC, is the Greek translation of "Canaan," land of purple-red. The color probably referred to the important Phoenician export of textiles dyed "royal purple" with secretions from the murex shellfish found at Sidon and Tyre. The coastal city-states of Tyre, Sidon, Beirut, and Byblos used the famous Cedars of Lebanon for shipbuilding and for export from Byblos to Egypt before 2400 BC. By the thirteenth century BC, the Phoenicians had also developed, probably for use in their active maritime trade, an alphabet that was gradually adopted, adapted, and diffused throughout the ancient world. Despite repeated invasions and later control by the Seleucids, Romans, and Byzantines, the area thrived, as monuments and ruins in every part of modern Lebanon attest.

The strength of the Christianity that developed during the centuries of east Roman-Byzantine control plays a key role in contemporary Lebanon. The Muslim conquest

Lebanon

Long-form official name, anglicized: Republic of Lebanon

Official name, transliterated: al-Jumhuriyah al-Lubnaniyah

Form of government: multiparty republic with one legislative house (National Assembly)

Area: 4,016 miles^2/10,400 km^2

Population, 1999 (rough estimate): 3,506,000. **Literacy (latest):** 92%

Ethnic composition (%): Lebanese 81, Palestinian 9.0, Armenian 6.0, Syrian, Kurd, and others 4

Religions (%, estimated): Shii Muslim 34.0, Sunni Muslim 20.0, Maronite Christian 19.0, Greek Orthodox 6.0, Druze 8.0, Greek Catholic 5.0, Armenian Christian 6.0, other 2.0

GDP, 1998: $15.8 billion; per capita: $4,500

Petroleum reserves: none

Main exports (% of total value, 1997): foodstuffs and tobacco 20, textiles 12, chemicals 11, metals and metal products 11, electrical goods 10, jewelry 10, paper and paper products, 8

Main imports (% of total value, 1997): foodstuffs 29, machinery and transport equipment 28, consumer goods 18, chemicals 9, textiles 5, metals 5, fuels 3

Capital city: Beirut 1,600,000; other cities: Tripoli (Tarabulus) 500,000; Zahlah 200,000; Sidon (Sayda) 100,000; Tyre 50,000

---

after 636 slowly altered the confessional balance and, later, the linguistic pattern. Nevertheless, the dominance of Christianity in Mount Lebanon persisted through thirteen centuries under the Umayyads, Abbasids, Crusaders, Mamluks, and, after 1517, the Ottomans. Under the *millet* system of the Ottomans, Mount Lebanon enjoyed a high degree of autonomy from the sixteenth century onward. After fighting between Christians and Druzes in 1860, Mount Lebanon had a special status that continued until World War I.

Lebanon emerged as a separate entity as a mandate of France under the League of Nations after World War I. Its territory was detached from the basic mandate Syria and was enlarged so as to create *Grand Liban,* "Greater Lebanon." This Greater Lebanon included not only the coastal plain and Mount Lebanon, but also the Bekaa paralleling Mount Lebanon on the east and the separate Anti-Lebanon mountain ridges beyond the Bekaa trough (Map 13-1).

After two decades under French tutelage, Lebanon was declared independent by the Free French on November 26, 1941, although a reaffirmation of independence was required on November 22, 1943, the official independence day. As in Syria, French forces did not finally evacuate the country until 1946.

Lebanon and the Lebanese

Lebanon is synonymous with cultural diversity, as virtually every major ethnic or religious group in the Fertile Crescent is represented. However, the diversity among Lebanon's peoples that underlies the country's factionalism is not so much ethnolinguistic as sectarian. Moreover, emphasis on the conflict between Christians and Muslims neglects the antagonisms among more than a dozen Christian subgroups and half a dozen Muslim subgroups. Intercommunal tensions are so great that all sects have opposed a census since the 1932 numeration, which showed a Christian majority and, under the system arranged with French guidance, gave majority government and military power to the Christians. This political arrangement was not adjusted, in the absence of a new census, until 1990, even though there has been an obvious Muslim majority for years.

The estimated 1999 population of 3.5 million represents only a modest increase in the 1975 estimate of 3 million, the lowest population growth in the region during those years. However, during the worst years of fighting, including the 1982 Israeli invasion, the population decreased sharply, especially in Beirut. When the 1989 accord seemed to be holding, Lebanese gradually began returning in the early 1990s.

Ethnolinguistic Groups

Ethnolinguistically, about 92 percent of the Lebanese are Arabs in that their mother tongue is Arabic. In spite of this similarity, however, the variations among Arabs seen in many parts of the Middle East are especially wide and critical in Lebanon. Some Maronite Christians, for example, even deny Arab ancestry and claim descent from the Phoenicians or Byzantines. By contrast, Palestinian refugees in Lebanon find their identity, in addition to their Palestinian status, in their Arabism and in Islam, or as Palestinian Christians. Yet other Lebanese Arab Christians consider themselves Arab and advocate mutual Christian-Muslim tolerance.

By far the most numerous non-Arab minority are the Armenians, estimated to number more than 210,000, about 6 percent of the national population. The Kurds are the second-largest minority, constituting as much as 1 percent of the population. The formerly sizable Jewish minority—estimated to have numbered more than 20,000 at the turn of the century and more than 7,000 in the 1950s—was smaller than 100 by the late 1990s.

Although not a separate ethnolinguistic group in Lebanon, the Palestinians were at the

MAP 13-1 Map of Lebanon. Circled numbers identify regions discussed in text. In May 2000, Israel withdrew from its "security zone," occupied since 1978.

focus of the fighting in Lebanon for much of the period 1975–1991 and therefore are a significant element in the complex pattern of the country. Of the 800,000 Arab refugees who fled Palestine or Israel during the 1947–1949 fighting, about 150,000 crossed into southern Lebanon, most of them expecting to return to their homes within a short time. Additional thousands came to Lebanon during the 1967 Arab-Israeli war and after the 1970 fighting in Jordan. Most of them crowded into seventeen refugee camps (now reduced to twelve) built with help from the United Nations Relief and Works Agency (UNRWA) near Tyre, Sidon, Tripoli, Beirut, and Baalbak in the Bekaa. By 1999, estimates of the number of Palestinians in Lebanon were as high as 375,000.[1] Some Palestinians, especially professionals, have obtained Lebanese citizenship, but most of the Palestinian refugees have remained stateless, destitute refugee camp dwellers. The Lebanese

MAP 13-2 Patterns of religions for latest year with reliable data. Circles are in proportion to population involved, and pie graphs indicate percentages of adherents to the various sects. Figures have, of course, changed during 40 years, as discussed in the text, but the graphs still reflect the complexity of communal structure in this small country.

government and a majority of the Lebanese have consistently rejected the local settlement or assimilation of the Palestinians; the rejection is primarily based on the sociopolitical threat that their settlement would pose to the delicate demographic power balance in Lebanese politics and to the already stressed social fabric. Having witnessed the "Palestinization" of Jordan and having suffered repeated Israeli invasions and bombing raids because of Palestinian and pro-Palestinian activity on their soil, the Lebanese reject further perpetuation of the half-century-long turmoil.

Confessional Groupings

Among the multidimensional, interactive factors in the matrix of Lebanon, religious affiliation is the single most vital identity among the Lebanese. Christian and Druze mountaineers enjoyed special status under the Ottomans, and Christians were the core sect around which

France created mandate Lebanon. Distinct from the Sunni Muslim lands around it, Lebanon—first as a mandate and then as an independent state—evolved under a carefully constituted balance of confessional elements: The majority of Christians held key positions, but power sharing and confessional distribution of offices were designed to produce stability and effectiveness. The breakdown of the system can be better understood through a review of the basic religious groupings. Map 13-2 shows the proportional distribution of the major confessional groups prior to the outbreak of the civil war in 1975, and although the information is outdated, it is still instructive.[2]

Muslims. Making up about one-third of the population, Shiis (Shiites) are now the largest single sect in Lebanon. Formerly and occasionally still referred to as Mutawalis, the Shiis have traditionally been the most oppressed people in the area. Emerging from their passive role in the 1970s, the Shiis matched other groups in Lebanon with their own militias—first, Amal (Hope) in 1974 and then, in 1980, Hizballah (Hizb Allah, Party of God), the latter a more militant and extremist fundamentalist Islamic group than Amal. Hizballah (or Hezbollah, in transliteration from Farsi) is supported by Iran and others. As is mentioned elsewhere, Hizballah fielded the uninvited main fighting force opposing operations by Israel and its proxy South Lebanon Army in southern Lebanon. It also fired rockets into northern Israel; the retaliatory attacks by Israeli aircraft and artillery included bombing attacks on Lebanon's power stations, as in February 2000. The Shiis have three main concentrations in Lebanon—the south, Beirut, and the northern Bekaa.

Sunnis (Sunnites), 20 percent of the population and formerly the largest and most influential Muslim group in Lebanon, are widely distributed in the country, with concentrations in Beirut, Tripoli and the Akkar, the southern Bekaa, and the Shuf (see Map 13-1). More than any other sect, the Sunnis resented being separated from Syria in 1920 when mandate Lebanon was detached from Greater Syria. In many respects, the quiet sympathies of this conservative and mostly middle-class Muslim group lie more with some of the more moderate Christian groups than with militant fellow Muslim Shiis.

Druzes, despite their relatively limited share of the population (8 percent), have figured significantly in the sociopolitical dynamics of the Lebanon area for several centuries. Concentrated in the mountains southeast of Beirut (Druzistan) and especially in the Shuf, the Druzes played a key role in the fighting of both 1958 and 1975–1991 but also in the everyday political life of the state.

Alawis number around 60,000 in Lebanon, most of them in Tripoli. A few thousand Ismailis round out the Muslim groupings in Lebanon.

Christians. Maronites, formerly the largest and most influential single sect in Lebanon, had diminished to 19 percent of the population by the late 1990s. They considered themselves creators and developers of the Lebanese state and assumed the role of guardians of its sovereignty and Christian character. In both mandate Lebanon and independent Lebanon into the early 1970s, Maronites guided, dominated, and enjoyed the unique polity that had evolved. Fearing for the integrity of Lebanon, during the 1975–1990 war the Maronite Phalangists, with broad Israeli support, formed the core of the militias opposing the Palestinians and associated Muslim groups. A split among the Maronites in 1989–1990 over Syria's role, leadership of Christian militias, and the presidency of Lebanon led to internal Maronite warfare and additional tragic death and destruction in Beirut. Maronites now lack leadership and share power with the Sunnis and Shiis.

In addition to the Maronites, another dozen Christian sects claim separate identity and roles in the Lebanese political structure. Most of them appear in Table 6-2. The Greek Orthodox make up about 6 percent of the population and are widely distributed in Lebanon. They urge accommodation with other groups. None of the remaining groups play a major role in the state's politics.

Disrupted Economic Patterns

From Phoenician times, the major economic activities of Lebanon have taken advantage of locational and physiographic assets: (1) the country's central location on the eastern Mediterranean coast, which has permitted the Lebanese to serve as middlemen between the hinterland to the east and Mediterranean lands to the west; (2) its central location in the Middle East, making it an intraregional and interregional crossroad; (3) its well-watered coastal plain and somewhat indented coastline, facilitating development of port cities; (4) its likewise well-watered mountain background, which has passes that lead inland; and (5) its original forest cover and present agricultural (horticultural) development.

Despite the foregoing advantages, mandate Lebanon had a limited population, small size, no extensive granaries, and virtually no mineral resources; the enterprising Lebanese therefore revived their earlier skills as Levantine traders and middlemen. Further expanding their service economy after 1950, they developed financial services, education facilities, medical services, a modern port and airport, consultative expertise, recreation areas, and other services that were then inadequate in most of the Middle East. Foreign companies and embassies based their regional representatives in "the Paris of the East." Beirut functioned for decades as an efficient regional central place for the emerging oil areas of the Gulf. When fighting erupted in this Middle East nerve center in 1975, however, Lebanon rapidly lost its role, further motivating the oil states to expand their own service functions.[3] By the time relative peace and stability returned in the early 1990s, Lebanon had little to offer its former patrons.[4] In theorizing about the revival of the country's economic viability, some traditional patterns as well as certain current trends can be meaningfully examined.

Services

Before 1975, Lebanon offered a full modern range of services, from personal services to banking operations to aircraft engine maintenance. It had excellent educational and medical facilities: In addition to the second-oldest university in the Arab world and one of the best, the American University of Beirut, there was the French Jesuit Université St. Joseph, Beirut Arab University, Lebanese University, Armenian Hagazian College, and Beirut University College (formerly Beirut College for Women, now Lebanese American University). Medical facilities, especially the American University Hospital and the French Hotel Dieu, both connected with good medical schools, served patients from Lebanon and much of the Arab Middle East. These facilities remain and offer high-quality expertise, but the Gulf states enjoy larger and more highly technological facilities.

Lebanon's label of Switzerland of the Middle East before 1975 also applied to the formerly extensive banking system. Not only were deposits and trusts attracted from Saudi Arabia, Kuwait, and other Gulf oil states, but also flight capital came to Lebanon from the less stable economies of Syria, Egypt, Iraq, and Jordan. This capital helped fuel the remarkable development of Lebanon during the period 1955–1975. The Lebanese pound, 90 percent goldbacked and freely convertible, was one of the world's most stable currencies for three decades after World War II. However, the steady loss in the value of the pound during the 1980s caused it to drop from 3.2 to the U.S. dollar to as low as 800–900 to the dollar and then plummet to a disastrous 3,000 to the dollar in late 1992. It was a stable 1,513 to the dollar in mid-2000.

Before 1975, more than 1.5 million visitors annually were attracted to Lebanon, partly because of its wide variety of historical monuments and ruins, from prehistoric and Phoenician through Crusader to Ottoman times. The massive Roman ruins at Baalbak were a major tourist site. More than 300 hotels, numerous beach resorts, beautiful scenery, both summer and winter mountain resorts, the striking Casino du Liban, a wide range of goods, a varied night life in Beirut—in general, a palpable joie de vivre—and easy access by land, sea, or

air contributed to the attractions of Lebanon as a center for tourism. Lebanon is working hard to regain this source of foreign exchange and is steadily rebuilding the physical facilities for tourism and restoring tourist confidence. One confidence-building development occurred in 1997 when the United States lifted its decade-long ban on travel to Lebanon by U.S. citizens. Direct air traffic between Lebanon and the United States was still prohibited in early 2000. Neighbors competing for the tourist dollar will slow Lebanon's return to its former premier tourist role.

Regional embassy offices and offices of major companies cannot be expected to return to Beirut until the city and country have recovered further and security is assured.

Trade and Transportation

Along with services, trade was formerly and probably will again be Lebanon's main economic activity. Significant from Phoenician times, Lebanon's trade started its modern growth after World War I and burgeoned after the region's oil industry began its rapid development in the later 1950s. The country's economic liberalism spurred a lively export trade and other commercial transactions, facilitating customs clearances and the operation of a free port (duty-free zone) in Beirut; and the stability and free convertibility of the Lebanese pound was an additional stimulus. Beirut's port became a break-in-bulk point and an entrepôt to warehouse products for later onward shipment. Large stores and small shops handled widely varied articles from Western Europe, the Middle East, and South Asia. Lebanon's foreign trade picture has undergone major alteration over two decades, but it still has much to offer the national economy. The variety of commodities involved in the export-import trade is shown in the country summary.

A sign of the economic distress and the demand for foreign exchange during the 1980s was that Lebanon produced large amounts of illegal hashish and opium in the Bekaa intermontane valley, which even in normal times produces some of these two drugs. During the war years, 12–15 tons of hashish was shipped annually—20 percent of the world consumption. After 1992, both Syrian troops and Lebanese police enforced prohibitions against growing either hashish or opium plants.

Because of the importation of quantities of consumer goods, the balance of Lebanon's trade in tangible goods has long been negative. However, the country's pre-1975 overall balance was normally well on the profit side because of services and other income that reflected the wide range of Lebanon's economic activities. Beirut's seaport and airport were ideally situated to serve as gateways to the Levant and beyond. The port, sixteenth busiest in the world in the early 1970s, is being rebuilt, modernized, and expanded. In the changed regional commercial dynamics of the new millennium, Beirut port can be expected to play only a modest role. Much the same future may be forecast for Beirut International Airport, although it formerly served as the Middle East aviation hub for both passengers and cargo and was the busiest civil airport in the region during the 1960s. Many airlines used Beirut's excellent catering services for their onward flights. Often nonoperational during the 1980s, BIA has received a $500 million modernization and expansion, including a new runway built on a ramp reclaimed from the Mediterranean. A new terminal opened in early 1998 can accommodate 8,000 passengers per day. Quasi-national Middle East Airlines has been considerably trimmed, now having ten operational aircraft and shorter routes, but the airline is seeking financing for restructuring. Lebanese rail lines are antiquated and are either abandoned or little used, and most goods and passengers move by road. The road net is relatively dense (Map 13-3), considering the rugged terrain in much of the country. Although many mountain roads are narrow and steep, most are well surfaced to withstand the winter rains and, at higher elevations, the deep snows. The Beirut-Damascus highway and the coast road are scenic routes, both of

MAP 13-3   Economic map of Lebanon.

which during the 1990s were being upgraded better to carry the heavy traffic in this automobile-minded country. Lebanon has a very low 2.9 persons per vehicle.

Manufacturing

Lebanon's modest production of specialized craft products and textiles developed and diversified after the early 1950s until manufacturing surpassed agriculture in the economic hierarchy. Although it was severely disrupted during the 1975–1990 warfare, the resilient manufacturing gradually recovered during the 1990s. Although not yet having attained its earlier level, it constitutes 23 percent of the GDP. Most manufacturing establishments, like most shops and service institutions, are small—85 percent employ fewer than 25 people. The main light industries cluster around Beirut, producing clothing, textiles, processed foods, jewelry, oriental handicrafts, printed materials, cigarettes, paints, and furniture. Three cement plants and two steel plants operate near Tripoli. The small

FIGURE 13-1   Agriculture on the coastal plain of southern Lebanon, north of Sidon. This fertile strip has been cultivated for millennia *(note foreground)* and now has hundreds of plastic hothouses like those shown here to aid early yields of horticultural crops.

oil refineries in Tripoli and Sidon originally used crude from the pipelines from Iraq and Saudi Arabia, respectively, but shifted to crude delivered by tanker when the pipelines were closed in the early 1980s. The Tripoli plant is being restored to use crude from Syria delivered through the last segment of the old Iraq Petroleum Company (IPC) lines. The agriculturally productive Bekaa has several food-processing plants, including beet sugar mills and, in Ksara, wineries. In addition to furniture and metal products, Tripoli produces soaps from olive oil and other local raw materials.

Agriculture

Lebanon's combination of physical assets creates conditions for horticulture par excellence. Generations of farmers harvest fruits, nuts, and vegetables that are scarce in the Arab Middle

East, certainly in the premium quality of the Lebanese products. Even though precipitation is concentrated in the cool season, hydrogeological conditions permit collection of the runoff, directly or indirectly through springs, for irrigation purposes well into the summer. Meltwater from heavy winter snows in Mount Lebanon is particularly useful. Elaborate terracing both protects the slopes from erosion by the runoff from heavy rainfall (50–60 in./1,270–1,525 mm) at this elevation and also spreads water from the runoff and artificial irrigation to the crops in the terraced beds.[5]

The upslope of Mount Lebanon offers ecological conditions suitable for subtropical crops along the coast and for progressively cooler-environment crops at increasing elevations—a vertical zonation of crops on the principle that "altitude equals latitude." In the alluvial soils immediately along the coast, there are irrigated groves of bananas, lemons, oranges, grapefruit, and similar tender fruits. Plastic hothouses proliferated during the 1990s; the vegetables they produce are in high demand during the winter and early spring in the wealthy oil states (Fig. 13-1). Slightly higher and on rocky soils are extensive olive groves and smaller almond groves that need little or no irrigation. Still higher, from 2,000 to 5,000 ft./610 to 1,525 m is a vertical succession of irrigated orchards of peaches, apricots, pears, plums, cherries, and similar soft fruits and vineyards, primarily producing table grapes, at several levels (Fig. 13-2b). At still higher elevations are apple orchards, which were greatly expanded after World War II. Vineyards for wineries also thrive on the lower and drier eastern slopes of the Lebanon range, around Zahlah and Ksara. Otherwise, crops in the Bekaa are normally of four types: nonirrigated wheat and barley; irrigated fruits; semi-irrigated sugar beets, onions, potatoes, and melons; and irrigated tomatoes and a wide range of other vegetables, especially in the Shtawrah (Chtoura) "oasis."

A Subregional Perspective

Looking down at Lebanon from 10,000 ft./ 3,050 m, an air passenger flying eastward from Beirut can clearly see the four distinct parallel regions that extend south-southwest to north-northeast: a narrow coastal plain, the core area of the Lebanon Mountains, the linear flat-bottomed depression of the Bekaa, and the complex Anti-Lebanon Mountains on the border with Syria (see circled numbers on Map 13-1).

[1] Coastal Plain

Extending the full length of the country's 140-mile/225-km Mediterranean shoreline, the narrow plain along the coast is partly wave-cut rock platform and partly alluvial, comprising fan deposits of streams debouching from their deep mountain valleys. Interrupted in five places by mountain ridges that reach the sea, the plain is only wide enough in some places to

accommodate a highway and a parallel rail line. Between Tyre and Sidon it is carpeted by citrus groves for more than 1 mile/1.6 km back from shore; in the extreme north, it opens into the 20-mile-/32-km-wide triangular Plain of Akkar.

Urban sprawl up and down the coastal plain is rapidly supplanting many of the fruit groves and market gardens that characterized the coast for so long. Greater Beirut extends more than 20 miles/32 km from Juniyah north of the capital to Damur to the south. Scenically located on a separate low structural peninsular plateau, one of the few significant protrusions from the eastern Mediterranean coast, Beirut has been occupied since the Neolithic. A minor Phoenician port and city-state, Beirut achieved greater stature as a Roman city, which, with its great law school, was destroyed in an earthquake and tidal wave in AD 551.

As both capital and primate city of Lebanon, Beirut developed rapidly after the early 1950s. High-rise luxury apartment buildings and hotels (Fig. 13-2) contrasted with slum settlements on the fringes, particularly the Palestinian refugee camps. Later slums comprise the spontaneous district of Ouzai in southern Beirut, occupied primarily by Shii refugees from the precarious Israeli-occupied south. The city emerged from sixteen years of division between "Christian East" and "Muslim West" to face unaccustomed ambiguities and uncertainties. The old "Beirut élan" is somewhat elusive but slowly reviving. The city's return to normalcy is highly dependent on the elaborate and high-cost plan to reconstruct the city center, the former Central Business District and heart and soul of Beirut. Under the Lebanese Company for Development and Reconstruction (French acronym, Solidere) of Beirut's Central District, the multi-billion-dollar plan has provoked sharp debate among city leaders, with modernists and traditionalists taking opposing sides.[6] Excavation for new construction in the city center has confirmed that for 5,000 years Beirut was indeed the historic nucleus of successive Canaanite/Phoenician, Roman, Byzantine, and Ottoman cities. The most significant

FIGURE 13-2   High-rise apartment houses in mainly Muslim southern Beirut *(top)* along Ramlat al-Bayda beach, and Juniyah *(bottom),* Christian area north of Beirut. Juniyah was a village before 1975 that developed extraordinarily during the fighting 1975–1990. The vineyard in foreground is a remnant of the former extensive agricultural exploitation of this west-facing slope.

remains of each city level are being preserved on a below-street-level "Archaeology Trail."

Toward the north end of the coastal plain lies Lebanon's second city and second port, Tripoli (Arabic, Tarabulus),[7] a Sunni Muslim stronghold. On the southern plain is the Phoenician port of Tyre (Arabic, Sur), and adjoining it are extensive Greco-Roman ruins. The Phoenician port of Sidon (Arabic, Sayda) lies north of Tyre, with a Crusader castle offshore. Also worth noting is the small northern port of Jubayl (better known as Byblos), with its renowned excavations showing a profile of civilizations from Neolithic times to the present (Fig. 2-1).

[2] Mount Lebanon

The traditional core of Lebanon is Mount Lebanon (Arabic, Jabal Lubnan), technically called Jabal al-Gharbi (Western Mountains). This range of mountains has played a profound role in the historical-cultural development of the area. Like rugged mountains in many humid areas, Mount Lebanon provided isolation and security to several groups, notably the Maronites and Druzes. Lying west of the great Yammunah Fault (see Chap. 3), the range's sedimentary strata were arched up by relatively gentle east-west compressional forces during the Miocene-Pliocene. The resulting arch is a rather open anticlinal structure aligned southwest-northeast and extending from the low Homs Gap at its northern end to the complex tectonic junction in southern Lebanon. The range is affected by several faults along its axis and by many cross faults. Highest elevations are toward the north, reaching 10,129 ft./3,088 m at Qurnat al-Sawda, east-southeast of Tripoli; however, elevations around 6,500 ft./2,000 m continue southward along the ridgeline to east of Sidon.

A significant hydrogeological feature of Mount Lebanon is the outcropping of extensive aquifers, bringing groundwater to the surface in lines of springs along the outcrops. Some of these springs are exceptionally large, feeding short, swift rivers that erode and dissolve spectacular canyons in the western slopes and thus add to the rugged relief. The springs also supply water for irrigation on the terraces and more gentle slopes, as well as pure drinking water, some of which is bottled for consumption in Beirut and for export.

The western slopes were originally heavily forested with oak, pine, fir, cedar, and juniper, with the famous Cedars of Lebanon (*Cedrus libani*—the national symbol) forming a belt between 4,600 and 7,200 ft./1,400 and 2,200 m. Exploitation for at least 4,000 years has degraded the vegetation primarily to maquis, although a few small stands of Cedars of Lebanon are preserved. The main group is in central Lebanon on Jabal Baruk, but the more famous is at the Cedars, in the north, near the ski resort area of Bsharri. Plantations of stone pine (*Pinus pinea*) and Aleppo pine (*P. halepensis*) give small areas a wooded aspect (Fig. 13-3), and stone pine yields the edible piñon nut (Arabic, *snubar*).[8]

Maronites and Druzes gradually intensified and diversified agriculture on the western slopes, building thousands of terraces (Fig. 13-3). Villages developed on spectacular sites, some formerly occupied by Phoenician and Roman settlements. Particularly after World War II, many towns in the 2,000–4,500-ft./600–1,475-m zone evolved as summer resorts. At upper levels, around 6,500 ft./2,000 m, ski resorts such as the Cedars and Laqluq thrive between mid-December and late March (see also Fig. 4-2).

[3] The Bekaa

The Bekaa—al-Biqa ("the valley")—is a young tectonic intermontane trough, a segment of the Levant Rift System. Along the western side of the Bekaa, the Yammunah fracture slices off Mount Lebanon on its eastern side and creates a vertical displacement of several thousand meters and a left-lateral horizontal displacement of about 4.4 miles/7 km. It is the most active of the many fractures in the Levant. Perceptible earthquakes result from displacement along one or another of Lebanon's fault planes every few years. Severe tremors strike once every 100–150 years, with the most recent

FIGURE 13-3   Typical western slope of Mt. Lebanon, showing scattered villages, terraced agriculture, low pine woodlands, and interspersed maquis and garigue flora. The main village shown is Baqlin, located in the Druze area west of Bayt ed-Din.

being in 1956, when 7,000 buildings were destroyed east of Sidon by slippage along the Roum Fault.

The main drainage of the Bekaa, the Litani River flows southward from near Baalbak, with a flow of 700–900 million m³ a year at Qirawn (Qaraoun). It has been dammed to create a reservoir at Qirawn, and the water is diverted to produce a considerable amount of hydroelectricity and also to supply water for a limited amount of irrigation.[9] The Litani is a Lebanese river from its source to its mouth in the Mediterranean; note, however, that Zionist water planners as early as 1919 sought territorial access to the Litani as an additional water source for the proposed future Jewish state.

A low, barely perceptible divide near Baalbak separates the watershed of the Litani from that of the Orontes (Asi) River to the north. The Orontes follows the Bekaa northward into Syria past Homs and Hamah and through the Ghab. Both rivers are fed by numerous springs on both sides of the Bekaa. These water sources

attracted Paleolithic wanderers, and at least 30 Neolithic villages were established, their tells prominent features on the Bekaa floor.

Although the northern Bekaa lies in the rain shadow of the highest segment of Mount Lebanon and receives only 9 in./230 mm of rain a year, the central area around Shtawrah receives 24 in./610 mm, the south even more. Wheat and barley production, recorded from Roman times, has declined as more area is irrigated for fruit trees, sugar beets, and market gardening. Seen from the adjacent heights, the Bekaa floor in spring is colorful with fruit blossoms, cultivated flowers, and green fields.

[4] Anti-Lebanon

Properly the Jabal al-Sharqi (Eastern Mountains), the Anti-Lebanon Mountains are folded linear highlands east of the Bekaa and along the frontier with Syria; indeed, only the western ridges lie within Lebanon. An anticlinal structure similar to Mount Lebanon, these eastern highlands have several ridges exceeding 6,500 ft./ 2,000 m, and the summit of volcanic Mount Hermon, a southerly extension of the eastern highlands, reaches 9,230 ft./2,813 m. They are the least exploited part of Lebanon and in the north, are virtually uninhabited.

Factions and Territories

State Idea and Its Failure

When the French determined in 1920 that they would detach the formerly semiautonomous Mount Lebanon from Greater Syria, the intention was to create a separate mandate around the Maronite Christians, the dominant sect in the mountains. Pleased though the Maronites were to be given "their" sovereignty, Mount Lebanon alone was not an adequate base for a viable state. To enlarge Lebanon and fragment Syria further, the French appended the coastal plain, the Bekaa, and part of the Anti-Lebanon, with their Sunni Muslims, Shii Muslims, Druzes, and non-Maronite Christians. The additional territory may have enhanced the new mandate's economic viability, but it concomitantly diminished Lebanon's political viability. The detachment of additional Syrian territory increased Syrian resentment and engendered long-lasting animus among the Sunnis, Shiis, and Druzes who were separated from "Muslim" Syria and included in "Christian" Lebanon.

With some help from the French, the several groups who were merged in the Lebanese confessional confederation after 1920 evolved a unique political structure of pragmatic, representative government. Lebanon's raison d'être expanded to embrace the pluralistic society; power sharing, checks and balances, and compromise were the inherent pledges to preserve the state idea.

The mechanisms of the Lebanese system were codified less in the formal constitution than in the informal National Pact of 1943. This unwritten 1943 "gentlemen's agreement" specified the method of power sharing through the distribution of political offices among confessional groups according to their proportions in the 1932 census: Maronite president, Sunni prime minister, Shii president (speaker) of parliament, Druze and other groups in cabinet posts, and, not least, a Maronite commander of the Lebanese Armed Forces. This power-sharing formula institutionalized Maronite leadership, but it worked reasonably well so long as economic prosperity melded the vigorously competing factions. The formula gradually lost its applicability as the Christian-to-Muslim ratio obviously decreased over the years; Christians attempted to disregard the decrease by rejecting a census—even as late as 1999.

The National Pact and other agreements also failed to come to grips with the territorial aspects of the confessional groups, each of whom possessed a fairly defined "turf" and core area (see Map 13-2). When the political equilibrium broke down, the territorial patterns solidified and evolved into a mosaic of ministates, each with its clan zaim (group leader). Lebanese territorial sovereignty became as fragmented as its body politic. The system cracked in the 1958 civil war, again in 1968–1969, once more in the 1973 Palestinian-Lebanese Army firefights, and broke down in 1975. The influx of Palestinian guerrilla groups expelled from Jordan in 1970–1971 was a catalyst to the increasing domestic stresses that contributed to the explosion. Many Lebanese rejected the Palestinians' attempt to create a "state within a state"; indeed, not only had such an attempt been the flash point for Jordanian military action against the guerrillas, but also a Maronite-Palestinian engagement had precipitated the full-scale fighting in 1975. The fragmented Lebanese, however, were unable to replicate the Jordanian military success against the guerrillas.[10]

Proxy "Civil" War in Lebanon

For sixteen years after 1975, Lebanon suffered weeks of terrible killing and destruction that alternated with weeks of tense, uncertain cease-fires. More than a dozen or so factions fielded heavily armed militias. Unrestrained by the powerless Lebanese, Fatah guerrillas in the south conducted strikes into northern Israel; these led to Israeli reprisals, some major, as in March 1978 and the full-scale invasion in June 1982. Named "Operation Peace in Northern Galilee," the air, naval, and ground assaults on already war-weary Lebanon killed more than 17,000 and destroyed hundreds of structures. By August, street battles in Beirut between Israelis and Palestinians and mediation by Western powers forced the sea evacuation of thousands of PLO troops and Syrians.[11] The Multi-National Force (MNF), including U.S. Marines, arrived to help stabilize a chaotic situation, but they soon withdrew. With the MNF gone, Maronite Phalange (Kataib) forces, with indirect Israeli support, massacred more than 800 civilians in the Sabra-Shatila Palestinian refugee camps in Beirut in mid-September.[12]

In the virtual anarchy, MNF troops were redeployed, and newly assembled anti-Israeli and anti-Western militants assumed the role of the departed PLO fighters. In a new dimension of suicide-extremism, truck bombs destroyed the American Embassy in April 1983, killing 46; the U.S. Marine barracks and a French barracks in October, killing 241 Americans and 56 French troops; and Israeli military headquarters near Tyre in November, killing 60. Although Fatah/PLO fighters left in late 1982, substitute groups—especially the Shii Hizballah—took over guerrilla action against Israelis in southern Lebanon and northern Israel. They, as well as Druzes, also fired on MNF troops, particularly U.S. Marines. In November and December, U.S. and French aircraft attacked Syrian and Hizballah positions in the Bekaa and mountains, and a U.S. battleship lobbed heavy shells into Druze positions. Such raids came in response to attacks on U.S. Marines. The kidnappings of Western, and particularly American, journalists and officials during the late 1980s became a serious concern.

But the Lebanese themselves suffered egregiously from the outbreaks of full-scale warfare.

By early 1991, about 140,000 Lebanese had been killed and as many wounded. Two presidents had been assassinated. The center of Beirut was in ruins, and thousands of buildings around Beirut, in Tripoli, in towns and villages in the mountains, and in the south were in a shambles—more than $50 billion in structural losses. A dubious Israeli-Lebanese peace accord brokered by the United States was signed May 17, 1983, but was predictably abrogated in 1984.[13]

Asked to supply the greater part of the 1976 Arab Deterrent Force, Syria sent large contingents into eastern Lebanon to maintain equilibrium and to discourage potential Israeli incursions into Syria through Lebanon. President al-Asad exploited the ambiguity of the situation to prolong the Syrian occupation of Lebanon and apparently to test the possibility of reattaching *Grand Liban* to "Greater Syria." The idea of outright reattachment was eventually dismissed; nevertheless, 35,000–40,000 troops were maintained in Lebanon to guarantee Syrian hegemony, and they were still there in mid-2000. Inter alia, they may also serve as a piece in the complex regional chess game played between Israel and Syria and their respective partisans.

Finally, in October 1989, under the aegis of the Arab League and with strong pressure from Syria inside Lebanon, a majority of the remaining members of the 1972 Lebanese Parliament met in Taif, Saudi Arabia, and agreed on a Document of National Understanding. Weary of death and destruction, the militias agreed to disarm, and a more representational political structure was put in place. The Maronite president, the Sunni prime minister, and the Shii speaker of parliament were given powers more in balance; and parliamentary seats were apportioned 50–50 between Christians and Muslims. Thus, confessionalism is still a political factor, although the hope is to phase it out in the long range. The revived Lebanese Army is more effective now and helps stabilize central government control in most of the country, including the far south after Israel's withrawal in May 2000 (see

Chap. 11, Arab-Israel Problem). There for 22 years the most militant remaining groups (Hizballah, rejectionist Palestinians, Amal, Iranian volunteers, and other militias) confronted occupying Israeli forces and their proxy South Lebanon Army (SLA).[14] The frequent encounters between opponents of Israeli occupation on one side and Israelis and the SLA on the other, as well as Hizballah/Amal rocket attacks on northern Israel countered by Israeli attacks into Lebanon, became a persistent cycle of violence. Israeli retaliations included successive air raids well into Lebanon, and occasionally in Beirut. Two campaigns are worth noting. The first, a six-day blitz in July 1993 dubbed "Operation Accountability" caused massive destruction and provoked an exodus of 400,000 refugees to the north, overwhelming Beirut. One account described the operation as "punishing the civilians in order to pressure the politicians."[15] Despite a restraining agreement, the attacks soon resumed;[16] cumulative casualties were in the hundreds.

Second, after an unusually heavy Hizballah rocket attack on northern Israel, in April 1996 Israel launched operation "Grapes of Wrath," sixteen days of the heaviest shelling, bombing, and gunship fire since 1982. An Israeli artillery attack on a UN observer camp in Qana on April 18 killed 102 civilians taking refuge in the neutral camp area. Although Israel called the attack accidental, it was considered deliberate by first-hand observers and in an official UN report.[17] In a counterresponse, Hizballah fired dozens of rockets in successive daily attacks on northern Israel; Israeli sources reported that the attacks were ineffective and had caused only a few wounded.[18] For its part, Lebanon, having endured sixteen years of warfare and having learned its limitations, could not attempt to satisfy Israel's demands by rekindling conflict on its soil. Unwillingly subject to Syrian hegemony, Lebanon is presently largely neglected by its former and logical supporter, the United States. Meanwhile, until May 2000, Lebanon, unable to reclaim its territory in the south and unable to restrain the militias attempting to do

so, continued to be the unhappy venue for the only active warfare in the Arab-Israeli conflict. After Israel's withdrawal of its forces and cessation of its support for the SLA, Lebanon could, in mid-2000, finally hope for some semblance of peace and stability. The hope would be much greater if Syria would end its political dominance of its smaller neighbor.

Cyprus

Two geographical facts—that Cyprus is an island and that it is located in the eastern Mediterranean—are the most important aspects of Cyprus's existence. Occupied during the Neolithic period, nearly 9000 BC, it has been fought for and used as an intermediate base for more than 3,500 years, with its former mineral wealth and its agricultural resources valuable bonuses. A third current basic fact, primarily a consequence of location, is the contemporary conflict on the island between two ethnic groups, Greek and Turkish, and the unilaterally forced division of the island between them in 1974. The imposed division installed an ambiguous Turkish polity in the northern one-third of the island, while the internationally recognized and overwhelmingly Greek[19] Republic of Cyprus continued in the south.

Two Mountains, Three Plains

About the size of Puerto Rico, Cyprus is the third largest, after Sicily and Sardinia, of the Mediterranean islands. Its mountains are clearly visible across the 43 miles/69 km of water that separate it from Asia Minor, and it lies 65 miles/105 km from Syria and 475 miles/765 km from mainland Greece. Its coastline exhibits several semiprotected bays in which harbors have sheltered ships for millennia. The island was formed during the Tertiary mountain-building period along the arcuate boundary between the African and Eurasian plates (see Map 3-2). Seismic repercussions from continuing plate convergence produce periodic earthquakes in Cyprus, some of them occasionally catastrophic.

Cyprus

Long-form official name, anglicized: Republic of Cyprus (ROC, south): (Turkish Republic of Northern Cyprus [TRNC] in the north not recognized except by Turkey)

Official name, transliterated: Kipriakí Dimokratía (Greek), Kıbrıs Cumhuriyeti (Turkish) in the south; (Kuzey Kıbrıs Türk Cumhuriyeti in the north)

Form of government: unitary multiparty republic with a unicameral legislature (House of Representatives) (south)

Area: 3,572 miles^2/9,251 km^2 (entire island); 2,277 miles^2/5,896 km^2 (south); 1,295 miles^2/3,355 km^2 (north)

Population, 1999: 861,000 (entire island); 673,000 south, 188,000 north. Literacy (latest): 95% (south)

Ethnic composition (%): Greek 97 (south), Turkish 99 (north), other 4

Religions: predominantly Greek Orthodox (south), predominantly Sunni Muslim (north)

GDP, 1997: $10 billion (south); per capita: $13,000 (south)

Petroleum reserves: none

Main exports, 1996: citrus, potatoes, grapes, wine, cement, clothing and shoes, ships' stores (south); citrus, potatoes, textiles (north)

Main imports,1996: consumer goods, petroleum and lubricants, food and food grains, machinery (south); food, minerals, chemicals, machinery (north)

Capital city: Nicosia (capital for both south and north) 225,000; other cities; Limassol 148,000; Larnaca 63,800; Paphos 36,000 (all in the south); Famagusta (Magosa) 21,500; Kyrenia 15,000 (north)

The island has five regions: east-west mountain ranges to the north and south, a broad basin in between, and narrow plains along both the north and the south coasts (Map 13-4). Toward the southwest are [1] the Troodos Mountains, the oval geomorphic nucleus of the island and a true massif, with an intruded granite core now exposed by erosion and Mt. Olympus, the highest elevation on the island, reaching 6,400 ft./ 1,951 m. Extensive mineralization accompanied the intrusions, and breakdown of the Troodos rocks produced fertile soils. Stretching the full length of the northern edge of the island is [2] the Kyrenia Range, a narrow, steep mountain ridge primarily of Cretaceous limestone that attains 3,360 ft./1,024 m. Some igneous patches occur, and metamorphism has produced marble in places. Much of the range is porous because of

solution cavities and is a source of springwater. Its ridges are rough and craggy, appropriately wild for the Crusader castle ruins that cling to its pinnacles.

Nestled between the Kyrenia Range and the Troodos is [3] the Mesaoria, the island's breadbasket, primarily an alluvial plain with fertile soils but with a platform of upturned sedimentaries between the Kyrenia ridge and the lower basin. Open at both its east and west ends, the Mesaoria slopes primarily eastward, from about 700 ft./215 m to sea level on the eastern coast. Nicosia, the primate city of the island and the capital of the Republic of Cyprus (and also designated as the capital of the self-proclaimed Turkish Republic of Northern Cyprus), nestles in the center of the Mesaoria. North of the Kyrenia Range, [4] a narrow coastal plain separates

MAP 13-4   General and economic map of Cyprus, showing dividing line between north and south Cyprus. Circled numbers indicate the regions.

the steep northern slopes of the range from the shore, with citrus groves in irrigated areas and rainfed crops in the remaining segments. [5] The coastal plain south of the Troodos is generally wider but more irregular. It is also more densely populated and more industrially developed, with two main centers, Limassol and Larnaca, as well as both British sovereign base areas.

Mediterranean Climate, Mediterranean Crops

Cyprus has a typical Mediterranean climate, with hot, dry summers and mild, moist winters. The island receives 75 percent of the possible sunshine in an average year, and it attracts thousands of northern European tourists to its warmth, scenic sites, and well-developed resorts. With 13 in./340 mm of rainfall at Nicosia on the open Mesaoria,

crops other than the dominant grains must be irrigated. The upper slopes of the Troodos exert the typical orographic effect and wring up to 45 in./1,145 mm of moisture from the westerly winds in winter, much of it as snow, which is sufficient for a modest skiing season in most winters. Much of the runoff from the impermeable igneous rocks is captured in reservoirs or aquifers to be used for irrigation during the dry summer. With cool temperatures and appreciable moisture, Troodos slopes are appreciably forested with pine, cedar, cypress, and poplar. These woodlands contrast sharply with the typical low, open maquis and garrigue typical of Mediterranean lowlands in much of Cyprus. Scenic Troodos resort centers do double duty as summer and winter attractions.

With assets of climate, relief, and soils, the island has had a good agricultural base for many centuries, and its farmers cultivate a high

FIGURE 13-4   Typical landscape on south-facing slopes of the Troodos, western Cyprus. A well-varied area, with olive groves *(right foreground)*, vineyards *(left foreground)*, terraced cultivation in middle distance, and scrub oak and pine forest on slopes in the distance.

percentage of the total area (see Table 7-1). The island's agriculture includes several tree crops—olives, carobs (Cyprus leads the Middle East in carob bean exports), almonds, citrus and other fruits—and especially grapevines. Cyprus wine, although not of premium quality, is very good, and extensive vineyards occupy the southern midslopes of the Troodos (Fig. 13-4). Table grapes, raisins, and wines are major products and major exports, as are citrus fruits of all types. Potatoes rank with citrus and grapes in tons produced and are also a major export. Wheat and barley are major crops, but production is insufficient to meet local demand. More than half of the farms in Cyprus have some form of irrigation, although only 28 percent of the cultivated land is irrigated. A prolonged drought during the 1990s seriously upset the island's water balance, reducing the level in the numerous artificial reservoirs to less than 15 percent of normal in 1997–1999.

Nonagricultural Economy

Mineralization in the Troodos during the igneous intrusions and the accompanying metamorphism gave the island major resources of copper, iron pyrites, chrome, asbestos, and iron oxide pigments as well as lesser sources of gold, silver, and zinc. The deposits of copper, the main metal in bronze alloy, were exploited as early as the third millennium BC and became a major source of the metal during the Bronze Age. Indeed, the Greek and Latin words for copper are related to the island's name. In modern times, mining was second only to agriculture in Cyprus during the 1950s–1960s, but intensive methods of extraction had virtually exhausted the larger deposits of copper and chrome by the late 1970s. In the late 1990s, the island produced only modest tonnages of pyrite, iron oxide pigments (for paints), bentonite clays, celestite, and gypsum. Exploiting the large reserves of asbestos in the high Troodos, the Amiantos mine operated for many years before closing in 1989 because of decreased world demand. Recently, the island's once considerable income from metallic mineral exports has been at a negligible level, although the resource base of commodities such as asbestos, bentonite, celestite, chromite, copper, iron oxide pigments, pyrite, and salt are still significant. Further exploitation must await more favorable economic conditions.

Diversification after independence in 1960 encouraged tourism and other services, light manufacturing, and transportation and trade. Even with grave political-economic difficulties between the Greek and Turkish Cypriot groups, Cyprus developed rapidly and solidly during the 1980s, achieving a well-rounded economy in the south, with a thriving tourist industry. With the economy divided, the per capita GDP of the rather isolated north Cyprus is only one-third that of the bustling south.

Before Division

Six crucial events in the long history of Cyprus are fundamental to the contemporary situation on the island. First, consequent to the mining of copper and exploitation of the forests for shipbuilding during the Bronze Age, thriving ports and other cities were established by Minoans from Crete and Mycenaeans from Greece, a fact underscored by Greek Cypriots. Successive masters ruled Cyprus until the Greco-Roman period, during which the second important event occurred: conversion of the island's population to Christianity by Paul and Barnabas (AD 45), as related in the New Testament. Christianity was reinforced during the 800 years, beginning in AD 364, that Byzantium ruled Cyprus. The third main event was the assertion of Ottoman control over the island in 1570–1571, after which several thousand Muslim Turks settled on the island. These developments set the stage for conflict between Cyprus's Greeks and Turks and their respective

supporters. A fourth crucial event was the coming of the British in 1878 under agreements among the powers at the Congress of Berlin. For well or ill, Britain influenced Cyprus fortunes for most of a critical century.

Annexed by Great Britain in 1914 and made a crown colony in 1925, Cyprus demanded independence after World War II. Behind the sometimes savage attacks of the guerrilla group EOKA, and with support from mainland Greece, the Greek Cypriots opened a paramilitary revolt against British colonial control. The aim of a majority of them was, in fact, union with Greece (*enosis*) rather than actual independence for the island. However, after nearly five years of the revolt, the Zurich-London Agreements among all parties—Britain, Greek Cypriots, Turkish Cypriots, and the Greek and Turkish governments—led to the independence of the Republic of Cyprus (ROC) on August 16, 1960, the fifth crucial event. An indication of the island's strategic location is the United Kingdom's retention of two sovereign base areas on the south coast (see Map 13-4).

The creation of an independent Cyprus entailed predictable dilemmas because of internal ethnic division. Of a total population of 550,000, 79 percent of the Cypriots were Greek speaking, practiced the Greek Orthodox religion, and, generally, strongly desired *enosis*. About 18 percent were Turkish speaking, adhered to Sunni Islam, and desired autonomy under some system of confederation or partition (*taksim*); and 3 percent were descendants of Armenian and Maronite refugees, all Christians, plus a few thousand British and other expatriates who had retired to the pleasant life of Cyprus. All these ethnic groups were intermingled over the island, and although most villages tended to be either Greek or Turkish, some villages were mixed.

Upon independence, a power-sharing agreement prorated political positions at a ratio of 7 Greek Cypriots to 3 Turkish Cypriots (even 6 to 4 in the proposed army), although the population ratio was about 8 to 2. The power-sharing compromise was not successful. By November

FIGURE 13-5   Pleasant outdoor café on Kyrenia harbor, Northern Cyprus' premier resort area.

1963, friction arose over the shortage of qualified Turkish Cypriots to fill the allotted quotas, as well as over Greek Cypriot impatience to move the new sovereign Cyprus forward. A month later, with many Turkish Cypriots "behind the barricades," conflict on Cyprus—and corollary tensions between Greece and Turkey—became so serious that the UN Security Council established the UN Peacekeeping Force in Cyprus (UNFICYP) in 1964. It was still in place in early 2000. For the next decade, the Greek Cypriots operated the government and economy virtually by themselves, with an increasing division between those who wanted *enosis* with Greece and those who were content with an independent Cyprus republic. Following additional intercommunal violence in 1967–1968, Turkish Cypriots formed their own provisional administration.

When the intra-Greek struggle culminated in an attempted coup in 1974 and a series of confused events, Turkey invaded northern Cyprus in July, declaring that it was protecting the Turkish Cypriot population pursuant to the 1960 Treaty of Guarantee. Backed by a strong military presence, the Turks drew the Attila Line, named after the Turkish commander, to divide their area from the ROC. This split gave the Turkish region 36 percent of the island territory and 18 percent of the population. Again, the Turks declared that they were offsetting the strength of the Greek Cypriots so as to protect their minority ethnic kin against continued oppression by the majority Greek Cypriots. During the Turkish invasion, 150,000–200,000 Greek Cypriots fled to the south, and about 45,000 Turkish Cypriots fled to the north. Possibly 6,000–8,000 died during the fighting and the population exchange. This sectioning of the island is the sixth and most climactic crucial event affecting contemporary Cyprus.

Divided Cyprus

The Autonomous Turkish Cypriot Administration established in late 1974 north of the Attila Line was replaced on February 13, 1975, with a unilaterally declared Turkish Federated State of Cyprus (TFSC) (Fig. 13-5). The name implied a future creation of the kind of island federation the Turkish Cypriots had demanded 20 years earlier. The TFSC became the Turkish Republic of Northern Cyprus (TRNC) on November 15,

1983, countering the southern zone's continued use of the original official name, Republic of Cyprus. The TRNC has not received recognition by any country other than Turkey.

North Cyprus is, in certain respects, little more than an autonomous province of Turkey. It is tied to the mainland in various ways: It uses Turkish currency, depends upon Turkey for protection (including up to 30,000 Turkish soldiers), conducts half of its import-export trade with the mainland, and receives a subsidy of several million dollars annually from Turkey. During the late 1990s, the mainland has assisted north Cyprus to further disengage from the south by integrating the north's telephone system with Turkey's; building a large electric power plant in the north; shipping potable water in huge plastic balloons from the mainland; and planning to lay a water pipeline under the 43-mile/70 km stretch of the Mediterranean that separates the island from Asia Minor.[20] An estimated 20,000–30,000 Anatolian Turks have migrated to north Cyprus, their arrivals partially offset by the emigration of several thousand Turkish Cypriots. Political and economic uncertainty have discouraged investment in the north, which has experienced limited development compared with the south. An influx of casinos in 1997–1998 that was supposed to create a local Las Vegas has shown only a limited benefit.

The Republic of Cyprus in the south is still considered by the international community to be the legitimate government of the island. Having lost a high percentage of the island's productive capacity, the republic has, nevertheless, long had many more tourists, more industrial output, and more income from services than the pre-1974 state did with most of the island included in the economy. Both the public and private sectors have aggressively pursued diversified economic development, particularly in tourism, transportation, and light manufacturing. During the later 1990s, per capita GDP in prosperous ROC was equal to that of Spain, more than that of Greece, three times that of the TRNC, and, with the exception of Israel and the two Gulf oil states of Kuwait and the UAE, the highest in the Middle East. A significant stimulus

to the development of southern Cyprus was the use of the area as a neutral adjunct of Lebanon during the Lebanon fighting in the period 1975–1991. Non-governmental organizations, foreign governments (including the United States), and international business have adopted the ROC as a base, hopeful that pragmatism would prevail in the intercommunal bitterness to preserve the general calm.

Attempts have continued since 1968 to devise institutional arrangements acceptable to both the Greek and the Turkish Cypriots and also to Greece and Turkey. The UN has sponsored successive rounds of negotiations; the EU has hosted discussions between the parties and has held out the inducement of membership of a peaceful Cyprus in the EU; and the United States has brokered additional meetings between the sides. Efforts were especially vigorous in 1997–1998; these followed violent killings at the Attila Line in August 1996, the first real violence since 1974.[21] An even greater incentive for mediation was to persuade the ROC not to make the planned purchase of a battery of Russian S300 ground-to-air missiles. After two years of intense negotiations, the ROC canceled the order and signed an accord to have the missiles placed on Crete, thus sparing the already overly militarized Cyprus an additional burden of weapons and a threatened war.[22] Tension between Turkish and Greek Cypriots and friction between Turkey and Greece are correlative. A reciprocal resolution would be of momentous benefit, but basic agreements require determined, patient negotiations with help and guarantees from U.S., UN, and EU mediators. (See the epilogue.)

Notes

1. Estimates of the Palestinian population vary widely for any country but especially for Lebanon (and, after the early 1990s, for Kuwait). The UNRWA figures for their Field of Operation—where they maintain official refugee camps—are based on registered Palestinians and are given as 370,144 for Lebanon, of whom 204,999 are in the 12 UNRWA camps. See <http://www.un.org/unrwa/refugees/me.html>.

2. See also Cobban 1985, "Thinking About Lebanon," *Lebanon* Country Study 1988, and Meir Zamir, "From Hegemony to Marginalism: The Maronites of Lebanon," in Bengio and Ben-Dor 1999.

3. See el Khazen 1985 and *Lebanon* Country Study 1988.

4. Although the fighting in Lebanon was not across international boundaries and was "internal" or "civil" in many ways, one or another faction was continually and openly stimulated and supported by outside states and groups, especially Israel, Syria, Libya, Iraq, Iran, Saudi Arabia, and other Gulf states, not to mention most of the Great Powers.

5. N. N. Lewis 1953.

6. Ragette 1983; *New York Times,* Feb. 23, 1997; *Christian Science Monitor,* Jan. 5, 1999; and the elaborate Gayin and Maluf 1996.

7. Gulick 1967. Maps in the book show the differences between street patterns of the old city and modern developments.

8. Mikesell 1969.

9. Hudson 1971.

10. Many studies analyze Lebanon's problems leading to and during the civil war of the 1970s and 1980s, although readers must beware of some authors' biases. Useful are Haddad 1985, which is concise and philosophical but insightful; Khalidi 1979, by a moderate Palestinian intellectual; Rabinovich 1984, giving a moderate Israeli scholar's analysis; the entire issue of the *Middle East Journal* 38, no. 2 (Spring 1984); Friedman 1989 and Fisk 1990, two very good journalistic accounts, one American and one British; Gordon 1983, a concise

general study of Lebanon, as is Salibi 1988; and Norton 1987.

11. See Sahliyeh 1986, Friedman 1989, Fisk 1990, and Rabinovich 1984.

12. See Kahan Commission 1983.

13. The U.S. role and related events are traced in detail in Parker 1993, Part III.

14. *Lebanon Report,* Spring 1998, 28–42.

15. *Christian Science Monitor,* Aug. 2, 1993.

16. *Economist,* July 15, 1995, 27.

17. See *New York Times,* Apr. 19, 1996; also Apr. 28, May 1, and May 8, 1996.

18. The depressing cycle of violence is seen in the detailed *MEJ* chronology. For events in "Grapes of Wrath," see issues 50, nos. 3 and 4 (Summer and Autumn 1996).

19. Even straightforward geographical writings on Cyprus by Cypriots show how viewpoints often differ sharply between Greek Cypriots and Turkish Cypriots. See Attalides 1979 for a moderate Greek Cypriot view. Denktash 1982 is an opposing view by the leader of the Turkish Cypriot community. See also the *Cyprus* Country Study 1993, the brief presentation in CIA 1973 for a concise coverage of the island before the emergence of north Cyprus, and Reddaway 1986. Stasis and Mavrocordatos 1989 is a secondary-school-level book but is still useful. Karouzis and Karouzis 1997 is actually a practical geography of Cyprus written by Greek Cypriot geographers.

20. *Christian Science Monitor,* July 31, 1998.

21. *New York Times,* Aug. 12, 16, and 18, 1996.

22. *New York Times,* Jan. 6, 1997, and Dec. 30, 1998.

14
Jordan:
The Land Beyond

During its long history, the area of the contemporary Kingdom of Jordan has undergone many changes in name, political status, and economic level. One result of these shifts, especially during the twentieth century, is confusion regarding Jordan's political geography, specifically its territorial base. Further uncertainty has been added in terminology because of the use of "Jordan" as the name of the famed river and valley and also as the name of the country.

The autonomous polity of Transjordan was created in the early 1920s, in former Ottoman Empire lands taken from the Turks during World War I, as a League of Nations mandate to Great Britain. The Amirate of Transjordan, as it was officially known for 25 years, became an independent kingdom on May 25, 1946, when Britain withdrew as mandatory power. Attachment of the West Bank, part of the former Palestine mandate, to the kingdom in 1948 (officially 1950) made "Transjordan" a misnomer (see below). A final change of name produced the Hashimite Kingdom of Jordan, commonly shortened to "Jordan." Occupation of the West Bank by Israel in 1967 placed both the West Bank and Jordan in an ambiguous situation that continued until Jordan announced its disengagement from the West Bank in August 1988.

For the sake of clarity, terms referring to the area east of the Jordan Valley may be distinguished in this way: The expression trans-Jordan basically indicates direction, "beyond the Jordan River," as opposed to cis-Jordan, "this side of the Jordan River"—both from the European perspective. The term Transjordan is a specific political designation referring only to

the polity that occupied a specific area east of the Jordan River between 1923 and 1948/1950, first as a mandate and then as a kingdom. A third designation, trans-Jordania, revives an old regional name that has no political implications. It could be said that Transjordan was a trans-Jordan polity in trans-Jordania.

Four major general aspects of spatial relations regarding the Kingdom of Jordan are noteworthy. First, whatever the name or status of the area, its location "beyond the Jordan" has been a significant factor in its geography and history. The physical barriers of the deep Jordan trench to the west and the desert expanses to the east were once serious obstacles to the movement of peoples and goods, although camel caravans found some useful routes. Second, the rather narrow, better-watered and most densely populated highland zone squeezed between trench and desert in the trans-Jordan region nevertheless functioned as a north-south transit land, the eastern counterpart of the Trunk Road or Via Maris (Way of the Sea), which extended northward from Egypt through Gaza, Lydda, and Megiddo to Damascus. Caravans followed either of two ancient routes in trans-Jordania: the King's Highway through the hill country past Petra, Karak, Madaba, and Amman, then northward to Damascus; or the generally level Desert Road, 18 miles/29 km farther to the east out on the plateau (Map 14-1).

The transitional character of the area is the third major geographical aspect. It has never been a power center, nor has it served as a significant part of a power center. Conflict between "the desert and the sown," between nomads and

MAP 14-1 General and economic map of Jordan. Circled numbers indicate regions discussed in text. Note concentration of settlement and development in western Jordan.

Jordan

Long-form official name, anglicized: Hashimite Kingdom of Jordan

Official name, transliterated: al-Mamlakah al-Urdunniyah al-Hashimiyah

Form of government: constitutional monarchy with two legislative houses (Senate, House of Deputies)

Area: 34,489 miles^2/89,326 km^2

Population, 1999: 4,682,000. Literacy (latest): 86.6%

Ethnic composition (%): Arab 98, Circassian 0.9, Armenian 0.9, Turk 0.1, Kurd 0.1

Religions (%): Sunni Muslim 96.5, Christian 3.5

GDP, 1998: $15.5 billion; per capita: $3,500

Petroleum reserves: negligible

Main exports (% of total value, 1996): chemicals 25.7; phosphate fertilizers 9.9; potash 9.8; vegetables, fruits, and nuts 6.4

Main imports (% of total value, 1996): machinery and transport equipment 26; food 22.5; mineral fuels and lubricants 12.2; chemicals 10

Capital city: Amman 1,755,800; other cities: al-Zarqa 450,000; Irbid 275,000; al-Salt 72,000

settlements, has inhibited development east of the Jordan Valley. Although the area embraced petty kingdoms such as Rabboth-Ammon and Moab 3,000 years ago and although small areas had sustained regional identity (Gilead, for example), the general trans-Jordan area lacked a specific regional unity from earliest times until its establishment as an entity after World War I.

The *raison de création* of mandate Jordan, beyond the purely political goals mentioned in the next section, encumbered the amirate and the successor kingdom with the destiny of a buffer state. Designed to keep the French north of the Yarmuk, to hold back the Saudis from the Jordan Valley, and to keep the Iraqis focused on Mesopotamia, the mandate was designed, delineated, and operated by the British as a buffer. With the advent of the state of Israel in 1948, independent Transjordan—slightly smaller than the U.S. state of Indiana—became the archetypal buffer for all three of its adjacent neighbors, and its fate became inextricably linked to the vagaries of the conflict between Israel and the Palestinians

and other Arabs. Contemporary Jordan not only has the longest border with Israel of all the Arab states, but it is in the unenviable position of being targeted by extremist Israelis as the preferred future homeland for all Arabs remaining in Israel and the occupied territories.

The fourth aspect concerns Jordan's territorial stability and integrity. During the mandate and its first few years as a kingdom, Jordan's territory lay entirely east of the Jordan River, as was suggested by its common Arabic name of that time, Sharq al-Urdunn (East of the Jordan). In 1950, incorporation of the central Palestine hill country (the West Bank) expanded Jordan's territorial base by a very important 2,270 miles^2/5,880 km^2, but for all practical purposes the West Bank was lost to Israeli conquest and occupation in the June War of 1967. After 21 years of uncertainty and crisis, Jordan renounced claims to the West Bank; therefore, description, data, and analysis of Jordan in this book pertain only to the East Bank—in effect, to virtually the same territory as that of the 1923–1946 mandate.[1]

Historical Evolution

From Early Times to the Muslim Conquest

Vestiges of the history of the trans-Jordan area are sharply etched into the landscape of the western fourth of contemporary Jordan. In this settled part of the country, one is rarely out of sight of some reminder of Jordan's past—a dolmen, tell, ruined building, Roman milestone, or the partially excavated ruins of an entire city such as Jerash, Umm al-Jimal, or Petra.

Trans-Jordania's golden age began under the Seleucids of Syria and continued through the Roman era and into the Byzantine period (about 200 BC–AD 600), when the area was the setting for successful trade routes, trade centers, and caravan towns. Prime movers in the trade through Jordan were the Semitic Nabataeans, who operated from their extraordinary capital and caravan center of Petra.[2] The modern Jordanian capital of Amman was the Rabboth Ammon of the Old Testament and the Greco-Roman Philadelphia. It and Jerash (see Fig. 2-4b), north of Amman, were two principal members of the Decapolis, a ten-city league formed to resist nomadic attacks. Mosaic floors from Byzantine Christian churches and other buildings of the fifth and sixth centuries are found in many sites. Outstanding are the numerous mosaic floors in the small highland town of Madaba, south-southwest of Amman. One such floor preserves the famous Madaba Map of the sixth century, which shows in intricate mosaic the Palestine area and adjacent parts of the region, including a recognizable plan of Jerusalem.

From Muslim Conquest to the Present

The golden age of Trans-Jordania waned with Byzantium's withdrawal to Anatolia before the invading Arabs 634–636. Lacking stability and security along the traditional route, the profitable land trade had dwindled and virtually disappeared by the ninth century; it was especially undermined as maritime traders increasingly linked the Indian Ocean and the Mediterranean. Cities declined, villages vanished, and

Bedouins overwhelmed the settled areas. Not until the Ottoman Hijaz Railway reused the corridor in the early 1900s was the area economically reawakened even marginally.

World War I action in the Middle East and, a few years later, the memoirs of T. E. Lawrence, *Seven Pillars of Wisdom*, reintroduced trans-Jordania to the West. This vague, undefined area east of the Jordan trench sprawled beyond its highland backbone out into its desert realms, merging into the barren wildernesses of the future Syria on the north, the future Iraq on the east, and areas to the south that were later consolidated into the Kingdom of Saudi Arabia.

Great Britain, as the mandatory power for both sides of the Jordan Valley, declared to East Bank shaykhs and notables at al-Salt in August 1920 that it favored self-government for them. British Middle East experts meeting with Colonial Secretary Winston Churchill in Cairo in March 1921 agreed that the inchoate trans-Jordan realm should become a League of Nations mandate under British tutelage, ruled by the Hashimite Amir Abdullah. The decision was intended both as a token fulfillment of the British promises to the Arabs in the Husayn-McMahon correspondence of 1915–1916 (see Chap. 11) and a desire to placate the Hashimite family (direct descendants of the Prophet Muhammad) in the person of Amir Abdullah ibn Husayn, son of the sharif of Mecca and brother of Amir Faysal, who contemporaneously became king of Iraq. Churchill personally met Abdullah in Jerusalem and informed him of the plan, which was regularized in mid-1923 in time for the official entry in force of all Middle East mandates in September 1923.[3] The amirate continued as a struggling, penurious mandate until it became an independent kingdom on May 25, 1946, with Abdullah automatically becoming king.

The political-geographical, demographic, economic, and social character of the kingdom altered dramatically and permanently with the advent of the State of Israel on May 14, 1948: Scores of thousands of Palestinian refugees crossed over the Jordan River to Transjordan, King Abdullah annexed the West Bank, and

Jordan was pulled into the conflict vortex that characterized Arab-Israeli relations well into the new millennium. Abdullah was assassinated in al-Aqsa Mosque in Jerusalem in 1951 and was succeeded briefly by his son Talal, who was in turn succeeded in 1952 by his eighteen-year-old son, Husayn. King Husayn (sometimes "Hussein") deftly balanced the many conflicting forces impinging on his vulnerable realm, having learned from his grandfather the skill of walking the geopolitical tightrope. Husayn usually chose the moderate and often mediating role, seeking consensus sometimes at great risk. In 1967, however, he made the first of two costly strategic mistakes when he agreed to join Egypt and Syria against Israel in the 1967 June ("Six-Day") War. Jordan suffered heavy military and territorial losses in the debacle, and the kingdom lost all areas west of the Jordan River in the territorial readjustments after the war. As a result, Jordan lost more than a third of its most educated population, much of its arable land, and its Holy Land sites. Territorially, the kingdom returned to its trans-Jordan status of pre-1948, a status confirmed by King Husayn when he renounced all legal ties with the West Bank in August 1988.

Cyclic turbulence has characterized Jordan's development from its independence to the present: the 1948–1949 wars with the new state of Israel, the disastrous 1967 war, periodic border clashes, several internal engagements between the army and insurgent groups, and a series of internal coup attempts. One persistent government effort to maintain stability was the imposition of martial law during the period 1967–1989. The most serious of the confrontations within Jordan was the showdown between the government and Palestinian fedayeen in September 1970 (called "Black September" by some Palestinian insurgents), when an estimated 3,300 were killed on both sides. In this civil war, which flared up again in 1971, the Jordan Arab Army definitively asserted control of the kingdom and forced the withdrawal of the fedayeen, mostly to Lebanon (see Chap. 13). King Husayn was later reconciled with PLO leader Yasser Arafat, but their relations remained strained, especially regarding their respective roles vis-à-vis Jordanian Palestinians and regarding Jordan-Israeli connections and the modalities of the peace process. King Husayn attempted several times to introduce democracy, always having to balance his "guest" Palestinian constituents and his still somewhat tribalized East Bank subjects. In parliamentary elections in 1989 and 1993, the King held out promises; but while expanding the political boundaries, he still controlled the process and restricted available space.[4] In 1990, Saddam Husayn's invasion of Kuwait placed King Husayn in a grave dilemma. The king would risk widespread condemnation from the international community and economic disaster if he avoided censure of Saddam Husayn and urged further diplomatic negotiation. More important, he would risk his throne and probably his life if he denounced Iraq and joined the Gulf coalition. Having appraised the emotional response of the Palestinian two-thirds of his population to Saddam Husayn's posing as champion of Arabs and Palestinians, King Husayn opted for the first choice. He was, indeed, sharply criticized by his neighbors and by the West; all aid from Gulf states, the United States, and Europe was canceled; Jordanian/Palestinian expatriate workers in the Gulf were expelled by the scores of thousands; and Jordan was isolated for about four years. But domestically King Husayn's popularity was affirmed and the national consensus solidified—even under the stresses his choice had imposed. After skillfully conducting the 1993 parliamentary elections, Husayn again made a risky choice by signing a peace treaty with Israel, under the moderate prime minister Yitzhak Rabin, on October 26, 1994. This choice refurbished his image with the United States and brought modest direct economic rewards. Signing the peace treaty also promised great peace dividends to all sectors of Jordanian society, but the returns proved disappointing: Exacerbating growing poverty, lack of the peace bonanza, and unemployment, government cutbacks and subsidy reductions provoked riots in Karak and other cities in August 1996 and brought suspension of the parliament. Both for economic and, increasingly, political reasons, popular opposition to the treaty mounted, especially during the apparent Israeli stalling tactics under prime minister Binyamin Netanyahu.[5] By 1999, a solid antinormalization movement in Jordan was speaking out and taking action against those who collaborated with the Israelis.[6] As this movement was gaining momentum, King Husayn died on February 7, 1999, at age 63; he had ruled for 47 years—longer than any other contemporary head of state except Queen Elizabeth of Britain. King Husayn was succeeded by his 37-year-old son Abdullah.[7] King Abdullah II reaffirmed his father's stance for peace and moderation, ties to the West, and lines to Arab neighbors.

Peoples:
Arabs, Minorities, Refugees

During the millennium prior to World War I, the people of trans-Jordania were, as now, overwhelmingly Arab, Arab language speakers, and predominantly Sunni Muslim. When the people were incorporated into the new mandate, they were overwhelmingly villagers and Bedouins, but they gradually became appreciably urbanized and sedentarized. Jordanians are now 79 percent urbanized, and the villagers now enjoy most modern amenities and often commute to nearby towns.

Most of the urbanized Jordanians live on one or another of the *jabals* ("hills") of Amman, the capital and primate city on the East Bank (Fig. 14-1). This group, many of whom are Palestinians, evolved after World War II along with the rapid growth and development of the Jordanian economy. Many of them have been educated abroad and speak English as a second language, and an appreciable number of them are Christian. Rusayfah and Zarqa to the east of Amman are actually large suburbs of the capital. Irbid, Jordan's third-largest city, is the population node in the northwest, and steadily expanding Aqabah is the kingdom's single port in the southwest.

Before 1900, tribal Bedouins made up the majority of the trans-Jordanian population and constituted a major segment of the Jordanian social structure, bringing Bedouin codes and traditions. During the mandate years, tribal shaykhs wielded decisive political influence and regularly attended national council meetings with Amir Abdullah in Amman. But after World War II, the Bedouins in Jordan became increasingly sedentarized and detribalized, as did Bedouins in neighboring areas. Nevertheless, a general sense of tribal identity and Bedouin heritage remains significant in both society and political culture. Bedouins in the army during internal crises repeatedly showed their traditional loyalty to their paramount chieftain, King Husayn, thereby helping to maintain the kingdom's political structure.

Of the score of Bedouin tribes in modern Jordan, noteworthy are the Bani Sakhr, Huwaytat, Bani Atiyah, Adwan, and the Bani Hasan. Much larger tribes, wandering over more extensive *dirahs* and thus not exclusively Jordanian, include the Rawalah, Anazah, and Shammar.[8]

Both ethnic and religious minorities play noteworthy roles in the Jordanian political and social systems. About 30,000 Circassians (see Chap. 6) populate villages around Amman and are numerous in the capital itself. Perhaps as many as 15,000 Chechens (sometimes called Shishanis) preserve their Caucasian language and culture, brought with them a century ago. The second-largest community of ethnic Chechens in the world, they fled to Ottoman Lands to escape the same sort of conflict with the Russians that afflicted Chechnya during late 1999 and early 2000.[9] Several hundred Armenians sought refuge in Jordan between the 1880s and 1920s, and their descendants continue to be unassimilated in Jordanian society. The western expatriate community, almost entirely British before World War II, is growing steadily and now includes not only British but also Americans, Germans, Yugoslavs, and others.

Jordan's social fabric is not torn by intercommunal conflict, as is that of Lebanon, since relations between the Sunni Muslims (more than 90 percent of the population) and the Christians (about 4 percent, mostly Eastern Orthodox) have always been good. Amir Abdullah demonstrated cordial relations with Christian families, and

FIGURE 14-1   Amman, capital of Jordan. The amphitheater was the heart of Roman Philadelphia. Beyond the theater is a modern residential area on Jabal al-Jawfa; to the right is Jabal al-Ashrafiyah. This older area of the city is yielding to the post-1980 urban development farther west in Amman.

King Husayn followed suit. Distributed among several sects, Christians constitute a community that dates back to the earliest spread of Christianity in the second and third centuries. Almost two-thirds of the East Bank Christians are Greek Orthodox, but there are also a dozen other sects. Certain towns are primarily Christian centers— Karak, Madaba, and al-Salt—and Amman has a high percentage of Christian inhabitants.

Ethnic and religious distinctions aside, it is the division between native "East Bankers" and "Palestinians" that is the crucial dynamic in all aspects of the Jordanian sociopolitical system. Both Palestinians and East Bankers are Arab, speak Arabic, are mostly Sunni Muslim, and have other characteristics in common. But the essential difference is that the Palestinians were dispossessed of their homeland, property, and national identity and have, therefore, profoundly different national sentiments and aspirations from those of the indigenous Jordanians.

Problems of Population

The 300,000 population of the Transjordan mandate in 1921 had increased to only 433,000 by the 1946 independence date. However, this figure increased dramatically in 1948–1949 with the influx of about 132,000 Palestinian refugees to the East Bank. Another 365,000 took refuge among the 400,000 permanent Arab inhabitants of the West Bank area, which was defended against Israeli attacks by the Jordan Arab Legion and its allies. In a matter of weeks, the East Bank population increased nearly one-third, and subsequent annexation of the West Bank area increased the population of the kingdom by 765,000. Jordan's population total thereby jumped during that brief period from about 435,000 to about 1,332,000, which obviously resulted in the original East Bankers' finding themselves suddenly outnumbered two to one by Palestinians. Furthermore, half of the West Bankers were also refugees, displaced by Israelis from their lands and livelihood, and both the refugees and the natives in the West Bank resented annexation by a neighboring polity.

Jordan's demographic—and territorial— status again altered radically with Israel's 1967 conquest of the West Bank. This action not only deprived Jordan of the territory, along with its tourist attractions and agricultural lands, but also reduced the population of the kingdom by half. More than 125,000 West Bank "old refugees" became twice-displaced as they fled invading Israeli military forces and joined their fellow Palestinian refugees on the East Bank. An additional 100,000 West Bank residents and another 45,000 Palestinians from the Gaza Strip also fled eastward as "new refugees" or "displaced persons." Thus, 270,000 new Palestinian immigrants augmented the 132,000 refugees of the late 1940s, their children, and casual immigrants during the period 1949–1967. A small population flow from West Bank to East Bank has continued since 1967, and Israeli extremists declare that all Arabs west of the Jordan must eventually be expelled to Jordan. Of the total 4,682,000 population in 1999, about two-thirds are Palestinians, 275,000 of whom live in ten official UNRWA camps. Most Palestinians in the kingdom have accepted citizenship in Jordan, the only country to offer blanket citizenship to its Palestinian population. This review of the Palestinian demographics of Jordan is a reminder both of the Palestinian *nakbah* and also of the crucial dichotomy in the Jordanian population that dictates a continuing national political balancing act.

Physical Resource Base

Jordan has exhibited remarkable flexibility during the changes in its territorial base and population, particularly in view of its limited physical resource base. A brief survey of this base and the state's exploitation of its resources will aid in understanding the challenges to this buffer kingdom.[10]

Regions of Jordan

An east-west cross section of Jordan shows a threefold physical division (see circled numbers on Map 14-1): [1] Along the western edge is the Jordan Valley and its continuation southward in the Wadi Arabah, a major segment of the Levant Rift System, which contains the lowest continental elevations on earth along the shores of the Dead Sea. [2] Immediately east of the Jordan Valley is a north-south belt of highlands, with elevations of 4,100 ft./1,250 m in the north and the highest elevations in the Palestine-trans-Jordan area, 5,575 ft./1,700 m, in the south. [3] Extending eastward at a general level of 2,625–2,950 ft./800–900 m is the Eastern Desert, which occupies about 85 percent of the country and has a surface that is variously flat, rolling, or exhibiting erosional remnants.

[1] Jordan Valley. The Jordan Valley (Arabic, *al-Ghor*), 65 miles/104 km long, may be subdivided into four narrow parallel belts. (1) The Jordan River itself (see Fig. 3-4), winding in tight meanders in its narrow bed, descends from the confluence of the Yarmuk River just south of the Sea of Galilee (Lake Tiberias) to the river's mouth in the Dead Sea, 1,310 ft./ 400m below sea level. (2) The river floodplain (Arabic, *zor*), with a mantle of rank vegetation called "thicket of the Jordan" in biblical passages, has a level surface that is just a few meters above the river level. (3) The upper terrace level (Arabic, *ghor*) is several hundred meters wide and is divided from the *zor* by a narrow eroded slope. The King Abdullah Canal (originally East Ghor Canal) was constructed on the gently sloping upper terrace level (see "Water" section below), enabling development of the most productive farmland in Jordan. The East Ghor is an archaeologist's paradise, with 224 sites having been identified. (4) A high, ruggedly eroded escarpment—with a total rise of more than 4,265 ft./1,300 m within 1.2 miles/2 km—forms the eastern wall of the great trench that extends from the Sea of Galilee to and beyond the Gulf of Aqabah (see Chap. 3 and Fig. 3-1).

[2] **Highland Belt.** Extending from the Yarmuk River on the north to the Gulf of Aqabah in the south, the highland belt receives the most precipitation of all the regions of Jordan and therefore has always served as the core of settlement, development, and culture east of the Jordan Valley. The hill zone varies markedly in width and relief, and there are fundamental differences in rocks and structure among its northern, central, and southern thirds. Because of their basic significance and their clear differentiation, the five principal subregions of the highland belt are examined in some detail.

(1) With an average 24–30 in./600–750 mm of precipitation, moderate slopes, productive soils, and a remarkable number of flowing springs, the Ajlun Highland is the best-watered and most naturally productive part of Jordan. It extends from the Yarmuk southward to the deep, broad valley of the Wadi Zarqa, the biblical River Jabbock. The Ajlun supports the densest population in the greatest number of villages outside the Amman metropolitan area. Along with cultivated crops, natural woodland has been legendary since ancient times, when resin of trees on these hills yielded the celebrated "balm in Gilead" (Fig. 14-2a).

On the plateau north of the Ajlun Dome lies Irbid (ancient Arbela), Jordan's third-largest city, now the site of a promising new industrial park. East of Irbid is Ramtha (ancient Ramoth or Ramoth Gilead), an old caravan station that served for several decades after World War I as the main border crossing point between Syria and Jordan. The principal north-south motorway now crosses the border east of Ramtha. Along the eastern flank of the dome, on the main highway, is the extensive ruined city of Jerash, with its well-preserved gate, colonnaded main street, forum, theaters, and temples from Hellenistic, Roman, and Byzantine times (see Fig. 2-4b). The southern boundary of the Ajlun subregion is the deep but broad valley of the Wadi Zarqa, the biblical River Jabbock, which cuts through a long sequence of geological strata.

Rising in springs near Amman, the Zarqa joins the Jordan River after a descent of 3,580 ft./

1,090 m. The King Talal Dam, Jordan's largest, was built across the lower Zarqa in 1977 and creates a reservoir that supplies water to Amman.

(2) South of the Wadi Zarqa is the Northern Balqa Highland, sometimes called the Amman Highland. On its western slope is al-Salt, the main center of trans-Jordania before the mandate. On its southeastern edge is Amman, the capital and also the administrative, economic, communications, industrial, and cultural center of Jordan. With buildings of limestone and chalk dimension stone covering the steep slopes of the several *jabals,* the city's morphology is dramatic (Fig. 14-1). From a population of about 6,000–7,000 in the 1920s, Amman was edging toward 2 million inhabitants in early 2000.

(3) The Southern Balqa lies south of the Northern Balqa/Amman Highland on a partly dissected plateau, sometimes called the Karak Plateau, a realm of grain cultivation and semi-nomadic pastoralism. This is the biblical Land of Moab and the classical Peraea ("on the other side"), bounded on the south by a spectacular gash in the plateau, the Wadi Mujib, the biblical River Arnon (Fig. 14-2b). Winding across the plateau is the scenic modern equivalent of the historic King's Highway, connecting the cities of Hisban (ancient Heshbon), Madaba, Dhiban (ancient Dibon), and Karak (ancient Kir Hareseth, chief city of the Moabites)—all mentioned in biblical accounts. Northwest of Madaba is the eminence of Mt. Nebo, from which Moses viewed the Promised Land.

(4) The most rugged part of Jordan, the Shara Mountains (from Seir, meaning "rock," of the biblical period) traverse the ancient land of Edom ("red"). The King's Highway continues southward along the crestline of the Shara to the Hisma, passing diminishing numbers of villages as aridity increases. The village of Wadi Musa adjoins the fantastic archaeological site of Petra, referred to by a British poet as the "rose-red city, half as old as time," hidden in the colorful mesas of Nubian sandstone on the western edge of the Shara (Fig. 14-3). Petra is justifiably Jordan's most frequented tourist site, once a much greater adventure to visit than it is now.

FIGURE 14-2   Jordan—the humid northwest and dry south: contemporary scrub oak and pine woodland in the formerly forested moist Ajlun Highland, biblical Gilead *(top)*, in northwest Jordan, and modern highway winding its way down into the Wadi Mujib, the biblical River Arnon *(bottom)*, in the semidesert near Karak.

(5) The Hisma landscape includes the Hisma Depression itself, with broad sand corridors winding their way among vertical-sided mesas and buttes of red Nubian sandstone, the dramatic, silent land of the Wadi Ram (sometimes Rum). From the Wadi Ram, a rugged corridor for highway and railway reaches Jordan's only seaport at Aqabah. The town has grown from a fishing village of fewer than 2,000 people in 1945 to 69,000 in 1999. Although it, like the adjacent Israeli port of Elat, is off the main sea lanes, Aqabah has expanded into a bustling modern port, especially for the export of phosphate rock and potash. It also now has chemical fertilizer plants and a thriving tourist trade, with its own international airport. Aqabah is the anchor center for Jordan's short coastline, 16 miles/26 km.

[3] Eastern Desert. Stretching eastward from the highland belt is the Eastern Desert, the Badia, a dry table-land that is the northwestern corner of the Syro-Arabian Desert. Except in one or two depressions, the tableland is everywhere over 2,000 ft./610 m. Lying nearly 1,000 ft./305 m below the general level of the highland belt, thus in its rain shadow, the tableland receives only 2–8 in./50–200 mm of precipitation a year. The western margin of the dry realm is Jordan's phosphate belt, and a small oil field and natural gas field are found farther east. One notable cultural feature of former and now renewed economic importance is the Hijaz Railway, which was constructed by the Ottoman Turks in the early 1900s along the dividing line between the sown region on the west and the desert on the east.

Of the Eastern Desert's several subdivisions, two have served historic roles: The depression of the Wadi al-Sirhan, which extends southeastward along the Jordan-Saudi Arabia boundary, was a traditional route for caravans for many centuries and is still used for Bedouin migrations. Azraq Oasis is a complex of shallow pools and marshes that forms the only permanent body of water in the Jordan desert and provides sanctuary for enormous flocks of migrating birds during the spring and fall flights through

the great Levant flyway. Much of the north-central desert is a barren lava plain (Map 14-1), a *hamadah*, in which angular lava boulders constitute the surface.

Water: The Vital Resource

As in other Middle East countries, Jordan's water balance is increasingly becoming a high-priority national issue, not just in agriculture but in human survival. The country is entirely dependent on its own limited and variable winter rainfall, with no major rivers to dam or draw from (but see section on Yarmuk below), and with no aquifers bringing artesian water from well-watered areas. Each of two perennial streams worth noting flows along a sensitive border and is controversial—the Jordan on the west and the Yarmuk on the north.[11] With average annual precipitation generally less than 5 in./125 mm, Jordan calculates its average annual water resources at less than 1 billion m³. Daily per capita domestic water consumption has averaged 85 liters per day in recent years, compared with 300 in Israel and 600 in Europe and America. Jordan's total annual per capita use is less than half the widely recognized "water poverty line" of 500 m³ per capita per year. Periodic severe droughts, such as that of 1996–1999, cause not only crop failures but also industrial emergencies and domestic water interruptions during the dry summer season.

The government has undertaken projects to conserve available water and to increase the water supply. Because irrigation consumes most of the water, farmers are being required to use more efficient systems, particularly drip irrigation. The 1994 Israeli-Jordanian peace treaty provides for Jordan to receive specific amounts of water from the Sea of Galilee; and improved Syrian-Jordanian relations have revived cooperative planning on a jointly operated dam on the Yarmuk. Considered since 1964 as the Mukaybah Dam, later Muqarin, original work began in the late 1980s but ended under the tensions among Israel, Syria, and Jordan. The resurrected project, termed

FIGURE 14-3   Its original name and purpose unknown, this famous monument in Petra was carved out of a vertical red sandstone cliff about 2,000 years ago. It is fancifully referred to in modern times as al-Khaznah ("The Treasury").

al-Wahdah (Unity), calls for a dam 328 ft./100 m high across the deeply entrenched river, impounding a reservoir of 225 million m3. Financing the $400 million cost is a significant hurdle.

Drawing water directly from the Yarmuk, the King Abdullah Canal waters about three-fourths of the country's irrigated area. Opened in 1964, it diverts a share of Yarmuk water into a canal along the level *ghor* between the Jordan River floodplain and the eastern wall of the Jordan Valley. The canal takes advantage of the greater hydraulic head at the elevation at which the diversion takes place and uses Yarmuk water before it mixes with the much saltier Jordan River water. By the mid-1980s, the canal had been extended, in three stages, to reach a length of 72 miles/116 km to the Dead Sea, and the irrigated area was steadily increasing (see next section).

Economic Geography

The independent Transjordan of 1946 that was soon overwhelmed with scores of thousands of destitute refugees faced bleak prospects. The country had very limited agricultural development or potential, minimal water supplies, virtually no other developed resources, no industry, an overwhelmingly poor population, and a penniless government. Nevertheless, with large inflows of grants and other aid, vigorous effort from refugees and indigenous inhabitants, and stimulus from the annexation of the West Bank, the renamed Jordan developed into a politically and economically viable polity. In 50 years it has achieved remarkable economic progress, although it still struggles under many of the same persistent constraints. It now exploits phosphate and potash resources (the major exports), enjoys a modest manufacturing sector, promotes tourism to several excellent sites, participates in major water projects, confronts its high unemployment (and high population growth rate), and cooperates in regional trade agreements and schemes to share electric power.[12]

Agriculture

Less than 6 percent of Jordan is arable, but three-fourths of this area is rain-fed, producing low-yield and highly variable crops of wheat and barley.[13] By far most food, and 90 percent of exported food, is produced in the irrigated 1.5 percent of the area, mostly in the Jordan Valley. The exceptional climate of the valley permits intensive production of such horticultural crops as citrus and bananas, and specialty crops are grown in plastic hothouses (Fig. 14-4). Although agriculture accounts for only 5.5 percent of the GDP (1997) and employs only 5.7 percent of the labor force, it is still a significant sector in the economy. High-value horticultural products provide 6 percent of exports, but foods make up 22 percent of imports. For example, domestic wheat production provides only one month's consumption (and less than half that in the drought year of 1999); imports must meet all other requirements.

Mining

Phosphate-bearing horizons underlie extensive areas of Jordan, generally along the alignment of the Hijaz Railway, and are believed to total almost 1 billion tons of high-grade phosphate rock. Since beginning open-cast mining of phosphates in 1934, Jordan has increased its exports of phosphate fertilizers in response to growing world demand—and steadily higher prices—until it is now third in world exports, shipping about 6 million tons annually to 30 countries, especially India. Mining from the original pits in Rusayfah, east of Amman (farthest from Aqabah but closest to Beirut, the export port for Jordan during the 1950s), was suspended in 1985 in favor of operations at Jordan's largest deposit at al-Shidiyah (sometimes Eshidiya), north of Aqabah. Production from this site alone is being expanded to 7.5 million tons per year; this will increase to a planned 10 million tons by 2005, when mining at the al-Hasa and Wadi al-Abyad sites will be phased out.

Although Israel set up a huge processing operation to recover chemicals from brines in

FIGURE 14-4   Irrigated citrus groves south of Karamah on East Ghor, Jordan Valley, Jordan. White structures in distance are hothouses for producing early vegetables.

the southwestern corner of the Dead Sea in the early 1950s, Jordan began another processing operation only in October 1982, with a $425-million plant on the southeastern shore of the Dead Sea. The plant produces about 1.8 million tons of potash and associated bromine and magnesium annually from evaporated Dead Sea brines. Exports of these chemicals and of phosphates and chemicals from them comprise nearly half of Jordan's exports by value.

A half-century of exploration for hydrocarbons and drilling of about 50 wells have resulted in the discovery of few fuel resources. The small Hamzah oil field, near Azraq, has only insignificant production. Natural gas found in the Rishah area, near the Iraq border, has raised hopes for further energy finds; and Jordan and Iraq have discussed joint development of oil deposits near their common border. These possibilities have frozen preliminary plans for a gas pipeline from Egypt to Jordan under the Gulf of Aqabah. Formerly fed by

Saudi crude via Tapline but cut off after 1990, the Zarqa refinery (90,400 bpd capacity) is now supplied by Iraqi crude. Under dispensation from the UN embargo, Jordan transports its 98,000 bpd requirements 600 miles/965 km by highway from Iraq with a fleet of 1,500 tanker trucks because a more efficient pipeline could not be financed. Producing Jordan's oil shale resources, perhaps up to 40 billion tons, is becoming more nearly cost-effective under higher crude prices.[14]

Manufacturing

Better to accommodate the vast number of refugees economically and to emerge from a preindustrial agricultural economy after the 1950s, Jordan sought diversification and the opening of appropriate manufacturing plants. The small and simple initial enterprises produced processed foods, detergents, paper products, batteries, and similar items; they clustered around the Amman-Zarqa area, which soon added cement plants and an oil refinery. By the 1980s and 1990s, larger and more complex plants burgeoned in Irbid (diversified industries) and Aqabah (fertilizers, other chemicals), as well as in greater Amman. Of special importance is the al-Hasan Industrial Zone being developed near Irbid; this is similar to the industrial parks established near Zarqa-Mafraq and Sahab, in the Jordan Valley. The result of an effort to deliver some of the "elusive peace dividend," the Irbid park is a special Qualifying Industrial Zone; its controversial Israeli joint ventures manufacture products that then have free trade access to the U.S. market—electronic components, textiles, ready-made clothing, and similar items. The labor force is well educated and motivated, but insecurity and limited investment capital have slowed Jordan's attempts to reach its industrial potential.

Transportation

Jordan's highway system admirably serves the kingdom's needs. With basic routes established during the 1950s and 1960s, roads were significantly extended and upgraded during the 1980s and 1990s. The main north-south route is a well-engineered four-lane divided motorway that runs from Syria almost to Aqabah. More recent highways extend from Aqabah through the Wadi Arabah and along the east shore of the Dead Sea; another serves as a shortcut connecting the main highway to Baghdad with Azraq, Maan, and Aqabah.

The historic Hijaz Railway (or Pilgrim Railway), inherited from the Ottomans and made famous in the Lawrence of Arabia legend, has been upgraded and is now a valuable transport asset; because it happens to run right through phosphate-mining areas, it is a significant link in the phosphate export system. Although the line has for many years been used for freight only, passenger express rail service was opened between Amman and Damascus in 1999. The present southern terminus of the railway is Aqabah, where territorial exchanges with Saudi Arabia permitted extension of Jordan's coastline

and expansion of the port. Aqabah has large, modern phosphate-handling facilities and general cargo equipment. The kingdom's national air carrier, Royal Jordanian Airlines, is headquartered at Queen Alia International Airport, south of Amman, and operates a score of jets with worldwide routes. RJA plays a major role in Jordan's important tourism industry, built especially around the country's archaeological treasures, notably Petra and Jerash.

Finances and Aid

From the founding of the mandate, domestic funding was woefully inadequate. Britain provided basic budgetary support 1921–1957, after which the United States was Jordan's main financial supporter for a decade, although other countries contributed also. The kingdom's role in the 1967 June War brought major funding from Saudi Arabia, Kuwait, and other Arab states; and hundreds of millions of dollars in aid promoted astonishing relative development during the 1970s and early 1980s. Foreign aid ceased, however, in late 1990 after King Husayn's perceived tilt toward Saddam Husayn in the Gulf crisis.

Jordan suffered three serious negative financial setbacks after August 1990: the loss of all foreign aid; the loss of billions of dollars in remittances, trade, and services; and an influx of about 300,000 Jordanians/Palestinians forced to return to Jordan after their expulsion from Gulf states, especially Kuwait. Unemployment soared to 35 percent—and to 83 percent among returnees. To help offset his isolation, King Husayn accelerated plans for a peace treaty with Israel, and after the mid-1990s, Jordan experienced an economic upturn; this accelerated perceptibly after the accession of King Abdullah II in early 1999.

International Relations

Close ties between mandate Transjordan and Britain continued after the amirate's independence, and they continue still, despite occasional disagreements. Tension followed King Husayn's dismissal of Glubb Pasha, a British citizen, as commander of the Arab Legion in 1956, and after Jordan's stance on Iraq in 1990. However, Britain has regularly given economic aid, and in 1958 it sent paratroopers to Jordan to help stabilize the kingdom after the coup in Iraq. After 1956, the United States became the main benefactor of the "plucky little king." U.S. support helped preserve the kingdom during the 1970–1971 pitched battles between government forces and Palestinian fedayeen insurgents. U.S.-Jordanian rapport cooled in the late 1970s as perception mounted that the United States—especially the U.S. Congress—gave Jordan only minimum support, enough to keep it viable, yet pliable in the Arab-Israel problem. The good relations of the 1980s lapsed in 1990 but warmed after the 1994 Israel-Jordan peace treaty, again after King Husayn devoted his last days to promoting the peace process, and still more with the new king. Military assistance was well along in 1997; Peace Corps volunteers returned in 1997; and large aid grants were resumed in 1999.

Both King Abdullah I and King Husayn pragmatically and realistically conducted periodic clandestine contacts with Israel, Jordan's most powerful neighbor. Despite two costly multilateral wars in which the two states fought each other, their historically generally correct relations culminated in their 1994 peace treaty. Of the several mutual low points, the most disquieting was the bungled attempt by agents from Mossad, Israeli intelligence, to assassinate Hamas leader Khalid Mashal in Amman, September 25, 1997.[15] Three years to the day later, Jordan closed Hamas offices in Amman.[16] But Jordan's associations with the West and with Israel notwithstanding, it is as an Arab state in an Arab world that Jordan must maintain its national consciousness, despite the fragmentation involved. Jordan's unhappy dilemma in the 1990 Gulf crisis is a case in point.

Although not a prime mover in the Arab world, Jordan has periodically moderated frictions in the region. It is one of the seven charter members of the Arab League and is interlinked with its neighbors in economic, political, and cultural associations. Relations with Syria, with whom affiliation should be very close under geopolitical logic, have been bewilderingly uneven (see Chap. 13); in 1999, relations appeared to be unusually warm.[17] Because the Saudis had seized Mecca and the Hijaz from the Hashimites, Saudi Arabia and Hashimite Jordan viewed each other with suspicion for several decades; however, Saudi Arabia aided Jordan magnanimously during the 1970s and 1980s with not only monetary grants and crude oil through Tapline but also with small military forces. Relations with Kuwait were very close, with Kuwait supplying Jordan hundreds of millions of dollars and employing 250,000 expatriate Jordanians/Palestinians, but aid ceased and the workers (most in professional or semiprofessional capacities) were expelled in August 1990. However, Kuwait reopened its embassy in Amman in March 1999, and in September 1999 signaled an opening to normalcy under King Abdullah.[18]

From the inception of the mandates of Transjordan and Iraq, relations between the two were special because Hashimite brothers occupied the two thrones. Successor Hashimite cousins united the kingdoms in the Arab Federation in 1958, but the union soon collapsed when King Faysal II of Iraq was assassinated in a violent coup. With encouragement from the West and its neighbors, Jordan established a symbiotic economic relationship with Iraq during the Iran-Iraq war and served as a prosperous transit land for Iraq's imports and exports. This was one reason for King Husayn's reluctance to judge Iraq in 1990.

An emotional political issue exploded among the majority Palestinian population in Jordan in August 1990 when the United States promptly organized military action to oppose Iraq's seizure of Kuwait. Such action against Iraqi president Saddam Husayn—who claimed to oppose imperialism, to champion Palestinian rights, and to condemn Israel—was emotionally and widely perceived as the application of a double standard: Whereas the United States has long acquiesced in Israel's seizure of adjacent Arab lands, America immediately fashioned a coalition to fight against an Arab country that invaded adjoining Arab land. At massive street demonstrations and in the media, militant Palestinian leaders in Jordan and elsewhere assailed the United States for its contradictory standards vis-à-vis Israel and anti-Israel Arabs. Some spokesmen emphasized that they did not approve of the Iraqi seizure of Kuwait but that they condemned the U.S. and Western application of a double standard.

Finally, a major political consideration remains as it began a half-century ago—the Jordanian government's ability to balance its obligations to its Palestinian population, its indigenous East Bankers, the West Bank Palestinians and the Palestinian Authority, the Palestinian diaspora, and other Arabs, as well as the United States and Israel. The idea of a confederation between Jordan (the "East Bank") and the Palestinian Authority (the "West Bank") periodically reappears. In any case, Jordan and its more than 2 million Palestinians will have at least a marginal role to play in the final peace settlement. Meanwhile, the kingdom will continue to seek the equilibrium essential to its survival and prosperity.

Notes

1. In addition to my own extensive field research during more than a score of visits to Jordan over a period of 40 years, for this chapter I have drawn on *Jordan* Country Study 1991, Naval Intelligence Division 1943, Salibi 1998 (with a strong geographical approach), Fathi 1994, Baly 1957, and Orni and Efrat 1980. See also <http://www.nic.gov.jo/>.

2. Useful for information on this period are G. A. Smith 1935, Naval Intelligence Division 1943, Baly 1957, and Aharoni 1967.

3. See Naval Intelligence Division 1943, R. Allen 1974, and Wilson 1987.

4. Adams 1996, 527.

5. *Christian Science Monitor,* Oct. 30, 1997.

6. *New York Times,* Oct. 15 and 20, 1999.

7. Lengthy coverage, including extensive background material, is given in the *New York Times,* Feb. 8, 1999. See also Jan. 26 and Feb. 6 and 19, 1999.

8. Tribalism is discussed at some length in *Jordan* Country Study 1991. See also Salibi 1998 and Fathi 1994.

9. The Chechen community in Jordan is discussed in the *Christian Science Monitor,* Nov. 29, 1999.

10. Again, I have supplemented my own field research with Salibi 1998, Naval Intelligence Division 1943, Baly 1957 and 1987, Orni and Efrat 1971, and G. S. Smith 1935.

11. See Salameh 1990, Kolars 1990, Wolf 1995, Elmusa 1997, *Water for the Future* 1999, and Soffer 1999.

12. Economic aspects are discussed in Gubser 1983; *Country Commercial Guide: Jordan,* FY 2000; *Background Notes: Jordan,* 1995; *Jordan* Country Study 1991; and *EIA: Jordan,* Aug. 1999.

13. This analysis is partly from *Agricultural Situation Report: Jordan,* 1997.

14. See *Minerals Yearbook: Jordan,* 1997; *EIA: Jordan,* Aug. 1999; and al-Zoubi and Batayneh 1999.

15. *Christian Science Monitor,* Oct. 3, 1997, and *New York Times,* Oct. 17, 1997.

16. *New York Times,* Aug. 31, 1999.

17. *Christian Science Monitor,* Apr. 23, 1999.

18. *New York Times,* Mar. 5 and Sept. 7, 1999.

15

Israel, "Palestine," and Disputed Territories

Of the world's 117 or so newly independent states (since 1943) and the Middle East's 10 new states, Israel has stimulated an unprecedented level of international involvement, both in support and in opposition. Chapter 11 examines the Arab-Israeli problem, the geopolitical aspects of the Jewish state and of the territories Israel has occupied since 1967, and the problem of the use of names regarding these areas. This chapter focuses on Israel itself, with sections on the local aspects of the territories it has occupied. In July 2000, negotiations were still in progress regarding the parameters of the Palestinian, Authority/Palestine, and talks on the political status of the Golan Heights had made little headway.

One of Israel's leaders once commented that Israel is in but not of the Middle East. The state is, indeed, distinct from its neighbors by virtually every criterion on which differentiation might be made—political, ethnographic, geographic, economic, military. Because of the interacting circumstances of its advent and early evolution, the state was a virtual island of isolation; it related to its neighbors only in military operations. Regionally perceived as having been founded in a partially European nationalistic colonial enterprise, the Jewish state that evolved from Zionist settlements on a segment of the Islamic-Arab Levant was for decades considered a pariah state by its neighbors. Yet a half-century later, Israel had signed peace treaties with Egypt and Jordan, was working toward a final settlement with the Palestinians and Syria, and was accepted—although with reservations, by other regional states.[1]

Historical Note

The long history of Palestine[2] holds a special significance for Christians and Muslims as well as for Jews because of biblical and Quranic associations with the land. For many Jews, the Old Testament accounts buttress modern Zionist claims to the land, whereas more recent history underlies the often conflicting claims of Muslims and Christians (see Chap. 2).

Defeat of Turkish forces in the Middle East in 1917 was followed by British occupation of Palestine and the Transjordan area and later by establishment of the British mandate over Palestine in the early 1920s. After absorbing scores of thousands of Jewish immigrants, the mandate was theoretically partitioned by the United Nations in 1947 (see Chap. 11). However, when the new State of Israel was proclaimed on May 14, 1948, fighting between Jews and Arabs erupted, and Israel—the Jewish-controlled area of Palestine—expanded by 50 percent after the Arabs were defeated (see Map 11-4). Israel occupied Sinai briefly in October 1956, in coordination with the British and French attack on the Suez Canal. Eleven years later, when President Nasser of Egypt closed the Strait of Tiran to Israeli shipping and mobilized troops, Israel responded with an attack on Egypt in the June War (or Six-Day War) of 1967; and after defeating Egypt and its allies Jordan and Syria, Israel controlled Sinai, Gaza Strip, West Bank, and Golan Heights. The Sinai was returned in 1982, but Israel still controls, directly or indirectly, part or all of the other three territories; therefore, the West Bank, Gaza Strip, and Golan Heights are included within the area discussed in this chapter. Discussions regarding the status of the Golan

Israel

Long-form official name, anglicized: State of Israel

Official name, transliterated: Medinat Yisrael (Hebrew); Israil (Arabic)

Form of government: multiparty republic with one legislative house (Knesset)

Area: 7,992 miles^2/20,700 km^2

Population, 1999: 5,740,000 (Israel Government, late 1999: 6,200,000). Literacy: 96%

Ethnic composition (%): Jewish 80.1, Arab and other 19.9

Religions (%): Jewish 79, Muslim (mostly Sunni) 14.8, Christian 2.1, Druze 1.6, other 2.5

GDP, 1998: $101.9 billion; per capita: $18,100

Petroleum reserves: 3.93 million barrels

Main exports (% of total value, 1996): machinery 29.5; diamonds 25.6; chemicals 11.8; apparel 4.9; food, beverages, and tobacco 3.9; rubber and plastic 3.9; ores and minerals 2.5

Main imports (% of total value, 1996): investment goods 17.7; diamonds 14.1; consumer goods 13.2; fuel and lubricants 7.1

Capital city: Jerusalem (seat of government) 650,000 (Jerusalem conurbation 950,000); other cities: Tel Aviv-Yafo 348,000 (Tel Aviv conurbation 2,100,000); Haifa 265,000 (Haifa conurbation 480,000); Rishon LeZiyyon 190,000; Beer Sheva (Beersheba) 170,000; Holon 164,000; Petah Tiqwa 161,000; Ashdod 159,000; Netanya 157,000

and of the Palestinian Authority took place in early 2000.

Varied Landscapes

Regions and Climate

Long latitudinally and narrow longitudinally, Palestine is 265 miles/425 km long and 47 miles/ 76 km wide (Map 15-1). Although the area is relatively small, it extends over such critical latitudes that it lies astride varied climate zones; and with the addition of contrasting landforms, it displays a great range of environments in relation to its size.[3]

The area exhibits a basically simple regional pattern, with three parallel linear belts extending along most of the north-south axis (see circled numbers on Map 15-1): [1] a moderately broad coastal plain along the Mediterranean, [2] a broad arch of limestone hills down the center, and [3] the deep Jordan-Dead Sea-Arabah

trench on the east. In addition, [4] the desertic Negev in the southern triangle is a complex area of cross-folds and basins, with a summit elevation of 3,390 ft./1,035 m on the highest anticline. In the north, from sea level at the coast, the hills rise to 3,963 ft./1,208 m in Upper Galilee (highest summit in Palestine) and to 2,500 ft./762 m at Jerusalem. Eastern slopes descend to the Jordan trench and Dead Sea, with the Sea of Galilee surface at 692 ft./211 m below sea level and the Dead Sea surface at 1,310 ft./400 m below sea level, although both surfaces vary in level.

The latitude and resulting climate of Palestine are similar to those of southern California and Baja California, with a Mediterranean climate (Koeppen Csa) phasing southward into low-latitude steppe (BSh) and desert (BWh). Although summers are hot and dry, with literally no rainfall, the coast around Tel Aviv is uncomfortably humid in late summer. Higher elevations are hot during the clear, cloudless days of summer, but they have low humidity and are cool at night. January is comfortably cool in the lowlands but can be raw in the hills, and snow falls nearly every winter in the Jerusalem area and especially in Upper Galilee. In occasional years, colder and wetter winters dump heavy snows in the highlands, as in 1991–1992, when four snowstorms paralyzed Jerusalem. At one time, 3 ft./1 m of snow blanketed the area, and heavy rains flooded some lower elevations. The coastal plain has a long season for crops, and frosts are rare.

As in Syria and Lebanon, rainfall decreases from north to south and from the coast inland: Acre receives 26 in./650 mm, Tel Aviv 20.8 in./ 529 mm, Gaza 10.5 in./263 mm, and Elat 1 in./ 26 mm. A locality halfway up the western slopes of the Samarian Hills receives twice the rainfall that a station at the same elevation and latitude records on the eastern slopes, in the rain shadow. An unusual element and bonus for agriculture are the 200 dew nights in coastal areas that contribute an additional average 1.2 in./30 mm of moisture. Thus, much of the area suitable for agriculture receives moderate to appreciable rainfall, with only the southern Negev and the southern Jordan Valley having an actual desert climate.

Soils and Vegetation

Patterns of soils and vegetation in Israel and in all of Palestine are, because of the area's varied environments, notably complex.[4] Characteristic *terra rossa* soils developed on most of the hard carbonates (limestone and dolomite) in the hills, but many soils have long ago been eroded away. Similarly, Rendzinas that formed on the softer carbonate outcrops (marls and chalks) east and west of the main *terra rossas* have also been seriously eroded. Loss of these hill soils has exposed the bare rock, often exhibiting lapies (fluting and grooving by solution processes), the common landscape in the hills of the Holy Land.

Alluvial soils dominate in the Huleh Valley, Jezreel Valley, and much of the coastal plain, with *hamra* ("red") clayey-sandy soils alternating with alluvials on the coastal plain. Many

MAP 15-1   General and economic map of Israel, without transportation. Major archaeological sites are indicated because of their historical significance. Circled numbers indicate regions mentioned in the text.

basins in the uplands, especially in the Galilee and Samarian hills, contain alluvial soils derived from *terra rossas* and Rendzinas eroded from the slopes above. Productive loessal soils (loess is fine windblown material) occupy the

Beer Sheva (Beersheba) Basin and adjoin a belt of moderately fertile but dry steppe soil; however, most of the remaining soils of the Negev are sandy or stony desert soils, including *hamadahs*. Dark soils on basaltic lava occupy small areas north and southwest of the Sea of Galilee. Partly owing to reclamation work since World War I, the best agricultural areas are in the coastal plain and other plains areas, including the northern Negev, the plains and valleys of Jezreel and the Huleh, and the major basins.

The maquis, garigue, and *batha* vegetation (see Chap. 5) of the Palestine hills is the Mediterranean vegetative landscape most familiar to tourists. However, Palestine as the meeting ground of three major phytogeographical zones—Mediterranean in the more humid areas, desertic Saharo-Sindian in the southern Negev and in the southern rift valley, and transitional Irano-Turanian in between—displays an exceptional variety of plants. About 2,500 plant species are known in Israel, compared with, for example, 1,700 in Great Britain. The vegetative landscape has been greatly modified in the twentieth century by the planting of pine trees in the humid north and center and of eucalyptus trees on the lower slopes and plains, including the northern Negev. However, the realm of the true desert remains generally barren, with widely scattered bean caper bushes, broom, and, where more moisture is available at depth, acacia trees.

Water

As we have seen, water is a crucial element throughout the Middle East (see Chap. 11). Because Israel has keyed its planning and development to a high level of water consumption, its water supply is of particular significance, involving not only major technical challenges but also significant political and military encounters.[5]

In discussing the future Palestine mandate with British officials in 1919, Zionist leaders solicited possession or control of maximum water resources for the mandate and its successor Jewish state. In partial response, the boundaries of the mandate were extended well to the north to encompass the Sea of Galilee, Lake Huleh, and some of the Jordan headwaters. However, the border delineation apportioned some headwaters among the new mandates concerned and excluded the upper headwaters of the Jordan as well as the lower Litani, which the Zionists had sought but which was left undivided along with the upper Litani in Lebanon. However, with the conquest of the Golan in 1967 (and unilateral annexation in 1981), the occupation of the West Bank and Gaza also in 1967, and control of southern Lebanon between 1978 and 2000, (tightened after 1982), Israel gained command of virtually all the water it had originally sought in 1919. Achieving such water control was, indeed, a major objective of taking and holding these four areas, under the general rubric of ensuring greater security for the state.[6] Israel's negotiations with Jordan, the Palestinians, and Syria in the peace process include meticulous details regarding access to and apportionment of water.

So heavy are Israel's water demands that even with efficient utilization of all the water of the state and of the occupied areas, Israel's annual water use is exceeding average supply by 15 percent. An increasing population, especially with the influx of 900,000 former Soviet Jews, and ever-increasing water use inexorably signify that unless proper action is taken promptly, "Israel is on the threshold of a catastrophe."[7] Some planners urge that the state abandon its emphasis on agriculture, which uses more than 75 percent of the water. Industrial applications—now accounting for only about 5 percent of water use—yield a higher return per unit of water consumed, and manufacturing produces export items to exchange for food at a good profit. To help alleviate its water shortage, Israel plans a facility near Ashqelon for desalinating Mediterranean water, despite its acute deficit in domestic energy supplies. Corollary facilities at Ashqelon are in advanced planning for receiving contracted-for water in large tankers from Turkey's Manavgat River, another benefit of the Israel-Turkey cooperation. Imports of piped water from Egypt are also under discussions (but see Chap. 20).

Furthermore, since the coastal plain aquifers are extensions of strata underlying the West Bank, where they receive most of their water charge, the apportionment of underground water in the hill country is increasingly a critical issue of contention between West Bank Arabs and Jewish settlers supported by Israeli authorities, who control water allotment. In both the West Bank and Gaza, Jewish settlers are allotted and use substantially more water per capita than the indigenous Arabs, who claim that they are at least systematically deprived of their rightful share of water—or of all water—and are often being forced out of their lands and villages. The claim is denied by some Israeli officials but confirmed by some extremist Jewish settlers.

Among a number of major water projects, the state's greatest undertaking has been the National Water Carrier. Partly a canal but primarily a massive underground concrete pipeline 8.86 ft./2.7 m in diameter, it conducts water from Tabagha at the northwestern corner of the Sea of Galilee down the coastal plain to the northwestern Negev (see Maps 15-1 and 15-2). Opened in 1964, the project spans 140 miles/225 km and delivers an average of nearly 400 million m^3 per year, most of it during the summer months, from the water-surplus north to the water-deficient south. Drought years and overuse can reduce delivery to only 160 million m^3, as in the summer of 1986 when the level of the Sea of Galilee was 20 in./0.5 m below the acceptable minimum. However, the following wet winter refilled Galilee to its maximum. The same cycle was repeated in the drought years of 1987–1990, when the Sea of Galilee was at its lowest level in 30 years but refilled during the extraordinarily wet winter of 1991–1992. The cycles are another reminder that climatic conditions in these marginal areas swing widely from period to period. The summers of 1999 and 2000 brought the worst drought since the state was founded. The Sea of Galilee was again at the "red line," considered to be the minimum level below which further lowering would irreparably damage the ecosystem.

MAP 15-2   Water situation in Israel, the occupied territories, and adjacent areas. (Adapted from map in *Geographic Notes*, no. 13, U.S. Department of State)

On the coastal plain, groundwater is pumped from shallow aquifers that are fed by the area's moderate rainfall and runoff from the slopes to the east (see Map 15-2). These substantial groundwater supplies augment water piped from Galilee and the Yarqon River for the intensive irrigation agriculture on the plain and for urban consumption. Potential dangers in the delicate balance were emphasized in 1986 when a decade of overpumping had lowered the water table more than 8 ft./2.5 m below any previous level. The drop occurred despite increasingly efficient use of irrigation water and despite a vigorous program of recycling urban wastewater for storage in the underground aquifers. However, the natural cycle temporarily remedied much of the problem with unusually heavy rains in the winter of

1986–1987. As with the Sea of Galilee, the underground aquifers experienced the same cycle of four dry years and one wet year in the years 1987–1992. In mid-2000, Israeli government officials warned of dire consequences of continuing drought.

Population and Peoples

Immigration

The goal of Zionism, the creation of a Jewish state in the territory of Palestine, required a rapid increase in the *yishuv* ("settlement," the Jewish community in Palestine) in order to create a Jewish majority by the end of the mandate period. The First Aliyah ("ascent," in this case to Palestine) in 1880–1904; the second, until 1919; and the third, until 1923 brought several tens of thousands of *olim* ("ascenders"). The numbers were much larger in the Fourth (1924–1928) and Fifth Aliyahs (1929–1939, which brought more than 250,000 *olim*). Unrestricted Jewish immigration, an essential in the Zionist program, was a serious problem for British mandatory authorities, who were as obligated under the Balfour Declaration to protect the rights of the indigenous Arabs as they were to permit specified Jewish immigration. The inflow was regarded by the Palestinian Arabs as an invasion and displacement by European outsiders.

"Ingathering" After Independence. After May 15, 1948, when Israel became independent, Jews around the world were importuned to immigrate to the new state to fulfill the basic Zionist ideological goal of "the ingathering of the exiles." The resulting influx had long been anticipated, and exceptional organization and preparations permitted the flood of 686,748 arrivals by the end of 1951 to be processed, housed, and fed. Special operations were undertaken to fly in virtually entire Jewish communities by chartered aircraft or aircraft lent by friendly governments. More than 121,000 of the 130,000 Jews in Iraq, descended from an ancient community including those who stayed behind after the Babylonian Captivity, were

flown to Israel, as were 44,000 of the 45,000 Jews in Yemen. Thousands more flooded in from all continents—an additional 810,000 during the two decades between 1952 and 1972.[8] Until the mid-1970s, immigrants constituted more than half of the population, but a decade later they represented less than 40 percent. Their percentage decreased until the flood of Former Soviet Union (FSU) immigrants restored it to nearly 40 percent in 1999, by which time the population had been drawn from more than 100 countries.

Inevitably, the huge influx of immigrants during the early years of the independent Israel diminished as the supply of would-be Israelis decreased and as word spread about the difficulty of life in Israel. The total of *olim* fell from 239,076 in 1949 to an average of 25,000–35,000 annually for the next several years. Along with reduced immigration, Jews inside Israel—including "Sabras," native-born Jewish Israelis—emigrated in large numbers, about 500,000 by 1981, most to the United States.[9]

Jews from the FSU. Thus, it was of compelling importance for Israel to arrange for the immigration of large numbers of Soviet Jews, whose inflow could help offset the outflow. Their free emigration had been demanded of the USSR for more than 25 years, with the United States pressed to include the topic on the agenda of virtually every negotiating session with the Soviets. Once the restrictions were lifted, Jews poured out of the USSR area—overwhelmingly the Russian area, both before and after the disintegration of the Soviet Union—and into Israel by the scores of thousands, totaling about 350,000 between late 1989 and early 1992 and peaking at 35,000 in December 1990. By 1992, when both Israel's absorptive capacity and the urge to leave the FSU had abated, immigration dropped to one-third of the 1990 peak.[10] Annual arrivals of FSU *olim* decreased steadily for the next several years, yet by 1999 nearly 900,000 of them had settled in Israel. In its determination to accommodate the newcomers, Israel turned to its longtime supporter, the United States, for a $10 billion loan guarantee, which was granted in October 1992 after the new Labor government reversed the Shamir-Sharon policy of expanding Jewish settlement on the West Bank. However, as happened regularly, the building pace soon resumed and continued.

Present Population Structure

Immigration of Jews to Israel from numerous and varied countries has generated a rich and complex social structure and vigorous, not always amicable, sociopolitical relationships. The six countries that have supplied the greatest number of immigrants are, in order, the Former Soviet Union, Morocco, Romania, Poland, Iraq, and Iran. However, many more languages persist in Israel, reflecting both the national origins of earlier immigrants and the perseverance of mother tongues: Russian (along with Ukrainian and other Slavic languages), Romanian, Western and Eastern Arabic, German, French, Spanish, Ladino (the basic language of Sephardic Jews), and, of course, Yiddish and English. This accounts for the large number of periodicals in various languages displayed on Israeli newsstands. In addition to language and sometimes costume, the wide range of physical characteristics—the Ethiopian features of the Falashas, the southern Arabian appearance of the Yemeni Jews, and the blond hair and blue eyes of the German Jews (nicknamed *yeckis* because of their characteristically formal male jacket attire)—attests to the varied origins of Israelis.

Multi-Cultures: Who Is a Jew?

In 1950 the Knesset (parliament) passed a Law of Return, which authorized immediate Israeli citizenship for any Jew settling in Israel. However, internal conflicts arose over the criteria for citizenship, and debate on the so-called Who is a Jew? question continues officially and informally in Israel. Landmark court cases have narrowed the issue but have not resolved it. A 1970 amendment to the Law of Return includes non-Jewish spouses, children, and grandchildren of Jews. Professed Jews with Jewish mothers or those who have converted to Judaism in accordance with religious law satisfy the criteria. However, some converted Jews, especially those converted by nonorthodox rabbis, face barriers, as do those who have converted from Judaism to another religion. The practice of Judaism as a religion is not a criterion for citizenship—Israeli studies show that more than half of the country's Jews are "nonobservant" (secular)—and it is significant that family descent has become the primary standard, reinforcing the ethnicity of Jewishness. The influx of FSU *olim* brought, for the first time, thousands of non-Jews—Russians who envisioned greater promise in the more affluent society of Israel. Most of them were spouses of acknowledged Jews. About 208,000 of the 900,000 Russian/FSU immigrants as of 1999 were not Jewish, and more than half of those arriving in the late 1990s were non-Jewish.[11]

Inter-Group Conflicts. Imbued with European nationalism, secularism, and socialism, European Jews—the *Ashkenazim* (from the Hebrew for "Germany")—organized Zionism to establish a state in Palestine based on European principles. As the founders promoted large-scale immigration, however, groups from dozens of other regions and subcultures brought new and different political and cultural concepts with them and tenaciously maintained them. The melting-pot idea dissipated. The unified, monocultural Jewish society envisioned by the Ashkenazim soon became variegated multidimensionally and was transformed into a factionalized and contentious body politic on the one hand and a vigorous, stimulating society seeking viable answers on the other. The cleavages were ethnic: Ashkenazi–Sephardi–Mizrahi–Russian–Ethiopian–Arab; political: left–right–center; religious: ultra-Orthodox–Orthodox–Conservative–Reform–Cabalist–secular; economic: rich–middle class–poor; philosophical: western–eastern and modern–traditional; and, cutting across all the above categories, peace process approaches that are hawkish–moderate–dovish. All of these polarizations become acute in Israeli elections, when more than a score of parties embodying the various elements just mentioned elect members to the Knesset. Although the cleavages should not be overemphasized, neither should they be underestimated. Three dichotomies are particularly worth noting: The Ashkenazi– Mizrahi, the Jewish–Arab, and the Orthodox– secular.

As immigration into Israel increased, Oriental Jews from North Africa, the Middle East, and southern Asia came to outnumber the Ashkenazim. Sometimes grouped under the term *Sephardim* (from the Hebrew for "Spain"), and after the early 1990s often called *Mizrahim* (Hebrew for "Orientals" or "Easterners"), Oriental Jews failed for almost three decades to achieve a meaningful role in the political and economic life of Israel. After 1948, many incoming Mizrahim were assigned to frontier settlements, either in the Negev or in vulnerable border towns. By the late 1980s, they composed 54 percent of the population but were represented far below their proportion in upper ranks of employment and education. "Jews in the form of Arabs" were "imported" in large numbers to outnumber Palestinian Arabs and to serve as cheap labor for the elite Ashkenazim. The further supposition was that the superior Ashkenazim could gradually raise the "primitive" Mizrahim to the Euro-Zionist level, whereas the Oriental Jews believed that such a process "hijacks the Jews of Islam from their own geography and subsumes them into the history of the European-Ashkenazi shtetl."[12] They protested their second-class citizenship not only by demonstrating in the 1970s but also by right-wing bloc voting against the traditional, liberal Ashkenazi establishment (Labor party).

By the election period in 1992, Sephardi leaders were also at odds with the Likud leadership. Sephardi alienation and frustration remain serious problems, and Ashkenazi apprehensions remain that the higher Sephardi birthrates will combine with the still-higher Arab birthrates to relegate the European-North American Jews to an increasingly minor role.

Mindful of the necessity to amalgamate immigrant groups from diverse cultural backgrounds, the Israeli government relies on compulsory military service for immigrant absorption and national integration, along with intensive training in Hebrew as a national language for all *olim* and general education to "Israelize" the newcomers, which Mizrahim understand but resent when "Israelization" means dismembering their Islamic-Jewish identity.

Not unrelated but having a different genesis is the interethnic conflict within Israel between the majority Jews and the minority Palestinian Arabs.[13] Although most of the Palestinians fled in 1947–1949 (see Chap. 11), about 160,000 remained, with major concentrations in Galilee. With a higher average birthrate than that of the Jews, the Arabs within Israel numbered nearly 1 million in early 2000, about 17 percent of the population.

Mutual distrust and resentment, as well as mutual preference for segregation, generally characterize contemporary Jewish-Arab attitudes, although there are individual exceptions on both sides. Most remaining Arab population centers have been surrounded by "mirror" government-planned Jewish housing. Inequities in budget allocations (five times higher for Jewish communities than for Arab communities) and government grants to municipalities (three times higher for Jewish municipalities) have resulted in consequent inequities in housing, economic development, employment, welfare, and general services. Arab university graduates who live in Israel experience difficulty in finding suitable employment, and they are discriminated against in many other ways. Eventually, entrepreneurial Arabs developed their small industries in the Arab areas of Israel; and despite handicaps in the business context in which they operate, they have become reasonably successful (see Map 15-3). The percentage of Israeli Arabs in agriculture, for example, dropped from 58.2 in 1954 to 4.6 in 1994.[14] Some Israeli Jews call for equal treatment of Israeli Arabs and mutual tolerance. However, some Jewish extremists, such as the Kach party followers of the former U.S. rabbi Meyer

Arab settlements by population
- ● above 25,000
- ● 10,000–25,000
- ● 5,000–10,000
- • 1,000–5,000
- · under 1,000

△ Jewish town

LEBANON

Qiryat Shemona

SYRIA

Fassuta

Zefat

Akko

Sakhnin

Haifa

Sea of Galilee

Tiberias
Kafr Kanna

Hadera ISRAEL

Afula

Bet Shean

Mediterranean Sea

Umm al-Fahm

JORDAN

Netanya

WEST BANK

Taiyiba

Tel Aviv

Kafr Qasim

MAP 15-3   Areas of continued Palestinian Arab settlement in Israel, indicating centers of Arab manufacturing enterprises. (Adapted from Schnell et al. 1999, with permission)

Kahane, express a candid determination to "cleanse" Israel of all Arabs.[15]

Another emotionally charged debate erupted among Israeli intellectuals in the late 1980s and quickly became a national conflict: the "New History." The issue was ventilated by some younger Israeli historians who examined government documentation from the 1940s and 1950s newly declassified and made available in the 1980s. After studying these extensive new sources, the "New Historians" reported that the events and developments surrounding the birth and evolution of the state had for 40 years been misrepresented and mythologized for nationalistic purposes. Distortions reported by the writers concerned inter alia the motivations of early Zionist leaders, the 1948–1949 warfare, the advent of the Palestinian refugee problem, and other issues long embedded in the traditional "mythology" of Israel's early years. The New History's reinterpretation of traditional Zionist historiography had a major impact on the country and in world Jewry. In the late 1990s, some Israeli schoolbooks were rewritten to incorporate the revised history, and *Tkuma* (Rebirth), a 22-part series produced by and shown on Israeli television for the Fiftieth Anniversary celebration, included many New History segments.[16]

Religions and Religious Frictions. Among religious groups in Israel in 1999, 79 percent were Jews and 15 percent were Muslims (mostly Sunni). Other groups are indicated in the country summary. Frictions between Jews and Muslims (and Christians) are manageable, since the Jews hold the balance of power, but frictions among Jewish groups are much more serious and sensitive. Somewhat as in Lebanon, religious communities, sects, and subsects are critical per se and are also critical in the governmental structure, as was demonstrated in the government crisis of July 2000. Especially fragile is the relationship between religious groups that are pro-Zionist and those that are anti-Zionist, and "post-Zionism" was added to issues vigorously debated in the Jewish state in the 1990s. The unusual Samaritans are discussed in Chapter 6.

Conflict between religious conservatives and liberals, evident in diverse religious groups throughout the region, also intensified in Israel in the 1980s. Increasingly noteworthy, particularly in view of the crucial support given the State of Israel by the U.S. Jewish community, is the growing rift between the American Conservative and Reform Jews—the great majority in America—and Israeli Orthodox rabbis. Orthodox leaders reject conversions, weddings, and other rites performed by non-Orthodox rabbis, a stance that the more liberal U.S. Jews reciprocally find offensive. Reconciliation of the viewpoints in the foreseeable future was still problematic in early 2000, one of the factors in the dichotomy between a particularistic and a pluralistic society in Israel.

Public confrontations occasionally occur in major cities between ultrareligious Israelis (*haredim*) and secular Israelis. Some *haredim* attempt to impose traditional Jewish religious law (*halakah*) on all phases of life in Israel

while secular citizens demand freedom of choice, including secularism. One small group of ultra-Orthodox Jews, the Neturei Karta (Guardians of the City) of the section of Jerusalem known as Mea Shearim, emphasize spiritual redemption and oppose Zionism and the existence of a political state of Israel. They also reserve the use of Hebrew, language of the Bible, for religious purposes only. Yet leaders of another ultra-Orthodox group, the Hasidim, believe that the Torah (the Pentateuch) provides the Jewish claim to the land of Israel.

Religions of Non-Jews. Of the non-Jews in Israel, most are Arabs, of whom three-fourths are Muslims, primarily Sunni. Recognized as a separate religious group since 1957, the 98,000 Druzes stand out because they remained through the hostilities in both 1948 and 1967 (especially in Golan), and they are allowed to serve in the Israeli Defense Forces. A few thousand Shiis who came from Lebanon several decades ago inhabit the northern hills, along with a few hundred Alawis. About 3,000 Circassians, speaking their own Circassian language and practicing Islam, live primarily in two Galilee villages, Kafr Kamma and Rihaniya, and also serve in the army. The eclectic Bahais, originally quasi-Shiis, have their world center on Mt. Carmel, overlooking Haifa, but number only a few hundred members of varied ethnic backgrounds within Israel.

Because of the close ties between Christianity and the Holy Land, at least 30 different Christian sects, representing several nationalities, are found in Israel. They congregate especially in Jerusalem, where thousands of them maintain centuries-old churches, monasteries, hostelries, and schools. The Christians are predominantly Arabs, although the Christian category also includes most of the non-Arab, non-Jewish population of Israel. Perhaps 25,000 longtime resident Europeans and Americans, most of them connected with ecclesiastical or charitable institutions, reside in Israel. Many, however, are actually in East Jerusalem, not a de jure part of the state of Israel.

Nearly three-fourths of the Christians are Greek Orthodox and Greek Catholics (Melkites). Roman Catholics (Latins), third in number, have a patriarch in Jerusalem and supervise many of the Christian holy sites through several orders. A bewildering variety of other Christian churches maintain at least small congregations in the Holy Land. Major Protestant groups include Anglicans and Lutherans; several other Protestant groups, from Baptist to Mormon, have "missions" or small offices in Jerusalem. Draft laws by the Knesset have sought to make proselytizing efforts among Israeli Jews by Christian groups illegal.

Settlements

Patterns of settlement are particularly relevant in Israel because of the quintessential role of settlement of the land in Zionist ideology. They are also significant in the rapid transformation of the landscape and because of the unique aspects of settlement preplanning, design, functions, and interrelations with inhabitants. The societal organization foreseen by Zionist planners called for collective and cooperative rural settlement types. Groups of similar cultural background could be assigned to one settlement, producing a maximum group effort, and the land, title to which was held by the Jewish National Fund (JNF), could be leased to groups rather than to individuals.

Three Rural Types

Three rural settlement types evolved: the kibbutz, moshav, and *moshav shittufi* ("collective moshav"). The kibbutz, the first of which was established in 1921 as an outgrowth of the twelve-year-old *kvutza* settlement concept, is a commune based on agriculture but with the potential to become an industrial collective. Eventually numbering more than 300 but now reduced to 267 with a total population of 118,300, kibbutzim became one of the two main forms of Jewish rural settlement in Israel. Originally conceived as an agricultural commune in

every respect—holding land and other property in common, dining in a common mess hall, maintaining a common child-care center—the kibbutz was a great attraction. But as Israeli society evolved, kibbutzim became less communalized, and few now maintain common dining facilities and child-care centers. Although some are still agricultural, many have developed specialized industries—polishing diamonds, producing electronic goods, catering to tourists, or simply serving as bedroom towns for commuters near major cities.

The moshav is a smallholders' cooperative agricultural settlement on JNF or government land, in which a member family has an individual home and a plot of ground worked by the family (Fig. 15-1). Marketing of produce, however, is done cooperatively. Moshavim became the main rural settlement type, reaching 424 in number in the early 1970s and increasing to 454 in 1998 with a total population of 194,800.

In the *moshav shittufi,* combining features of the moshav and the kibbutz, members have individual homesteads but conduct agriculture and economy as a collective unit. Two other agricultural settlement types, the *moshava* and *moshav ovdim,* are found in limited numbers.

Urban Planning

Of more than 650 Arab villages before and during the mandate years, 394 were destroyed by the Israelis in 1948, and only a modest number remain in Israel within the pre-1967 boundaries. Many had few residents after the flight and expulsion of Palestinian refugees in 1947–1949, and an uncertain number of occupied villages were sequestered by Israeli military authorities after independence. Since the older settlement sites usually had a locational asset—water supply, good soil, defensibility, transportation—new Jewish settlements were usually built adjacent to an older site (Fig. 15-1).

Although early Zionist planning emphasized rural settlement, the flow of immigrants to towns made urban planning also necessary. Zionists established separate quarters for Jews outside the older sections of existing towns in

FIGURE 15-1   Margaliyot, 1958 and 1990. A moshav founded in 1954 on a dramatic site on the Galilee Heights overlooking the Huleh Valley, Margaliyot replaced the old Arab village of Hunin, ruins of which are seen in the background of the photograph on the top. By 1990, the moshav had been largely rebuilt two or three times, and Hunin had virtually disappeared *(bottom)*. It had been further changed by 1997.

the late 1800s, and in 1909 they founded the new town of Tel Aviv, the planned modern hub of the state of Israel, north of Jaffa. New and planned extensions of Haifa and Jerusalem followed. Major institutions and monuments were planned for hilltop sites in Jerusalem: Hebrew University, Knesset (the Parliament), other government buildings, memorials, and similar structures. The government built mass high-rise apartments in strategic locations around East Jerusalem after Israel took the West Bank in 1967 and extended the municipality boundaries of the city.

The Jewish Quarter inside the walls of the Old City of Jerusalem was, after 1967, also largely cleared of the centuries-old houses and rebuilt; one large block of ancient houses was bulldozed to make the Wailing Wall plaza. As in many historical cities worldwide, new construction often occurs at the expense of traditional older architecture, and the disproportionate demolition of Arab buildings and homes aggravates interethnic hostility. In Haifa, several sites on Mt. Carmel have been built up with Jewish residential areas, resorts, and institutions, including two universities. As more than a million new *olim* poured into an already densely populated but outwardly affluent Israel during the 1990s, housing in towns and cities became increasingly inadequate. Construction outran planning. Apartment buildings became increasingly multistoried, although in the West Bank individual houses were built by the hundreds to attract settlers, most of whom, however, preferred the greater certainty of towns inside Israel proper.

Economic Patterns

A General Economic Perspective

Israel's economic distinctiveness is as marked as its political and religious differentiations in the region. Initial economic plans predate the Zionist immigration begun at the turn of the century. The basic institution was the World Zionist Organization (WZO), founded in 1897 by the First Zionist Congress. The Jewish National Fund (Hebrew, Keren Kayemeth Leisrael) was founded in 1901 to purchase land for Zionist colonies in Palestine. The Keren Hayesod was founded in 1920 as the main Zionist international fund-raising agency, although the United Jewish Appeal serves this function in the United States. The Jewish Agency, founded in 1919, served as an informal government for Jews under the British mandate in Palestine, and it continues to act, along with WZO, as a basic Zionist institution, working hand in hand with the government of Israel.

Specialized planning and research agencies directed or coordinated virtually every phase of the economy in Israel before the marked socioeconomic changes of the 1990s. Similar planning addressed defense, science, education, and the arts. Such centralized planning rested on participation of interlocking national institutions (government, JNF, Jewish Agency) and the central labor organization (Histadrut), which until its diminishing status in the mid-1990s controlled not only labor activities but also industries and other economic establishments. This diverse expertise has contributed to an economic development in Israel that, even without a petroleum sector, but with the comparable advantage of receiving billions of dollars yearly in aid, has achieved the highest general standard of living in the Middle East. This achievement is also based partly on the complex politico-economic agreements that Israel, supported by the U.S. government, has arranged with the EU, Turkey, and other entities, now including Egypt and Jordan, and particularly the United States. Another stimulus was the great economic impetus of the nearly 1 million FSU immigrants as highly trained producers and eager consumers. The early peace treaty with Egypt, the progress of the peace process—including negotiations with Syria in early 2000—and the peace treaty with Jordan in 1994 converged to produce an economic boom in Israel during the mid-1990s. Its former regional isolation has now largely dissipated, and its once heavy dependence on aid from the United States, from Jewish organizations, and from individual donors has lessened, although aid continues in large amounts. Such aid permits Israel to maintain not only its high GDP per capita (see country summary) but also its military-industrial establishment, ambitious technological research and development more characteristic of a world power (nuclear weapons and energy, space rocketry, missiles and antimissile weapons, biological and chemical R and D), wide-ranging intelligence and diplomatic agenda, massive welfare programs, and extensive bureaucracy.[17]

Agriculture

Agriculture in the original Zionist plan to colonize Palestine was not just a routine economic activity nor just a necessary process to provide employment and food to the immigrants. Above and beyond these, it represented an ideological and mystical bonding of the Jewish people to the Land of Israel, as we have seen in the discussion of settlements. Nevertheless, the practical aspects of farming were very much emphasized, with the usual Israeli stress on research, experimentation, and efficiency. Thus, Israel's agriculture has become the most scientifically planned, organized, systematized, modernized, and mechanized in the Middle East (see Chap. 7) and ranks among the most productive in the world.

The basic range of crops, however, differs little from that in other Mediterranean areas. As in Lebanon, citrus fruits are outstanding: Along with grapefruit, Jaffa oranges, famous for centuries on the irrigated coastal plain, supply one of Israel's noteworthy exports, although citrus exports are decreasing. Market-oriented horticulture is especially highly developed, systematized by area, growing techniques, and exact dates so that specialty crops, including flowers, can be rushed to European markets earlier than those from other producing areas. In the relentless quest for maximum yield from each unit of land, Israeli agricultural researchers have urged adoption of new varieties of plants, use of best patterns of planting (such as growing tender crops on gentle slopes for cold air drainage), and, above all, maximum extension

of irrigation and most effective use of water, as in drip irrigation (see Chap. 7).

As in crop growing, the state's dairying, fishing, and forestry are also scientifically planned and conducted. For example, the milk yield of Israeli dairy cows is twice that of any other Middle East country and ten times that of Iran. In forestry, more than 115 million trees have been planted in forest and woodland as well as along roads, in windbreaks, and along frontiers and in other security areas.

Whereas virtually all Jewish agriculture is institutionalized and cooperative, Arab farms, located primarily in Galilee, are generally individual and traditional. Lacking the funding given the Zionist rural communities and without access to Jewish marketing cooperatives, Arab farms remain less mechanized, more conservative, and less prosperous. Several thousand nomadic Arab pastoralists in the Negev have resisted forced settlement in an effort to preserve their Bedouin way of life. However, they have had to surrender much of their *dirahs* for use as airfields, settlements, and mining areas.

Mining

Mining is not a major activity in the Israeli economy, although two aspects contribute appreciably to the country's GDP: phosphate mining and Dead Sea water evaporation. A third aspect, technically a mineral industry, is diamond polishing, which forms the basis for a leading export. Petroleum production now plays a negligible role (see Chap. 8), although exploration efforts continue. In early 2000, exploration for natural gas offshore from southern Israel and Gaza offered some hope for a possible extension of the rich offshore gas reservoirs north of the Nile Delta. Discovery of major gas fields in this offshore area would transform the energy equation for both Israel and the Palestinian Authority. Meanwhile, Israel and Egypt have tentatively agreed that natural gas might be piped from the Nile Delta across the Sinai to Israel, as well as to the PA. The state's only known hydrocarbon deposit is lean oil shale in the Negev, where there are an estimated 12 billion mt. Meanwhile,

Israel imports 99 percent of its petroleum consumption of about 210,000 bpd, from Mexico and Western Europe. Although most of Israel's electric power plants were formerly oil-fired, they are now primarily coal-fired, using 11 million mt of imported coal, about half from South Africa, per year (1998). Completion in 2000–2001 of Israel's fourth major coal-fired power plant, at Ashqelon, could rachet up annual coal imports to 12 million mt. The use of coal is, in turn, raising questions about adding to the pollution of the normally clean, crisp air in the area.

Israel's major subsurface resource is phosphorite (phosphate-bearing rock), part of the great regional belt of late Cretaceous phosphates. Extensive open-pit mining of high-grade phosphorites is concentrated in the northern Negev, where Oron is the main center (see Map 15-1). Phosphate production of 4 million mt in 1996, seventh-largest in the world, was shipped by rail to Ashdod for export.

Evaporation of Dead Sea water in extensive ponds at Sedom at the southern end of the lake yields large quantities of bromine, potash, and magnesium chloride as well as smaller amounts of related chemicals. Israel is the world's second-largest producer of bromine and bromine compounds and sixth largest producer of potash. Continued evaporation of the lake's water, combined with a curtailed inflow of the Jordan River, is drying up the southern third of the lake (Map 15-2).

Manufacturing

Even more than agriculture, manufacturing differentiates Israel from its neighbors in its organization, scope, technical level, and markets. In spite of a limited resource base and an import dependence for energy, Israel's industrial development is by far the most diversified and most technologically advanced in the Middle East. Expertise brought by European and FSU Jewish immigrants, along with imported technology and subsequent Israeli research and engineering advances, yielded rapid development. Initial industries produced basic items: processed

food and beverages (notably wine), textiles, clothing, and similar light articles. Increased population, with its notable brain gain, and transfers of both capital and technology led to far more complex production than Israel's age as a state, population, size, geographical area, and resource base would suggest. Institutional research in the universities—especially research carried on by Technion, the Weizmann Institute, Soreq nuclear reactor, Dimona nuclear facility, Nes Ziyyona Israel Institute for Biological Research, the several military research facilities, and similar agencies—carried scientific and industrial technology well beyond that learned from immigrant researchers and outside sources.[18]

Israeli industry is now producing not only the predictable household appliances, vehicle tires, plastics, and similar routine items but also medical equipment, advanced optical and other precision goods, and high-technology electronic equipment—with a booming emphasis on computer software and hardware. Israel's special industry of diamond cutting gives the country one of its most important single export items. The diamond industry is diminishing under competition from Asian technicians, but the computer software industry is expanding rapidly. Numerous ex-military computer specialists are applying the high technology they learned in the Israeli Defense Forces to commercial manufacturing by becoming entrepreneurs in newly created companies. On a much greater scale, and increasingly controversial, is the state's production and export of large quantities of some of the world's most sophisticated armaments and military support equipment. Although it failed to fulfill Israel's commitment in a mid-1980s project to produce the Lavi fighter aircraft, in which the United States invested nearly $1.5 billion, the Israeli Aircraft Industries (IAI), with South Africa, produced a Lavi-type aircraft and reportedly sold the Lavi electronics system to China. U.S. objections regarding such Israeli sales to China surfaced again in late 1999, this time involving sophisticated radar systems.[19] The IAI does produce combat and civil aircraft, as well as armored cars, missiles, patrol boats, and similar military items. Israel has become one of the world's main exporters of armaments, including the Uzi submachine gun, missiles, artillery shells, armored vehicles, and naval craft.

Israel's most famous weapons facility is the Dimona nuclear establishment, built secretly in the mid-1950s in the northern Negev with French assistance. The uranium found in the phosphorite rocks near Dimona is extended with ore imported from South Africa, with which Israel cooperated in weapons development. Israel's nuclear capability and its possession of a considerable number of nuclear devices were revealed in 1986 when an Israeli who was a former technician at Dimona handed photographs and details of the underground operations to a London newspaper.[20] As a member of the exclusive nuclear club— although it refuses to sign the Nuclear Non-proliferation Treaty—Israel is now recognized as being far more technically advanced and militarily powerful than any of its neighbors and than many other states in the industrialized category.

Israel's main concentration of industry lies on the coastal plain from the Haifa area south to Ashdod, with outliers in Ashqelon and the Negev centers of Beer Sheva, Dimona, Arad, Sedom, and Elat. Haifa has the greatest single concentration in Israel: oil refining, production of chemicals (including fertilizers), shipbuilding, and many other industries (Fig. 9-1). Tel Aviv has a variety of lighter industries, and Israel Aircraft Industries, the largest single employer in Israel, operates near Ben Gurion Airport.

The bulk of the country's domestic production comes from large manufacturing enterprises, some of which are being privatized, but most of which are either state owned or owned by a combine of government and quasi-government agencies. However, a significant proportion comes from small establishments. Many of the small industries develop in kibbutzim that turn from agriculture to light industrial activities. Manufacturing is increasingly being dispersed, for reasons of

both security and local employment, into and around small settlements literally from Dan to Beer Sheva.

Transportation

Palestine functioned as a land bridge from early times; by contrast, independent Israel was largely isolated along its land boundaries until tentative connections were opened with Egypt in the 1980s and then with Jordan after 1994. Traffic flow with both neighbors is still limited, although increasing; and negotiations between Israel and Syria in early 2000 were expected eventually to establish at least qualified movement between the two countries, as well as between Israel and Lebanon. Indeed, Israel's isolation before 1980 underscored the essentiality of extensive and efficient air and sea connections with the outside world. Those connections are still maintained: Israel has developed a superb integrated system of transportation for moving people and goods efficiently; and although the great increase in commuter traffic in the Tel Aviv area has strained facilities, upgraded mass transit is in planning. Urban buses as well as intercity bus lines are exceptionally efficient. The Negev corridor to the head of the Gulf of Aqabah gives Israel an outlet to the Red Sea, and thence to the Indian Ocean, and also a land link between the Gulf of Aqabah and the Mediterranean (Map 15-4). That link has been used since 1969 for a 42-in./107-cm oil pipeline (see Map 15-1), and Israel plans eventually to use it for a rail line as well. Conversely, the Negev corridor divides the Arab states of the Fertile Crescent-Arabian realm from those of North Africa, a matter of immense economic and strategic significance.

Highways. North of Beer Sheva, Israel maintains an extraordinarily dense road net that is entirely paved, and heavily traveled sections east and north of Tel Aviv are divided throughways. The main north-south trunk route extends southward from the Ladder of Tyre, north of Akko in the northwest, along the coastal plain through Haifa, Tel Aviv, and Ashqelon to Gaza, then cuts southeastward across the Negev to Elat. A parallel north-south route 30 miles/48 km to the east runs from Metullah at Israel's northern tip down the west side of the Jordan rift to Elat. Similarly, a main-crest road runs the length of the occupied West Bank hill country, whose roads are integrated into the highway net of Israel. In the late 1990s, an ambitious plan for a Trans-Israel multilane freeway was being debated among officials and engineers. Excellent though the present highway system is, the great increase in population and the higher standard of living have combined to overcrowd the roads with more than 1.7 million vehicles.

Railways. Rail lines are used primarily for transporting heavy, bulky freight—phosphates and other minerals, grains, fuel, and citrus. Building on the modest rail net of mandate Palestine, Israel has constructed new standard gauge lines—from Hadera (south of Haifa) to Tel Aviv in 1953, to Beer Sheva in 1956, on to Dimona in 1965, then to Oron and the phosphate pits in the Har Zin area. A final extension to Elat was in planning in the late 1990s.

Ports and Shipping. Supplanting Jaffa (Yafo), which had served as a major harbor since the Bronze Age, the Bay of Haifa became the dominant port after 1900 and has evolved into one of the busiest general-cargo ports in the Middle East. Ashdod, 20 miles/32 km south of Tel Aviv and formerly of negligible importance, has been developed by Israel as a second major Mediterranean deep-water port to handle exports of phosphates and Dead Sea chemicals and imports for south-central Israel. Ashqelon, south of Ashdod, is primarily a specialty port for handling coal and petroleum. Elat, the country's fourth major port, serves the Indian Ocean trade and handles the decreasing amounts of petroleum moving through the Trans-Israel Pipeline from Elat to Ashqelon.

Airlines. As was mentioned earlier, full and effective air service was for several decades of particular importance for Israel because of the

MAP 15-4 Israeli transportation facilities. Note the "safe passage route" between Gaza and the West Bank Palestinian Authority areas.

state's relative isolation from its landside neighbors. Continuing to be important for strategic reasons, it early became the channel for Israel's immense flow of tourists. A commercial airport built at Lydda (Lod) on the coastal plain southeast of Tel Aviv in 1936 became Lod Airport, later renamed Ben Gurion International Airport. The installation handles all of Israel's international air traffic and ranks sixth in the region in the number of passengers processed. El Al is the Israeli national airline for international flights, and ARKIA is a primarily internal airline.

Commerce and Services

Israel has become one of the most trade-dependent countries in the world and has evolved a remarkable ensemble of trade agreements and export-import procedures. It receives preferential treatment for its exports to the United States, the EU, and many other countries, and Israel has agreed to remove customs duties on imports from these countries. Most of its merchandise trade—$48.2 billion in 1998—is with the EU, but the United States is Israel's leading single trade partner. Exports and imports are listed in the country summary early in this chapter, and other data are given in Tables 9-3 and 9-4. In most years during the middle and late 1990s, the trade deficit ranged between $7 billion and $10 billion. The unique role of diamonds in the country's international trade picture is noteworthy: In recent years, rough diamonds have made up about one-fifth of imports; cut and polished diamonds (worth more than $5 billion) have been about one-fourth of exports. In the late 1990s, the role of high-technology items—especially software—in Israel's manufacturing output and export trade is shown by the one-third share of such items in export value. Domestic trade is predictably significant in a nation of traditional business operators: Small businesses are still thriving, but larger stores are gaining ground, and more than 30 large western-style shopping malls have appeared since the mid-1980s.

A full range of services has been developed, with banking and tourism as major segments after public services. The state's banking system has worldwide connections, and two of the banks are in the world's top 100 banking institutions. Branches of such Israeli banks as Bank Leumi Le-Israel are located in the United States and Western European countries. The highly restricted, formerly all state-owned banking sector is easing restrictions somewhat, and a controlling stake in the largest bank, Bank Hapoalim, has been privatized. Other large banks are also being sold.

With some of the world's most important religious, historical, and scientific sites (Figs. 15-2 and 15-3), Israel has developed a vigorous tourist industry. From 4,000 in 1948, the number of tourists rose to 1.5 million in 1985 and 2 million annually during the late 1990s, contributing $3 billion to the Israeli economy. Both the hotel system and the tour bus transportation system are highly organized. Although the restaurants serve a variety of national foods, most practice *kasrut,* religious dietary practices for observant Jews.

Reflecting traditional Jewish emphasis on education and medical care, Israel has built major universities and hospitals. Supported both by the government and by contributions from abroad, there are seven universities in Israel (excluding occupied territories), the largest in Tel Aviv and Jerusalem. Hebrew University of Jerusalem is best known and is one of the finest universities in the Middle East. Israel Institute of Technology (Technion) in Haifa was founded in 1924, a year before the Hebrew University. Hadassah Hospital, on a hilltop in West Jerusalem, is the major medical facility.

Relations

Because of hostilities between Israel and its neighbors over the circumstances of Israel's establishment and expansion, relations between the Jewish state and its neighbors continued to be antagonistic for more than four decades (see Chap. 11). Only after the U.S.-mediated Israeli-Egyptian peace treaty in 1979 did Israel have diplomatic relations with any adjacent state. Once the peace process was set in motion in 1991, the level of regional animus decreased, and the 1994 peace treaty with Jordan opened Israel's

FIGURE 15-2 Jerusalem, looking west from the Mount of Olives. Eastern wall of the Old City at bottom, Dome of the Rock and other buildings of the Old City in middle ground, and ever-increasing new high-rise buildings of the burgeoning West Jerusalem in distance (1997).

longest border. As was mentioned above, if peace talks with Syria resumed in 2000 eventually succeed, Israel will then enjoy open relations with all four contiguous neighbors.

Even while shunned by its neighbors, Israel steadily developed diplomatic relations with more distant states and is now linked with the overwhelming majority of the world's nations. These include longtime holdouts China, India, and the Soviet Union before it disintegrated, and all the FSU states afterward. Pursuing every opportunity to ensure its security, Israel seeks to maintain patterns of relations that not only strengthen its own national well-being but also weaken its foes and potential foes, particularly neighboring opponents. Iraq is Israel's main regional adversary, and the U.S.-Israel lobby urges continued American harnessing of Iraq. Iran is a second main foe, although Israel gave Iran some support during the Iran-Iraq war and

later (see epilogue). It was in one of the elaborate schemes to aid Iran that the United States became involved in the infamous Iran-Contra scandal that received such intense and prolonged attention in 1987.[21] Once Iraq was defeated, Israel and its supporters advocated the U.S. policy of "dual containment" of Iraq and Iran. In addition to the vehemence of condemnation of Israel by Iran, Iranian support of the Hizballah guerrillas in south Lebanon was a specific factor in Israel's determination to keep Iran "contained." Relations with Lebanon have posed a frustrating problem, as was shown in Chapter 13; Israel's withdrawal from southern Lebanon in 2000 will open opportunities for détente. For many years, Israel categorically refused to have relations with the Palestine Liberation Organization (PLO), and in 1986 the Knesset passed legislation that made dealing with members of the PLO even by private individual Israeli citizens a

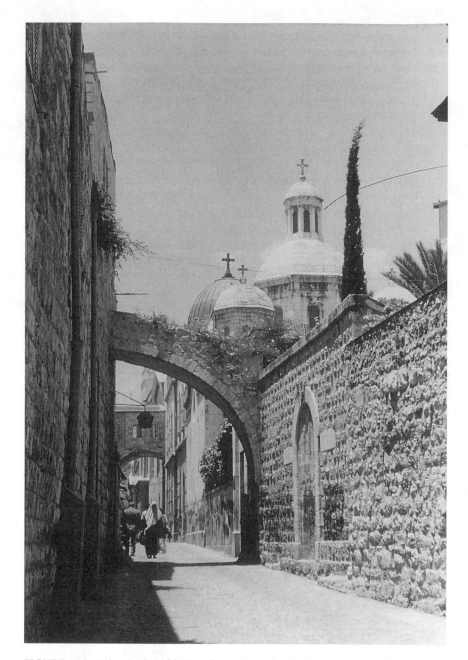

FIGURE 15-3   View in the Old City of Jerusalem: the Via Dolorosa in the Christian Quarter. To the left is the Ecce Homo Arch. The church is part of the Convent of the Sisters of Zion. (Photograph by Mildred M. Held)

criminal offense. However, the act was repealed in January 1993 in the context of the ongoing peace talks and in recognition of the more moderate stance of the PLO vis-à-vis that of Hamas. In September 1993 Israel and the PLO exchanged mutual recognition, and the peace process was then well under way (Chap. 11). Certainly, the relations between Israel and the Palestinian entity will be the critical external issue in Israeli politics for the foreseeable future.

Great Britain. Among European states, the United Kingdom was formerly the most involved with Zionist agencies and independent Israel. The British government issued the Balfour Declaration in 1917 (see Chap. 11), and Britain was the mandatory authority in Palestine from the early 1920s to 1948. In 1956, the British, French, and Israelis cooperated in the Suez invasion. Since that time, because of its varied interests in the Gulf, petroleum affairs, and other economic sectors in the Middle East, Britain has maintained a balanced policy in Middle East affairs and has been wary of identification with U.S. support of Israel.

Germany. The enormous loss of life by Jews in Nazi World War II concentration camps remains an overwhelming political, ethnic, and religious event affecting Israel's policies. Postwar West German authorities not only expressed guilt and regret but also gave more than $4 billion in reparations to Israel as the center of the Jewish people, restitution to individual Israelis who suffered under the Nazis, and development loans. United Germany continued the policy of making amends for Nazi atrocities, donating $163 million to Israel in 1991 to help compensate Israel for damage it suffered from Scud missiles and economic dislocation during the Gulf crisis.

France and Others. The French Jewish banking family of Rothschild gave the first large-scale financial support to Jewish colonization in Palestine (early 1880s). After World War II, the French government assisted the Israelis in construction of their Dimona nuclear facility

and sold fighter aircraft and other military equipment to Israel. More recent French-Israeli relations have been temperate and even nettlesome. The Netherlands is often bracketed with the United States as Israel's strongest supporter on the world scene. However, one grievance by Holland arose consequent to the flaming crash of an El Al cargo plane into an Amsterdam apartment building in 1992, when 39 Dutch residents were killed and hundreds injured. Later, when hundreds of residents and rescue workers contracted inexplicable illnesses, Israel admitted that the plane had carried components to make sarin gas, along with 114 tons of weapons and other chemicals. For "state security reasons" Israel still refuses to detail the plane's cargo.[22] Belgium has major trade ties with Israel through the diamond industry.

Israel and South Africa were originally linked in their pariah status in their respective regions, but they shared genuine economic interests in military cooperation and in South Africa's supplying rough diamonds and coal to Israel. Longtime antagonists Russia and China now enjoy mutually beneficial relations with Israel, which sends and receives sophisticated arms to and from both. The ties with Russia are particularly interesting in view of the years of nonrecognition (1967–1990) between Israel and the Soviet Union and the decades of Soviet support of Israel's Middle East enemies. A centuries-long conflict between Jews and Roman Catholic papal leadership over certain biblical interpretations has carried over into relations between Israel and the Vatican. Accusing the Vatican of sustained anti-Jewish policies and actions, Israel has demanded that the papal leadership apologize for and renounce those policies. The Vatican has modified certain issues but has refused to meet all the Israeli demands. A major element in Israel's foreign policy evolved during the 1990s in the rapid enhancement of relations with Turkey (see Chap. 21).

The United States. Although no formal alliance between the United States and Israel has ever been signed, the so-called special relationship between them has been far closer than any long-term alliance with which the United States has been associated. Zionist aspirations received U.S. support as early as 1917, when the U.S. government responded to Zionist lobbying and endorsed the Balfour Declaration. President Truman extended U.S. recognition of the State of Israel 11 minutes after Israel was declared independent. During the 52 years since U.S. recognition of Israel, U.S. support has rarely faltered and, overtly and covertly, has escalated quantitatively and qualitatively. The United States extended direct loans and grants totaling more than $78 billion between 1949 and 2000 and transferred all funds as free grants after 1984. These transfers were made "up front," in cash at the beginning of the fiscal year. In 1999, one-fourth of all U.S. direct foreign aid went to Israel and more than one-fifth to Egypt as a continuing reward for maintaining peace with Israel.[23] In addition, various grants and subsidies to Israel from U.S. government agencies for research and development—such as that on the Lavi fighter and recent joint work on missiles and antimissile missiles—are estimated to exceed $26 billion. During the 1990s, several U.S.-Israeli cooperative institutions have evolved: bilateral commissions and foundations in science and technology and in political and military affairs. The United States has underwritten intelligence activities conducted by Israel, sometimes as U.S. surrogate, especially during the cold war.[24] Moreover, tax-deductible private donations to Israel by individual Americans and by organizations such as the United Jewish Appeal, along with sales of Bonds for Israel, are estimated to have totaled $22 billion during the period 1949–1999.

The several issues on which the United States differs with Israel, even when they are serious, are almost invariably discussed quietly; they are carefully professed not to be allowed to disturb the special relationship between the two governments. (See the epilogue mention of Israel radar sales to China.) Divisive issues usually arise from broad global contexts, often in connection with earlier UN commitments involving overarching U.S. strategic interests. For example, the United

States maintains its embassy in Tel Aviv, as do virtually all other states, in conformity with basic UN resolutions and opposing Israel's unilateral declaration of Jerusalem as its capital. Under strong pressure from the Israel lobby, the U.S. Congress has repeatedly attempted to force the relocation of the embassy to Jerusalem. Second, the United States rejects Israel's unilateral annexation of the Golan Heights. Third, it warned Israel about annexing the West Bank and Gaza Strip, which would be a violation of several declarations by the United States and of the Fourth Geneva Convention. The U.S. position helped promote Palestinian rights in the occupied territories so that the peace process could proceed.

After the 1990–1991 crisis in the Gulf, both the United States and the United Nations as an institution were morally and logically obligated after 25 years of waiting for progress on UN Resolution 242 to press for the definitive initiation of regional peace talks. The United States was also obligated to pursue a firm position on Jewish settlements in the occupied territories in order to substantiate its long-term but formerly subdued policy of opposing such settlements. However, Israel continued to expand Jewish settlements and to establish new ones, especially under Prime Minister Binyamin Netanyahu, 1996–1999. Despite its verbal censure of Israel's settlement policy, the United States carried out no meaningful action against it, and the policy was still in force in early 2000.

The most comprehensive joint effort by the United States and Israel during the 1990s was the historic peace process initiated in Madrid in 1991. The major steps in the process are discussed in Chapter 11. The Arab-Israeli peace process is also discussed in Chapter 11 and in the epilogue.

Occupied Territories

As was shown in Chapter 11, Israel took three separate pieces of land, one from each of its foes, in the 1967 Six-Day War: Sinai with the Gaza Strip from Egypt, the West Bank from Jordan, and the Golan from Syria. Neither Sinai nor Golan had ever been part of mandate Palestine; hence, they were not involved in the 1947 UN partition of Palestine. However, both the West Bank and the Gaza Strip had been integral parts of Palestine, and both had been included in the half of the mandate allotted to the potential Arab state in the 1947 partition. As part of the philosophy of "exchanging a piece of land for a land of peace" urged upon Israel from several sides, Israel withdrew in stages from the largest area, Sinai—which is two-thirds larger than Israel itself—pursuant to the peace treaty with Egypt.

For 26 years, however, Israel continued to occupy all three of the remaining areas. Not until the aftermath of the Gulf crisis in 1990–1991 motivated the peace process and until the Oslo agreement emerged did the status of the West Bank and Gaza begin to change. The Golan Heights issue was in stalemate in early 2000 as one major aspect of Israel-Syria peace discussions. One achievement was the ending of the 22-year-long Israeli occupation of southern Lebanon. The West Bank and the Gaza Strip, which were recognized as solidly Arab in the 1947 partition plan, have become a microcosm of the Arab-Israeli problem; and it was in Gaza that the *intifadah,* the Palestinian uprising, exploded during 1987–1992. They thus underscore the fundamental fact that not only the Arab-Israeli problem but also many other regional problems are essentially geopolitical. West Bank and Gaza have emerged as the geographical and human symbols of the struggle between Arabs and Israelis for the land itself, with Israeli extremists claiming the areas as part of Eretz Israel and asserting that Jews have a right to settle in any part of Eretz Israel. Hardliners thus insisted on "creating facts on the ground" so that by creeping annexation, Israel would achieve permanent control without having to declare outright annexation. These hardliners rejected the applicability of the Fourth Geneva Convention of 1949 to Israeli settlement, but the United States and others adhere to the convention's relevance.[25]

From West Bank and Gaza to Palestinian Authority

During the 1990s, the West Bank and the Gaza Strip underwent a dramatic and historic transformation. Change came in slow, small steps after 1993, but by early 2000 both of them were constituent parts of a fragmented Palestinian Authority (PA), a quasi-state and state-in-becoming. The new PA, which is scheduled to become a State of Palestine during 2000, can be examined by an analysis of each of its two parts.

West Bank

During the past 50 years, this area has progressed from being (1) part of mandate Palestine to (2) a remnant of Palestine annexed by Jordan to (3) one of the territories taken and occupied by Israel in 1967 to (4) a fragmented self-governing area under the PA en route to statehood. Its final status was under discussion in mid-July 2000.

The West Bank received its name in 1948–1949 when its area was defended by Arab forces against Israeli capture and was annexed by Transjordan (the East Bank), officially in 1950. Its shape is deeply indented on the west by the Jerusalem salient; the area's northern half includes the Samarian Hills, with Nabulus as a center, and the southern half embraces the Judean Hills, with Hebron as center (Fig. 15-4). The kidney-shaped 2,270-miles^2/5,900-km^2 area (see Map 11-5) was militarily occupied and generally administered by Israel after 1967, but it is neither de jure nor de facto under Israeli sovereignty. The boundary of the West Bank with Israel is the Armistice Line agreed to by Israel and Jordan after the 1948–1949 fighting.

Severed by the 1949 Armistice from the rest of Palestine, the West Bank was annexed by King Abdullah of Transjordan reportedly to be kept in trust for the Palestinian people pending an eventual treaty disposition of the area. When Israel took the area in the 1967 war, it referred to the West Bank as Judea and Samaria and placed it under strict military occupation. Jordan

FIGURE 15-4   Barbs of discord: where Jewish settlement impinges on indigenous Palestinian neighborhood in Hebron. Kiryat Arba, across the road in distance, is one of the most controversial of all Jewish settlements in the occupied areas and is expanding into area to right in foreground. Israeli soldier to left.

continued to claim the territory until August 1988, when King Husayn renounced all claims to it. This renunciation, the impact of the *intifadah,* and the aftermath of the Gulf crisis— especially the progress of the peace process— brought the beginnings of self-government to the West Bank (see more below).

Demography

The 1947 population of the area, estimated to be 400,000, was increased in 1948 by the influx of 365,000 refugees from the area occupied by Israel. A May 1967 estimate gave the area a population of 845,000, despite an outmigration, primarily to the East Bank, of more than 400,000. The census of September 1967 showed a drop to 596,000, mostly reflecting the flight of refugees across the Jordan River to the East Bank as Israeli forces approached in June. The first census, conducted in 1997, indicated a population of

1,873,476 in the West Bank, excluding Jewish settlements. The Arabs live in about 450 towns and villages, with about 10 percent of the population in 8 UNRWA refugee camps and 30 percent in 25 towns. Main towns include Ramallah, Nabulus, Hebron (al-Khalil), Bethlehem, Jericho, Janin, al-Birah, Tulkarm, and Halhul.

As is recounted under "Arab-Israeli Problem" in Chapter 11, the establishment of Jewish settlements virtually without interruption in the West Bank has been at the center of the dispute over the territory. Successive accords from Oslo I to Wye II included arrangements involving settlements and water. By late 1999, about 200 Jewish settlements in East Jerusalem, the West Bank, and Gaza had a total population of nearly 400,000. Strategically and meticulously patterned to consolidate Israeli holdings and to fragment long-time Palestinian lands, the settlements are also connected by strategic "access and bypass roads" to create discontinuity among Palestinian areas (see Map 15-5). Overwhelming world opinion sees the settlements in violation of the Fourth Geneva Convention—a violation reaffirmed in Geneva on July 15, 1999—but Israel rejects the convention's applicability. With the status of Jerusalem, particularly of East Jerusalem, being the acme of the territorial quandary, Jerusalem and the settlements will certainly be the major sticking points in the final negotiations.[26]

Water and Land.   In addition to land itself, water is the basis for many of the conflicts between Israelis and Palestinians, whether at the official level or at the individual level on the ground. Also, the friction concerns not only the allocation of daily water supplies but also potential control of aquifers that supply both the West Bank and the densely populated Israeli coastal plain. Runoff from the considerable winter rainfall accumulates in underground aquifers, some yielding water in springs where they outcrop, others retaining underground water for wells. Controlling the technical hydrogeological information, the technology, and the government, Israel and Israeli settlers increasingly control the water resources, leaving many of the original Arab farmers with little or no water for farming or even for domestic use.[27]

Concomitantly, increasing amounts of land are being taken by Israelis, through various techniques. Large blocks of state-owned land have been requisitioned or declared security areas or nature reserves, on much of which the 200 settlements have been built. Without sufficient water for farm and family use, encircled by Israeli settlements, and living under a military government that gives preference to Jewish settlers, some Arab farmers eventually sell their family lands to Israeli purchasing agents. Land is also taken over by Jewish settlers on the basis that some Arab farmers have no legal proof of their long landownership, because of the failure of past governments—Turkish, British, Jordanian—to establish complete and accurate cadastres (official landownership registers). A former Israeli official in the West Bank wrote:

Redemption of the land (*geulat haqarqa*) is a fundamental Zionist concept.... The history of the Zionist enterprise is an account of physical *faits accomplis* through land acquisitions and settlement, created to achieve national, political, and military objectives.... The Palestinians, attaching the same macronational and symbolic value to the land, resist Israeli land acquisition efforts with whatever means they can muster. The unequal strength of the conflicting parties, however, dictates the results.[28]

The Economy

Since its inception, the West Bank has suffered economic uncertainty and instability, minimal private investment and governmental inputs, constrained industrial development, high unemployment, and, consequently, limited economic development. Obviously, an occupying power could not only impede "enemy" economic progress but also choose to contribute little to the occupied territory. From 1950 to 1967, Jordan could add only limited inputs to the West Bank because it had only limited financial resources for both segments of the state. Gaza suffered even more economic restraints, and UNRWA has been a financial lifesaver in both areas. The modest agricultural sector faced a shortage of markets, and farm lands were steadily lost to Israeli requisitioning. The only employment for a high percentage of West Bankers and Gazans was menial labor in Jewish settlements and in nearby Israeli towns, or construction work in the very Jewish settlements that were consuming their territorial heritage. The irony of such labor was addressed in the late 1990s when the Palestinian Authority began prohibiting Palestinians from working as construction laborers in Jewish settlements. Because Israeli authorities had in any case periodically placed curfews on both territories after acts of terrorism in Israel, the Israelis imported an estimated 300,000 foreign workers as menial laborers. Although the West Bank and Gaza emerged as fractionally autonomous areas of the Palestinian Authority,

MAP 15-5   The West Bank: A, B, and C Palestinian Authority areas, 200 Jewish settlements, and strategic roads. Situation as of March 1999. (After a map by Jan de Jong in *Report on Israeli Settlement in the Occupied Territories,* 9, no. 2, Mar.–Apr. 1999, p. 7)

pledges of several billion dollars by European and American governments gave some promise of reasonable economic advancement. The next section puts some specific economic aspects of the area in the new context.

A Palestinian State-in-Becoming

Pursuant to the Declaration of Principles signed by Israel and the PLO September 13, 1993, ("Oslo I") and to the Cairo Agreement signed eight months later, preliminary steps toward self-rule in the West Bank and Gaza were initiated in May 1994. The Palestinian National Authority emerged from Oslo I and has evolved into a virtual government and quasi-state. The first areas involved were the Gaza Strip (excluding the Jewish settlements) and the Jericho area on the Jordan River. The two parties signed the "Oslo II" Interim Agreement on September 28, 1995; this agreement initiated a long process of Israeli troop withdrawals from West Bank areas, which were given interim designations as the Palestinian Authority (PA) extended its control. In the fall of 1995, six main cities and scattered rural areas were categorized in Area A, full Palestinian autonomy; category B, joint control by Israeli Defense Forces (IDF) and Palestinian officials; and category C—the largest areas, continued full IDF control. In the first-ever Palestinian elections, on January 20, 1996, PLO Chairman Yasser Arafat was elected president of the PA. Also elected were members of a Palestinian National Council, a tentative parliament. Following the assassination of Yitzhak Rabin in 1995, Binyamin Netanyahu was elected Israeli prime minister in May 1996; for the next three years, Netanyahu actualized his long-declared views of noncooperation with the Palestinians. Although he signed several agreements, notably the Wye River Memorandum of October 23, 1998, he equivocated on implementation of many of the major provisions. When Ehud Barak defeated him in the May 1999 elections, movement toward a comprehensive settlement resumed.

Emerging as a completely new quasi-state, the Palestinian Authority encountered all the complexities of a political entity aborning. Revolutionaries were forced to readjust to the modalities of governance, including the balancing of authority with democratic processes. In the early years, graft and corruption were common; but gradually the signs, symbols, and institutions of statehood appeared as the PA evolved—flag, anthem, expanding territory, elections, officials, parliament, courts, stamps, recognition by growing numbers of foreign governments (100 by late 1999), passports, auto license plates, census, international area telephone code (970), Internet domain (—.ps—), and so forth. However, as of mid-2000, the PA was not a state; it had observer status at the UN (not membership), could not issue its own currency, and had no credit history with which to obtain loans. Nor was there the reassuring support of either the PA or the peace process by some former Palestinian resistance leaders. However, citizens joined in the state-building efforts as the entity progressed. A small but bustling casino opened in Jericho, along with a new soccer stadium, an elaborate Jericho Beach Resort, and an aerial cable car up to the Mount of Temptation. A new international airport opened in Gaza in December 1998, and Palestinian Airlines opened for business with three aircraft. The PA will save the taxes and delays at Israel's Ashqelon port with the opening of a modest but highly symbolic seaport now under construction in Gaza. With the financial and political support pledged by the United States and European states, and with mutual accommodation between Israel and the PA, the PA quasi-state should find its footing and be able to make the transition to full statehood.

Gaza

The Gaza Strip is a small area along the Mediterranean coast, sandwiched between Egypt and Israel, that Egyptian military forces were able to hold until after the armistice that ended the 1948–1949 fighting. Separated from settled Egypt by the full width of Sinai, it remained under Egyptian military occupation until it was captured by Israeli forces in the abortive tripartite Suez invasion in 1956. It reverted to Egyptian military occupation after Israel was forced to withdraw from Sinai and Gaza in early 1957, but it was again taken by Israel in the 1967 assault on Sinai and remained under Israeli military occupation for the ensuing 26 years.

Because of its small size and isolated location, the Gaza Strip (see Map 11-5) and its human and political importance were often overlooked until clashes between Gaza Palestinians and Israeli troops in late 1987 provoked the outbreak of the widely publicized *intifadah*. The Gaza Strip is only 25 miles/40 km long and 5.6 miles/9 km wide—about twice the size of the U.S. District of Columbia—yet it shelters a large population of more than 1,100,000, giving it the markedly high density of 7,730 people per mile^2/3,000 per km^2. Such densities usually characterize urban areas or extraordinarily rich agricultural lands, whereas Gaza conforms to neither category. With an extremely circumscribed economy, high unemployment, and little industry, the crowded Gaza Strip has been described as "concentrated misery."

The Gaza Strip is part of the Sinai-Palestine coastal plain, with high sand dunes along the shore backed by areas of good soils of sandy clay, silt, and loess. Marginal annual rainfall of 12 in./300 mm is supplemented in extensive areas by irrigation from wells tapping the appreciable groundwater supplies. With the need to support the overcrowded population, intensified irrigation agriculture has overpumped the aquifers, endangering both the amount and the quality of the groundwater. Lowering of the water table near the seacoast reduces aquifer resistance to seawater intrusion, raising the groundwater's salinity level.

The Gaza area has been agriculturally productive for centuries. Citrus is a primary crop; other tree products include dates, almonds, grapes, and olives; and there are also vegetable and other field crops. With 45 percent of the area under crops, agriculture is still a major sector of the economy. It has, however, been surpassed as employer and contributor to the GNP by public and other services and by construction. Much of the GNP is supplied by remittances from workers employed abroad, UNRWA minimal support of refugees, private charities, and wages earned by 30,000–35,000 Gaza day laborers in Israel, mostly in construction and agriculture.[29] Tensions consequent to the *intifadah* provoked periodic Israeli curfews and periodic prohibition against Gaza workers' entry into Israel. Unemployment rose to 40 and 50 percent even during normal circumstances. The UNRWA program has saved Gazans from starvation: More than two-thirds of the inhabitants are registered with UNRWA as refugees, and half of these live in eight UNRWA refugee camps in Gaza, thus eking out a living. No visitor to this concentration of human misery can disagree with one writer's characterization of Gaza as "a pressure-cooker ready to explode"— which indeed it did in initiating the *intifadah*— with "overcrowding, poverty, hatred, violence, oppression, poor sanitation, anger, frustration, drugs, and crime."[30] Full of despair and feeling dispossessed, many Gazans turned to radical fundamentalist Islam, the Islamic Resistance Movement (Hamas), and the Islamic Jihad, which in turn generated Israeli suppression. It was with some relief that Israel turned the Gaza quagmire over to the Palestinian Authority. Gaza was transformed through the "implementation" of the Oslo and Wye agreements: It gained the admirable international airport, became connected to the West Bank by direct link for the first time in October 1999, and observed the construction of a seaport beginning in 1999.

Whereas the West Bank was integrated into its contiguous Arab neighbor, Jordan, in 1948, the Gaza Strip was placed under Egyptian military occupation and experienced little economic development during its eighteen years of Egyptian occupation. Gazans were not accorded any of the privileges of Egyptian citizenship, nor were they allowed into Egypt itself. Seizure by Israel in 1967 led to the Israeli military occupation that continued with increasing bitterness on both sides until the 1993 accords called for Gazan autonomy. As in the West Bank, and despite serious overcrowding, Jewish settlements have been established in the Gaza Strip, with a total of approximately 6,000 settlers in 24 communities by 1999, with 30 percent of the Gaza area appropriated for the 0.4 percent of the Gaza Strip population in the Jewish settlements. For Gazans, one of the embittering aspects of the Israeli settlements is that each Jewish settler is allowed 85 times as much land area as each Palestinian resident; and in contrast to the crowded Arab areas, Jewish settlements are spacious, with paved and lighted streets, irrigated green lawns, swimming pools, and several riding stables.[31]

Gaza presents a number of challenging problems, but the marked improvements in the Strip during the later 1990s promise some hope of approaching solutions through local self-control supported by outside pledges of technical and financial aid.

Golan

Of the three territories in addition to Jerusalem that are still occupied by Israel, Golan is the only one that was and is indisputably a de jure segment of another existing sovereign state, Syria (see Chaps. 11 and 12). Yet Golan is the only one of the three territories captured in 1967 that Israel has annexed to its state territory, by announcing in December 1981 that Israeli law is applicable to the Golan. This unilateral declaration, like the declaration of annexation of East Jerusalem and of its detachment from the West Bank, has not been accorded international recognition and has been internationally condemned. Having simmered mostly in the background of the more acute aspects of the Arab-Israel conflict, the Golan problem was seriously discussed during the regime of Prime Minister Rabin but was then put aside until late 1999. At that time, Prime Minister Ehud Barak and Syrian President Hafiz al-Asad

agreed to conduct negotiations regarding normalization of relations in tandem with Israeli withdrawal from Golan territories. Negotiating sessions were held in Washington in late 1999 and early 2000, with President Clinton offering encouragement and mediation over impasses.[32] However, negotiators reached no agreements, and talks were suspended. With the death of Hafiz al-Asad in June 2000, his son and successor needs time to adjust to the circumstances before resuming negotiations.

Israel's settlement and annexation of the Golan occurred after the flight of more than 90 percent of the area's 93,000 Syrian inhabitants—some estimates were as high as 250,000—from the 1967 fighting. Their flight left only 5,875 Druzes, 385 Alawis, and a few hundred others, mostly Circassians, in Qunaytirah. By late 1999, about 17,000 Israelis occupied 33 settlements, including 10 kibbutzim and 6 religious moshavim. In addition, 16,500 Druzes resided in four other towns. With heavy financial support, the Jewish population developed the considerable water resources, expanded vineyards, installed a winery, and intensified agriculture. The Israeli Defense Forces constructed sophisticated radar equipment on the occupied shoulder of Mt. Hermon to monitor military movements inside Syria.

The present eastern border of the Golan Heights was determined in the 1974 disengagement agreements between Israel and Syria after the 1973 war. The border is actually a variable-width buffer zone, up to 5.5 miles/9 km wide and as narrow as 0.2 mile/0.32 km, between lines A and B (see Map 11-5). The agreement also called for Israeli evacuation of Qunaytirah, which lay within the buffer zone and which the Israeli forces demolished prior to their pullback. These lines would become irrelevant in the event that Israel evacuates the Heights.

Extending about 40 miles/64 km north-south and 8–16 miles/13–26 km east-west, the Golan covers about 445 miles^2/1,150 km^2. Mainly a basaltic plateau rising from 985 ft./300 m to 3,935 ft./1,200 m, highest in the north, the Golan Heights is a tilted tableland sloping toward Israel. A high escarpment, 1,310–2,625 ft./400–800 m—

again, highest in the north—overlooks Israel on the west, matched by the Galilee escarpment across the Huleh Basin and the Sea of Galilee.

The Golan Heights thus possesses a traditional strategic advantage. During the 1950s, the Syrians installed fortifications, including both gun emplacements and bunkers, on the brow of the heights in anticipation of an eventual conflict, but the fortifications did little to impede the Israeli advance when Israeli-Syrian fighting broke out in June 1967. Syrian gunners on the Heights and Israeli artillery periodically exchanged fire, usually over Israeli construction or agricultural work in the forbidden Demilitarized Zones (DMZs). Claims and counterclaims regarding these hundreds of exchanges accumulated into a significant narrative and eventually escalated into a major motivation of the 1967 war. In a 1976 interview, General Moshe Dayan, who later held several ministerial portfolios, put the exchanges in context when he commented that 80 percent of the attacks were provoked by the Israelis and that the Golan was seized to add land to the state.[33] Israeli control of the area after 1967 denied Syria the elevation advantage and, in contrast, gave Israel the benefit of a *glacis,* a territorial cushion. Such control emplaced Israel on the shoulder of Mt. Hermon and gave it command of the whole tristate junction—southeastern Lebanon, southwestern Syria, and, of course, northeastern Israel.

Syrian-Israeli negotiations over the Golan Heights clearly must grapple with profound issues—settlements, water, mutual security, economic implications, precise border demarcations, national emotions, historical claims, geopolitical strategy, and quid pro quo. Some arguments may appear trivial to outsiders; indeed, grand strategy sometimes devolves to centimeters of horizontal or vertical earth and to cubic centimeters of water.

Notes

1. The highly complex history of Israel's development has been covered in unprecedented detail by thousands of books and articles. The problem is to distinguish the polemics for and against from the reasonably balanced accounts that also put the story in context. See Sachar 1976/1987, Goldschmidt 1998, Peretz 1994, Peretz 1997, and Reich 1993.

2. "Palestine" is universally used to apply historically to the general area between the Mediterranean Sea and the Jordan River and from Metulla in the north (at the northern tip of Israel) to Elat at the head of the Gulf of Aqabah.

3. Few of the books on Israel focus on regional coverage. *Survey of Israel* (*Atlas of Israel*) 1985 is invaluable, and it is complemented by Orni and Efrat 1980 and Baly 1957. Also useful is Wolffsohn 1987 and the small but authoritative Israel Pocket Library 1973.

4. Best coverage of this topic is Zohary 1962.

5. Israel's water problems are treated in many studies, but see Kolars 1990; Dillman 1989; Wolf 1995; Rogers and Lydon 1994; Hof 1997; Rouyer 1999; *Water for the Future* 1999; Soffer 1999; and *Near East Report*, Sept. 6, 1999.

6. *Near East Report*, Feb. 17, 1992, 44; and Dillman 1989.

7. University of Haifa geographer Arnon Soffer, quoted in *Christian Science Monitor*, Mar. 14, 1990. See also Dillman 1989.

8. See sections 3–5 in the Israel Pocket Library *Immigration and Settlement* volume. Sachar 1976, 395–424, gives slightly different figures. See also Friedlander and Goldscheider 1979. For current data see the annual *Statistical Abstract of Israel*.

9. See Sachar 1987, 833–835 and 232–234; *Israel Country Study* 1990, 88–91; and the Israel Pocket Library *Immigration and Settlement* volume, 59–61.

10. See the five-part series on Soviet Jewish immigration in the *Christian Science Monitor*, July 25–August 1, 1991.

11. *New York Times*, Dec. 6, 1999, and *Jerusalem Post* No. American Ed., Nov. 5, 1999.

12. These passages are from Shohat 1999, an Iraqi Jew who writes from bitter experience as an "Arab Jew" *olah* in Israel. An early prescient study of sociopolitical cleavages is Leslie 1971. Elazar 1989 examines the Sephardim in detail.

13. See Lustick 1980.

14. Compare Falah 1992 and Graicer 1992 re "mirror housing" and other discrimination. For discrimination in employment, see the *Jerusalem Post*, International Edition, Nov. 23, 1991. For Arab industries, see Schnell et al. 1999.

15. Kahane 1981 voices a radical view but articulates demands by many Israeli extremists that all

Arabs must be expelled from Eretz Yisrael. Kahane, who was formerly leader of the U.S. extremist Jewish Defense League, was assassinated in New York in 1991.

16. An early revelation by the New Historians was Morris 1989 (first published 1987). Morris followed with several other critical writings, including "Falsifying the Record," *Journal of Palestine Studies* 24, no. 3 (Spring 1995): 44–62. Efraim Karsh led the attack on the New Historians in Karsh 1997, and his article, "Benny Morris and the Reign of Error," *Middle East Quarterly* 6, no. 1 (March 1999): 15–28. On the related issue of a growing critical reassessment of Zionism, see the defense of traditional Zionism in the same number of *Middle East Quarterly* Wurmser, 1999. See also Sternhell 1998. *Tkuma* is discussed in the *New York Times,* Apr. 10, 1998. For a lengthy analysis, see "The Battle over History," *Jerusalem Post* No. American Ed., Nov. 5, 1999.

17. The Israeli economy requires close monitoring because of its rapid changes. Information is available in the *New York Times, Christian Science Monitor,* and *Washington Post* daily and in the weekly North American Edition of the English-language *Jerusalem Post* and in the London *Economist.* See also the annual *Country Commercial Guide: Israel, FY 2000,* as well as the annual *Statistical Abstract of Israel* <http://www.cbs.gov.il>.

18. The subject is discussed in detail in *Israel* Country Study 1990, especially in Chapters 3 and 5; see also Black and Morris 1991, Hersch 1991, Cockburn and Cockburn 1991, and, on the secret Israel Institute for Biological Research, *Jerusalem Report,* Dec. 21, 1998, 16–21. This institute was the intended destination of the sarin gas components that were aboard the El Al cargo plane that crashed in Holland Oct. 4, 1992, also covered in the same source.

19. *Israel* Country Study 1990, 316; Cockburn and Cockburn 1991, 291–292; *New York Times,* Mar. 14, 1992; and, on later sales, *New York Times,* Nov. 11 and Dec. 2, 1999.

20. The revelations were widely covered in news media at the time. See Hersch 1991; Black and Morris 1991, 437–443; *Israel* Country Study 1990, 317–318; *Jerusalem Post* No. American Ed., Dec. 3, 1999; and Cohen 1996 and Cohen 1998.

21. Fully reported in the news media during late 1986 and early 1987, the affair may be studied in *The Tower Commission Report,* Bantam Books, 1987.

22. First reports of the crash in early October 1992 included nothing about the cargo inventory. For information that finally emerged six years later, see *Jerusalem Report,* Dec. 21, 1998, and *New York Times,* Jan. 29, 1999.

23. Collins 1990. The subject is examined in more detail in el-Khawas and Abed-Rabbo 1984, as well as in a six-part series in the *Christian Science Monitor,* June 20–21, 24–25, and 27–28, 1991. U.S.-Israeli relations are examined—praised or damned—in numerous studies. Spiegel 1985 is also an academic study of relations, examined administration by administration. Lenczowski 1990, written by a longtime scholar of Middle East affairs, looks at successive presidential policies also academically but from a somewhat different viewpoint than Spiegel. Among his several well-balanced studies, Quandt 1986 focuses on the critical Camp David arrangements. For later analyses see Zunes 1996; "Still Special? The U.S.-Israel Relationship," *Middle East Quarterly* 5, no. 4 (Dec. 1998): 53–65; and Chap. 3, *Congressional Quarterly 2000;* Ball 1992; and Lewis 1999. An editor of *Near East Report,* published by the American Israel Public Affairs Committee (AIPAC), the Israeli lobby in Washington, recounts AIPAC's achievements in Bard 1991. An opposing view is Curtiss 1990, written by the editor of the *Washington Report on Middle East Affairs,* as is Findley 1989, by a former Republican congressman from Illinois whose reelection is widely considered to have been defeated by AIPAC-coordinated efforts. Opposing views on U.S.-Israeli relations are given in the biweekly *Near East Report* and the American Educational Trust's monthly *Washington Report on Middle East Affairs.*

24. See Cockburn and Cockburn 1991 and *Washington Report on Middle East Affairs* 11, no. 5 (Nov. 1992): 12, 86.

25. See Aronson 1990, Benvenisti 1986, and *Israel* Country Study 1990. The several useful studies of the West Bank that appeared in the early and middle 1980s preceded Jordan's dramatic renunciation of ties with the West Bank in July and August 1988. Although economic details have changed, basic aspects are still relevant in Peretz 1986, Benvenisti 1984 (and his later reports), and Richardson 1984. Figures for the precise area of the West Bank vary among sources, depending upon segments included (East Jerusalem, Metropolitan Jerusalem, Latrun, "No Man's Land," Mount Scopus as well as West Bank proper).

26. Like data on Palestinians, those on Jewish settlers and settlements are problematic. Inclusion or exclusion of figures on East Jerusalem makes a huge difference. Israel insists that the East Jerusalem as enlarged unilaterally by Israel in 1967 is part of Israel itself, but the claim is rejected by the United Nations

and virtually all of its members except Israel. Settlements are monitored in detail in the bimonthly publication by the Foundation for Middle East Peace, *Report on Israeli Settlement in the Occupied Territories,* and URL <http://www.fmep.org>. Much of the same material appears in the quarterly *Journal of Palestine Studies* under "Settlement Monitor," usually prepared by FMEP editor Geoffrey Aronson. See also *New York Times,* Mar. 17, 1999. Regarding Jerusalem, see Lustick 1997, Rempel 1997, Abu Odeh 1992, and Emmett 1996.

27. Nakhleh 1988; *Christian Science Monitor,* Sept. 14, 1992; *Water for the Future* 1999; Rouyer 1999; Soffer 1999; and Ventner 1998.

28. Benvenisti 1984, 19.

29. See Gharaibeh 1985 and Roy 1995.

30. Nakhleh 1988, 210.

31. Roy 1995.

32. For a full account of Rabin negotiations, see Rabinovich 1998. For basic considerations in both earlier and 1999–2000 talks, see Alon BenMeir, "The Israeli-Syrian Battle for Equitable Peace." *Middle East Policy* 3, no. 1 [Issue 47] (1994): 70–83, and his "Why Syria Must Regain the Golan to Make Peace." *Middle East Policy* 5, no. 3 [Issue 57] (Sept. 1997): 104–112. Regarding the importance of water in the Golan context see Hof 1997. The same scholar examines the delicate issue of a new border (based on previous lines) in Frederic C. Hof, "The Line of June 4, 1967," *Middle East Insight,* Sept.–Oct. 1999, 17–23. For news accounts of the 1999–2000 meetings see *Christian Science Monitor,* Dec. 15, 1999, and Jan. 13, 2000; and *New York Times,* Jan. 16, 2000, for an in-depth account, with map.

33. Dayan's comments have been extensively covered. See the Hof 1999 article cited in Note 32 above.

16

Iraq:
Modern Mesopotamia

Iraq and Its Antecedents

Modern Iraq emerged as an independent kingdom in 1932, its boundaries and major institutions having been defined while it was a League of Nations mandate under British tutelage. As constituted in the early 1920s in accordance with the 1920 San Remo talks and the 1923 Treaty of Lausanne, mandate Iraq generally incorporated the three former Ottoman *vilayets* ("provinces") of Mosul, Baghdad, and (partially) Basrah. With the possible exceptions of the western panhandle and the northeastern mountains, the mandate was generally coextensive with the traditional geographical region of Mesopotamia ("between the rivers"). The Arabic name *al-Iraq* ("the cliff") had sometimes been applied as a geographical term to lower Mesopotamia but had not previously designated a state occupying the Mesopotamian Basin.

Whether traditional Mesopotamia or the modern state, Iraq is the land of two rivers, the Tigris and Euphrates, two of the three great rivers of the Middle East (Map 16-1). This eastern limb of the Fertile Crescent was the cradle of the earliest known civilizations and served as the culture hearth from which the first ideas of sedentary agriculture, domestication of animals, the wheel, writing, and urban development are believed to have diffused westward to the Nile Valley and eastward to the Indus Valley. Evidence of the Neolithic agricultural revolution is scattered along the Zagros piedmont east of the lower Tigris Valley, and ruins of the world's first cities have been uncovered on the interfluve south of Baghdad (see Chap. 2). It should be noted,

however, that ruins of a city of 3500 BC were found at Tell Hamoukar on the Euphrates in northeastern Syria, according to an annoucement in early 2000. Sumer, Akkad, Babylonia, and Assyria are part of the historical and cultural heritage of Iraq, and their material remains constitute a major element in the Mesopotamian landscape, normally attracting modern scientists and tourists alike.

Mesopotamia has periodically functioned as one of the major political and military power bases of the Middle East (see discussion of power cores in Chap. 2). For 2,000 years after Cyrus the Great, the Tigris-Euphrates Basin was usually linked with the adjacent power on the plateau to the east. While linked, the basin served as the core of the combined areas from the Persian Achaemenids to the Arab Muslims in AD 633. Twice in the five decades after 633, the Euphrates Valley served as the locus for conflicts over the Islamic caliphate (see Chap. 6), which resulted in the martyrdoms of Ali and his son Husayn.

Reduced to a province of the Umayyad Empire in 661, Mesopotamia reasserted itself in 750 to supplant Syria as the Muslim imperial heartland. As the center of the Abbasid Empire, it became the nucleus of a cultural efflorescence under Caliph Harun al-Rashid (r. 786–809) of *Arabian Nights* fame. However, decline following the Islamic golden age eventuated in the sacking of Baghdad by the Mongols. Mesopotamia was first overrun in 1258 by Hulagu, grandson of Genghis Khan, then in 1393 by Tamerlane, who killed or enslaved most of the intellectual cadre of savants, artisans, writers, and engineers. Both conquerors destroyed Mesopotamia's extensive irrigation systems,

Iraq

Long-form official name, anglicized: Republic of Iraq

Official name, transliterated: al-Jumhuriyah al-Iraqiyah

Form of government: unitary single-party republic with one legislative house (National Assembly)

Area: 167,975 miles^2/435,052 km^2

Population, 1999: 21,722,000. Literacy (latest): 58%

Ethnic composition (%): Arab 77.1, Kurd 19.0, Turkmen 1.4, Persian 0.8, Assyrian 0.8, Armenian and other 0.9

Religions (%): Muslim 96.3 (Shii 60.0, Sunni 35.8), Christian 3, other 0.7

GDP, 1998: $52.8 billion; per capita: $2,400

Petroleum reserves: 112.5 billion barrels (second-largest in Middle East and world)

Main exports (% of total value, 1998): fuels and other energy 99.5; food and agricultural raw materials 0.5

Main imports (% of total value, 1998): foodstuffs 6; medicines and medical supplies 28; machinery and spare parts 10

Capital city: Baghdad 5,348,117; other cities: Mosul 650,000; Irbil 500,000; Kirkuk 475,000; Basrah 425,000; Sulaymaniyah 325,000

Note: Several data are only rough estimates. Some data not available inside Iraq, others not made available outside Iraq.

developed over millennia, as well as its cities, craft shops, and trade routes. The ravaged basin then was subjected to Ottoman and Persian contention, in which the Ottomans finally triumphed in 1638. Thus ended the long politico-economic symbiosis between the Mesopotamian Basin and the Iranian Plateau. Since then, the Zagros piedmont has been the fault line of discord between Arab and Iranian culture and territorial aspiration. Ottoman control of the basin continued until World War I, when British and Indian forces drove the Ottomans back into Anatolia, and Great Britain was given the mandate over the newly created Kingdom of Iraq in the early 1920s.[1] Iraq was the first mandate to become an independent state (1932).

The independent kingdom of Iraq became a republic through a military coup d'état led by General Abd al-Karim Qasim (Kassem) in July 1958, when the young King Faysal II and his closest advisers were murdered. The Qasim revolutionary government fell in turn to a coup in 1963 that first brought to power the Baath (Arab Renaissance Party), although the Baath was soon ousted briefly. Coup attempts in 1965 and 1966 failed before a decisive Baath coup succeeded in July 1968. The Baathists have since retained political power under a one-party government in Iraq, maintaining leadership under strongman Saddam Husayn (Hussein) after 1979.[2]

From its creation as a mandate, Iraq has felt marginalized and deprived of its proper place in the Middle East and Arab sun. It resented its mandate status and clamored for independence until receiving it in 1932. Iraq objected to continued British influence in its affairs until the overthrow of the pro-West monarchy in 1958, when it finally felt independent.

MAP 16-1   Iraq: main cities, economic aspects, and antiquity sites. Circled numbers identify regions. The 33rd and 36th parallels marked UN "no-fly zones" after the 1990–1991 Gulf war. Zones were still being enforced in mid-2000.

Iraq has pursued many avenues to demonstrate its political potency to offset perceived external denigration. As Chapter 11 explained, from the first, Iraq has repeatedly asserted its claim to Kuwait and a fairer share of coastal outlet. The government accused oil companies in Iraq of discrimination against Iraqi interests—not a groundless charge—and later led in the

successful organization of OPEC. When Britain withdrew from the Gulf in 1971, Iraq promptly asserted its claim as the rightful leader of the Gulf. However, it was challenged by Iran and prudently yielded to its more powerful neighbor, which was under the rule of the shah and was supported by the United States at that time. However, the claims served notice of Iraqi ambitions—which, indeed, were reexhibited in the war against Iran and in the invasion of Kuwait.

Iraq during the 1970s benefited from a period of maximum oil prices and rapid development in the Gulf, and it achieved marked progress during the decade. When the Baath leadership acknowledged a fact of some years and selected Saddam Husayn as president in 1979, Iraq became personified in the most ambitious and aggressive leader of the country since its creation in the early 1920s. Within a year Iraq was at war with Iran as a result of miscalculation by President Saddam, and before it could extricate itself in 1988, it suffered not only hundreds of thousands of casualties among its young men but also the destruction of many of its new industrial plants, transport facilities, and buildings. Much of southern Iraq lay in ruins. Iraq received billions of dollars in aid from Gulf oil states during the war, and the country continued development during the 1980s. After the cease-fire with Iran, Iraq undertook an aggressive rebuilding and redevelopment program, using oil production as collateral for major projects and otherwise contracting for goods and services from countries and companies that provided generous long-term financing. It continued amassing a staggering foreign debt that was estimated to exceed $25 billion in the late 1990s.

In August 1990, the leadership once again miscalculated and invaded Kuwait (see Chap. 11). When Iraq refused to withdraw and coalition aircraft attacked Iraqi targets in mid-January 1991, the damage inflicted on Iraq's main cities and infrastructure was enormous (see Chap. 11)

Facing a decade-long stalemate with the UN—and specifically with the United States—over conditions for the lifting of sanctions, Iraq in early 2000 survived under its lowest standard of living since 1920. Apparently by choice, Iraq prefers pride and penury over perceived submission and prosperity. Whether the support of the Iraqi people for national defiance of the sanctions is voluntary or is forced upon them by the leadership is a crucial question for the world in the new millennium.

Regional Patterns

Cradled in the land segment of the great tectonic trough downfolded between the Arabian Platform to the southwest and the Zagros ridges to the northeast, Iraq embraces four distinct natural regions, each of which plays and has historically played identifiable roles in Mesopotamian political and economic life: [1] western and southwestern desert plateau, [2] Jazirah or northern Mesopotamian upland, [3] southern Mesopotamian alluvial plain, and [4] northeastern uplands and Zagros Mountains (see circled numbers on Map 16-1).

[1] Western and Southwestern Deserts

This extension of the Syrian and Arabian deserts lies west of the Euphrates Valley and comprises the barren western third of Iraq. It is the realm of Iraq's few thousand remaining Bedouins and is the least populated and least developed part of the country. In the far west is a continuation of the Jordanian desert platform and the Arabian area of al-Widyan, furrowed with numerous east-west wadis and traversed along its northern edge by the major express motorway from Baghdad to Amman, Aqabah, and Damascus. Rutbah as a way station has developed from a dusty village in the 1970s into a bustling highway junction and trading center. The highway became a vital link with Aqabah port for Iraq during the Iran-Iraq war and during the aftermath of the 1991 Gulf war. Farther east is al-Hajarah, a limestone platform strewn with flint and chert, crossed by the old caravan trail of the Darb Zubaydah for pilgrims to Mecca. Farther southeast is the sandy, gravelly plain of Dibdibah, cut by the prominent Wadi al-Batin, which forms the western boundary of Kuwait. The open desert west of the Wadi al-Batin was utilized by coalition ground forces in late February 1991 to outflank and encircle Iraqi forces in Kuwait. The far west panhandle of Iraq gained a place in history when it was used by the Iraqi military as the launch area for nearly 80 Scud missiles into Saudi Arabia and Israel during the Gulf war.

[2] Jazirah: Northern Mesopotamian Upland

Most of the Jazirah upland, extending from Syria into central Iraq, is a desert plateau descending from 1,475 ft./450 m in the northeast to 260 ft./79 m at Baghdad. Except for the river flood-plains and for the segment northwest of Mosul, population is sparse and development relatively limited. In the extreme north a prominent outly-ing ridge of the Zagros–Anti-Taurus folds, the Jabal Sinjar, extends westward from Mosul.

The region is drained from north to south by the steep-banked Wadi Tharthar, which emp-ties into the extensive Tharthar Depression midway between the Tigris and Euphrates. A major project in the 1950s developed an artifi-cial lake in the depression into which Tigris floodwaters can be diverted by the Samarra Barrage and from which overflow can be spilled southward into the Euphrates. North of Jabal Sinjar, the undulating plateau is devoted to rainfed cultivation of wheat and barley, a great granary that was a major asset to the ancient Assyrian empires and their successors. The plateau is now bisected by the main rail line from Europe to Basrah. Iraqi development plans envision later development of the Jazirah, including appreciable irrigation, comparable to that undertaken by Syria in the extension of that same region into the neighboring state. Mosul, located in the heart of ancient Assyria—and, indeed, partly developed on the site of ancient Nineveh—has developed steadily dur-ing the last 50 years; during a recent spurt it became the second-largest city in Iraq. It lies on the northeast periphery of the Jazirah but serves as the main center for the northern third of the country.

[3] Southern Mesopotamian Alluvial Plain

Extending southeastward from near Ramadi on the Euphrates and from just south of Samarra on the Tigris is the flat alluvial plain that has in recent geological time been built Gulfward by the accumulated silt in the coalesced deltas of four rivers: Tigris, Euphrates, Karkheh, and Karun. The original shoreline is marked by a sin-uous cliff, probably the feature for which Iraq is named, which extends from Ramadi to near Samarra. Along and between these lower courses of the Tigris and Euphrates, where ancient empires thrived and the ruins of the most ancient cities of the world still stand, the cultural and economic core of modern Iraq has evolved. On the area's western periphery lie the two most sacred shrines of Shii Islam, in Karbala and al-Najaf, the former the tomb of the martyred Husayn and the latter the tomb of Ali, Husayn's father and the fourth caliph and first Shii imam.

Temperatures during the dry summers aver-age 95°F/35°C for July and soar to daytime highs of more than 122°F/50°C. Winter rainfall aver-ages only 5.5 in./140 mm. Elevations and relief are low. Heights range from 80 ft./25 m in the north to sea level in the south, but some areas beyond the rivers' natural levees are actually below sea level upstream from the Shatt al-Arab.

The northern end of the alluvial plain, where the Tigris and Euphrates make their closest approach to each other, constitutes one of the historically most strategic sites in the Fertile Crescent. Its importance is manifested by the transit of the narrow interfluve by a major trade route since Neolithic times; by the loca-tion of successive capitals and primate cities in the immediate vicinity—Akkad (although its exact site is uncertain), Babylon, Seleucia, Cte-siphon, and Baghdad; by its development for irrigation agriculture for many centuries; and, of greatest current significance, by its multiple advantages and attractions for the development of modern industry, including production of weapons and other armaments. Modern Bagh-dad, heir to famed capitals of the past, was founded as an Islamic Abbasid capital in 754. It became legendary in the so-called *Arabian Nights* (see Chap. 2) and thrived for 500 years before being sacked in 1258 and again in 1401 and sinking into 500 years of obscurity. Until Iraq's defeat in 1991, Baghdad was a vibrant, multi-faceted capital (Fig. 16-1) astride the middle Tigris, with a major university and one of the world's finest antiquities museums. The

FIGURE 16-1   Liberation Monument, by Iraqi artist Jawad Salim, erected in central Baghdad following 1958 revolution.

current leadership's emphasis on military might is manifested in the number and size of monuments with martial themes. In the late 1990s, Baghdad struggled to maintain an interim existence.

Southeast of the Baghdad area, the central interfluve was for centuries mostly wasteland or saline marshes because of the high water table and inadequate drainage. To facilitate drainage and reclaim the area, the Iraqi government in 1992 constructed a major 350-mile/563-km Main Outfall Drain (MOD) along the axis of the central interfluve (see Map 16-2). Sometimes termed the Third River, the MOD is designed to drain both the central marshes and the southern marsh homeland of the Madan (see below).[3] Also following the axis of the deltaic interfluve is Iraq's north-south express motorway.

Multiple traces of abandoned channels of the Tigris and Euphrates indicate radical course changes by the rivers, as do the present locations of ancient cities—Kish, Nippur, Uruk, Ur, and others—now far from the riverbanks along which they originally lay. Both settlement and cultivation tend to exhibit a ribbon pattern, since they are concentrated along the banks of rivers and canals, including the Third River and the Shatt al-Gharraf. Such concentration of cultivation is due both to the proximity of irrigation water and, more important, to the better drainage on the low, broad natural levees built up on both banks during regular river overflow. Where the stream has bifurcated, as the Euphrates has in several places below Hit, both naturally and artificially, irrigated agriculture and settlement have become especially intensive.

Between Nasiriyah and the confluence of the Euphrates with the Tigris at Qurnah lies an area formerly possessing unusual ecological relationships, the lower Euphrates marshes occupied by the Marsh Arabs, the Madan. For thousands of years, these marshland dwellers utilized the local reeds (*qasab*) growing in the marshes to build their shelters on artificial

MAP 16-2   Southern Iraq, drainage schemes, early 1990s. (Adapted from several maps)

reed-mat islands and to construct their council houses (*mudhifs*), all of which are shown in Fig. 16-2. They caught the plentiful fish in the surrounding waters; raised water buffalo for milk, yogurt, and hides; and moved between houses and villages by the typical local boats, the high-prowed *mashhuf*, which they pole through the shallow water.[4] Shii fugitives from Iraqi military persecution took refuge in the marshes in 1991–1992, which accelerated Saddam Husayn's project to drain the marshes and corral the Madan. Scores of thousands of Madan fled to Iran, and the remainder were forced into collective government settlements, as were Kurds in the late 1980s.[5] Thus ended within a few years a remarkable group's millennia-old and unique way of life.

East of the marshes and the Hawr al-Hammar, the confluence of the Tigris and Euphrates creates the Shatt al-Arab, through which the combined rivers flow 100 miles/160 km to the Gulf. For much of the Shatt's length, a broad belt of date palm groves had long paralleled both riverbanks, naturally irrigated by an intricate network of canals in which the fresh water rises and falls with the daily tidal backup of the river

FIGURE 16-2   A disappearing marsh culture: typical *mudhif,* an all-reed guest house *(top),* and all-reed village *(bottom)* in the lower Euphrates marshes east of Nasiriyah. The boat is a typical *mashhuf.* Government drainage of the marshes has transformed the ecology of the area, killing the reeds and displacing the Marsh Arabs *(al-Madan)* from their unique homes of many centuries.

water. This formerly well-ordered and productive landscape was obliterated during the early years of the Iran-Iraq war, leaving shattered stumps where the great groves once stood. Midway up the Shatt and on its west bank lies Basrah, formerly Iraq's main port and second city. This historic trade center has long been a Shii stronghold, and older quarters and buildings attest to the strong influence of India on the city's development over the centuries. Basrah was heavily damaged in repeated battles during the Iran-Iraq war, was again devastated in military operations in 1990–1991, and suffered still further destruction during the Shii insurrection in 1991 and 1992 after the end of Desert Storm operations. In revenge for rebellion by the Basrah Shiis against the central government, Baghdad has made only minimal repairs to damaged bridges, buildings, and the port. Such neglect not only leaves the formerly thriving port city shabby but intensifies the animosity between the southern Shii and the central Sunni. In the desert west of the Shatt is one of Iraq's main groups of oil fields, notably Zubair and Rumaila, the latter involved in the acrimonious dispute between Iraq and Kuwait. West of the mouth of the Shatt al-Arab is Iraq's narrow "window" on the Gulf, 36 miles/58 km of Gulf coastline at this lower end of the Iraq "funnel." In this strategic outlet of Iraq's corridor to the sea is an increasing concentration of oil activity, heavier industries, and multiple port development (discussed later in this chapter under "Economic Patterns and Problems"). Also in this strategic corridor is focused Iraq's historic grievance against Britain's allocation of territory and delineation of boundaries in the early 1920s. The strip is thus the focus of Iraq's territorial and boundary complaints and claims against Iran and Kuwait, and it is from here that Iraq lashed out in 1980 and 1990. The details of Iraq's claims regarding the Shatt al-Arab boundary and the Kuwait boundary are given in Chapter 11 (see Map 11-6).

The physical geography of extreme southeastern Iraq is as much influenced by the southwestward-building deltas of the Karun and Karkheh rivers as by the southeastward-building deltas of the Tigris and Euphrates and their common outlet, the Shatt al-Arab. The building of the Karun-Karkheh deltas has had three geomorphic effects: It has aided in filling in the head of the Gulf, it has forced the Tigris and Euphrates together into the Shatt al-Arab, and it has simultaneously blocked some of the combined drainage and thus contributed to the formation of the lakes, intermittent lakes, and marshes that sprawl over much of the landscape of the combined deltas of the four rivers.[6] Some of these marshes were among those drained or partly drained during the 1990s.

[4] Northeastern Uplands and Zagros Mountains

Uplands, piedmont, and rugged mountains rising northeastward from the upper Tigris in Iraq exhibit a sharp contrast to the desert plains areas that cover most of the rest of the country and that typify perceptions of Mesopotamia and Iraq. Except for a few prominent ridges near the Tigris (Jabal Hamrin, for example) the major highlands lie northeast of a line connecting Zakhu, Mosul, Irbil, Kirkuk, and Khanaqin. Elevations rise from 655 ft./200 m on the lower piedmont just east of the Tigris to 3,000 ft./915 m in the foothills, then reach 5,900 ft./1,800 m on the typical ridge tops and 11,808 ft./3,600 m in a summit elevation on the Iranian border east of Ruwanduz. Lying at 36° N Lat, only 6° farther north than Iraq's torrid desert Gulf coast, these elevations are blanketed with snow half the year and can be cool at night in summer. In the lower elevations, Mosul and Kirkuk are still hot in summer, but they receive 15 in./385 mm of winter precipitation compared to Basrah's 6.5 in./164 mm.

Ridges in the far north extend east-west, following the trend of folding in the Taurus and Anti-Taurus mountains, whereas tectonic trends south of Ruwanduz turn southeast and thence combine with the dominant Zagros folds. The same tectonic forces that created the folded mountain ridges and linear foothills also produced the subsurface structures in which petroleum and gas accumulated. Several

FIGURE 16-3   Western entrance to the dramatic and strategic Ruwanduz (sometimes Rawanduz or Rawan-
doz) Gorge, northeastern Iraq. The gorge carries the main road from Irbil to Iran—the only route linking the
two countries through the rugged northern Zagros Mountains.

streams follow deep gorges that are parallel to
the folds in their upper courses and then cross
the grain of the folded ridges to join the Tigris:
the Khabur, Great Zab, Little Zab, Udhaym, and
Diyala. The highest ridges contain Iraq's only
forests, some of them quite extensive, preserved
by the isolation and ruggedness of the area.
Most of the mountain slopes permit only grazing, lower and more gentle slopes support fruit
and nut trees, and the broad lower valley bottoms are intensively cultivated. Access to the
higher areas is limited, and passes through the
rugged Zagros summit ridges into Iran are few.
Most famous of these routes is the Ruwanduz
River gorge (Fig. 16-3), with the spectacular Spi-
lak Pass and Ali Beg Gorge west of Ruwanduz
and the Shinak Pass near the Iranian border.

Some of Iraq's earliest and largest hydraulic
projects were developed in the late 1950s in
these well-watered, rugged mountain areas,
where deep gorges and solid rock offered ideal
sites for dam construction. The Dukan Dam
and accompanying large reservoir were built on
the upper Little Zab, the Darbandikhan Dam
and reservoir on the upper Diyala, and, later,
the Dibs Dam on the Little Zab. The Great
Zab's potential was finally under exploitation in
the late 1980s with the construction of a large
dam in its upper course.

Apart from its landforms, northeastern Iraq
is also noteworthy for its role as a human
minority refuge, a political-cultural buffer and
frontier, and an underground reservoir of
hydrocarbons. It is the Iraqi segment of
Greater Kurdistan, in which Kurdish tribesmen
normally move freely among Iraq and Iran and
even Turkey. Kurds are overwhelmingly the
dominant group (see Chap. 6), using the
ruggedness and isolation of the elevated
Zagros as their fortress and refuge in their successive wars for autonomy against the Arab
central government—including the widely

publicized fighting of 1991–1992. In the lower hills are many Turkmen, smaller numbers of Assyrians, and small groups of Sarliyyas, Yazidis, and other groups.

Population and Peoples

Population Patterns

Iraq's estimated population of 21.7 million in 1999 marked a growth of 321 percent over 1950. This growth has occurred primarily through natural increase, unlike the much greater percentage upsurges, primarily from immigration, in the southern Gulf amirates. Map 6-2 shows that Iraq's population is concentrated in linear patterns along the banks of rivers and canals on the plains but is more generally distributed in the villages and towns of the northeastern uplands and mountains.

The greatest single concentration of population, about half of the total for the country, begins north and west of Baghdad, sprawls westward and southward across the mid-Iraq interfluve, and then follows the Euphrates and its various branches along the west side of the alluvial plain to Samawah. Metropolitan Baghdad alone has about one-fourth of Iraq's population. Other major nuclei in the concentration include the shrine city of al-Najaf; Hillah, one of the main date-producing centers in Iraq; Diwaniyah; Karbala, with the shrine to Husayn; and Fallujah.

Secondary concentrations of population are found in the south, where population fluctuated wildly after 1980 and is now reduced; in the north around Mosul; and in the northeast piedmont, around the oil developments of Kirkuk and the ancient city of Irbil. The Kurdish "capital city" of Sulaymaniyah, in the heart of the Iraqi Zagros east of Kirkuk, is probably Iraq's sixth-largest city.

Ethnolinguistic Groups

Some groups within Iraq's borders have maintained their separateness for many centuries, to the extent that their group identities compete with Iraqi nationalism. Although the primary ethnic conflict is between Arab and Kurd, also significant is the religious rift between Sunni Muslim and Shii Muslim, discussed below. Smaller ethnic minorities—Turkmen, Assyrian, Armenian, Yazidi, Lur and smaller Persian-speaking groups, Mandaean, and others— remain distinctive but, except for the Assyrians between the world wars and some of the Persians in the 1980s, are not actively separatist or anti-national.

The geographic pattern of the three dominant adversarial groups in Iraq creates an issue crucial to the country's internal and external policies. With the highly nationalistic Kurds concentrated in the north and the restive majority Shii dominant in the south, the minority Sunni elite in between has historically ensured its control of the state's territorial unity and its dominance among the three constituent groups. A corollary concern has faced the United Nations, and particularly the United States, in their policies since 1991 to force Iraq to comply with UN resolutions: Operations must not risk fragmenting Iraq into three rump states—a northern Kurdish, a southern Shii, and a central Sunni.

Arabs. Composing more than 77 percent of the population, Arabs have been the dominant group numerically and politically for 1,000 years. During most of that period, they have considered themselves the eastern bulwark against non-Arab influences. The Iraqi Arabs represent a biological mixture of many peoples over thousands of years.

Although only about 20 percent of the Arabs in Iraq are Sunni, they have been the dominant economic and political group for many centuries. Since Shiis have long been associated with Iran and Iranians, Sunnis have considered themselves the Mesopotamian "loyalists," with a reciprocal affinity for the predominantly Sunni Arab neighboring countries. During the centuries of Sunni Ottoman control of the basin, Shiis became alienated, isolated through endogamy, and suffered decreased cultural and economic opportunities. Virtually all of the

Kurds are also Sunni, so that the combined Sunni groups make up approximately 36 percent of the total population.

Shiism, the original partisanship for Ali, emerged in southern Iraq during the seventh century. Shii strength in southern Iraq has continued to the present time, although the greater concentration of the sect evolved in neighboring Iran during the sixteenth century. The proportion of Shiis in the Iraqi population exceeds 60 percent, with their major strength in the areas in which population is most concentrated.

Kurds.[7]   The approximately 4.3 million Kurds in Iraq live primarily in the northeast uplands and Zagros Mountains, the Iraqi sector of Kurdistan (see discussion of Kurds in Chap. 6). After 1927, petroleum development around Kirkuk, on the periphery of traditional Kurdish territory, prompted a new interaction between plain and mountain. However, the inability of the central government and Kurdish leaders to achieve mutual accommodation has led to a seemingly unending cycle of internecine conflicts between the two groups. They extended from the mandate period at least intermittently through such periods as 1919–1930, 1943–1946, 1961–1970, 1974–1975, during much of the Iran-Iraq war, the crucial late 1980s, and then the fateful months in 1991–1992 after the Gulf war when more than 1 million Kurds fled Iraqi military attacks. The normal cycle is that the Kurds make demands for regional autonomy, sometimes even for independence; the national government rejects such demands, fearing that autonomy might lead to separatism, which might in turn involve loss of the area oil fields; and fighting breaks out that ends indecisively and sets the stage for the next cycle.

Each of the two cycles in the late 1980s and in 1991–1992 was unique. The first was a climax to bitter fighting along the border with Iran east of Darbandikhan Reservoir in early 1988, when local Kurdish *peshmergas* (guerrillas) supported an Iranian attack inside Iraq. As they had on previous occasions when they were seriously threatened, according to UN charges during the early 1980s, Iraqi forces used poison gas both in the battle and against civilians in the neighboring Kurdish town of Halabjah, where several thousand died.

The Iraqi government then undertook a wide-ranging program of razing Kurdish villages and resettling populations from several villages together in cement-block collective settlements. The towns were built by the Baghdad government in open plains areas, each heavily guarded by a military garrison. The administration expected the resettlement program to solve the Kurdish problem definitively.[8]

Inevitably, Kurds took advantage of Iraq's military engagement in the south in 1990–1991 and again sought control of their "homeland." Iraqi forces using helicopter gunships and bombers responded ferociously after withdrawing from Kuwait, driving more than 1 million Kurds to seek safety in Turkey and Iran, neither of which wanted them. Coalition forces expelled government troops from the North, and by extension of UN resolutions, in April 1991, the United States and Britain declared an air exclusion zone (no-flight or no-fly zone) for Iraqi aircraft north of the 36th parallel. The zone has been regularly patrolled for more than eight years and, along with the southern no-flight zone, was the theater of a war of attrition during 1999.

After Iraqi forces withdrew in 1991 and Iraqi-Kurdish talks broke down, the Kurds held elections in May 1992 and attempted to achieve unity and finally to set the stage for autonomy within Iraq. However, a power struggle between two major groups competing for leadership generated an intra-Kurdish civil war in 1994–1996. In a 1996 low point, the Kurdish Democratic Party (KDP) under Masoud Barzani even accepted help from the Iraqi army against the Patriotic Union of Kurdistan (PUK) under Jabal Talibani, who was supported by Iran. To punish Iraq for taking military action in the north, the United States launched 44 cruise missiles against southern targets and enlarged the southern no-flight zone by unilaterally shifting the boundary from the 32nd parallel to the 33rd. Both actions were severely criticized by

UN members, including most Arab countries.[9] At the opening of the new millennium, Iraqi Kurds faced a brighter future than they had in past years (see the epilogue).

Turkmen. Making up about 1.4 percent of the Iraqi population, Turkmen live in the piedmont and foothills of the northeast. They form an ethnic transition between the Arabs of Mesopotamia and the Kurds of the Zagros and are numerous in both Kirkuk and Irbil as well as in villages on the piedmont. Turkmen are Sunni and middle class, and many have become integrated and serve as government employees.

Other Ethnic Minorities. Smaller ethnic minorities include Persian-speaking Shiis with strong ties to Iran, many of whom were expelled to Iran in the early 1980s when they voiced pro-Iranian sentiments. Their strongholds were Karbala, al-Najaf, and al-Kazimiyah (near Baghdad) as well as Basrah. Another Persian-speaking group, the Lur, are concentrated in tribally organized villages near the Iranian frontier.

Jews numbered 118,000 in the 1947 census but were undoubtedly more numerous, since in 1951 about 121,000 emigrated to Israel and several thousand went to Iran. Before 1951, Iraqi Jews generally lived in urban areas, often as merchants, professionals, and government officials in Baghdad. A few thousand remained in Iraq in the mid-1980s, but most of them emigrated later.

The Christian Armenians are estimated to number about 20,000 and are usually urban. The small group of Mandaeans—also called Sabians, Subba, or John the Baptist Christians—are an interesting ancient people of uncertain origin who are differentiated primarily by religion but who are also physically distinct (see Chap. 6). The Yazidis, an extension of the Yazidis in Syria, live in villages along the Jabal Sinjar west of Mosul.

Christian Minorities. In addition to the Christian Armenians, several other distinctive Christian groups are significant in Iraq. Most of them are in the north, particularly in the Mosul area, but there are others in the Baghdad area. The largest group is the Chaldeans, in Mosul and villages on the surrounding plain but also numerous in Baghdad, seat of their patriarch. Assyrians, sharing a common origin with the Chaldeans, are concentrated mainly in the extreme north around Zakhu and Dahuk, in Kirkuk, and in Baghdad.

Economic Patterns and Problems

Economic Interrelations

Mandate Iraq was, like its Arab neighbors, overwhelmingly agricultural. Despite its enviable agricultural potential, its actual land development and production were retarded. Manufacturing was limited to such handicrafts as metalworking, weaving, and food processing.

Emerging from centuries of colonial control by the Ottomans, the new Iraq, with British help, steadily evolved a more diversified economy. Discovery of large—later enormous—oil fields in 1927 added a preeminent complementary dimension to the state's economy; Iraq now possessed a superior economic potential, balanced between plentiful water and arable land on the one hand and enormous energy resources on the other, with a growing supply of productive labor to exploit them. Independent Iraq after 1932 gradually took its place in the emerging political pattern of the region and steadily developed its infrastructure: roads, railways, ports, dams, schools, and related structures. After the 1958 coup, major industries were transferred to the public sector (later called the "socialist sector"), especially in 1964, and nationalization of the petroleum sector began in 1972. By the late 1970s, Iraq had achieved an admirable level of development but was squandering huge sums on military armaments and weapons industries. As was explained earlier, the 1980–1988 Iran-Iraq war consumed capital and labor, diverted national energies to a destructive war, and destroyed some of Iraq's new infrastructural and industrial developments.

Iraq's geographical vulnerability was exposed in the late 1970s as relations with Syria and Iran deteriorated. Syria shut down Iraq's export oil pipelines to the Mediterranean, and, although Iraq had gained an outlet through Turkey in 1977, it still needed its export terminals in the Gulf. Engaging in war with Iran provoked the destruction of those facilities. A new pipeline outlet through Saudi Arabia in 1985 was promptly lost consequent to the 1990 invasion of Kuwait and the threat to Saudi Arabia. It seemed that every prospect for an Iraqi economic takeoff was nullified by some miscalculated costly political or military confrontation. Before the country had caught its economic breath from the Iran-Iraq war, Saddam Husayn turned on his Arab benefactors and provoked the further destruction of his economic base by seizing his small Arab neighbor of Kuwait. Given every chance to withdraw, he defied the UN coalition; indeed, Saddam Husayn paid heavily for this third major miscalculation. Since 1991, Iraq's economic recovery has languished in a battle of wits and wills between the Iraqi government and the UN, which Iraq claims is dominated by the United States (discussed later under "Relations").

Agriculture

From the country's major economic activity in the 1920s, agriculture dropped to 16 percent of the GDP in 1988, rose to 20 percent in 1990, and doubled the 1988 rate in 1992 with 35 percent as Iraq attempted more nearly to feed itself and to employ more of its workforce. Having to reemphasize its great agricultural potential under the abnormal conditions of the 1990s was one of the compensations of the difficult times. With regard to the number of workers in the sector, it must be noted that the figures for agricultural workers in the late 1980s were skewed by the fact that most of the 2 million expatriate workers—1.5 million Egyptians, 300,000 Sudanese, and 200,000 South and East Asians—were farm laborers.

Of the country's total area, about 13 percent is arable. A surprising 53 percent of the arable land is rainfed, nearly all of it in the mainly Kurdish north and northeast, although most of the agricultural production is from the more intensively cultivated areas of the irrigated plains.

Iraq's major crops are grown in both the irrigated plains and the rainfed northern uplands—barley, wheat, cotton, potatoes, tobacco, millet, and sorghum. Wheat and barley are winter crops, utilizing the winter rainfall of the Mediterranean climate, whereas the other plants are summer grown, with some irrigation in the north. Other crops, especially rice and dates, are restricted to the southern irrigated areas along the rivers and canals, with citrus often grown in the shade of date palms. Thousands of date palms, which formerly supplied an important export, were destroyed during Iraq's two wars, 1980–1988 and 1991–1992. A complete range of temperate and subtropical fruits and vegetables is produced in Iraq.

By the 1970s Iraq had shifted from net food exporter to food importer. This shift was prompted by several factors, including population increase, a rising standard of living, increased industrialization, migration of farm workers to the cities (and to military service), and a loss of soil productivity in poorly drained irrigated areas of the south. Ambitious land reclamation and irrigation projects were accelerated after 1988, especially in the Jazirah along the East Euphrates channel and in the Third River Project in the southern interfluve. Irrigated area was thus greatly increased in the late 1980s, and agricultural efficiency has improved as collectivized farms have been privatized. Turkey's increasing preemption of Euphrates water (Chaps. 11 and 21) has challenged Iraq's inventiveness and may yet create serious problems for portions of the irrigated agriculture in Iraq. Baghdad must always balance the Euphrates water problem with Turkey's current accommodation of Iraq's only major export oil pipeline outlet. Further agricultural development may at last permit Iraq to approach its great crop production potential.

Petroleum

The first well drilled in Iraq, by the Turkish Petroleum Company or TPC (later renamed the Iraq Petroleum Company or IPC), struck a major reservoir with enormous gas pressure at Baba Gur, north of Kirkuk, in 1927. However, shipment of Kirkuk's output was delayed for seven years pending completion of export pipelines. The government of Iraq believed—correctly, as records later showed—that IPC sacrificed oil developments in Iraq for British political-economic interests, and Iraq-IPC relations remained discordant until Iraq nationalized its oil operations in 1975. Iraq had already joined OPEC as a charter member in 1960, passed Law 80 in 1961 reclaiming all concession area not in production, and created the Iraq National Oil Company (INOC) in 1964. These frictions in the country's oil operations continued even after nationalization of the industry and retarded economic development in Iraq.

Long ranking among the regional "big four" in reserves and production—Saudi Arabia, Iran, and Kuwait are the other three—Iraq finally achieved a peak production of 3.4 million bpd in 1979, only to fall sharply the next several years during the price collapse and the war with Iran. It approached the 3-million-bpd level in 1989, but in 1991 fell to 283,000 bpd, its lowest level in 40 years. Under UN sanctions it averaged less than 600,000 bpd until 1997, when major production was permitted under the UN Security Council Resolution 986 "oil-for-food" program. Iraq had refused a similar compromise in 1991 and had rejected the terms of Resolution 986 a year earlier. Output doubled in 1998 and might have gone higher had worn-out handling facilities not constrained production. Under several six-month renewals of Resolution 986, Iraq was allowed to use some oil income to import food and medical supplies for humanitarian purposes (later to receive critical machinery and equipment). The balance of the income went to pay compensation for Gulf war victims, funding for UN teams, transit fees for pipelines through Turkey, and similar costs (see the epilogue).

Iraq's refining capacity of 347,500 bpd throughput—about half the pre-war level—comes from nine installations, geographically well distributed between Kirkuk and Basrah. The two largest are in the center: Bayji with a throughput of 150,000 bpd north of Baghdad, and Dawrah with 100,000 bpd in Greater Baghdad. Basrah refinery, with 70,000 bpd normal capacity, needs repair and upgrading—as do all eight facilities in Iraq to varying degrees.

Details of the several Iraqi pipeline complexes are given in the "Pipelines" section of Chapter 8. A brief review shows that the old IPC multiple lines through Syria have been shut in since 1982, although Iraq and Syria conducted talks in 1998 regarding reopening them. The dual lines from Kirkuk across southeastern Turkey to Yumurtalık, one opened in 1977 and the other in 1987, saved Iraq's economy during the Iran-Iraq war, although Turkey shut them in after August 1990 at the UN's demand. The lines were reopened under UN Resolution 986 in 1996. The large IPSA line through Saudi Arabia was also a major "back-door" outlet but has been shut in since August 1990. Two large trestle tanker export terminals that Iraq opened off the Shatt al-Arab in the late 1970s were damaged in the 1980s fighting; they were back in partial operation only in the late 1990s. Mina al-Bakr has four 400,000 bpd berths for VLCCs, whereas Khawr al-Amaya's export capacity is 1.2 million bpd.

Thus, Iraq has all the essentials for a highly productive and profitable petroleum industry: 112.5 billion barrels of proved reserves—second-largest in the world (after Saudi Arabia); a well-distributed pattern of more than 70 fields, from the Turkish border to the Gulf coast; a normal producing capacity of 4 million bpd, expandable to 5 million bpd; an export capacity of 6.4 million bpd if all pipelines and terminals are operating; and an institutional system (which needs improving) to oversee operations. As of late 1999, the petroleum industry is receiving significant exemptions from UN sanctions and, as the favored sector, is driving the Iraqi economy.

However, it—like the economy and polity in general—desperately needs the necessary agreements among parties concerned to be reached so that sanctions can be lifted and normality restored.

Other Minerals

Nonfuel mineral resources of Iraq have so far proved to be relatively limited, compared with those of neighboring Turkey and Iran; and only sulfur and phosphates outputs are noteworthy. In addition to by-product sulfur from its refineries, Iraq also mines mineral sulfur at Mishraq from one of the world's largest deposits—130 million mt, located south of Mosul—and derives a range of acids and other products from it in nearby plants. Phosphate mining at Akashat (near al-Qaim, on the Euphrates near the Syrian border) was expanded several times to exploit these large reserves after the late 1970s, and an enlarged plant at al-Qaim processes some of the phosphates for acids and enhanced fertilizers. Both the sulfur and phosphates, along with products derived from processing them, normally supply important exports.

Manufacturing

Most of Iraq's industrial development has occurred since 1960. Concentrations of industries evolved around Baghdad, because of its market and labor supply, and around Basrah, because of its import-export advantages and the availability of oil and gas for energy and raw materials. Increased production of oil and gas in the north stimulated growth of population and industry in the Mosul-Irbil-Kirkuk triangle, giving Iraq its third manufacturing belt (see Map 9-1). The more important manufacturing centers are underlined on Map 16-1, although many smaller towns pursue various crafts.

Textiles have been a Mesopotamian product for centuries, with Mosul—which gave its name to muslin—a continuing textile center. Food and beverage processing were major activities in Iraq's early years, and still are.

Increased oil production in the 1950s generated many enterprises exploiting energy or using hydrocarbons as raw materials. Industrial concentration in central Iraq intensified as additional plants produced a wide range of items—pharmaceuticals, paper and plastic products, household appliances, clothing, assembled automobiles and trucks, and, before 1991, large amounts of military weaponry and support systems. When intelligence reports indicated progress in the Osiraq nuclear reactor, Israel bombed it in 1981.

The mid-Iraq interfluve continues to be the country's industrial heartland. However, before being bombed by Iran during the 1980s and by the coalition in 1990–1991, the strategic southern corridor was developed as a center for heavy industry and petrochemicals. Iron and steel, steel fabrication products, oil pipe, salt, fertilizers, and other chemicals are usual products. Profits from oil exports permitted generous government funding of heavily socialized industries, giving rise to several large parastatals.

Increasing emphasis on military strength, with cooperation from the then Soviet Union, generated a sophisticated weapons industry. For more than seven years, the nature, location, capacity, and level of readiness of this industry were the issues involved in a grim cat-and-mouse game between UN weapons inspectors on the UN Special Commission (UNSCOM) team and Iraqi authorities. UNSCOM inspections were conducted under UN Security Council Resolution 687 of April 3, 1991, which set the terms for the cease-fire between Iraq and the coalition, for Iraq's disarmament, and for prohibition of Iraqi possession or production of chemical, biological, and nuclear weapons. Following a serious confrontation between the two parties in December 1998, Iraq expelled UNSCOM, and the United States and Britain launched a punishing four-day air attack December 16–19.[10] Thus, during 1999 little could be learned about the details of Iraqi industrial development. With oil output already obligated for the near future, not only will government financing for industry be limited but private investors and foreign financing will be wary until Iraq stabilizes and emerges from its pariah status.

Transportation and Trade

Roads. Iraq's physical geography and early development—mostly along the two northwest-southeast axes of the Tigris and Euphrates—imposed an early pattern on road and railroad development. Major roads generally parallel both the Tigris and the Euphrates rivers, the main north-south motorway following the Tigris from Mosul to Baghdad but then taking the interfluve directly to Basrah and Kuwait (Map 16-1 shows main highways). In addition to the motorway from Mosul, three highways converge on Baghdad from the north and west: from Sulaymaniyah, from Irbil through Kirkuk, and from the Jordan border. The road from Jordan is an express motorway joined by the Euphrates highway from Syria. Southward from Baghdad, in addition to the express motorway, are the highways following both rivers. The links to north, west, and south brought in essential food and military matériel during the Iran-Iraq war, especially the route from Jordan's port at Aqabah through Rutbah and Ramadi to Baghdad. Again during the Gulf crisis in 1990–1991, this motorway was Iraq's one ground link with the outside world, and it continued to serve as a vital artery during the lengthy period of Iraq's relative isolation after the crisis. Dozens of bridges destroyed or damaged in 1990–1991 were gradually repaired during the 1990s.

Railways. A railway from Berlin to Baghdad was a goal of the Germans and other Europeans during the heyday of railroad building, and the southern segment of the realized line enters Iraq northwest of Mosul, parallels the Tigris to Baghdad, then follows the Euphrates to Basrah and the Gulf. It was the country's only railway until development of the phosphate deposits near al-Qaim prompted construction of a 318-mile/512-km railway, completed in 1984, down the Euphrates and across to Baghdad. Built in 1987, a second line, 156 miles/252 km long, parallels the major pipelines from Kirkuk to Hadithah on the Euphrates, where it joins the line from al-Qaim

to Baghdad. A third line into Baghdad links Irbil and Kirkuk with the capital. During the 1990s, after the two Gulf wars, the main lines were repaired, upgraded, and double-tracked between Baghdad and Basrah. Like those in Egypt, Iraqi railways carry a heavy passenger load.

Ports. The narrowness of Iraq's window on the Gulf restricts the country's ports to a small area. So limited is its actual Gulf coast that only the exploitation of existing indentations (drowned estuaries, called *khawrs* or *khors*) for port development has enabled Iraq to develop useful ports. Despite the geographical constraint, several ports are normally essential because of the scale and variety of Iraq's imports and exports. Basrah long served as Mesopotamia's only port. Its location on the relatively shallow Shatt al-Arab, however, limited growth and led to congestion. Oil development and Iraq's economic expansion after the 1950s occasioned construction of an oil terminal at al-Faw, down the Shatt al-Arab from Basrah; two general-cargo ports, Khawr al-Zubair and Umm Qasr, on the Khawr al-Zubair drowned estuary near the Kuwait border, with Umm Qasr also serving as a naval base; and two oil export terminals—Mina al-Bakr and Khawr al-Amayah—on trestle causeways into the deeper water at the head of the Gulf. Even before the Iran-Iraq war, Iraqi ports were overloaded, and Iraq imported through Aqabah and Kuwait as well as other Gulf ports. Virtual destruction of Iraq's ports by Iran in the early 1980s necessitated greater reliance on Kuwait and especially Aqabah, neither of which was accessible to Iraq during the 1990–1991 Gulf war. Iraq's aggressive search for its own sovereign and secure ports was one motivation for its repeated confrontations with and attack on Kuwait.

Trade. For many years, crude petroleum has constituted 98–99 percent of Iraq's exports. The remainder has been primarily processed dates and fertilizers. Like other aspects of the Iraqi economy, foreign trade was profoundly affected by the war with Iran and much more so by the aftermath of the Gulf crisis of 1990–1991. UN Security Council Resolution 661, August 6, 1990, imposed sanctions on trade with Iraq and was still in effect in early 2000. Only a trickle of goods—some smuggled—entered or left Iraq, although 80,000–100,000 bpd of oil went to Jordan by truck under special UN exemptions. Importation of some food and medical supplies was encouraged, but Iraq's perverse refusal to accept some UN parameters prevented the inflow of such items. By 1996, the internal situation became desperate. Because Saddam Husayn could no longer blame the West entirely for the hunger and collapse of health care, he finally agreed to the terms of the UN food-for-oil Resolution 986 of April 14, 1995. Large oil exports generated funds for food and medicine, which began arriving in March 1996, along with much of the wheat bought on the Iraqi account supplied by the United States. The trade picture brightened appreciably for more than three years as the program was repeatedly renewed for six months. Otherwise, the country's trade remains under UN sanctions, as firmly demanded by the United States in the atmosphere of decreasing international support. The once-strong Iraqi dinar collapsed after the two Gulf wars, dropping from 1 dinar=$3.20 in 1990 to 1 dinar=$0.0008 in late 1999. Thus, for two decades Iraq's foreign trade has been abnormally skewed, and its pattern for the foreseeable future is impossible to forecast.

Relations

Iraq's external political and economic relations have fluctuated widely since 1958, both because of internal politics and because of regional changes. After August 1990 and continuing in early 2000, Iraq, under President Saddam Husayn, was a pariah state with only very tenuous relations with its neighbors, its former trading partners, its one-time supporters in the Former Soviet Union, and certainly North America and Western Europe.

Iraq's long political and economic relationship with Britain, steered for many years by the pro-Western Nuri al-Said, linked Iraq with Europe internationally until 1958. One consequence of this link was that Iraq became the sole Arab country to join the Baghdad Pact. However, the revolutionary republican government reversed the trend, withdrew from the pact in 1959, and accepted a breach with the West.[11] Successive governments brought in by coups have maintained a generally ambiguous attitude toward the West at best, and usually have been contentious.

Iraq between 1958 and 1990 has made its primary foreign policy concern the reaffirming and strengthening of its links with the Arab world but also the assertion of a leadership role in the region. Iraq had supplied troops in the 1948–1949 war between Arabs and the new state of Israel, and it did so again in 1967. It has consistently supported the Palestinian Arab cause within the context of Arab unity. It has accepted a minimum number of Palestinian refugees. However, Iraqi government leaders— particularly President Saddam Husayn—have issued calls for a remedy of the Palestinian problem, usually involving confrontation with Israel. It is this prominent rhetorical support that won Iraq appreciation among Palestinians and other Arabs on the street, especially in Jordan and Yemen. Thus, as implacable opponents and genuine threats to each other's security, Iraq and Israel view each other as mutual major foes. Iraq made its most militant move against Israel in 1991 when it fired 39 Scud missiles into Israel during the coalition's response to the invasion of Kuwait. Iraq declared that the Scuds were, inter alia, a response to Israel's bombing raid on Iraq's Osiraq nuclear reactor in 1981. Israel also gave military assistance to Iran during the Iran-Iraq war, has undercut Iraq's economic development, wages an effective war of words against Iraq, and is a major factor in the U.S. stance against Iraq as well as Iran.

Since World War II, and especially since the 1958 revolution, Iraq has emphasized its historical role in Islam (Fig. 16-4) and has considered itself the eastern anchor of the Arab world and the natural eastern flank of the Mashriq, the Arab Middle East, of which Egypt is the western

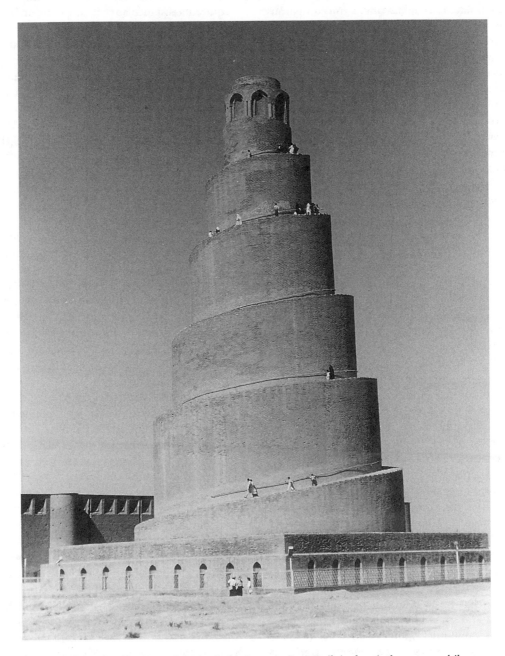

FIGURE 16-4 Spiral minaret *(al-Mawiyah)*, Samarra, Iraq. Built in the ninth century while Samarra was the capital of the Abbasid Empire. Figures at base give scale of this unusual minaret, 171 ft./52 m high, which served the Friday Mosque glimpsed at lower left.

flank. As a member of the Arab League, it is regularly militant, often advocating more vigorous stands than do the majority of the members. It is a "rejectionist" state on many political points. Its direct relations with Egypt have blown hot and cold since 1958 but reached their nadir in 1990 when Egypt, greatly moderated since the radical years of Gamal Abd al-Nasser, joined the coalition to force Iraq to withdraw from Kuwait. Other Arab states of the Mashriq are ambivalent toward Iraq: They condemn its aggression against Kuwait and its firing Scud missiles into Saudi Arabia, as well as other acts by Saddam Husayn; but they still recognize its role in attesting to Arabism, its stand against Iran, its defiance of vestiges of imperialism, and its opposition to Israel. Yemen has voiced support for Iraq for these reasons. Because of rifts between Syrian Baathists and Iraqi Baathists, relations with Syria deteriorated after that country's 1963 Baath coup. Iraq, Syria, and Egypt have contended for leadership of the Mashriq.

Iraq's relations with Jordan between 1923 and 1958 rested on the fraternal relationship of the Hashimite kings of the two countries. Although meaningful implementation of the proposed Arab Federation between the two kingdoms was prevented by the 1958 revolution, mutual interests restored relations. The link has proved critical to Iraq, as well as economically beneficial to Jordan, as has been shown in Chapter 14 and earlier in this chapter. Close Jordanian-Iraqi relations are certain to be resumed when UN sanctions are removed because of the compellingly reciprocal advantages that cooperation between these neighbors provides.

It is with its Arab neighbors of the Gulf region that Iraq's relations become the most critical and sometimes ambiguous. Those relations became prickly after the overthrow of the monarchy in the 1958 revolution in Iraq, and each Iraqi reassertion of claim to Kuwait and of dominance over the Gulf region heightened the tensions, as occurred in 1971. When the Gulf states, including Saudi Arabia, organized the Gulf Cooperation Council, they discouraged

Iraq's inclusion. Yet when Iraq desperately required assistance after its invasion of Iran in 1980, proclaiming itself the bastion of Arabism against Persian designs, all the Gulf states came to its aid with billions of dollars and other assistance. Kuwait and Saudi Arabia were especially helpful. In addition to their financial aid, they helped with proxy shipments of oil on Iraq's OPEC quota and account, and Saudi Arabia agreed to the construction of the IPSA pipeline to the Red Sea. Iraq's about-face invasion of Kuwait and attacks on Saudi Arabia during the Gulf war were, therefore, all the more inexplicable and completely contradicted Iraq's vociferous claims to be a leading supporter of Arab unity. As the two main victims, Kuwait and Saudi Arabia feel profoundly betrayed by Iraq and are the most reluctant to forgive their attacker for the 1990–1991 invasion (see Chap. 11). But, along with other Arab states, even they are skeptical about the motivation of the United States regarding its role in the Gulf and especially its persistent war of attrition against a sister Arab state—even one that has attacked them.

Following its alienation from the West after 1958, Iraq turned to the USSR, accepting USSR military supplies denied by the West. Iraq intermittently retreated from other relations with the Soviets. Iraqi-Soviet relations were strained by the Soviet Union's support of Syria and even Iran, and cautious relations between Iraq and the West were resumed after 1980, affording Iraq a more balanced support system during its life-or-death struggle with Iran. Iraq also thus positioned itself to receive assistance from the West in the mid- and late 1980s just as the Soviet Union disintegrated.

Although relations with Turkey had been passive for decades, they were reinvigorated in the mid-1970s by the agreement on the pipeline from Kirkuk to Yumurtalık. Further agreements regarding the pipelines and Turkey's receiving oil supplies through the system afforded increasingly close relations and greater trade between Iraq and Turkey. However, this mutually beneficial rapport collapsed overnight in August 1990 when Turkey reluctantly agreed to abide by the UN sanctions against Iraq. Relations between Turkey and Iraq were on a roller-coaster in the early 1990s, especially regarding the Kurds and the role of the PKK in Turkey. With the UN suspension of some sanctions and implementation of the oil-for-food program in 1995–1996, relations warmed again as oil flowed through the pipelines to Yumurtalık. Underneath the symbiotic warmth regarding oil, running tension persists over Turkey's reduction of Euphrates water to downstream riparians.

The historical antagonism between the people of the Mesopotamian Basin and those of the Iranian Plateau intensified after the Iranian revolution in 1979 and finally broke out in open warfare between Iran and Iraq in September 1980 (see Chap. 11). After the eight years of fighting, it was ironic that in 1990, President Saddam Husayn should renounce in Iran's favor all that Iraq had gained by its Pyrrhic victory, in order to keep Iran neutral in the second Gulf war and thus avert the danger of having to fight on two fronts. Curiously, Iraq's relations with non-Arab Iran during the 1990s were warmer than those with its Arab neighbors. In the later 1990s, Iran and Iraq exchanged some prisoners of war from the 1980s and discussed other issues of common interest.

U.S.-Iraqi relations following the 1958 revolution in Baghdad were little more than "correct," and Iraq broke relations with the United States after the 1967 Arab-Israeli war on the basis that the United States had assisted Israel during that conflict. Quiet improvements in contacts during the late 1970s finally led, in December 1984, to a resumption of full diplomatic relations. The détente survived both the revelation of the U.S.-Israeli arms sales to Iran and also the May 1987 Iraqi nighttime Exocet missile strike on the U.S. Navy frigate *Stark* while it patrolled Gulf waters. The United States made many gestures toward Iraq in the late 1980s in an effort to "build bridges"; it provided food shipments and badly needed machinery and other goods on favorable credit terms, then bought 100,000 bpd of Iraqi crude oil for cash. Opponents in both countries minimized the attempts at rapprochement, and U.S. efforts were heavily criticized, especially after Iraq invaded Kuwait; however, such efforts are standard approaches and have been used with considerable success with other countries. The policy did fail in Iraq, and hindsight shows that this failure was traceable largely to the quixotic President Saddam Husayn. Whereas U.S.-Iraqi relations were patently low in 1990–1991 because of the U.S.'s leading role in the coalition opposing Iraq, they sank much lower as sanctions remained in force year after year, largely at U.S. insistence. By 1998, when the United States virtually coopted the UN role in responding to Iraqi actions, it came under increasing criticism from its fellow UN Security Council members and other leaders. Even the declaration of the no-flight zones in 1991 and 1992, which the United States demanded under UN Resolution 688, was met with reservations. Also criticized was the severity of U.S. (and sometimes British) enforcement in the zones, as well as expansion of the southern zone from 32° to 33° in 1996. After the climactic contretemps regarding UNSCOM in late 1998, the almost daily bombing by U.S. planes became a war of attrition. Iraq gained appreciable, if grudging, sympathy from its Arab neighbors as well as from other countries when it labeled the attacks "unreasoning United States hostility."[12] As the bombing intensified—27,000 sorties in ten months in 1999—a thoughtful analysis of the campaign commented that the feeling across the Arab world held that U.S. policy was "something more sinister, drawing its energy from the sheer savage vigor of supremacy."[13] U.S. statements have increasingly and firmly demanded Iraq's full compliance with all UN resolutions before sanctions are lifted. Other statements imply that only a "regime change" would satisfy all requirements, and official U.S. government support for opposition groups has been publicly announced.[14]

Iraq continues to be a country with many assets but beset by major problems and challenges. It cannot afford morally or economically to resume the internecine struggle that has absorbed its energies, humanity, and treasure for so many years.

Notes

1. The creation of Iraq is recounted in several studies (see Note 2 below), but the background given in Klieman 1970, Chapter 7, is especially relevant and includes the story of installing Faysal ibn Husayn as king of Iraq in 1921.

2. Among several good modern histories of Iraq see Marr 1985, Penrose and Penrose 1978, and Helms 1984. Several useful essays are included in Niblock 1982. *Iraq* Country Study 1990, like all volumes in this series, gives excellent broad coverage. Unfortunately and curiously, few commendable, balanced general studies of Iraq have appeared during the 1990s. One useful study of the post-1991 military situation, effect of sanctions, and some political aspects is Cordesman and Hashim 1997.

3. See *New York Times,* Jan. 24, 1993.

4. The fascinating story of the former ecological symbiosis between marsh and Madan is recounted in the classic account Thesiger 1964. It has been republished and reprinted several times.

5. The following remarks on the current situation are partly based on Edwards and Yamashita 1999.

6. Discussed in Lees and Falcon 1952.

7. Journalistic reports on the Kurds appeared daily during the spring and summer of 1991. A good study by a veteran journalist is Randal 1998. More scholarly studies include Jwaideh 1960, Ghareeb 1981, Pelletiere 1984, and Entessar 1992.

8. During field observations in Kurdistan in mid-1990, I visited the ruins of scores of the razed Kurdish villages and observed several of the new settlements. The sight left no doubt as to the scale of the project or about the government's determination to subdue the Kurds through reversing the geographical advantage.

9. Fully treated in Cordesman and Hashim 1997 70–97. See also *New York Times,* Sept. 5, 1996.

10. See *New York Times,* Dec. 29, 1998. For a detailed analysis of Iraq's weapons industry see Cordesman and Hashim 1997, chaps. 7 and 15. For a partisan account by an UNSCOM member see Ritter 1999.

11. The subject is well covered in Penrose and Penrose 1978.

12. *New York Times,* Sept. 5, 1996.

13. *New York Times,* Dec. 20, 1998

14. *Christian Science Monitor,* Nov. 30, 1998; *New York Times,* Nov. 2, 1999; "Overthrow Saddam? A Debate."

17

Saudi Arabia: Development in the Desert

The Arabian Peninsula (Arabic, *Jazirat al-Arab*—Island of the Arabs) has played a significant role through 7,000 years of Middle East history and into the present. Three especially important roles should be emphasized. One, it served as the source area for Semitic peoples who migrated into the Fertile Crescent as Akkadians, Amorites, Assyrians, Aramaeans, and Chaldeans; as smaller groups that included Canaanites, Hebrews, Edomites, and Nabataeans; and, of particular interest, as Arabs in the seventh century. Two, it is the cradle of Islam, the religion of more than 1.25 billion people, and the destination of more than 2.5 million pilgrims to Mecca every year. Also, hundreds of millions of Muslims face toward Mecca for prayers five times daily. Three, under its eastern margins lie 46 percent of the world's known petroleum reserves. Seven states occupy the Arabian Peninsula: Saudi Arabia, the four Gulf states (see Chap. 18), and Oman and Yemen (see Chap. 19).

Saudi Arabia: A Preview

Saudi Arabia figures prominently in international rankings for both geographical and economic reasons. It is the largest country in the Middle East as delineated in this book (Sudan is a larger Arab country) and ranks twelfth in size in the world. Among the countries of the world, it possesses the largest reserves of petroleum, largest single oil reservoir, largest-capacity oil export terminal, largest oil storage tanks, longest natural gas liquids pipeline, largest-capacity seawater desalination plant, and largest airport.

Saudi Arabia possesses significant contemporary characteristics other than those related to petroleum and to the religion of Islam. Although politically conservative and internationally oriented toward the West, the country's economic power reinforces its independence and the development of its distinctive assets. It possesses the longest Red Sea coast of all the littoral states; its Gulf coast is second longest after that of Iran. It adjoins every state on the peninsula plus Jordan and Iraq. Although it maintains a comparatively low profile politically and militarily, it has worked toward internal stability and a modest defense capability.

Funded with petrodollars, Saudi Arabian development proceeded rapidly after about 1960, requiring millions of foreign consultants, managers, and laborers, yet the kingdom preserved its deeply conservative and religious character. The Saudis demonstrated a socioeconomic resilience in their adaptation both to two decades of affluence and to the years of recession after 1982, as well as to the disturbing years of the eight-year Iran-Iraq war and the traumatic Gulf war of 1990–1991. Six five-year development plans have included major focus on "Saudiization," the development of human services and resources—planners, managers, and workers—to replace at least some of the expatriate technicians by a new generation of educated Saudis who are trained in the skills needed in the country's economy.

Saudi Arabia is a young nation—dating from only 1932, although it was developing for 30 years prior. It was born of a special combination of circumstances and has adhered to many of the traditions that were and are an integral part of its raison d'être. Such conservatism has

Saudi Arabia

Long-form official name, anglicized: Kingdom of Saudi Arabia

Official name, transliterated: al-Mamlakah al-Arabiyah al-Saudiyah

Form of government: traditional monarchy, with Council of Ministers and, since 1993, Consultative Council

Area: 868,000 miles^2/2,248,000 km^2 (area imprecise, since some land boundaries undelimited)

Population, 1999: 21,500,000 (estimate; includes 5,500,000 expatriates). Literacy: 63%

Ethnic composition (%): Arab 90 (includes Egyptian, Lebanese, Yemeni, other Arab expatriates); African-Asian 9 (includes Indian, Pakistani, Filipino, Thai, Korean, Sri Lankan expatriate workers); American-European expatriates 1

Religions (%): Muslim (mostly Sunni) 98.8, Christian 0.8 (expatriates), other 0.4

GDP, 1998: $186 billion; per capita $9,000

Petroleum reserves: 259 billion barrels (world's largest)

Main exports (% of total value, 1998): petroleum and petroleum products 93; foodstuffs and others 7

Main imports (% of total value, 1998): machinery and appliances 21.0; transport equipment 15.3; metals and metal articles 10.0; chemicals and chemical products 8.1; foodstuffs 12.3; textiles and clothing 7.3

Capital city: al-Riyadh 2,800,000; other cities: Jiddah 1,600,000; Mecca 1,500,000; al-Taif (summer capital) 525,000; Medina 400,000; Dammam–al-Khobar–Dhahran agglomeration 1,000,000

strengthened the Saudi social fabric and, conversely, has both weakened the nation's social evolution and attracted foreign criticism. This contradiction received widespread attention when Saudi Arabia played host to several hundred thousand foreign troops, support groups, and media personnel from 33 countries, along with thousands of planes, tanks, and vehicles, during the Gulf crisis and war in late 1990 and early 1991. Although the Saudis were well aware that the forces were present in a protective role, which they deeply appreciated, they were also apprehensive that most of the forces represented many social mores and values to which the conservative Saudis had long been antipathetic. Strict Saudi rules, policies, and customs—which were considerably exaggerated in early media reports—were soon adapted and adjusted, and goodwill on all sides permitted reasonably smooth relations for the six months of the crisis.

Historical-Political Geography

Limited archaeological exploration of the peninsula before the mid-1970s found evidence of widespread ancient occupation, settlement sites, and burial mounds. Dramatic discoveries in the mid-1980s confirmed that bands of *homo erectus* had brought their Developed Oldowan tool culture from the Olduvai Gorge area in East Africa to western Arabia more than one million years ago (see Chap. 2). Late Paleolithic and Neolithic tools found in the now-barren Rub al-Khali were left by hunters or settlers along old lakeshores more than 17,000 years ago and again 10,000–5,000 years ago.[1] Finds along the northeastern coast and on Tarut Island reveal ties with Mesopotamian civilizations of 2500 BC and earlier (see Map 2-1).

A retracing of old trade routes has shown that many towns depended economically on serving one of the several main caravan tracks. The major ancient route from Aden led northward through Asir and the Hijaz to the caravansary and watering point of Mecca before continuing northward. Traffic along this route in the early seventh century influenced the emergence of Islam.

When the focus of political and military power of Islam passed from Mecca and Medina to Damascus in the seventh century and later to Baghdad, the role of the Hijaz and of Arabia diminished for several centuries. Most of Arabia remained a frontier zone, isolated and tribally fragmented. With the breakdown of the Abbasid caliphate (1258), Mamluk Egyptian control extended to the Hijaz holy places. Mamluk control passed in turn to the Ottomans when the Turks conquered Egypt in 1517. The peninsula's interior evolved separately, leading to the emergence in the eighteenth century of the family of Al Saud. Battling other tribes and clans, the Sauds achieved a leading role in Najd, the central plateau core of the Arabian Peninsula. Najd has continued to be the Saudi power nucleus.

In the mid-eighteenth century, Al Saud leader Muhammad ibn Saud allied the family with a religious reformer, Muhammad ibn Abd al-Wahhab, linking Saudi political-military power and Muslim puritanism. The connection persists as a strong symbiosis until the present. The resulting religious belief is sometimes called "unitarian" and sometimes, inappropriately, Wahhabi. From their center in al-Diriyah near Riyadh, the two leaders had expanded Saudi control of most of the peninsula by the early 1800s. Wary of the growing Saudi strength, the Ottomans ordered Muhammad Ali of Egypt to overthrow the Sauds and to reestablish Ottoman authority over the holy Hijaz. The Egyptians captured the Saudi capital of al-Diriyah in 1818, destroyed its forts, and interrupted Al Saud dominance but failed to eradicate Saudi power. The Egyptian invasion of the peninsula heartland was one of the very few successful penetrations in history, and even it was only briefly effective. A few years later, the Sauds regained their lost territories, except

in the Hijaz, and established a new capital in Riyadh, where it has remained.

With Saudi leadership weakened by family disputes, the Ottomans occupied al-Hasa in the eastern part of the peninsula; and the Rashids, a family contending against the Sauds, asserted control over much of the Najd. Al Saud leaders took refuge in Kuwait, from which a young Saud, Abd al-Aziz ibn Abd al-Rahman, regained control of Riyadh and Najd in 1902. As the new family leader, Abd al-Aziz organized many of the Bedouins into groups of *ikhwan* ("brethren") and gradually reclaimed control over most of the peninsula. He annexed the last major area in 1924–1925 when his *ikhwan* warriors conquered the Hijaz—the western highlands and coast of the peninsula. This former Ottoman province, governed by the Hashimite family of the Sharif Husayn of Arab Revolt fame, included the holy cities of Mecca and Medina; and control of them gave Abd al-Aziz the distinction of being Custodian of the Two Holy Mosques. Each royal successor has maintained that custodianship as part of his official title, comparable to the British monarch's partial title of "Defender of the Faith."

In January 1927, Abd al-Aziz was officially proclaimed King of the Hijaz and Najd and Its Dependencies, with Mecca and Riyadh as his capitals. In the Treaty of Jiddah (1927), Great Britain recognized the status quo in Arabia. On September 22, 1932, Abd al-Aziz, who became known in the West as Ibn Saud, renamed the country the Kingdom of Saudi Arabia, still the official designation.[2]

Abd al-Aziz accepted the concept of modernization of the country and persuaded the ultraconservative religious leaders to accept new technologies: automobiles, radio, telephone, aircraft, and television. After 50 years of rule, Abd al-Aziz died in 1953 and was followed by a succession of sons—Saud ibn Abd al-Aziz (1953–1964), Faysal ibn Abd al-Aziz (1964–1975), Khalid ibn Abd al-Aziz (1975–1982), and since 1982, Fahd ibn Abd al-Aziz.

Reflecting the joint power structure, Saudi Arabia is controlled by the Saud family, specifically represented by the Al Saud member serving as king, and by the religious leaders of the country, the ulama. The ulama influence the choice of the Saud family member to be named as the next king, and they intervene if the king departs from conservative Islam. In 1953, King Abd al-Aziz appointed the first cabinet; the Council of Ministers—now numbering 30—continues as a basic organ of the state. In 1993, King Fahd responded to escalating pressures for liberalization and appointed a Consultative Council (*Majlis al-Shura*), which he renewed and expanded from 60 to 90 members in July 1997. Similar provincial councils were also designated. Although the Council is a limited step forward, it is a significant one, as it has demonstrated in its frequent meetings and relations with the king and his ministers.[3] The king thus faces constraints on policies and actions, with respect to modernization, for example.

The steps taken to broaden the political institutions have been not only characteristically cautious and limited but consistent with the Saudi practice of pursuing evolution rather than revolution, which the Sauds consider to have been so disruptive in Iraq, Iran, and the former South Yemen. There are no political parties or national elections, and the king leads as a shaykh of shaykhs in a male-dominated, largely tribal society. Women are severely limited socially, with some exceptions for foreigners: They may not dine alone in a restaurant, may not drive an automobile, may not work in an open public office, must be segregated in schools, and must be completely covered in public. Under the kingdom's very raison d'être, there is no concept of the separation of religion and state. The religious police (*mutawwain*) enforce adherence to Islamic norms by monitoring public behavior. "Saudi law severely limits freedom of speech and press. Authorities do not countenance criticism of Islam, the ruling family, or the Government."[4] Time will tell whether sociopolitical adjustments in the Saudi kingdom can be made quantitatively and qualitatively at the pace demanded by sociopolitical developments.

Physical Patterns

Diversity in the Desert

Despite the preponderance of desert in the country, Saudi Arabia's landforms exhibit great diversity, even in the sizes, shapes, and colors of dunes in the extensive sand deserts.[5] The relatively green mountains of Asir in the southwest are especially differentiated from the rest of the country. Scarped sedimentary Najd in the center, crystalline shield Najd farther west, lava-covered areas in the north and the west, and immense sand seas in north, south, and east contrast with one another in both geomorphology and cultural character.

The gross geomorphological characteristics of the peninsula are influenced by its formation as a separate tectonic plate that split from northeastern Africa along the Red Sea rift during the Tertiary period (see Chap. 3). The west-central third is a massive crystalline block of Precambrian igneous and metamorphic rocks, with extensive young basalts on the west. Eastward, sedimentary layers cover the rest of the peninsula, except in al-Hajar in Oman, with strata dipping generally eastward and with successively younger outcrops toward the Gulf. Sand seas and sand dunes blanket more than one-third of the peninsula, including the Nafud in the north, the vast Rub al-Khali in the south, and the arc of the Dahna dunes connecting the two.

Regions

[1] **Tihamah.**   Starting on the west, the first natural region (see circled numbers on Map 17-1) consists of a sandy-gravelly coastal plain, Tihamah, which extends virtually the full length of the Red Sea coast. Squeezed between the coastline and the rugged Hijaz range, Tihamah varies in width from only a few meters at the Gulf of Aqabah to more than 25 miles/40 km near Jaizan in the south. The plain is referred to in the north as Tihamat al-Sham, in the center as Tihamat al-Hijaz, and in the south as Tihamat Asir. Although it is naturally barren and forbidding, almost waterless between infrequent rains, and lacking

MAP 17-1 Reference map of Saudi Arabia. Circled numbers refer to regions discussed in text. Petroleum, solid minerals, transportation, and other topics are shown on maps in relevant chapters (Maps 8-1, 8-2, 8-5, 9-2, and others).

significant harbor indentations, Tihamah has been a major route of passage for centuries. Small ports—Wajh, Yanbu, Jiddah, Jaizan— somehow persevered, supported by fishing and limited trade, with Jiddah serving as a passenger port for Mecca pilgrims after the seventh century. Jiddah is now the kingdom's leading general port, and the once-small fishing villages have become huge industrial ports. A first-class highway now extends

along the ancient caravan route from the Jordan border to the Yemen line.

[2] **Hijaz-Asir Mountains.** To the east of the coastal plain is a mountain belt ranging in width from 25 to 87 miles/40 to 140 km. It is generally low in the north but increases in elevation toward the south, with crest elevations reaching 6,987 ft./2,130 m northwest of Medina and 9,840 ft./3,000 m near Abha. A gap in

the mountain belt near Mecca has been used for a travel route for centuries. It is from this formidable uplifted crystalline mountain block that the name for the western region—al-Hijaz ("the barrier")—is derived. The elevated southern segment constitutes Asir, the best-watered area of Saudi Arabia, receiving 12–20 in./300–500 mm of precipitation annually, much of it during the summer monsoon. Moderate slopes echoing the dramatic terraces farther south in Yemen have long been terraced (Fig. 17-1a) to permit production of warm-season crops (Fig. 7-4). In addition to the Asir rainfall, the Hijaz crestline receives the most winter rainfall of any part of the kingdom. Nestled in barren volcanic basins in the central Hijaz are the two most sacred cities in Islam, Mecca and Medina, and also the summer capital city, al-Taif. In the unique and fascinating Asir are found the rapidly expanding agricultural and resort area around Abha, the military area of Khamis Mushayt, and the pleasant Najran district. National parks west of Abha attract thousands of visitors, with spectacular views down the great seaward-facing escarpment and hundreds of hamadryas baboons scampering through the wooded uplands.

[3] **Najd.** Continuing eastward from the central segment of the uplifted Hijaz-Asir highland and extending to the middle of the peninsula is the main crystalline block of the Arabian Shield. It comprises granites, gabbros, gneisses, schists, marbles, and related rocks. Like most shield areas, the Arabian Shield has mineralized areas, with deposits of copper, gold, silver, lead, zinc, and other metals. Most of these mineral occurrences are limited, although numerous ancient gold and silver workings have been found through intensive searches by U.S., French, and Saudi geologists. Persistent exploration has found more than a score of deposits worth large-scale exploitation.

Along the western edge are six major lava fields, 390–7,720 miles^2/1,000–20,000 km^2 in extent, which are dotted with numerous lava cones and cinder cones in north-south alignments (Fig. 3-3). One of these relatively young

basalt flows near Medina dates from as recently as AD 1250. As Map 6-2 shows, extensive areas of the crystalline shield between the Hijaz Mountains and central Najd are virtually uninhabited.

East of the shield and distinctly contrasting with it is sedimentary Najd, a part of the central plateau with outcropping sedimentary rocks in a great curved belt around the eastern edge of the crystalline basement. Escarpments, ridges, and buttes, each with a resistant cap, are characteristic features around this Central Arabian Arch. One particular escarpment, an Upper Jurassic limestone cuesta extending along a 1,000-mile/1,600-km crescent, forms Jabal Tuwayq, the most prominent physiographic feature of central Arabia (Fig. 17-1b). All of these outcropping strata dip eastward and are found at depths several thousand feet below the surface in the oil fields of eastern Arabia. The outcropping layers of sedimentary rocks in eastern Najd both serve as catchment rocks for aquifers that are tapped in the Eastern Province and also provide conditions for many local contact springs. These springs gave rise to numerous ancient and still-persisting Najd settlements, and their presence prompted the drilling of water wells in modern times.

Groups of villages around several central places and coordination of agricultural activity have resulted in the evolution of a subregional consciousness along the Jabal Tuwayq. The main subregion in the north is al-Qasim, located west of the Tuwayq cuesta and centered on the large towns of Buraydah and Unayzah, southeast of Hayil.[6] South-southeast of al-Qasim and still west of Jabal Tuwayq is the Washm subregion, embracing several small towns and a vastly expanded agricultural economy. East of al-Qasim, on the backslope of the Tuwayq escarpment, is the Sudayr, centered on Majmaah (Fig. 10-1b) and less populated than al-Qasim. All three districts experienced remarkable development of irrigation agriculture during the 1980s, as well as road net intensification, population increase, and extensive urban development. Southeast of Riyadh is the subregion of al-Kharj, which has significant

FIGURE 17-1 Contrasting landscapes in Saudi Arabia: terraced agriculture in the Asir *(top)*, best-watered region of the kingdom, just north of Yemen, and dissected back-slope of the resistant Tuwayq cuesta *(bottom)* in the desert south of Riyadh.

solution springs and has long been one of the largest oases in the peninsula. For several decades it has accommodated one of several concentrations of U.S. military training personnel. Extending southward from al-Kharj along a secondary cuesta are two well-defined subregions: al-Hawtah, with the villages of al-Hillah and al-Hilway, and, farther south, al-Aflaj, centered on Layla. Al-Aflaj refers to the irrigation system that formerly supported extensive gardens around Layla. The Hawtah subregion was launched into a local oil boom in the period 1989–1991 with the discovery of completely new super light petroleum fields extending 47 miles/75 km from the southern Hawtah to al-Dilam, south of al-Kharj.

[4] **Dahna, Summan, Coastal Plain.**   Between Najd and the Gulf coast lie three belts that generally parallel the arcuate Jabal Tuwayq. All are generally considered to be in the Eastern Province, and they contain most of the Saudi Arabian oil fields: the Dahna, a great arc of rust-colored sand dunes 30 miles/48 km wide and extending 800 miles/1,290 km from the Nafud in the north to the Rub al-Khali in the south; al-Summan plateau, with escarpments and buttes on its eastern margins; and near the Gulf coast, an irregular plain terminating in a ragged coastline of *sabkhahs* (Fig. 5-1b), sand spits, and offshore sandbars.

Under the plateau and coastal plain, as well as offshore, are the world's greatest petroleum reservoirs, now well delineated and intensively exploited. Except for the Hofuf and Qatif oases and a few small coastal villages, this vast realm was the haunt of the Bedouins and their camels prior to World War II. Now it throbs with hundreds of oil wells flowing under high pressure, gas-oil separator plants, flow lines, pump stations, heavy traffic on a dense road net, oil-related industries, sprawling cities, bustling ports, and a still-expanding general economy. The nerve center of the vast operation is the oil-company headquarters in Dhahran, near which are located the University of Petroleum and Minerals, the older international airport and the huge new airport, and, on the coast, the

ever-expanding cities of Dammam (the provincial capital) and al-Khobar and its residential suburb of Thuqbah, creating an agglomeration of varied population and economy. North of Dammam is the great oil-export terminal and refinery of Ras Tanura (Fig. 8-3), farther north the newer and equally large export terminal of Juaymah, and north of that the recently (since the late 1970s) developed industrial city of Jubayl.

[5] **Rub al-Khali.**   Vast seas of sand in the north and south of the country constitute two of the most distinctive physical features on the peninsula. The largest single dune field in the world, the Rub al-Khali (Empty Quarter) covers more than 230,000 miles^2/600,000 km^2. Referred to simply as al-Riml ("the Sands") by Bedouins, the Rub al-Khali comprises almost entirely loose, dry sand shaped into dunes that vary from one sector of the desert to another depending upon the wind. Three types of dune predominate: numerous linear or longitudinal dunes (*uruq;* singular, *irq*), some of them 60 miles/100 km long, in the western half (see Fig. 1-1); barchans or crescentic dunes in the northeast; and giant dunes, the remarkable Sand Mountains, along the eastern and southern margins. Formless "sand seas" fill other areas. Although limited areas exhibit some vegetation, the Rub al-Khali's loose sands are relatively barren, and because so few wells exist in the area, even Bedouins generally avoid the vast desert. Al Murrah and occasional other tribesmen move along the edges and infrequently cross it.[7] The formerly remote and isolated eastern Rub al-Khali has now been opened consequent to development of the rich Shaybah oil field on the UAE border.

[6] **The Nafud.**   In the northwest is the great Nafud, called by the Bedouins simply *al-Nafud,* the northern term for "sandy desert." Characterized by complex dune forms including deep pits, the reddish sands of the Nafud cover 45,000 miles^2/116,550 km^2. The sediment source for the sand is an extensive area of poorly cemented Paleozoic sandstones that lie upwind from the Nafud. The Nafud is sparsely

inhabited but constitutes an important sea-sonal grazing area.

[7] **Northern Regions.** To the northwest, north, and east is a sequence of varied land-scapes, each with its own identification. In the extreme northwest, at the northern end of the Red Sea, is the rugged area of Midyan (biblical land of Midian), which drops eastward to the plain around the steadily developing military cantonment town of Tabuk. Farther east is the mountain mass of al-Tubayq, which sinks north-eastward to the Wadi al-Sirhan, the great depres-sion extending from al-Azraq in Jordan to the oasis of al-Jawf in Saudi Arabia. The depression is more than 200 miles/322 km long, about 25 miles/40 km wide, and 1,000 ft./305 m below the level of the plateau. The Wadi al-Sirhan gives way on the northeast to the extensive lava fields and cinder cones of al-Harrah, southeast of which extend al-Hamad, al-Widyan, and al-Hajarah, stony plains traversed by the now mothballed Trans-Arabian Pipe Line (Tapline). Southwest of Kuwait is the well-marked Wadi al-Batin and the great gravel plain of the Dibdibah.

Most of these vast northern regions had vir-tually no permanent inhabitants prior to 1950, when the great Tapline spanned the desert wastes and gradually opened the sandy-gravelly plains to development. Towns grew up around the pump stations, and international travelers followed the pipeline track, which was later blacktopped and then upgraded to a major highway. Each of the pump-station towns now exceeds 25,000 in population and functions as a service center for traffic along the long stretches of the highway. The military cantonment of Hafar al-Batin built near Qaysumah has attracted special development and served as a key center for ground forces during the buildup and operations in the Gulf war in 1990–1991.

Population and Peoples

Census-taking in Saudi Arabia is both a com-plicated procedure and a sensitive matter: It is complicated because the population is widely scattered over a large area, Bedouins move frequently and avoid government attention, urban populations shift rapidly, and expatri-ates present special problems of enumeration. Expatriates ("expats") change fairly fre-quently, both individually and in total num-ber, yet Saudis are reluctant to recognize that millions of foreign professionals and workers have been brought in to help develop the king-dom. Also, this land, the cradle of Islam, is averse to acknowledging that perhaps 10 per-cent of the population—however temporary—is non-Muslim. A 1963 sampling suggested a population of about 3.3 million; a 1992 census showed a total of 16,929,294, about 30 percent expatriate; a 1999 estimate indicated more than 21,000,000, including more than 5.5 mil-lion expatriates, and with a growth rate of more than 3 percent.

Saudi Arabia has three principal population nuclei and a few outlying foci, all separated by relatively empty or sparsely settled desert. Most populous of the three population nuclei is Najd, the Saudi heartland, with its node in greater Riyadh, which now has about 2.5 mil-lion inhabitants (Fig. 17-2). Relatively concen-trated Najd settlements extend from Hayil and Buraydah in the north southeastward to al-Kharj in the south, and there are a score of towns of small to medium size in the irrigated depressions on the plateau and along the escarpments, as was mentioned in the para-graph on Region 3, Najd.

In the west, the Hijaz-Asir nucleus aligned on the Jiddah-Mecca-Taif (al-Taif) axis con-tains nearly 4 million people. The extended area reaches from Yanbu and Medina in the north to Jaizan and Najran in the south and includes Abha and Khamis Mushayt in the rapidly developing resort and agricultural Asir. Across the peninsula, the Eastern Province population centers on Dammam Municipality (which includes Qatif, Dammam, Dhahran, al-Khobar, and al-Thuqbah) and has a popula-tion of more than 1.3 million. The extended agglomeration extends from the new indus-trial port city of Jubayl on the north to Hofuf in al-Hasa Oasis on the south and includes

FIGURE 17-2   New Ministry of Interior building, Riyadh. The structure was not quite completed when photographed in 1990. Many of the government and office buildings in the Saudi capital exhibit unusual architectural design.

Qatif Oasis, the oil terminals of Juaymah and Ras Tanura, the coalesced populations of al-Khobar, al-Thuqbah, and Dhahran, and the oil-producing center of Abqaiq.

Outlying centers with sizable populations include Tabuk, in the northwestern corner of the kingdom, with more than 200,000 population; the Hayil Oasis, south of the Nafud, with about 100,000; al-Jawf Oasis, north of the Nafud; settlements along Tapline; and the smaller settlements of al-Khamasin and al-Sulayyil toward the southern end of the Jabal Tuwayq.

Although the indigenous Saudi population is relatively uniform ethnically, it includes diverse tribal affiliations. The number and ethnic variety of expatriate workers and managers also diversify the population. During the thirteen centuries of annual pilgrimage seasons in Mecca, some pilgrims have remained, adding to the Saudi ethnic mixture such cultures as those from the East Indies, Bengal, Punjab, Iran, Morocco, and other Muslim areas. Such diversity is evident in the Hijaz. In coastal Asir, the inhabitants display some African traits, combined with characteristics that are neither typically Arab nor African. In the Qatif and Hofuf oases of the Eastern Province, some inhabitants are descendants of Iranians who settled on the Arabian Peninsula several centuries ago, bringing Shii Islam to the predominantly Sunni peninsula.

Clothing is also traditional and is very much maintained despite material modernization. Males wear the loose-fitting, ankle-length white *thawb* (see Fig. 6-1), similar to the *dishdashah* worn in the Gulf area. In cool weather and on more formal occasions, the flowing cloak (*bisht* or *mishlah*) is worn over the *thawb*. The head covering for both outdoors and indoors is the ubiquitous *ghutrah* and *igal*, the headcloth and double ring of black cord to hold the *ghutrah* (called a *kufiyah* in the Levant) in place. Workers in the oil industry and other industrial plants commonly wear Western-style work pants and shirts during the day. A female in public wears the loose, floor-length *abayah* over her head and body. The *abayah* may cover a dress similar to the male *thawb*, except that it is usually colorful, or it may cover the latest Paris fashion. Any of several types of veil or partial face covering may be added to the *abayah*.

The marginal economy and lack of population unity and security in past centuries prompted many kinship groups to seek localized order in tribalism. Although modernization since the 1950s has weakened this tribalism, a diminished tribal identity retains its validity among many Saudis, especially Bedouins. In this highly traditional society, village organization and tribal affiliation remain basic social factors among both settled and nomadic populations.

Foreign workers were drawn to the oil fields and cities of Saudi Arabia as early as the 1940s, but they arrived in large numbers after the early 1970s. They make up a significant proportion of the population and have exceeded 30 percent of the total for several years. The government meticulously controls who enters, for what reason, and for how long; those entering the kingdom must be sponsored by a responsible local person, company, or institution that the government can hold accountable. The early expatriates were invited to develop the petroleum resources, then later other expatriates were brought to develop the infrastructure and to maintain the going concerns—especially service enterprises—that could not find qualified or willing Saudi employees. Rising standards of living created a demand for millions of custodial and domestic workers, who were available in seemingly unlimited numbers from southeast Asia. For many decades, a rewarding symbiosis had existed between Saudi Arabia and the large Yemeni labor pool, which probably supplied 1.5 million workers to the kingdom in 1990, before they were expelled because of the Yemeni official stance on Iraq's invasion of Kuwait. The Saudi government still maintains a strict policy of denying entry to casual salesmen, fortune seekers, or random tourists; hence the uneasiness of the Saudis over the presence of nearly half a million foreign troops in the kingdom in 1990–1991. Restrictions were, however, lowered in late 1998 to permit organized tour groups to visit the country.

Settlements

Although traditions of nomadism are strong in the Arabian Peninsula, sedentarism preceded nomadism. Until after World War II, the typical pattern of settlement consisted of widely scattered oasis villages and occasional towns in a symbiotic relationship with nomadic Bedouins living in their long rectangular tents. Nor were the two lifestyles mutually exclusive: During severe droughts, Bedouins moved into villages; conversely, villagers—especially former nomads—sometimes moved into the desert. Before the petroleum age in Saudi Arabia, an estimated 60 percent of the population was nomadic. Settlement of the Bedouins has been a deliberate policy of the government of Saudi Arabia since the time of King Abd al-Aziz. The petroleum age also stimulated sedentarization of the nomads, contributing to urbanization. By the 1990s, Bedouins had decreased to less than 4 percent of the population. Permanently settled nomads consider themselves *hadar,* that is, no longer Bedouins.

Since World War II, urbanization has accelerated in Saudi Arabia as elsewhere, with increased growth of cities after the development of the petroleum industry. By 1999, nearly 80 percent of the population was urban. No extensive preindustrial cities had developed in Arabia, and even the largest settlements—Mecca and Medina, for example—were moderate-sized towns of 30,000 population each in the 1930s. Nevertheless, few towns or cities in Saudi Arabia of 2000 exist on completely new sites; even the "new towns" of Jubayl and Yanbu are extensions of earlier villages. Transformation of the Saudi landscape, epitomized in the metamorphosis of the urban landscape, has occurred with minimal outside cognizance; such is one of the drawbacks to the Saudi policy of admitting few Western scholars and reporters. Those who visited Jiddah, Riyadh, and Dammam in the 1950s when all three were small towns with few amenities can only be staggered at what unlimited funds and intelligent planning have accomplished. Many unique, charming, and historic

FIGURE 17-3   Modern high-rise apartment buildings in complex in Jiddah.

structures—palaces, forts, walls, and houses—were unfortunately swept away in the rush to modernize and exploit central locations; many of the buildings, especially in Riyadh, were of mud and could not be saved, although a few major sites have been preserved, most of them in Riyadh and Jiddah. Usually, there was more than enough space in the surrounding desert into which cities could expand.

Traditional Islamic architectural themes have frequently been employed in new urban centers, universities, and museums. A wide variety of contemporary designs have characterized major new structures that, with generous funding, need not employ monotonous modular techniques (Fig. 17-3). Indeed, Saudi structures are a great architectural success when Islamic traditions are combined with other Arabian features in a contemporary mode. In the mountain villages of Asir, exterior house walls typically show alternating courses of mud and projecting rock, with the rock ledges deflecting rain to prevent erosion of the primarily mud walls. Typical building walls in Najd are topped by decorative battlements, vestiges of military architectural features. In Najd, but also in other parts of the country, the wooden doors of many houses are decorated with elaborate geometric designs.

Economic Patterns

Economic patterns in Arabia had remained stable for centuries when discovery of petroleum in 1938 initiated a literally fabulous transformation. Prior to 1938, the remote and generally poor Arabian realm survived on limited pastoralism and oasis agriculture, profits from the Mecca pilgrimage, and meager trade. With modest but increasing oil production after 1945, during the 1950s and 1960s the kingdom caught a glimpse of things to come, then exploded with development during the

1970s. National income from oil sales alone exceeded $300 million per day between 1977 and 1981, supplying billions of dollars for perhaps the most complete transformation of a large country on a grand scale and in a short time in history. Drawing on urban and systems planners, design engineers, architects, contractors, educators, and workers from Western Europe, North America, the Middle East, and South Asia, Saudi Arabia virtually built an entire country from infrastructure to complete university campuses to U.S.-style fast-food shops. Private financing and investment contributed the retail centers, many of the smaller industries, and much of the agricultural expansion.[8]

Much of the development has taken place under a series of five-year plans, with a peak during the $195-billion second plan, 1975–1980, when 28 dams, 4 ports, 175,000 new homes, 15,000 miles/24,000 km of roads, and the Jiddah airport (the world's largest until the opening of the Riyadh airport) were completed. Before and after this period, water projects, industrial developments, petroleum operations, infrastructure, the billion-dollar causeway to Bahrain, and other operations were constructed or greatly expanded. The fourth plan, 1985–1990, had to be curtailed because of the recession that followed the sharp drop in the world oil market in 1982. Saudi oil sales dropped from 9.6 million bpd in 1980 to 3.3 million bpd in 1985, and the price per barrel plummeted from $35–40 per barrel in 1980 to $10–12 per barrel in 1985—both occurring at a time when the value of the U.S. dollar was shrinking. The fifth plan, 1990–1995, budgeted for $100 billion, focused especially on the country's defenses during the Gulf war and only to a lesser extent on improving government social services, developing regional areas, and expanding private-sector employment for Saudis. The sixth plan, 1995–2000, emphasized more efficient government, more training, a more diverse economy—especially in industry and agriculture—and greater Saudiization of the labor force. Each plan sought greater economic diversification to reduce the country's dependence on the oil industry, to increase self-sufficiency and reduce imports, and, in the long range, to develop national viability for the inevitable end of petroleum prosperity when the wells run dry. A secondary goal is to ensure that the enviable and highly efficient infrastructure, systematically developed at the cost of many hundreds of billions of dollars, is properly maintained, repaired, and upgraded.[9]

Agriculture

The percentage share of agriculture in the economy of Saudi Arabia decreased sharply after 1960, falling to only 3 percent in the mid-1970s. It increased to 13 percent a decade later under encouragement of subsidies but gradually slid to 9 percent in the late 1990s. The Saudi government seeks greater self-reliance in agriculture, aiming for a long-range agricultural sufficiency. Such an aim is unrealistic not only in terms of cost-benefit ratio but also in terms of water availability, since Saudi crop production relies overwhelmingly on irrigation. Indeed, over-enthusiastic irrigation in the Najd has already lowered the water table detrimentally (see below). However, rain-fed agriculture dominates in Asir, where highlands intercept summer monsoon rains and the water is efficiently utilized on terraced plots (Fig. 17-1a). As a result of agricultural planning and heavy government subsidizing of wheat and barley crops, the cultivated area increased from 704,000 acres/285,000 ha in 1973 to 3 million acres/1.2 million ha in 1990, with much of the expansion coming in wheat acreage. With the government offering many times the world market price for wheat produced domestically, wheat acreage rocketed from 370,650 acres/150,000 ha to 2.3 million acres/0.93 million ha in 1992. In 1981, wheat production was only 4,000 mt, but in 1992, it was 4.1 million mt.[10] Because only 800,000 mt was needed domestically, the excess was exported or donated. The Najd landscape was completely transformed in the 1980s as hundreds of startlingly green circles of wheat

irrigated by self-propelled center-pivot sprinkler systems appeared against the tawny desert
as large-scale farmers responded to funding by
government subsidies and made the desert
bloom. When the aquifer water level plum-
meted from overuse of water, and cost
accounting showed the real costs involved, the
government decreased subsidies and reduced
quotas. Area in wheat fell by nearly two-thirds
and in 1997–1999 was steady at 830,256 acres/
336,000 ha and production at 1.8 million mt.

Of the many oases in the kingdom, the two
largest—both in the Eastern Province—are classic examples. Hofuf (al-Hasa) Oasis,[11] the largest
on the peninsula and considered to be the largest
groundwater-fed oasis in the world, is watered
by 159 springs, including 8 major artesian
springs (*ayns*) that flow a total of more than
1,900 gal./7,190 l per second. The largest single
spring has a flow of 475 gal./1,800 l per second.
A major project in the early 1970s modernized
and systematized the oasis irrigation and
drainage, replacing ditches with concrete conduits. Qatif (or al-Qatif) Oasis, a few miles north
of Dammam, received much of the same modernization achieved in al-Hasa. Both oases have
been improved and upgraded in successive
development projects. Large areas of former date
palm groves are now devoted to fruit trees and
vegetable production in plastic greenhouses.

Although their number is decreasing, many
thousands of Bedouins still pursue a nomadic
life-style and continue to supply animals and
animal products to the Saudi economy. Increasing numbers of Bedouin families divide their
time between desert nomadism and crop raising or other economic pursuits in villages on
the perimeters of their tribal *dirahs*. As have
nomads in other parts of the Middle East,
many Saudi Bedouins have installed electric
generators and television sets in their tents,
their pickup trucks parked alongside.

Water resource studies have yielded approxi-
mations of the water balance, permitting systematic efforts for more effective use of
renewable water resources. Hydrogeological
studies reveal that much of the deep aquifer
water in the Najd is "fossil water," stored as long

ago as 40,000 years, and that water in the relatively shallow aquifers of the Eastern Province
is 18,000–28,000 years old. Thus, withdrawing
water from such aquifers amounts to "mining"
nonrenewable resources, and systematic efforts
must be made to substitute renewable water for
fossil water, in the production of subsidized
wheat, for example.

Fundamental to the agricultural development program has been a series of water development projects that added more than 200
dams, several hundred deep wells, and many
miles of irrigation conduits. Most of the dams
were constructed in the regions of Najd, and
particularly Asir, where the Wadi Bisha dam is
one of largest in the Middle East outside Turkey
and Egypt.

Domestic supplies and irrigation systems
rely also on the desalination of seawater. Availability of large amounts of fuel prompted the
initiation in 1965 of a massive construction
program of large-scale desalination plants, of
which there were 26 by the end of 1999 (20 on
the Red Sea and 6 on the Gulf) with a capacity
of 2 million m³ (529 million gals/2 billion l). By
1999, desalted water, blended with brackish
groundwater, supplied about 70 percent of
home use in major cities. The Jubayl plant on
the Gulf coast is the biggest in the world and
pumps millions of gallons per day of distilled
water to Riyadh. Saudi Arabia leads the world
in the production of potable water by desalting
seawater. Nevertheless, in some cities, prodigal
use of domestic water creates severe shortages
in the summer months. In Jiddah, for example,
water has been unavailable for days at a time in
some quarters, although increased capacity has
been added. One problem is that potable water,
like many commodities, is heavily subsidized,
often not metered, and often wasted.

Fishing

Important on both coasts, fishing has been
especially developed on the east coast. Traditional fishing methods have been replaced by
modernized techniques and equipment, with
ships operating primarily out of Dammam, and

there are processing and freezing plants in Dammam and al-Khobar. Additional facilities are opening in the new port and industrial city of Jubayl. With all of the Gulf littoral states intensifying fishing efforts, overfishing has occurred, and the total Gulf catch peaked in 1967–1968.

Petroleum Industry

Beneath the deserts of eastern Arabia, the world's largest petroleum reserves lay unrecognized until the 1930s.[12] King Abd al-Aziz granted a concession for oil exploration to a British financial syndicate in 1923, but the syndicate did not pursue exploration and lost the concession. In 1933, the king granted Standard Oil of California (Socal) the exclusive right to prospect for and produce oil in eastern Arabia, along with preferential rights in other parts of the kingdom, for a period of 60 years—later extended for an additional six years. A new subsidiary, California Arabian Standard Oil Company (Casoc), was assigned the concession in 1934 and was converted to 50–50 ownership by Socal (which later became Chevron) and the Texas Company in 1937. In 1944 Casoc was renamed Arabian American Oil Company, with the now world-famous acronym Aramco, which is still used even for the Saudi-owned company. In 1948, the Standard Oil Company of New Jersey (later renamed Esso and still later Exxon) and the Socony-Vacuum Oil Company (later named Mobil) joined in the Aramco ownership. The four owner companies remained the all-U.S. capital and technical forces behind oil development in mainland Saudi Arabia until 1973.

Socal started drilling in April 1935 in Dammam Dome, near the Gulf coast, and production began in March 1938. The first oil was loaded in May 1939 at Ras Tanura, which was later developed into one of the world's great oil export terminals. Exploration for new fields—which still continues—soon showed that the Eastern Province contained the leading fields in the world. The first segment of Ghawar, the world's largest oil field, was found in 1948;

Safaniya, the largest offshore field in the world, in 1951. By 1998, 72 commercial fields had been discovered (see Maps 8-1 and 8-2), five in 1990 alone. More than 80 billion barrels had been produced just by Aramco since 1938, yet reserves were 259 billion barrels in 1999 and were expected to increase; reserves of nonassociated natural gas exceeded 204 trillion ft.^{3}/ 15.8 trillion m^3 (fourth-largest in the world); and major projects were under way to upgrade scores of facilities all over the kingdom.

In 1973, Saudi Arabia assumed 25 percent ownership of Aramco's rights and facilities. Government participation increased to 60 percent in 1974 and to 100 percent in 1980. Officially designated the Saudi Arabian Oil Company, or Saudi Aramco, in 1988, Aramco continues to be known in the industry by its familiar 48-year-old acronym. Aramco continues as operator for Saudi production and as intermediate contractor for a range of engineering and construction projects. The company served such a function as early as 1949, overseeing construction of the Saudi government Dammam-Riyadh railway, and more recently by overseeing implementation of the Master Gas Plan. Aramco took its first major step into overseas downstream operations in 1988 through a joint venture with Texaco for refining, distributing, and marketing petroleum products in the eastern and Gulf Coast regions of the United States. It has since purchased or joined enterprises in South Korea and other Asian countries. The fundamental structure and function of Saudi Aramco changed greatly during the 1990s consequent to a Royal Decree of July 1, 1993. Because it was entirely government-owned, it was charged with all government oil operations in the kingdom, upstream and downstream, from exploration to marketing. It took over Tapline (originally a separate company), Petroline, and all government-owned refineries and Petromin marketing outlets formerly under Samarec. Saudi Aramco's reserves, production capacity, production facilities, transport lines, markets, and work force size (58,000) make it one of the four largest integrated oil companies in the world.

Although Aramco manages 95 percent of the production for Saudi Arabia, two other companies operate in the Saudi half of the Divided Zone, the former Kuwait-Saudi Neutral Zone. The U.S.-owned Texas Company holds the concession for the land area (formerly held by Getty Oil Company), and the Japanese-owned Arabian Oil Company (AOC) holds the offshore concession. The territory of the zone, which was partitioned in 1965 and demarcated in 1970, was divided roughly equally between Kuwait and Saudi Arabia. On a similar basis, the two countries agreed to share equally the oil reserves of the zone and to divide proceeds from oil produced there. Proved reserves of the entire zone total 5 billion barrels, and production averaged 521,000 bpd in 1996–1998.

As sole operator in its concession area, Aramco needed to drill and produce only the optimum number of wells; even after 60 years, none of the wells requires pumping. One reason for maintenance of reservoir pressure is the use of a huge water injection system, in which more than 10 million bbl of nonpotable water a day is pumped into major reservoirs as oil is withdrawn; much of the water is brought by three large pipelines 60 miles/100 km from the Gulf. Only about 1,400 flowing wells produce up to 9 million bpd in Saudi Arabia, thus averaging approximately 6,425 bpd each. The kingdom actually produced an average 7.5 million bpd in mid-1999, down from 8.5 million a year earlier.

Handling, transporting, and processing the petroleum require a complex of facilities distributed across eastern Arabia—strung together with more than 13,050 miles/21,000 km of pipelines. Each of more than 60 gas-oil separator plants (GOSPs) serves several wells in a considerable radius via flowlines, each showing its fiery flare—now reduced to conserve natural gas—against the sky. Stabilizers in Abqaiq and Juaymah "sweeten" sour crude, and natural gas liquids (NGL) plants produce propane, butane, and natural gasoline. There are also numerous large petroleum-related industrial plants along the Gulf coast, especially in the new industrially specialized city of Jubayl. Huge oil-export terminals operate at

Ras Tanura and Juaymah, with crude and product storage capacities of 30 million bbl and 25 million bbl respectively, as well as at Yanbu on the Red Sea, with 12.5 million bbl storage capacity—twice the average daily production of the United States.

In the east, large refineries operate in Ras Tanura, 300,000 bpd, and Jubayl, 292,999; in the west, in Rabigh, 325,000; Yanbu—with two plants—366,000 and 190,000; in Najd, Riyadh, 140,000. Including two smaller refineries in Jiddah and Ras al-Khafji, the kingdom has eight facilities with a total throughput of 1,685,000 bpd.

As Chapter 8 explained, the great Trans-Arabian Pipe Line (Tapline) that opened in 1951 was beset by political problems and became unprofitable during the 1970s. It ceased delivering 450,000 bpd to Sidon in 1983, but continued small deliveries of 60,000 bpd to the Zarqa refinery in Jordan; these also ceased in 1990, and Tapline has been mothballed since then. However, the Saudis revived the concept of an outlet to the west for strategic insurance against the potential dangers of Gulf shipping and the Hormuz choke point. This led to billion-dollar spanning of the peninsula, from the eastern fields to Yanbu on the Red Sea, with three pipelines during the 1980s: The East-West natural gas liquids (NGL) pipeline, 726 miles/ 1,170 km long and 26–30 in./66–76 cm in diameter, was commissioned in March 1981; and the East-West crude oil pipelines, one 48 in./122 cm in diameter, was commissioned in July 1981, and a "loop" of this line that is a huge 56 in./ 142 cm in diameter was commissioned in 1987—both are 745 miles/1,200 km long. (The IPSA pipeline is a separate Iraqi project; see Chap. 16.) The addition of pumps and the expansion of facilities at each end of this East-West crude oil system in 1991 raised its capacity to nearly 5 million bpd—ten times Tapline's capacity and half of Aramco's production capacity. The parallel NGL line carries 270,000 bpd of ethane and natural gas liquids. These transpeninsula systems afford the Saudis an entirely domestic, secure route that reduces the threat of a cutoff of Saudi exports. The Saudis are, however, still subject to an interdiction of their exports from Yanbu at either end of the Red Sea.

In the late 1970s, Saudi Arabia undertook the ambitious Master Gas System. Associated gas that was formerly flared after being separated from oil in gas-oil separator plants (GOSPs) now supplies power generating stations, water desalination plants, numerous factories, and domestic lines. Huge reservoirs of nonassociated gas—including deep Khuff gas under the great Ghawar oil field—are increasingly yielding gas for the new industrial cities of Jubayl and Yanbu as fuel and feedstock for oil refineries, petrochemical and fertilizer plants, steel plants and rolling mills, and other industries, as well as for large-scale exports. Now collecting and processing more than 4.5 billion ft.^{3}/130 million m^3 of gas per day, the system can add the equivalent of more than 1 million barrels of crude oil a day to the world's supply of energy.

Saudi Arabia was a charter member of both OPEC and OAPEC (see Chap. 8) and has played a particularly major role in OPEC since its founding. As Saudi production constituted an increasingly greater share of the OPEC and world totals, the country played a "swing role" in influencing the world price of petroleum by varying its output for several years. However, the kingdom now presses for fruitful adherence to OPEC quotas by all members, which successfully stabilized the price during late 1999 in the range of $22–$25 per barrel. The price spiked to more than $33 in early 2000, which led OPEC to increase production and induced Saudi Arabia to pump an additional 500,000 bpd. The price slowly decreased in July.

Other Industries

In the 1950s, manufacturing expanded after four key developments: expansion and diversification of oil operations and the industry work force; rapid increase in population and consumer demand; growing availability of private and government capital; and increasing foreign company joint ventures with Saudi partners—including the Saudi government. Successive decades saw a marked increase in the number, size, and diversity of producing establishments. At first they turned out processed foods, paper and plastic items, clothing, and basic furniture. After the early 1970s, they added items such as paints, air-conditioners, aluminum prefabricated buildings, steel rods, and an increasing number of products using oil and gas as feedstocks and fuel. These latter items include fertilizers, petrochemicals and other chemicals, and by-product sulfur. The country still lacks sophisticated industries in such fields as electronics, optics, and other precision goods.

Saudi Arabia, with an earlier shortage of indigenous technological experience and trained labor, relied on overseas contractors for technology, equipment, services, and labor for construction and industrialization projects—often on a turn-key basis (see Chap. 9). For many major projects, the contracts were on a build-operate-maintain (BOM) basis. However, educational and vocational programs by contractors have provided more trained local workers, and "Saudiization" of establishments is raising the percentage of Saudis in the labor force. More important is the large-scale development of education, including technical training, under the six five-year plans. The University of Petroleum and Minerals in Dhahran (Fig. 17-4) is a major example of the several universities established during the last four decades.

Investing the high petrodollar income of the 1970s, Saudi Arabia constructed the two model industrial and port cities mentioned earlier, Jubayl on the Gulf coast and Yanbu on the Red Sea coast. Focusing on industries based on oil and gas, both cities have oil refineries and plants producing petrochemicals and other chemicals, fertilizers, plastics, steel, and plastic and metal goods. Facilities at Jubayl and Yanbu now include ports and airports, huge dual-purpose systems that combine seawater desalination and power generation, and satellite industrial and consumer goods plants. Integrated planning and construction included both service and residential sectors in contemporary architectural designs.[13]

FIGURE 17-4   University of Petroleum and Minerals in Dhahran, Eastern Province. Built in the 1960s on a stretch of sand and rock south of Aramco headquarters, it was the first of several new universities built in Saudi Arabia with some of the rising oil income and represents the plans for a modernized and technological segment in Saudi society.

By the early 1990s, manufacturing contributed more than 9 percent to the GDP. Many incentives attracted both local capital and joint ventures by foreign companies. A government agency, the Saudi Arabian Basic Industries Corporation (SABIC), was established in 1976 to develop large petrochemical and steel plants; it has achieved major goals. By 1999, the government reported that 2,537 factories were capitalized at $42 billion and that petrochemical facilities were the most rapidly expanding industry.

Transportation

Highways.   With sparse population and a preindustrial economy, Arabia before the mid-twentieth century had no road network to move people and goods over the deserts. The camel continued to be the common mode of transport, especially of goods, until after World War II. A limited number of automobiles drove across the open deserts, following old caravan routes, but they often foundered in deep sand before the development of four-wheel drive and sand tires.

Increasing petroleum development called for an expanded road net, and the first surfaced roads linked the main towns and oil facilities in the Eastern Province. Highway construction reached a peak during the early 1980s; by the early 1990s highways extended to every town, and remote villages were tied into the network by branch rural roads (see Map 9-2). A four-lane divided highway connects the Red Sea and Gulf (Jiddah-Mecca-Riyadh-Dammam), with a spur to Medina in the west and another to Unayzah and Buraydah in the northern Najd. At the Gulf end, the highway crosses a 15.5-mile/ 25-km causeway from al-Khobar to Bahrain that was opened in 1986 (see Fig. 9-5a). The causeway carries unbroken lines of cars on Thursdays and Fridays, the Saudi weekend. It has been so successful that preliminary planning is under way for a 9.2-mile/14.9-km causeway across the Strait of Tiran to connect Saudi Arabia and the Sinai Peninsula of Egypt. Tiran Island would serve as the midway connection.

Air Facilities. Population concentrations widely separated by barren deserts encouraged the use of air transportation in preference to railways and roads in the early years of the country's development. Saudia, the national airline, founded in 1945 and evolved originally under a management contract with the U.S. airline TWA, has expanded to become the largest airline in the Middle East, with more than 80 jet aircraft serving a worldwide traffic net. A ten-year airport building program has supplied all cities and major towns in the country with modern airports, their runways accommodating at least medium-sized jet aircraft. By the late 1990s, more than 200 airports, 25 with regular commercial service, served Saudi cities and towns.

Between 1981 and 1984, Saudi Arabia opened two new international airports, the first in Jiddah, the second in Riyadh. They are the two largest airports in the world: Jiddah's covers 40 miles^2/103 km^2 and includes a separate facility for the more than 2 million pilgrims who arrive by air for the annual ten-day religious pilgrimage to nearby Mecca. Nearly three times the size of the Jiddah airport, the opulent Riyadh airport was opened in 1984. They are the two busiest air hubs in the Middle East after Cairo. In 1999, a huge new airport opened in the Eastern Province, 22 miles/57 km northwest of Dammam, replacing the kingdom's first modern airport in Dhahran.

Railways. The Saudi Government Railroad, opened in 1951, links the port of Dammam with Riyadh via Hofuf, Harad, and al-Kharj. This 360-mile/580-km link was the sole operating rail line in the kingdom—and the entire peninsula—for 30 years. In 1985, the government's General

Saudi Railways Organization opened a new dual line that ran directly between Dammam and Riyadh, avoided the Harad loop, and shortened the trip by 20 percent. An additional 62-mile/100-km rail line is under construction between Dammam and Jubayl, and other lines are under consideration. The legendary Hijaz Railway is disused in Saudi Arabia (see Chap. 9).

Ports and Shipping. Beginning in the 1950s, the earliest infrastructural preparation for the enormous development ahead was the expansion of ports on both sides of the peninsula. Jiddah had for centuries served as the entry port for pilgrims to nearby Mecca as well as for cargo for the Hijaz towns. When dredging through coral reefs and the manifold expansions of docks, handling facilities, and storage areas were completed, Jiddah became one of the leading ports in the Middle East for containerized and bulk cargo. A new pilgrim terminal, Jiddah Islamic Port, has been added to its facilities. Dammam evolved into the Gulf coast equivalent of Jiddah. Large, newer specialized ports were built during 1975–1985 in the Industrial Cities of Jubayl on the Gulf and Yanbu on the Red Sea. As was noted earlier, two of the world's largest oil export terminals were developed in Ras Tanura and Juaymah, followed by Yanbu on the west.

Trade

Formerly limited by the sparse and low-income population, domestic trade in Saudi Arabia has become a significant segment of a large economy involving an affluent population of avid consumers. The traditional Middle East *suq*, with multiple small, specialized shops, characterized Saudi Arabian marketing into the late 1950s. As consumer spending boomed, stimulated by Western retailing practices, outlets also changed; urban shops became larger and typical of those in Western cities. The Jamjoon Center in Jiddah and two new opulent complexes in Riyadh, Faysaliyah and Kingdom Center, are the equal in facilities and inventory of almost any shopping mall in North America.

True, Westerners find it disconcerting when shops, including restaurants, close for about 30 minutes several times a day for prayer time. In small settlements, open-air *suqs* still thrive. The large, well-stocked supermarkets that operate in every city offer most brands of products on the international market as well as many specialty products favored by expatriates from southeast Asian countries. Fresh fruits and vegetables arrive by road and air from horticultural centers as far as 1,500 miles/2,410 km away. As in the Gulf area, large automobile dealerships offer major makes of cars, and Saudis are very much an automobile-minded society.

Saudi Arabia's imports are diversified by both type and source. Imports range from heavy equipment used by oil companies and contractors to large amounts of armaments and military support equipment to a wide variety of consumer products including automobiles, electronic equipment, and food. Saudi exports were formerly 99 percent petroleum and petroleum products but are becoming increasingly diversified (see country summary). Saudi Arabia now ranks as both the world's leading producer and the world's leading exporter of petroleum. The United States imports more than 1.5 million bpd from Saudi Arabia, equaling imports from Canada and Venezuela. Oil exports, which are about 700,000 bpd less than production figures (see Chap. 8), rose from about 2 million bpd in the early 1960s to an average of nearly 9 million bpd in 1979–1981, fell to less than half that total in 1988, then averaged about 7 million bpd in late 1999. Major export destinations were the United States, Japan, Singapore, France, and others. Major suppliers of the kingdom's imports are the United States, Japan, and Britain. In 1999 Saudi Arabia was negotiating accession to the World Trade Organization (WTO).

Relations

The Kingdom of Saudi Arabia has, since its inception in 1932, maintained generally peaceful relations with its eight neighbors, although not uniformly so. Prior to the 1990–1991 Gulf crisis,

the most notable exceptions were a short war with Yemen in 1934, a dispute with Abu Dhabi and Oman over the Buraymi Oasis during the 1940s and 1950s, and tensions over Saudi support of the imam of Inner Oman against the sultan of Oman during the late 1950s and 1960s. The kingdom has also had running disputes with Qatar over their mutual boundary. Border problems have similarly created periodic tensions with the UAE, Oman, and Yemen, but they have been smoothed out (see Chap. 11). Saudi co-membership in the Gulf Cooperation Council (GCC) and other shared developments have warmed relations with Qatar, UAE, and Oman. In addition to tensions (eased in mid-2000) over the 1,300-mile/2,100-km border, frictions with Yemen arose from Saudi Arabia's having supported the royalists during the 1962–1969 civil war, as well as from Saudi efforts to hinder unification of the two Yemens in 1990. Border discords flared during the 1990s; there was even a one-day battle in July 1998 over the tiny island of Duwaima.[14] Yemen's refusal to condemn Iraq's invasion of Kuwait (Yemen was a rotating member of the UN Security Council at the time) caused Saudi ire, and hundreds of thousands of Yemeni workers in Saudi Arabia were forced to return home. Similarly, Jordan's ambivalent stance regarding Saddam Husayn derailed the rapport that had evolved between the two moderate monarchies. Saudi Arabia ceased large-scale financial support of Jordan, major purchases from Jordan, supplying crude oil via Tapline, and the hiring of thousands of Jordanians.

Saudi Arabia is an active participant in and headquarters for the GCC. Saudi support for Iraq in its war against Iran beginning in 1980 was both financial and political, including the agreement for the IPSA pipeline from southern Iraq to extend across the kingdom to the Red Sea just south of Yanbu. Saudi Arabia turned bitterly against Saddam Husayn after he invaded Kuwait in 1990, and it closed the IPSA line, supplied bases for the coalition forces against Iraq, and joined in the coalition. During the 1990s Saudi Arabia supported general enforcement of sanctions against Iraq but balked at the heavier attacks in December 1998 and during much of 1999. Conversely, Saudi Arabia has had good relations with Kuwait, sharing the Divided Zone and assisting Kuwait on a grand scale when it was invaded by Iraq in 1990. Good Saudi-Bahraini relations are evident in the fact that modest amounts of Saudi crude oil have been pumped to Bahrain for refining from the early years, as well as the facts of a 1960 agreement to divide the income from the offshore Abu Safah field near their median line and the agreement on a causeway, financed by Saudi Arabia and completed in 1986, linking Bahrain to the mainland.

Financial support from Saudi Arabia and the other Gulf states had for several years been the Palestine Liberation Organization's main source of income, although some of the actions conducted under the PLO umbrella contrasted with Saudi Arabia's basically nonviolent political philosophy and moderate stance. Although the PLO lost that support when PLO Chairman Yasir Arafat chose not to condemn Saddam Husayn's invasion of Kuwait, an outward rapprochement was later reached between the Saudi government and the PLO.

Saudi Arabia plays a low-key leadership role in the Middle East, based on religious, economic, and political influence. In addition to its role of protecting the holy cities of Mecca and Medina and administering the annual pilgrimage, Saudi Arabia provides funding for Islamic institutions, including a new Islamic University in Asyut, Egypt. The country also contributes from its oil income to less wealthy countries of the region, and the rapid development in Saudi Arabia provides employment and worker remittances for other economies.

Overall, British-Saudi relations have remained good, with Britain filling multibillion-dollar Saudi arms contracts after U.S. sales to Saudi Arabia halted because of pressure by pro-Israeli groups. Increasing numbers of British are serving in a wide range of professional, managerial, and technical capacities, especially as more British military equipment is utilized in the kingdom. British are also steadily replacing Americans in many such positions. In addition,

Saudi Arabia through the GCC is drawing closer to the EU in general.

Saudi Arabia's close relations with the United States began with Aramco's exploration for and production of petroleum after the late 1930s. Thousands of U.S. employees and their dependents have lived in Aramco camps for decades, devoting their entire working lives to the ongoing project. Both Aramco and its four U.S. corporate owners before 1973 maintained excellent relations with the provincial and central government.

The United States and Saudi Arabia also cooperate in other technical areas: The United States Geological Survey (USGS) conducted geological and mineral studies in the western shield area for many years and cooperated in the production of geographical and geological maps of the shield. In 1974, a U.S.-Saudi Arabia Joint Commission for Economic Cooperation, funded by the Saudi Arabian government and still operating, was established for research into economic issues of mutual interest and for technical economic assistance. The United States depends on Saudi Arabia for an appreciable percentage of its oil imports, averaging 14 percent in late 1999. As many as 65,000 U.S. citizens lived and worked in the kingdom in the early 1980s, but the number fell to half that in the late 1980s before rising again to about 40,000 after the Gulf war.

In 1942, King Abd al-Aziz agreed to the construction of a U.S. air base south of Dhahran, which became a combined military-civilian airfield, replaced in 1999 by a huge new airport farther north. In 1953, the United States Military Training Mission (USMTM) began training elements of the Saudi air force, army, and navy, and that program continues. The United States has also been the kingdom's major supplier of military equipment and services—amounting to billions of dollars annually— including consultant and supervisory services by the U.S. Army Corps of Engineers for military construction. As is mentioned elsewhere, the Saudi government compensated the U.S. government $16.8 billion in war costs during the 1990–1991 Gulf crisis, in addition to supplying airfields, facilities, and millions of gallons of drinking water without charge. After the end of the Gulf war, about 5,000 U.S. troops remained in the kingdom as rapid deployment forces in case Saddam Husayn attacked again. The ambivalence of the regional reaction to a non-Muslim military presence, especially American, in Muslim lands has been demonstrated in various ways. Car bomb attacks on U.S. military facilities killed 7 Americans in Riyadh November 14, 1995, and 19 Americans in the Khobar Towers June 25, 1996. U.S. forces have been rather segregated, some in remote areas, for security reasons and to avoid cultural conflicts. Moreover, inevitably, there have been misgivings on both sides because of the "special relationship" between the United States and Israel. The kingdom supports a peaceful resolution of the Arab-Israeli conflict but is firm in its support of justice for the Palestinians and UN Resolution 242 calling for Israel's withdrawal from territories occupied in 1967.

Saudi Arabia's intentions to broaden its contacts in the world were demonstrated in the early 1990s when the kingdom established diplomatic relations with the long-shunned former Soviet Union and China; reestablished relations with Iran, which had been broken off in 1988; and indicated plans to exchange diplomats with East European countries. Saudi Arabia was also a charter member of the United Nations, and it is particularly active in some of that organization's specialized affiliated agencies such as the International Monetary Fund and the World Bank.

Notes

1. One of the first Saudi monographs on the country's archaeology is the elaborately illustrated al-Ansary 1982. Whalen and Pease 1992 discusses the Developed Oldowan tool findings.

2. The history of the interior of the Arabian Peninsula was little known until oil developments brought Arabia to world attention, and accurate, detailed history of the area is still limited. Useful concise accounts are in *Saudi Arabia* Country Study 1995 and Saudi Arabian Oil Company 1995. For more details, see Holden and Johns 1982 and Lacey 1981. Some popular accounts are fanciful or spiteful.

3. These reforms and the Council are analyzed in Dekmejian 1998.

4. *Country Commercial Guide: Saudi Arabia,* FY 1999.

5. Coverage of Arabian regions and physical aspects is in Ministry of Agriculture and Water 1984; U.S. Geological Survey 1966–1967, 1975, and 1989; McKee 1979; Holm 1960; Brown and Coleman 1972; Brown 1972; Scoville 1979; Saudi Arabian Oil Company 1995; and Farsi 1989.

6. Shamekh 1975 discusses Bedouins in the Qasim, and Altorki and Cole 1989 discusses development connected with Unayzah.

7. The readable Thesiger 1959 on the Rub al-Khali realm has become a classic.

8. The rapidly changing development of Saudi Arabia must be followed closely in relevant periodicals. It is well covered in the *Middle East Economic Survey* and the *Middle East Economic Digest. Country Commercial Guide: Saudi Arabia,* FY 1999, is excellent. Comprehensive statistics are given in the Kingdom of Saudi Arabia *Statistical Year Book.* Oil developments are given in the authoritative *Saudi Aramco,* 1995; *EIA: Saudi Arabia,* 1999; *Minerals Yearbook: Saudi Arabia,* 1997; Exxon 1984; Woodward 1988; Ali 1987; Nabir 1988; and Saudi *Aramco Annual Report.*

9. See Krimly 1999 and *Background Notes: Saudi Arabia,* Sept. 1998.

10. Krimly 1999 and <http://apps.fao.org/>.

11. See the well-regarded Vidal 1955, although the oases have been greatly transformed since the study was made.

12. The history, development, and current situation of the Saudi oil industry is authoritatively covered in *Saudi Aramco* 1995. Other sidelights are in Yergin 1991. For current information see *EIA: Saudi Arabia,* 1999.

13. See Pampanini 1997.

14. *New York Times,* July 26, 1998.

18

The Gulf
and Its Oil States

The body of water almost enclosed between the Arabian Peninsula and the Iranian coast is variously designated as the Persian Gulf, Arabian Gulf, Persian/Arabian Gulf, or increasingly, simply the Gulf. By whatever name, it has become well known because of its regional oil resources and because of its place in news headlines during the tanker war of 1987–1988 and the Gulf crisis of 1990–1991. Whatever else may be said of them, Desert Shield and Desert Storm left no doubt about the explosive significance of the geopolitics of the Gulf region. However, prior to the 1930s, the Gulf region was little recognized in the Western world other than by a few British officials and adventurers. Remote, isolated, and poverty-ridden, the area was characterized in 1928 by one British official: "The amenities of life are few and far between. Nature is in her fiercest humour and man has done little to improve upon her handiwork."[1]

Nevertheless, between 1960 and 1985, the span of one generation, the coast of the Arabian Peninsula from Kuwait to Muscat underwent a dramatic transformation. Former villages mushroomed into cities with populations 50, 100, and 150 times those of 1928, including Kuwait, Dammam, al-Khobar, Doha, Abu Dhabi, Dubai, Sharjah, and Muscat-Matrah. Once-impoverished indigenous peoples along that coast now have some of the highest per capita incomes in the world.

Although "nature is in her fiercest humour" even yet, "man" has done a great deal to improve upon nature's handiwork. Billions of petrodollars have covered the huge costs of building impressive new cities and ports and, which is more amazing, finding (or "manufacturing") and

transporting water for urban domestic supplies and for irrigating parks and gardens. With enormous amounts of energy available from local gas and oil supplies, air-conditioning makes the temperature inside virtually any structure comfortable. Albeit most of the commodities and much of the labor are imported, few of the conveniences and comforts of contemporary living are lacking along the Gulf littoral.[2]

Earlier chapters covered several functional aspects of the Gulf: its physical characteristics, influence on climate, role in the petroleum industry, strategic aspects, organization in the GCC, and maritime function. Now it is time to examine the regional characteristics of the smaller states along the western coast of the Gulf: Kuwait, Bahrain, Qatar, and the United Arab Emirates (UAE).[3]

A Glance at History

Neolithic sites have been found in several locations around the Gulf, including a number of presently barren desert areas of the Qatar Peninsula, and artifacts from rather intensive archaeological explorations conducted since the 1950s are now on exhibit in handsome museums in all the Gulf littoral states. Archaeological finds substantiate an established sea traffic through the Gulf and eastward to the Indus Valley from about 2300 BC, with another peak during Babylonian times. With its gushing artesian springs, Bahrain was an important way station in ancient times for Gulf mariners sailing between the Indus Valley and Mesopotamia. A famous transit of this same sea-lane was made by Nearchus, Alexander the

Great's military commander, as he returned from Alexander's expedition to the Indus Valley in 325 BC. Romans mastered the difficulties of sailing with the monsoons to and from India but utilized the Red Sea rather than the Gulf.

Islamic civilization and its maritime trade reinvigorated the economic significance of the Gulf after the eighth century. From this period came the tales of Sinbad the Sailor, woven around voyages that began and ended in the Gulf. The basin's economic importance relapsed in the thirteenth century but revived with the arrival of Portuguese ships in the Gulf in 1514, after the opening of the route around southern Africa. Drawn by the wealth of Persia under the Safavid shah, Abbas the Great, Dutch and British ships supplanted those of the Portuguese. Expanding Ottoman power coalesced with the Dutch and British bridgeheads in the Gulf, and Basrah, Bushehr (Bushire), Bahrain, Bandar-e Abbas, Hormuz, and other Gulf ports were thriving trade centers and entrepots during most periods after the early 1600s. By the early 1800s, British economic, military, and political dominance extended along almost the entire Gulf littoral, with the exception of the stretch of coast from Kuwait Bay south to the Qatar Peninsula.

By the end of the 1920s, southwestern Iran was a British "sphere of influence"; Iraq was a British mandate; and Kuwait, Bahrain, Qatar, the Trucial States, and Muscat and Oman were all either official British protectorates or under British influence. The British installed navigational aids (Persian Gulf Lighting Service) and undertook surveying, charting, and mapping of both the Gulf and its coasts and the Tigris and Karun rivers. The later British role and withdrawal from the Gulf, as well as the emergence of independent Gulf states, are discussed in Chapter 11 and in following sections.

A Glance at Gulf Oil

In 1999, oil reserves in the eight producers facing the Gulf totaled 662 billion bbl, 64 percent of the world's reserves; and average daily output of the eight during the late 1990s totaled 20

million bbl. Of these totals, the four smaller Gulf states covered in this chapter show reserves of 200.66 million bbl during the decade 1976–1985, and an average production of 4.4 million bpd during 1999. The numerous producing oil and gas fields in and around the Gulf are shown in Map 8-2, which in addition indicates the large number of fields that are completely or partially offshore. Map 8-2 also shows the numerous Gulf oil terminals, several of which rank among the world's largest: Ras Tanura, Juaymah, Mina al-Ahmadi, and—before the Iran-Iraq war and again after 1992—Kharg Island. A general discussion of the Gulf petroleum industry is included in Chapter 8, and additional details are given in Chapter 17 and under the individual countries below.[4]

A Geopolitical Perspective

Intra-Gulf Relations.   Regionally, the Gulf has long served both as an arena of contention and conflict and as a theater of peaceful trade and regional intercourse. For most of the past 150 years, partly under the aegis of the *Pax Britannica,* the littoral states have usually been willing to seek nonmilitary resolutions to discord in the Gulf. Most of the clashes that have taken place have occurred in the hinterland—over water sources, grazing rights, dynastic disputes, or territorial consolidation—rather than over the Gulf as such. However, Gulf states have periodically disputed control of offshore islands, access to pearl beds, and freedom of navigation. Rulers of the city-states of the southern Gulf shore have clashed over access to and control of wells and springs in the desert, and Bahrain and Qatar have contended for two centuries over dynastic and territorial questions. The Buraymi Oasis dispute is one of the classic conflicts among the modern Gulf states.

The extensive petroleum fields of the Gulf trough frequently lie astride political boundaries, onshore and offshore, but conflicting claims regarding land and maritime boundaries affecting parts or all of certain fields have been settled surprisingly amicably. Britain has sometimes served as arbiter, and the United States conducted a cross-Gulf survey in the mid-1960s for peaceful delineation of a median line in the central Gulf. One unsettled offshore boundary problem—affecting Kuwait, Iraq, and Iran—involves the equitable division of offshore oil resources at the head of the Gulf. In a second such conflict, Bahrain and Qatar dispute ownership of islands and waters between them.

By far the most serious conflicts in the Gulf region since World War II have been the protracted Iran-Iraq war, 1980–1988, and the Gulf crisis of 1990–1991, both sparked by Iraqi aggression that backfired (see Chap. 11). The beginnings of the Iran-Iraq war continued the historical land conflict along the line of disjunction between the Zagros Mountain belt and the Mesopotamian Basin, two major power foci of the Middle East. The Iraqi invasion of Kuwait was more complicated, but, inter alia, it was one of a series of events that manifested a resurgence of the Mesopotamian power focus.

Global Perspective. However, because the Gulf Basin countries possess 64 percent of the world's petroleum resources and produce between one-fourth and one-third of the world's daily oil output to energize much of the world's industry and transportation, the Gulf's geopolitical interactions extend to virtually every part of the inhabited world. Such extension was clearly demonstrated when nearly 30 governments joined the coalition to liberate Kuwait and restore stability in the upper Gulf in 1990–1991. The troubled waters of the Gulf are an unstable chessboard on which every energy-dependent country must try for at least checkmate. This subject has been examined in Chapters 8 and 11 and will be touched on again in this chapter.[5]

Kuwait

Kuwait Fort and Port

Originally a small port and trade center, the town of Kuwait historically took advantage of its geographical location on a deep coastal indentation that facilitated maritime activities and a modest land trade (Map 18-1). Its name is from the Arabic *kuwayt* ("little fort," from *kut*, "fort"). Landward, overland trade and pastoralism supported 10,000–15,000 townspeople and several thousand Bedouins.[6] More important was its maritime economy of pearling, fishing, boatbuilding, and sea trade with India and upper Gulf coastal towns. Its excellent harbor on Kuwait Bay gave it the greatest port potential in the northern Gulf, which, however, was never realized because of its lack of fresh water. Basrah, on the Shatt al-Arab, had better links with its hinterland and had plentiful fresh water. In view of its water shortage, Kuwait's population of 100,000 after World War I was surprisingly large. However, the world depression of the 1930s and competition from Japanese cultured pearls combined with changing technology and trade patterns to undermine Kuwait's traditional livelihood. By 1936–1937, the shaykhdom's economic future looked bleak, as the 700 pearling boats of 1921 decreased to 320 in 1933, 125 in 1939, and 40 in the 1940s.[7] Many pearling dhows joined the growing fleet of "booms" transporting fresh water from the Shatt al-Arab to Kuwait, supplying up to 100,000 gals/378,500 l each day. The depressed economy recovered and expanded dramatically when the discovery of petroleum in 1938 led to increasing oil exports after World War II, which brought immense wealth and rapid development in little more than a decade.[8] By 1961, Kuwait had achieved economic and political viability; and it gained independence from Great Britain, its protector since 1899, reaffirmed in 1914.

Sovereignty for the amirate, including withdrawal of British protection, brought its own problems, as Kuwaitis quickly discovered. Extremely wealthy but small and weak, and long coveted by a strong neighbor to the north, independent Kuwait was immediately claimed once again by Iraq, now a three-year-old revolutionary republic. However, Britain promptly revived its protection policy—later assumed by Arab League forces—and Iraq withdrew its threat and its border troops. The Iraqi claim

Kuwait

Long-form official name, anglicized: State of Kuwait

Official name, transliterated: Dawlat al-Kuwayt

Form of government: constitutional monarchy

Area: 6,880 miles^2/17,818 km^2

Population, 1999: 1,866,104 (Kuwaiti 766,954, non-Kuwaiti 1,099,150). Literacy: 78.6%

Ethnic composition (%, 1998): Kuwaiti Arab 38, non-Kuwaiti Arab 31, Asian (mostly Pakistani and Indian but also Sri Lankan, Thai, and Filipino) 21, Iranian 4, other 6

Religions (%, 1998): Muslim 85 (Sunni 45, Shii 40), Christian, Hindu, Parsi, and other 15

GDP, 1998: $43.7 billion; per capita: $22.700

Petroleum reserves: 94 billion bbl (9% of world total)

Main exports (% of total value, 1996): crude petroleum and petroleum products 95

Main imports (% of total value, 1996): machinery and transport equipment 41.6; manufactured goods 19.8; food and live animals 14.0; miscellaneous manufactured articles 12.9; chemical products 7.2; beverages and tobacco 1.1

Capital city: Greater Kuwait City 1,475,000; al-Jahra 185,00

and threat were periodically renewed, provoking several border incidents, some of the most serious in 1973.

For three decades Kuwait enjoyed almost unparalleled economic development and redevelopment. Billions of dollars of income from oil exports and investments permitted the hiring of outside expertise and labor for development, as well as the purchase and importation of foreign goods and equipment. As has been explained elsewhere, the Iran-Iraq war created eight years of problems and fears for the Kuwaitis, who negotiated for and bought what they needed, including security. Then, on August 2, 1990, Kuwait's complacency was shattered when Iraq invaded the coveted territory. The little-known, even though very wealthy, small amirate suddenly dominated world television screens, radio, and headlines.

Although the Gulf crisis is discussed in Chapter 11, the impact inside the amirate may be examined briefly here. Significantly, at the time of the invasion (early August), as is true every year, scores of thousands of

Kuwaiti residents were on vacation—wealthy citizens in the cooler lands of Western Europe or elsewhere and expatriates in their homelands. The absence of so many residents made the invasion easier for the Iraqis and complicated the situation for the Kuwaitis both during and after the occupation.

Destruction in Kuwait City and environs was extensive and often savagely senseless, but most buildings remained structurally sound and were reparable. The greatest damage inflicted on the country resulted from Iraqi looting of transportable items and sabotaging of fixed facilities. The value of looted materials can be only approximated but has been roughly estimated to be between $70 and $100 billion.[9] Fortunately, some of the most valuable items were later returned by Iraq under UN cease-fire resolutions. Nearly 17,000 items stolen from the Kuwait National Museum were returned, as were 3,216 gold bricks weighing 27.56 pounds/ 12.5 kilograms each.[10]

More obvious was the sabotage of Kuwait's oil wells, tank farms, oil-export terminals,

MAP 18-1   General and economic map of Kuwait. The Divided Zone is the former Saudi-Kuwait Neutral Zone, depicted with dashed line boundaries.

pipelines, and refineries, which not only caused direct losses of billions of dollars in resources and facilities but also despoiled many aspects of the local and regional environment. In an act sometimes called environmental terrorism and ecocide, Iraq blew up 749 wellheads of Kuwait's 935 wells, leaving more than 690 wells afire or blowing wild, causing millions of barrels of oil to flow out onto the desert around wells and tanks, and burning other millions. In addition, in late January 1991, Iraq dumped 150,000 bpd of oil from Kuwaiti storage tanks into the upper Gulf, a spill that exceeded 4 million bbl before it was staunched. This amount may be compared

with the 258,000 bbl spilled by the Exxon *Valdez* in Alaska in 1989. Enormous as the environmental damage was, an appreciable amount has gradually healed; however, large areas of the Kuwaiti landscape will remain despoiled for many years. More serious is the loss to the world of perhaps as much as 3 billion bbl of petroleum reserves through wanton sabotage.[11]

Immediately after Iraqi forces were expelled, Kuwait contracted with 27 oil-well damage control teams from 10 countries to fight the runaway wells and roaring well fires. After paying out more than $1.5 billion, the amirate was grateful to see the last fire extinguished on

November 6, 1991. Thanks to plentiful funds and to the high priority given to recovery, much of the physical damage had been repaired within three to four years. Meanwhile, in response to pressures that built from the early days of the occupation, government and public attention was devoted to social and political reforms. Various levels of Kuwaiti reaction to the invasion and to the brutality of the occupation had revealed serious weaknesses and deficiencies in the body politic; the imperative for reform was patent, and pressures were exerted from within and without. Change has been slow in coming, but Kuwait had achieved progress at the beginning of the new millenium.

In one definitive step to preclude future Iraqi boundary and territorial pretensions, the UN delimited and precisely demarcated the long-controversial line between Kuwait and Iraq in 1992–1993. The boundary generally confirmed the line described in two earlier documents exchanged between Kuwait and Iraq, in 1932 and 1963 (see Chap. 11, "Boundary and Territorial Disputes").[12]

Oil and Oil Industry

A surface showing of asphalt spurred the first interest in Kuwait's oil potential in 1911, and the first geological survey, conducted in 1914, yielded encouraging results. Without its promise of oil production, Kuwait would probably not have been maintained as a separate polity by the British after World War I and would likely have been incorporated into the mandate of Iraq. Certainly, petroleum has been the axis around which the amirate has revolved since the initial discovery. After World War I, the Anglo-Persian Oil Company and the Gulf Oil Corporation[13] of the United States combined to create a jointly owned local subsidiary, Kuwait Oil Company (KOC), and in 1934 that company obtained an oil concession from the government of Kuwait. After a dry hole in the north, KOC struck a gusher in the Burgan Dome south of Kuwait Bay in 1938 and later proved that Burgan, with oil in several relatively

shallow horizons, was the world's greatest field of its time. It is still the world's richest field for its areal extent, credited with 70 billion bbl. Delayed by World War II, the first commercial exports of crude from the Burgan Dome were lifted in 1946. Continued exploration during the 1950s opened a half-dozen new fields—Ahmadi, Magwa, Raudhatain (with 6 billion bbl), Bahra, Sabriya (with 3.8 billion bbl), and Minagish.

The Kuwait government awarded concessions to the U.S. Aminoil group for the Kuwaiti half of the Kuwaiti-Saudi Neutral Zone in June 1945, and four years later it extended the concession to include several offshore islands. Aminoil discovered the considerable Wafra Field in 1953 and developed Umm Gudair after KOC found the field in 1966. In 1958, Kuwait followed the lead of Saudi Arabia and awarded a concession for its offshore half of the Neutral Zone to the Japanese group, Arabian Oil Company. AOC discovered the Khafji Field offshore in 1960, and Hout Field in 1963; it also found the Lulu and Dorra fields in 1967, but neither has yet been produced. Later, concessionary exploration was conducted by the Spanish at Raudhatain, in northern Kuwait, where both more oil and the amirate's only sweet groundwater were found in 1955.

As oil production mounted rapidly, Kuwait became increasingly cognizant of its dependence on a single depletable resource. Upon the advice of a young group of "technocrats," the Kuwait government moved toward conservation of the country's source of wealth by reducing petroleum output. It also moved to reduce the wasteful flaring (because no economic market was available) of gas separated from the crude prior to further handling. After having increased its production each year to a peak output of 3 million bpd in 1972, Kuwait reduced output sharply to less than 2 million bpd during the late 1970s. By this time, the amirate had amassed such enormous wealth for its small size and population and had been so intensively developed economically that conserving its oil resources was more logical than accumulating additional millions of dollars. Although requesting an OPEC quota of not less than 1.25 million bpd in late 1986, Kuwait moved to balance production with conservation objectives. Ironically, Kuwait's allegedly exceeding its OPEC production quota was claimed by Iraq as one basis for its invasion of the amirate.

Like other OPEC countries, Kuwait sought participation in its concessionary companies and by 1975 controlled KOC. It nationalized Aminoil and its operations in the Neutral Zone (by that time the Divided Zone) in 1977. In 1980, Kuwait Petroleum Corporation (KPC) was created to serve as the umbrella organization, covering Kuwait Oil Company, KOC (domestic exploration and production); Kuwait National Petroleum Company, KNPC (domestic refining and marketing); Kuwait Oil Tanker Company, KOTC (marine transportation); Petrochemical Industries Company, PIC (petrochemicals); and a half-dozen additional companies and agencies for operations outside Kuwait, from exploration to marketing. In 1998, KOC and KNPC reportedly merged to streamline costs. Now a completely vertically integrated corporation in domestic operations, KPC also competes with the multinationals, having purchased the former Gulf Oil facilities in Benelux, Scandinavia, and Italy in 1983–1984, as well as 157 outlets from BP in 1998. In 1999, KPC subsidiaries operated more than 5,000 service stations under the "Q8" banner in ten Western European countries. KPC also has refineries in Western Europe and North America, it expanded its downstream operations abroad in 1997–1999 to South Asia and the Pacific Rim. In Kuwait, three main KNPC refineries at Mina al-Ahmadi, Mina Abdullah, and Shuaybah have been restored to their pre-1990 capacity levels to total nearly 900,000 bpd throughput (see Table 8-2).

At century's end, Kuwait's petroleum industry rests on 94 billion bbl of reserves (fourth largest among world countries and 9 percent of world total), an average 1.8 million bpd production from 790 wells, and a workforce of about 16,000 (1 percent of the Kuwaiti workers). Projects are already under way to drill a modest number of new wells for judicious

expansion of some fields; construct new gathering centers to handle a rise in output; expand production capacity from the present 2.4 million bpd to 3.5 million bpd by 2005; relax its policies concerning activity by foreign oil companies and thereby gain the advantage of special expertise; and expand the petrochemicals industry substantially. Overall, the oil industry accounts for half of GDP, 90 percent of export revenues, and 75 percent of government income. The amirate's dramatic development after about 1960 and its rapid urban and economic recovery after 1991 are based largely on its huge oil resources, along with intelligent use of outside expertise and a resilient indigenous population. Additional discussion of the broader economy follows.

Other Industry and Trade

Government goals for industrial development focus on capital-intensive and energy-intensive industries, as opposed to labor-intensive manufacturing, in the fields of petroleum, petroleum by-products, construction materials, consumer goods, and electronics. Diversification of industry and the shift to domestic production of basic commodities that have been traditionally imported are deterred by the small size of the consuming population, regardless of the high per capita income. The relatively few nonpetroleum Kuwaiti industries currently include cement, pharmaceuticals, nonalcoholic beverages, processed and frozen fish, building materials, plastics, paper products, furniture, and milled flour.

With less than 4.5 in./114 mm of annual rain—and none for the five summer months, no surface streams, and only small amounts of underground water, Kuwait imported its water before the 1950s and "manufactures" it now. Utilizing its plentiful energy supplies to generate electric power and offset its water deficiency, it produces 7,000 megawatts; and in the same process, it supplies more than 265 million gallons/1 million m^3 of sweet water per day.

With one of the highest per capita incomes in the world, Kuwait has developed a consumer-oriented economy to match the oil export sector. From a tradition of trading, shipping, fishing, and pearling, the knowledgeable Kuwaiti merchants moved rapidly into importing, retailing, appliance service, electronic products, furniture and other household furnishings, and automobiles. The shops in the quaint old town *suqs* have long since been replaced by modern Western-style shopping centers and individual merchandising outlets. Increasing numbers of banks at one time ranked among the leading independent financial houses, as investors sought to place surplus funds. However, four events during the decade after 1981 seriously impacted Kuwait economically—and politically: (1) a scandalous collapse in August 1982 in the extraofficial Suq al-Manakh "stock market" that resulted in more than 500 bankruptcies; (2) the 50 percent drop in oil prices during the early 1980s; (3) the Iran-Iraq war, which further depressed economic activity in Kuwait; and (4) most traumatic of all, the devastating Iraqi occupation between August 2, 1990, and February 27, 1991. Kuwait's total financial wartime costs can be estimated at nearly $200 billion.

In 1976, when Kuwait decided to reduce oil production to extend the life of its one main resource, it also set up a Reserve Fund for Future Generations, to which 10 percent of ordinary revenues is allocated each year. This fund is complemented by a portfolio of normal investments, the General Reserve Fund. About $100 billion of the two funds was invested abroad by 1990; the government drew on these reserves during and right after the Iraqi occupation for operational and reconstruction expenses. Some of the expenditures from these funds became issues in complaints against the government in 1991–1992.

The Kuwait Fund for Arab Economic Development (KFAED), created in 1961, has lent or granted several hundred million dollars a year to other Arab states. Since 1974, its potential recipients have included all developing countries. Kuwait also made separate grants of huge sums to the "Front Line States" of Egypt, Syria, and Jordan, as well as—ironically—loans of $4–5 billion (never repaid) to Iraq during its 1980s war against Iran.

From the time of its initial settlement, Kuwait has experienced minimal agricultural development; today the amirate imports 95 percent of its food. The 12,000–15,000 Bedouins of a century ago supplied appreciable meat, but the few remaining Bedouins contribute little to the food supply. Small date groves persist around some of the brackish wells, and new dairy and chicken farms, along with limited hydroponic vegetable production, add to the fresh food supply. Although a negligible number of workers are employed in agriculture, 50 percent work in public administration, 40 percent in services, and 9 percent in industry.

Society and Settlements

Kuwait town was settled in the early eighteenth century by Arabs from the Najd (central Arabia). Although the environment was niggardly, especially because of its shortage of water, benefits of the excellent harbor sustained the tenacious population. Gradually, numbers of Arabs from Mesopotamia, the peninsula, and Oman, as well as Iranians, joined the small settlement, which was ruled by Al Sabah shaykhs. By the early 1900s, the population was estimated at 35,000 and was double that size in 1946, when the first commercial oil was exported from the shaykhdom. Increasing oil production attracted immigrants by the thousands, until the population reached 206,473 in the first census, taken in 1957, and 2.1 million—ten times that of the first census—in mid-1990.

By 1965, the aliens ("non-Kuwaitis," or immigrants or expatriates) outnumbered the native Kuwaitis and the alarmed indigenous population jealously imposed rigid nationality criteria that restricted citizenship to those indigenous residents who had been inhabitants prior to 1920 and their offspring. Stringent conditions for naturalization effectively precluded attainment of Kuwaiti nationality by immigrants except for about 50 per year. Of the 1.87 million inhabitants in 1999, fewer than 770,000 were citizens, and only they were entitled to the full range of extraordinary social benefits extended by the government. Criteria for suffrage are even more restrictive. Only adult males who lived in Kuwait before 1920 and their male descendants, totaling about 113,000, were politically franchised until 1996. Beginning in that year, male citizens who have been naturalized for 30 years or more are allowed to vote. In May 1999, the ruler decreed that women in the same categories as male voters could also vote and run for office in 2003. However, exercising its constitutional rights, Parliament repeatedly refused to enfranchise women during the following year.

Kuwait's population fell precipitously after the Iraqi invasion as expatriates especially, but also Kuwaitis, fled the terror and hardships of the occupation. Many thousands of residents already on vacation in August when the invasion occurred extended their visits abroad. The number remaining in Kuwait may have been as low as 500,000 by early January 1991. After liberation of the amirate in late February 1991, scores of thousands of citizens and expatriates sought reentry, but many lifelong resident expatriates were dismayed to find themselves turned away. Further, many expatriates who had remained during the occupation were expelled. Seizing the opportunity to achieve a social and political restructuring, government authorities then embarked on a firm restoration of Kuwait for the Kuwaitis, announcing a postwar population goal of about 1.2 million. Such a rigid restriction was unrealistic and did not permit staffing a return to national viability and prosperity; as a result, by the late 1990s more than 1 million expatriates had been admitted and constituted 60 percent of the population.

Especially numerous among expatriates before 1991 were the Palestinian refugees, who came by the thousands in search of livelihood and home following their loss of both to Israelis during and after 1948–1949. Arabs and mostly Muslims, educated and motivated, the Palestinians became available just as Kuwait had a critical need for the skills and characteristics they possessed; and by the late 1980s, they and their descendants in the amirate numbered nearly 400,000, contributing their skills as civil servants, engineers, technicians, middle managers, and teachers. However, when some

Palestinians became politically and journalistically activist, the entire group became suspect to the authorities, and Palestinians were no longer welcome as newcomers. During the Iraqi occupation, the perceived support for President Saddam Husayn—or at least for his expressed ideals—by many Palestinians in Jordan and by some in Kuwait created bitter resentment among many Kuwaitis (and other peninsula and Gulf Arabs) against the longtime Palestinian resident aliens. Such was the stimulus for the expulsion by Kuwait of hundreds of thousands of Palestinians—with other expatriate inhabitants—until fewer than 40,000 Palestinians remained.

A serious consequence was the loss of scores of thousands of the amirate's most effective workers on several levels, thus prolonging the area's recovery. Kuwaiti authorities were also systematically selective in permitting the return of several other expatriate groups, reducing non-Kuwaiti Arab groups in favor of Asian groups, who are less politically active and more manageable. Thus, the structure and texture of the Kuwaiti population and society were fundamentally altered in a period of months.[14]

A leading tribal family, Al Sabah, furnished the ruling shaykh of the amirate (principality) of Kuwait beginning in the 1750s. The latest Sabah, Jabir Ahmad al-Jabir Al Sabah, became amir in 1977. Under the 1962 constitution, which stipulates the process of succession, the ruler enjoys broad powers, including the final word on most government policies. However, the National Assembly—the only elected parliament among the Arab states of the Gulf—possesses and exercises real powers in the governing process. Although the amir suspended parliament in 1976–1981 and again in 1986–1992, the powers of the parliaments elected in 1992, 1996, and 1999 are understood to be stronger after the national trauma of 1990–1991. Ideological representation in the assembly is broad, a large percentage of members having an "opposition" orientation. Opposition members candidly criticize government actions and propose different policies in the assembly meetings. Sooner or later,

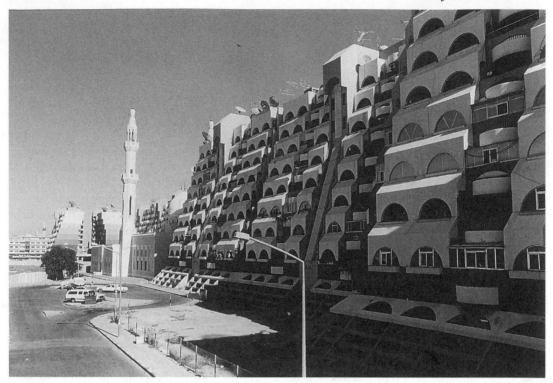

FIGURE 18-1   Sawabar Residential Complex, Kuwait City, a modernistic adaptation of Islamic architectural themes.

women will be elected to parliament, as was debated in late 1999 and early 2000; when this occurs, Kuwait's already leading position among the Gulf amirates concerning citizen participation in government will be enhanced. Of the Shii 35–40 percent of the population, many of Iranian descent, some of the more radical were attracted to Iranian revolutionary ideology before 1990. Several thousand were deported, but in the reformist atmosphere after 1991, the Shiis were given a greater role in the government and now enjoy an increasing approach to equality.

Kuwaiti citizens have profited especially from the rapidly expanding political and economic systems of the oil-rich state; however, expatriates have also enjoyed great benefits from the obviously wide distribution of wealth among the general population, although they are not entitled to certain privileges. Full benefits include virtually guaranteed employment, free medical service, housing subsidies,

marriage bonuses, free education at all levels, and retirement income. Resident foreign nationals are entitled to basic welfare services. Thousands of Kuwaitis, mostly men, have been sent to Britain and the United States for free university education, although most Kuwaiti university students now attend the impressive University of Kuwait, opened in 1967. In a significant break with local tradition, increasing numbers of Kuwaiti women also attend the university, where they have outnumbered men since the early 1980s.

Kuwait City, once a small port on the southeastern coast of Kuwait Bay, now is an elaborately planned metropolis covering much of the center of the state. Some of its ultramodern buildings echo traditional Islamic architecture (Fig. 18-1), and each of the carefully planned sectors suggests the traditional Islamic urban "quarter" and includes a mosque and shopping area reminiscent of the traditional *suq;* otherwise, few features reflect the typical Islamic

FIGURE 18-2   Kuwait water towers, the Kuwaiti capital's hallmark, serving an identifying function similar to that of the Eiffel Tower in Paris. The highly colored and decorated spheres store municipal water, and the tower on the right includes a luxury restaurant. Trees indicate scale.

city. Serving as a city symbol, the three unique Kuwait Towers on the tip of Ras Ajuzah are a dominant feature of the landscape (Fig. 18-2). The southwest-northeast axis of the built-up area and most streets follows the trend of coastline that forms the northwestern boundary of the city. The historic mud wall was dismantled during the expansion of the city in the late 1950s, but two of the old gates have been preserved. The central business district covers most of the old *madinah,* the pre-1945 walled town (Fig. 10-5). Three harbors retain features of the old Kuwait along the bay, and traditional dhows still anchor inside the breakwaters. Concentric ring roads centered on the old town carry residential sectors southeastward and industrial sectors southwestward. Kuwait's main general-cargo port is an extensive state-of-the-art facility at Shuwaykh on the western side of the city.

Relations

Like the shaking of a kaleidoscope, the disarray caused by the Gulf crisis forced Kuwait into certain new patterns of regional and world relations. Bonds with such traditional friends as Saudi Arabia and other GCC neighbors, Britain, the United States, Japan, and others were greatly strengthened. Indeed, Kuwait owes its rescue primarily to them. Connections with Iraq fell to an absolute nadir after Saddam Husayn's invasion in 1990 and were little improved nine years later. During the 1990s, Kuwait was a vigorous supporter of continued sanctions against the Iraqi government while expressing concern for the welfare of the Iraqi people. Relations with brotherly Arab states Jordan and Yemen were strained after the ambivalent reactions of those governments to Saddam Husayn's rationalization for his assault on Kuwait. However, Kuwait and Jordan renewed diplomatic relations in 1999. Ironically, relations with Iran improved from the low level of 1980–1988. Relations with the United States became extraordinarily close, building on the U.S. Navy's convoying of Kuwaiti tankers in 1987–1988. After the coalition rescued Kuwait in 1990–1991, the amirate recognized that its security ultimately depended on Western military power. It pragmatically acquiesced to cooperative security measures and became a major base for and supporter of U.S. and British air operations against Iraq; it also hosted thousands of U.S. ground troops during the 1990s. The United States has become not only the main arms supplier for Kuwait but also the largest supplier of goods and services and the leading trading partner.

Bahrain

An Overview

Bahrain (Arabic for "two seas") is the main island of a group of 33 small low-lying islands, also called Bahrain, which is the smallest of the 16 Middle East states.[15] It is located 15 miles/ 24 km off the east coast of Saudi Arabia, with which it is connected by a causeway, and 18 miles/29 km from the Qatar Peninsula

(Map 18-2). Only six of the islands are inhabited. Of the archipelago's total area, the main Bahrain Island covers 221 miles^2/572 km^2; second-most important is Muharraq, with the state's second-largest city (also called Muharraq), international airport, and dry dock. A new causeway that replaced the original one built in 1929 connects Muharraq with Bahrain. Other islands include Sitra, locus of the state's oil export terminal, linked to Bahrain by bridge and more recently by a causeway to Manama; Nabih Salih, its date palm groves fed by artesian springs; Umm Nasan, private island of the ruler and a link in the new Arabia-Bahrain causeway; and Jiddah, with the state prison. The Hawar group of islands off the southwestern coast of Qatar is disputed between Bahrain and Qatar. The dispute evoked a diplomatic crisis and alleged gunboat fire in the fall of 1991, when Qatar took its claim to the World Court, and King Fahd of Saudi Arabia attempted mediation (see Chap. 11). Most urban development has taken place on the *sabkhahs* in northern Bahrain and southern Muharraq, and these areas are surrounded by oases, which give way southward to rocky and gravelly barren desert.[16]

Despite its island situation, Bahrain is very hot in summer, with regular afternoon temperatures exceeding 106°F/41°C. Consistently high humidity makes the high temperature especially uncomfortable. November to March is a milder period, the season when Bahrain receives its average annual 3 in./76 mm of rainfall.

The main island of Bahrain is fringed by a shallow rock platform and by extensive coral reefs. The island is a surface expression of a breached asymmetrical anticline with a north-south axis in which oil and gas have been trapped at several depths. Erosional breaching of the anticline has produced a shallow basin in the center of the island that is surrounded by a low, oval-shaped, inward-facing escarpment of resistant limestone. Several erosional remnant hills that mark the former crest of the arch rise 100–200 ft./30–60 m above the inner basin.

Bahrain

Long-form official name, anglicized: State of Bahrain

Official name, transliterated: Dawlat al-Bahrayn

Form of government: Monarchy (amirate), with a cabinet appointed by the amir

Area: 267 miles^2/692 km^2

Population, 1999: 633,000. Literacy: 85.2%

Ethnic composition (%): Bahraini Arab 63.0, Asian (mostly Indian, Pakistani) 13.0, other Arab 10.0, Iranian 8.0, European 2.5, other 3.5

Religions (%): Muslim 92.0 (Shii 75.0, Sunni 25.0), Christian 7.3, other 0.7

GDP, 1998: $8.2 billion; per capita: $9.776

Petroleum reserves: 160 million barrels

Main exports (% of total value, 1997): petroleum products 61.0; aluminum products 7.0

Main imports (% of total value, 1997): nonpetroleum products 59; crude petroleum products 41.0

Capital city: Manama 151,500; other cities: al-Muharraq 82,000; Jidd Hafs 55,000; al-Rifa 49,000; Isa Town (Madinat Isa) 47,000

Most prominent of the hills is Jabal Dukhan, near the center of Bahrain's oil field, the highest elevation on the island at 440 ft./134 m. Oil company headquarters are at Awali, in the northern part of the basin and north of the field itself.

Important as oil became after 1932, another liquid resource attracted visitors and settlers as early as the Neolithic and especially during the Bronze Age: the plentiful supply of sweet artesian water from numerous *ayns* in the northern part of Bahrain Island and on adjacent islands. Other freshwater springs that erupt from the floor of the Gulf between Bahrain and Saudi Arabia have supplied mariners with drinking water for centuries. Bahrain's central location on the Gulf's long axis and the fact that it is the largest and best-watered of the Gulf islands south of Kuwait made it a transit point for Sumerians sailing between Mesopotamia and the Indus Valley. The same basic advantages, plus the oil industry, pertain today.

Excavations near the ruins of Bahrain Fort on the northern coast of Bahrain Island uncovered an ancient temple complex where artifacts were found that link Bahrain with Sumer and the Indus Valley. Archaeologists conclude that Bahrain is the Dilmun mentioned in Sumerian inscriptions[17] and that it also had ancient cultural links with Faylakah Island off Kuwait Bay and with settlements in Abu Dhabi. Grave mounds, estimated to number more than 100,000, in a huge necropolis in northwestern Bahrain date from as early as 2400 BC and from every period after that through the Sassanian. Such prominent landscape features have caught the attention of visitors and writers for 2,300 years. Unfortunately, thousands of the tumuli have been bulldozed to clear ground for highways and new and expanding settlements.

Transit trade, dhow building, fishing, and pearling underpinned the island's economy for centuries as Bahrain was occupied or controlled by Sassanians, Umayyads, Abbasids, Hormuzis, Portuguese, Persians, mainland Najdis, and Ottomans. The leading shaykhs, Al Khalifah—who had tribal affiliations with the Al Sabah in Kuwait—came to be accepted as

MAP 18-2   General map of Bahrain and Qatar, an island and a peninsula in the middle Gulf.

rulers in the eighteenth century and threw off Iranian control in 1783. Soon after, they were included under the umbrella of British Gulf protection, which continued for 150 years. The decline of pearling during the 1930s coincided, fortuitously, with the discovery of oil. Bahrain emerged from British protection in 1971, 40 years after it became the first oil producer on the west side of the Gulf, just in time to enjoy an economic boom as a sovereign state.

A new constitution in 1973 afforded more political participation by the inhabitants through the creation of an experimental National Assembly, but the fledgling parliament was disbanded by the ruler in 1975. With escalating oil prices and explosive development in the Gulf during the first decade of the independence of the Gulf amirates, Bahrain profited in many ways from its geographical location, relative stability, diplomatic finesse, and able work force. As its economic development expanded, its traditional strategic importance also increased (see below). Its balancing act during the Iran-Iraq war preserved its links with all sides, and during the Gulf war in 1990–1991, the main island played a significant role as an insular aircraft carrier for British and U.S. warplanes. Indeed, Bahraini pilots also flew strike missions in Iraq.

Descendants of the Khalifah family have continued to rule the island amirate; Shaykh Isa bin Sulman Al Khalifah led the impressive economic development and the activity of Bahrain in the two Gulf crises. He died March 6, 1999, and was succeeded without incident by his son, Amir Hamad bin Isa Al Khalifah. After disbanding the National Assembly in 1975, Shaykh Isa had given no date for reintroduction of representative institutions. Although he appointed a 30-member Consultative Council in 1993, the reform was unpopular, and it kindled riots in 1994. In 1996, he strengthened the Council's powers and increased its members to 40. Shaykh Hamad has generally followed his father's political philosophy. Prosperity on the island seems to have subdued most of the opposition.

People and Population

During Bahrain's long history as a center for traders and seafarers, many ethnic groups settled on the islands, producing a characteristic indigenous mixture. Earlier Iranian influence induced the present 75 percent adherence of Bahrainis to Shii Islam, although the ruling family of Al Khalifah and most members of the power structure are Sunni. Although the distinctions are becoming less important, three main social groups among the Shii include the Baharna, descendants of the original inhabitants of the island; the Hassawi, descendants of settlers from oases in the Eastern Province of modern Saudi Arabia; and the Ajami, whose families migrated from Iran in more recent times. Sunni Arabs originally from Arabia who migrated to Iran and then back to Bahrain are called Hawala. The ethnically complex population also includes large numbers of Indians and Pakistanis, other Gulf Arabs, some Europeans, a few Jews, and a few black Africans. Although not socioeconomically stratified, the groups tend to concentrate in certain areas of Bahrain or in certain quarters of Manama and Muharraq. By 2000, more than one-third of the population was non-Bahraini.

Population increase in Bahrain has been steady since World War II, rising from 90,000 in 1941 to 633,000 in 1999, somewhat larger than that of Qatar, which has the Middle East's smallest population. The main concentration of population is around the capital and primate city of Manama and its suburbs, with a secondary node on the island of Muharraq (see Fig. 10-4). Manama displays an interesting mixture of old and new, its Indian-style bazaars contrasting with surrounding new high-rise office buildings and luxury hotels (Fig. 18-3). A few miles southwest of Manama is a completely new settlement, Isa Town, begun in 1968 as a model town for the growing population. Hamad Town, in western Bahrain, was added in 1982 and has expanded rapidly. In eastern Muharraq Island, the Shii city of al-Hidd is now developing as an industrial area. In central Bahrain, the Amir's palace and its appurtenances have evolved into

FIGURE 18-3   New buildings in Manama, capital of the island state of Bahrain. (Photograph from Bahraini Ministry of Information)

the desert town of al-Riffa. The oil company center of Awali in the island's central basin developed much like a small American suburban town.

Economic Patterns

The petroleum industry and related activities have dominated Bahrain's economic patterns since the 1930s, but such traditional activities as trade, shipping and servicing Gulf shipping (including entrepôt services), dhow building, fishing, and agriculture are still important sectors. Only pearling, in which Bahrain led the world in the early 1900s, has virtually disappeared, although trade in pearls is still important in the Manama *suq*. Recognition in the 1950s of the limited amount of oil reserves prompted the government to diversify the economy through long-range planning and to attract activities not based on resources or a large labor supply. The planning was well-conceived and by the 1980s

was paying high dividends (see below). Even so, oil and gas still dominate the economy, providing about half of government revenue.

Oil.   The first oil well in Bahrain, and the first in the Gulf proper, was drilled by Bahrain Petroleum Company (Bapco) in 1931–1932 at Jabal Dukhan and produced 9,600 bpd from 2,008 ft./612 m. It is still producing. Using mostly Saudi crude, received through undersea pipelines, as feedstock, a small refinery opened in 1936 and expanded to handle a 248,000-bpd throughput, producing more than 80 products, most of them exported from Sitra. Oil from Saudi Arabia still supplies 50 percent of Bahrain's imports.

Steady at only 30,000 bpd for many years, Bahrain's oil production then rose steadily to a peak of 76,600 bpd in 1970 before declining to the 40,000-bpd range during the 1980s. Output dropped to 36,000 bpd in 1993, but then statistically tripled in the mid-1990s when Saudi

Arabia began giving Bahrain 100 percent of the 140,000-bpd output from their joint offshore field of Abu Safah. Bahrain's onshore oil reserves are expected to be exhausted early in the new century; however, depending on production, nonassociated gas reserves in the deep Khuff formation (about 10,000 ft./3,048 m) should last several decades beyond that time. New industries were developed to make use of the considerable supply of Khuff gas.

Bapco, which held the Bahrain concession for more than four decades, was incorporated in Canada but was originally a wholly owned subsidiary of Standard Oil of California (Socal), now Chevron. In 1936, Texaco bought 50 percent of Bapco and joined Socal in the California-Texas Oil Corporation, which became Caltex Petroleum Corporation in 1968 and which owned Bapco as a subsidiary. The company was for many years the main employer and income earner in the islands, and, enjoying an amicable partnership with the government, played a long, vital role in the development of the country. In 1975, Bahrain, which considered itself too minor a producer to join OPEC, assumed 60 percent participation in Bapco and took over the other 40 percent in 1980, administering control through Banoco (Bahrain National Oil Company), founded in 1976.[18] After some ownership shuffling during the 1980s, the government bought Caltex's share in the industry in 1997; and in 1998, it merged Bapco and Banoco into a single company. In addition to the Sitra refinery—which is being modernized and expanded—oil-based industries include a liquefaction plant and a sizable petrochemical plant.

Other Industry. Using the island's large gas resources, a joint venture opened a large aluminum complex (ALBA) in 1971. Alumina is imported from Australia as raw material, and during the late 1990s the smelting operation had an output of 500,000 mt. ALBA, of which the Bahraini government owns 77 percent, is the second-largest single-site aluminum smelter in the world. The complex now includes several downstream operations, including a rolling mill, an extrusion plant, a cable plant, factories producing aluminum powder and wire mesh screening, and two automobile wheel factories. A second large installation is the Arab Ship Repair Yard (ASRY), completed in 1977 on an artificial island linked to Muharraq. Owned jointly by Bahrain and six OPEC states, ASRY's huge facility services supertankers up to 500,000 dwt. Smaller vessels are serviced in an older yard and slipway. The facilities proved to be of great value during the tanker war in the 1980s and during the 1990–1991 Gulf crisis. The large industrial area behind the main port of Mina Sulman and the naval base of Jufayr, in northeast Bahrain, embraces a score of smaller plants. Electric power and desalination plants are increasing, with a large installation to be built in al-Hidd. Elsewhere on the island there are food-processing plants, clothing factories, potteries, and similar light industries. Dhows are still constructed for both utilitarian and recreational use.

Other Economy. By the 1960s, Bahrain sought to supplement its very modest petroleum industry with service-centered economic sectors, particularly entrepôt facilities, trade of various categories, financial services that would attract large banking houses, education and training, and tourism. Coincidentally, the convergence of regional dynamics directed billions of petrodollars toward the Bahraini efforts when the traditional Beirut financial functions were displaced by warfare in Lebanon. The government and private capital simultaneously developed systematic infrastructure for the expected commercial boom—state-of-the-art communications and information technology; a modern and efficient international airport in Muharraq with excellent service by 30 airlines; spacious, modern office quarters; luxury hotels and upscale residential areas; a broad choice of restaurants; good roads and automotive maintenance facilities; a full inventory of consumer goods at competitive prices; and a hospitable administrative climate. Reasonable regulation is complemented by a stable currency, no personal or corporate taxation, unrestricted currency flow, a capable labor force, encouragement of the private sector, and a friendly, efficient government. The general commercial atmosphere is cosmopolitan, yet informal in the highly concentrated business district of Manama. By 1999, the Bahrain Monetary Agency had licensed 180 financial institutions, including 19 commercial banks comprising 81 branches. About 40 U.S. companies have regional headquarters in Bahrain. Tourism has grown along with the rapid commercial development of the island; most of Bahrain's 2.4 million annual visitors arrive by way of the 15.5-mile/25-km causeway that has linked the island with Saudi Arabia since 1986 (Fig. 9-5a). The more relaxed island atmosphere and availability of alcoholic spirits and female companionship are special attractions to mainland visitors.

Relations

Despite its small size and small population, Bahrain has multidirectional foreign relations. Its intimate connections with its larger Gulf neighbors are complemented by its close relations with Britain and the United States. Bahrain must obviously maintain good rapport with Saudi Arabia, with which it has long had many close ties. For many years from the mainland has come 75 percent of the feedstock for the Bapco refinery; Saudi Arabian money paid for the new causeway and fuels much of Bahrain's industrial development, banking operations, retail trade and entrepôt operations, tourism, and even its basic budget, since much of the island's income derives from Saudi-produced oil from the offshore Abu Safah field. With many Persian families among its mainly Shii population and with past ties to Iran, Bahrain maintains correct relations with revolutionary Iran and hopes that Iran will continue to honor the late shah's repudiation of Iran's long-standing claim to the archipelago. The state is cautious about involvement with Arab and Islamic issues and maintains strict control over militant groups on the islands, whether pro-Palestinian, pro-Arab nationalist,

or pro-Iranian. The shaykhdom carefully maintains good relations with the other Gulf amirates except for Qatar, with which it contends over ownership of the Hawar Islands. Currently, Bahrain focuses on Gulf affairs through the Gulf Cooperation Council (GCC).

Ties with Britain during the decades when Bahrain was a British protected state have continued as a basic aspect of the state's political, commercial, and cultural relations. Relations with the United States have been numerous and extensive, beginning with the fact that Bapco was first a U.S. company, even though it operated under British (Canadian) charter and had mainly a British managerial staff. Bahraini-U.S. military ties increased during the 1960s and later, as Bahrain served as the low-profile home port of the U.S. Navy's Middle East Forces (MIDEASTFOR) until 1977. Bahrain also gave quiet but significant assistance to the U.S. and European convoys during the 1987–1988 tanker war in the Gulf, and it actively participated in the coalition fighting Iraq in 1990–1991. It now is host to the U.S. Navy's Fifth Fleet and receives modest military assistance from the United States.

Qatar

Peninsula State

The State of Qatar lies on a mitten-shaped peninsula midway down the east coast of the Arabian Peninsula (Map 18-2). Formed by a broad, gentle anticlinal upfold, the peninsula is a generally flat, low-lying area of mostly barren Tertiary carbonate rocks (primarily Middle Eocene limestones, dolomites, and marls), with much of the surface overlain by aeolian sheet and dune sands and *hamadah* (gravel-like desert pavement). Elevations in most of the peninsula are less than 130 ft./ 40 m, with limestone ridges in the west and Miocene-Pliocene mesas in the south. The main western ridge is Jabal Dukhan, the surface expression of a tight north-south anticlinal fold that lies parallel to the main peninsula upwarp and to the similar Bahrain and

Qatar

Long-form official name, anglicized: State of Qatar

Official name, transliterated: Dawlat Qatar

Form of government: traditional monarchy, with unicameral Advisory Council

Area: 4,416 miles^2/11,437 km^2

Population, 1999: 579,000 (U.S. Govt.: 723,542). Literacy: 79.4%

Ethnic composition (%): Qatari Arab 22.0, other Arab (Palestinian, Lebanese, Omani, Syrian, Egyptian) 23.0, Pakistani 18.0, Indian 18.0, Iranian 10.0, European and other 9.0

Religions (%): Muslim (mostly Sunni) 92.8, Christian 5.9, Hindu 1.1, Bahai 0.2

GDP, 1998: $12 billion; per capita: $17,100

Petroleum reserves: 3.7 billion barrels

Main exports (% of total value, 1997): crude petroleum, petroleum products, and liquefied gas 82.0; chemicals 10.4; manufactures 5.9

Main imports (% of total value, 1999): machinery and transport equipment 39.7; manufactured goods 21.8; food and live animals 13.2; chemicals and chemical products 7

Capital city: Doha (Dawhah) 360,000; other cities: al-Rayyan 155,000; al-Wakrah 32,000

Dammam folds to the northwest. The ridge also reflects the subsurface structure that contains Qatar's Dukhan oil and gas field, the amirate's only onshore producer. Sterile sand dunes and *sabkhahs* characterize the base of the peninsula. The remarkable northwest-southeast lineation of aeolian sand ridges in all parts of the peninsula connotes the prevailing northwest wind, the *shamal*.[19] Of the several islands included in the state, Halul, to the east of the peninsula, is of particular importance in oil operations. The Hawar Islands off the west coast of Qatar are disputed with Bahrain. The long-running dispute between Qatar and Saudi Arabia over the precise delineation of their boundary at the base of the peninsula is finally being resolved (see Chap. 11).

The desert climate is reflected in the widely spaced and stunted flora, and temperatures and precipitation are similar to those in Bahrain. Qatar has no streams or springs, and only in recent years has well drilling found modestly productive underground aquifers.

The groundwater is pumped to irrigate scattered small agricultural plots that utilize generally circular surface depressions (*rawdahs; often rodas*) that are surface expressions of underground collapse of solution structures in limestone and evaporites. Irrigation of the *rawdahs* by groundwater has led to dangerous over-pumping, diminishing the water supply for Doha and necessitating desalination of seawater at a plant near Doha.[20]

Shallow Gulf waters in the bay west of the peninsula prevent maritime approaches; thus, despite the location of the Dukhan field just inland from the west coast, port and urban development has taken place on the eastern shore. Land has also been reclaimed along the eastern shore north and south of the capital city, Doha (Dawhah), which takes its name from the same Arabic word for a small crescent bay.

Several Neolithic sites have been found in northern Qatar, but later occupation appears to have been limited, presumably because of increasing desiccation of the climate. By the eighteenth century, Qatar was controlled by the family of Al Khalifah in the west and Al Thani clan, originally Bedouins from Najd, in the east. When the Al Khalifah family moved to Bahrain, the Al Thani assumed control in Qatar, and it is still the ruling family. Qatar became a British protectorate in 1916 and achieved sovereignty in September 1971, when the British withdrew from the Gulf.[21]

From Poverty to Prosperity

Qatar was isolated, sparsely populated, and poor before the late 1930s. Prior to that time, limited fishing and pearling, with bits of irrigation agriculture, supported fewer than 20,000 people. Petroleum Development (Qatar), renamed the Qatar Petroleum Company (QPC) in 1963, an Iraq Petroleum Company subsidiary, received a petroleum concession in 1935, found oil in the Dukhan fold in 1940, and began exporting in 1949. Shell received the concession for Qatar's offshore areas in 1952 and discovered the Idd al-Shargi field in 1960, Maydan-Mahzam in 1963, and Bu al-Hanin in 1970. By the early 1990s, Qatar's proved reserves exceeded 4.5 billion barrels. In 1971, Shell drilled into the Khuff zone in Qatari waters 165 ft./ 50 m deep and 44 miles/70 km north of the peninsula and discovered the North Field gas reservoir, its 300 trillion ft.^{3}/8.5 trillion m^3 in proved reserves, making it the world's largest known single nonassociated gas reservoir. The North Field gives Qatar the third-largest proved gas reserves in the world, after Russia and Iran.

Qatar assumed ownership of QPC in stages and held 100 percent by 1976, added 100 percent of Shell operations in 1977, and consolidated both in the Qatar General Petroleum Company. Qatar and Abu Dhabi share production from the offshore Bunduq field, located astride their median line. Qatar's oil output rose to 664,000 bpd in 1998 and then slid to 600,000 bpd in mid-1999 to meet its OPEC quota. Thus, the substantial production continues to afford the small population of Qatar a very high per capita income.

In modernizing and industrializing, Qatar faced shortages in most factors except energy.

In order to gain access to technical and managerial skills for its industrial diversification, it arranged joint ventures with the Norwegians, Japanese, French, and others for a fertilizer plant, a direct-reduction iron and steel plant, and a petrochemical complex that is one of the largest in the Middle East. All were constructed in a heavy-industry park at Musayid (Umm Said), 25 miles/40 km south of Doha. The concentration also has a 57,500-bpd throughput refinery (being upgraded to 83,000 bpd), twin joint-venture natural gas liquids (NGL) plants that utilize North Field gas and that are among the world's largest, and several support activities.

Creating the infrastructure to exploit North Field gas and constructing the two huge NGL plants absorbed more than $6 billion in loans, mostly from Japanese banks. Because of the sharp drop in oil prices and the Asian economic crisis, servicing the large debt was difficult for Qatar, which sharply reduced government outlays; however, the increase in oil prices in late 1999 appreciably relieved the financial pressures. Because of the supergiant scale of the North Field gas reservoir, numerous large-scale projects to utilize the resource have been broached, including piping the gas to Europe. A mammoth plan projected ultimately to cost $10 billion is in advanced planning—the Dolphin initiative, proposed by UAE Offsets Group, Abu Dhabi. In Phase I, Qatar gas is to be piped under the southern Gulf to Dubai and Abu Dhabi to feed gas-supply projects and large gas-based industries there. Later, the pipeline is to be extended to Suhar, Oman, to supplement Omani supplies. Finally, plans call for the Dolphin net to reach Pakistan by pipeline under the Gulf of Oman, perhaps by 2005.[22] A light-industrial zone near Doha supplies processed foods and small manufactured items for Qatar's limited number of inhabitants.

Qatar's small population has increased by more than 33 times since the 1930s, rising to more than 579,000 (723,000 by U.S. Government estimate) in 1999 as the economy attracted thousands of Pakistanis, Indians, Iranians, Baluch, and Arabs from Egypt, Jordan, Lebanon, Yemen, and Oman. As one consequence of the

FIGURE 18-4   Royal Palace, Doha, Qatar, one of several structures in the capital with striking architecture.

influx of immigrants, only one-fifth of the population is now indigenous Qatari. More than four-fifths of the state's population live in Doha and its immediate suburbs. Little more than a fishing village before World War II, Doha has been completely redeveloped around successive ring roads into an admirably modern capital, as in Kuwait City. The new (late 1980s) marble palace of the ruler sits amid scores of handsome structures on the shore of Doha Bay (Fig. 18-4). A former traditional palace now houses the well-developed national museum. The interior of the peninsula is very sparsely inhabited but supports a varying number of small *rawdah* farms and a few hundred Bedouin families, whose numbers decrease yearly.

The ruling Al Thani, Amir Hamad bin Khalifa, deposed his father, Shaykh Khalifa bin Hamad, on June 27, 1995, in a bloodless coup. The progressive new amir is encouraging democratic institutions; for example, he appointed a committee in July 1999 to draw up a constitution within three years. Qatar television "al-Jazira," is attracting attention for opening the medium to ideas and personalities uniquely liberal in the region.[23] Qatar was briefly in the world spotlight in November 1997 when the Middle East/North Africa (MENA) Summit met in Doha; however, MENA virtually collapsed by the date of the meeting because of Arab states'

anger over Israel's intransigence in the peace process at that time. Shaykh Hamad has indicated that Qatar will continue the relations it formerly enjoyed with other GCC members and with Britain and the United States.

United Arab Emirates (UAE)

A Survey

Most recent of the Middle East states to achieve independence, the United Arab Emirates[24] comprises seven desert component polities: Abu Dhabi, Dubai, Sharjah, Ajman, Umm al-Qaywayn, Ras al-Khaymah, and, the only amirate not facing the Gulf, Fujayrah (see Map 18-3). Thus, the UAE occupies coasts on both sides of the Musandam Peninsula (the "Horn of Arabia") in the eastern corner of the Arabian Peninsula. Formerly an aggregation of British-protected tribal shaykhdoms known as the Trucial States, the amirates moved abruptly from isolation and poverty in the 1950s to oil wealth and dramatic development in the 1970s and 1980s.[25]

Neolithic and Bronze Age settlements and tombs, found especially in Abu Dhabi and Dubai, reveal ties with the Dilmun and Sumerian cultures in the northern Gulf and Mesopotamia. The coastal area became familiar to Europeans—the Portuguese in the early

United Arab Emirates

Long-form official name, anglicized: United Arab Emirates

Official name, transliterated: Ittihad al-Imarat al-Arabiyah al-Muttahidah

Form of government: federation of seven monarchies (amirates or shaykhdoms)—Abu Dhabi, Dubay, Sharjah, Ajman, Umm al-Qawayn, Ras al-Khaymah, and Fujayrah—with specified powers to the central government and remaining powers to the individual rulers

Area: 32,000 miles^2/82,880 km^2

Population, 1999: 2,744,000. Literacy: 79.2

Ethnic composition (%): Emirian 19.0, other Arab (Egyptian, Lebanese, Palestinian, Sudanese, Omani) 23.0, South Asian (Baluchi and other Pakistani, Indian, Sri Lankan, Bangladeshi) 48.0, Iranian 5.0, African 0.8, European and other expatriates 4.2

Religions (%): Muslim 95.0 (Muslim 80.0, Shii 20.0), Christian and other 5.0

GDP, 1998: $40 billion; per capita: $17,400

Petroleum reserves: 97.8 billion barrels (third-largest in Middle East and world)

Main exports (% of total value, 1997): crude petroleum 45.0; natural gas 9.0; reexports, fish, dates 25.0

Main imports (% of total value, 1997): manufactured goods 34; machinery and transportation equipment 29; foods 15; chemicals 5

Capital city (population as of 1999): Abu Dhabi 725,000; other cities: Dubai 675,000; Sharjah (al-Shariqah) 330,000; al-Ayn 300,000; Ras al-Khaymah 175,000

1500s and then the British in the 1700s. The series of coastal islands and indentations, offering shelter to Gulf fishing and pearling dhows, were dotted with coastal villages that, through a series of treaties, were placed under British protection. After several British naval operations in the southern Gulf, the British imposed the first coastwide maritime truce in 1820 and followed it with other treaties and imposed agreements in 1835, 1839, and 1847.[26] The Treaty of Maritime Peace in Perpetuity (1853) gave the British navy supervision over maritime relations in the lower Gulf, leaving land relations to the shaykhdoms. From this 1853 truce evolved the official designation of the coastal settlements as the Trucial States (sometimes Trucial Shaykhdoms, Trucial Coast, or even Trucial Oman), a designation that lasted for more than a century. Out of these "village states," whose

patterns of independence shifted as ruling families altered relationships and domains, developed the post-1971 United Arab Emirates.

In 1951, the British persuaded the rulers of the shaykhdoms to create a Council of Trucial State Rulers, and in the same year the Trucial Oman Levies were organized to suppress slave traffic and maintain law and order. These forces later became the storybook Trucial Oman Scouts (TOS), who, under a handful of British officers seconded to them, were responsible for security in the area. Disbanded after independence, the TOS supplied cadres to the new military units of the UAE.

The landscape along the UAE coast has been dramatically transformed in one generation. Formerly, cross-country tracks and wadi bottoms served as roads until the mid-1960s (see Fig. 9-4), and a few small generators supplied

MAP 18-3   General map of the seven United Arab Emirates (UAE), with neighboring Bahrain and Qatar. Numbers in the UAE refer to exclaves belonging to the respective amirates. See maps in Chapter 8 for petroleum and gas fields. Recent boundaries are depicted.

electricity only part of the time in the towns. After the decline of pearling, the hardy inhabitants relied on a primarily subsistence economy of fishing, herding, date culture, and a growing dhow trade. In the early 1960s, the oil boom began in Abu Dhabi, later in Dubai, and then in the other amirates. Within a few years after independence, the UAE achieved a level of economic development that could be described only as spectacular, its people enjoying the world's highest per capita income.

Preliminary to their withdrawal from the Gulf, the British delineated shaykhdom boundaries for the first time, partly to inhibit later boundary conflicts and partly to prevent dissension over oil and gas exploration. With British warnings against political fragmentation, the Trucial States explored confederation with Bahrain and Qatar but finally remained separate, becoming independent under a provisional constitution on December 2, 1971. Ras al-Khaymah originally held back but relented and joined the federation in February 1972.

Despite British efforts, boundary disputes among several shaykhdoms jeopardized the success of federal integration in the early months. However, Dubai and Abu Dhabi resolved their boundary problem by agreeing to a Neutral Zone, and Dubai and Sharjah tentatively settled their dispute in 1976 and finally in 1997. Although the federation envisioned in the provisional constitution encountered certain difficulties, especially the reluctance of local rulers to surrender their traditional powers to a central government, the UAE soon evolved into a vigorous and prosperous polity. The overriding question was whether the individual rulers could accept the surrender of certain of their jealously guarded monarchical powers. To the relief of the people, other Gulf states, and the British, centripetal forces were stronger than centrifugal forces; and the UAE emerged as a political-geographical oddity, a republic in which the federal units are monarchies. After 25 years, the right balance had been reached in the allocation of powers (and funds) between constituent principalities and the federal institutions. Criteria for the distribution of offices proved acceptable; in June 1996, the Federal National Council approved a permanent constitution and designated Abu Dhabi the permanent federal capital. The extraordinary transformation has been handled extraordinarily well.

Population

Development in the amirates stimulated growth of the population from about 75,000 in 1950 to about 223,000 in 1970, followed by an explosive twelvefold increase between 1970 and 1999, when the total exceeded 2.7 million. By far most of the population is concentrated in the UAE provisional capital city of Abu Dhabi and in the coalescing cities of Dubai and Sharjah. Additional nodes of population mark the other amirate capitals, several scattered oasis towns, and especially the merging villages and towns in al-Ayn, the UAE section of the Buraymi Oasis. The ethnic composition of the population is noteworthy, not only because it is the most complex of the varied population mixtures of the Gulf states but also because only 19 percent of the UAE population is indigenous Emirian.

The sparse local population of the early 1960s, although intelligent and energetic, could not meet the demand for labor, either in numbers or in technical skills, that erupted in the early boom years; not only the expertise and materials to handle the boom had to be imported, but also the scores of thousands of workers. The rate of migration created housing shortages, forcing many workers, some with families, into *barasti* ("palm frond") huts, tents, and other spontaneous housing until the wealthier amirates erected extensive block after block of houses. By the early 1980s, when the construction boom had slowed, the economy began the ups and downs imposed by rising and falling oil prices. Like all the major Arab petroleum producers, the UAE is attempting to reduce its need for outside personnel—90 percent of its workforce. Various regulations call for more rigid "Emirazation" of the labor force's managerial levels, and a 1996 law severely restricts further immigration.

Economic Development

Oil and related industries dominate the economy of the UAE as they do in Qatar and Kuwait. For example, exports of crude and processed oil and gas supply 77 percent of export earnings, and 86 percent of government revenues are from oil.[27] It is noteworthy that Abu Dhabi produces 84 percent of the UAE's oil and contributes nearly three-fourths of the federal government's income. As in the other Gulf oil producers, especially Bahrain, the UAE has followed a vigorous program of diversifying industries that are energy-related and several that are only indirectly related. Although most of the plants are export-oriented, some of them cater to the affluent population distributed over the union area.

However, as important as the oil industry is, the several amirates have expanded their traditional economic activities: trade and transit trade, shipping, and modest but increasingly important agriculture that includes dairy, poultry and egg production, horticulture, animal herding, and fishing. Successful industrialization and diversification have helped cushion the periodic low-oil-price recessions. Even more important is the role of administrative, financial, commercial, and personal services—government, banking, insurance, export-import, retailing, hotel and restaurant operation, and general tourism. Thus, the diversified and vigorous economy in a larger territory gives the UAE an outward and genuine air of energy and a lively bustle. Different centers have developed specializations and characteristics: Abu Dhabi is an oil, financial, industrial, and administrative center (Fig. 18-5). Dubai is a recreational, trade, industrial, financial, and shipping center; Sharjah is a cultural center with two universities and also complements Dubai as a diversified transportation, manufacturing, and business center; and Fujayrah is a beach resort. Al-Ayn is a productive agricultural oasis, as are Sharjah's Dhayd and Ras al-Khaymah's Diqdaqah (Digdagga) Oasis.

Oil, Gas, and Related Industries. Ranking third in both the Middle East and the world in proved petroleum reserves, the UAE possesses a known 97.8 billion barrels. New discoveries tripled the reserves between 1987 and 1988. The UAE thus modestly surpassed Kuwait and Iran (see Table 8-1) and has far more reserves than any of the next three oil giants—Venezuela, the former Soviet lands combined, and Mexico. It has more than four times the oil of the United States and could produce 2 million bpd for 135 years. In addition, as a result of the new discoveries in 1986–1988, the UAE has the fourth largest gas reserves in the world. (Russia leads all others). Abu Dhabi alone has 94 percent of the federation's oil reserves and 93 percent of the gas (see Table 8-1). Each member amirate in the federation retains full rights to its individual oil and gas resources, sharing with other states only that income unanimously agreed upon.

Petroleum Development (Trucial States), an Iraq Petroleum Company subsidiary that became Abu Dhabi Petroleum Company in 1962, conducted initial exploration in southwestern Abu Dhabi in 1939, found oil in 1958, but exported only in 1963. Produced in the great Bab field (originally Murban), the oil was lifted from a major new terminal at Jabal Dhanna in extreme western Abu Dhabi. Meanwhile, oil had been found by Abu Dhabi Marine Areas in the offshore Umm Shaif field, which began production in 1962. A second offshore field, Zakum, went on stream in 1967, with production pumped to the Das Island terminal, along with output from Umm Shaif and from Bunduq, jointly owned with Qatar. By 2000, more than a score of offshore fields had been found in Abu Dhabi's waters (some of which have not been put on stream), along with ten major onshore fields. One such field was found to extend under the border with Saudi Arabia as an extension of the large Shaybah light-oil reservoir. Deep drilling into the Khuff zone in search of nonassociated gas below already-producing oil horizons (a concept pioneered in Bahrain) discovered immense gas reservoirs beneath Umm Shaif and Abu al-Dukhush offshore and Bab onshore. The discoveries gave Abu Dhabi the huge gas reserves mentioned earlier and prompted a major industry. Even so, Abu Dhabi and Dubai are pursuing the Dolphin project to bring Qatar gas to the UAE and Oman (discussed under Qatar, above). The Abu Dhabi National Oil Company (ADNOC), operating mainly onshore, and Abu Dhabi Marine Areas (ADMA), mainly offshore, are the principal operating and service companies in Abu Dhabi.

Although exploration was begun by Petroleum Development (Trucial Coast) in Dubai in 1937, it was unsuccessful. Not until 1966 did Dubai Marine Areas (DUMA, a consortium of U.S. and European companies) find the moderately large field of Fateh, 56 miles/90 km offshore (see Fig. 8-2). Associated fields were found a few years later, and Dubai's total production rose to 469,000 bpd in 1990 before declining to 300,000 bpd in the middle and late 1990s. Dubai is importing gas from both Sharjah and Abu Dhabi to feed its considerable industries, but it still promotes the Dolphin project for Qatar gas.

Sharjah and Ras al-Khaymah found oil still later. After onshore wildcat wells in Sharjah proved dry, a new concessionaire (Crescent

402

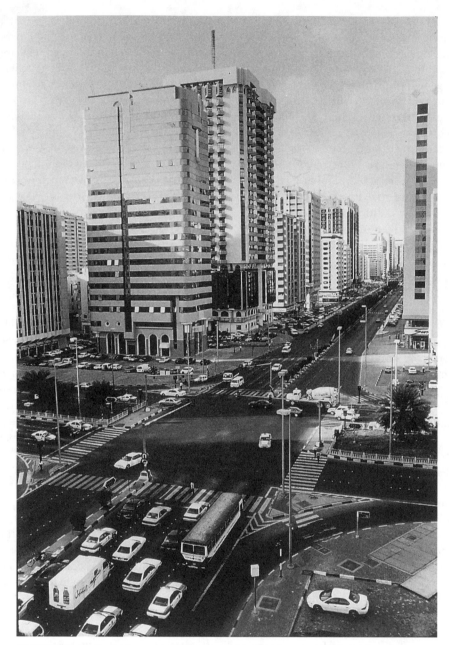

FIGURE 18-5   Typical street in downtown Abu Dhabi, capital of the United Arab Emirates (UAE). When I first visited Abu Dhabi in 1964, it had less than a dozen permanent structures, none more than two stories high.

Petroleum Company, with Buttes Gas and Oil of the United States as operator) found the small Mubarak field near Abu Musa Island, 45 miles/72 km offshore, in 1972. Oil from this field was first exported in 1974, and revenues were shared with Iran as a result of accords regarding Iran's claim to Abu Musa and therefore to its territorial waters. Mubarak production rapidly declined from 38,300 bpd to less than 2,850 bpd in 1996. However, an onshore gas condensate field found (by Amoco and Sharjah Petroleum Department) in 1980 at Saja, 5 miles/9 km inland, along with later condensate and dry gas discoveries, are bringing Sharjah significant revenues. Sharjah is now supplying gas to several of its neighbors. Ras al-Khaymah also produces small amounts of gas condensate from its offshore Saleh field, opened in 1983–1984 and lying 26 miles/42 km into the Gulf. Petroleum explorations in Ajman, Umm al-Qaywayn, and Fujayrah have been commercially unsuccessful, but some gas has been found in Umm al-Qaywayn.

The UAE opted not to engage in large-scale refining, but it is steadily expanding other energy-related industries. The main refinery, with a capacity of 132,000 bpd, operates in the western Abu Dhabi industrial zone of al-Ruways, near Jabal Dhanna. That zone also includes petroleum-based plants producing fertilizers, petrochemicals, and, increasingly, natural gas liquids (NGL). As the UAE steadily exploits its enormous gas reserves, gas processing plants using 3 billion ft.^{3}/85 million m^3 per day are being developed offshore and onshore. The increasing condensates exports are not subject to OPEC quotas. The future for UAE oil, gas, and associated industry is certain to be bright.

Other Industries. In addition to the petroleum-processing plants, the al-Ruways industrial zone contains other plants, including a steel mill producing iron bars for construction. However, in the mid-1970s, Dubai developed a man-made port and industrial zone at Jabal Ali in an isolated desert area southwest of Dubai City that eclipsed al-Ruways. Despite skepticism around him, the enterprising ruler of

Dubai, the late Shaykh Rashid bin Said Al Maktum, deep-dredged a channel and constructed a major port, put in a large power plant and desalination facility, invited dozens of industrial companies, and opened a free port area. Two decades later, as the imaginative Shaykh Rashid predicted, Jabal Ali is a multi-billion dollar regional economic node. Like the still larger aluminum smelter in Bahrain, the Dubai plant at Jabal Ali utilizes the plentiful energy of the area to produce 245,000 tons of ingots per year; some of the aluminum is rolled or extruded in adjacent operations. The main power plant, regularly expanded, not only feeds the smelter but desalinates 30 million gals/113.6 million l of water per day. The booming zone includes other power and water plants; 200 factories, including refineries and gas-processing facilities, petrochemical plants, cement plants, a steel fabrication plant, fertilizer factories, paint factories, food processing establishments, grain silos, tank farms, and metal fabricators; an ever-expanding free zone with comprehensive private rights of operation for 700 companies from 59 countries; and the world's largest manmade port, a state-of-the-art facility. Modest but impressive industrial parks have also been developed in Sharjah and tiny Ajman. As in other energy-rich Gulf states, desalination is a major and expanding industry. More than 40 plants generate large amounts of electricity plus 500 million gallons/1.9 million m^3 per day of desalted water. Desalination plants provide more than three-fourths of nonagricultural water in the UAE. Overuse of groundwater has caused aquifers to drop significantly, and many wells have run dry; encroaching seawater has caused other groundwater to become saline.

Trade and Transportation. Crude petroleum and refined products constitute the bulk of the UAE's exports, most of which go to Western Europe, Japan, and the United States. However, reexports and such UAE-fabricated products as aluminum are becoming increasingly important and constitute more than one-fourth of exports. Dubai especially has a highly developed reexport system in the free zones at both main seaports and at its airport. International operators shipping between Europe and the Far East send goods to Dubai, where they are offloaded, broken down, and reloaded as reexports for specific distribution. A special service in Dubai offloads sea cargoes from the Far East or South Asia, breaks them down, and reexports them by air to European destinations. The varied imports include decreasing percentages of food as the UAE expands its own agricultural output. Machinery, much of it for oil operations, and many consumer goods together constitute more than half of imports. A centuries-long tradition continues in regional maritime trade and in extensive commerce with India, Iran, and East Africa. Ras al-Khaymah, Sharjah, and Dubai were successively involved in the exchange, with Dubai later predominating. The picturesque dhow operations from the Creek in Dubai smuggle gold and consumer goods to the subcontinent and to Iran. The vigorous local retail trade satisfies a lively demand for consumer goods by a wealthy upper class and an affluent middle class; most imported goods are customs free or are taxed at a flat 4 percent, and there is no tax on retail sales. Sharjah and Dubai are crowded with "vacation shoppers" who come on special charter flights from Eastern Europe and other areas short of consumer products. The shoppers fly in specifically to buy large quantities of electronic items, watches, jewelry, photographic equipment, and other low-bulk, high-value goods to take back to their home countries and sell at handsome profits. The trade is highly organized, from shopping flights to discount hotel rates to shopping buses to the huge new magnificent *suqs* of Sharjah, Dubai, and Ajman. These extraordinary shopping malls feature world-class architecture (Fig. 18-6) and are brimming with inventories of highly varied consumer goods.

Large, planned ports in Dubai, Abu Dhabi, and Sharjah contrast with their tiny predecessors, which were used only by dhows for Gulf and Indian trade, fishing, and pearling. Port Rashid in Dubai is one of the largest ports in the Middle East, enclosing more than 500 acres/200 ha within its breakwater. The Jabal Ali port in southern Dubai has steadily increased its cargo handling. Even so, the small-scale port facilities in Khawr Dubai ("The Creek") still attract scores of dhows each day. The number of vessels calling at Dubai's ports increased three and one-half times between 1980 and 1998, when 11,316 vessels called; dry cargo handled increased more than eight times to 28 million tons during the same period. In a manner typical of the competitiveness among member amirates, Abu Dhabi has expanded its Port Zayyid, especially its container facilities. Abu Dhabi is also installing a large free zone facility on Saadiyat Island, adjacent to Abu Dhabi Island, to compete with Jabal Ali. Sharjah has vigorously pushed its smaller Port Khalid in Sharjah town and its container port of Khawr (Khor) Fakkan on the east coast, facing the Indian Ocean. Khawr Fakkan—as well as the small port of Fujayrah—has grown steadily in response to its major locational asset: its situation on the Gulf of Oman, outside the entrance to the Gulf. An international cargo ship can save up to 24 hours and insurance costs by avoiding the trip through the straits and into the Gulf. Ajman and Ras al-Khaymah also promote their small ports.

Of the federation's four larger airports (Abu Dhabi, Dubai, Sharjah, and Ras al-Khaymah), the first three vie for handling the most aircraft and passengers. Dubai has a large transit traffic; Sharjah receives a large number of arrivals in its "shopper vacations" program—and also enjoys great admiration for its aesthetically attractive terminal; and Abu Dhabi receives governmental and oil-business travelers. Again, competitiveness led Ajman and Fujayrah each to open its own airport. Thus, the UAE is oversupplied with both seaports and airports. All towns and villages in the UAE are now integrated into an excellent national highway network (see Fig. 9-4b).

Agriculture and Fishing. Although their relative contribution to the economy is now minor,

FIGURE 18-6   Sharjah City's old *suq (top, 1964)*, with palm frond (*barasti*) roof for shade, and one of the city's new *suqs (bottom, 1979)*. In the background are high-rise buildings of the city's new central business district (CBD). In 1990, an ornate "new new *suq*," al-Majarrah, opened in Sharjah.

fishing (including pearling) and agriculture (including nomadic herding) were, along with trade, the main bases of the Trucial States economy prior to World War II. Agriculture in this desert environment, with only 3 inches of rainfall, was then confined to small oases and date palm groves around the coastal villages, and the limited water resources were minimally developed. After the mid-1960s, the greatly increased availability of capital and the greater demand for fresh foods stimulated development of the few potentially productive agricultural areas.

Increased production has come especially from the three extensive oases of al-Ayn, located in eastern Abu Dhabi (see Map 18-3); Dhayd, in Sharjah and east of Sharjah City; and Diqdaqah, in Ras al-Khaymah. All three lie at the western foot of the Oman Mountains and tap aquifers fed by runoff from the mountain slopes. Al-Ayn is an exceptionally extensive oasis and, as the original bailiwick of UAE President Zayid bin Sultan Al Nahyan, has been intensively developed to produce a variety of dates, fruits, and vegetables.[28] Dhayd, somewhat farther away from the mountains, uses groundwater irrigation; the unexpectedly large and varied oasis produces crops from strawberries to lemons. Diqdaqah, south of the town of Ras al-Khaymah, contains an agricultural experimental station established in the oasis in 1956; fruits and vegetables from Diqdaqah supply many of the needs of the cities to the south. Al-Ayn, Diqdaqah, and Dhayd exemplify the marvels that can be wrought with huge inputs of capital and technology. Large dairy farms also operate in all the large oases, as do air-conditioned chicken farms marketing several million chickens each year. More than 50 small groves of date palms extend along an arc of tiny oases in al-Jiwa (or al-Liwa) in southwestern Abu Dhabi.

Relations

With some of the world's largest petroleum and gas reserves in a crucial location, yet with a small population and negligible military strength, the vulnerable UAE must walk a strategic tightrope. It follows a pragmatic but skillfully diplomatic balancing act by maintaining, for example, mutually beneficial "correct" relations with Iran on one side and Saudi Arabia on the other. It ensures that, as a former British protectorate, it can rely on British assistance in a crisis; and, for double insurance, it has since independence in 1971 maintained good relations with the United States—close private commercial ties and friendly government-to-government relations, including U.S. security assistance. Relations with the United States became much closer after the Iraqi invasion of Kuwait, and the UAE contributed more than $4 billion to the coalition fighting Iraq. Locally, the UAE places much of its diplomatic emphasis on the GCC and regionally on the Arab League.[29]

Sketches of Individual Amirates

Abu Dhabi.   Largest (86 percent of the total UAE area), most populous, and by far the wealthiest of the seven component amirates, Abu Dhabi (or Abu Zaby) is the dominant member of the UAE. Located on a low near-shore island of *sabkhah* and sand, Abu Dhabi City, the population core, grew from a small village of *barasti* huts and a fort in the 1950s to a wealthy, bustling, planned city of 725,000 in 1999, with high-rise office buildings, luxury hotels and palaces, divided boulevards, mosques and schools, housing estates, and irrigated plantings bordering and dividing boulevards and ornamenting large traffic circles (Fig. 18-5). It also serves as the capital of the UAE. A secondary core is in the oasis of al-Ayn, seat of the UAE's first university, and other clusters are in the al-Ruways-Jabal Dhanna oil and industrial area and in the arc of al-Jiwa (al-Liwa) oases (Map 18-3).

Dubai.   Next-largest polity and next in location to the north of Abu Dhabi is the amirate of Dubai (sometimes Dubay or Dubayy), population 710,000, with about 45 miles/72 km of sand and *sabkhah* coastline. The commercial and shipping center of Dubai (population 675,000) developed on both sides of Dubai Creek, which affords an ideal and picturesque harbor for dhows engaged in fishing, pearling, smuggling, and other maritime trade (see Fig. 18-7). Dubai proper, more of an administrative center, lies south of the creek and has a carefully preserved group of older structures topped by *badgirs,* Persian wind towers (see Fig. 4-3); Dayrah, with more of the commercial and tourism functions, developed north of the inlet. The two banks of the Creek are connected not only by two bridges and a tunnel for automobiles but also by *abras,* picturesque small passenger ferries. With a laissez-faire commercial philosophy, Dubai predominates as the commercial center of the coast, with a lively nightlife. On the southern coast lies the remarkable Jabal Ali port and industrial park described earlier; between it and Dubai City is a coastal hotel claimed to be the world's largest.

Sharjah. Third-largest amirate and adjacent to Dubai on the north is Sharjah (al-Shariqah), and the cities of Sharjah and Dubai virtually coalesce. The amirate's 10-mile/16-km coastline formerly included a small dhow harbor, which developed into a modest modern port after 1970. Sharjah's territory, with a population of 410,000, is the most fragmented of all the amirates (see Map 18-3). With three exclaves on the Batinah coast of the Gulf of Oman (Diba, Khawr Fakkan, and Kalba), Sharjah thus has a common border with all six of the other polities in the federation. Dhayd Oasis and irrigated plots along the Batinah coast combine to give Sharjah a plentiful supply of fruits and vegetables. With only limited resources in hydrocarbons, Sharjah pursued a vigorous program of tourism and tour-shopping, and the city has an extraordinary number of four-star and five-star hotels and retail shops. The present ruler has encouraged cultural facilities, including two universities opened in 1997, one being the impressive American University of Sharjah. Farther into the desert beyond AUS is the Desert Park and Natural History Museum, with world class exhibits. Two Gulf islands, Abu Musa and Sir Abu Nuayr, are claimed by Sharjah, but Iran also claims Abu Musa, maintains troops there, and shares revenues from the offshore field in the island's territorial

waters. Sharjah, with 330,000 people, was the site of the coast's first airfield and also hosted a Royal Air Force detachment and, after the mid-1950s, the headquarters of the Trucial Oman Scouts.

Ajman. Next up the coast is the amirate of Ajman, the smallest unit in the UAE, with 120,000 people. It includes the town of Ajman, a strip of desert behind the town, and two tiny exclaves in the interior. In competition with Sharjah, Ajman has developed a small but lively industrial park in its port area and in 1990 opened a large, gleaming white shopping mall, Suq al-Ajman. It retains seafaring traditions in a large dhow-building yard and in a fish-trap fabricating facility.

Umm al-Qaywayn. North of Ajman is the second-smallest and the least populated (35,000 people) of the amirates, Umm al-Qaywayn. With a population of 33,000, the town occupies a site on the tip of a narrow peninsula, reached by a spur from the coastal highway. With negligible energy resources, Umm al-Qaywayn has lagged behind the other members of the federation in developmental growth, but it installed an "aquapark" in the early 1990s. In addition to its traditional fishing, it has attracted a few clothing-manufacturing and printing establishments.

Ras al-Khaymah. Northernmost of the polities and occupying a triangular area west of the mountain spur that reaches the sea at the village of Sham, Ras al-Khaymah, population 210,000, exhibits appreciable diversity. The town itself, with 179,000 people, lies on a peninsula and has a long seafaring tradition. The Diqdaqah agricultural station and half a dozen other towns and villages are distributed around the amirate. In the mountains at the northern tip of Ras al-Khaymah lives a small but interesting non-Arab ethnic group, the Shihuh. The two offshore islands of Little Tunbs and Great Tunbs were long claimed by Ras al-Khaymah but were seized by Iran in 1971. Ras al-Khaymah's only known oil comes from its

408

FIGURE 18-7   Fabled Dubai Creek (*Khawr Dubay*), 1964 and 1997, from same hotel roof. In middle distance, note wind towers (*badgirs*) to left and dozens of dhows at anchor to right. The inlet long served as the city's port and helped make Dubai the main commercial center of the lower Gulf.

off-shore field of Saleh, but it also has some modest gas reserves.

Fujayrah. The only federation member located on the eastern, or Gulf of Oman, side of the peninsula, Fujayrah, now with 171,000 people, was isolated until federal highways made it easily accessible and encouraged a beach-resort development. Having only a limited fishing economy and a few date palms until the 1960s, Fujayrah's resort facilities include stretches of clean, sandy, and still uncrowded beaches. The success of the beach resort encouraged the building of other resort facilities, making Fujayrah unrecognizable compared to its pre-1960s condition. The emirate is also pursuing development of its port to compete with Khor Fakkan. Huge chicken farms with air-conditioned hen houses and a major dairy have also been developed inland from the resort.

Notes

1. L. S. Amery, in his foreword to Wilson 1928, ix.

2. After development in the Gulf boomed, scores of studies on the subject appeared. For development and general coverage see Cottrell 1980, Long 1978, Niblock 1980, Crystal 1990, Zahlan 1998, *Persian Gulf States* Country Studies 1993, and Netton 1986. Netton also contains an excellent essay on source materials. The Gulf Cooperation Council is analyzed in Twinam 1992.

3. Refer to Scoville 1979 and to Lorimer 1915.

4. Studies of the fabulous Gulf oil industry are also legion. Gulf petroleum is discussed in the studies already cited and also in Akins 1981, PennWell's annual *International Petroleum Encyclopedia,* Exxon 1984, and Yergin 1991.

5. Many studies understandably link oil and Gulf security. In addition to the works cited in Notes 2 and 4, see Peterson 1983, Cordesman 1984, Cordesman, *Bahrain ...,* 1997, Ramazani 1979, Doran and Buck 1991, and Sindelar and Peterson 1989. Atherton 1985 pertains to the entire Middle East.

6. The classic work on the old Kuwait is the massive compendium Dickson 1949, followed by his *Kuwait and Her Neighbors.*

7. Crystal 1990, 39.

8. See Middle East Research Institute (MERI) report on Kuwait (1985), Abu-Hakim 1983, Al-Sabah 1980, Ffrench and Hill 1971, *Persian Gulf States* Country Studies 1993, and Crystal 1990.

9. *Christian Science Monitor,* Mar. 19, 1991. For a popular pictorial account of the Iraqi destruction, see Al Rashoud 1992. An "inside story" of the invasion and occupation is Levins 1997.

10. Return of stolen items is discussed in the *Washington Post Weekly,* Mar. 1, 1992, and *Christian Science Monitor,* June 17, 1991.

11. Among the many articles on the environmental catastrophe engendered by the oil spills and well fires in Kuwait, useful and easily available coverage, including ground photographs and space imagery, is given in Williams 1991, Canby 1991, and Earle 1992. An authoritative assessment with more perspective is given in *International Petroleum Encyclopedia* 1992, 222–229.

12. See Note 12, Chap. 11, especially Schofield 1993, Brown 1994, and Rahman 1997.

13. See Note 12, Chap. 11, especially Schofield 1993, Brown 1994, and Rahman 1997.

14. The problem is examined in detail in Lesch 1991; and in articles in *Christian Science Monitor,* Mar. 26, 1991; Apr. 17, 1991; June 26, 1991; Aug. 2, 1991; and Feb. 27, 1992. See also Ffrench and Hill 1971, 1–50, and Le Troquer and al-Oudat 1999.

15. The main island was called al-Awal in the past, hence the name Awali for the oil field and oil town. Believed to have been the ancient Dilmun, Bahrain was the classical Tylos; and, to add to the confusion, the name Bahrain was long applied to eastern Arabia as well as to the islands.

16. See Brunsden et al. 1979. For a popular but useful illustrated account of Bahrain well into its current development, see Abercrombie 1979. For more detailed examinations, see *Persian Gulf States* Country Studies 1993, Lawson 1988, and Nugent and Thomas 1985. For current information I have drawn on the *Country Commercial Guide: Bahrain,* FY 2000.

17. Bibby 1969. The finds are on display in the small but interesting Bahrain museum.

18. Clarke 1990 covers the history and status of Bahrain oil in minute detail and includes very useful appendixes and bibliography.

19. See the detailed Landsat images in Yehia 1983, which also includes sectional topographic and geologic maps of Qatar.

20. Batanouny 1981 gives good, concise coverage of the Qatar environment, as well as detailed scientific

coverage of the flora. Yehia 1983 discusses and illustrates the *rawdahs* and coastal features.

21. Among the growing number of studies on Qatar, see Zahlan 1998, Crystal 1990, Moorehead 1977 (popular, with photographs), *Persian Gulf States* Country Studies 1993, and Cottrell 1980.

22. See *Oil and Gas Journal,* July 19, 1999, 28. For information on Qatar's oil and gas industry and other economic developments, see *Country Commercial Guide: Qatar,* FY 2000, and "Qatar," *EIA: Qatar,* Aug. 1999. The *New York Times,* July 23, 1997, has an in-depth article on the gas industry.

23. See *New York Times,* July 4, 1999.

24. Although "amir" and "amirate" are the preferred transliterations and are generally used in this book, "emirates" is more widely accepted in the name of the UAE and is, at the risk of some confusion, used in this specific application. As for the "most recent"

Middle East state, unified Yemen might claim that distinction, since its two components combined in 1990, as opposed to the UAE's independence in 1971. However, each of the constituents of the new Yemen had previously been independent.

25. Khalifa 1979, the MERI report on the UAE (1985), el Mallakh 1981, Peck 1986, Taryam 1987, and Zahlan 1998. Peck is concise and broad in scope and also has a handy list of references.

26. The traditional claim that the British assumed control of the Gulf to suppress Arab piracy is disputed in al-Qasimi 1988.

27. For further details see *EIA: United Arab Emirates,* Dec. 1998; *Country Commercial Guide: United Arab Emirates,* FY 2000; and Gabriel 1987.

28. See Shahir and Nasr 1999.

29. Rugh 1996 gives a good analysis of UAE foreign relations.

19

Oman and Yemen: The Southern Fringe

Extending from the Strait of Hormuz to the Bab el-Mandeb along the southern fringe of the Arabian Peninsula are Oman and Yemen, the two largest of the six peripheral states of the peninsula. Since 1971, Oman has developed increasingly close relations with the Gulf states (with which it is often grouped because of its exclave on the Strait of Hormuz) and with neighboring Saudi Arabia. In 1990, the long-separated North Yemen and South Yemen merged to create a unified Republic of Yemen.[1]

Oman and the two formerly separate parts of Yemen maintain individually distinct characters physically, culturally, economically, and politically. Oman is a sultanate, the formerly almost absolute monarch now advised by two councils. Conservative and stable, it maintains cautious links with the West and has had 25 years of well-planned development, financed by its moderately large oil income. The Republic of Yemen, on the other hand, emerged in 1990 as a unification of the Marxist former People's Democratic Republic of Yemen (South Yemen) and the Yemen Arab Republic (North Yemen). The new unified Yemen confirmed its raison d'être after a 1994 civil war and continues haltingly to develop the necessary institutions of a politically viable entity.

Oman

Termed Muscat and Oman prior to 1970, the Sultanate of Oman was also sometimes confused with Trucial Oman, an alternate name for the Trucial States, now the UAE. Among other things, the several names reflect the regionalization of Oman into two basic parts: Inner Oman, west of the mountains, and the Batinah coast along the Gulf of Oman (Map 19-1).

The only sultanate in the Middle East, Oman exhibits many of the same types of development and modernization seen in the other oil states of the Gulf region. However, Oman has evolved in its own distinctive way, modernizing while maintaining much of its traditional culture. Caution and conservatism, therefore, characterize the Omani approach to development, and the sultanate deliberately maintains modest growth rather than allowing the explosive expansion of Kuwait, Abu Dhabi, and Dubai.[2] For example, the population is estimated to have grown less than 220 percent between 1960 and 1992, compared with an increase of more than 1,900 percent in the UAE during the same period.

Oman lies on the Tropic of Cancer; it is exceptionally hot in summer and is warm even during the low-sun season. It is a desert land except in a few higher elevations and in the highlands of southern Dhufar. Muscat, the capital city, lies virtually on the Tropic of Cancer, has an average annual temperature of 84°F/29°C, and receives less than 4 in./100 mm of rainfall annually. Along with the Yemen Mountains, highland Oman receives appreciable amounts of summer monsoon rain, particularly in the mountains around Salalah in the extreme south, as well as orographically enhanced winter cyclonic storm rain, exceeding 18 in./457 mm in parts of the northern ranges. Runoff from such rains in the northern mountains supplies the irrigation water for crops along the Batinah coast and in the interior oases.

Oman

Long-form official name, anglicized: Sultanate of Oman

Official name, transliterated: Saltanat Uman

Form of government: monarchy with elected consultative council and appointed state council

Area: 119,500 miles^2/309,500 km^2, within recently agreed boundaries (U.S. government: 82,030 miles^2/212,460 km^2)

Population, 1999: 2,364,000 (1993 census: 2,018,074)

Ethnic composition (%): Omani Arab 73.5, other Arab 3.5, South Asian (Indian, Pakistani, Baluch, Bangladeshi, Sri Lankan) 20, other 3

Religions (%): Ibadhi Muslim 75.0, other Muslim 11.0, Hindu 13.0, other 1.0

GDP, 1998: $18.6 billion; per capita $7,900

Petroleum reserves: 5.28 billion barrels

Main exports (% of total value, 1996): crude petroleum and gas 80.2; reexports 13.7; food and live animals (including fish) 1.9; fruits and vegetables 1.9

Main imports (% of total value, 1996): machinery and transport equipment 41.5; manufactured goods 17.3; food and live animals 12.9; miscellaneous manufactured articles 9.0; beverages and tobacco 4.2

Capital city: Muscat (Greater Capital Area) 625,000; other cities: Salalah-Raysut 100,000; Suhar 80,000; Ibri 80,000; Nazwa 52,000

Physical Regions

Oman comprises five distinct physical regions, each of which possesses its individual cultural character: [1] the Batinah coast, [2] al-Hajar (or Oman Mountains), [3] Inner Oman, [4] Central Oman, and [5] Dhufar (see circled numbers on Map 19-1).

[1] **Batinah Coast.** The Batinah coast is a coastal plain 6–18 miles/10–30 km wide that extends for 168 miles/270 km along the arc of the Gulf of Oman coast. The name implies "front" or "belly," as opposed to "al-Dhahirah" (Inner Oman), which suggests "back." Composed primarily of coalesced alluvial fandeltas of gravel, sand, and silt, the plain is squeezed between mountain chain and seashore and is Oman's primary agricultural area, cultivated for thousands of years. Crops are irrigated in a strip

about 1.8 miles/3 km wide, using the appreciable groundwater stored in the sandy gravels of the alluvial fans that have been built at the mouths of the streams after descending the mountain slopes. Date, lemon, lime, and banana groves extend along both sides of the highway, alternating with "strip settlements" only one household wide on each side of the road—the Omani version of the classic *strassendorf*. At the debouchment of the larger wadis, the major fans support more extensive agriculture and, usually, more populous settlements. Some towns are of considerable antiquity, for instance, Suhar, the largest town in al-Batinah; and many coastal settlements still engage in traditional fishing. With the exception of the Capital Area, al-Batinah is the most densely populated region in Oman and is rapidly developing its commerce and industry. Sib International Airport and its associated facilities are

MAP 19-1 General and economic map of Oman, with circled numbers indicating regions explained in text. Note the widespread distribution of petroleum fields, most of them small. International agreements have been recently reached on all of Oman's boundaries, a historic achievement.

located at the southern end of the plain; major industrial estates lie at each end, the earliest at Rusayl, near Sib, and a new one near Suhar in the north.

[2] **Al-Hajar.**   Often referred to as the Oman Mountains, al-Hajar ("the Rock") is a high, rugged chain of mountains that parallel the Batinah coast in a 435-mile/700-km arc from the northern tip of the Musandam Peninsula to Ras al-Hadd. They form the "backbone" between the Batinah "belly" and Inner Oman, or Dhahirah, "back." The northern end of the mountains overlooks the Strait of Hormuz and constitutes Ras Musandam, a striking desert fjord-type land that forms a maze of isthmuses and islands with coastal cliffs dropping sharply to sea-filled valleys. Politically, this tip of the Musandam Peninsula on the Horn of Arabia is an Omani exclave, separated from the rest of the sultanate territory by a wedge of the UAE. As such, it may be considered a subregion of al-Hajar. Much of the main mountain chain exceeds 4,800 ft./1,463 m. Peak elevations reach nearly 10,000 ft./3,048 m in the central block, the very rugged Jabal al-Akhdar (Green Mountain), a name sometimes mistakenly applied to the entire Hajar range. As was mentioned in Chapter 3, the Oman Mountains are a virtually unique geomorphic feature, both scientifically and scenically. Two sets of nappe complexes, one of ophiolite oceanic crust, have been thrust from former ocean deeps into stacked thrust sheets thousands of feet thick. Gigantic "windows" *(fenêtres)* carved into the nappes through erosion have exposed multiple overfolded strata of different ages, origins, and colors. Some almost vertical window walls are more than 6,500 ft./2,000 m high.[3] The one major pass through the chain is Samail Gap, just east of Jabal al-Akhdar, which is traversed by the main route connecting the Muscat area to Inner Oman. Oman's lifelines—large oil and gas pipelines—parallel the highway and carry the sultanate's entire production to the export terminal west of Matrah. Created by erosion along a major tectonic fault, the trough divides the Hajar range into the larger, scenically

rugged Western Hajar (Hajar al-Gharbi) and the smaller Eastern Hajar (Hajar al-Sharqi). The northern end of the Samail Gap intersects the southern end of the Batinah coastal plain, where structures of al-Hajar push to the coast and embrace two harbors. Muscat, on the western bay, evolved as the earlier main port and capital, but its small basin in the rugged ophiolites and pillow lavas curtailed development. Matrah, in the next depression eastward, had a larger basin and is now the main port (Fig. 19-1). Urban development has leapfrogged over the lava ridges and has spread up the southern Batinah to Sib airport and beyond. Thus, the Greater Capital Area is a second subregion of al-Hajar.

[3] **Inner Oman.**   Inner Oman (al-Dhahirah—"the back") is an amorphous foreland area extending southwestward from al-Hajar to the sands of the Rub al-Khali. The pattern of long-settled villages—Izki, Nazwa, Bahlah, Ibri, Dank, and others, as well as the oasis town of Buraymi—along the internal piedmont and belt of alluvial fans resembles the string of settlements on the eastern side of al-Hajar in al-Batinah, "the front." Watered by hundreds of small canals and *aflaj* (sing. *falaj*—see Glossary), extensive date palm groves, deep green against the barren mountains, mark the several oasis towns and dozens of villages on the alluvial fans along the piedmonts of al-Hajar. However, the interior settlements are less endowed with water resources and have traditionally been isolated because of their remote location, wedged between the rugged mountains to the east and the barren sands to the west. Even so, Inner Oman has long had ties with the Gulf shaykhdoms, especially through the Buraymi Oasis, as well as with Muscat and the Batinah via the Samail Gap. Subregional designations reflect a certain variety even in this seemingly uniform area: The northern extension of Inner Oman toward the large Buraymi–al-Ayn oasis is al-Jaw, with Ibri—largest town in al-Dhahirah—as the center. The subregion of the piedmont of Jabal Akhdar is the traditional heart of Inner Oman,

FIGURE 19-1   Waterfront of Matrah, the port extension of Muscat. Qaboos Port to right.

al-Dakhiliyah, supporting the major oases of al-Hamra, Bahlah, Nazwa, and Izki. All the oases cultivate extensive date groves, but they are diversifying into fruits and cotton. Nazwa, with its well-preserved fort, is the major center, having served as an older caravan town and political and cultural capital for centuries. East of the Samail Gap, the piedmont of the Eastern Hajar is usually referred to as al-Sharqiya (the East) and has its string of oasis towns in Ibra, al-Mudayrib, al-Mintirib, and al-Kamil, as well as the ancient small port of Sur and the eastern tip of Oman at Ras al-Hadd. Modern highways and excellent telecommunications now facilitate closer relations in both directions, integrate the interior economically, and strengthen political ties with the sultanate core around Muscat. Inner Oman is associated with the special Islamic group in Oman, the Ibadhis, who enjoyed a militant autonomy under their own imam for several decades prior to 1959. It is also the location of Oman's first and main producing oil fields.

[4] **Central Oman (al-Wusta).** Central Oman, locally called al-Wusta ("the middle"), extends from Inner Oman southward as a large, virtually barren area that for centuries has been little more than the realm of less than a dozen small Bedouin tribes. In the east, wedged between the Arabian Sea coast and the eastern Oman Mountains is an unusual dune field, the Wahibah Sands. The Wahibah contains a range of dune formations, including fossil sand seas, of such interest that it was the object of an intensive multidisciplinary investigation by the Royal Geographical Society (London) and Omani counterparts in 1985–1987. Otherwise, Central Oman is a monotonous land of sand and gravel, much of it dissected by wadis in former pluvial periods, and it had little to offer until more than a score of oil fields were discovered beneath its surface (see Map 19-1). Continued exploration found another 60 small pocket fields, some of which are actually in Dhufar. A high-speed highway completed in 1986 traverses the region, connecting Muscat

and Salalah. This formerly remote and isolated area is not only traversed by a major highway but also has been carefully mapped and is intensively crisscrossed by tracks of oil-exploration vehicles and well-maintenance trucks, although it is still devoid of significant settlements.

[5] Dhufar.   Dhufar (sometimes Dhofar) is an ill-defined area that merges imperceptibly with Central Oman to the northeast and with Yemen to the west. Primarily a rough, barren, sparsely inhabited desert area inland, it has mountains just back of the south coast with green slopes and monsoon forests, some producing frankincense, that contrast spectacularly with the inland desert. Dhufar was poorly known until intensive exploration opened more than a dozen producing oil fields centered 100 miles/ 160 km northeast of Salalah, the provincial capital. Southern Dhufar was contested between Dhufar rebels and Oman in the early 1970s (see next section). Mountain areas and some coastal villages are inhabited by several ethnolinguistic groups that are believed to predate Arab occupation of the area. Lying offshore are the Khuriya Muriya Islands. In 1991, amateur archaeologists guided by satellite imagery discovered and test-excavated the ruins of an ancient city 93 miles/150 km north-northeast of Salalah that is believed to be Ubar, famed center of frankincense trade from 2000 BC to late Roman times.[4] The obvious main center of Dhufar is Salalah, the southern anchor of Omani administration, commerce, transportation, and, recently, tourism. Salalah's unusual summer weather, unique in Oman, attracts thousands of Omanis to enjoy the cool, misty midsummer monsoon conditions on the mountain slopes (Fig. 19-2). The recently developed port of Raysut (now called Port Salalah) is being expanded and industrialized.

A Historical Sketch

Although incompletely studied, the antiquity of human occupation in the region has long been recognized in sites along the coast, in Inner Oman, and in Dhufar. Tombs in the village of

Bat, in al-Dhahirah, near Ibri, contain artifacts similar to those found in Abu Dhabi and suggest a relationship with Sumer at about 3000 BC. In the extreme east, in the Ras al-Hadd area, Phoenician artifacts suggest a link between the port of Sur and the Mediterranean Phoenician port of Sur (Tyre). Dhufar was a major source of frankincense and engaged in a significant trade for millennia.

Like the rest of the peninsula, Oman adopted Islam in the seventh century, but the theologically distinctive sect of Ibadhism, neither Sunni nor Shii, evolved in Oman in the eighth and ninth centuries and continues to be dominant. Ibadhis are the spiritual descendants of the Kharijis ("seceders"), a group that first supported Ali in his claim to be caliph but then separated from Ali during his conflict with the Umayyads. Oman has the only concentration of Ibadhis in the Middle East, although there are other Ibadhi communities in Zanzibar and North Africa.

Even more than in the Gulf amirates, Portuguese control for 142 years after 1508 left its mark in the forts and towers that are still prominent along the coast, especially around Matrah and Muscat, and on many hilltops elsewhere in the sultanate. With increasing British regional control after the Portuguese and Dutch were supplanted in the region, British influence in Oman remained strong for the next 300 years. However, the sultanate was technically independent after 1650, and Britain formally recognized Omani independence in 1951. Omani seafarers ranged the Indian Ocean and even established political control in Zanzibar and neighboring areas of East Africa and in the exclave of Gwadar on the Baluchi coast, near the present Iran-Pakistan border. Oman held Gwadar until 1958 and Zanzibar, at least indirectly, until 1964.

The Al Bu Said line, an Ibadhi dynasty, became the ruling power in 1744 and has retained the sultanate ever since. Inner Oman and the coast have been periodically disunited, suffering a particularly sharp division during the late nineteenth and early twentieth centuries, when the interior Ibadhis chose to have a

FIGURE 19-2   Fishing boats on the quiet beach of Mughsayl, west of Salalah. Raised reefs in distance. This area is the developing region of Oman.

theocracy ruled by their religious leader, the imam of Oman. The struggle was temporarily resolved by the Treaty of Sib, signed in 1920, which granted the imam autonomy in Inner Oman but recognized the nominal sovereignty of the sultan in the interior. However, when the latest imam, Ghalib ibn Ali, was elected in 1954, conflict erupted anew; the Imam Ghalib's rebellion against the sultan's control of the interior was defeated, with British help, only in 1959. The sultan of that period, Said bin Taimur Al Bu Said, prohibited use of private motor vehicles, refused expansion of the small electricity and telephone net in the capital area, and maintained a nighttime curfew in Muscat, having the city gates locked soon after dark. Sultan Said isolated himself in Salalah for self-protection. Oman at that time was the most backward and isolated area in the Middle East.

Four developments have dominated Oman's history since 1960. First, Oman's petroleum resources were discovered and have been developed into the leading industry, providing a national income of billions of dollars each year. Second, a separatist revolt by the communist-backed rebels of the Dhufar Liberation Front broke out against the sultanate in 1964. Third, the old sultan was forced to abdicate in favor of his son, the present ruler, Sultan Qabus ibn Said, in 1970. Fourth, Sultan Qabus (sometimes Qaboos) soon abolished many of his father's antiquated restrictions, urged educated Omanis to return home to a new regime, oversaw the defeat of the Dhufar rebellion, launched a major development program, and united Oman.

Success of the Dhufar rebellion would not only have meant the overthrow of the sultanate and the spread of the Aden communist regime into Oman, it would probably have also threatened other conservative regimes in the Gulf. The original Dhufar Liberation Front later merged with the Marxist-dominated Popular Front for the Liberation of Oman and the Arab Gulf (PFLOAG), which proclaimed its goal of overthrowing all traditional regimes in the Gulf region. In mid-1974, PFLOAG, renamed the

Popular Front for the Liberation of Oman (PFLO), was defeated and was finally driven out of Dhufar by the combined efforts of the Omanis, British officers, an Iranian task force, military forces from Jordan, and others.

During the next 25 years, Sultan Qabus led Oman in an entirely new direction, both economically and politically: While retaining the ultimate secular authority, he brought leaders of various segments of Omani society into the political process to balance tribal, regional, ethnic, and economic interests. In November 1996, he approved a Basic Statute, Oman's first written constitution—as well as the first in the Arab Gulf states. In October 1997, a limited electorate chose 82 members of the *Majlis al-Shura,* or Consultative Council. Moreover, two months later, Sultan Qabus appointed 40 members, including 4 women, to the new *Majlis al-Dawlah,* or State Council. In general, Oman, with its stable, conservative institutions, has the lowest level of politico-economic tensions in the region.[5]

The Omanis

Nearly one-fourth of the total population of 2.4 million is concentrated in the Muscat-Matrah-Ruwi core. Much of the rest lives in the belt of Batinah towns and the string of inner villages paralleling the southwestern piedmont of al-Hajar. However, major population outliers are the area of Salalah-Raysut and surrounding villages on the southern Dhufar coast and Sur at the eastern corner of the country. The sultanate's first-ever census, in 1993, statistically confirmed patterns of population distribution that had been estimated in past years.

Oman's basic Arab population differs perceptibly from that of neighboring Saudi Arabia and the UAE. The distinction arises partly because influences from southern Asia and East Africa entered along the Indian Ocean coast and partly because Arab influences from the interior diminished as they diffused into this most easterly projection of the Arabian Peninsula. Furthermore, fragmented by mountain ranges, highland masses, and desert belts,

Oman embraces many different ethnolinguistic and religious minorities, some still surviving in isolated mountain refuges. Strong tribal affiliations in the interior further diversify the Omani people.

Oman's maritime connections with southern Asia and East Africa and the sultanate's earlier political control of Gwadar and Zanzibar attracted immigrants from those areas. Indians, Baluch, Iranians, and Somalis and other East Africans settled in Oman, with many of the Africans being brought as slaves. The Shii Muslim Khojas (Arabic, Lawatias), a prominent minority, are members of a close-knit community of Hindu converts to Islam originally from India but resident in Oman as merchants for more than two centuries. The Khojas occupy a separate walled quarter in Matrah but also constitute communities along the Batinah. Other Shii Muslims include the Baharinah and the Ajam, of Persian background. A considerable Hindu community, the Binya (Arabic, Banyan), similar to the Khojas in their occupations and areas of residence, came from Gujarat in India and have resided in Oman for several centuries. Several minor ethnic groups, including some unassimilated pre-Arab peoples, occupy remote mountain areas. To the above must be added the nearly 600,000 expatriates—about one-fourth of the population—now employed in the sultanate. These non-Omanis include several Arab groups, South Asians, Filipinos, and Western Europeans and Americans. As other Gulf states are doing, and in a systematic program of "Omanization," Oman is seriously pursuing a reduction of its expatriate force.

Indigenous Omanis are divided into two basic tribal lines. The Hinawi, the older of the two, migrated from the Yemen highlands more than 1,800 years ago, and the Ghafiri arrived later from northern Arabia. This basic division, although less significant now than a few decades ago, cuts across socioeconomic groupings and is accepted as a fundamental fact of Omani society.

Although Islam is the predominant religion in Oman, the sultanate's major sect, the Ibadhi, is distinct from all other Islamic sects in the

Middle East. Oman was established as an Ibadhi state and has evolved an Ibadhi particularity. Whereas Inner Oman has long been the main concentration and theological stronghold of Ibadhism, the Al Bu Said ruling dynasty, while Ibadhi, has its power base in the southern Batinah. Conservative, fundamentalist, and simple in their principles, without being extremist, Ibadhi norms have strongly shaped Omani culture. Sunnis constitute the largest non-Ibadhi sect in Oman and are dominant in Salalah, distinguishable by their dialect. Shiis form the third-largest religious group, concentrated in the Batinah and especially in Muscat-Matrah, where the Khojas form a significant Shii community. The main non-Muslim group is the Indian Hindu community on the coast.

Most Omanis of both sexes can be immediately differentiated from other Middle Easterners by their national costumes. The standard male attire is the white, calf-long *dishdasha,* comparable to the ankle-length *thawb* in Saudi Arabia. The headgear is of one of two types: Dominant is the *kumma,* a fitted, brimless, round cap that is typically colorfully embroidered and usually expensive (see Fig. 6-5). It is unique to Oman. More formal is the elaborate modified turban, the *amamma,* a large square of light Kashmir wool artfully wound around the head. Traditionally, the well-dressed Omani male also wore a *khanjar,* a curved dagger with a highly decorated scabbard, frequently worn in the southern peninsula. Omani women also dress distinctively, with articles from both Arabia and India. Under a colorful *dishdasha* they wear ankle-length trousers, the *surawal,* and usually add one or more decorated filmy scarves or shawls.

Economy

Oman's preindustrial economy of seafaring, fishing, and irrigation agriculture rested on a broader base and supported a larger population than did similar economies in the Gulf shaykhdoms. For example, Oman has nearly twice the cropland of all the other four Gulf states combined, with most of its agricultural areas divided between the Batinah coast and the inner piedmont of the Hajar. Two-thirds of the agricultural area is in permanent crops, primarily dates, bananas, mangoes, and limes. Fishing remains a significant economic activity, much of it still traditional, although an increasing percentage is being modernized and systematized to take advantage of the rich fisheries in the upwelling waters along the coast.

As elsewhere in the general Gulf region, Oman's economy has been revolutionized by oil developments, although Oman was the last of the Gulf region countries to discover petroleum.[6] After several years of unsuccessful exploration in the late 1950s, the Iraq Petroleum Company (IPC) surrendered its concession, later taken up by Petroleum Development (Oman) (PDO). PDO, with Shell as its major partner, made its initial strikes at Natih, Fahud, and Yibal, 140–185 miles/225–300 km southwest of Muscat, in 1962–1964. A pipeline from the discovery area was laid through the Samail Pass to an export terminal at Mina al-Fahal, just west of Matrah, and all subsequent producing areas have been linked to this same terminal. Oman's single refinery is also at the terminal (see Table 8-2). By the late 1990s, intensive exploration by PDO and a score of other companies had discovered more than 110 fields, many of which are too small to tie into the system. Main output is still from the original discovery area—Yibal, al-Khuwayr (Lekhwait), and Fahud fields—but appreciable production comes from fields in Central Oman and Dhufar (see Maps 8-1 and 19-1). Oman's very complex geology makes exploration, drilling, and production difficult and expensive. Reservoirs also tend to be scattered, small, less productive, and quickly exhausted, with the result that production per well is less than that of the UAE and Saudi Arabia. Oman has increasingly been making use of enhanced oil recovery (EOR) techniques to raise production and lower costs—horizontal and multiple drilling, water injection, and gas injection. The state has also recently emphasized production, use, and export of the natural gas it is increasingly finding and producing. As is shown in Table 8-1,

Oman requires half again as many producing wells as Saudi Arabia to yield about 11 percent as much oil. Petroleum revenue is 75 percent of the total government revenue, 91 percent of the value of exports, and 42 percent of the GDP. By 1999, Oman's reserves were a moderate 5.3 billion barrels, sixth largest in the Middle East and comparable to those of the Divided Zone, and production was about 895,000 bpd. Since it is not an OPEC (or OAPEC) member, Oman is not subject to OPEC quotas or restrictions, but it coordinates closely with OPEC.

Few of the many minerals found in the complex rocks of al-Hajar are worth commercial exploitation; however, ancient copper workings near Suhar, in the northern Batinah, have been reopened and mined for several years but are mostly exhausted. Also recently exploited are deposits of chromite, manganese, asbestos, and marble.

Starting its development after the 1970 coup as the most backward country in the region, Oman under the new sultan moved deliberately, with guidance from competent, experienced consultants. Following a series of well-designed five-year plans that began in 1976, Oman first installed its basic infrastructure. For example, in 1970 only 6 miles/10 km of surfaced roads existed in the sultanate, since private vehicles were prohibited, and there was minimal electric and telephone service only in Muscat and Matrah. Oman then improved its agriculture and fishing, initiated education and other social programs, and finally undertook a modest import-substitution industrial program. By the late 1990s, more than 311,000 vehicles of all types utilized thousands of miles of well-surfaced roads. With elaborate consideration, the fifth development plan, imaginatively termed "Vision 2020," was launched in 1995 to give direction for the next 25 years.

As one major step in industrialization, in 1983 Oman established its first industrial estate in Rusayl, near Sib International Airport (Fig. 9-3a). By 1999, 100 privately owned factories were producing a wide range of basic products for the local market, from car batteries to air-conditioning units. Industrial estates are also being opened at opposite ends of Oman, one in Suhar, in the northern Batinah, and one in Raysut, west of Salalah. Others are planned for the center—Nazwa, Buraymi, Khasab, and Sur.

Because of the small size of the picturesque old harbor of Muscat, the new and modern port of Mina Qabus was constructed in the larger harbor at Matrah, a few miles west of Muscat, in the early 1970s. With development of southern Oman, a new port was also opened at Raysut, a few miles west of Salalah. Now redesignated Port Salalah, the facility is being greatly expanded to serve as the dominant container-transit port on the Indian Ocean coast of the peninsula; to compete successfully, it must surpass the UAE's Khawr Fakkan and Yemen's Aden. In 1974, a large new airport was opened at Sib, west of Matrah. Oman's only other airport with scheduled service is at Salalah. The Sultanate operates its own airline, Oman Air, and participates in the regional Gulf Air.

While pushing aggressively ahead with modernization, Oman has taken remarkable care to preserve important archaeological and cultural monuments. Most noteworthy are the picturesque sixteenth-century Portuguese forts overlooking Muscat and Matrah, the fine old mansions inside the former Muscat wall, the splendid fort of Rustaq (old capital of Oman) north of Jabal Akhdar, and the Nazwa fort. The grand mud fort of Bahlah (Fig. 19-3, top) is in restoration. Worthy in themselves, these conservation measures are also intended to serve the expanding tourism program—a remarkable contrast to the pre-1970 period when virtually no outsiders were permitted to visit the sultanate. Excellent new hotels also cater to tourists, with al-Bustan Palace Hotel, in a spacious setting east of Muscat, one of the most sumptuous hostelries in the region (Fig. 19-3, bottom). The Capital Area has greatly expanded west of Matrah toward the Sib airport, with a commercial and banking center in Greater Matrah-Ruwi, residences in Qurum and Madinat Qabus, and ministries and embassies in al-Khuwair.

FIGURE 19-3 Old and new in Oman: ruins of the splendid old mud fort in Bahlah, in Inner Oman *(top)*, and the magnificent al-Bustan Palace Hotel, near Muscat *(bottom)*. The fort dates from the eighteenth century, the hotel from the mid-1980s.

Yemen

Long-form official name, anglicized: Republic of Yemen

Official name, transliterated: al-Jumhuriyah al-Yamaniyah

Form of government: unitary multiparty republic with one legislative house (House of Representatives)

Area: 214,300 miles²/555,000 km² (U.S. Government: 203,850 miles²/527,970 km²) (area imprecise, since some land boundaries undefined)

Population, 1999: 16,388,000. Literacy: 38%

Ethnic composition (%): Arab 90.0, Indian, Somali, Afro-Arab mix, European, other 10.0

Religions (%): Muslim 99.9 (Sunni 53.0, Shii 46.9), other 0.1

GDP, 1998: $12.1 billion; per capita: $740

Petroleum reserves: 4 billion barrels

Main exports (% of total value, 1998): crude oil 90–95%; cotton; coffee; fish

Main imports: food and live animals; machinery and transport equipment; manufactured goods; chemicals and other

Capital City: Sana (political capital) 1,100,000; Aden (economic capital) 650,000; other cities: Taizz 400,000; al-Hudaydah 350,000; al-Mukalla 110,000

Relations

During the many decades that the sultanate was a British protected state, most of Oman's relations were handled by His Majesty's Government. After the abdication of the reactionary former sultan in 1970, and British withdrawal from the Gulf region in 1971, Oman broadened its relations. In the West, it retained friendship with Britain but turned especially to the United States, with which it has maintained a moderately close relationship. Having sovereignty over the tip of the Horn of Arabia on the Strait of Hormuz opposite Iran, Oman pursues a balance in the uneasy relations among Gulf powers. It maintains a correct posture with Iran, and it sustained diplomatic relations with Iraq during the Gulf crisis. However, it quietly but firmly supported the coalition against Iraq in 1990–1991, a continuation of its cooperation with the Gulf states, Britain, and the United

States during the Iran-Iraq war. Omani cooperation includes permitting Britain and the United States to use Masirah Island as a military base. Oman grounds much of its moderate foreign policy on its membership in the Gulf Cooperation Council—it was a founding member in 1980—and is one of the fourteen members of the Indian Ocean Rim Association for Regional Cooperation. It continues a centuries-long friendship with India. Already cordial with the UAE, Oman has drawn increasingly close to Saudi Arabia, and it has settled its long-uncertain boundaries with both, as well as with Yemen. Oman has not become intimately involved in Arab nationalist movements.

Yemen

The most recent state to appear in the Middle East, contemporary Yemen emerged as the Republic of Yemen on May 22, 1990, from the

MAP 19-2   General and economic map of the Republic of Yemen. Note former boundary between North and South Yemens. Circled numbers indicate regions discussed in the text.

fusion of the two formerly separate states of the Yemen Arab Republic (YAR, often informally referred to as North Yemen) and the People's Democratic Republic of Yemen (PDRY, often South Yemen).[7] The united Yemen is the second-largest state and has the second-largest population on the Arabian Peninsula. Indeed, the size of the indigenous population in Yemen apparently exceeds the number of indigenous Saudi Arabs.

The country occupies the area of the classical Arabia Felix (Fortunate Arabia), the southwest corner of the vast Arabian Peninsula. The former PDRY was the poorest Middle East country and, as a radical client of the former Soviet Union, was virtually a pariah state in the region and in the world. The former YAR was the second-poorest Middle East country and was ambivalent in its East-West relations. United Yemen is still the poorest state in the region, certainly in terms of development and productive capacity. Indeed, unification leaves

many problems unsolved and has created certain new ones; however, it was of great mutual benefit and instantly reduced many redundant expenses, numerous points of inter-Yemeni conflict (such as control over Karaman Island north of Hudaydah and Perim Island in the Bab el-Mandeb), and certain obstacles to economic and social development. Yemen started at a low developmental level, and it still has a long way to go—with limited capital—to reach the regional average. Moderately promising petroleum production raises optimism for the future; however, the forecast for oil income does not encourage large investments. Two related problems combine to challenge Yemen's greatest efforts: an alarming population growth rate—3.7 percent in the late 1990s—and an increasingly serious shortage of water. The impact of these developments is examined later, following a review of the country's regions (Map 19-2).

Five Regions

The Republic of Yemen (ROY) extends from the border with Oman on the east along half of the southern peninsula coast and around the corner at the strategic Bab el-Mandeb and northward along the Red Sea coast to the border with Saudi Arabia. With greatly contrasting rocks and rock structures, as well as sharp variations in relief, its dramatically rugged volcanic landscapes, including actual craters of extinct volcanoes (as in Aden), have quite different aspects from the flat-lying limestones of the Hadramawt Plateau and from the coastal plains. Most spectacular is the steep but highly dissected escarpment towering over the Red Sea Tihamah coast. Circled numbers on Map 19-2 indicate Yemen's five geographic regions.

[1] **Tihamah.**   The Red Sea coastal plain, al-Tihamah, is a segment of the coastal fringe that reaches the full length of the western edge of the Arabian Peninsula. Averaging approximately 40 miles/65 km in width and sandy-gravelly along most of its length, it extends 325 miles/523 km from the Saudi border to the Bab el-Mandeb. Although climatically a desert, the extremely hot, humid Tihamah is traversed at intervals by large wadis that carry heavy runoff after spring and fall monsoon rains on the high escarpment above. The broad bottoms of the wadis crossing their own alluvial fans are cultivated for cotton, melons, bananas, papayas, and similar crops; and the underground water in the wadi gravels is tapped by shallow wells for domestic use, as well as for irrigation. Smaller settlements have a distinct African appearance, with many round dwellings built of thatch, and an appreciable population percentage of Ethiopians and Sudanese from across the Red Sea. Formerly isolated from the rest of Yemen, Tihamah now connects with the highlands by way of two highways and frequent air flights. The centuries-old port of Mocha and the growing modern port of Hudaydah have given the coastal plain new vitality, as has the oil-export facility at Salif.

[2] **Central Highlands.**   From the Tihamah's inner margin, an escarpment rises abruptly and steeply through block-faulted and ruggedly eroded topography to the plateaus and shallow basins of the Central Highlands. Elevations commonly exceed 7,000 ft./2,135 m, with one summit elevation of 11,877 ft./3,620 m, located southwest of Sana and only 80 miles/130 km from the Red Sea coast. Facing west-southwest, the upper slopes of the escarpment intercept the monsoon winds in April–May and August and wring from them 20–35 in./500–900 mm of orographically enhanced rainfall, with more than 40 in./1,000 mm falling on the southern highlands around Ibb. The escarpment is almost vertical in places but in many other places has slopes that permit terraced agriculture (see Fig. 19-4), making this scenic subregion the most productive part of Yemen and one of surprisingly high population density.

Farther east is the backbone of Yemen, the Central Highlands or High Yemen. With a width varying from 40 to 75 miles/65 to 120 km, this subregion extends as an elevated plateau with several flat-floored basins from the northern border of Yemen to the former boundary between the pre-1990 Yemens. The plateau aspect is broken toward its northern and southern ends, and irregular mountain masses rise above it near and south of Sana. The relatively dense population of the upper western escarpment laps onto the high plateau and concentrates in and around Sana, the capital and primate city of the former YAR and now the political capital and still the largest city of unified Yemen. With the highest elevation of any Middle East capital, Sana lies at 7,250 ft./2,210 m, so that at this latitude it has moderate temperatures with a large diurnal range and cool nights all year round. More accessible and better known than the distinctive architecture of the Wadi Hadramawt (see [5] below) is the building and ornamental style of the High Yemen, well preserved in the old walled core of Sana (Fig. 19-5). The practice of whitewashing the surrounds of windows and doors gives a unique character to the multistoried houses of

FIGURE 19-4 Typical village and terraced agriculture in the ruggedly dissected escarpment of western Yemen. Crops include mainly *qat* and coffee. Compare Figures 7-4 and 10-3.

basalt dimension stone or mud in the urban landscape.

Noteworthy towns serve as population nodes along the plateau backbone, all of them with the distinctive Yemeni architectural styles and most with picturesque old walls, towers, forts, and mosques. From north to south, they include Sadah, the central place for extreme northern Yemen and focus of road traffic with Saudi Arabia; Amran; Sana, anchoring the center; Dhamar, old Himyaric city and agricultural center; Yarim; Ibb, an especially picturesque old city that has become a major development center; and, former capital of Yemen and central place of the southern plateau, Taizz, clinging to a rugged volcanic slope. Indeed, the evidence of volcanism is rarely out of sight anywhere on the plateau. Much of the highland itself is built up of successive lava flows, and extending northward from Sana is a striking series of cinder cones.

From the plateau summit, the eastern escarpment descends to the interior less steeply and with much less relief than does the western escarpment. By wadis and spurs it steps down from more than 7,000 ft./2,135 m to the eastern desert general level of 3,300 ft./1,000 m. Lying in the rain shadow of the Central Highlands, the escarpment contrasts climatically with the west and is dry and sunny. It also contrasts lithologically and primarily displays dissected Jurassic and Cretaceous sedimentary strata—mostly limestones—as opposed to predominantly lava flows on the west. Like the vegetation, population is sparse.

[3] **Mashriq.** Toward the bottom of the escarpment, volcanic forms reappear, then both the sedimentary layers and the lavas lose themselves under the sands of the southwestern Rub al-Khali, where locally the dune fields are

FIGURE 19-5   Sana, capital of Yemen, with its unique architectural styles (note the painted surrounds of the windows) and with a small plot of irrigated horticulture in foreground.

known as the Ramlat al-Sabatayn. This eastern region, the Mashriq ("the east"—not to be confused with the same term used for the entire eastern Arab world), was well developed 3,000–1,500 years ago when Marib was a main station on the Incense Trail during a more pluvial period and when the Sabaeans maintained the famed Marib Dam. The dam (actually, a system of dams) retained floodwaters in a large wadi and permitted intensive irrigation downstream during several centuries. Shifts in trade patterns, final collapse of the main dam, and diminution of Sabaean vigor ended the local civilization in the sixth century, and the area was isolated and little known during the last millennium. Excavations in the early 1950s revealed temples of the Marib heyday, but it was exploration for and discovery of substantial oil fields in the early 1980s that opened the Mashriq once again. A new Marib Dam

impounds floodwaters once more, and extensive irrigation has created a green oasis in the otherwise barren landscape. The future of Marib, the Mashriq, and all of the republic now that Yemen has joined the other regional petroleum producers is more promising than could have been imagined by the ancient Sabaeans.

[4] **Indian Ocean Coastal Plain.**   The south coastal plain along the Gulf of Aden and the open Indian Ocean is separated from the Tihamah by the volcanic masses at Aden and by the right-angle intersection of two sets of ocean-spreading rifts (see Chap. 3, especially Map 3-2). It is a generally flat, sandy coastal strip varying from 5 to 10 miles/8 to 16 km in width. Reddish-black volcanic hills and other ragged, barren masses of lava frequently rise above and interrupt the plain, overlooking

numerous fishing villages that fringe the shore. Occasional wadis cross the plain, bringing runoff from the inland hills, with irrigated cultivated plots along the wadis. The entire coast east of Aden formerly supported only occasional fishing villages and the one small picturesque port of Mukalla. Development since 1985, and more so after 1990, has stimulated growth in most coastal settlements, especially in Bir Ali, west of Mukalla, the terminus of the pipeline from the Shabwah fields; Balhaf, just west of Bir Ali, where a multibillion dollar LNG plant is under construction; Riyan, just east of Mukalla, the regional airport; Shihr, east of Riyan, the terminus of the pipeline from the Masila fields; and especially in Mukalla itself.

With its complex of harbors created by its location on one side of an old volcanic crater, Aden has been used as a port and an entrepôt for millennia. As a modern city, its several sections—Crater, Maala, Khormaksar, Steamer Point, Tawahi, Little Aden with its refinery— play hide-and-seek with one another behind dark, barren, pockmarked volcanic masses. Nearly 300 miles/480 km to the east, Mukalla, seat of the former sultanate of Quaiti, has also functioned as an important port. It has served the eastern areas for centuries, specifically the Wadi Hadramawt, with which it is connected by a well-surfaced road up and over the intervening plateau. Its port facilities have been expanded and upgraded during the past decade. The large, strategic island of Socotra, 215 miles/346 km off the coast of eastern Yemen (not included on Map 19-2, but see Map 3-1), is of particular interest: Because it was a separate fragment formed during the tectonic separation of Arabia from Africa, it displays a biological complex differentiated from the mainland since Tertiary times.[8]

[5] Hadramawt.   Stretching over most of the eastern reaches of Yemen and inland from the coastal plain is the extensive Hadramawt, which includes several plateaus and the great flat-floored valley famed as the Wadi Hadramawt. The plateau proper that lies between the

wadi and the coastal plain is the Jawl, an extensive tableland of flat-lying reddish-brown limestones, moderately dissected by wadis a few feet to 200–500 ft./60–150 m deep. All of the wadis were eroded primarily during earlier pluvial periods and now appear oversized for the amount of water presently draining down the system. The Jawl flats lie at 3,300 ft./1,000 m and, on the south, fall abruptly to the coastal plain 10–12 miles/16–20 km back from the shore and, on the north, drop by vertical cliffs into the Wadi Hadramawt. After the valley was initially eroded, silt, sand, and gravel later partially filled the bottom of the wadi, giving it a flat floor that has been irrigated and cultivated along much of the wadi course for thousands of years. The irrigated agriculture supports scores of small villages and several towns— particularly neighboring Shibam, Saywun (locally Sayoun), and Tarim—that are remarkable settlements with architectural treasures constructed of mud bricks by local builders (see Saywun palace, Fig. 19-6, top). Centuries-old "skyscraper" mud-brick houses in Shibam were added to the UNESCO World Heritage list in 1982 (Fig. 19-6, bottom). Although rare, devastating floods can play havoc with the mud structures, as happened during the May monsoonal rains in 1989.

The Wadi Hadramawt was little known even when it was theoretically accessible under British control, and it was virtually a closed area during the PDRY period. One result of this inaccessibility is that it retained its special character, its unique architecture, its distinctive ethnic mix, and its social and religious conservatism, although tourism and other modernization will probably change it in many ways after it was opened to tourists in the early 1990s. An especially unusual custom among the Hadramis was the practice of sending young men to Malaysia and Indonesia to work for and with fellow Hadramis who had been established in these countries before them. A smaller number went to East Africa for the same purpose. Virtually all of these men returned to the wadi to retire, many of them

FIGURE 19-6   Remarkable mud architecture in the Wadi Hadramawt, eastern Yemen: palace of the former sultan of Kathiri *(top)*, in Saywun (Sayoun), built entirely of mud that has been painted white, and western facade of the all-mud city of Shibam *(bottom)*. These unique mud "skyscrapers" earned Shibam inclusion on the UNESCO World Heritage list in 1982.

exceedingly wealthy, and built mansions in a mixed Hadrami-Malay-Javanese style. Many such handsome homes contribute to the special character of the town of Tarim.

Historical Sketch

During the first millennium BC and until the sixth century after Christ, southwestern Arabia gave rise to several kingdoms: Saba (Sheba), with the famous dam at its capital of Marib; Main (Minaea) farther north; Himyar, still flourishing as late as the sixth century, south of Saba; Qataban southeast of Himyar; and Hadramawt well to the east. All of these kingdoms (shown on Map 19-2) thrived on the flourishing and long-lived transit trade.

Islam swept southwestern Arabia during the time of Muhammad and remains virtually the exclusive religion of the area. Local rulers, Abyssinians (Ethiopians), Persians, Muslim empires, Egyptians, Portuguese, and Ottoman Turks controlled part or all of the area politically before the British took Aden in 1839 and gradually extended control in the south up the wadis and across the plateaus. From that time until 1990, the High Yemen and the southern coast and plateaus experienced separate historical development. In the hinterland of the south, the British maintained the fragmented pattern of local control by shaykhs and sultans by declaring a Western Aden Protectorate (with nineteen sultanates), an Eastern Aden Protectorate of Hadramawt, and other entities. To maintain a strong control center, the British declared Aden and its environs a crown colony in 1937. This three-way pattern continued until the late 1950s, when Britain prepared to withdraw from the area.

What later became the PDRY, 20 years before it merged with the YAR, evolved through a complicated series of political and name changes. Preparatory to withdrawal from the region, Britain sponsored the creation of a Federation of Arab Amirates of the South in 1959, which, after some expansion, became the Federation of South Arabia. However, violently radical groups caused the disintegration of the fledgling federation. Rival nationalist groups seeking domination of South Yemen after independence in 1967 engaged in a costly civil war and in terrorist attacks against the British prior to their departure in 1968. Renamed the People's Republic of South Yemen, the new state became more radical and assumed the name People's Democratic Republic of Yemen in 1970. Partly reflecting the centuries-old mosaic of tiny shaykhdoms and sultanates in the complex terrain of the region, bitter enmities emerged in successive coup attempts: 1978, 1980, and 1986. Having thrown off British imperialism, the state embraced communist ideology under appreciable Soviet and Chinese influence, adopting regionally incongruous radical centralized control of political and social structures. Despite becoming more disciplined and progressive in some ways, the PDRY was generally isolated for the next two decades.

In the north, however, the historical evolution during most of the past two millennia has followed quite different courses. Although both north and south grew wealthy from early trade between Aden and the Levant, particularly in frankincense and myrrh, northern Yemen enjoyed better climate and soil and hence more developed agriculture and a larger population.

Highland Yemenis embraced Islam in the mid-seventh century and served with distinction in Muslim armies from North Africa to central Asia. Having been under Muslim control, from the Hijaz, Damascus, and Baghdad, in 897 the High Yemen came under the rule of a descendant of Zayd, great-grandson of Ali. For most of the next 1,100 years, until 1962, the Shii Zaydi dynasty continued to rule all or part of the area as imams, with periodic interruptions. During much of the Middle Ages, the Highlands and Tihamah were fragmented into scores of small shaykhdoms, sultanates, and kingdoms perched on mountainsides or mountain peaks. Elevated and protected sites of many contemporary villages, though picturesque and even spectacular in today's landscape, reflect this period of disorder and insecurity (see Figs. 7-4, 10-3, and 19-4). More serious is the persistence of tribal feuds and disputes over lands, water, and political influence. Ottoman Turks exercised varying degrees of suzerainty in the Highlands and Tihamah until the last full Turkish occupation in the period 1872–1918.

Two very conservative Zaydi imams, Yahya (1904–1948) and his son Ahmad (1948–1962), ruled independent Yemen until the country became a republic. Increasing Nasserist influence persuaded Ahmad in 1958 to lead Yemen into a loose association with Egypt and Syria (the UAR, 1958–1961) in the virtually meaningless United Arab States.

When the reactionary and isolationist Imam Ahmad died in 1962, the army opposed the succession of his son Badr and, with massive military support from Nasserist Egypt, staged a coup and declared a republic under strongman Colonel Abdullah al-Sallal. Revolutionary republican forces, mainly from the Sunni Shafii population south of Sana, were joined by scores of thousands of Egyptian troops in a civil war against royalist forces supporting Imam Badr. Royalists were primarily tribesmen and other primarily Zaydi groups north of Sana, who were in turn aided by Saudi Arabia and Jordan. More than 200,000 were killed as the civil war dragged on until 1969, although President Nasser, embarrassed by Egypt's defeat in the June War, withdrew his forces in 1967. Significantly, in the mid-1960s the political capital was shifted back from Taizz, in the southern plateau, to Sana, in the more neutral center, where the capital had been before 1948.

In 1971, North Yemen's first nationwide elections marked a reconciliation between republican and royalist forces that has remained in effect despite various underlying tensions. During the following 20 years, the north walked tightropes internally, externally, and with the "other Yemen." With moderately large capital transfers and technical assistance from many countries—Saudi Arabia, the United States, China, Britain, the former USSR, Kuwait, and others—Yemen installed a basic infrastructure, especially a highway net, that moved it beyond the level of South Yemen and that stood it in good stead when development accelerated in the 1980s.

Republic of Yemen

Highland Yemen to the north and Aden and the Hadramawt to the south and east have each opposed the other and resisted control by the other for centuries. After the north declared itself a republic in 1962 and the British left an independent south in 1967, the two areas outwardly declared a desire for unity but in reality sparred for dominance. They engaged in brief but savage bilateral warfare in 1972 and 1976, further wasting both human and financial resources already depleted by a decade of fighting in both areas.

The Marxist-Leninist ideology of the south promoted secularization, especially in Greater Aden; and "progressivism" altered the traditional status of religion, social classes, women (less so in the Hadramawt), education, and, of course, government. Influence of the USSR, China, and North Korea increased as Western influence decreased. Revolution and progress in the north were sharp departures from imamate days, but Highland Yemen retained many conservative customs and resisted communism. It sought political nonalignment and profited by accepting aid from all quarters. A higher percentage of the women remained veiled there than in the south.

Despite the obvious advantages of unity, practical obstacles remained, especially the difficulty of merging scores of disparate elements with their historic respective ambitions, ideologies, traditions, and other politico-socio-economic factors. After a process of lengthy discussions, preparation of a draft constitution, and votes in each parliament, the two Yemens united on May 22, 1990, creating the Republic of Yemen (ROY).[9] Inevitably, many parties had to make compromises and unforeseen adjustments in the new polity. Some obstacles were external. Three months after unification, Yemen made the costly decision not to condemn Saddam Husayn's invasion of Kuwait. Many donors canceled financial support, and Saudi Arabia (as well as other Gulf states) expelled nearly one million Yemeni guest workers; the expellees returned to Yemen only to face 40 percent unemployment in a tenuous economic environment. Saudi Arabia, Kuwait, and other states raised stresses by playing on Yemeni internal tensions. In the heightened friction, the south initiated hostilities to withdraw from the four-year-old union; civil war returned to Yemen between May and July 1994. The secessionists were defeated, the unified republic was restored—stronger than before—and the government has generally emerged from the pariah status it was in after 1990.[10]

The Yemenis

The population of Yemen is estimated to be 16,388,000, about 83 percent of whom are in the former North Yemen area, with growth rate traditionally high throughout Yemen. The Sana area has by far the greatest concentration of people, the Aden area the second largest, and Taizz and Hudaydah the third and fourth largest, respectively. Basic ethnic uniformity is high: The overwhelming majority of the people are "Yemeni Arabs," although biological differences and descent characteristics differ appreciably among regions. For example, an upper-class inhabitant of Sana is shorter and has lighter skin than an upper-class Hadrami. Many Hadramis are descended from dark-skinned migrants from the subcontinent, probably Dravidians, and are mixed with both Malay-Indonesians and East Africans. Many villagers along the Tihamah are of African descent. Accents and dialects may vary, but nearly all Yemenis speak Arabic as a mother tongue. Tribal affiliations are paramount in the north and east, including towns and villages. The remaining actual Bedouins are found primarily in the Mashriq and the Jawl. The Bedouin tradition is not a significant influence in the republic.

Ethnic relative uniformity is partly offset by persistent tribal distinctions and conflicts (which, however, are slowly diminishing), by the sectarian division of the north into a Shii Zaydi northern two-thirds and a Sunni Shafii south of Dhamar, and by sharp political groupings in the Adeni south. The greater power in the highlands region has traditionally been

wielded by the tribally conscious Zaydis, from whom came the ruling imams; but Shafiis, with some ties to the south, have gained strength under the republics. Although always powerful, tribal leaders in the north periodically reassert their prowess to remind the central government of their needs and aspirations. During 1996–1998, several tribes kidnapped tourists or oil company representatives to reinforce demands for government funds and projects—roads, housing, irrigation, vehicles, or similar items.

The western escarpment and the Central Highlands especially exhibit a surprisingly dense pattern of villages distributed over landscapes that would appear to limit human settlement. Although only a small percentage of the Yemenis continue to be nomadic, less than one-quarter of the population is urban. The half dozen cities are growing rapidly as urban pull attracts job seekers from the more impoverished rural areas. Another 70 towns have more than 2,000 inhabitants each. Yemen as a country of villagers is confirmed by data on the former YAR, which are also applicable to the south: 11,000 villages have 100–500 inhabitants, and an astonishing 41,000 hamlets have fewer than 100 residents. This pattern of settlement is consistent with most of Yemen's topographic and climatic environments, which offer few sites for extensive settlement possessing adjacent cultivable area for supporting agriculture. Further limiting settlement size was the traditional siting in medieval times of fortress-type villages on peaks and ridges for protection during the frequent local wars (see Fig. 19-4).

A sizable minority of Jews lived in the cities—especially Sana, Sadah, and Aden—some for more than 2,500 years. According to tradition, they came in several waves and were an integral part of Yemeni life. In 1949–1950, about 50,000 Yemeni Jews were airlifted to Israel on special flights, and only a few hundred remain in the country.

As with their landforms and historical evolution, the Yemenis' costumes are also distinctive. Unlike virtually all other Arabs, males in all parts of Yemen wear a calf-length, patterned wraparound skirt (*lungi* or *futah* or, in the Wadi Hadramawt, where Malay-Indonesian influence is considerable, *sarong*); a colorful turban headdress similar to the Omanis' but wrapped differently; and, often, a folded shoulder shawl, especially in the higher elevations where temperatures can suddenly drop below the comfort level. More than anywhere else in Arabia, men also traditionally wear a *janbiyah,* a curved dagger in a decorated scabbard, comparable to the Omani *khanjar.* Western wear is steadily becoming more common in Yemen, as it is in most of the Middle East. Female attire is more similar to that in southwestern Saudi Arabia.

A particularly detrimental social problem common among highland Yemenis especially is the daily pastime of chewing qat (*Catha edulis*), a mild stimulant. About 60 percent of the men—and 20 percent of the women—of all social classes participate in the old, deeply rooted ritual that is a socially accepted custom. The consumer packs several *qat* leaves inside one cheek in the early afternoon and maintains them as a prominent wad for two or three hours, much as some people chew tobacco. Long-term effects are not clearly understood, but the reduction in productivity among millions of Yemenis during the daily *qat*-chewing period slows economic progress and is a matter of grave concern to many responsible Yemenis. If nothing else, the leaves must be picked fresh daily and rushed to the nearest *suq,* where they are quite expensive, especially those of premium quality. A daily supply can absorb one-third of a low-income worker's earnings. The *qat*-chewing routine is receiving mounting criticism from President Ali Abdullah Salih and others; while recognizing the plant's ubiquity, they denounce as destructive of soil and society both the growing of *qat* and the all-afternoon chewing sessions.

Emerging Economy

The more populous north has historically possessed the greater agricultural potential—indeed, recent findings indicate that advanced irrigated farming in the Dhamar area dates from before 2500 BC. In the south, Aden and its environs have been the overwhelming focus of economic activity for millennia. The primary asset has been Aden's excellent and protected harbor and its location at the junction of land and sea routes to and from several directions. Aden port gained particular primacy after Britain took control in 1839 and made it the regional coaling station for the increasing number of steamships plying the Indian Ocean. Its importance was greatly enhanced with the opening of the Suez Canal in 1869, when Aden became the midway port of call for ships sailing between the Mediterranean and India and points east. That importance was further augmented when fuel oil replaced coal in steamships and Aden, declared a British colony in 1937, served as a key oil-bunkering port. Increasing production of petroleum in the Middle East after World War II added to the importance of routes passing Aden and encouraged the British to construct a major refinery in 1954 on the western arm of the harbor, in Little Aden. By the late 1950s, Aden thrived as one of the world's busiest ports, with as many as 250,000 transit passengers annually generating a booming trade in the duty-free shops; by the late 1960s, Aden was languishing. The Suez Canal was closed, and civil conflict besieged the several quarters of Aden. The port served only local interests during the Marxist PDRY years; it did not revive until unified Yemen designated Aden as the "economic capital" of the ROY (Fig. 19-7).

More rural and with less European influence before 1970, northern Yemen desperately needed and sought large-scale aid abroad, and it received substantial help from its neighbors and from both the West and the communist world. The Central Planning Organization coordinated the foreign aid, focusing first on infrastructure, then on social services, public administration, and agriculture. With relations between Yemen and Saudi Arabia variable, aid from the Saudis was sometimes uncertain but in some years exceeded $100 million. U.S. assistance was modest but was responsible for Yemen's first modern highway up the escarpment. Chinese, British, Dutch, German, Swiss,

FIGURE 19-7   Port of Aden, "economic capital" of Yemen. The Aden harbor is nestled in a breached volcanic crater.

Soviet, and especially UN technical assistance combined to endow northern Yemen with a badly needed basic network of paved highways, planned urban expansion, a number of small industries, and fair educational and health systems. The largest industry in highland Yemen is a cotton textile mill north of Sana that was built in 1967 by the People's Republic of China (PRC). The PRC also constructed, with its own Chinese labor force, the vital and scenic highway from Hudaydah up the escarpment to Sana, as well as roads in southern Yemen.

Much of the economic growth after 1975, especially in the north, was fueled by remittances from the more than one million Yemenis working abroad, mainly in Saudi Arabia. Employment, salaries, and therefore remittances diminished after the drop in oil prices in 1982–1983. Aid from Saudi Arabia and other oil producers likewise decreased, slowing development. With union of the north and south

approaching, several contributing states raised their level of aid to encourage an obviously beneficial step forward. It was unfortunate that the reactions of the newly unified republic to the 1990–1991 Gulf crisis prompted the array of economic penalties mentioned earlier. Not only would the national economy have been immeasurably better during the 1990s but the costly 1994 civil war would probably not have been precipitated.

Two sectors of the economy deserve special attention: agriculture, the traditional mainstay, and the petroleum industry, the current driving force. Highland Yemen and Tihamah have been overwhelmingly agricultural. Well into the 1950s, agriculture engaged 90 percent of the economically active population, and it still engaged more than 70 percent in the late 1990s, by far the highest level among Middle East states (Table 9-1). Once self-sufficient in food, Yemen now imports significant percentages of its wheat, rice, animal feed, and other food-stuffs. Extensive rainfed agriculture is practiced in the highlands by virtue of the centuries-long practice of terracing the slopes and thus conserving soil (virtually creating it in some ways) and making maximum use of runoff from the seasonal rains (see Fig. 19-4). The degree of slope that has been terraced and the extent of the terracing are astonishing in parts of the escarpment. The terrace walls must, of course, be carefully maintained, especially after heavy rains; and the exodus of so many young men from the terraced farms has been a cause of concern. More active irrigation is necessary on Tihamah, in the south, and in the extraordinary Wadi Hadramawt.

In addition to the expected crops of wheat, barley, maize, grapes, several fruits, and various vegetables, Yemen produces cotton and dates on the coastal plains and in the Wadi Hadramawt; and three other crops are unusual among Middle East countries: sorghum (*durrah*), coffee, and *qat*. *Durrah* is especially well adapted to the double-monsoon rainfall regime and formerly occupied up to three-fourths of the cultivated land. Yemen held a virtual world monopoly on coffee during the period 1500–1775, giving it appreciable local wealth. Because for many decades most of the coffee beans were exported from Yemen's Red Sea port of Mocha, one name for coffee has long been *mocha*, as another name, *java*, was adopted after production shifted to Indonesia. Although Yemeni coffee continues to be a premium product, the output of less than 3,000 mt is negligible on the world market, and production continues to decline.

Unfortunately, coffee and *qat* plants have the same ecological demands, and coffee trees are steadily being uprooted from the high terraces of the western escarpment and being replaced by *qat* bushes. Coffee trees require several years to reach optimum bearing age, and they then yield only one crop a year. *Qat* bushes begin producing marketable leaves after only a few months, and they yield a high-value crop every day, averaging 20 times the annual income of

coffee. Thus, Yemen loses the value of an export commodity while sustaining the social and economic losses associated with *qat* chewing. In addition, major food crops are being replaced in some areas by *qat*, so that Yemen is becoming less and less able to feed itself.

With decreasing remittances and foreign aid reducing Yemen's GNP, oil finds in the Mashriq and the adjacent Shabwah area of the south came at a particularly auspicious period. In the former YAR, the first strike came on July 4, 1984, in the Alif field in the Marib–al-Jawf Basin 37 miles/60 km east-northeast of the town of Marib in the Mashriq. Discovery was made by the Hunt Oil Company, a U.S. firm, which later, as Yemen Hunt Oil Company, became the operator of a production-sharing agreement with participation by Exxon and a Korean consortium. During the same period, exploration near Shabwah on the PDRY side of the border was under way by Soviet technicians, who were later joined by other companies and then replaced by an Arab group.

Marib production quickly reached 175,000 bpd, by which time a small 10,000-bpd refinery was in operation near the Alif field and a 24–26-in./61–64-cm pipeline had been completed to Salif on the Red Sea, a total of 257 miles/414 km (see Map 19-2). Further exploration in the Mashriq led to the discovery of several new fields, some yielding significant amounts of nonassociated gas (see below).

Farther southeast, in the Ayad and Amal fields near Shabwah, early limited production increased after the completion in 1991 of a 20-in./51-cm pipeline to the small port of Bir Ali on the Gulf of Aden, 130 miles/210 km distant.

In the early 1990s, Canadian Occidental (Canoxy) discovered a new block of fields in the Masila area in the plateau north of Mukalla. With completion of a pipeline to Shihr in 1993, the Masila fields became Yemen's most productive. A score of major and independent oil companies explored Yemen in the late 1990s. Production curves suggest that the Marib block output peaked in 1995 and that overall production—406,000 bpd during

1999—may well have peaked unless significant new reservoirs are found. Like its neighbors, Yemen is focusing its hydrocarbon hopes on processing gas from substantial nonassociated gas discoveries. Its finds are in the Marib basin, whence a gas pipeline is being laid to a large joint-venture liquefied natural gas (LNG) plant on the Gulf of Aden coast at Balhaf. The multibillion dollar venture, exporting to South and East Asia, will be Yemen's largest single industrial project. Yemen's two refineries, already mentioned, have capacities of 110,000 bpd (Aden) and 10,000 bpd (Marib). The obsolescent Aden plant is being upgraded, inter alia, to restore its design capacity of 170,000 bpd throughput. A third refinery is tentatively planned for Ras Isa (Salif), north of Hudaydah, the terminus of the Marib-Salif pipeline.[11]

Finally, regarding economic activity, it can be noted that fishing is an important source of food and income along both seacoasts. Hudaydah has appreciable fish-processing facilities. In another economic sector, air transportation has opened Yemen's links with the world more than anything else has done. International airports operate in Sana, Taizz, Hudaydah, and Aden, although they urgently need upgrading and equipping with adequate navigational aids. The necessity for such upgrading also applies to many aspects of Yemen's infrastructure if economic development is to be successful and sustained. Increased tourism, for example, would give a considerable boost to the national economy.

Relations

Unification eliminated one of the most persistent problems in relations faced by each of the Yemens, and the collapse of both Soviet influence and the status of communism provided a more salutary climate for the merger. The unfortunate retribution some of Yemen's financial supporters exacted from the state after 1990 has gradually subsided, and the republic critically needs capital transfers from

any quarter. With augmented income from the greatly increased oil prices of late 1999 and of 2000, Yemen will enjoy higher income and can hope for more generous aid from its neighbors. Of three border/territorial questions, Oman and Yemen have definitively settled their boundary; and Eritrea and Yemen were reconciled over control of the Hanish Islands after arbitration in 1998 divided the islands between the claimants.[12] The long Yemen-Saudi Arabia boundary east of the Asir was the last remaining disputed border on the peninsula, but the two disputants signed a treaty in mid-2000 that promises resolution of the conflict. U.S. relations with the former PDRY were uniformly bad and with the YAR were ambiguous; the YAR broke those relations in 1967. Restored in 1972, they segued with the Republic of Yemen in 1990, were ambivalent for several years after the Iraqi invasion of Kuwait, then were reasonably balanced in the late 1990s.

Notes

1. These two peninsula rimland states were the last to receive intensive attention after the opening of the region but are now becoming the subject of an increasing number of studies.

2. Sources for developing Oman include Townsend 1977, C.H. Allen 1987 (with good references for further reading), Anthony 1976, Zahlan 1998, Janzen 1986, Al Taie 1997, Mandaville n.d., O'Reilly 1998, Riphenburg 1998, *Persian Gulf States* Country Studies 1993, and *Country Commercial Guide: Oman*, FY 2000.

3. See details in Hanna 1995.

4. *New York Times,* Feb. 5, 1992; and *Christian Science Monitor,* Feb. 19, 1992; Nicholas Clapp. *The Road to Ubar,* New York: Houghton Mifflin, 1998.

5. Al-Haj 1996 and "Interview with Sultan Qaboos bin Said Al Said," *Middle East Policy* 3, no. 4 (April 1995): 1–6, and Kechichian 1995.

6. For an authoritative study, see Al-Yousef 1995. Also see the *EIA: Oman,* Feb. 1999.

7. The former North Yemen is covered in Steffen et al. 1978, which is highly geographical as well as demographic; Daum 1988, Bidwell 1983, and *The Yemens* Country Studies 1985 cover both former Yemens authoritatively; Dunbar 1992 examines the

unification of the two Yemens. (Dunbar was U.S. Ambassador to Sana at the time of the merger.) See also Dresch 1989. The former PDRY (South Yemen) is discussed in Stookey 1982, as well as in Bidwell 1983. For more current coverage of unified Yemen, see *Country Commercial Guide,* FY 1999: Yemen.

8. See Tim Mackintosh-Smith. "The Last Place in Yemen." *Aramco World,* Sept./Oct. 1999: 8–21.

9. See Dunbar 1992.

10. Dunn 1994 examines what went wrong to contribute to the civil war.

11. See *EIA* report on Yemen, July 1999. I am also grateful to Yemen Hunt Oil Co. for a briefing and visit to the offshore tanker at Salif.

12. *New York Times*, Oct. 14, 1998; and Lefebvre 1998.

20

Egypt:
A River and a People

A View of Egypt

"Egypt is the gift of the Nile," wrote Herodotus 2,500 years ago. Kipling, in turn, described the Nile as "that little damp trickle of life." Both comments emphasize the role of a single river as a fundamental element in the existence of this ancient land.

In few countries are the basic geographical factors and their direct influences so plainly imprinted as in Egypt. The Nile Valley is unique in its singular symbiosis of people and environment and in its remarkable history and contemporary development. Flanked by desert ramparts, the Nile Valley kingdoms flourished for millennia, with only occasional major disruptions. Egypt's location on the nexus between Africa and Eurasia has long given it a pivotal position in the World-Island, whether in ancient, medieval, or modern times, right up to the start of the new century.

Inscriptions, carvings, bas-reliefs, statues, and monuments—all well-preserved for millennia in the dry climate but now under stress from contemporary pollution—provide detailed documentation of everyday life and beliefs in Pharaonic and Ptolemaic Egypt. Both tourism and archaeological scholarship focus on such ancient works as well as on the numerous pyramids, temples, tombs, and colossi, with their hieroglyphics and distinctive arts. History is an essential ingredient of everyday life in Egypt (see Figs. 2-2 and 20-1).

Although the imperial domains of ancient Egypt were less extensive than those of Persia or Assyria, they periodically extended well into the Levant, and the Nile Valley has persisted as one of the four major power cores of the Middle East (see Chaps. 2 and 11). Ensconced behind its desert glacis (buffer zone) and well supplied with military resources, it has suffered fewer conquests than the Fertile Crescent states. Domestic stability and protected location contributed to a historical continuum that, although several times disturbed, was not devastated as was the development of the Hittites, Assyrians, Israelites, and Byzantines, for example. Similarly, evolution along a riverine ribbon has made Egypt a linear geographical unity that, once integrated about 3000 BC, has rarely been seriously ruptured. The city-states that were so adapted to the environments of mainland Greece, western Asia Minor, and Phoenicia contrast with the integrated polities of the Nile Valley and Delta. The productive agricultural economy that developed along the river has always supported a relatively large population, and Egypt now has one of the three largest national populations in the region (see Table 6-1 and Graph 6-1).

Located near the center of the Islamic and Arab worlds in more recent centuries, Egypt has long played an influential role in both realms, partly because of the influence of Cairo's al-Azhar University on religious affairs and partly because of the country's long intellectual tradition. Similarly, Egypt has exercised a dominant influence in the Arab world, particularly since World War II, sometimes contending with Syria and Iraq (and occasionally with Saudi Arabia) for leadership. Egypt's cultural output—motion picture films, television productions, radio programs, and publications—has long exceeded that of all other Arab countries combined. In 1988 an Egyptian novelist, Naguib Mahfouz, received the first Nobel prize for literature awarded to an Arab writer.

Egypt

Long-form official name, anglicized: Arab Republic of Egypt

Official name, transliterated: Jumhuriyat Misr al-Arabiyah

Form of government: republic with one legislative house (People's Assembly) with a Consultive Assembly

Area: 385,229 miles^2/997,739 km^2

Population, 1999: 63,261,000. Literacy: 51.4%

Ethnic composition (%): Egyptian 99.8 (including some Nubian, Berber, Beja), other (Greek, Italian, Syro-Lebanese) 0.2

Religions (%): Sunni Muslim 90.0, Christian (mostly Coptic) 10.0

GDP, 1998: $83.8 billion; per capita: $1,294

Petroleum reserves: 3.5 billion barrels

Main exports (% of total value, 1996): petroleum and petroleum products 48.5; cotton yarn, textiles, and clothing 12.5; basic metals and manufactures 5.4

Main imports (% of total value, 1996): machinery and transport equipment 29.7; foodstuffs 20.9; iron and steel products 9.5; chemical products 3.9

Capital city: Cairo (al-Qahirah) 7,000,000 (Greater Cairo exceeds 14,000,000); other cities: Alexandria (al-Iskandariyah), 3,800,000; Giza (al-Jizah) 2,250,000; Shubra al-Khaymah 834,000; al-Mahallah al-Kubra 408,000

Egypt has moved from persistent power core to colonial possession to political leader of the Arab world to regional pariah for several years after 1979 and, finally, back to qualified political eminence in the Arab world in the 1990s. These changing roles have accompanied variations in Egypt's own stability and in the regional environment. In adapting to its changing roles, Egypt has sought security and economic viability—survival—within new relationships and new internal and external patterns.

A Rich History

Historic Continuity

Over the millennia, Egyptian civilization developed a stability that enabled it to survive, if not always to repel, incursions by foreign forces. Although defeated militarily upon occasion, resilient Egypt not only preserved its population and sustained its culture but also absorbed the conquerors, sometimes adapting part of their religious or political concepts.

Once Upper Egypt (i.e., up the Nile River Valley, to the south) merged with Lower Egypt (the delta) about 3000 BC, the two physically different but interdependent parts of Egypt remained integrated most of the following centuries. The unifying of Upper and Lower Egypt after a major cleavage in the seventeenth century BC was celebrated in numerous contemporary symbols, including the form of the royal crown, and in thousands of hieroglyphic inscriptions. Unification prevailed even though the river civilization could not entirely overcome the incompatibility between valley and delta with their cultural and environmental differences. The centripetal-centrifugal relationships between Upper and Lower Egypt remain

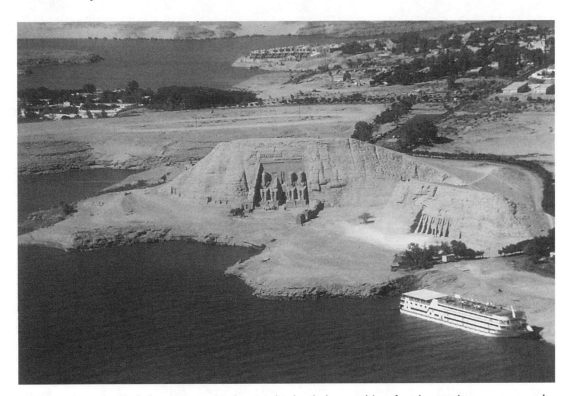

FIGURE 20-1　Abu Simbel monument, a prime tourist site, in its repositioned setting: cut into segments and moved from its original cliffside location, now under water. The mound behind the monument is actually an empty shell of disguised concrete. Note cruise ship in lower right and tourist facilities in right distance.

meaningful, although modern communications and increased interregional dependence have reinforced the sense of unity.

The shifting of royal capitals and religious centers between north and south in ancient times reflected shifts in the political center of gravity. Memphis, the first capital of the united kingdom of Upper and Lower Egypt, was established at an intermediate location, at the apex of the delta, a location to which the capital returned periodically after shifts to Thebes (opposite Luxor), other valley cities, and delta cities (see Map 2-3). It is significant that Cairo, the political center of Egypt for the past 1,300 years, is located—as was Memphis—at the precise junction of delta (Lower Egypt) and valley (Upper Egypt).

Despite periodic incursions over many centuries by Hyksos, Libyans, Nubians, Ethiopians, Assyrians, Persians, and others, Egypt has maintained an unmistakable Egyptian character and unity. The Persian conquest in 525 BC began a series of conquests by more distant powers: Greeks under Alexander the Great, 332–323 BC; successor Greek Ptolemies, 304–30 BC; Romans 30 BC–AD 476; and Byzantine successors to the Romans, AD 476–640 (see Chap. 2). A major modification of the ancient Egyptian culture was introduced during the east Roman-Byzantine hegemony, when Christianity became the dominant religion (see Chap. 6). It persists today among the minority Copts.

Arab-Islamic Transformation

In AD 642, the Muslim Arab conquest brought a momentous and permanent transformation of Egypt. The Arabs not only overwhelmed Egypt militarily but also immigrated into Egypt by the thousands, intermarrying with the indigenous population. Their intangible contributions included a proselytizing religion (Islam), a new language (Arabic), and a concept of strong ties between religion and government. Islam supplanted Christianity, and by 706 Arabic had been decreed the language of official transactions.

Once ingrained, Islam has never been challenged. Sunnism, however, was displaced for two centuries under the Shii Fatimid state, 909–1171, which supplanted Abbasid control in most of North Africa. Sunnism returned permanently with the Ayyubids, 1171–1250, whose dynasty included Salah al-Din (Saladin), a Kurd who became one of the most honored heroes of the Arabs. Under the succeeding Mamluk ("slave") sultans, who ruled Egypt for more than 250 years, Cairo gained architectural treasures, underwritten mainly by income from the rich Red Sea-Mediterranean trade. Mamluk buildings, especially mosques with characteristic minarets and fluted domes, are some of the contemporary city's most distinctive monuments. Loss of the profitable Red Sea-Mediterranean trade routes to Portuguese merchantmen sailing around the Cape of Good Hope after 1497 deprived Mamluk Egypt of its main revenues, and Egypt fell to the Ottoman Turks in 1517. Although Ottoman control was tenuous after the late 1700s, it technically continued until 1914. After 1805, Egypt was locally ruled by the Muhammad Ali dynasty under Ottoman suzerainty, but in fact British control prevailed after 1882.

Contemporary Republic

Contemporary Egypt was born in a bloodless military coup on July 23, 1952. King Faruq (Farouk), last of the Muhammad Ali line, was sent into exile, and the present republic emerged, led by members of a revolutionary junta. The following two decades brought a sequence of historic events that shook the Middle East and, in some cases, the world. Many of the events were orchestrated until 1970 by Gamal Abd al-Nasser (al-Nasir), the charismatic coup leader who became president in 1954.

Among his more memorable actions, Nasser forced the withdrawal of Britain from Egypt 1954–1956, negotiated a Czech-Soviet arms deal in September 1955, nationalized the Suez Canal in July 1956, preached and promoted aggressive pan-Arabism and Arab nationalism, oversaw the merger of Egypt and Syria in the United Arab Republic (UAR) in February 1958 (which was dissolved in September 1961), and escalated tensions that encouraged Israel's invasion of Egypt in June 1967. He was attempting to reconcile the Palestine Liberation Organization and the government of Jordan in September 1970 when he suffered a fatal heart attack.

Nasser's successor, Anwar al-Sadat, brought increased pragmatism to and a changed direction in Egyptian policies. After he initiated a joint Egyptian-Syrian surprise attack on Israeli lines at the Suez Canal and in the Golan Heights in 1973, he downgraded relations with the Soviets and established close relations with the United States. As one step to remedy the country's growing economic malaise, he minimized the Nasserist socialism and declared an economic "open door" policy (*infitah*). To escape continued entanglement in military adventures and with U.S. promises of support, he made a dramatic visit to Jerusalem in November 1977 to address the Israeli Knesset and signed the Camp David accords with Israel in September 1978 and the Egyptian-Israeli peace treaty on March 16, 1979. After having championed Arab resistance to Israel for 35 years, Egypt embittered its former allies and supporters by making peace with Israel, and it was expelled from the Arab League (see Chap. 11). Domestically, the treaty was received with ambivalence, with some extremist opponents especially vocal. Although Sadat was praised in the West as a man of peace and, in 1978, had been awarded the Nobel Prize for Peace (along with Prime Minister Begin of Israel), he was assassinated by disaffected Egyptian extremists in October 1981.

Sadat's successor, President Husni Mubarak, has taken a low-key approach and has achieved the longest tenure among leaders of Egypt since World War II. Pragmatic and politically shrewd, he has skillfully maintained the country's interests and security through engaging in a delicate balancing act. Although he had many domestic critics and faced a seven-year campaign of anti-government and anti-foreigner terrorist attacks by extremist Islamist groups, he succeeded in restoring general internal stability by 1998. Some observers condemned his countermeasures as excessively severe and questionably broad, but the methods were effective. Mubarak was commended for economic openness and development but was also reproved for political repression. Parliament chose him in mid-1999 as the sole candidate for president in September, when his election was confirmed in a plebiscite. Mubarak has conducted foreign relations with even greater skill: He has balanced his role in the Arab and Muslim worlds with his close ties with the West, especially the United States, and his treaty relationship with Israel.[1]

River, Delta, and Deserts

Egypt comprises five regional elements: [**1**] Nile River Valley, [**2**] Nile Delta, [**3**] Western Desert, [**4**] Eastern Desert, and [**5**] Sinai Peninsula (see circled numbers on Map 20-1). It is worth noting that whereas Egypt has long been considered a seismically stable region, a 5.9 earthquake centered 20 miles/12 km southwest of Cairo occurred on October 12, 1992, causing more than 400 deaths and 3,000 injuries. Not having been built according to earthquake-resistant codes, many buildings collapsed; for several years afterward, post-1950s and older structures showed earthquake damage and were condemned and sometimes razed. However, major ancient monuments seem to have escaped serious damage.[2]

[1] Nile River and the Aswan Project

Egypt is the Nile, and the Nile is Egypt. The headwaters of the river rise far to the south, fed by runoff from heavy summer rains in the East African lake district and the Ethiopian highlands. These headwaters form the White Nile and Blue Nile rivers, which in turn join at Khartoum in the Sudan, whence the single Nile

flows to enter Egypt through Lake Nubia/Lake Nasser. It then flows 938 miles/1,510 km across the entire length of Egypt, including Lake Nasser, before debouching into the Mediterranean.[3]

Nile Valley: Upper Egypt. Below the first cataract at Aswan, the Nile flows in a relatively narrow, flat-floored valley, eroded as much as 1,000 ft./300 m below the flanking plateau near Qena (Qina). The valley floor continues to be flat but broadens downstream below the Qena bend, until it is 6–11 miles/10–18 km wide as it approaches Cairo. The valley walls are reduced to less than 165 ft./50 m high at Giza before they disappear entirely as the river flows out onto its delta. It is the lush ribbon of irrigated, cultivated fields on the flat floodplain along the Nile Valley that is the quintessence of traditional Egypt (see Fig. 7-5).

Just upstream of the delta, a prominent feature west of the valley is the Fayyum, a circular depression in the limestone plateau of the Western Desert. Nile waters formerly poured into the Fayyum, at least during flood, through the Hawara channel, which used to feed a large lake (Moeris). However, later diversion of the river from the basin reduced Lake Moeris to a remnant, now called Lake Qarun, with a present surface 147 ft./45 m below sea level. Most of the bed of old Lake Moeris is now intensively cultivated and supports a dense population in a significant subregion of the country.[4]

The evolution of the Nile Valley is extremely complex. Stream flow, valley erosion, and deposition of sediment both within the valley and in the delta have varied greatly with alternating periods of pluvial and arid conditions in the Nile watershed. On top of thousands of feet of earlier valley fill, an average of 30 ft./9 m of silt has been deposited in the valley since beneficial silt deposition began approximately 10,000 years ago.[5]

Although some important archaeological sites are found in the delta and in the desert, the vast majority of the great monuments are located along the valley (see Map 20-1). Few stretches of the river between Aswan and Cairo

MAP 20-1   General and economic map of Egypt. The five major geographic regions
are identified by circled numbers. Note new Tushka (Toshka) Project in the south.

exhibit no ruins of some period or other, and remarkable new finds have recently emerged in Luxor and on the Giza Plateau. Modern cities, some with large populations, have developed around some of the monuments: They include Aswan, Luxor, Qena, Asyut, al-Mina, Helwan, and Giza.

Aswan High Dam.   Inaugurated in 1971, the Aswan High Dam (Sadd al-Aali) has had the greatest physical and symbolic impact of any construction project in Egypt in modern times.[6] In its technical transformation of the country's vital resource, the dam altered the equilibrium of the Nile below Aswan, changed

the rhythm of valley life, and had significant impact on crucial aspects of the valley's ecology. One example is the effect of Lake Nasser on the Nile's silt load: Now that the upper Nile empties into Lake Nubia (the Sudanese segment of Lake Nasser), the 50 million mt of silt formerly spread annually along the valley and dumped into the Mediterranean is deposited in a new delta that is building northward in the lake.

The constricted valley of the Nile at Aswan, where it crosses resistant granites and other basement rocks, had long been considered as a site for a high dam. The original low Aswan Dam, constructed in 1902 and raised in 1912 and 1934, had demonstrated the benefits of

FIGURE 20-2   Egypt's two main water projects: Aswan High Dam *(top)*, with large hydroelectric power station, and Suez Canal *(bottom)*, with freighter in transit.

control of the river, and its usefulness stimulated discussion of a higher structure. Work began on the multipurpose high dam in 1960, and teams of environmental impact specialists studied the potential effects of the project during the decade it was under construction.

The completed dam, power station, and impounded lake are among the world's largest. A few statistics indicate the impressive scale of the project: The dam is 365 ft./111 m high, 2.36 miles/3.8 km long at the top, and 0.62 miles/1 km thick at the base, and it contains 17 times the volume of the Great Pyramid of Giza. The impounded reservoir is 297 miles/478 km long and an average of 6 miles/10 km wide. The power station doubled Egypt's generating capacity in 1970 but supplies 25 percent now (see Fig. 20-2a).

On the positive side, the dam permits flood control and, by regulating river flow for optimum benefit to downstream agriculture, permits perennial irrigation and thus multiple cropping. In addition, the dam allows for economical hydrogeneration of enormous amounts of electricity. The lake supports both commercial and sport fishing, and the lake and the dam are major tourist attractions.

Negative impacts, many of which were projected in the feasibility studies, are of serious concern to Egyptian authorities and others. The water table under the cultivated fields in the floodplain has risen, and resulting poor drainage threatens salination of productive valley and delta soils, a risk that can be minimized by the installation of underground drains. Fields formerly naturally fertilized during the annual Nile flood must now be treated with chemical fertilizers, which are changing the chemical balance of much of the valley. The number of acres reclaimed as a result of the Aswan project has, disappointingly, been one-third less than the projected total.

Cessation of sedimentation at the outer limit of the delta by the now-clear river has caused the delta coast to be eroded back as much as a mile, and the related loss of nutrient-rich materials in the southeastern Mediterranean has reduced fish life, especially sardines, by as much

as 90 percent. In the exceptionally dry climate of southern Egypt, evaporation from the extensive surface of Lake Nasser is enormous, totaling several hundred billion cubic meters each year. More manifest is the impact of severe drought that periodically affects the Nile's upper catchment basin. Such drought reduces river flow; in 1988, it lowered the level of Lake Nasser as much as 75 ft./23m following the 1980s drought that caused widespread starvation in Ethiopia. By contrast, good rains in the late 1990s overfilled the lake. Such variations have, of course, beset the Nile watershed throughout history, but the balance is now so delicate that the potential scale of catastrophe is very much greater.[7]

[2] Nile Delta: Lower Egypt

The Nile Delta encompasses a total area of about 8,495 miles²/22,000 km² and includes more than half of the cultivated area of the country (Fig. 20-3). A classic delta deposit, it was built up by continued sedimentation of Nile silt in a former embayment in the northeast African coast. (The earlier coastline reached to present-day Cairo.) Although distributaries of the river have varied in number and in their courses during the past several thousand years, two main branches of the Nile traverse the delta at present: the Rosetta on the west and the Damietta on the east.

As is typical of deltas, the alluvial area is very flat, with a low gradient to the distributaries as they cross the plain. Many of the low mounds scattered over the surface are tells (archaeological mounds) marking the sites of ancient settlements. The delta is one of the most intensively cultivated areas in the world, and it also contains thousands of agricultural villages and several of Egypt's larger cities: Alexandria, an ancient city at the northwest corner of the delta, Egypt's second-largest city and most important port; the large central-delta textile-manufacturing cities of Mahalla and Tanta; and other cities such as Zagazig, Rashid (Rosetta), and Damietta. With rural population densities of 3,500–4,000 per mile²/1,350–1,545 per km², the delta has one of the highest agricultural

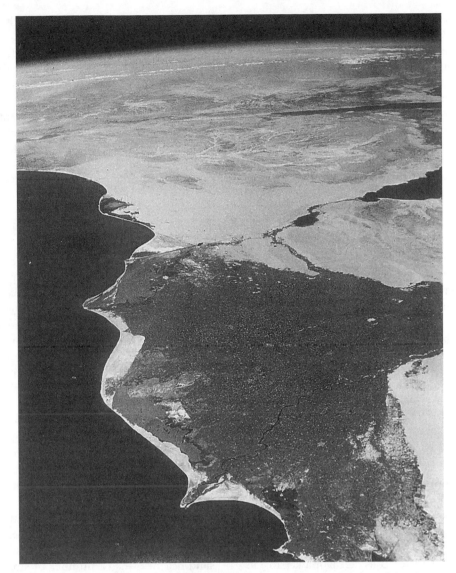

FIGURE 20-3   Nile Delta and the Sinai. The Suez Canal crosses the center of the photograph; sand-choked wadis crisscross the central Sinai. View from space looking southeast. Compare Figure 3-1. (NASA photograph)

population densities in the world. The thousands of small settlements show as gray dots in the space photograph in Figure 20-3.

[3] Western Desert

The huge Western Desert region covers 263,000 miles^2/ 681,000 km^2, an area slightly smaller than the state of Texas and more than two-thirds the total area of Egypt. Reaching from the western edge of the delta and valley to Libya, it is an extension of the Libyan Desert, itself part of the Sahara. Although the Western Desert is basically a low plateau with a cover of generally horizontal sedimentary rocks, landforms vary moderately from section to section in response to changes in rock types, wind erosion, and occasional faulting.

Nubian sandstones prevail in the south but are overlain by Tertiary limestones to the north, with an extensive Great Sand Sea in the west blanketing nearly half of the Western Desert region. Several strata of the Nubian Formation that underlie much of the northern Sahara serve as aquifers and have large amounts of artesian water, most of it fossil water. Egypt plans to exploit these "water deposits," as Libya does in its Kufrah Oasis, but only limited progress has been achieved because of budgetary constraints.

Overlying the Nubian sandstone, Tertiary limestones form a barren plateau tableland that extends eastward to the Nile Valley and slopes gently northward to the Mediterranean. Along their southern edges, the limestones form prominent ragged escarpments 985–1,640 ft./ 300–500 m high.

Embayments along the escarpments embrace several large semi-enclosed depressions watered by contact springs. In the depressions lie five historic oases: Siwa, al-Bahriyah, al-Farafirah, al-Dakhilah, and Kharijah (see Map 20-1). The four historic and scenic inner oases that lie along what is believed to be an ancient channel of the Nile are currently being revitalized (see below). Geomorphically, the Fayyum Depression mentioned above may be included in the same category as the western oases.

In the northwest is the largest of the Western Desert depressions, the forbidding and uninhabited Qattara Depression, about the size of the state of Delaware. With an irregular floor 436 ft./133 m below sea level in its lowest part, the depression has been considered for a key role in an ambitious but risky project to generate hydroelectricity. The plan, now in abeyance, proposes that Mediterranean Sea water be piped to the depression's edge and then down through penstocks to drive turbines located halfway down the basin wall. In addition to the Qattara Depression itself, towns along the northern coast became internationally known during World War II because of their roles in North African campaigns—Sallum, Sidi Barrani, Matruh, and al-Alamayn (el-Alamein). The stretch of Mediterranean shore west of Alexandria toward al-Alamayn and beyond was developed during the 1990s as a mixed resort area and belt of exclusive summer luxury villas. Such mansions were traditional in Alexandria in past decades, but the coastal estates permit extensive gardens and secluded swimming pools as well as inhibit the evolution of planned resorts that might generate tourist revenues. Farther south, recent exploration for oil and gas has opened several scattered fields with modest but increasing production.

[4] Eastern Desert

The two deserts divided by the Nile Valley are markedly different in character. In contrast to the Western Desert just described, the Eastern Desert consists essentially of a backbone of elevated and mostly rugged mountains running parallel to and just inland from the Red Sea coast. These Red Sea Hills are an elevated and faulted edge of the Nubian Shield composed of igneous and metamorphic rocks of the basement complex (see Chap. 3). Overlapping the western and northern portions of the hills is a relatively low, maturely dissected, extensive Eocene limestone plateau; the resistant crystalline hills farther to the south reach 7,175 ft./2,187 m.[8]

More elevated and slightly better watered than the Western Desert, the Eastern Desert is less inhospitable and is traversed by several routes between the Nile and the Red Sea. The crystalline rocks of the Red Sea Hills contain numerous mineral occurrences, but few are commercially exploitable. The Red Sea coast—fringed by extensive stretches of pristine white sand beaches—has a number of small ports, some dating from ancient times. As part of its extensive tourism promotion program, Egypt is developing these coastal beaches into a major resort area for swimming, scuba-diving, and collecting seashells. Farther north, the Gulf of Suez coast is also a scuba-diving attraction, its surrealistic offshore oil-production platforms and flares visible from the beaches.

[5] Sinai

The large triangular Sinai Peninsula, 23,590 miles²/61,100 km² in area, belongs geomorphically to the Red Sea Hills but has been separated by vigorous faulting along both sides of and beneath the Gulf of Suez (see Fig. 3-3). Such tectonics have in some stretches created structural conditions for accumulations of petroleum. The southern extent of Sinai is composed of uptilted igneous and crystalline rocks that reach 8,650 ft./2,637 m in Jabal Katherina, highest elevation in Egypt, and 7,495 ft./2,285 m in nearby Jabal Musa (Mount Sinai). Nestled in a dramatic site in these rugged igneous highlands lies the famous Greek Orthodox Monastery of St. Katherine, with its unique collection of ancient manuscripts. Formerly remote and isolated, Sinai has increasingly been opened to the outside world since 1980. It has undergone rapid development by oil companies in the west of the peninsula, resort building—complete with airfields—on both gulf coasts, solid mineral mining, and several new roads. In the south, recently opened national parks and natural protectorates will encourage international tourism, protect the unusual environment, and help raise the Bedouins' standard of living.[9]

Sinai's landforms are easily seen in Figure 3-1: The northern two-thirds of the peninsula is a great northward-draining limestone plateau that rises from the Mediterranean coast and terminates southward in a high escarpment, Jabal al-Tih, on the northern flanks of the igneous core of Sinai. The backslope of the limestone is relatively open country that drains to the Mediterranean through numerous sand-choked tributaries that merge into the Wadi al-Arish, the River of Egypt of the Old Testament. The northern reaches of the plateau have been traversed through the centuries by armies and migrating peoples, including Egyptian and Israeli armies in 1948–1949, 1956, 1967, and 1973. The peninsula is connected with Africa by the sandy Isthmus of Suez, through which the Suez Canal was cut by 1869 (see Fig. 20-2 and discussion under "Waterways" below). Anchoring the northern end of the canal is Port Said, on the Mediterranean, and at the southern end is Suez. The midway city is Ismailiyah.

The Egyptians and Their Society

Population

With a 1999 population of 63.2 million, Egypt adds 1 million people every ten months, a projected increase that will double the population in 28 years. An Egyptian baby is born every 18 seconds. The large population and high rate of increase involve several significant geographical relationships. That a population of 63.2 million could evolve and mostly be supported until recently on such a limited amount of cultivated land is a tribute to the productivity of this great river oasis and its people. However, the increasing population is shrinking the amount of available cultivable land per capita and, under foreseeable financial conditions, threatens to overwhelm the national capacity to supply basic services and even food and water. Increasing percentages of the food consumed are being imported each year. A broad spectrum of systematic projects to meet the daunting challenges, underway since the mid-1980s, is discussed later.

Peoples

The dominant group in the Egyptian population, Egyptian Arabs, represents a mixture of the already mixed indigenous Egyptians and the immigrant Arabs who entered the area during the seventh to ninth centuries consequent to the Muslim conquest. Egyptians long considered Bedouins as "the Arabs" and viewed the majority of the population as "the real Egyptians." Fellahin (literally, "tillers of the soil") in many isolated Nile Valley villages have maintained features and many customs of ancient Egyptians, as those are shown in ancient representations. By the late 1800s, Egypt identified increasingly with the Arab world and stimulated some of the main currents of Arab nationalism; and after the mid-1950s, Arabism reciprocally impacted and defined Nasserist Egypt and its regional relationships.

Egypt does not exhibit the complexity of distinct ethnolinguistic groupings of Iraq or Iran.

Most of the ethnic groups that immigrated into Egypt in the past have been absorbed into the population, although some small groups have emigrated en masse. Significant minorities, including Greeks and Jews for millennia and Europeans for shorter periods, were at home in Egypt for centuries, but many left during the Nasser period. One group prominent among Egypt's growing social and economic elite are descendants of the former ruling class, the Turks.

Copts, by far the largest minority, genetically preserve an ancient Egyptian lineage, more so than any other group. Although most Copts are clearly differentiated physically from other Egyptians, their major distinction is that they are Christians, remnant of a community that included most Egyptians prior to the Arab Muslim invasion (see Chap. 6). Estimates of their number vary, but Copts apparently make up less than 10 percent of the total population; they are concentrated in Luxor and the Asyut and Minya provinces of Upper Egypt and in Cairo and Alexandria. They formerly held many influential positions in the government and in business, but thousands have emigrated to escape discrimination since the mid-1950s and even periodic violence against them, as late as the early 1990s.

The second-largest minority is that of the Nubians, numbering possibly 200,000, now concentrated around Kom Ombo, north of Aswan. Formerly living in villages along the Upper Nile Valley southward into the Sudan, the Nubians were resettled in the early 1960s because their villages were to be submerged under Lake Nasser after completion of the Aswan High Dam. Although compensated for their lost property and given new lands and new homes, the Nubians have found the dislocation and loss of their traditional houses culturally disruptive.

The Bedouins in Egypt have been moving away from nomadism and toward sedentarization for more than a century. However, several thousand nomadic Beja people (non-Arabs) migrate into and out of southeastern Egypt from and into northeastern Sudan. A small Bedouin tribe, the Maaza, with probably 1,000 members, wanders the hills and wadis of the Eastern Desert.[10] The Jabaliyya and associated tribes in the southern Sinai are especially involved in touristic and other economic development of the St. Katherine area.[11] A few other small groups are also elements in the mixture of peoples in Egypt. Berbers are the main group in several villages in the Western Desert, especially in the Siwa Oasis in the northwest of the country, having inhabited the area for many centuries. Several thousand Armenians live mostly in Cairo and Alexandria.

Although Old Testament sources recount that Hebrews lived in Egypt in serfdom as Bnai Yisrael (Children of Israel) about the thirteenth century BC, that group left in the emigration described in the book of Exodus. A thousand years later, in Ptolemaic times, Jews settled in Alexandria and started a Jewish community in Egypt that expanded by immigration of Spanish and central European Jews until World War I. Growing Zionism, the later emergence of the State of Israel, and periodic wars between Israel and Egypt created a backlash against Egyptian Jews, most of whom gradually emigrated to Israel and elsewhere. Of about 80,000 Jews in 1947, only about 1,000 remain in Egypt. The number of Western expatriates decreased during the Nasser years, but the expatriate community was again expanding by the late 1980s and at the turn of the millennium included thousands of oil and gas technicians, general contractors, aid personnel, diplomats, and consultants.

The pluralistic coexistence in Egyptian society fractured during the revolutionary Nasser period and was further fragmented by growing Islamic fundamentalism beginning in the late 1960s. Sociopolitical readjustments in Egypt during the Sadat regime contributed to the growth of a number of militant opposition groups (associations or fraternities). The older Muslim Brotherhood (Ikhwan al-Muslimun), founded in 1928, continued to agitate for an ultraorthodox Islamic basis for society and government. As the Brotherhood moderated its methods, more extreme and clandestine associations emerged, an estimated 50 of them in the

Islamic Fraternity (Jamaat al-Islamiyya). The most violent and secretive group styled itself al-Jihad (literally, Arabic "struggle," often translated "holy war"), the group that assassinated President Sadat. During the 1970s, Christian Copts were attacked by militants, evoking retaliation by Coptic students. The Mubarak administration generally rectified this problem, but terrorism by the jamaa against governmental authorities, and often against Western tourist groups—to weaken the Egyptian economy and therefore the government—became shocking between 1992 and 1998. During scores of terrorist attacks, more than 1,000 persons were killed, including security personnel, terrorists, and foreigners; 20,000 accused were imprisoned and dozens executed. The violence ceased when the country, the civilized world, and even most of the militants recoiled over a Jamaat al-Islamiyya atrocity in November 1997. In a planned surprise attack in the Temple of Hatshepsut in Luxor (Fig. 2-2), fanatics massacred 58 European and Japanese tourists and 4 Egyptians before 6 perpetrators were shot.[12] The attack devastated the vital tourist industry for several months, but greatly increased government security gradually restored confidence, and by early 1999 tourism was virtually normal.

Settlements

In its population distribution, Egypt has historically and traditionally been predominantly a land of small agricultural villages. Despite steadily increasing urbanization, thousands of villages are still scattered the length of the valley and in the delta. Valley villages are usually sited just beyond the edge of irrigation, in order to conserve irrigable land, and are located for most of the length of the Nile on the western edge of the floodplain. Most of these valley villages are linear in morphology. Until recently, houses have been constructed of mud from the clay-silt that is in plentiful supply along the Nile or from a nearby canal. Two or three villages can be seen from any given point along the river, and predictably there is a regular pattern of spaced market towns that function as service centers for several surrounding villages. In turn, cities of 150,000–200,000 population have evolved every 40–50 miles/65–80 km as hierarchical central places.

Villages in the delta, on the other hand, display a nucleated morphology and, in the absence of the stone that is available on the valley fringes, were formerly even more likely to have houses constructed of mud bricks. Obviously, as the rapidly increasing population necessitated greatly increased numbers of houses, continued use of mud from nearby fields turned former productive plots into useless pits. A farmer could earn more from the sale of the top 3.3 ft./1 m of his land for making mud bricks than he could earn from the sale of the land. So much of the best arable land was being lost that in 1982, a law was passed prohibiting use of mud for building construction. The change entirely altered village architecture and the appearance of Egyptian villages, where all new construction is of generally reddish fired brick. Because special brick clay can be extracted in only a few places, and must therefore be brought from a distance, and because the fired brick is appreciably more expensive, village homes have become more costly but more permanent—if less attractive.

The dominance of the village has been diminishing since the early 1950s, and the percentage of urban population has increased from less than one-third in 1950 to 45 percent in 1999 (see Table 6-1). Despite the marked growth of several cities, especially Cairo, Egyptian social structure retains village roots more than the urban migration would indicate. Increasing hundreds of thousands of landless and displaced fellahin have flooded into the cities since the 1950s, often grouping themselves by place of origin and thus preserving their village identity. Indeed, this kind of urbanization, the virtual displacement of village to city, has been referred to as the "ruralization of Cairo." Incoming migrants typically have little education, almost no money, and no relevant skills.[13]

Cairo has for many years been the largest city in Africa and the Middle East. During some recent years, it has added a million people annually; by 1999, the population of the Greater Cairo Region (GCR) exceeded 12 million. Including fringe suburbs, the population probably surpassed 15 million, nearly a quarter of Egypt's total. In contrast to Cairo's impressively modern front yard along the Nile in Garden City, Zamalek, and Qasr al-Nil (Fig. 20-4), seething squatter slums lie to the east. More than 1.5 million of the city's poor have taken refuge in the tombs and monuments in the City of the Dead, the extensive Cairo cemeteries east of the capital. Although unable to supply adequate municipal services, the government is making major efforts to clean up the slums and to reduce the serious pollution from automobiles, potteries, cement factories, and lead smelters.[14] Traffic in the central business district was becoming virtually immobile until a new subway system, opened in 1987 and considerably expanded during the 1990s, appreciably relieved the tangle of surface circulation. Engineered and partly financed by the French, the Metro has been such a success that early planning is well along on a subway in Alexandria.[15]

With nearly half of its population urbanized, Egypt has 26 cities with populations exceeding 100,000 and more than twice as many with 50,000–100,000 inhabitants. Growth far outruns the census taker. Most of the larger cities are located in the delta, where urban sprawl consumes vital agricultural land. The vital necessity for relief of urban crowding in the Greater Cairo Region prompted some corrective action as early as the 1960s. Plans called for fourteen new urban centers—some satellite cities and some new towns—to be built well away from Cairo and well away from farmland. Fourteen had been constructed by 1989, and more are planned in the hope of their accommodating several million people. Progress on developing infrastructure and services has been uneven; indeed, many migrants prefer living in a Cairo slum with old friends to adopting an unfamiliar lifestyle in a strange environment.[16]

Changing Economic Patterns

An Economic Perspective

The historical riches of Egypt are proverbial— the productivity of the irrigated soil, the creativity of the Egyptian artisans, the gold from the Pharaonic and Ptolemaic tombs, the trade between Red Sea entrepôts and Mediterranean coastal states. However, the ever-increasing population of modern times presses on the maximum limits of even Egypt's fabled resources. The agricultural productivity is several times greater today than in centuries past, but demographic demands on that productivity have increased even more. Once a net food exporter, then at least self-sufficient, Egypt now imports growing percentages of its food consumption— more than 60 percent in the late 1990s.

The political revolution of 1952 brought a correlative economic revolution. Economic efforts of the revolutionary junta included land reform, controls over agriculture, nationalization of industries and institutions (notably the nationalization of the Suez Canal in 1956), sequestration of foreign businesses and agencies, an inflow of bilateral and multilateral loans and grants, and construction of the Aswan High Dam system. Progress toward these well-intentioned goals was impeded by administrative problems, by bureaucratic inefficiency, and by Egypt's military buildup and three wars with Israel. President Nasser's insistence on a socialist approach to state management repelled both foreign and domestic investment. Originally, his statist-paternalistic approach had domestic popular appeal, since land reform, widespread nationalization, and tight control over the economy broke the power of the large landowners, foreign capitalists, and wealthy Egyptians. Nasser's revolution was, indeed, a watershed event in modern Egyptian history. Many of his reforms brought long-range benefits, but some apparent gains soon revealed serious flaws. For example, Nasser's "social contract" improved the lot of the average Egyptian, but only through price controls, heavy subsidies, and unselective

FIGURE 20-4   View down the Nile River at Cairo, with major bridges in foreground and buildings of Zamalak in center distance.

guaranteed employment. Such broad paternalism and free university education, along with the assured employment of graduates, seemed progressive; but they loaded the bureaucracy and large public sector enterprises with redundant employees, depressed the wage scale, degraded the quality of the educational system, and resulted in a downward economic spiral.

President Sadat reversed the trend when he opened Egypt's economic doors by means of his moderate *infitah* policy of 1974, which reduced earlier restrictiveness. However, conditions in Egypt and in the Middle East as a whole countered some of the goals of *infitah*,[17] resulting in a certain amount of deindustrialization and increased indebtedness. Falling incomes and government austerity measures produced riots in Aswan and Alexandria and intensified the immediacy of Sadat's initiative to seek peace with Israel and to request the contingent greater assistance from the United States. After partly implementing reforms in 1991, Egypt finally acceded in 1996 to stringent recommendations of the International Monetary Fund and World Bank. Thus, during the 1990s, the macroeconomy witnessed a remarkable turnabout as the Cairo government sought to integrate the country into the global economy. One key move was to mobilize the private sector, reversing the Nasserist philosophy by privatizing 25 percent of the public sector enterprises and arranging to sell off the remaining 239. The GDP has regularly increased at 5 percent per year, inflation is a modest 4–5 percent, subsidies have been decreased, government spending has been kept in check, taxation has increased, and the rate of exchange for the Egyptian pound has been stable. However, unemployment is still high—officially 10 percent, but actually closer to 18 percent—and GDP should increase by about 8 percent to absorb the 700,000 annual additions to the labor force. The country's infrastructure is developing rapidly but continues to be overtaken by increasing population and economic expansion. The most notable remaining deficiencies and choke points include port facilities and services.

By 1998, tourism was the leading foreign exchange earner, at $3.6 billion, and was a major component of the GDP. Remittances from the 2 million or more Egyptians working abroad, mostly in the Arabian Peninsula, were $3.4 billion in 1997, up 11.3 percent from 1996. Although losing ground, agriculture is still the most important single sector in the GDP, followed by industry and mining, trade, oil and gas products, transportation, tourism, and revenues from the Suez Canal.[18]

Agriculture and Water

The Nile Valley has supported a flourishing agriculture for more than 8,500 years, and much of the valley and delta was under cultivation soon after the union of Upper and Lower Egypt about 3000 BC. Once the cultivable area had been cleared of forest and brush, increasing portions of the area that is now cropland were farmed under the natural flood-irrigation system that was dominant in Egypt until after AD 1800.

The irrigation system so long practiced was basically simple. It utilized the runoff from the heavy summer rains in the East African highlands that poured down the Nile channel and raised the water level 20–25 ft./6–8 m, covering the entire floodplain with several feet of silt-laden floodwaters. When the floodwaters receded after several weeks, the silt loam soils, built up by past floods, were water soaked and were also covered with a fresh few millimeters of nutrient-rich new silt. Thus the valley soils were watered, fertilized, and renewed annually by natural means, without human intervention. Crops were then planted to mature before the soil dried out some months later. Perennial tree and vine crops, carefully sited as to elevation—somewhat lower than village locations—could also be maintained; otherwise, only one crop in a flood season could be harvested. In later centuries, water was retained in basins to prolong irrigation; still later, canals were installed by Pharaonic engineers. As experience was passed from generation to generation, the fellahin of the Nile Valley became expert hydraulic farmers, and their traditional culture was as immutable as the annual Nile flood.

For many centuries, virtually all crop production was restricted to the level and the area of the natural annual flooding. Not until application of modern technology in the mid-1800s was the irrigable area significantly increased through the construction of barrages at the head of the delta (in 1860) and later at Asyut. Completion of the first Aswan Dam in 1902, and later additions to its height, extended perennial irrigation. The Aswan High Dam, discussed earlier, introduced the single most momentous program for perennial irrigation and attendant year-round cropping virtually everywhere in the "old" settled area; despite bringing several major problems, the dam set the stage for the potential engineering of major "new" areas for settlement.

The Tahrir (Liberation) Project west of the delta, undertaken in the 1950s, failed to meet expectations but offered hope for other such schemes. More ambitious was the New Valley Project (al-Wadi al-Jadid) for revitalization of the once-productive and even wealthy oases of the Western Desert described earlier. Recent discovery and excavation of a Roman-period necropolis in Bahriyah in 1996 reveals evidence of a thriving community of 2,000 years ago that grew prosperous by making wine from dates and grapes.[19] The New Valley Project seeks to restore such affluence to the area. After twenty years of planning and delay, agriculture has been vigorously expanded by using deep Nubian Formation groundwater; production centers on such high-value crops as dates, olives, fruits, and vegetables for shipment to Cairo and the urban markets of the delta. Complementary infrastructure has accompanied the crop expansion, with roads, electric power, schools, and housing for the expected new settlers, plus hotels for the growing number of domestic and foreign tourists.

The New Valley Project is expected to receive enormous impetus during the first decade or two of the new century when the program merges with the grandiose Tushka (or Toshka) Canal Project. After several years of study and planning, the Tushka Canal venture began construction in 1999. (It is unrelated to the Tushka

Spillway, opened in 1980, to drain excess flood waters from Lake Nasser into a desert depression southwest of Aswan.) The canal project will require one of the world's largest pumping stations, under construction in mid-1999, to lift lake water 175 ft./53 m to the level of the canal. The concrete-lined channel will extend 150 miles/240 km northwest across empty desert in the first stage.[20] It will be extended to Kharijah Oasis and possibly on up the arc of depressions sheltering the other Western Desert oases (Map 20-1). Thus, the present New Valley Project will be expanded and merged with the Tushka Canal Project, planned eventually to open about 3.5 million acres/1.4 million ha for irrigated cultivation. Such a planned expansion would increase Egypt's cultivated area by about 40 percent, to 11.6 million acres/4.7 million ha, and would accommodate several million new settlers and perhaps a million new jobs by 2017. Completion is expected to take twenty years and more than $80 billion in investment.[21] However, many outside technicians consider government expectations highly optimistic.

Complementing these South Valley projects is another major reclamation scheme in the northeast, the North Sinai Agricultural Development Project. Irrigation will use Nile water delivered through the Peace (al-Salam) Canal, which in turn is fed with water siphoned under the Suez Canal through four tunnels. Plans call for the initial cultivated area to be 170,000 acres/69,000 ha, with an eventual potential expansion well beyond that.[22] One controversial aspect of the Peace Canal is that it might be extended eastward into Israel. Other reported plans call for some water to be channeled to Gaza. It might be claimed that such sharing is in violation of the basic treaties allotting Nile water among the riparian states.[23]

The pattern of cropping is complicated by two factors: the growing of two and three crops a year on many plots, and the differences in production in "new lands" and "old lands." However, overall, the main crop in both area and tonnage is clover (berseem), with cereals continuing to occupy 40–50 percent of the total cropped area. Wheat and maize lead in cereal acreage and tonnage,

with the new high-yield wheats increasing output per acre nearly 50 percent since 1985. Rice ranks third among cereals, and the famous Egyptian cotton is the leading nonfood crop. Such fruits as citrus, dates, and grapes, and a wide variety of winter and summer vegetables, vie with rice in area, and all of these crops are important exports. Sugar cane maintains its place as a major crop. Figure 20-5 shows a typical mix of crops in the Nile Valley.

Egyptian long-staple cotton has been the preferred cotton fiber on world markets since its development by a French agronomist in the 1820s. Although long-staple cotton is increasingly produced elsewhere, Egypt still produces more than one-third of the world crop. The main cotton area is in the central delta, where long expertise and government extension work and control ensure quality. With the more realistic government pricing policies that have recently aided cotton farmers, production and marketing changes can be expected. The cotton produced is increasingly being used in the important domestic textile industry, and cotton textiles and yarns now constitute Egypt's second-leading export by value. Raw cotton is of only minor importance as an export.

Animals have been an integral element in the activities of virtually every Egyptian farm since ancient times. Tomb paintings depict the role of cattle and other animals in early Egyptian agriculture, and the cow and the bull were venerated in the ancient Egyptian pantheon. Sheep, goats, and ducks have also been of prime importance for more than 4,500 years, as has the donkey. Cattle, buffalo, and donkeys are still multipurpose farm animals, pulling plows and carts, carrying loads (the donkey serving also for individual transportation), supplying manure for fields and fuel, and furnishing milk. The useful camel came later and is still common. The Indian buffalo (*gamus* or *gamush*) was imported in the Middle Ages and is now the most numerous farm animal. It is well adapted along the river and canals, yielding milk, meat, manure, and hides and serving as a plow animal.

Fishery production in Egypt was 305,000 mt in 1994, only half that of Turkey, the Middle

FIGURE 20-5   Typical view of the timeless Nile Valley: intensive cultivation in the fertile alluvial soils, date palm grove and fruit trees, sugar cane, village under the shade trees, and fellahin still laboring by hand as they have for centuries.

East leader. The fish catch has increased in recent years, with Lake Nasser replacing the Mediterranean as the main source.

Industry

Oil and Oil Processing.   The first oil well in Egypt was drilled in 1886, although commercial production came only in 1913. After World War II, several foreign companies, most of them American, conducted oil explorations, primarily under concession agreements. Oil operations in Egypt expanded in the 1960s, and production averaged 882,750 bpd in 1994–1997, reaching an all-time high of 992,000 bpd in 1995. Although Egypt is a member of the Organization of Arab Petroleum Exporting Countries (OAPEC), it is not a member of OPEC and is, therefore, not subject to OPEC production quotas. However, it usually exhibits a willingness to follow OPEC's trend.

Egypt's increasing petroleum production during the 1980s and its growing oil exports have had a major impact on the national export economy. In 1974, a low-production year for Egypt, oil sales constituted only 4 percent of the country's revenues from commodity exports.

By 1981–1982, with the price between $29 and $34 per barrel, oil was Egypt's leading export, and, with some variations, after 1996, petroleum and petroleum products constituted about half of its exports.

The most important oil field developments have been in and along both coasts of the Gulf of Suez (see Map 20-1). Intensive exploration in the Western Desert has found several fields in the northern sector, although output has been modest. However, the possibility remains that oil fields in Libya extend into western Egypt.

Whereas new oil discoveries have been modest and production has been somewhat flat, nonassociated natural gas finds and output have increased dramatically. Gas reserves in 1991 were 12.4 trillion cubic feet and in 1999, were 31.5 tcf; however, later discoveries reported by the government in early 2000 hinted at reserves of 120 tcf. When major gas fields were found in three different Tertiary zones in the northern delta after 1993, offshore exploration opened several more major fields. Thus the northern delta and the adjacent offshore area, now a world-class gas province, possess more than 67 percent of Egypt's gas reserves. By using its natural gas for power plants and industries, which burn 95 percent of the gas used domestically, the country can export more of its crude oil and product. Plans are now under consideration for exporting gas by pipeline either under the Gulf of Aqabah to Jordan or by LNG tankers to Turkey. Similar tentative plans have been discussed for supplying gas to Israel by pipeline across northern Sinai, with Gaza another potential customer. These plans must await results of seismic surveys taken in 1999 that suggested offshore gas structures extend from Egyptian waters into the Israeli and Gaza exclusive economic zones.

Egypt was credited in 1999 with having oil reserves of 3.5 billion bbl, about the same as in 1982, although Egypt claimed in early 2000 that new finds upped its reserves to 8.2 billion bbl. About 70 percent of the oil production is from the Gulf of Suez, the oldest fields, and about 15 percent from the Western Desert. Exploration and production are carried out by more than 30 European and North American companies, particularly BP-Amoco, under contract with the government, usually with the Egyptian General Petroleum Corporation.

Two Egyptian pipelines are noteworthy: The 200-mile/320-km Sumed (Suez-Mediterranean) line, from Ayn Sukhnah on the Gulf of Suez to Sidi Krir just west of Alexandria, is a dual 42-in./107-cm line with an original capacity of 1.6 million bpd, increased to 2.4 million bpd in 1995. Egypt owns it jointly with Saudi Arabia, Kuwait, the UAE, and Qatar. Sumed was opened in 1977 to bypass the Suez Canal, both because the largest tankers exceeded the capacity of the canal and also because the canal had been shut down between 1967 and 1975 after the June War with Israel. Because competition from the line is now to the canal's disadvantage, negotiations are in progress to redress the imbalance through fee adjustments. The second line, opened in 1981, extends from Ras Shuqayr on the Gulf of Suez to refineries at Suez and Cairo. Ras Shuqayr is the export terminal for the adjacent offshore fields.

Of eight refineries processing a total of 578,000 bpd in 1999, the largest is at Mostorod near Cairo, with a throughput of 145,000 bpd. Noteworthy among refineries being expanded or newly constructed is the Egyptian-Israeli joint-venture MIDOR refinery in Alexandria, scheduled for a throughput of 100,000 bpd, especially oriented toward export. Principal petrochemical plants are near Alexandria and Suez.[24]

Other Mineral Industry. Contemporary commercial solid-mineral mining is extensive and involves a considerable range of minerals, but it is only a modest contributor to the Egyptian national economy. Iron ore and phosphate rock are the most important non-fuel minerals produced in Egypt. Iron ore from Aswan was used in the Helwan iron and steel mill, south of Cairo, from its opening in 1958 until the mid-1970s; however, somewhat better and more plentiful sedimentary ore from al-Bahriyah Oasis now feeds the Helwan mill via a railway constructed for this purpose. A recently discovered high-grade iron ore deposit in an empty desert area 50 miles/80 km southeast of Aswan is the basis for a new Aswan Iron and Steel Company complex. Scheduled to start initial production in mid-2001, with an eventual output of 1.4 million mt per year, the plant will provide 3,000 jobs and will be the centerpiece for a completely new community. Its products will include seamless tubing for export to the regional oil industry. The Alexandria National Iron and Steel plant was expanded to a capacity of 1.5 million mt per year in 1998; thus, Helwan, Alexandria, and Aswan will give Egypt an impressive iron and steel industry.

Phosphate rock is mined near Isna (south of Luxor), near Bur Safajah on the Red Sea, and at the railhead near al-Kharijah Oasis. Production averaged 1.6 million mt in the late 1990s, about the same as Syria's. Other non-metallic minerals produced were of relatively low value and included large tonnages of gypsum, fire clay, kaolin, and salt, as well as all varieties of dimension stone, including Aswan granite. As is true elsewhere in the Middle East, cement production is a major minerals industry. Egypt's first coal mine was opened in late 1995 at al-Maghara in the northern Sinai and is producing 650,000 tons per year.[25]

Other Manufacturing. Egypt experienced delayed industrial development before World War II and suffered uneven development after the 1952 revolution. The unskilled labor supply was more than adequate, and skilled labor was moderately available; however, large supplies of capital were limited, as were planning and management skills, thereby constraining industrial growth in Egypt during the 1950s and 1960s. Petroleum development, benefits of the High Dam, *infitah* policies, strong donor support, and Egypt's realistic economic and political policies after 1991 finally stimulated a significant and consistent growth of the manufacturing sector.

However, earlier policies for industrial development under state socialism resulted in virtually all of the larger and medium-sized establishments having evolved in the public sector. The 314 most important establishments were saddled with bloated employee rolls, bureaucratic mismanagement, and inefficient administration. Economic reform after 1991 had as one principal aim the privatization of these key industries, of which more than 75 had been partly or wholly shifted into the private sector by 1998.[26] An additional 50 were added by mid-1999. Another goal of the reform is geographical diversification. At present, nearly half of Egypt's manufacturing is centered in the Shubra al-Khaymah industrial area north of Cairo and in Helwan south of the capital, contributing to serious air and water pollution in the Greater Cairo Region. Major industrial areas outside the GCR are Naj Hammadi (west of Qena, processing imported bauxite to produce aluminum); the major delta cities of Tanta and Muhallah al-Kubra (textiles); Alexandria (refineries, petrochemicals, iron and steel, shipyards); Suez (fertilizers); and several middle-Nile cities. Medium-sized armaments industries, including the assembly of jeeps, tanks, helicopters, and other weaponry, are located in Lower Egypt. By 1998, industry supplied 18 percent of the GDP and employed 13 percent of the workforce.

Traditional private sector establishments are small and generally artisan in character. They are located primarily in and around Cairo, especially in the old *suqs* of the Muski and Khan al-Khalili, but also in other main cities and towns. They produce food products, textiles, leather goods, jewelry, artistic glass objects, copper and brass ornamental and utilitarian items, and furniture and other wood products, including intricately inlaid boxes and other household items.

Transportation and Trade

Roads. With settlement highly concentrated in the Nile Valley and Delta, transportation by river, road, and railroad is equally concentrated (see Map 20-1). A medium-speed paved highway extends the full length of the Nile Valley between Cairo and Aswan and also extends from Cairo to Alexandria and other terminal points along the northern delta. At right angles to the valley-delta routes is the Mediterranean coastal highway between the Libyan border on the west and the Israeli border on the east. Successive military operations in Sinai and increasing development of the area have prompted the construction of other transpeninsular and circumpeninsular roads in Sinai, opening an area that was isolated as late as the mid-1950s.

A recently completed north-south Red Sea coastal highway connects Suez and the Sudan border, opening a new area for beach resorts and secondary ports and relieving traffic on the Nile route. The Suez Canal is paralleled on both sides by roads that are linked by the 1-mile/1.6-km Ahmad Hamdi Tunnel, which passes under Bitter Lake. The two main north-south routes, Nile Valley and Red Sea coast, are connected by several east-west roads. The Delta Road between Cairo and Alexandria and the Desert Road between the same two cities reveal a marked and interesting contrast in Egyptian landscapes.

Railroads. Unlike many national rail systems, Egyptian lines are heavily used by passengers, giving Egypt half of the total passenger-kilometers for the Middle East. Indicative of the pressure of population on facilities, trains into and out of Cairo are so overloaded that hundreds of passengers must either stand inside or cling precariously to the outside of trains. This hazard is being relieved by the new mass transit system between al-Marg, a northern suburb of Cairo, and Helwan to the south. In two major rail construction projects, a 620-mile/1,000-km railroad was opened in 1996 between Safajah and al-Kharijah Oasis; it will carry phosphate rock from Abu Tartu, just west of al-Kharijah, to the export port on the Red Sea, and bring bauxite for processing at Naj Hammadi. Double-tracking the line from Asyut to Aswan is also planned.

Waterways. In addition to the Suez Canal, Egypt has 2,175 miles/3,500 km of inland waterways, half along the Nile River itself and half along several major canals, especially in the delta. Sailing on the Nile was the only north-south method of travel in Egypt until completion of the railway to Aswan and the later construction of a motorable road. The Nile between Aswan and the Mediterranean is still used by hundreds of the typical Nile sailing boats, *faluqas* (feluccas), as well as by rapidly increasing numbers of motor-powered tourist boats. *Faluqas* are a practical and inexpensive means of north-south shipment of heavy and nonperishable goods.

Since its opening in 1869, the Suez Canal has been both a significant symbol and an integral economic element for Egypt (see Chap. 11). Operated by an Anglo-French company until it was dramatically nationalized by President Nasser in 1956, the canal quickly became Egypt's leading foreign exchange earner; however, as tanker traffic and revenues steadily declined for various reasons, the canal's earnings fell to $1.76 billion in 1998, behind tourism, oil exports, and remittances. It was closed by the 1967 Arab-Israeli war but was reopened in 1975, then dredged in 1980 to a draft of 52 ft./16 m to permit transit of larger tankers. It was further deepened to 58 ft./17.7 m ten years later. (See additional details under "Suez Canal," Chap. 11.)

Ports. Alexandria, Egypt's most important port, was founded by Alexander the Great, and for much of 23 centuries it has functioned as one of the largest and busiest general-cargo ports in the eastern Mediterranean and the Middle East. It fills so many functions—port, resort, industrial center, commercial center—that traffic is increasingly being spun off to satellite ports in Dikhaylah and Marsa Matruh to the west and in Damietta to the east. Port Said and Suez, at opposite ends of the Suez Canal, are thriving industrial centers as well as major ports; they enjoy free zones, as do Alexandria and Damietta.

Air Transportation. The government-owned airline, Egypt Air, was founded in 1932 and operated for many years as Misr Air (Arabic *Misr* = Egypt). Egypt Air flies an extensive network from Western Europe to the Far East and into Africa, operating 55 jet aircraft, third-largest civil aviation fleet in the area, after Saudia and Iran Air. Along with its civil fleet, Egypt has a large air force and also maintains a significant number of medium-sized combined civil and military airports. Cairo's airport is the busiest in the Middle East and sends frequent flights to the country's main tourist centers in Upper Egypt, Luxor and Aswan.

Trade. Still almost entirely in the private sector, most domestic retail trade follows the Arab commercial tradition, in which outlets tend to be small, often operated only by the owner and perhaps one or two family members. Central Cairo and Alexandria have relatively large Western-style "department" stores. Country-wide, food shops predominate, but other retail stores offer clothing, textiles, small household items, and jewelry and other items handcrafted in Egypt for the tourist and internal trade. Such items include a wide range of inlaid wood pieces, hand-engraved brass and copper, turned and carved alabaster, jewelry and costume jewelry, tooled leather, traditional screens of turned wood (*mashrabiyah*), and paintings on Egyptian-grown handmade papyrus.

Cairo preserves the traditional *suq* in addition to its modern, Western-style central business district. The Khan al-Khalili, located in a fourteenth-century Mamluk caravansary or khan, has been famous for centuries throughout the Middle East. Traditional Egyptian goods and certain types of specialty goods from around the world are on sale in the primarily small stalls. The adjacent Muski sells similar items but also has sections for utilitarian and lower-value items. Both bazaars are a paradise for leisurely shopping for the curious and the unusual, especially if the shopper is a skilled bargainer.

Foreign trade has been a major factor in the Egyptian economy for thousands of years. Exchange between Lebanon and Egypt, for example, flourished before 2400 BC; and medieval Cairo was probably the world's greatest trade center, relaying shipborne products from the Indian Ocean to the Mediterranean. Shifts in commodities traded and in directions of trade both historically and recently reflect significant changes in the routing of trade, within Egypt, and in Egypt's foreign relations. For example, exports of long-staple cotton during the American Civil War brought Egypt instant but short-lived prosperity, petroleum exports during the early 1980s offset increasing trade deficits until the world oil price collapsed, and Egypt's trading partners shifted in accordance with its political orientation between 1970 and 1980 and shifted again during the mid-1990s, when it joined the World Trade Organization.

For many years, Egyptian exports were overwhelmingly agricultural raw materials, chiefly food products and cotton. The share of agricultural products is now not only down to 10 percent of the value of exports but is about 30 percent of the value of imports. Other foreign trade data are given in the country summary at the beginning of this chapter and in Tables 9-3 and 9-4.

Relations

Egypt's relations both with its neighbors and with the major powers have been of crucial importance since 1947.[27] Under Nasser, relations were confrontational and erratic. Under Sadat, they involved complete reversals in policies with Israel, the USSR, and the United States. They then stabilized and followed a relatively consistent policy under Mubarak after the 1980s.

A watershed in Egyptian relations was President Sadat's turning away from the USSR in the early 1970s, establishing close ties with the United States, and signing a peace treaty with Israel in 1979. His making peace with Israel prompted most Arab countries to break diplomatic relations with Egypt and precipitated expulsion of Egypt from the Arab League (Chap. 11). Egypt's regional role, however, was and is too vital to be denied: The Organization of the Islamic Conference (OIC) reinstated Egypt in 1984; most Arab states reestablished diplomatic relations with Mubarak's government after the Arab Summit meeting in Amman in 1987; and the Arab League welcomed Egypt back as a leading member in 1989 and returned League headquarters to Cairo in 1990. Also in 1989, President Mubarak took the chair of the Organization of African Unity (OAU). Thus, Egypt was restored to both Arabism and Africa and retained its position within Islamic world affairs. In February 1989, Egypt, Iraq, Jordan, and the then Yemen Arab Republic joined to form the Arab Cooperation Council (ACC), an unlikely regional grouping similar to the GCC with aims comparable to those of the European Common Market. In the regional reaction to the watershed Iraqi invasion of Kuwait in 1990, Egypt led the opposition and vigorously supported an international coalition to liberate Kuwait. In addition to its critical political efforts, Egypt contributed 35,000 men and their equipment—third largest after the United States and Saudi Arabia—to the coalition armies. During the crisis, the fledgling ACC collapsed, as has every union Egypt has attempted. Egypt's overall internal situation markedly improved under the aegis and financial support of the United States.

Egypt's relations with its upstream neighbor, the Sudan, have been important since the dawn of history. During the period of Britain's de facto hegemony over Egypt, the Sudan was an

Anglo-Egyptian condominium. These long relations found expression in a friendly 1982 agreement, a ten-year Charter of Integration, calling for close cooperation in foreign policy, security, and development. However, relations deteriorated in the late 1980s under increasing threats by the Sudan to dam the Nile, ascendancy in 1989 of a new confrontational government in Sudan, and Sudan's siding with Iraq after the invasion of Kuwait. Relations with President Qadhdhafi (Qaddafi) of Libya have been spasmodic. Tentative plans for political unity in 1971 were abrogated in 1984, giving way to conflict and brief border warfare. After more years of tension, Egypt and Libya were reconciled in mid-1989, although proof of détente in the resumption of full diplomatic relations was slow in coming.

Relations between Egypt and Israel have been the mainspring of the post-World War II geopolitical evolution of the Levant and northeastern Africa (see Chap. 11 and other country chapters). Despite having been Israel's main foe in four wars, Egypt was the first Arab country to sign a peace treaty with Israel. Although suffering a decade of ostracism by most of its neighbors after 1979, Egypt increasingly profited from the "peace dividend." Among several inevitable ups and downs between the treaty's signatories, one setback concerned Israel's disputed claim on Taba, in the Sinai across the border from Elat. After arbitration in Egypt's favor returned the enclave to its long-time owner in 1988, reciprocal confidence increased. As the Egyptian-Israeli relationship and Mubarak's role matured, Egypt frequently served as mediator among diverse players in regional disputes. Not only did it strongly support the successive stages of the Palestinian/Arab-Israeli peace process, it found mutual benefits in its various dealings with Israel and the United States. Only during the highly controversial regime of Israeli prime minister Binyamin Netanyahu did the relationship move into a "cold peace." By mid-1999, with relations correct again, Egypt resumed its support of the peace process. Thousands of Israeli tourists visit Egypt annually, but few Egyptians visit Israel.

Relations with the United States after 1974 became a key factor in Egypt's political-economic position. Cut off by Nasser after Israel's attack on Egypt in 1967, U.S.-Egyptian relations resumed in 1974 after the United States brokered the Sinai disengagement agreements. In other efforts to foster détente between Egypt and Israel, the United States established the Sinai Support and Field Missions after 1976 and sponsored the Camp David accords and the Egyptian-Israeli peace treaty. Financially, the United States first supplanted then supplemented Arab aid with U.S. aid, eventually committing nearly $55 billion in economic and military grants, credits, military training, economic support, and food aid between 1974 and 1999. Egypt continues to be the second-largest recipient (after Israel) of U.S. aid.[28] Egypt, in turn, maintains peace with Israel and has provided facilities for use by U.S. forces in the region and for joint military exercises. U.S.-Egyptian relations became particularly close during 1991–1992, when the United States forgave $7 billion of Egypt's debt.

Relations between the former Soviet Union and Egypt are primarily of historical interest, although the Aswan High Dam remains as a long-term testament to Egypt's benefits. After seventeen years of close Soviet-Egyptian relations on a basis of mutual advantage, those relations deteriorated. In July 1972, President Sadat expelled 15,000–20,000 Soviet advisers and repudiated the 1971 friendship treaty with the Soviet Union. In September 1981, the Soviet ambassador and several aides were expelled on charges of espionage, but relations were restored in July 1984.[29] Soviet-Egyptian relations remained correct after the reestablishment of U.S.-Egyptian ties. After the breakup of the USSR, Egypt pursued good relations not only with Russia but also with the new Muslim republics—Azerbaijan and the five republics in central Asia.

Despite having exercised imperialist control over Egypt after 1882 and having participated in the 1956 tripartite invasion of the Suez, Britain retains good relations with Egypt.

France also had imperialist interests in the area and assumed an especially important role in the construction and operation of the Suez Canal. Because of the involvement of Britain and France in the 1956 Suez affair, Nasser sequestered British and French properties in Egypt. European cultural influence carries over, however, and both English and French are second languages for many educated Egyptians.

Thus restored to a pivotal role in Arab and Islamic world affairs, and once again demonstrating the continuing advantages of its major power core location, Egypt strives to pursue a moderate course among its trilateral ties with the Arab world, the West, and Israel. President Mubarak also restored relations with Iran in 1991 after four years of mutual distrust. With Naguib Mahfouz winning the Nobel Prize for Literature in 1988 and the former Egyptian foreign minister Boutros Boutros-Ghali, a Coptic Christian, having served as secretary-general of the United Nations 1992–1996, Egypt has achieved positive recognition on the world stage.

Notes

1. Egypt is one of the best-analyzed countries in the Middle East. Recommended studies of post-1952 Egypt include Waterbury 1983, Cooper 1982, Hopwood 1982, Harris 1988, Makram-Ebeid 1989, Lorenz 1990, and *Egypt* Country Study 1991. An appraisal of Mubarak and his government is given in the *Economist*, June 12, 1999, 40. The article errs in saying that Mubararak is Egypt's longest serving ruler since 1850.

2. Although technical in many aspects, Said 1962 is useful for the landforms of Egypt. Dr. Said was formerly director of the Geological Survey of Egypt. For the 1992 Cairo earthquake see *New York Times*, Oct. 13, 1992.

3. Details are given in Elhance 1999 and Rogers and Lydon 1994.

4. Several studies of the Fayyum (often spelled Fayoum) are outdated or difficult to find, but see Hewison 1989.

5. The evolution of the Nile is well covered in Said 1981, which is less technical than Said 1962.

6. See Benedick 1979.

7. Nile water problems and some details of the High Dam are discussed in Elhance 1999. See also

Fahim 1981, Haynes and Whittington 1981, and Waterbury 1979.

8. The excellent Hobbs 1989 discusses the physical environment of the Eastern Desert and focuses on the Bedouins of the area.

9. Scholarly but readable accounts of these developments are in Hobbs 1996 and Hobbs 1999.

10. Hobbs 1989 is an in-depth study of the Maaza.

11. Hobbs 1996.

12. *New York Times*, Nov. 19, 1997. For a retrospect see *Economist*, May 1, 1999, 43–44.

13. Saqqaf 1987, 227 and 234. Saqqaf 1987, Part V, analyzes urbanization in Egypt, especially Cairo. The readable Rodenbeck 1998 gives an intimate view of Cairo. See also Abu-Lughod 1971.

14. *Christian Science Monitor*, Mar. 20, 1998.

15. See details *Christian Science Monitor*, Aug. 13, 1997.

16. Stewart 1996.

17. See Moore 1986.

18. This section draws partly from *Country Commercial Guide: Egypt*, FY 99; *Economic Policy and Trade Practices: Egypt*, 1998; and *Agricultural Situation Report: Egypt*, 1997.

19. Hawass, Zahi. "Oasis of the Dead." *Archaeology* 52, no. 5 (Sept./Oct. 1999): 38. The find is also reported in *New York Times*, Aug. 24, 1999.

20. See additional details in *New York Times*, Jan. 10, 1997.

21. See article by David Hirst in *The Washington Times*, Aug. 4, 1999. Further details are given in the Foreign Agriculture Service (FAS) report for Egypt for 1997: <www.fas.usda.gov>.

22. See FAS report for Egypt 1997, as well as Bleier 1997 and *Christian Science Monitor*, Oct. 22, 1997.

23. See Bleier 1997 and *Al-Ahram*, July 22, 1999.

24. Updating is from *EIA: Egypt*, July 1999, and *International Petroleum Encyclopedia* 1999 and earlier years.

25. See U.S. Bureau of Mines *Minerals Yearbook: Egypt*, 1996, for details on Egypt's solid minerals.

26. See *Country Commercial Guide: Egypt*, 1999, plus FAS report on Egypt 1997.

27. Lorenz 1990 gives an excellent discussion of the subject, including an introductory chapter entitled "The Geographic and Historical Setting."

28. U.S. aid to Egypt increased dramatically after Camp David and is analyzed in Weinbaum 1983 and Clarke 1997.

29. See an insider's analysis of this subject in El Hussini 1987. The author was a commodore in the Egyptian navy.

21

Turkey: Bridgeland in Anatolia

Between Europe and Middle East

With its geopolitically strategic bridgeland location, Asia Minor has functioned as a transit land and transition between Europe and southwest Asia for more than 3,000 years. Traversing that bridgeland millennia ago, Europeans worked their way down the valleys and over the passes of the Balkans and into the Anatolian basins and beyond. Similarly, other peoples from the Caucasus and the Iranian Plateau traversed the rugged mountains of eastern Anatolia and mingled with Europeans in the central basins. Later empires were centered in Constantinople and ruled lands from central Europe in one direction to the Arabian Peninsula coastlands in the other. Post-World War I republican Turkey has retained its tenacious foothold in Europe and, now connected to the continent by actual bridges over the Bosporus, links Europe with the eastern reaches of Asia Minor. The only Middle East state adjoining Europe, contemporary Turkey is also the only Middle East Muslim state that openly pursues Europeanization, that uses the European (Roman) alphabet, and that belongs to the North Atlantic Treaty Organization (NATO). Also, in December 1999, the European Union finally voted to make Turkey a "candidate state" for EU membership.

Turkey's geographical assets include not only its location in the geopolitically major Anatolian power center but also its control over the strategic straits of the Bosporus and the Dardanelles. Facing imperial Russian lands then later the Soviet constituent republics and now the successor republics across the Black Sea and in the Caucasus Mountains, Turkey has been involved in more wars with Russia than any other nation. One reflection of Asia Minor's strategic location is Turkey's function as an anchor on the southeastern flank of NATO; evidence of its transitional function was shown in its simultaneous membership in NATO and CENTO (Central Treaty Organization) before CENTO collapsed in 1979. The disintegration of the USSR diminished the importance both of NATO and of Turkey's role in NATO, but Turkey's intermediate location thrust it once again into a geopolitical vortex vis-à-vis the former Soviet satellites and successor republics in the trans-Caucasus and in central Asia. Moreover, Turkey is the only country that bordered both contestants in the 1980–1988 Iran-Iraq war, and it was one of the six immediate neighbors of Iraq in the 1990–1991 Gulf crisis.

Although it ranks fourth in absolute size among Middle East states, Turkey is endowed with a much greater proportion of habitable and productive environments than the larger Saudi Arabia, Iran, and Egypt. It leads the region in a wide range of agricultural products and, with the notable exception of petroleum, a range of both mineral resources and production. Turkey's development has focused on human, agricultural, mineral, and industrial resources; and after several decades of lagging progress, it showed evidence after the mid-1980s of a growing realization of its national potential. Serious problems remain, but the country has advanced dramatically toward modernization, democratization, and Westernization.[1]

Turkey

Long-form official name, anglicized: Republic of Turkey

Official name, transliterated: Türkiye Cumhuriyeti

Form of government: multiparty republic with one legislative house (Grand National Assembly)

Area: 300,948 miles^2/779,452 km^2

Population, 1999: 64,567,000. Literacy (latest): 82%

Ethnic composition (%): Turk 78, Kurd 18.5, Arab 1.5, other (Laz, Georgian, Circassian, Jewish, Armenian, Greek) 2

Religions (%): Muslim (mostly Sunni) 98.0, other (mostly Christian and Jewish) 2.0

GDP, 1998: $425.4 billion; per capita: $6,600

Petroleum reserves: 299 million barrels

Main exports (% of total value, 1998): textiles 30; agricultural products 16; iron and nonferrous metals 13; food 5; leather and hides 4; machinery 3

Main imports (% of total value, 1998): machinery and transport equipment 26; iron and steel 6; electrical equipment 7.1

Capital city: Ankara 3,250,000; other cities: Istanbul 8,000,000 (Greater Istanbul more than 13,500,000); Izmir 2,600,000; Adana 1,800,000; Bursa 1,350,000; Konya 980,000; Gaziantep 800,000

Physical reminders of Asia Minor's rich history are found not only in Istanbul and other cities but also along the coastlands and in the remote valleys of Turkey. Sites of the numerous successive civilizations in the diverse environments of the peninsula are becoming increasingly accessible and well known.

For clarity in nomenclature, it should be noted that "Turkey" refers to the contemporary state, the Republic of Turkey, which includes the 3 percent of its territory that lies on the southeastern tip of Europe (eastern Thrace). "Asia Minor" refers to the broad peninsula of southwest Asia that lies between the Black Sea and the northeastern Mediterranean and east of the Aegean. "Anatolia" (Turkish, Anadolu), although frequently considered as synonymous with Asia Minor, technically refers to the interior plateau and traditionally excludes the coastlands on three sides of Asia Minor. Both Asia Minor and Anatolia exclude Turkey-in-Europe, with Anatolia implying the antithesis

of Europe. "Ottoman," of course, refers to the empire or aspects of that empire (dynasty, culture, territory) that centered in Constantinople and Asia Minor prior to 1918.

Complex Regional Patterns

A Physical Interlocation

The rugged and often picturesque landscapes of Turkey are the product of particularly complex and powerful earth forces that have shaped Anatolia for millions of years and still manifest themselves in frequent and major earthquakes and related seismic events (see Map 3-3). Like Iran, ancestral Asia Minor lay in the former Tethyan geosyncline and has been literally squeezed between the African and Eurasian tectonic plates (see Chap. 3). It is one segment of the huge belt of Alpine folding during the Tertiary period that extends from the Atlantic to the eastern Himalayas. Anatolia and Iran are the two halves of the Mobile Belt Province (see Map 3-2), and both—Turkey more so than Iran—exhibit exceedingly complex geomorphology that has a strong impact on other patterns.[2]

The massive tectonism that shaped Asia Minor created a virtually continuous belt of folded mountains across northern Anatolia and a similar belt across the south. This pattern is replicated in Iran. In both Turkey and Iran, the diastrophism and volcanism accompanying the plate convergence induced widespread mineralization (see Map 8-5). The compression enclosed resistant blocks in between, and accompanying forces raised and depressed masses in the east and west. In the west, the alternating raised blocks (horsts) and depressed basins (grabens) create the irregular coastline along the Aegean. In the east, the confused mountain mass comprises some of the most rugged topography in the Middle East (see Fig. 3-2), with lofty volcanoes including the well-known Mount Ararat. Other volcanic cones rise high above the central Anatolian plateau in symmetrical grandeur.

At least three blocks in southern Turkey are allochthonous terrains—segments of the earth's crust rafted in from some considerable distance and literally rammed into place in the process of compression between the African and Eurasian plates.[3] Thus, relatively recent folding, faulting, and volcanism have combined with interrelated soils, vegetation, and climates to endow Turkey with a wide variety of landscapes and environments. These, in turn, have been utilized and shaped by successive civilizations to produce modern Turkey.

A Mosaic of Regions

[1] **Pontus and Black Sea Coast.** The northern fold belt comprises principally the Pontic Mountains (or North Anatolian Mountains), which include a variety of sedimentary rocks, some igneous intrusions, and large areas of lava flows (see Map 21-1, on which circled numbers indicate regions). Topographically, the mountains comprise long, narrow chains and lengthy troughlike valleys and basins, with

rivers following the structures for part of their courses toward the Black Sea. Some of the trenches mark the strike of the North Anatolian Transform Fault. Slippage along this very active fault zone caused several devastating earthquakes in the twentieth century between Erzincan in the east and the Marmara area in the west. In addition to those mentioned below, the 7.4 magnitude quake of August 17, 1999, on the Gulf of Izmit, and its aftershocks, followed by another 7.2 quake at Düzce on November 12, combined to be one of Turkey's greatest natural disasters. Nearly 20,000 died, 25,000 were injured, and 600,000 were made homeless in this densely populated area. Several ridges in the west and one toward the east form an almost unbroken wall between the Black Sea and the interior, with ridge elevations of 5,000–6,000 ft./1,525–1,830 m in the west and higher summit elevations in the east, 10,000–13,000 ft./3,050–3,960 m (see Fig. 1-2). The upper and steeper slopes, especially those facing northwest, support Turkey's densest forests, primarily hardwoods in the west and evergreen softwoods in the east.

Features with major historical, economic, strategic, and seismic significance include the down-faulted basins now flooded by the Sea of Marmara and its eastern extensions into the gulfs of Izmit and Gemlik. Comprising almost a separate geographic region, the eastern Marmara area has the greatest concentration of population in the country, including the historic city of Istanbul (formerly Constantinople) and its suburbs. Especially in European Turkey (Thrace), the countryside has orchards and market gardens near the cities, with fields of sunflowers beyond.

North of the Pontic Mountains, a narrow coastal plain extends most of the length of the Black Sea shore, with the Kızıl and Yeşil rivers forming prominent deltas west and east of Samsun. Except where mountain shoulders push against the shore, the plain is densely populated, with the major coal-mining and industrial town of Zonguldak toward the west and one of Turkey's two main tobacco areas toward the east, around Samsun. East of the tobacco

464

MAP 21-1   Turkey, with major cities, main highways, spot heights, main mountain ranges, and geographic regions identified by circled numbers.

belt lies a strip of citrus groves and, east and west of the ancient city of Trabzon, the world's leading area for the production of hazelnuts (filberts). Farthest east, beyond Rize, extensive tea plantations were developed after World War II, and the southeastern Black Sea is Turkey's highest-yielding fishery.

[2] Taurus, Anti-Taurus, and Mediterranean Coast.

Embracing approximately the southern one third of Asia Minor, the Taurus Mountains (Toros Dağları) stretch from the southwestern corner of the peninsula eastward to the upper Seyhan River Basin to the north of Adana. From there, the Anti-Taurus Mountains extend to the region of Lake Van. The complex Anti-Taurus also embrace extensive nappe structures but differ from the Taurus in having deep ocean crust masses (ophiolites, as in the Oman Mountains), South Anatolian Suture structures, faulting along the South Anatolian Transform Fault, and thrust-faulted masses east of the transform fault. Mineralization in these complex structures has enriched the area; around Ergani lies one of the most important mining and metallurgy areas of Turkey. In the area around Elazığ and Malatya, the rugged topography, drained by the Euphrates and Tigris rivers, has become the flourishing focus of Turkey's most ambitious development scheme, GAP (see below). High atop the isolated peak of Nemrud Dağ stands the remarkable burial complex of a Commagene king from the middle of the first century BC (Fig. 21-1). The eastern Anti-Taurus merge with the East Anatolian Accretionary Complex (see 5 below). The upper elevations of the broad mountain belt of the Taurus vary from 7,000–9,000 ft./2,135–2,745 m. Primarily limestone, and including several nappes and fenêtres (see Glossary) like those in the Swiss Alps, the maquis-clad highland separates the Mediterranean coast and the Anatolian interior. The few rivers that cut through the limestone mass follow almost vertically walled canyons, and only three or four major routes connect coast and interior. The most famous of the routes passes northwestward from Adana through the dramatic Cilician Gates (Gülek Boğazı), at 3,444 ft./ 1,050 m.

Along the southern coastal bulge from Alanya to Mersin, mountain shoulders drop steeply into the sea, separating eastern settlements from those to the west around Antalya. Impressive karst features are common—collapsed caverns, sinkholes, and dolines and poljes (larger solution basins)—and several are spectacular tourist attractions. Many of the dolines and poljes are floored with alluvial soils on which wheat, barley, and sometimes grapes and figs are grown. Where a coastal plain exists, or on small deltas formed by rivers slicing through the Taurus, citrus and banana groves, early vegetables, and other tender plants are cultivated.

At the eastern end of the coast is the flat Çukurova (Çukur Plain), on the extensive coalesced deltas of the Seyhan and Ceyhan rivers. The Çukurova, sometimes called "smooth Cilicia," is the best-developed agricultural area in Turkey, with primarily irrigated cotton fields. Cotton gins, cottonseed mills, textile mills, and clothing factories employ part of the dense population of the plain. Adana, the central place, is Turkey's fourth-largest city, and near it is the huge NATO airbase of Incirlik. The Gulf of Iskenderun, rapidly developing as the complex of outlets for petroleum from three directions and for agricultural products from the southeast, lies to the east of the Çukurova. Yumurtalık serves as the outlet for the dual oil pipelines from Iraq, and its area may become the terminal for the vigorously discussed pipeline from the Caspian oil fields. Dörtyol is the terminus for the pipeline from Turkey's Batman oil fields. Iskenderun (formerly Alexandretta) is the main import-export facility for the greatly developed southeast Turkey area, including GAP, and is the site of a major iron and steel mill. West of the Çukurova lies Turkey's largest port, one of the three busiest, at Mersin (recently renamed İçel). Still farther west as far as Manavgat is the "rough Cilicia" coast, and farther to Antalya is the Pamphylian coastal plain. Between Mersin and Antalya, along this Turkish riviera, the ruins of ancient settlements, most from Hellenistic and Roman

FIGURE 21-1   Two of Turkey's many famous archaeological sites: Huge stone heads from a Commagene monument on remote Nemrud Dağ *(top)* date from the second century BC. Hollowed-out volcanic-ash stacks in the Göreme Valley *(bottom)* were used as dwellings and churches by early Christians.

times, attest to an obviously dense, rich, and thriving seaward-facing population in classical times. Castles, theaters, and other vestiges attract archaeologists and tourists to Anamur, Alanya, Side, Aspendos, Perge, Termessos, and, especially, to Antalya, the western core of the coast.[4]

[3] **Aegean Area.** The Aegean area of Turkey resembles much of Greece in topography, climate, soils, and even the numerous ruins of classical cities along the coast. Until the early 1920s, much of the population of the area was Greek. The up-thrust horsts and down-dropped grabens follow the predominant east-west structure of Asia Minor, offering easy access to climatic and cultural influences. Grabens afford deep eastward penetrations of valleys, some drowned by the sea, and horsts form extensions of the land westward as mountainous peninsulas. Rivers such as the Büyük Menderes drain the alluvium-filled grabens and have built deltas westward into the narrow bays. Some deltas advance several meters per year and in doing so, have silted up ancient harbors, leaving ruins of classical port cities such as Ephesus and Miletus several miles inland.

These and the ruins of other Greco-Roman cities combine with modern resorts and the scenery to give Turkey some of its most outstanding tourist attractions.[5] Major classical sites include Pergamum (modern Bergama, Fig. 2-4), Izmir (formerly Smyrna), Sardis, Colophon, Ephesus, Priene, Miletus, Didyma, and Halicarnassus (modern Bodrum). The central place of the Aegean region is Izmir, Turkey's third-largest city, site of NATO's largest naval base in the eastern Mediterranean and of the annual Izmir International Trade Fair. Among the newly built coastal resorts, Kuşadası is one of the best developed. The alluvial-filled grabens are prime agricultural areas, planted in olive groves next to the coast, then fruit and nut trees (citrus toward the south and almonds toward the north), and tobacco and cotton. Aegean tobacco complements Black Sea tobacco and helps supply one of Turkey's traditional exports. The broad grabens have long provided access between the Aegean and the productive interior.

[4] **Interior Anatolia.** Immured between the Pontic wall on the north and the Taurus barrier on the south is the inner Anatolian Plateau, technically the true Anatolia. Its surface, except in the heart of the region surrounding Tuz Gölü, displays a greater variety of relief than might be suggested by the term *plateau*.

Western Anatolia, which is hilly to mountainous, exhibits evidence of continuing tectonism, with numerous earthquakes, lava flows, and hot springs. The thermal springs indicate molten rock intrusions close to the surface. Hot springs near Denizli served as a spa for classical Hieropolis, and its calcium-carbonate travertine terraces at Pamukkale attract scientists and tourists. Still more volcanism can be seen in the city of Afyon, which has developed around a prominent mountain that peaks in a volcanic plug. Wheat and corn grow over large areas, and uncommon specialty crops are produced in selected localities—for example, opium poppies around Afyon (Turkish *afyon* = "opium"), tobacco in several areas, and roses near Isparta, north of Antalya. From roses is derived an essential oil for rose water, used both as an essence in desserts and for fragrant hand washing on special occasions throughout the Middle East.

This transitional area between the Aegean and central Anatolia was the major battleground for the Greek-Turkish fighting in the early 1920s. The same area, then underpopulated, later received many of the Turkish immigrants from the Balkans in the population exchange with Greece and Bulgaria in the 1920s. Industry has developed steadily in the area, bringing factories to Isparta, Kütahya, Eskişehir, Afyon, and elsewhere. A scenic lake district between Isparta and Konya includes twelve larger lakes that occupy grabens and solution basins and serve as local sumps. Most of the lakes have no outlet and are saline.

Farther east, in the central and eastern parts of the interior plateau, lies the quintessential Anatolia with its vast flat to rolling treeless steppes devoted to the region's characteristic wheat fields. Climatic stress typical of steppe conditions brings rain-deficient years that reduce the grain yield sharply, as in 1928, when the harvest was less than one-tenth the average yield. This semiarid core, with less than 12 in./ 300 mm of rainfall, produces primarily wheat and barley, whereas the more humid peripheral areas grow fruits, cotton, sugar beets, grapes, and tobacco.[6]

Formerly poorly developed, central Anatolia benefited economically from the focus of national attention on the area after the breakup of the Ottoman Empire following World War I. A particular stimulus was the shift of the political capital from Istanbul to Ankara in the 1920s, when Ankara was little more than an unprepossessing Anatolian village in a hilly volcanic area; however, it enjoyed a central, interior, protected location and was a major route junction. Now the second largest city in Turkey, Ankara is the central place for the Anatolian Plateau; it has spread upwards on its original basin slopes and onto the surrounding plateau (Fig. 21-2). Economic growth brought the subsequent development of such infrastructure as dams and paved highways in the region. Hirfanlı Dam was constructed on the Kızılırmak northeast of the Tuz Gölü in the mid-1950s. Scholars and tourists frequent Hattusa, the ancient Hittite capital east of Ankara; Göreme, with unique early Christian churches and homes hollowed out of volcanic ash pinnacles west of Kayseri (Fig. 21-1); remarkable underground cities, excavated in the soft volcanic tuff and used by early Christians for refuge, at Derinkuyu and Kaymaklı; Konya, the Seljuk capital; and other sites. Tuz Gölü is a shallow salt lake at the bottom of the enclosed central Anatolian sump. With a surface slightly below 3,000 ft./900 m, the lake varies greatly in area, depending on local precipitation and runoff.

[5] **Eastern Anatolia.** The rugged eastern Anatolian mountains comprise the eastern end of the Anti-Taurus and also the complex folding and volcanism resulting from the junction of three tectonic units (see Map 3-2 and Fig. 3-5). Several extensive Tertiary lava flows and volcanic cones testify to vigorous volcanicity attending the interplate compression, with Mount Ararat towering to 16,948 ft./5,166 m. Several peaks reach 8,000–10,000 ft./2,440– 3,050 m. Lake Van, the largest of Turkey's lakes, has a surface elevation of 5,400 ft./1,646 m and so completely blocks transit routes that the railway to Iran must cross the lake on a ferry from Tatvan to Van. The massive and frequent earthquakes in the area are the result of slippage along two fault systems that intersect west of Lake Van. Erzincan, located near the intersection of the North and East Anatolian faults, has suffered three earthquake disasters in the last 50 years—45,000 people died in the 1939 quake, 1,330 in the one in 1983, and 1,000 in the one in March 1992.

These rugged highlands have afforded refuge for several peoples, especially the Armenians (after whom the mountainous area of Armenia was named) and, south of the Armenian area, the Kurds. Covered with heavy snowfalls during the long winters, these mountains serve as a major hydrographic center, and their melting snows and some spring rains supply the headwaters of several rivers: both the Tigris and Euphrates, flowing southward to the Gulf; the Aras, flowing eastward to the Caspian; and several small streams that empty into the Black Sea or into the enclosed Lake Van basin.

Numerous villages lie among the valleys and on the steep slopes, but towns are widely separated; Erzurum is the major central place. To the northeast, Kars and Ardahan anchor territory long contested between Turks and Russians.

[6] **The Southeast: The Arabian Platform.** Lying south of the Anti-Taurus and the Arabian Fold Belt is the Arabian Foreland, which extends far south into Syria. The broad plateau surface exhibits gentle relief and elevations between 1,640 ft./500 m and 2,625 ft./800 m. The main center is Urfa—awarded the honorific title "Şanlıurfa" in 1983 and now one of the fastest-growing cities in Turkey—once the capital of the Crusader kingdom of Edessa. Gaziantep, sixth-largest city in the republic, serves as a center west of the Euphrates, and Mardin serves the area toward the east. Toward the northern edge of the platform, on the upper Tigris, is the ancient basalt-walled Kurdish city of Diyarbakır. Traditionally a wheat

FIGURE 21-2   View of Ankara, capital of Turkey, from the Hisar (ancient citadel), on a volcanic remnant in the center of the city. The view looks northeast along Etlik Caddesi to the northeastern suburbs of Ankara.

and barley area, the region had achieved only limited development until recent major irrigation projects brought Euphrates water to farmlands in the western section. The region is experiencing an economic boom and a transformation of the landscape in response to development of the Southeast Anatolia Project. About 600,000 Arabs inhabit the area, along with Kurds who have moved from mountain villages in the north to the southeastern cities. As in the general area of southeastern Turkey, the Kurdish insurrection has destabilized the Arabian Foreland region for 15 years.

A Historical Tapestry

Like Egypt and Iran, Asia Minor reflects a long history of cultures and empires (see Chap. 2), and recent intensified field research has pushed back both the beginnings and the scope of early

Anatolian cultures. The increasingly rich physical evidences of this history may be seen in the thousands of tells (*hüyüks* or *tepes*), tumuli, towers, tombs, and ruins. World-famous national museums in Istanbul and Ankara contain superb collections of prehistoric implements and later pottery, statuary, cuneiform tablets, jewelry, and other artifacts.

Caves near Antalya show evidence of Upper Paleolithic occupation. Hacılar, the earliest agricultural settlement in Asia Minor, has been dated to 7040 BC, and Çatal Hüyük with its remarkable artworks flourished 6500–5650 BC (see Map 2-1). The fabled city of Troy, guarding the entrance to the Dardanelles, has early layers predating 2500 BC, although the legendary Trojan War was associated with events of about 1200 BC. The Hittites evolved in central Anatolia and maintained a great capital at Hattusa. A score of other peoples waxed and waned in the fastnesses of Anatolia and along the rugged coastlines. Lydians in the west had Sardis as their capital and Croesus (fl. 550 BC) as their most famous king. Aeolian, Ionian, and Dorian Greeks ensconced themselves along the Aegean coast. Among the many peoples in the interior were the Galatians (Gauls), of European descent, to whom the apostle Paul wrote epistles later included in the New Testament. Indeed, Asia Minor nurtured first-century Christianity, harboring the "Seven Churches of Asia"—Pergamum, Smyrna, Ephesus, Sardis, Laodicea, Philadelphia, and Thyatira—and emerging as the area in which Christianity was then strongest.

A watershed geopolitical event occurred in AD 330, when Emperor Constantine transferred the Roman capital from Rome to Byzantium, which was renamed Constantinople and later Istanbul. Constantinople served as the capital of the eastern Roman, Byzantine, and Ottoman empires for nearly 1,600 years. With the steady decline of the once-mighty and once-extensive Byzantine Empire, Arab Muslims from one direction and Seljuk Turkish Muslims from another carved away at Byzantine territories. Crusader efforts to help protect the Christian Byzantines delayed but hardly prevented Turkish inroads. The Seljuks established the central Anatolian Sultanate of Rum (*Rum* = Rome— i.e., Europe), which was soon joined by other Turkish and Turkmen principalities that rose and fell for two centuries. Finally, the Ottoman Turk principality achieved dominance and, after encounters with a second wave of invading Mongols, established control of Asia Minor and extensive areas beyond (see Chap. 2).[7] The Ottomans seized Constantinople in 1453 and made it their capital until the end of the Ottoman Empire after World War I.

Contemporary republican Turkey arose on the ruins of the Ottoman Empire, the "sick man of Europe," defeated in World War I.[8] Led by the charismatic Mustafa Kemal, later surnamed Atatürk ("Father Turk"), the young republic asserted a new Turkish viability in the early 1920s. It resisted partition of the Turkish Anatolian homeland and achieved substitution of the Treaty of Lausanne in 1923 for the onerous

Treaty of Sèvres (1920). The aggressive Kemalist program for national resurgence called for republicanism, nationalism, populism, reformism, secularism, statism (state capitalism), and economic development. Atatürk insisted on Turkishness, the modernization of Turkey, and economic and cultural Europeanization. One fundamental and symbolic change, for example, was the abandonment of the Arabic alphabet for writing Turkish and the adoption of a modified Roman alphabet (1928). Also replaced were several items of traditional Turkish clothing, notably the fez (or tarbush) worn by Turkish men. Most men then adopted the visored cap, common in America and Europe during the 1920s, a headgear that still gives Turkish workingmen a characteristic appearance. The veil formerly worn by women was forbidden, a proscription that angered conservative families, especially in inner Anatolia, and that has rekindled debate in the 1990s. The magnetic Atatürk served successive terms as president until his death in 1938. By this time, progressive Kemalism had been institutionalized into a quasi-religion countering some conservative aspects of Islam; it continued to provide the ideological base for Turkey for decades and is still the basic rationale for the more liberal Turkish policies. The relevance of Kemalism a half-century later, however, was vigorously debated in the Turkey of the 1990s.

Turkey was neutral until the final days of World War II, when it declared war on Germany and became a charter member of the United Nations. Soviet assertiveness immediately upon the end of the war prompted a mutuality of policies between Turkey and the United States. Under the 1947 Truman Doctrine, U.S. military and economic aid was extended to Greece and Turkey, and Turkey joined NATO in 1952. Most Turkish concerns for the next 40 years revolved around Soviet intentions. Lacking an Atatürk-like authority figure, governments repeatedly failed to manage the faltering economy and the domestic conflict—often violent—between left and right. The Kemalist-minded military establishment staged coups in 1960, "by memorandum" in 1971, and in 1980; each temporarily stabilized a disintegrating situation. Thus, for decades Turkey's democratic tradition was regularly marred by episodes of instability and authoritarian rule. After 1984, the insurrection by the Kurdish Workers Party (PKK) in the southeast, the poorest and most neglected part of the country, became the dominant quagmire for every administration.[9] Capture of the PKK leader, Abdullah Öcalan, in February 1999, and his death sentence in June provoked Kurds into violent demonstrations, but Öcalan's request to his followers for cooperation with the state suppressed the domestic rebellion. EU pressures and an appeal to the European Court of Human Rights delayed a final decision as of early 2000. Turkey and the Cyprus problem, as well as Turkey and EU developments, are discussed under Relations. During the 1980s and 1990s, Turkey forged ahead economically and was in an enviable economic position at century's end.

The Turkish Population

Turkey has the largest population among all Middle East states (see Table 6-1 and Graph 6-1), and Turks are, after Arabs, the second-largest ethnolinguistic group in the entire region (see Table 6-3). Because of the percentage annual growth rate, the population has more than doubled since 1960. Population growth exceeded employment growth, and thousands of excess workers took temporary jobs in labor-short Western Europe during the 1960s. This migration of labor later ceased, but in the late 1990s Germany alone hosted 2 million Turks, about one-quarter of them Kurds.

Among the larger of the states of the Middle East, Turkey has the geographically most nearly evenly distributed population. Lacking desert areas, Turkey shows reduced densities only in the more rugged mountains and on the central steppe. As Map 6-2 shows, the highest densities are in the Istanbul area and its surroundings, along the Black Sea coast, along and inland from the Aegean coast,

around Ankara, and on the highly developed Çukurova around Adana.

A multiethnic empire in Ottoman times, Turkey sought greater ethnic homogeneity in the new republic. Under the Ottoman *millet* system, which permitted ethnic groups maximal autonomy, some groups developed separatist sentiments that evolved into anti-Turkish nationalism. Supported by European powers, various groups did gain independence. The republic renounced the multinational state and, downplaying ethnic differences, proclaimed "Turkey for the Turks and the Turks for Turkey."

Ethnic Turks are basically descendants of central Asiatic nomadic Turkish tribes who intermarried with more than a score of identifiable groups during the centuries. In the Ottoman golden age, the designation "Turk" was a term of disdain for Anatolian peasants as opposed to the cosmopolitan "Ottomans" of Constantinople. However, republican leaders acclaim Turkishness with national pride and have systematically "purified" the Turkish language of many of its Arabic and Persian loanwords.

Census reports minimize ethnolinguistic differences, grouping most citizens as Turks. As a result, the size of the several known minority groups can only be estimated. As a transit land with rugged mountains sheltering valleys and basins, Asia Minor inevitably gave refuge to passing peoples. The obviously large Kurdish population is believed to be as much as 20 percent, and the Arab minority may be between 1.5 and 2 percent. Smaller minorities include Circassians, Abkhaz (related to Circassians), Georgians, Laze, Armenians, Greeks, and Jews (including Dönme—see below). Turkmen and Tatars, like the Yoruk, are grouped with Turks.

More than 10 million Kurds, about 16 percent of the population and sometimes referred to as "mountain Turks," are firmly entrenched in the southeastern Turkey extension of their mountain homeland. Kurds, Armenians, Turks, and Russians were involved in fighting in eastern Anatolia in 1915, with Kurds and Armenians each fighting for independence from both Turks and Russians and Kurds and Armenians sometimes fighting each other. Once Turkey had achieved a certain stability in the mid-1920s, it specifically rejected Kurdish identity and ensured that Kurds made no progress toward separatism, as it had earlier done with Armenians. Southeastern Turkey was kept under martial law for many years, and use of the Kurdish language in schools, publications, broadcasting, and courts was made illegal—although some use of Kurdish was permitted after 1991. As Kurds in Iraq were increasingly suppressed under Saddam Husayn, the Marxist Kurdish Workers Party (PKK) in Turkey initiated open rebellion in southeastern Anatolia in 1984. By the time of the trial of the PKK leader, mentioned above, nearly 30,000 rebels, Turkish military, police, and civilians had died in the 15-year-long insurgency. The war against Kurdish separatism has been one of Turkey's two costliest recent ventures—GAP, also in the southeast, being the other. Turkey's human rights record, especially with the Kurds, has evoked wide international censure and delayed the invitation from the EU for Turkey to apply for membership.[10]

Also noteworthy in the southeast are the Shii Alevi, (many of whom disguise their religion) a sect akin to the Alawis, the heretical Shii sect in northwestern Syria (see Chap. 12). Blurred differentiations caused Alevi to be considered as including all Shii, although in actuality the Alevi are only one—the largest—of four Shii sects in Turkey. Numbering several million, Alevi constitute between 10 and 25 percent of the population and include Arabs, Kurds, and Turks. Originally concentrated in the southeastern area, some Alevi have migrated to urban areas in western Turkey.

Relatively small minorities of peoples from the Caucasus include Circassians and the related Abkhaz, with many of the Circassians living in the Adana area; Georgians, a group that actually embraces several different minorities; and the Laze, a small group of primarily fishermen in the southeastern Black Sea area (see Table 6-3).

Greeks and Armenians are the major Christian groups in Turkey. Both are heavily concentrated, primarily in the business sector, in the Istanbul area, and both are fractional remnants of much larger pre-World War I groups (see Chap. 6). Armenians were formerly dominant in the eastern Anatolian area, generally known as Armenia, but now are a small minority of about 40,000 found only in the northwest. Details of the Armenian problem are given in Chapter 6.[11]

Of an estimated 90,000 Jews in Turkey at the end of World War II, fewer than 20,000 are believed to remain. About 30,000 emigrated to Israel in the late 1940s, and several thousand more have left Turkey since then—some of them also going to Israel. Most remaining Jews are in business in Istanbul or Izmir. Nonhomogeneous, they include Sephardim, who speak Ladino; Ashkenazim, who speak Yiddish; and some Karaites, viewed by other Jews as heretics, who speak Greek. All speak Turkish (and often French) as a second or equal language. Dönme are Jews who converted to Islam but are now merging with the general population and are considered neither Jews nor Muslims by most of their compatriots.

Village and City

Although Turkey is becoming more urbanized, it is still very much village oriented, with more than 40,000 villages well distributed over the country. The widespread pattern of humid climates and rainfed agriculture enables Turkish villages to be located on upper slopes and hilltops, thus presenting landscapes more typical of the humid Levant or Europe. Widely differing house construction and materials appear in different environments: wooden houses in forested areas, masonry houses on barren limestone slopes, and often houses of mud brick or with mud walls in river bottoms.

Mosque, public bathhouse, small fruit and vegetable market, and the village teahouse (*halkevi*—literally, "people's house") form the village center. The *halkevi* continues to be ubiquitous in city and village, where the clientele is virtually all male, and village attitudes remain conservative regarding the role of women.

Except where they have become urban enclaves of expanding cities, villages also remain politically conservative, religious, and stable. An important element in village life is the weekly market, conducted in centrally located larger villages.

The rapid growth of the rural population in the 1950s and 1960s drove hundreds of thousands of landless villagers to larger cities. Whereas the rural component of the total population was nearly 80 percent in the early 1950s, it had dropped to 40 percent by the late 1990s. Migrants to Istanbul, Ankara, Izmir, and other larger cities found shelter in the rapidly spreading *gecekondus* ("built overnight"), the squatter settlements that were made possible by a Turkish law that prohibits the forced removal of habitations having completed roofs (see Chap. 10). The Muslim tradition of urban "quarters" for respective groups carried over to the *gecekondus,* which are clustered according to ethnic and sectarian affiliations.[12]

Turkey's cities exhibit great variety, especially those that were former capitals of kingdoms or principalities. Istanbul, as an imperial capital built on the peninsula overlooking the Bosporus, Sea of Marmara, and Golden Horn, has a unique architectural skyline because of its numerous magnificent domes and minarets. Bursa, the Ottoman capital before Istanbul, preserves some of its medieval monuments and, as a major silk-producing center, is Turkey's fifth-largest city. The old Seljuk capital of Konya, its ruins mixed with modern buildings rising from the plain in interior Anatolia, preserves a concentration of structures in the old Seljuk style. By contrast, Turkey's current capital city of Ankara has a core of primarily contemporary government buildings.[13]

Economic Development

Statism and After

Having lagged in its national economy during the declining years of the Ottoman Empire, Turkey made slow progress toward a modern economy after World War I. To counterbalance the shortage of private capital and to protect against the dominance of foreign capital, Atatürk adopted statism (state capitalism) as the country's basic economic philosophy. This emphasis on government participation in industry had certain advantages for planning purposes, but it also constrained development because of its bureaucratic approach carried over from the Ottomans. Nevertheless, persistence finally brought the country to a level of appreciable development through a series of five-year plans under the State Planning Organization, created in 1961. Reforms during the 1980s under the progressive economist Turgut Özal, prime minister then president, finally generated the acceleration needed for Turkish economic development.[14] Gradually, the government abandoned the insulated, state-directed economic policies of Atatürk, reformed the state economic enterprises (SEEs), and adopted a vigorous program of privatization. By 2000, Turkey enjoyed enviable economic prosperity: It had averaged an annual 5 percent growth in GNP for fifteen years; had the world's eighteenth largest economy; was the OECD's fastest growing economy, the largest economy in the Middle East and one of the world's top 20 tourist destinations; and was a U.S.-designated "big emerging market." It was a member of the World Trade Organization (WTO), and, after 1996, a partner in the EU customs union. Energy, telecommunications, transportation, and textile sectors were especially vigorous; and the share of manufacturing and services in the labor force had risen steadily.

On the downside of the national economy in the late 1990s, the continuing runaway inflation—99 percent in 1997, 70 percent in 1998—resulted primarily from public sector deficits. (To illustrate the problem: The Turkish lira dropped from 7 to $1 in 1957 to 2,618 in mid-1990, to 9,262 in early 1993, to 172,593 in September 1997, and to 624,000 to $1 in mid-2000.) These deficits manifest the urgency for accelerated privatization; indeed, the dynamic private sector is driving the vigorous economic development. In a 1998 accord with the IMF, Turkey is obligated to speed up the selling of its

SEEs to reduce subsidies and price supports, to raise the retirement age (which averages age 43 in the three separate social security systems), and to cut the budget deficit. Also, despite the general adequacy of its infrastructure, Turkey needs to upgrade its ports, some of its airports, and its railways.[15] Statistically, its infrastructural achievements are impressive: Turkey leads the Middle East in length of roads, length of paved roads, length of rail lines (one-third of the total for the Middle East), and number of ports, as well as number of automotive vehicles. Turkey also leads in most aspects of agriculture, forestry, and fishing. Thus, with the exception of its deficiency in petroleum resources, Turkey has the most nearly balanced economy in the Middle East (Map 21-2).

Turkey is also credited with the highest potential for hydroelectric power among all European countries except Norway and Sweden. Lacking significant petroleum resources, Turkey turned to its hydropower potential to help solve its energy shortage.[16] Dams had already been constructed before 1970 in widely separated river basins—the Kızılırmak, Yeşil, upper Gediz, Sakarya, Seyhan—and smaller dams elsewhere. However, it was the ambitious program of construction of the giant Euphrates dams after 1965 that established Turkey's major rank in hydropower and large-scale irrigation. The keystone of the huge program is the Southeast Anatolia Project (Turkish, Güneydoğu Anadolu Projesi—GAP).

Embracing thirteen interrelated subprojects distributed over 28,185 miles^2/73,000 km^2, GAP is one of the largest projects of its kind ever attempted and is the largest in Turkey. Included in the 13 subprojects—7 on the Euphrates and 6 on the Tigris—are to be 22 dams and 19 hydroelectric installations, as well as irrigation of 4.2 million acres/1.7 million ha of land—equivalent to about half of the total irrigated area of Egypt. The Euphrates is already dammed by three giant barrages, Keban (technically not included in GAP), Karakaya, and Atatürk (shown on Map 21-2). GAP's grand scale exploits the steep gradients of the rivers descending from the well-watered east

Anatolian mountains and the several deep canyons they have cut along their courses—especially the Euphrates. The Euphrates profile permits the construction of the series of three high dams that form successive reservoirs in a stairstep configuration, with a difference in elevation of 495 ft./151 m from one reservoir to the next.

The first dam upstream is the Keban precursor to GAP, completed in 1974 for power purposes only, 670 ft./204 m high. Located 103 miles/166 km downstream from Keban is the Karakaya Dam, completed in 1987—as with Keban, for power generation only. Another 112 miles/180 km downstream is the showpiece of Turkish development and of GAP, the Atatürk Dam and its 2,400-MW power station (see Fig. 21-3). In back of the dam is a ramifying reservoir 315 miles^2/817 km^2 in area, largest in GAP and in Turkey. This dam, near the southern margin of the Anti-Taurus, is to supply water through canals, tunnels, and pipelines to irrigate about 1.8 million acres/730,000 ha of high-quality land in ten plains areas in the Arabian Foreland just north of the Syrian border. Turkey's interference in the Euphrates flow and its consumption of the river's water on a major scale have raised deep concern in both downstream riparian states Syria and Iraq (see Chap. 11).

Six other subprojects involve the Tigris between Diyarbakır and the Syrian border. All are on a smaller scale than those in the Euphrates Basin, but they will nevertheless affect the Tigris flow and have raised concern in Iraq. When completed, GAP will have an installed capacity of more than 7,500 megawatts and is to generate 27 billion kilowatt hours of electricity annually, slightly less than one-third of the national total; however, Turkey needs to double its capacity to maintain its pace of development.

Agricultural Development

Varied climate and productive soil have sustained agriculture in Anatolia for more than 3,000 years. Farming, which had made little technical progress in centuries, was encouraged

MAP 21-2   Economic map of Turkey, showing railways, ports, airports, numerous solid-mineral mining areas, pipelines, and other economic features. Note Atatürk Dam (Figure 21-3) on Euphrates River west of Urfa.

FIGURE 21-3   Atatürk Dam on the Euphrates River. Each of the eight giant penstocks of the power station *(center)* is 24 ft./7.25 m in diameter. This dam, completed in the early 1990s, is the centerpiece in Turkey's GAP. (Photograph from Turkish Government State Hydraulic Works [DSİ])

to modernize and diversify after World War II; Turkish agriculture is now an organized and productive sector. The most fruitful historically have been the Aegean and Marmara areas, but the irrigated Çukurova now vies with them. As more and more of the Arabian Foreland plains are irrigated in the GAP scheme, they too will become prime areas. In the late 1990s, 123,550 acres/ 50,000 ha were devoted to irrigated crops, mostly cotton, in the Harran Plain (south of Urfa) alone. Overall, irrigated area has increased from 2.72 million acres/1.1 million ha in 1962 to 5.5 million acres/2.22 million ha in 1989 and to 10.3 million acres/4.2 million ha in 1999.

Agricultural landholdings in the 4.5 million farms are generally small and fragmented, although central Anatolian wheat farms are medium-sized. Maintaining inherited land is traditional, and about 45 percent of the Turkish workforce is in agricultural production—more than in any other Middle East country with the exception of Yemen. Increasingly mechanized farming, the high rural birth rate, and the attraction of urban economy induces a rural-to-urban and east-to-west migration.

Animal husbandry has always been an essential part of Anatolian agriculture, both as animal raising on farms and as herding of sheep, goats, and camels by nomadic pastoralists (see Fig. 7-6). As in crop cultivation, breeds of animals, breeding practices, feeds, meat processing, and marketing are all being improved. Cattle have received particular attention, and dairying is a major aspect of agriculture in the high pastures of the northern Anatolian mountains. Grazing is by far the dominant type of agriculture practiced in the mountainous eastern fourth of the country. As elsewhere in the Middle East, poultry raising has expanded markedly; and Turkey continues to be second, after the United States, in world production of mohair, sheared from the famous Angora goat.

In its great variety of environments, Turkey produces a remarkable range of crops: bananas, dates, grapes, citrus fruits, and cotton along the southern coast; olives, cotton, tobacco, citrus, grapes, soft fruits, and figs in the west; tobacco, tea, rice, and hazelnuts along the Black Sea in the northeast; and, above all, wheat and barley in central Anatolia. Potatoes, sugar beets, pulses, melons, onions, and other crops are widely distributed. Sunflowers, grown for their oilseeds, flourish in extensive fields in the open landscapes of Thrace (European Turkey). An unusual aspect of Turkish agriculture is the regulated growing of opium poppies in the west-central basins. Maize has proved to be well adapted to the more humid areas of Anatolia (see Fig. 1-2) and is increasingly produced for both food and feed. Turkey leads the Middle East in the production of a score of crops and for many of them produces from 40 to 70 percent of the total for the entire region (see Tables 7-2, 7-3, and 7-4).

Forestry and Fishing

Turkey and Iran are the only two countries in the Middle East with well-developed forest industries. Of the two, Turkey possesses more extensive forests (45 million acres/18 million ha of all types) and has developed its production to an output level of almost two-thirds of the total roundwood output of the Middle East. Forests cover the steeper slopes of the mountains rimming the central Anatolian plateau and basins, with particularly dense forests in the higher Pontic Mountains in northern Anatolia.

As the leading fishing country in the Middle East, Turkey increased its annual catch by 11 times from 1975 to 1989 to 627.9 mt of fish and similar aquatic animals of several kinds, about 40 percent of the Middle East fish total. An estimated $55 million worth of fish is exported annually, mostly to Western Europe, including such specialty items as shrimp, lobsters, snails, eels, sponges, tortoises, and frog legs. Half of the Turkish fish catch is taken in eastern Black Sea waters, but virtually every town and village along all three coasts engages in fishing.

Industrial Development

An Overview. As we have seen, Turkey's range of industrial establishments and their total non-oil output already lead those of all other countries in the region and are growing under the liberalized policies developed in the period 1983–1989 under Prime Minister Turgut Özal, who continued economic liberalization after he became president in late 1989. The variety and quantity of agricultural products support the food-processing and agrobusiness sector, and the country's minerals industry—the most varied and highly developed in the Middle East—further contributes to the diversification of manufacturing. As it has from the early years of industrial expansion, the deficiency of energy sources, particularly petroleum and natural gas, has challenged the manufacturing sector to seek adequate sources of energy. However, Turkey's manufacturing sector steadily increases its contribution to the GNP, reaching 30 percent of the GNP in 1999.

As was mentioned earlier, the government has set aside the Kemalist policy of statism in favor of vigorous privatization of SEEs. To reduce spiraling public sector deficits further, the government encouraged foreign firms to submit proposals on the "build, operate, and transfer" (BOT) model, which in effect transfers much of the risk to project sponsors. Therefore, the share of private ownership of industries is increasing and is expected to mount under the recent liberalization of government policy.

As with agricultural production, mining operations, and population, which are unusually uniformly spread over the state territory, industrial concentrations are likewise well distributed over Turkey (see Map 21-2). The largest industrial complexes, especially those producing consumer goods, are in the main population centers. As a consequence, the half-dozen largest cities are also the leading industrial centers: Istanbul (which has more than half of the country's industries), Ankara, Izmir, Adana, Bursa, and Gaziantep. However, towns in specialty crop areas usually have industries to process foods, beverages, and industrial crops. Examples include Rize, tea packing; Trabzon, hazelnut shelling and packing; Tekirdağ, wine making; Afyon, opium processing; Bursa, silk articles; Isparta, rug making using local wool; and Adana, cotton milling and cotton textile manufacturing.

Minerals Industries. The tectonic and structural conditions in the Mobile Belt, extending across the Anatolian and Iranian plateaus, give rise to several zones of extensive mineralization. Unfortunately, Turkey possesses a relatively large number of small deposits and few large ones. Reserves for most metallic commodities are not large by world standards, although those for bauxite (aluminum ore), chromite, copper, iron ore, gold, and silver are appreciable. The most significant reserves are of such industrial minerals as boron, barite, magnesite, perlite, pumice, and dimension stone. Turkey ranks first in world production of boron and magnesite, second in chromite and pumice, and seventh in barite. The public-sector Etibank had long controlled mineral resources and mining, but during the 1990s it steadily sold off its holdings; private operations have now appreciably increased the profitability of mining. Mineral utilization has a long tradition in Anatolia: Ironworking—which is believed to have originated among the Hittites—was a profitable activity of the Hittite Empire 3,700 years ago, the wealth of Croesus came from gold taken from the rivers of the Aegean region, and obsidian (volcanic glass) from the volcanic area of central Anatolia was traded in the Fertile Crescent during the Neolithic period.[17]

Hydrocarbons. Turkey's mineral fuels include coal, lignite, and small amounts of petroleum.[18] Although Turkish coal and lignite production is more than 96 percent of the total for the Middle East, the country's petroleum output is only two-thirds that of tiny Bahrain

(see Table 8-1). Bituminous coal reserves, 1 billion mt, and lignite reserves, 7.5 billion mt, are sufficient for more than 200 years at the present rate of production. By contrast, known petroleum reserves of 300 million barrels indicate less than a 12-year supply, even at the low rate of production. Recent natural gas discoveries, primarily in Thrace, improve the energy outlook modestly. Turkey must import more than 90 percent of its petroleum needs and 50 percent of its total energy requirements. As one of the benefits of allotting right-of-way for Iraqi pipelines to Yumurtalık in 1977 and 1987, Turkey shared oil from the lines (see Chaps. 8 and 16) until it was obliged to shut them down in August 1990. After importing crude from several neighbors for seven years, Turkey was again allowed to share oil from the Iraqi lines in 1997, when the UN allowed Iraq to export specified amounts of crude under the UN Resolution "oil-for-food" program. In addition, more than 50,000 bpd of Iraqi oil was being smuggled by tanker trucks into Turkey in early 2000. As was examined in the "Pipelines" section of Chapter 8, Turkey has been deeply involved in the controversial discussions over the routing (and financing) of the critical main export pipeline (MEP) from the Caspian oil fields to a marine export terminal. When agreements were signed in Istanbul in November 1999, Turkey, having been strongly supported by the United States and Israel, appeared to be favored over Russia and Iran. The plan calls for the MEP to cross eastern Anatolia to a terminal in the Ceyhan area, near the Yumurtalık outlet of the Iraqi pipelines. Inter alia, Turkey opposes an eastern Black Sea terminus for the MEP, since tankers loading there create a major environmental hazard when they must then transit the Bosporus, passing Istanbul, to reach western markets.[19]

In lobbying for the MEP, Turkey has also vigorously sought a major gas pipeline from the Caspian area. A Caspian source is just one of several options Turkey is pursuing in its major shift to primarily natural gas for power generation and space heating. Smog resulting from the former widespread use of low-grade coal convinced

Turkey to utilize its considerable hydropower and imported gas to generate environmentally clean energy. Although Turkey has been importing gas by pipeline from Russia through Bulgaria since 1986, it has discussed tentative plans for greatly increased imports with Egypt and Iran, as well as with Caspian producers.

Although 45–50 million mt of lignite is mined in most years in several areas, especially in east-central Anatolia, coal is mined almost entirely in the Zonguldak area on the western Black Sea coast (7 million mt of anthracite in an average year). Because the coal veins are thin and contorted, extraction is increasingly difficult and costly, and coal is now imported for industrial use in the western and southern parts of the country.

Petroleum. The first encouraging oil strikes in Turkey, in the Batman area between Diyarbakır and Siirt in southeastern Anatolia, were not made until 1940. Shell and Mobil have been the most successful of the several cooperating companies, but the public-sector petroleum company, TPAO, produces about half of the crude oil. Despite widespread exploration, discoveries have been virtually limited to the Fold Belt, where fields are small, scattered, and often deep and are found in complex geological structures. Production during the 1990s averaged 65,000–72,000 bpd, but jumped to 86,700 bpd in 1991 after the pipeline from Iraq was temporarily shut in. Output from the Batman-area fields moves by pipeline to Dörtyol on the Gulf of Iskenderun.

Oil Processing. Of Turkey's five refineries (see Map 21-2 and Table 8-2), the two largest—supplied by imports by sea—are located at Izmit and Izmir, the former damaged in the August 1999 earthquake. The Kırıkkale refinery, opened in 1986, is fed by Iraqi crude brought by a dedicated pipeline from Yumurtalık. Petrochemical production is limited, since feedstock would have to be imported.

Metallurgy. Many of Turkey's mineral processing plants and manufacturing establishments that use mineral raw materials are mine oriented, so that mining areas and mineral industry concentrations are locationally related (see Map 21-2). Steel mills are located in three widely separated areas: around Zonguldak, with large plants at Karabük and Ereğli; Iskenderun; and around the eastern part of the Sea of Marmara, where three small plants utilize primarily scrap metal. A small plant in Izmir also uses scrap steel. Aluminum ore (bauxite) is mined and processed in a large new complex at Seydişehir, southwest of Konya.

More important on the world scale is Turkish production of several ferroalloys, none of which is plentiful on the world market. They include chromite (6 percent of the world total, from Kütahya, Ergani, and Muğla), antimony (northwest of Sivas), manganese (Thrace, Eskişehir, Ereğli, and Denizli), and tungsten (near Bursa). Also significant is the production of such nonferrous metals as copper, from several sources but especially from the major metallurgical centers of Ergani and Murgul, as well as lead and zinc from several mines, especially those around Kayseri and Elazığ. Turkey produces significant percentages of the world's emery (50 percent), boron (35), magnesite (4), perlite (2), and barite. Near Eskişehir is the world's only commercial deposit of meerschaum, which is machined and carved in cottage industries and small plants in and around the city. It is used primarily for making smoking-tobacco pipes.

Other Industries. In addition to the crop-related and mineral industries, Turkey has developed a wide range of other plants and factories. Indeed, the range of manufactures may well be the widest in the Middle East. With a large domestic market, Turkey supplies consumer goods from automobiles through household appliances to electronic items. For its many farms it makes tractors (Turkey has more tractors than all other Middle East countries combined), combines, milking machines, and fertilizers. For its large military forces it manufactures weapons and ammunition, tanks, military vehicles, aircraft, and naval craft. It produces a variety of electrical equipment, railway rolling stock and other railway equipment, cement, and automotive spare parts. It makes steel from its own pig iron, in turn made from its own iron ore. Moreover, it exports a modest amount of its manufactures. Not to be overlooked are Turkey's well-regarded traditional crafts—ceramic tiles from Iznik and pottery from Kütahya, brass and copper items, leather products, and rugs.

Transportation

Turkey's large size, the country's well-distributed development, and planning have combined to produce Turkey's impressive transportation network. Although several links require improvement, the basic nets are the largest and best-balanced in the Middle East. Through rail and road nets, Turkey is well connected with all five of its neighbors, excluding former Soviet republics, and some traffic began moving between Turkey and the trans-Caucasus republics even before dissolution of the Soviet Union. Shipping and airlines also link Turkey with its neighbors and more distant states.

Railways. A trans-Anatolian rail line served Turkey as early as 1918, and an additional 2,052 miles/3,302 km of railway had been completed by the end of World War II. Major post-World War II additions have been made in the southeast and east, along the steadily developing Malatya-Elazığ-Diyarbakır-Siirt axis and on the CENTO- and RCD-supported line to Iran, which crosses Lake Van by ferry. All the Turkish trackage is standard gauge (4.7 ft./1.435 m) and is operated by Turkish State Railways (TCDD), which has scheduled a badly needed overhaul of much of the system. By 2000, Turkey possessed one-third of the Middle East's rail lines, especially adapted for shipping coal, other bulky minerals, and grain hundreds of miles to ports or internal markets.

Roads. Turkey entered the post-World War II era with a very limited road network, most of it poorly surfaced. Some of the financial aid supplied Turkey under the Truman Doctrine was devoted to road building, for economic and political purposes as well as for security reasons. Funding also later came from CENTO. By 1998, Turkey had 40 percent of the total length of all roads in the Middle East (see Table 9-2); and every town in Turkey had been integrated into a well-designed, well-constructed, and serviceable road network. Accelerated economic growth after 1985 overtaxed major routes, requiring construction of four-lane divided motorways. About 1,865 miles/3,000 km of motorways have been completed, approximately one-third of those planned. The Europe-Middle East route was first to be constructed: Edirne to Istanbul, across the second Bosporus bridge to Ankara, then to Adana and Gaziantep; sections around Izmir, Konya, and Ankara have also been completed. Turkey's goal is to build a net comparable to the German Autobahn or the U.S. Interstate Highway system. Unfortunately, many Turkish drivers disregard traffic laws, creating not only domestic safety problems but concerns for the EU.

Despite an efficient and colorful ferry service across the Bosporus, heavy and rapidly increasing automobile and truck traffic in the late 1960s necessitated construction of a bridge across the strait. Spanning the narrowest part (about 0.6 mile/1 km) of the lower Bosporus a few miles up the waterway from old Istanbul and high above the water level, the suspension bridge links Europe and Asia and enables traffic to avoid long delays at ferry crossings. The bridge so facilitated the rapidly increasing through traffic across the Bosporus that a wider, second span was opened in 1988 to carry long-distance traffic, leaving the 1973 bridge to handle local traffic. Despite early fears, the structures detract little from the beauty of the Bosporus (Fig. 21-4).

The new Trans-European Motorway (TEM) enters Turkey at Edirne, crosses the Bosporus by bridge and extends eastward through Ankara and Erzurum to the Iranian border opposite Maku, a stretch of 1,120 miles/1,800 km. Branch highways reach south to Adana (and beyond to Syria and Iraq) and north to the Black Sea at Trabzon, giving Turkey a total

FIGURE 21-4   Bosporus Strait, looking north toward Black Sea. Rumeli Hisar, built in 1453 by Ottoman Sultan Mehmet the Conqueror to facilitate his seizure of Constantinople, is to the left. The second Bosporus Bridge, opened in 1988 and named after Sultan Mehmet, spans the strait in the distance.

of 2,235 miles/3,600 km of the motorway. Having become an important transit land for vehicular traffic, especially tandem trailer trucks, between Europe and the Middle East, Turkey benefits appreciably from its inclusion in the TEM network. Tourist facilities also hope to attract larger numbers of European tourists from the northwest and vacationing Arabs from the southeast.

Ports and Shipping.   With 4,474 miles/7,200 km of coastline and intimate interrelations between land and sea in the west and northwest, Turkey has a long maritime history. The republic has maintained numerous ports, some active since ancient times, and also has sustained a vigorous maritime trade. In addition to numerous small ports for coastal shipping, Turkey operates a half-dozen major ports and a score of secondary and minor ports for international trade. Although the tonnage handled varies from year to year, leading ports include Mersin and Iskenderun on the Mediterranean, Izmir on the Aegean, Samsun on the Black Sea, and Bandırma, Derince, and Hydarpaşa (opposite Istanbul) on the Sea of Marmara. All are served by railway. Secondary ports from Alanya around Asia Minor to Trabzon are indicated on Map 21-2.

The total tonnage of general international cargo, excluding petroleum, loaded and unloaded through all Turkish ports exceeds that of any other Middle East country. Free zones were established at the two Mediterranean ports of Mersin and Antalya in the mid-1980s. Turkey operates the second-largest merchant marine fleet in the Middle East, about 880 ships; but their total deadweight tonnage is less than that of Iran and only one-fifth that of the fleet registered in Cyprus, which includes numerous tankers and other large ships using the Cypriot flag of convenience.

Airways. Turkish Airways (Türk Hava Yolları—THY), with more than 53 jet aircraft, is the third-largest airline in the Middle East. Turkey's 26 airfields with scheduled flights lead the region, followed by the 25 in Saudi Arabia. There are, however, 30 major airports, including NATO airfields, notably Incirlik (near Adana), Izmir, and Karamürsel (near Izmit). One of three busiest airports in the region, Istanbul opened a new showcase terminal in 1996. It is worth noting that Turkey has about 12 private airlines that operate on international routes. THY has a virtual monopoly on domestic routes.

Trade

With its intermediate location, extensive coastline and numerous harbors, and range of resources, Asia Minor has historically engaged in extensive commerce and transit trade. Although some of the medieval trade routes from India, China, and East Africa ended at the Levant coast, others continued northward across Asia Minor to Trabzon or westward to the entrepôt of Constantinople or to lesser termini on the Aegean coast. European countries maintained active trade with the Ottoman Empire even as it declined.

During its early years, the Republic of Turkey had little more to export than agricultural products and specialty raw materials, such as meerschaum. By the late 1980s, manufactured products had mounted to more than two-thirds of the country's exports. Exploiting the Arab League boycott of Egypt for 11 years after 1979, Turkey increased its exports to Middle East countries as part of its expanding economic and political ties with its neighbors to the southeast—most of which were coincidentally formerly Ottoman imperial possessions. However, Turkey's persistent and vigorous efforts to strengthen relations with the EU have directed most of the foreign trade in the direction of EU countries. All aspects of exports were sharply improved after the economic liberalization beginning in the early 1980s and after the Turkish lira was made fully convertible

in early 1990. One evidence is the escalation in the value of Turkey's exports from $2.28 billion in 1978 to $11.6 billion in 1989 and to $31 billion in 1998.

Relations

Turkey's location on the strategic bridge land of Asia Minor, with its geopolitical assets, inevitably creates multidirectional reciprocal relationships; these exist not only between the republic and its neighbors but also with several more distant powers concerned about this critical area. Interactions with imperial Russia were a mainspring of Ottoman Turkish foreign policy for centuries; periodically the Turks turned to the British or French—and, later, the Germans—to counterbalance Russian power. After Atatürk's revival of a defeated Turkey and his preservation of its Anatolian territory in the early 1920s, Turkey and the Western European states reached an uneasy détente. During World War II, Turkey remained neutral, as was mentioned earlier, but eventually declared war on the Axis and became a charter UN member. As Soviet aggression after 1945 replaced historical Russian imperialism, Turkey allied with the Western powers, especially with the United States in the Truman Doctrine, against Soviet hegemonism.

With the Straits a critical focus (see Map 11-7), Turkey, as a significant segment of the Northern Tier and the Eurasian Rimland, played a major geopolitical role during the Cold War: It participated in NATO (after 1952), the Baghdad Pact, and then CENTO (which headquartered in Ankara 1958–1979) as a regional military anchor. It later joined the Council of Europe, the European Free Trade Association (EFTA), and, in 1996, the EU customs union. After years of ambivalence, the EU accepted Turkey in December 1999 as a "candidate state" for membership—the only Muslim state so accepted.

Turkey will have to change hundreds of laws and regulations to conform to EU standards, and before it can be considered for actual membership (perhaps several years away), Turkey will have to alter several basic policies; for instance, it must improve its human rights record, curb the power of the military in politics, change its approach to minorities, and negotiate more openly with Greece.[20] Its status with the EU is profoundly important, since, inter alia, that acceptance would finally bestow the cachet on Turkey as a genuine European entity.

Along with its important relations with Western Europe, Turkey's relations with the United States remain close and a mainstay, although they cooled between 1975 and 1978 during the U.S. embargo on arms supplies to Turkey consequent to the Turkish invasion of Northern Cyprus in 1974. Since 1947, U.S. military aid to Turkey has totaled more than $14.5 billion and economic aid more than $4 billion. A large USAID mission coordinated civilian economic assistance; a Joint Economic Commission considered economic development after 1993; and the Joint U.S. Military Mission for Aid to Turkey (JUSMMAT) and the Turkish-U.S. Logistics Group (TUSLOG) coordinated military aid of equipment transfers. In reciprocity, Turkey accorded the United States access to more than a dozen major facilities, including military airfields; communications, naval, and intelligence-gathering installations; and, until 1963, nuclear storage facilities. The United States still conducted major operations against Iraq from the Incirlik air base near Adana in early 2000.

The focus by Turkey on the Soviet threat during the Cold War was in conflict with the focus by neighboring Arab states on the threat posed by Israel. Turkey's alliances with Western powers put it in further discord with neighbors' policies. During this period, Turkey practiced discreet disengagement from its Middle East environment and avoided involvement in inter-Arab disputes, the Arab-Israel conflict, and other regional conflicts. Yet it attempted to maintain cordial, if not close, political and diplomatic ties with all the Arab regimes and Iran—with the exception of Syria.[21] The end of the Cold War profoundly affected Turkey because its role in the Western alliance was suddenly ambivalent;

Turkey now sought a more participatory role in its own neighborhood—the Balkans, the Caucasus, Central Asia, and the Middle East. At that same time, the Iraqi invasion of Kuwait forced Turkey to adopt a prominently active policy regarding Middle East affairs, while also seeking links with the newly independent former Soviet republics.

Relations with its three contiguous Muslim neighbors—Syria, Iraq, and Iran—have varied markedly. Those with Syria have never been warm, primarily because republican Turkey both incorporated the Arabian Foreland plains inhabited by Arabs ("Syrians") and also accepted the disputed Hatay/Alexandretta area unilaterally ceded to Turkey by France in 1938 (see Chap. 11). Two more acute contentions in the 1980s and 1990s heightened tensions dangerously: Syria's umbrage over Turkey's alleged overutilization of Euphrates water in the GAP, along with Turkey's anger over Syria's support of Kurdish rebels, including its harboring the PKK leader, Abdullah Öcalan, during 1984–1999. Details of both disputes are given in other chapters.

Relations between Turkey and Iraq are of signal importance to both parties regarding several mutual concerns: their Kurdish minorities, the oil pipeline from Kirkuk to Yumurtalık, the waters of the Euphrates and Tigris basins, and communications and commercial relations. Cooperation between them during the Iran-Iraq war was of great mutual benefit, but after Iraq had invaded Kuwait, Turkey was obliged to close the Iraqi pipeline and generally work with the UN coalition. Both Turkey and Iraq have benefited from the conditional reopening of the pipeline in 1997, and both have made tentative overtures regarding closer relations; but Turkey still permits U.S. aircraft to operate against Iraq from Incirlik.

Turkish-Iranian links were very close for 25 years under the Baghdad Pact-CENTO, and even more so under the Regional Cooperation for Development (RCD), until such ties were loosened after the Islamic revolution in Iran. During the 1980–1988 Iran-Iraq war, Turkey managed to maintain mutually beneficial links with both combatants, and it still enjoys good, if not close, relations with the Islamic Republic.

Along with the more crisis-driven developments in Turkey's redirected foreign relations during the 1990s, links between Turkey and Israel quietly evolved until they became a major regional concern. Turkey as a Muslim state—albeit secular—had been cautious in its attitude toward the Arab-Israel conflict; but it had recognized Israel in 1949 and had maintained low-key diplomatic and economic relations with the Jewish state for four decades. Subsequent to the sea change in the regional dynamics after 1990, Turkey decided to de-emphasize its links with Arab states while pursuing closer ties with an increasingly more powerful Israel. Beginning with a tourism agreement in 1992, the two governments signed a series of additional agreements, including a military training arrangement in 1996, which permits Israeli air force jets to use Turkish airspace for training flights. In addition, the Muslim state signed a contract for $632 million for Israel to upgrade its 54 F-4 fighter jets and also for Turkey to purchase Israeli missiles. In another climactic development, Turkish, U.S., and Israeli naval units conducted joint maneuvers in January 1998 off Israel's Mediterranean coast. Thus, Turkey has outflanked Syria and has minimized the emerging relations between Syria and Greece.[22] One American columnist commented that Turks "…see America as making the world go round and Israelis as a key to American support. Israelis need a powerful friend in the Muslim world…."[23] Even so, Turkey has evinced openness toward Iran, Iraq, and Syria.

Across the Black Sea, in the Caucasus, and in Central Asia the burgeoning independent former Soviet republics immediately attracted Turkey's attention in 1991–1992, and Turkey quickly reached out to them. It especially sought close relations with the new entities that are not only Muslim but also Turkic—Azerbaijan, Turkmenistan, Kazakhstan, and Kyrgyzstan. In April 1999, the presidents of Turkey, Azerbaijan, and Georgia pledged to work for peace and to cooperate on aspects of the Caspian oil and gas pipelines. In June 1992, Turkey hosted in Istanbul a meeting of ten nations, including six former Soviet republics, who signed a declaration creating the Black Sea Economic Cooperation project.

As important as the foregoing relations may be, none are more critical than those Turkey has with Greece and Cyprus. Dating from ancient times, antagonisms between Greece and Asia Minor were manifested in modern times in the Greek war of independence from the Ottomans in the early 1800, the Greek-Turkish war of the early 1920s, the conflict over Cyprus, and, in more recent years, dispute over the Aegean seabed (see Chap. 11). Among all the tensions in Turkey's foreign relations, the Cyprus problem has been the most acute and the most difficult to resolve; however, late 1999 discussions regarding the membership of Cyprus and Turkey in the EU offer some promise of more successful negotiations over Cyprus. Rapport between Greece and Turkey was also improved in late 1999 through "quake diplomacy," when each country responded to the other's need for help after earthquakes struck in Turkey and then Greece. The rapport improved further in early 2000.

Notes

1. Several good general studies of Turkey are widely available. See *Turkey* Country Study 1995; B. Lewis 1968; G.S. Harris 1985; Schick and Tonak 1987; Ahmad 1993; and Mastny and Nation 1996.

2. A good, readable discussion is in Dewdney 1971, which also covers the general geography of Turkey. For technical geology, see Brinkmann 1976. For technical tectonics, see Dixon and Robertson 1984, which reveals the enormous complexity of Asia Minor's structure.

3. See Section 3, Dixon and Robertson 1984.

4. These and other sites are covered in Bean 1968.

5. For a detailed, scholarly, yet practical study of the many archaeological sites in Turkey see Akurgal 1970.

6. Erinç and Tunçdilek 1952.

7. See Pitcher 1972, a superb historical geography of the Ottoman Empire with excellent maps.

8. B. Lewis 1968 is a standard work on the evolution of modern Turkey.

9. See *Turkey* Country Study 1995 and *Background Notes: Turkey* 1999.

10. See Gunter 1997.

11. For opposing viewpoints on Turkish treatment of the Armenians, see Jernazian 1990 and Gürün 1985.

12. For a detailed study of the Anatolian village see Kolars 1968; for a study of the *gecekondu* see Karpat 1976.

13. An excellent guidebook on Turkey, intelligently written and superbly illustrated, is *Turkey*, 1989.

14. Development is concisely covered in G. S. Harris 1985. For more details and later coverage see Schick and Tonak 1987 (Part 3), Hershlag 1988, *Background Notes: Turkey*, 1999, and *Turkey* Country Study 1995.

15. See *Country Commercial Guide: Turkey*, 1999 and *Background Notes: Turkey*, 1999.

16. This section is based on briefings by officials of the Turkish State Hydraulic Works (DSİ) at Atatürk Dam in 1990 and in DSİ headquarters in Ankara in 1997, as well as on Kolars and Mitchell 1991.

17. Minerals and mineral industries are examined in detail in *Minerals Information: Turkey*, 1996.

18. Turkey's energy situation is examined in the *EIA: Turkey*, Aug. 1999.

19. Aspects of the Caspian MEP are discussed in the *Oil and Gas Journal*, Nov. 15, 1999, 23–28.

20. *New York Times*, Dec. 2, 1999. For an appraisal of attitudes between Turkey and Europe, see *New York Times*, Dec. 11, 1999.

21. See good study in Sayari 1997.

22. The subject is well appraised in Bolukbasi 1999.

23. William Safire, *New York Times*, Feb. 4, 1999. The column adds that Israelis need "...the large Turkish land mass over which to train their air force.... The Turks sell textiles and other commodities duty-free to Israel, which adds its labor to the product and sells it to the U.S. duty-free. This boosts the Turkish economy, which hires Israeli companies to construct power plants and develop irrigation projects. Meanwhile, the U.S. leans on oil companies to build a pipeline from the Caspian Sea through Turkey rather than Iran."

22

Iran: Complex Republic on the Plateau

Young State, Ancient Land

Iran's major rankings serve as reminders of the fundamental importance of the country: In the region, it is second in size, second or third in population, fourth in petroleum reserves, first in natural gas reserves, second in total area under cultivation, first in area under irrigation, second in wheat production, first in copper output, and otherwise a ranking producer (see tables in Chaps. 6, 7, and 8). Its natural gas reserves are second only to those of Russia, and its petroleum reserves rank fourth in the world, despite the fact that it was one of the earliest producers and has yielded billions of barrels since output began. Iran has been the core of Shii Islam for centuries and has appointed itself leader of the militant Shiism and even of militant Islam of the 1980s and 1990s. Ensconced in one of the strongest power foci in the Middle East (see Map 2-6), Iran has periodically demonstrated its viability and resiliency, the latest attestation coming in the Iran-Iraq war of the 1980s. Of especial historical-geopolitical significance is Iran's persistence in the concept of *Iran-zamin,* "the land of Iran." Somewhat comparable to the idea of *Greater Syria,* the concept is one of a broad area of former Iranian imperial domain, implanted Iranian culture, and historical Persian influence through millennia—an ancient relationship between a people and their cultural homeland.[1] Although contemporary sentiment regarding Iran-zamin may not reach the level of emotional irredentism, Iranian efforts to extend the Islamic fundamentalist revolution to neighboring lands suggest that the Iran-zamin idea is near the surface of Iranian revolutionary consciousness.

Certain aspects of ethnicity and terminology also suggest Iran's individuality. As one of the four states in the Middle East that is not Arab, Iran is the only major Middle East state whose national language is neither Semitic nor Turkic. Migrating Aryans brought their Indo-European language into the plateau in the second millennium BC and became the ancestors of the Persians and perhaps other peoples. The term *Iran* derives from "Aryan" and has always been preferred by the descendants of the Aryans as the general name for the area. Another toponym arose in the south-central part of the plateau. The local name Fars became the root for both "Farsi," the present designation for the main local language (Persian), and also the name "Persia," through consonant shift. The area was best known in the West as Persia until Reza Shah in 1935 demanded that "Iran" be applied to the state and the Western oil company operating there. Thus, the official name, Iran, is a reminder of the original Indo-European Aryans ("nobles") who laid the foundations for the future state.

Entrenched in its high plateau, Iran has played a powerful historical role for more than 2,500 years. Since the evolution of a regional empire under Cyrus the Great, Iran has maintained a vigorous national base century after century, even while temporarily succumbing militarily and politically to Greeks, Arabs, Mongols, and others. Over the centuries, migrating peoples settled in the less populated mountain basins and valleys, but, like the Chinese, Iranians assimilated many of the invaders and immigrants or tolerated other groups in

Iran

Long-form official name, anglicized: Islamic Republic of Iran

Official name, transliterated: Jomhuri-ye Eslami-ye Iran

Form of government: unitary Islamic republic with a single legislative house, the Majles (Islamic Consultative Assembly)

Area: 635.234 miles^2/1,645,258 km^2

Population, 1999 (est.): 61,531,000 (U.S. Government: 65,179,752)

Ethnic composition (%): Persian 51, Azeri 23, Gilaki and Mazandarani 8, Kurd 7, Arab 3, Luri 2, Baluch 2, Turkmen 2, Bakhtiari 1, other (Armenian, Qashqai, Afshar, Ilsavan, Jewish, many splinter groups) 1

Religions (%): Muslim 98.0 (Shii 90.5, Sunni 7.5), Christian 0.7, Jewish 0.3, other (Zoroastrian, Bahai) 1.0

GDP, 1998: $339.7 billion; per capita: $5,000

Petroleum reserves: 89.7 billion barrels

Main exports (% of total value, 1998): petroleum and petroleum products 80; carpets, fruits, nuts, hides iron, steel 15

Main Imports (% of total value, 1998): machinery 41, iron and steel 6, grains and other foodstuffs 6, transportation equipment 5.5

Capital city: Tehran 7,700,000 (Greater Tehran about 11,000,000); other cities: Mashhad 2,375,000; Esfahan 1,880,000; Tabriz 1,400,000; Shiraz 1,230,000

---

isolated parts of the plateau. Periodically absorbing powerful new elements that refreshed and reinvigorated it, the vibrant Iranian culture persevered and preserved its essence.

The 1978–1979 Islamic Revolution brought numerous radical social changes in Iran, none more radical than the shift in the ruling elite. Competing social groups have been a dynamic within the Iranian body politic for many decades: aristocracy, bazaar (merchants), clergy, tribal leaders, and army. Thought to be well under control, the clergy suddenly asserted itself in 1978–1979, and the Iran of the 1980s reversed the sociopolitical trends of the 1960s and 1970s. Peoples and environments once again renewed their traditional interaction in the human search for identity and control.

Iran enjoyed many years of generally good relations with the rest of the world before 1979. Its status as a pariah for more than a decade after that time sometimes obscures its long cultural traditions, enduring geopolitical significance, petroleum wealth, economic potential, and human resources. As is true in any political-geographical evaluation of a state, the short-term conditions must be balanced with the enduring factors. Such balancing is difficult in a Western estimate of Iran because of Iran's direct and indirect involvement in terrorism and other abnormal behavior after the Khomeini revolution of 1979. Nevertheless, the abiding factors in Iran's situation must be kept in focus, and those factors are emphasized in this chapter.

Plateau Palimpsest

The sequence of human occupance of Middle East lands over thousands of years is well preserved in the Iranian Plateau, and the antiquity of this settlement in Iran is neither inconsequential nor academic. Ruins and other evidence of ancient habitation are rarely out of sight in the more humid areas of the plateau. Numbering more than 250,000, archaeological sites in Iran include several Middle Paleolithic (Mousterian) sites from about 40,000 years ago, during the last glacial period. Thousands of tells containing successive Neolithic villages dot the valleys, piedmonts, and plains of western Iran. Also called *tepes* or *chegas* in Iran, mound sites of later villages are equally numerous,[2] and excavated examples have yielded elaborate pottery and ornaments of bronze, silver, and gold. On the flat Marv Plain (Marvdasht) before Persepolis, more than 1,000 tells have been enumerated, most appearing to date from 6000–5500 BC.

Following the succession of powerful early empires on the Iranian Plateau, the Arab Muslim invasion in the 630s introduced momentous changes in Iran. Although the collapse of the Sassanian Empire was at first staggering, a national revival demonstrated once again the Iranian vitality. Persian expertise, vigor, experience, and cultural vibrancy contributed to the effectiveness of the Umayyad Empire and then were major factors in the establishment of the Abbasid Empire in Mesopotamia, close to and associated with the Iranian core area. The Persian language diffused throughout the Middle East and exchanged hundreds of loanwords with Arabic, as well as with Turkish later on. Although Islam was cradled in Arabia and brought into the Fertile Crescent and Iran by Arabs, the Islamic civilization that evolved over the following several centuries was highly Persianized.

Iran suffered political fragmentation, cultural disruption, and physical destruction after the collapse of the Abbasid Empire in 1258; and Mongol and Tatar invasions under Genghis Khan, Hulagu Khan, and Tamerlane threatened Persian continuity and identity over three centuries. As in the seventh century, Iran absorbed and integrated disparate ethnic and cultural influences, preserved its "Persianality," and continued to thrive. This reinvigorated Iran incubated a late-sixteenth-century Persian golden age under the Safavid dynasty shah, Abbas the Great (1587–1629), whose lasting contributions to Persian culture are preserved in the splendid monuments of Esfahan.

Iranian power declined after Shah Abbas, and the Safavid dynasty ended in 1736, followed by the Zands until 1794. The mediocre Qajars, under whom Iran lost both vigor and territory, held the plateau until 1925, when Reza Shah founded the two-ruler Pahlavi dynasty and set the course for contemporary Iranian development. Because he refused to allow Iranian territory to be used by the Allies as a transit area for supplying the USSR with war material during World War II, Reza Shah was forced by the Allies to abdicate and was replaced in 1941 by his young son, Mohammad Reza. Reigning during a period of development and modernization, Mohammad Reza Shah was ousted briefly by the nationalistic, anti-Western Mohammad Mossadegh between 1951 and 1953 but regained power with controversial U.S. assistance. He continued a strong reign and rule until the political-religious revolution led by the Ayatollah Khomeini forced him out in January 1979.[3]

A Theocratic Republic

Having sought political control in times past, Shii clerics joined lay factions in the 1970s to fight foreign influences and the wide domestic corruption and repression in Iran. After Ayatollah Ruhollah Khomeini and his clerical supporters had ousted the shah and his regime and had gained control, however, some of their methods were no less harsh during the early years than those of the previous regime. Revolutionary courts convicted and condemned hundreds of opponents and critics on such a scale that the practice raised internal and external censure, which finally moderated the ruthlessness. One Iranian scholar stated that "Iran's Islamic Republic is a religious *oligarchy* of intricately overlapping relationships among the leading clerics.... At the apex of the political pyramid is the Supreme Leader (*rahbar*) who is the spiritual guide of the nation, the official head of state, the commander-in-chief of the armed forces and, as vali-e-faqih [Islamic jurist], the protector of the faith." He had earlier written, "Since Islam is a polity ruled by God, disobedience toward God's surrogate rulers is seen as not only a sin against the Almighty but a crime against the state, leaving no room for criticism, disagreement or dissent...."[4] Claims that political opponents are enemies of God have been used periodically for centuries and have been adapted in other parts of the contemporary Middle East, from the Iranian-backed Hizballah in Lebanon to Jewish militants in extremist movements in Israel.

The revolutionary government ended a secular monarchy and established a theocratic administration, and the new politics required extensive domestic and international adjustments. National cohesion became a priority for the new government, and, although some ethnic groups in Iran reasserted their separatist tendencies, the government suppressed the tendencies and preserved national unity. Internationally, revolutionary Iran reoriented its foreign relations, repudiating Western (especially U.S.) political and cultural influences. The seizure of scores of diplomatic persons, including 53 U.S. embassy staff members on November 4, 1979, by Iranian extremists was an unprecedented violation of diplomatic protocol and international norms, and such actions isolated Iran globally. Release of the hostages after 444 days did little to improve world perceptions of Iran, since irreconcilable hard-liners in Iran continued to flaunt world opinion.

The outbreak of the Iran-Iraq war in September 1980 (see Chaps. 11 and 16) led to many casualties (estimated at 1 million for Iran) and great physical destruction. Southwestern Iran, like southern Iraq, suffered widespread damage estimated by a UN team at $97 billion. Although Iraq received greater material and financial aid than Iran, the Iranians periodically received assistance at critical times, especially from Syria, Libya, Taiwan, and the People's Republic of China as well as from and through Israel and the United States, as was

disclosed in the Iran-Contra congressional hearings in Washington in 1986 and 1987.

During the two years between the Iran-Iraq cease-fire and Iraq's invasion of Kuwait, the Islamic Republic of Iran achieved basic domestic stability, despite the eight years of bitter warfare—and, indeed, partly by using the war as a centripetal factor. During the same period, it made an unexpectedly smooth transition to a successor administration following the death of the Ayatollah Khomeini at age 87 in 1989. The new regime was a dual leadership of Ayatollah Ali Khamenei and President Ali Akhbar Hashemi-Rafsanjani, both of whom, President Hashemi-Rafsanjani especially, were more moderate and pragmatic than the zealous and charismatic Khomeini. The Iraqi invasion of Kuwait created a dilemma for Iran, which condemned Iraq but also disliked the United States and other anti-Iraq coalition members. Iran received a bonanza when on August 14, 1990, Iraq finally accepted Iran's claims and conditions for an end to the eight-year Iran-Iraq war, primarily to obtain Iranian neutrality in the new Gulf crisis. During the entire decade of the 1990s, Iran's internal and external dynamics were generally impeded by two persistent stalemates. Politically, the conservative hard-line elite frustrated efforts by more moderate officials to ease manifold restrictions—on the press and on free speech, for example. Economically, governmental inexperience and mismanagement continued to repress development, add to inflation, and curtail employment. Popular election and re-election of the moderate President Hashemi-Rafsanjani and then the landslide election of the liberal President Muhammad Khatami in May 1997 ("the second revolution") manifested the public aspiration for a more open society and economic reform.[5] Riots in Tehran in 1992 and 1995 reflected grievances with the stagnant economy. The more significant and highly publicized student riots at Tehran University in July 1999 made the mood for change patently clear. Again, the conservatives suppressed further demonstrations and dampened President Khatami's efforts toward liberalization.[6] Another symptom of social malaise during the period was the spread of drug addiction—unusual in Iranian society. Heavy drug traffic from Afghanistan flows across Iran to Europe, carrying hashish, heroin, and opium; appreciable amounts are sold in Iran, despite major government efforts to interdict the traffic.[7]

At the beginning of the new century, Iran faced many interlaced problems, but it was also able to point to several noteworthy achievements: great rural economic development (electrification, water supply, road access, postal services); an almost doubled literacy rate; a great increase in higher education for women and governmental employment of women (while enforcing a strict female dress code); and the rebuilding of cities damaged in the Iran-Iraq war. Iranian society was also in a period of tremendous intellectual ferment and vigorous debate over the Islamicization of politics, the role and status of women, pluralism, foreign relations, and similar sociopolitical issues.

A Mountain-Rimmed Plateau

Iranian Landscapes

Variety and Contrasts. Even in a region of contrasts, the contrasts among Iranian landscapes are greater than those in any other Middle East country. Turkey and Israel display great variety, but only Iran has the range between lush, humid subtropical environments like the mountain-backed Caspian coast and totally barren, salt-encrusted deserts like the huge *kavirs* of Iran's interior basins. The country's landforms, climates, vegetation, and peoples are all of great variety.[8]

Landforms. The Iranian Plateau is a region of intermontane plateaus and mountains, with high and rugged mountains providing walls on three sides (Map 22-1). The land thus appears as a triangular bowl. The base of the low triangle extends from the northwestern corner to the southeastern corner, and the apex lies in the northeast near Mashhad. This basic form has influenced cultural evolution in the land from

earliest times. Coastlands and mountains frame the borders of the contemporary state of Iran and have historically served as ramparts.

Iran is the central segment of the Tethyan geosynclinal belt that extends from Morocco to Indonesia. It is the eastern half of the Middle East's Mobile Belt or Fold Belt (see Map 3-2) and was compressed between the Arabian Shield and the Russian Platform during the long period of intense folding from Triassic to Pliocene and Pleistocene times. The Zagros and Elburz-Kopet mountains were folded and buckled upward as a result of this tectonic compression, embracing between them a relatively inflexible block, a denuded shield forming the vast interior *kavirs*. This compression and thrust-faulting is continuing, creating numerous seismic events on all sides of Iran, some of them disastrous. Iran today has so many mountains and high plateaus that its average elevation is an unusually high 4,920 ft./ 1,500 m.

Drainage. Reflecting Iran's primarily Mediterranean precipitation regime, runoff reaches a maximum in late winter and early spring during seasonal rains and the melting of snow. The Karun River, tributary to the Shatt al-Arab and Iran's largest river, has ten times as much flow in April as in October. Farther east, the Zayandeh Rud, largest river in the Esfahan watershed, has a spring maximum discharge of 1,680 m³/sec with its load of meltwater but has less than 2 percent of that flow in late fall. Similarly, salty Lake Urmia, occupying a closed basin in northwestern Iran, covers one-third more area in May than in early October, since it receives snowmelt runoff from surrounding mountains in spring.

Large dams on several streams impound the seasonal runoff for use throughout the year, and many more dams are needed to increase the supply of water for irrigation purposes. Scores of smaller streams carry runoff from upper mountain slopes to piedmonts and alluvial fans on the inner sides of the many mountain chains and then dissipate in the sands, gravels, and saline crusts of the interior basins.

MAP 22-1   General map of Iran, with ostan (provincial) centers and other cities, highways, spot heights, and main mountain ranges. Regions are indicated by circled numbers.

More than half of Iran's drainage area lies in interior basins, from the vast *kavirs* to pocket-sized valleys in the Zagros. It is, nevertheless, these interior streams that are exploited in thousands of cases by *qanat* systems for irrigation water. Table 4-1 shows the seasonality and yearly average of precipitation in the four main climate areas of Iran.

Pattern of Regions

The pattern of regional physical and cultural features in Iran reveals especially significant

contrasts, and some understanding of the regional design aids in an appreciation of Iran's general character and problems. Several regional central places that are notably differentiated both historically and regionally and that are representative of their regions are included in the regional surveys.[9]

[1] **Zagros Mountains and Gulf Coast.** As part of the southern arc of the great Alpine folding system, the Zagros Mountains extend northwest-southeast from the Turkish border for 1,000 miles/1,600 km to the Strait of Hormuz.

Four parallel belts exhibit different lithology, structures, and landforms from west to east; and the southeastern Zagros features scores of salt domes, which pierce the entire folded sequence and form prominent landscape features in the desert climate (see Fig. 11-5).

It is in the four belts of the Zagros region that much of the population lives and most of the present and historical development of Iran has taken place. Winter precipitation intercepted by the considerable linear elevations provides irrigation water in the succeeding season. In the folds of the central-western Zagros are the great majority of the country's oil fields (see Maps 8-1 and 8-2), and in the volcanic belt and thrust-faulting of the eastern Zagros are most of the country's metallic mineral deposits, along the interplate zone of contact. Most of Iran's major and more famous cities are nestled in the valleys or along the piedmonts of the Zagros folds and along the Gulf coastal plain west of the Zagros (Map 22-1).

In the northwest is Tabriz, Iran's fourth-largest city, a former imperial capital and now the provincial capital of Azerbaijan Ostan (Persian *ostan* = province). Its bustling old bazaar and mosques have the distinct atmosphere of a dominantly Turkic Azeri metropolis, but other ethnic groups also jostle one another on the crowded streets. The central Zagros valleys, basins, and eastern piedmont embrace several of the republic's major centers, from Sanandaj and Qom in the north to Esfahan in the south. This group of cities includes former imperial capitals (Hamadan and Esfahan), noted carpet centers (Hamadan, Kermanshah, Qom, Kashan, Esfahan), contemporary industrial concentrations, and the important religious center of Qom. The status of Qom was enhanced after the Shii clergy gained power in 1979 and the Ayatollah Khomeini ruled like a sovereign from his home there. Esfahan especially preserves its former imperial status in its Safavid pavilions, picturesque main square, or *maydan,* and blue-tiled royal mosque, Masjid-e Shah, renamed Masjid-e Imam after the revolution

(Fig. 22-1). Third-largest city in Iran, Esfahan is credited with half the beautiful sites of the world in the Iranian proverb *Esfahan nesf-e Jahan* (literally, "Esfahan is half the world").

In the southern Zagros, Shiraz is the main center. It is the fifth-largest city in Iran and is yet another of the western cities that has the special aura of a former imperial capital. Climatic and soil conditions give Shiraz a particularly good ecology for growing roses, which crowd the hundreds of gardens that adorn the city. Two of Iran's most famous poets, Hafez and Saadi, are memorialized in impressive tombs in the city.

Iran's Gulf coast of more than 800 miles/ 500 km topographically and climatically formerly repelled dense human habitation and development. Along most of the shore, Zagros ridges rise precipitously from the Gulf, leaving no room for settlement. Elsewhere, marshy flats constitute the coast, and nowhere is fresh water plentiful. Nevertheless, Iran's very extensive oil operations in the southwest necessitate export facilities on the nearby Gulf coast and islands, and very considerable import needs require large-scale general cargo ports. The main terminal was developed on Kharg (Khark) Island, 25 miles/40 km offshore, opposite Kuwait. Gulf cargo ports are Bandar-e Khomeini (formerly Bandar-e Shahpur) in the north, Bandar-e Bushehr south of Kharg, and Bandar-e Abbas on the Strait of Hormuz (Persian *bandar* = port). The coast is being more closely integrated with the rest of Iran, especially as offshore oil and gas fields are further developed (see "Ports" below). Additionally, the small Gulf island of Kish has been transformed into a free port with liberalized social practices.

[2] **Elburz Mountains and Northeast Chains.** This region comprises not only the Elburz Mountain chain itself but also the eastern extension of the same compressional structures, as well as the piedmonts or forelands that lie north and south of the entire belt. The chain from the southwestern corner of the Caspian Sea to the northeastern corner of Iran beyond Mashhad is a segment of the northern belt of

FIGURE 22-1   Masjid-e Shah (Royal Mosque), Esfahan, from the reign of Shah Abbas the Great in the early 1600s, now officially called Masjid-e Imam. With its beautiful blue tiles, it is considered to be one of the world's most splendid mosques.

Alpine folding, splaying from the Zagros structures west of Tehran. Unlike the Elburz range proper, the eastern extension comprises several parallel ridges, which are usually referred to as the Kopet Mountains (Kopet Dagh), the name of the northernmost ridge along the Turkmenistan frontier.

Averaging about 60 miles/97 km in width, the Elburz range has numerous summits above 12,000 ft./3,658 m. It culminates in the impressive symmetrical volcanic cone of Mt. Damavand, 18,600 ft./5,671 m, in the central Elburz, highest elevation in the Middle East. The steep northern slopes of the Elburz descend to the Caspian plain and to the shore, which lies 92 ft./28 m below sea level. On the opposite side, the southern slopes terminate at the plateau level, 5,000 ft./1,525 m at Tehran, so that the total relief is less than on the northern side. Several small glaciers give an indication of the elevation of the higher peaks. Except for a few high

passes, traversed by three spectacular highways, the chain is a major impediment to transportation and to the flow of moisture-laden winds from the northwest. The Elburz are still building tectonically, as is indicated by the periodic sharp but rarely destructive earthquakes that strike Tehran. However, in the western Elburz, a devastating earthquake struck June 21, 1990, causing 50,000 deaths and 100,000 injuries and rendering 500,000 homeless. A moderate quake on February 28, 1997, near Ardabil in the Azeri area, killed nearly 1,000. Severe tremors have shaken areas across much of northern Iran as well as southwestern and eastern areas.

In northeastern Iran the folded Kopet ridges of northern Khorasan are appreciably lower than the Elburz proper and are more comparable to the folded Zagros. Open valleys are devoted to cereal cultivation and support a moderately dense population. Mashhad is the major city of the northeast. It is not only the

FIGURE 22-2   Northern Tehran (Shemiran and Tajrish residential suburbs) nestled at the foot of the towering snow-covered Elburz Mountains.

second city of Iran but also, like Tabriz, a center of ethnic complexity, with Persians, Turkmen, Baluch, Kurds, Hazaras, and other peoples mingling in the bazaars and mosques. Turkmen especially bring their Bukhara-style carpets for marketing in Mashhad. Like Qom, Mashhad has one of the holiest shrines in Iran. The opening of the border between Iran and Turkmenistan and the other new republics of former Soviet central Asia in 1991 has produced an appreciable influx of visitors from these long-isolated lands.

The large population of the Caspian coast is distributed in numerous small towns and villages rather than in a few metropolitan areas. Rasht, in the west, is noteworthy, along with the port of Bandar-e Anzali (formerly Bandar-e Pahlevi). In the east are Gorgan and the port of Bandar-e Torkeman (formerly Bandar-e Shah). Several coastal towns are much-frequented resort centers, including Ramsar and Chalus.

The piedmont and foredeep south of the Elburz-Kopet belt support not only the metropolitan area of Tehran but also Qazvin to the west, the ancient city of Rey immediately south of Tehran, and a series of towns along the present Tehran,-Mashhad railway, which follows the old Silk Road. A score of suburbs and former peripheral villages have coalesced to form greater Tehran, which sprawls along the alluvial fans on the southern side of the Elburz. About 20 percent of Iran's population resides in greater Tehran, which has an even higher percentage of the country's professional workers, office employees, and general labor force. Formerly, palaces, upper-class residences, and Western expatriates were concentrated on the higher slopes in northern Tehran, especially in the suburb of Shemiran (Fig. 22-2). These neighborhoods had first use of the water from the *qanats* that formerly supplied the city, and they both avoided the smog of lower Tehran and were cooler because of their higher elevation.[10] The city has an impressive concentration of government buildings, embassy compounds, banks, schools, and business establishments. Streets of the central business district have some of the most congested traffic of all Middle East cities, and the Tehran bazaar, in the crowded southern sector, is normally one of the major shopping centers of the Middle East. It is especially noted for gold jewelry, carpets, and decorative brass and copper wares.

[3] **Eastern Highlands.** Several separate complex ridges form the eastern rim of the Iranian "bowl." Runoff from the ridges supports a few scattered villages, some of which include ruins of ancient settlements. At the southern end of the eastern highlands is Iran's only recently active volcano, Kuh-e Taftan. A magnitude 7.1 earthquake on May 10, 1997, north of Birjand in this seismically unstable area, killed 2,000, injured 5,000, and devastated 200 villages. A 7.7 quake on September 16, 1978, killed 25,000. These eastern reaches of Khorasan, Iran's largest province, share a long, porous border with Afghanistan, most of which had been included in Iran-zamin for centuries. During the Soviet occupation of Afghanistan from 1980 to 1989, about 2 million Afghans sought refuge in eastern Iran, and many are still resident in the republic. This frontier zone was brought under central government control only in the 1960s and is now a battleground between drug smugglers and government forces.

[4] **Interior Basins.** This region is contained within the larger Iranian triangle and generally corresponds to the "Tabas wedge." Although it includes several smaller basins, its two major depressions are Dasht-e Kavir in the north-center and Dasht-e Lut in the southeast (Persian *dasht* = desert or plain).[11] The lowest part of the Dasht-e Kavir watershed is occupied by the Great Kavir (Persian *kavir* = playa or salt flat), an immense erosional surface with salt- and mud-filled depressions and extensive dune fields covering more than 20,000 miles²/51,800 km². Dasht-e Lut (*lut* = desert basin), lowest sump in interior Iran, and only 672 ft./205 m above sea

level, is somewhat smaller than the Great Kavir and is separated from it by a low divide. Dasht-e Lut is quite different from the Great Kavir. Its weird surface is etched by wind into yardangs, alternating ridges and grooves, some as high as 195 ft./60 m, and the wind-eroded material is piled into dunes to the south and east.

Neither the great salt expanse making up the Dasht-e Kavir nor the rough Dasht-e Lut is inhabited or even utilized by nomads. Neither the soil nor the meager precipitation permits growth of perceptible vegetation, although desert bush survives on the higher parts of the basins and in the courses of seasonal streams. These barren interior basins are the least useful parts of Iran.

People: Demography and Ethnography

Population

With one of the three largest populations in the Middle East,[12] Iran has far more people than all the other Gulf states combined, including Iraq and Saudi Arabia. Moreover, it has the region's most complex ethnic structure, both in the number of major groupings and in solid concentrations of those groupings. Its population includes at least eight peoples numbering more than 1 million each and another half-dozen of approximately 100,000 to 1 million each (see Table 6-3 and Map 22-2).

The areas with the most favorable environment for human occupation have long been densely populated: the Zagros valleys, Caspian coastlands, and inner piedmonts of the mountain frame. Along with the socioeconomic development and rising standard of living that began in the 1950s and faltered only in the late 1970s, Iran saw its net increase in population escalate to 46.3 per thousand, highest in the Middle East. Efforts initiated by the shah in the 1960s to slow the extraordinary birthrate were beginning to show modest results when the fundamentalist revolutionary regime reversed the government program. From a fairly high 2.9 percent population increase per year in the mid-1970s, the rate jumped to 3.9 percent—one of

MAP 22-2   Iran's complex patterns of ethnic groups.

the world's highest—before the new regime reacted and again encouraged birth control.

As in other Middle East states, as well as in most developing countries, the shift from rural to urban areas in Iran has been pronounced. Whereas the urban population was only 30 percent of the total in the mid-1950s, it was 57 percent in the late 1990s. The urban increase notwithstanding, millions of Iranians continue to reside in more than 55,000 villages along the piedmonts and valleys of the country-side (see Fig. 10-1). Since the villages contain concentrations of agricultural population, the pattern of areal distribution of villages correlates with patterns of available runoff and of higher rainfall. The Islamic city as examined in Chapter 10 is clearly identified in Iran, where it also possesses its own "Persianality."[13]

Peoples of the Plateau

Ethnic Complexity.   As an ethnic mosaic, Iran is
the most complex country in the Middle East.
Indeed, its pattern of people is so motley that the
central government through the centuries has
done well to maintain the state's national unity.
Although ethnic Persians (as distinct from Iranians in general) have played a prominent role in
Iran's development, events have also been influenced by minority peoples occupying valleys and
basins near the ethnic Persians. Both the location
of Iran and its complex pattern of landforms
have influenced the historical influx of various
groups and the resultant ethnic pattern.[14]

Over the millennia, groups have invaded or
migrated into the plateau from Asia Minor, the
Caucasus, central Asia, and the Indian subcontinent. Once they found themselves south of
the barriers of the Black Sea, Caucasus Mountains, and Caspian Sea, migrants were forced
through the mountain-ribbed Iranian "throat"
between the Caspian Sea and the Gulf. Some
westward-moving peoples pushed on into and
across Mesopotamia; others elected to settle in
the basins of the rugged Zagros Mountains.

The complexity of landforms, with elaborate
patterns of parallel and sometimes interconnected linear valleys and irregular basins,
imposed difficulties but also offered opportunities. There were opportunities for settlement,
for survival for those who developed a water
supply, and for protection from neighbors as
well as from a central authority. Some early
migrants have been partly or completely assimilated, but more than a score of peoples retain
separate identities in exclusive territories, as do
the Qashqai, Bakhtiari, and Lur. Several
minorities maintain a tribal organization, thus
structuring and protecting their culture. The
remarkable preservation of minority languages
provides a functional linguistic criterion to aid
distinction among groups. In a few cases, religion becomes the main basis for particularity.

Most of the peoples of Iran are discussed in
Chapter 6 and are included in Table 6-3, hence
only a few details need be added here to place
them in more specific context. A few smaller

groups are also mentioned. Map 22-2 shows the
generalized patterns of the ethnic groups of Iran,
and the identification numbers of the groups
discussed are keyed to that map. Estimated percentages of the major groups are given in the
summary data at the beginning of the chapter.

Persians and Related Peoples.   Persian (Farsi)
is the principal language in a subfamily of Indo-
Iranian languages that also includes Kurdish,
Luri, Baluchi, Gilaki, Mazandarani, and several
other tongues spoken by relatively small groups.

Although ethnic Persians (8) are the third-
largest people in the Middle East and the largest
single ethnic group in Iran, they are just 50 percent of the country's total population. Persians
are the most widely distributed of the Iranian
peoples, but they are found especially in an
almost unbroken broad ring around the interior basins. They comprise the great majority of
the upper class, the important government
employees, and the economic elite.

The main concentration of Kurds (5) is in
the Iranian segment of Kurdistan, in the western Zagros parallel to the Turkish and Iraqi
borders. Like related tribes in Iran and Turkey,
the Iranian Kurds have exhibited separatism,
rebelling unsuccessfully in 1919, during World
War II (the short-lived Mahabad Republic was
broken up in 1947), and in 1979. The Kurds are
mostly Sunnis and constitute the largest group
of Sunnis in the republic.

The Baluch (4) are concentrated in the
extreme southeastern corner of Iran and are the
least economically and nationally integrated of
the major minorities. They are still nomadic and
are known for their hand-knotted Baluchi rugs.

Divided by the main concentration of the
Bakhtiari (7), the Lur (2) have two clusters in
the central Zagros. Khorramabad is the center
of the northern area, Lorestan; the oil center of
Gach Saran lies on the southern edge of the
southern concentration. The Bakhtiari, concentrated between the oil center of Masjed-e
Soleyman and Shahr-e Kord, are considered
the most powerful of the southern tribes. Making and marketing Bakhtiari carpets are
important aspects of the tribal economy.

Secluded in high mountain valleys and basins in Khorasan (eastern Iran), a few tens of thousands of several tribal groups speaking Indo-European languages spill over from neighboring Afghanistan and the central Asian republics. A few other such groups live in scattered locations southwest and south of the Caspian. One of the largest is the Hazara or "Berberi" (3), living in and around Mashhad, who are a branch of a larger group in central Afghanistan. The Aimaq (9) include a score of tribal groups, a grouping that exemplifies the multiplicity of tribal divisions in this rugged area with its history of criss-crossing migrations.

Astride the northern segment of the Iranian-Afghan border live the Pushtun (6), who are also called Pashtun and are known farther east as the Pathan. A few tens of thousands of Tajik (9) live in the northern part of the Zabol salient. West of the Caspian, on either side of the international border, are several thousand Talysh (1); along the southern Caspian coast and on the slopes above are the Gilani (sometimes Gilaki) (9) in the west, around Rasht, and the Mazandarani (9) farther east. The Gilani have several times taken separatist action, most notably during the establishment of a short-lived socialist republic after World War I.

Turkic Peoples. The Azeri, or Azerbaijani (12), the largest ethnolinguistic minority in Iran, speak a Turkic language but adhere to Shiism and other Persian cultural traditions. Their center is Tabriz. While maintaining an Azeri identity and language, they join in Iranian nationalism as long as the central government accepts their informal autonomy. Their separatism was encouraged in the short-lived communist Tudeh Republic of Azerbaijan created under Soviet auspices at the end of World War II. Thwarting this Soviet effort was one of the first effective acts of the United Nations. After the former Soviet constituent republic of Azerbaijan became independent in 1991, the Iranian Azeris—to the discomfiture of the Iranian government—made several tentative declarations of hope for a union of Azeris in an enlarged independent state.

The Qashqai (11) have preserved one of the strongest nomadic traditions among the larger groups in Iran. They occupy two large areas in the Fars Province, one north of Shiraz and one to the south. With well-organized tribal confederations, the Qashqai have traditionally resisted central government control.

Turkmen (10), a tribally organized people, live in widely scattered groups in the northeastern mountains next to Turkmenistan. At one time they formed a strong military cavalry but are now nomadic pastoralists and settled farmers, known for hand-knotted carpets named after various descent groups—Tekke, Yomut, Salor, Saryk, and others. Their separatism, strong until the 1920s, reasserted itself after the 1979 revolution but was suppressed by the central government.

The 50 or more Ilsavan (formerly Shahsavan) nomadic groups occupy a dozen scattered areas from the Aras River southeastward to the steppes south of Tehran. The Qajars (14) form an enclave among the Mazandarani on the southeastern corner of the Caspian Sea. Afshars (13) primarily inhabit several separate areas in northwestern Iran. Other small tribal Turkic groups are scattered chiefly in the mountains of Khorasan and in the more rugged areas east of Shiraz, especially the Teymurtash and Qaragozlu.

Arabs. More than 1 million Arabs (15) live primarily in Khuzistan, the plain at the head of the Gulf, which Arabs refer to as Arabistan ("land of the Arabs"). They also live in the southern Zagros interior and even in widely scattered areas northeast and east of the Dasht-e Kavir. Descendants of Arabs who invaded in the seventh century and of later settlers, the Iranian Arabs maintain their separateness and have not assimilated, although they are predominantly Shiis.

Armenians and Assyrians. These two quite different peoples are grouped together as the two numerically significant Christian sects in Iran. The primarily Orthodox Armenians live in Tehran (about half), Tabriz, and Esfahan. As in Lebanon and Syria, they maintain their separate language, churches, and schools and have achieved marked success in professional and clerical positions in Tehran and in the Khuzistan oil fields.[15] The Assyrians are only one-tenth the number of Armenians and are concentrated west of Lake Urmia. They maintain their cohesion and preserve their Syriac vernacular and Nestorian Christianity.

Jews.   Long resident in Iran, at least as early as the Babylonian Captivity, Jews numbered about 100,000 in the 1970s, when they were prosperous and influential under the shah. Although less favored after 1979, they, along with Armenians, were respected as "People of the Book." They maintained their Jewish identity in their own schools, synagogues (there are 23 in Tehran alone), social institutions, and businesses. Many are wealthy merchants, especially in the rug trade, in Tehran, Esfahan, and Shiraz. The revolutionary government emphasized that it drew a distinction between the Jewish state, Israel—which it reviled—and the Jewish faith. Even so, more than two-thirds of Iranian Jews chose gradually to emigrate, mostly to the United States and Israel.[16] The approximately 30,000-member present Jewish community of Iran is the largest in the Muslim world, comparable with the 20,000 in Turkey (see Chap. 6). Iran's arrest of 13 Iranian Jews in early 1999, charged with espionage for Israel and the United States, incurred censure by Israel and the U.S. government. Iranian Jewish leaders urged the West not to exacerbate the situation and stressed that seven Muslims were also charged.[17] A verdict in July 2000 found ten Jews and two Muslims guilty; sentences ranged from 2 to 13 years.

Iranian Economic Patterns

Perspective

As in neighboring Gulf petroleum-producing countries, economic development and modernization have escalated in Iran since 1950. However, Iranian economic patterns exhibit comparatively greater complexity and subtlety of structure because of Iran's long economic history, early start in petroleum production, and combination—unique in the Middle East—of large size and large population with huge petroleum resources.[18] The patterns are further complicated in the recent context by the ramifications of the Islamic revolution.

Prior to development of the petroleum industry, Iran's traditional prosperity was based on a varied agriculture, trade, and widespread and artistic craftsmanship. Ordinary textiles, specialized hand-printed textiles called *qalamkar,* hand-knotted carpets, copper and brass items, decorated gold and silver items, enamel work, inlaid items, and hand-painted miniatures attracted buyers around the world. Although these traditional items form a modest percentage of the country's present production and exports, demand for them remains high; and for some isolated tribal groups, such artisan sales provide much of the cash income. Also, these products, rather than petroleum, symbolize Iranian traditions and creativity. Agriculture continues to be a major sector in the Iranian economy and in many regions is the only economic activity of any significance.

Having assured himself in the late 1950s that Iran had a major place in the petroleum market, Mohammad Reza Shah pursued an almost frenetic program of economic development of his country. During the period 1960–1977, Iran's real annual growth of 9.6 percent was about double the average of other developing countries. The very stable Iranian rial was virtually convertible. Every sector received attention, especially physical infrastructure—roads, railroads, ports, airports, communications, industries, trade, urban development. However, when the shah concomitantly attempted to give Iran military superiority and to transform it into an industrial power, a modern welfare state, and a secular, Westernized society, the effort became over-loaded for the economic base. When he further practiced widespread authoritarianism and denied basic freedoms to the citizens, disaffection set the stage for the revolution of 1978–1979. By coincidence and design, the revolutionaries reversed many developments that the shah had initiated, especially the framework of secular Westernization. Nevertheless, the new regime was able to cope for several years by coasting on the shah's accomplishments, including the military buildup.

The revolutionary government's initial economic efforts will always be ambiguous because of the almost immediate impact of the Iran-Iraq war.[19] The evidence is that the new regime had little comprehension of the complexities of economic development. All major industries were taken from their private owner-managers and placed in state hands. Thousands of a wide range of establishments were confiscated from supporters of the previous regime. Banking was "Islamicized," so that loans were made interest free and the banks were unprofitable. Both internal and external circumstances constricted development. The external impacts were especially serious—the war with Iraq, sharp decline of oil prices, Iranian assets being frozen abroad, Western economic sanctions, and other blows. The GDP of the late 1980s was no higher than that of fifteen years earlier. The revolution prompted the exodus of many entrepreneurs, managers, skilled professionals, and capital. The former privileged class was largely broken, but a new elite arose. The lot of the poor, for whom the revolution was theoretically launched, was little improved, especially that of the urban poor. However, as was mentioned earlier, rural development substantially improved the quality of life in tens of thousands of villages.

By the early 1990s, in its first economic five-year plan (1989–1993), the more moderate regime that succeeded the Khomeini ideology attempted to address economic realities. It was actively reprivatizing some establishments, attempting to restore confidence in government policies, inviting selected foreign firms (notably excluding U.S. companies) to enter both the oil and industrial sectors, and seeking foreign financing for new industrial production, including automobile assembly. However, efforts at liberalization were consistently derailed by conservative elements, so that, along with mismanagement, corruption, inflation,

and persistently high population increase, the economy remained stagnant. Indeed, 1976 per capita income had decreased 57 percent by 1994, and the gap between rich and poor had widened alarmingly. Unemployment was chronic, partly because, owing to the wage–cost-of-living imbalance, qualified employees held two jobs. Another major obstruction to economic achievement has been the role of the *bonyads*, independent and monopolistic religious conglomerates that control respective economic enterprises with few constraints. Extraordinarily generous subsidies on basic items—gasoline sold for 12 cents a gallon at the pump until the mid-1990s—were significant palliatives, but they added to the budget deficit. Lack of meaningful economic reform and progress in the late 1990s dampened some of the enthusiasm for the otherwise popular President Khatami. Also noteworthy is Iran's aggressive program of remilitarization, calling for an expenditure of billions of dollars for armaments from Russia, China, Pakistan, and North Korea.

Agriculture and Water Control

Although only a limited proportion of Iran is naturally suitable for rainfed agriculture, human ingenuity over thousands of years has created a broad agricultural base for a large population. Finding, conserving, and channeling water to cultivable soil areas in linear valleys and along piedmonts were the essential challenge and the main accomplishment. Iran's agricultural productivity, supplemented by imports, remained sufficiently effective during the 1980s so that even under wartime conditions, the population suffered no widespread hunger. Despite the dominance of the oil sector in the national economy, 22 percent of the economically active population still engages in agriculture, which contributes 25 percent of the GDP.

As in Syria and Iraq, the large landowners and tribal leaders controlled huge areas before 1960, maintaining sharecropping agreements with peasants working the land. Indeed, landowners controlled entire groups of villages

FIGURE 22-3   *Qanats* on Iran's northwestern plateau. These underground tunnels with their surface chain of wells have been the standard Iranian irrigation method for millennia.

along with the land and the village inhabitants. Two major land reform programs transformed the system. One was the highly publicized "White Revolution" carried out by the shah in 1963; the other was the revolutionary government's land reform in 1982. The two reforms curbed the power of the large landowners and reduced the size of their landholdings.

Extensive areas in the northwest and northeast support rainfed cultivation and arboriculture, as well as specialty horticulture in the distinctive ecology of the Caspian coast. However, typical Iranian agriculture relies on water management. Although several irrigation techniques are now employed, the ancient system of tapping and distributing water through a network of *qanats* remains the most important (see Chap. 7). These underground water channels, revealed on the surface as a chain of wells, are ideally constructed in alluvial fans that absorb runoff from adjacent watersheds on higher slopes that have intercepted rain and

snow. Scores of thousands of *qanats* in Iran, many constructed centuries ago and carefully maintained on northern and southwestern slopes, appear aerially as strings of beads on the long slopes of the fans (Fig. 22-3). Although all irrigated areas require local cooperation, *qanat*-watered basins demand an exceptionally high level of coordination and engender a complex and uniquely Iranian socioeconomic structure.

Crops.   The four tables in Chapter 7 clearly reveal Iran's high rank in the production of the various crops and animals listed. Iran competes with Turkey and Egypt in many other respects besides population, but, as noted earlier, among Middle East states, it leads in area under irrigation and in the production of combined fruits, oranges, dates, sheep, chickens, and goats; and it ranks second or third in many other crops. Nearly everywhere, except in the barren interior and southeastern corner, the dominant crops are wheat and barley, grown in both rain-fed and irrigated areas. Much of the wheat is rough-milled to make the unusual Iranian bread: large, flat, and dimpled from being baked on hot pebbles in a large oven. Rice is the third major cereal, grown in paddies on the alluvial plains on the southwestern Caspian coast. Much of the excellent rice is consumed in the favorite national dish, *chelo kebab*—flattened, grilled lamb kebabs on a bed of rice. Wheat and rice production, nevertheless, fail to meet demand, necessitating substantial imports. Potatoes are a fourth basic food grown in large quantities. Melons are grown everywhere, along with a wide range of vegetables. Also widely distributed are grapes used for raisins, table grapes, and in certain areas, wine.

Tree crops, common on the lower Zagros slopes, yield a wide range of nuts and fruits, with pistachios in great variety a particular specialty. Iran is the world's greatest pistachio producer, and the nuts rank third by value among exports, after carpets. Almonds and walnuts also grow well in subhumid areas. Fruits, from citrus along the Gulf coast to apples in the higher elevations, include all but humid tropical varieties. A specialty crop, tea grows along the south Caspian coast in the same protected environment that produces rice and other subtropical crops. Tea is the popular social beverage in Iran, far surpassing coffee, and must also be imported to meet demand.

Grown on the Caspian coast and in favored locations in the southern Zagros, cotton and tobacco are major industrial crops. Both sugarcane and sugar beets have been expanded in acreage, and sugar mills process these crops at refineries in central and northeastern Iran. Opium poppies, once prohibited, are now being grown under government supervision, as in Turkey.

Livestock, Fishing, Forestry. Vast areas are well suited for the grazing of sheep and goats, and cattle raising is of increasing importance. In addition to dairy products, cattle supply manure for fertilizer and for burning as domestic fuel (see Fig. 10-1). Fishing is important along the Gulf coast, along the Gulf of Oman, and on the

Caspian Sea coast. Iranian Caspian fisheries are especially famous for their superior caviar, the roe of the large Caspian sturgeon. Already very limited and therefore expensive, the caviar supply is threatened by chemical pollution, the fluctuating water level of the Caspian Sea, and overexploitation. Ranking second in amount of fish caught (see Table 7-3), Iran also ranks second in the export value of fish because of its caviar sales. Iranian forests, particularly in the Elburz, are the only commercially productive forest areas in the Middle East other than those in Turkey.

Hydrocarbons: A Major Producer

Iran became the first major petroleum country in the Middle East in 1908 with the discovery of the great Masjed-e Soleyman field in the folds of the middle Zagros, southeast of Dezful (see Chap. 8). Oil has long played a dominant role in Iran's economy and has undergirded the country's economic development for several decades.

Iran is credited with petroleum reserves of 89.7 billion barrels, fifth largest in the Middle East and in the world. More impressive are its natural gas reserves of 812.3 trillion ft.^{3}/ 23 trillion m^3, second in the world after Russia and nearly half of all those in the Middle East. As are neighboring countries and Egypt, Iran is placing priority emphasis on the exploitation of its gas resources. Petroleum production peaked in 1974 at more than 6 million bpd before decreasing to a minimum of 1.37 million bpd in 1981, early in the country's revolution and the Iran-Iraq war. Production returned to the 3.6 million-bpd level in the mid-1990s and has continued at that level, near its OPEC quota.

Historical Note. Early oil operations by Anglo-Persian (later Anglo-Iranian) Oil Company are traced in Chapter 8. After four decades of AIOC control of Iran's petroleum activity, one of the major crises in international oil industry history arose during the 1951–1953 dispute between the Iranian government under Prime Minister Mohammad Mossadegh and the AIOC. The crisis arose when the Iranian government rejected a draft agreement between the AIOC and Iran and nationalized the Iranian oil industry under the new National Iranian Oil Company (NIOC). During the dispute, Iranian oil sales fell to zero. In 1953, Mossadegh was displaced, and under a completely new accord the former AIOC concession passed to a new consortium of British, Dutch, French, and U.S. companies.

Operating under NIOC supervision, the Consortium produced and refined most of the Iranian output for the next 25 years. However, NIOC also formed partnerships with several other U.S., Italian, and Canadian companies in the late 1950s for exploration and production outside the original AIOC concession area, including offshore areas. NIOC attempted to be its own operator during the 1980s and succeeded reasonably well under the difficult circumstances. During this period, NIOC found giant nonassociated gas fields, especially offshore, the largest being an extension of the supergiant North Field off Qatar (see Chaps. 8 and 18). In the early 1990s, Iran decided to reinvigorate its hydrocarbon industry but faced two major obstacles: lack of the huge amounts of investment capital needed to implement its plans, along with depreciation of fields and facilities during the state's several years of isolation; both obstacles were exacerbated by the effects of the various sanctions imposed by the United States. Iran therefore actively sought participation by foreign companies; it invited bids for several major projects under the unusual "buy-back" system so that the projects would be financed by foreign company capital. Significant projects included opening the giant offshore gas fields (especially South Pars) and rejuvenating the over-exploited onshore Agha Jari oil field by a massive injection of gas from neighboring large gas fields. Iran has neglected such enhanced oil recovery (EOR) methods for the last two decades. The exploitation of a new oil discovery near the huge Iraqi Majnoun field on the Iran-Iraq border is an additional major undertaking.[20] More than a dozen European companies showed interest in bidding for the

buy-back projects, despite the U.S. government's extraterritorial attempt to preclude foreign companies from operating in Iran. Under strong EU censure, the United States has had to modify its sanctions; in early 2000, it sees its efforts hurting U.S. companies and foreign relations.[21]

Fields and Facilities. Most of Iran's oil fields are located in linear northwest-southeast reservoirs paralleling the Zagrosian fold structures in the original discovery belt (Maps 8-2 and 22-3). After nearly a century of exploration, 28 onshore fields extend 600 miles/966 km from west of Khorramabad to Bandar-e Abbas and 12 offshore fields are widely scattered the full length of the Gulf on Iran's side of the median line. Onshore gas fields are concentrated at the northwestern and southeastern ends of the oil belt (Map 8-2). Virtually no onshore reservoirs have been found outside the Zagros folds. As in Saudi Arabia, overall central control of operations permits drilling only the optimum number of wells, so that in 1999, Iran produced from just 1,120 wells, some of which still yield thousands of barrels a day after 80 years.

Oil and natural gas pipelines form a dense network in the closely packed fields of Khuzistan and adjacent areas. Most of the lines feed the Kharg Island export terminal northwest of Bushehr, which compares with Ras Tanura and Juaymah in Saudi Arabia as being among the world's three largest export terminals. Numerous other lines carry feedstock to the refinery on Abadan Island, on the east bank of the Shatt al-Arab, one of the two largest in the Gulf world, processing 400,000 bpd. Among the country's nine refineries, with a total capacity of 1.5 million bpd, the three next largest after Abadan are in Esfahan, Bandar-e Abbas, and Tehran.

Increasing wealth in natural gas gave new directions to the country's hydrocarbon industry and national economy. After installation of only a skeletal pipeline net, gas could replace oil for generating electric power, supply a major new export, permit widespread distribution of bottled LPG for domestic use and for use in automobiles, and, with more pipelines, gradually supply natural gas to cities and towns.

MAP 22-3 Economic map of Iran, showing major oil fields and facilities, solid mineral deposits, ports, and railways.

Some of this potential has been realized: Most of Iran's power plants now use gas. By the late 1990s, more than 300 cities were receiving piped gas, up from 6 before 1978. As one phase of the program to reduce serious pollution in the capital, more than 90 percent of Tehran's taxis run on LPG. Also, huge quantities of gas are reinjected into oil fields in EOR efforts.[22]

As early as 1970, Iran opened a 40–42-in./ 102–107-cm pipeline, IGAT-1, from its southwestern fields to northern Iran and onward into the southwestern areas of the former

USSR. IGAT-2, from the Kangan gas field on the Gulf south of Shiraz to Astara, where the Azerbaijan border meets the Caspian Sea coast, opened in 1992 under the aegis of the recently formed National Iranian Gas Company (NIGC). The IGAT-2 diameter is a huge 56 in./ 142 cm to Qazvin, northwest of Tehran, and 48 in./122 cm from Qazvin to Astara. In early 2000, Iran had tentative agreements with Turkey and Armenia for their importation of Iranian natural gas. Plans for an IGAT-3 line from offshore gas fields to Turkey are under consideration. However, Iran faces competition from Caspian Central Asia gas producers. Further to utilize its plentiful hydrocarbon wealth, Iran has inaugurated an extensive integrated program to construct ten new petrochemical plants, with Bandar-e Khomeini (sometimes Bandar-e Imam) as a special petrochemical economic zone. The National Petrochemical Company is offering attractive inducements to foreign companies to join the program over the next several years. Using petroleum and natural gas to produce petrochemicals has many advantages, including adding considerable value to plentiful raw materials and avoiding restrictions imposed by the OPEC quota for petroleum production.[23]

Non-Oil Resources

Scattered mineral deposits, especially copper, were mined in ancient times on the Iranian Plateau. However, few commercially significant deposits had been identified in recent decades until modern technology, including space imagery, was applied to the exploration of the highly mineralized volcanic belt in Iran near the tectonic plate boundary along the inner Zagros. In this intensive study, geologists discovered one deposit after another—copper, iron, chrome, lead, zinc, bauxite, manganese, coal, barite—approximately along the axis of the railway from Qom to Kerman. Numerous finds have been commercially exploited, some on a large scale. Iran possesses an array of mineral raw materials for eventual domestic use and export (see Map 22-3).

The most important discoveries were of copper, scattered along the entire length of the inner Zagros volcanic belt from the northwestern border to south of Bam in the southeast. Of total copper reserves of 2.6 billion tons, the largest deposits are at Sar Cheshmeh, southwest of Kerman, which some Western engineers claim are the richest in the world. An integrated mining, smelting, and refining operation that is one of Iran's major projects has exploited the resources, and a new smelter has opened at Khatounabad, near Sar Cheshmeh. Mining at

Ahar, north of Tabriz, has been expanded. Iran is aiming for an annual output of 250,000 tons a year in 2000.

Other metallic minerals found in quantity include ores of iron, chrome, zinc, lead, manganese, and aluminum. A remarkable concentration exists near Bafq, southeast of Yazd, and the same area is the location of Iran's main iron ores and major deposits of lead-zinc ores, not far from large coal resources. Iron is transported to the Esfahan steel works by rail from Bafq, and still richer iron ore resources of 1.13 billion tons at Gol-e Gohar, south of Sirjan, are being mined to feed both the Esfahan and the Ahvaz plants. Several major chrome deposits south and southeast of Kerman yield ores for export and for smelting near Bandar-e Abbas. The aluminum industry has burgeoned as smelters have expanded to 120,000 tons a year at Arak, southwest of Hamadan, and 220,000 tons a year at Bandar-e Abbas.

Important nonmetallic minerals include coal; the largest deposits are northwest of Kerman, but more than a score of collieries also extend across northern Iran from Lake Urmia to Mashhad. Fine turquoise from Neyshabur, west of Mashhad, is used in a variety of locally crafted jewelry, although some turquoise is exported; inexhaustible supplies of salt occur in the numerous salt plugs near Bandar-e Abbas, with native sulfur from many of the same structures supplying an important export item; and kaolin, near Qom, is used in the large ceramics industry. Decorative tiles made with Qom kaolin are used in walls, floors, and even house facades, giving Iranian houses a distinctive appearance.

Industries

Industrialization of Iran, under the shah's initiative during the 1960s, proceeded on a scale that observers considered unrealistic, demanding too much too fast. Plans produced large-scale projects with inadequate infrastructure, inducing Shii fundamentalist charges of "Westoxication" and anti-Islamic policies. Nevertheless, an appreciable number and variety of major industries were successfully established,

FIGURE 22-4   Hand-knotting an especially large and fine rug in an Esfahan workshop. Three young girls are guided by two adult women. Hand-made carpets are the second-ranking export of Iran.

from food processing to iron and steel production to automobile assembly. Joint ventures with foreign corporations brought transfers of technology and training programs for Iranian labor, even though few ventures achieved planned production levels.

After 1978, few of the new industrial establishments sustained production as a result of the unreliable labor supply and shortages of raw materials, spare parts, and other inputs. The war with Iraq also skewed production and forced emphasis on wartime requirements. Inauguration of the Five-Year Development Plan, 1989–1993, brought a shift in development strategy and economic policy, but significant strides came more in the next plan during the mid-1990s. By that time the government recognized the imperative need for industrial revitalization and the necessity to deregulate and deregiment the industrial sector. Privatization of at least one-fourth of the state-owned

enterprises was in progress, and selected foreign interests were cautiously being allowed to join the industrial development.

The industries of Iran are widely distributed in the western third of the country, including cities along the inner Zagros axis. Many of the manufacturing plants are concentrated around Tehran, and light industries and craft shops are found in dozens of towns and even villages. Major products include processed foods and beverages, cigarettes, home appliances, assembled automobiles, textiles, and machine tools. Iran is especially noted for its wide variety of hand-knotted Persian rugs, jewelry, metalwares, inlaid items, and decorated ceramic tiles (Fig. 22-4).

The Tehran region, including the western suburb of Karaj, is the dominant manufacturing focus of the country, including auto assembly plants, household appliance factories, and clothing factories. Esfahan, the second-largest industrial center, has the country's major iron and steel plant, cotton mills, and numerous small shops producing metal household items, including brass and copper trays (Fig. 9-2). Tabriz, with a major machine tool plant, is the industrial center of the northwest. Arak, southwest of Qom, has one of Iran's aluminum smelters, and about 60 percent of its output is exported. Still other cities with appreciable manufacturing plants are shown in Map 22-3, which emphasizes the concentration in the western third of Iran and the isolation of Mashhad in the far northeast. Noteworthy are the famed rug-producing centers of Tabriz, Ardabil, Hamadan, Qom, Kashan, Esfahan, Nain, Shiraz, Kerman, and Mashhad.

Transportation and Trade

Land Routes. Economic development in the 1930s and even after World War II was inhibited by a limited infrastructure, and construction of a transportation net was both difficult and expensive. Terrain, climate, and distance combine to constrain construction of transportation routes, even if financing and engineering skills are available. By the 1980s, however, all cities had been integrated into a systematic highway network, well engineered and well constructed by European companies under contract. The net penetrates all parts of the country except the virtually uninhabited east-central interior basins (see Map 22-1).

The railway through the Zagros between Dezful and Qom was extended during World War II through Tabriz to the then Soviet border for the shipment of war matériel by the Allies to the Soviet Union. As part of the CENTO and RCD (Regional Cooperation for Development) railway from Istanbul to Karachi in Pakistan, a link was constructed to the Turkish border in the northwest and from Qom through Kashan and Yazd to Kerman. After long delays, the extension from Kerman and Bam to Zahedan was recently completed, thus connecting Istanbul and Tehran with Quetta and Karachi. In addition, a major link has been constructed from Bafq (between Yazd and Kerman) through

the mountains to Bandar-e Abbas. In the extreme northeast, a short but strategic link in the late 1990s has extended the main line from Tehran through Mashhad to Sarakhs, on the Turkmenistan border. From there, the Trans-Asian railway continues along the old Silk Road to Mary, Bukhara, Samarkand, and Tashkent. Iran has thus positioned itself to serve as a strategic area connecting Central Asia to the Gulf and beyond.

Ports. Despite a coastline of 1,555 miles/ 2,500 km from the Shatt al-Arab to the Pakistan border, Iran has surprisingly few good harbors for large port installations. Since the main population and development centered near the head of the Gulf even in antiquity, most of Iran's major ports lie in the arc from Khorramshahr to Bushehr, including the main oil export terminal of Kharg Island. In the north, Bandar-e Khomenei (formerly Bandar-e Shahpur) was expanded during the 1990s to serve also as a burgeoning petrochemical center. Farther south, Bandar-e Bushehr is the site of Iran's 1,000-megawatt nuclear reactor, still under construction after many years. Bandar-e Abbas was expanded during the war with Iraq and is now connected by a branch rail link from the main line through central Iran; it serves as a major general cargo port, passenger port for cross-Gulf traffic, and Iran's main naval base, which guards the Strait of Hormuz. Chah Bahar (sometimes Bandar Beheshti) was developed during the 1980–1988 war as an outlet on the Indian Ocean for the southeast (see Map 22-3). On the Caspian coast, Bandar-e Anzali is the leading port for fishing and trade with the other Caspian Sea littorals.

Trade. Although in normal times Iran's imports include a range of contemporary industrial and consumer goods, the country's exports are overwhelmingly petroleum, petroleum products, and related items, by both volume and value (see Country Summary). Petroleum customers vary appreciably from year to year, but regularly include Japan, Britain, South Korea, Germany, and Turkey.

Imported products—machinery, iron and steel products, transport equipment, grains, textiles, and chemicals—come primarily from Germany, Japan, Italy and UAE. Weapons and ammunition have been a substantial share of imports during the last three decades, and armaments imports in the 1990s approached the high level reached under the shah in the 1970s. Despite its condemnation of the former regime for squandering Iranian wealth on weapons, the revolutionary government was importing a wide range of armaments, as well as machine tools for producing armaments, from Russia, China, and North Korea.[24] Russia and China also supplied nuclear technology.

Regional and Global Relations

Long before petroleum was found in southwestern Iran, the Iranian Plateau played an important geopolitical role both locally and internationally. On the contemporary scene, Iran's geopolitical position, place in world oil and global finances, human resources, and aggressively idiosyncratic approach to internal and external relations converge to make Iran a mutually vital partner in dozens of global relationships. The links are multidirectional and multifaceted, and some are global, involving governments from Washington to Brussels to Beijing to Tokyo. Internal struggles between militant conservatives and pragmatic moderates inhibit stable economic and diplomatic links with other governments.

United States.   Crucial as relations with Iraq and the GCC may be, those with the United States have been the most influential for half a century. The mutually hostile current U.S.-Iranian attitudes stand in marked contrast to those of the 25 years following the U.S. CIA's aiding the restoration of the shah to power in 1953. By the 1960s, Iran as "this island of stability" in the Middle East became the U.S. "chosen instrument"—as it was referred to at the time. It was the eastern anchor of the U.S. geopolitical position in the region; Northern Iran was a

vital U.S. intelligence listening post for Soviet rocket launches in Kazakhstan, for example. Thousands of American technicians, advisers, and commercial representatives and their families lived in Iran. Huge quantities of sophisticated U.S. military equipment poured into the country, along with training personnel to prepare Iran for a leading role in the Gulf. Some critics accused the United States not only of winking at widespread abuses of human rights by the shah but also of contributing to them. As the shah's main supporter and the main contributor to the "Westoxification" of Iran, the United States became the main target of the Islamic revolution in 1978–1979. In the backlash against the earlier U.S. role, the revolutionaries designated America as "the Great Satan" and seized the American Embassy, as was described earlier. The acrimonious break in U.S.-Iranian relations was further embittered by U.S. tilting toward Iraq during the 1980s and, in a tragic case of mistaken identity, by the shooting down of an Iranian civil aircraft in July 1988 by a U.S. naval vessel. Such acrimony has continued to characterize relations for 20 years. Iran is coupled with Iraq in the U.S. "dual containment" policy, which designates both states as rogue supporters of terrorism and as governments seeking to develop weapons of mass destruction. Under the more liberal President Khatami, elected in 1997, Iran and the United States have broached a détente several times, but side issues have revived mutual recriminations.[25] (But see epilogue.)

Regional.   Although revolutionary Iran withdrew from the Central Treaty Organization in 1979 and thereby precipitated CENTO's collapse, Iran continued to maintain ties with Turkey and Pakistan; it also loosely continued its participation in the Regional Cooperation for Development (RCD), later the Economic Cooperation Organization (ECO—see Chap. 11). ECO provides the Central Asian republics with more direct access to the sea through Iran and Pakistan than they had as constituent republics of the former Soviet Union.[26] Most members also signed the rail agreement involving the Trans-Asian railway mentioned above, and Iran finds a strong attraction toward the old Silk Road. The Caspian Basin states, resources, and problems are matters of priority in the Iranian grand strategy, and in early 1992 Iran promoted a new Caspian Council grouping Iran, Azerbaijan, Turkmenistan, Kazakhstan, and Russia.

Sunni, but secular, Turkey contrasts with contemporary Iran, but recent Turkish moves toward Islamism pleased Iran even if the moves were short-lived. Iran and Turkey share certain problems regarding their Kurdish minorities, and they compete in the Republic of Azerbaijan. Already well-linked by railway and highway, the two neighbors have tentatively agreed to Iran's eventually supplying natural gas to Turkey, although Iran objects to the growing Turkish-Israel military and economic cooperation (Chap. 21). Similarly, Iran maintains good relations with the contiguous Islamic Republic of Pakistan to the southeast, with whom it shares a tug-of-war between conservatism and moderation. One contention is Sunni Pakistan's support of the Sunni Taliban in Afghanistan and Shii Iran's strong opposition to it. Iran is concerned that the instability introduced into the Afghan situation by the Taliban jeopardizes Iran's security. Indeed, skirmishes between Taliban and Iranian forces on the Afghan border in October 1998 raised fears of open warfare, but Iran has no desire to replicate the Soviet experience in the Afghan quagmire.

But it is with its western neighbor, Iraq, that Iran has long had the bitterest and most persistent conflict, a prolongation of the millennia-old cleavage between the Iranian Plateau and Mesopotamian Basin; the bloody eight-year war of the 1980s was a resumption of the proxy war of the mid-1970s. Relations continue to fester, although Iraq permitted Iranian pilgrims to visit Shii holy shrines in Iraq in September 1997 (for the first time since 1980), and Iran and Iraq exchanged some prisoners of war in April 1998.

The GCC members are states with whom Iran should logically maintain intimate relations; but connections have been strained from the beginning of the GCC, especially since the GCC supported sister Arab state Iraq against Iran in the 1990s. Further, the Council was partly organized as a common defense against Iranian threats. Nevertheless, Iran sought cordial links with the GCC as a group and as individual states after 1988 and especially after 1990. Relations were broken with Saudi Arabia in 1988 because of violence involving Iranians in Mecca, but they were restored in 1991. In the late 1990s, the two neighbors restored civil air flights and maritime connections, made high-level visits, and in May 1998 signed agreements on trade and cultural exchanges. The UAE and Iran have long held close trade ties but have contended over Abu Musa and Tunbs islands, discussed earlier.

Iran's curious ties with Syria continue to be cordial, and relations with arch-enemy Egypt have even warmed under the deft handling of President Khatami. Israel, on the other hand, continues to be acrimoniously reviled at least in public, in contrast to the pre-1979 cordial informal relations between Israel and Iran, when Israel sent technicians to Iran and Iran shipped petroleum to Elat. (See the epilogue.) During the 1990s, Israel battled Iranian-supported Hizballah guerrillas in its strip of occupation in south Lebanon.

Global. Links with Russia are generally cordial, in contrast to the suspicions and tensions that marked relations during the Cold War; at that time, Iran was a vital geopolitical player as a key member of the Baghdad Pact/CENTO and the Northern Tier in concert with the United States to contain Soviet influence and expansionism. As an offset to its enmity with the United States, revolutionary Iran cautiously established a military-economic link with Russia, which supplies large amounts of heavy armaments and is engaged in completion of the Bushehr nuclear reactor. Iran maintains a similar link with China, which supplies arms and also constructs major industrial plants in Iran. Iran's long-standing mutually beneficial relations with Western European states and, more recently, with the EU as an entity, see-sawed during the 1990s but ended the decade as cordial. Ayatollah Khomeini's *fatwa* offering a huge reward for the assassination of Salman Rushdie, author of *The Satanic Verses,* was a major obstacle for several years. Iran withdrew the reward in 1999, but it later equivocated about the *fatwa.* Iran's role in the assassination of four Kurdish dissidents in a Berlin restaurant in 1992 placed another damper on relations for some time. Europe buys 60 percent of Iran's petroleum exports, and Germany is Iran's main trading partner.[27]

Notes

1. See Limbert 1987, Chapters 1 and 2.

2. For a focus on Fars, see Summers 1986. For general coverage of archaeological sites, see Matheson 1973.

3. Limbert 1987, covers these developments as well as Iran in general, including Iran-zamin. The role of the American CIA in the shah's restoration became and is still an issue of bitterness among Iranians, especially Khomeini revolutionaries.

4. Amuzegar "Islamic Fundamentalism ..." 1995, 26 and 22–23.

5. See Fairbanks 1997 and Amuzegar 1995. For later more specific developments, see *Economist,* Aug. 21, 1999.

6. *New York Times,* July 15, 1999, covers the crisis in detail. See also *Economist,* May 15 and July 17, 1999.

7. *New York Times,* Aug. 29, 1999, and *Christian Science Monitor,* Dec. 7, 1999.

8. An excellent, comprehensive coverage of Iran's geography is in W. B. Fisher 1968. A concise treatment is given in Limbert 1987, Chapter 1.

9. In addition to the standard Defense Mapping Agency 1985, see Adamec 1976–1988. Numerous place names were changed by the revolutionary Iranian authorities (see A Note on Transliteration). Some names seem to have been changed back to the originals. Kermanshah (city) was renamed Bakhtaran then re-renamed Kermanshah. Chah Bahar was renamed Bandar Beheshti, but is now shown as Chabahar. Other re-renamings can be expected.

10. Montaigne 1999 discusses this topic and pictures northern Tehran.

11. Detailed studies are in Krinsley 1970.

12. The populations given for Turkey, Egypt, and Iran are all estimates, and actual totals almost certainly shift periodically among the three in rankings.

Three reliable sources estimated Iran's population as 61.5 million, 65.2 million, and 67.3 million. It might be advisable to say that Turkey, Iran, and Egypt all have populations of about 63–65 million.

13. Useful studies regarding Iranian settlements are Bonine 1979, English 1966, and Kheirabadi 1991.

14. Concise discussion of peoples and their distribution is given in Limbert 1987 and *Iran* Country Study 1989.

15. So many Armenians were employed in the American Embassy in Tehran before 1979 because of their education and adaptability, that some wags referred to it as the Armenian Embassy.

16. *Economist,* Feb. 13, 1987, and *Christian Science Monitor,* Feb. 3, 1998.

17. *Christian Science Monitor,* Feb. 3, 1998, and Oct. 26, 1999; *New York Times,* June 10, 1999, and Oct. 17, 1999 (lengthy review); and *Economist,* June 19, 1999.

18. See Bonine and Keddie, 1981; Limbert 1987, Chapters 1, 5, and 6; and *Iran* Country Study 1989, especially Chapter 3.

19. The intricacies of the Iranian economy are followed in *Iran* Country Study 1989; Amirahmadi 1990; and Amuzegar 1992, a concise comparison of pre- and post-revolutionary conditions, updated in his Amuzegar 1995 and 1999; from all of which I have drawn.

20. These plans are detailed in *Oil and Gas Journal,* Sept. 13, 1999, 27–30, and Sept. 27, 1999, 28.

21. See, among many articles on the situation, the editorial in *Oil and Gas Journal,* Dec. 6, 1999, which notes that Iran and the United States "...mutually spoil potential for a relationship from which both would benefit." It ends commenting that "...neither side is right."

22. *Oil and Gas Journal,* Sept. 27, 1999, 28.

23. A detailed study is *Oil and Gas Journal,* Aug. 16 and Aug. 23, 1999.

24. *New York Times,* Nov. 7, 1992. See also Monshipouri 1998.

25. For a penetrating study of these relations by a leading scholar, see Bill 1988. *Middle East Policy* 3, no. 1 (1994) has a debate on "dual containment" in "U.S. Policy toward Iran and Iraq" among four experts. For later developments, see Amuzegar 1998, "Khatami's Iran"; "Next Steps with Iran," 1998; Monshipouri 1998; and Ramazani 1998.

26. See Ramazani 1992 and Monshipouri 1998.

27. Iran's foreign relations in general are discussed in the sources cited in Note 25 above. Relations with Israel are discussed in Sohrab Sobhani, "The Course of Iranian-Israeli Relations," *Middle East Insight,* Nov.–Dec. 1999, 39–40.

GLOSSARY

See Index for page number of main discussion of most terms. For names of geological time periods (Pleistocene, Cretaceous, etc.), see the geological time chart at the end of this glossary.

Abbasid: pertaining to the Muslim Empire ruled by the Abbasid dynasty from Baghdad AD 750–1258.

Al, al-: uppercased and not hyphenated, connotes "family of, belonging to," as in Al Saud, Al Jabbar. Lowercased, represents definite article "the," as in al-Khalij, "the Gulf" (usually connected to the noun by hyphen).

Aliyah: literally, "ascent, going up," the immigration of Jews to Eretz Ysrael, the Land of Israel (*see also* olim).

Allah: God.

Alluvial: pertaining to river-deposited materials, especially fine silt and silt-clay laid down on floodplains and deltas such as those of the Nile.

Amir (emir): commander, prince, ruler. May have, but need not have, territorial jurisdiction.

Amirate (emirate): realm of an amir. In lower Gulf, also called shaykhdom.

Ashkenazim: Jews from central or eastern Europe, directly or by descent.

Ayatollah: "the sign of God." Title of respect for upper-ranking Shii clergyman. One title for the late Ruhollah Khomeini, former Iranian revolutionary leader.

Ayn: flowing spring, open sinkhole water supply, or flowing artesian spring.

Baath: Arab Renaissance [Revival] Party, separate branches of which control the governments of Iraq and Syria.

Basalt: a common type of lava—dark, fine-grained, extrusive volcanic rock. In original molten state, flows readily from fissures; covers large areas of the Levant and western Arabia.

Basement (or basement complex): massive, very ancient igneous and metamorphic rocks, usually Precambrian, very complex and underlying sedimentary strata.

Bbl: barrel, barrels. Standard barrel of oil contains 42 U.S. gal. (34.97 UK or imperial gal.).

Bedouin: pastoral Arab nomad of the desert; corruption of Ar. for "desert dweller."

Bpd: barrels per day (usually oil production).

C°: temperature in degrees Celsius or centigrade. Temperature in C° = Fahrenheit° minus 32 times 5/9. Temperature in F° = C° times 9/5 plus 32.

Caliph: from Ar. *khalifah*, "successor"—i.e., successor to Muhammad as head of the community of Islam, the *ummah* (q.v.).

Cuesta: linear ridge with steep escarpment on foreslope and with gentle backslope. Asymmetry results from erosion of outcrop of gently dipping resistant stratum. Successive cuestas are prominent features of central Arabia.

Dağ (dagh): Turkish for "mountain."

Desert: any area with scanty rainfall, little vegetation, and therefore limited agricultural use. May be plain, plateau, or mountains at any latitude. Area in Koeppen's BWh group (see Map 4-3).

DFLP: Democratic Front for the Liberation of Palestine, one of the more aggressive Palestinian guerrilla groups.

Dhow: general term for several types of traditional coastal sailing ships plying the waters around the Arabian Peninsula and parts of Indian Ocean. Term not used by Arabs, who employ specific names for different types: boom, sambook, and others.

Diaspora: dispersion. Usually refers to the dispersion of Jews from Palestine after AD 70. Also, Jews now outside Palestine constitute the Diaspora. Palestinian refugees sometimes apply the term to

513

their dispersion and community outside Palestine.

Diastrophism: from Grk. for "distortion, dislocation." Processes that have deformed the earth's crust, producing continents, ocean basins, mountains, folded strata, and other major features. Orogeny (q.v.) is one type of diastrophism.

Dirah: traditionally accepted tribal range of the Bedouin tribe.

Diurnal: daily, occurring daily, or having a daily cycle; e.g., the range of high and low temperatures during a 24-hour period.

Dolomite: light-colored stratified sedimentary rock similar to limestone but high in calcium magnesium carbonate rather than the calcium carbonate of limestone.

Dunum: a unit of land area measurement common in Palestine and Jordan. Equivalency varies between 900 m² and 1,000 m² but is most commonly 919 m² (0.23 acre, 0.0919 ha).

Dwt: deadweight tons (maritime shipping).

Enosis: union of Cyprus with Greece.

Entrepôt: center—usually a city and often a port city—that receives goods in transit, warehouses them, and reships them.

Ethnolinguistic: pertaining to a distinct people (ethnic group) whose distinguishing characteristic is especially language, although other criteria may also make them distinctive (e.g., Armenians).

EU: European Union, successor to European Community (1993).

Expatriate: one who lives in a foreign country. Many Europeans, Americans, and South Asians work and live in several Middle East countries as expatriates (informally called "expats").

Extrusive: pertaining to pouring out of molten rock (lava) onto the earth's surface, where it solidifies; opposite is intrusive (e.g., granite). *See* basalt.

Falaj (**pl.** *aflaj*): *see* qanat.

Faluqa (**felucca**): traditional sailboat on the Nile and seas adjacent to Egypt, carries lateen sail.

Farsi: Persian, i.e., the language spoken by Persians.

al-Fatah (Fateh): palindromic acronym for *Harakat al-Tahrir al-Filastiniyya* (Palestinian Liberation Movement), a guerrilla group formed several years before the PLO. Power base for Yasser Arafat, one of Fatah's founders.

Fault: surface of fracture in rock involving vertical or horizontal (or both) displacement of rock on either side of the fault plane; result of tectonic strain in earth's crust. Faulting is a major cause of earthquakes (seismic crustal tremors). With horizontal shearing, a fault is left-lateral if displacement is to the left of an observer looking across the fault line. *See also* transform fault.

Fedayeen (*fidayyin*): From Ar. for "sacrificers," usually applied to Palestinian guerrillas or to Shii fundamentalist fighters.

Feddan: a unit of land-area measurement used in Egypt, equal to 1.038 acres or 4,201 m².

Feedstock: raw material for a processing plant, often applied to crude oil or natural gas for a refinery or petrochemical plant.

Fellah (pl. fellahin): roughly equivalent to peasant, from Ar. for "tiller of the soil."

Fertile Crescent: modern term for arcuate area extending from Gaza northward and northeastward across northern Syria and southeastward along Zagros piedmont (see Map 2-1), believed to be where Neolithic farming evolved.

Garigue: stunted evergreen dry scrub vegetation on limestone in drier areas of Mediterranean climate in Asia Minor and the Levant (cf. maquis).

Gawr (**gor, khawr khor**): river floodplain, narrow coastal indentation, or flat-bottomed valley.

GCC: Gulf Cooperation Council, short form of Cooperation Council for the Arab States of the Gulf, formed in 1981 and including Saudi Arabia, Kuwait, Bahrain, Qatar, the UAE, and Oman.

GDP: gross domestic product, total value of goods and services produced by residents and nonresidents within a given country in a given year.

Gecekondu: Turkish for "built overnight," applied to spontaneous settlements built illegally on the peripheries of Turkish cities.

Geomorphology: "earth form," the earth science dealing with the origin and development of earth landforms; somewhat related to the older term "physiography."

Gneiss: coarse-grained crystalline rock usually with streaked or banded black-white-gray appearance. The product of dynamic metamorphism of granites and other igneous rocks. *See also* schist.

GNP: gross national product, total value of goods and services produced both from within a given country and from external (foreign) transactions in a given year.

Gondwana: a conjectured single landmass in Paleozoic times from which the southern continents are theorized to have been formed. *See* plate tectonics.

GOSP: gas-oil separator plant, an oil-field facility serving several producing wells to separate dissolved natural gas from the crude petroleum.

Graben: narrow, down-dropped block of the earth's surface bounded by parallel faults; related to rift valley. *See* rift.

Granite: intrusive igneous rock of various colors and grain size.

Hajj: the Muslim pilgrimage to Mecca, an obligation required in the Quran and one of the pillars of Islam.

Halacha (halakah): generally, Jewish religious law.

Hamadah: a rock desert with barren, wind-scoured bedrock surface and little sand. There is an extensive *hamadah* where Arabia, Jordan, and Iraq meet.

Hamas: acronym for *Harakat al-Muqawama al-Islamiyya* (Islamic Resistance Movement), extremist group, one of several Palestinian resistance groups in West Bank and Gaza Strip.

Hammam: bath, bathing facilities, and/or toilet facilities.

Harem: quarters in a Muslim household set aside for women and children.

Hashimite (Hashemite): pertaining to descent from Hashim or the Hashimite clan, which included Muhammad's family and which was part of the Quraysh tribe; commonly pertaining to dynasty in Jordan and, before 1958, in Iraq.

Hectare: international unit of land area measurement, 10,000 m^2 or 2.47 acres.

Hegira (hejira): from Ar. *hijrah*, "flight"; the flight of Muhammad and his followers from Mecca to Yathrib (renamed Medina) in AD 622, which marked the beginning of the Islamic calendar.

Hizb Allah **(Hizballah, from Arabic; Hezbollah, from Farsi):** Party of God, a group in Lebanon comprising Shii extremists who were involved in seizing hostages in the late 1980s and then conducted guerrilla warfare against Israelis and their proxy South Lebanon Army in the self-declared Israeli security zone, from which Israel withdrew in May 2000.

Horst: opposite of graben (q.v.); an uplifted block roughly paralleled by faults.

Igneous: pertaining to molten or formerly molten rock material, either extrusive (on the earth's surface) or intrusive (underground rock masses). Types include lava (extrusive) and granite (intrusive).

Imam: Shii religious or, sometimes, political leader; commonly, the leader of Muslim worship services; technically, one of the succession of Shii leaders who, beginning with Ali, are accepted by Shii as the legitimate successors of Muhammad.

Infitah: Ar. for "opening," i.e., economic opening in post-Nasserist Egypt.

Interfluve: linear area lying between roughly parallel rivers, e.g., the location of Baghdad between the Tigris and Euphrates rivers.

Intermontane: between mountains, usually a plateau between mountain ranges, e.g., the Anatolian and Iranian plateaus.

Intifadah: Ar. for "uprising," the rebellion of young rock-throwing Palestinians in the Gaza Strip (especially) and West Bank during the period late 1987 to late 1992.

Iranian: pertaining to the country of Iran or to its citizens of whatever ethnic group (not equivalent to Persian).

Islam: "submission," the submission of the followers of Islam to the will of God (Allah).

Islamism: a complex ensemble of ideological extensions of Islam into political action, return to fundamentals ("Islamic fundamentalism"), resurgence or renaissance of Islamic ideals, revolutionary Islam, and others, sometimes through extremist and violent methods. A devotee is an Islamist.

Isobar: line on a map connecting points of equal barometric pressure.

Isohyet: line on a map connecting points of equal precipitation (see Map 4-2).

Isotherm: line on a map connecting points of equal temperature (see Map 4-1).

Jabal **(jebel):** Ar. for "hill," "mountain."

Jamii (camii): Ar. for "mosque," often for the main or Friday mosque in a city. *See* masjid.

Jihad: Ar. for struggle on behalf of righteousness, especially within Islam; translation as "holy war" is rather ambiguous and focuses on only one aspect.

Karst: limestone or dolomite landscape subjected to carbonation-solution and having underground drainage, caverns, sinkholes, and other typical surface features.

Kavir: Pers. for "salt flat," "salt waste," "playa." *Kavirs* are numerous and extensive in eastern, interior Iran.

Khawr (khor): *see gawr.*

Kilometer: international unit of distance measurement equaling 1,000 m, 0.6214 mile, 0.5399 nautical mile.

Knesset: Israeli parliament.

Kufiyah: common traditional male Arab headdress, a large square of cloth folded diagonally and worn with straight edge over the forehead. Usually white in Gulf area, red checkered or black and white in the Levant, but colors and patterns vary among localities. Called *ghutrah* in Saudi Arabia.

Lava: extrusive igneous rock that flows onto earth's surface while molten. *See* basalt.

Levant: eastern Mediterranean coastal region, roughly the maximum area held by the Crusader states; comprising western Syria, Lebanon, Palestine, and western Jordan.

Lingua franca: a language or composite language spoken as a common tongue among several language groups in a given region.

Lithosphere: outermost shell of the earth's layers, 10–30 miles/16–48 km thick, comprising several rigid "plates" floating on the partly molten asthenosphere. *See* plate tectonics.

Littoral: of or pertaining to the shore (of seas or lakes).

Loess: fine, coherent, porous yellowish dust believed to have been picked up from barren areas by the wind and redeposited in amorphous layers nearby. Serves as parent material for fine-textured, deep, well-drained soils.

LPG: liquefied petroleum gas, primarily propane and butane, derived from NGL (q.v.).

Madrasa (medrese): Muslim school, originally one attached to a mosque for religious training. Now used more generally.

Maghrib (Maghreb): Ar. for "west" and applied to the western Arab states in northwestern Africa: Morocco, Algeria, Tunisia, and sometimes Libya.

Majlis (mejlis): from general Ar.-Pers. term for gathering, gathering place, reception; hence, an official reception room or audience of a ruler or tribal shaykh. In some countries, the consultative or legislative assembly, e.g., Iran, Kuwait.

Mamluk: lit. "slave," but applied to Turkish and Circassian slave military oligarchy that ruled Egypt 1250–1517; also architecture and other aspects of the period.

Mandate: in the Middle East, a commission awarded by the League of Nations to Britain or France to administer an assigned territory toward timely independence; also the polity so administered under this commission (Palestine, Transjordan, and Iraq by Britain; Syria and Lebanon by France).

Maquis: a low evergreen scrub vegetation typical of better Mediterranean climate areas of western and southern Asia Minor and the Levant; includes oleander, rosemary, myrtle, and similar plants and is a higher-order plant association than garigue (q.v.).

Mashriq: Ar. for "east" and sometimes applied to the eastern Arab states in the Middle East as defined in this book. Less common term than Maghrib (q.v.).

Masjid: Ar./Pers. for "mosque." *See* jamii.

Massif: general term applied to a compact upland mass.

Mawali: "clients"; non-Arab converts to Islam during early period of the Muslim conquests; soon out-numbered Arab Muslims (*ummah,* q.v.).

Maydan: Ar./Pers. for an urban open area or city square, typical of the traditional Islamic city.

Mesolithic: Middle Stone Age, sometimes called Epipaleolithic; transitional between Paleolithic and Neolithic periods and dated roughly 12,000–8,000 BC.

Metamorphic: pertaining to rocks whose original structure has been altered by great earth pressures (dynamic metamorphism) and/or by heat (thermal metamorphism), producing compact and resistant rock types (e.g., gneiss, schist, quartzite, marble).

Meter (metre): the basic international unit of measurement equaling 1,000 mm, 100 cm, or 3.28 ft.

Millet **(mil-let):** under the Ottomans, self-administered non-Muslim religious community (e.g., Jews, Christians), a logical extension of the early Muslim concept of "people of the book."

Mina: coastal inlet and, by derivation, port.

Minaret: tower associated with a mosque from which the call to prayer for the Muslim faithful is intoned at least five times daily by a muazzin (q.v.).

Mizrahim: Eastern or Oriental Jew, recently adopted term to distinguish Middle East/North African Jews in Israel from Ashkenazim (q.v.) and Sephardim (q.v.). Formerly grouped with Sephardim.

Monsoon: from Ar. word for "season"; the seasonal reversal of pressure and winds, especially across southern and eastern Asia; generally applied to rains typical of summer season in Asia and to winds in both summer and winter.

Muazzin (muadhdhin, muezzin): especially trained man who intones calls to prayer for the Muslim faithful from a minaret five times daily.

Muhammadan: loosely applied to follower of Muhammad, but preferred term is Muslim (q.v.).

Muslim: an adherent of Islam (q.v.), "one who submits"—to the will of God.

Nakbah: Ar. for "catastrophe," the establishment of the state of Israel in Palestinian areas and the displacement of Palestinian Arabs from their lands and homes.

Neolithic: New Stone Age, beginning roughly 8,000 BC and ending 4,000–5,000 years later as copper and bronze came into use for implements.

NGL: natural gas liquids, derived from natural gas and yielding ethane, propane, butane, natural gasoline, and related substances.

Nomad: member of a social group that regularly migrates over a traditional realm in search of pasture for their flocks. Bedouins (q.v.) are the best-known true nomads of the Middle East.

OAPEC: Organization of Arab Petroleum Exporting Countries (see Chap. 8).

Olim (sing. olah): "ascenders," Jewish immigrants to the Land of Israel (*see* aliyah).

OPEC: Organization of Petroleum Exporting Countries (see Chap. 8).

Orogeny: a major tectonic process of fold-mountain building.

Orographic: pertaining to mountains; e.g., orographic rainfall is caused by the uplift, hence cooling, of humid wind blowing up a mountain slope—the process producing virtually all heavier rains in the Middle East.

PFLP: Popular Front for the Liberation of Palestine, extremist Marxist Palestinian group known for earlier aircraft hijackings.

Plate tectonics: theory that the earth's crust (lithosphere) comprises about six main and several other minor rigid "plates" that broke away from one main mass and are now "drifting" slowly in respective directions (see Chap. 3).

PLO: Palestine Liberation Organization, formed in 1964, which became the umbrella organization for Palestinian aspirations; Yasser Arafat, chairman. Finally accepted by Israel as legitimate representatives of Palestinians for negotiations over future of remaining Palestinian lands, first in Oslo then for continuing peace process and for administration of Palestinian Authority.

Pluvial: rainy—pertaining to moister periods during the recent geological past, with such periods in the Middle East usually correlating with glacial advances and related climatic changes; opposed to alternating dry periods.

PNC: Palestine National Council.

Primate city: A city much larger—even many times larger—than any other city in the country and with a much greater range of economic and social activities. Term suggested by Mark Jefferson, 1939. Cairo, Baghdad, and Tehran are examples.

Ptolemaic: the Egyptian kingdom under the Hellenized dynasty of the Ptolemies, 323–30 BC.

Qanat: ditch, canal, tunnel; specifically, an underground tunnel-canal marked by a surface chain of wells; thousands of *qanats* are found on alluvial fans in Iran (see Fig. 22-3).

Qat: *Catha edulis*, a leafy plant grown on terraced hillsides in northern Yemen. *Qat* leaves are chewed by highland Yemeni men during afternoon hours for mild narcotic effect.

al-Quran (Koran): Ar. for "recitation"; Muslim holy scriptures, believed by Muslims to be the exact words of God revealed (or "recited") to the Prophet Muhammad through the angel Gabriel.

Ramadan: ninth month of the Islamic calendar, considered a holy month because Muhammad received the first revelations from Gabriel in Ramadan. During entire month, Muslims are obligated to observe absolute fasting between dawn and dusk. Such fasting is one of the pillars of Islam.

Rift: a narrow linear trough between parallel faults or along linear fissuring, e.g., the Levant Rift, a segment of the great rift from northern Syria to southern Africa.

Riparian: pertaining to riverbanks, especially rights of access to the river ("riparian rights") or occurring along rivers ("riparian powers"). As noun, persons or polity along a river.

Sabkhah (subkha): a flat area of salty silt, whether a tidal flat, salt flat between dunes, or former tidal flat now cut off from the sea (see Fig. 5-1).

Sabra: from Hebrew for "prickly pear," term for a native-born Israeli Jew.

Sanjak: provincial administrative district of the Ottoman Empire, administered by a sanjak bey, later by a mutassarif (e.g., Sanjak of Alexandretta).

Sassanian (Sassanid): pertaining to the Persian Empire or its ruling dynasty named after its founder, Sassan; empire lasted AD 227–651 (see Map 2-4D).

Saudi: concerning the central Arabian Peninsula dynastic family of Al Saud, the kingdom founded and ruled by members of Al Saud, or political policies of the dynasty; hence Saudi Arabia—Arabia of the Sauds.

Schist: fine-grained, foliated crystalline metamorphic rock of varying color. *See also* gneiss.

Sedimentary: formed of sediments—materials laid down usually in seawater but also in lakes and rivers or by wind—and usually stratified (e.g., limestone, shale, sandstone).

Seismic: pertaining to earth tremors or earthquakes.

Semitic: of or pertaining to the subfamily of the Afro-Asiatic language family that includes Arabic, Hebrew, and Aramaic languages; also pertaining to certain aspects of speakers of these languages, excluding racial characteristics.

Sephardim: technically, Jews from Spain or descended from Spanish Jews; by extension, "oriental" Jews (from North Africa, Middle East, and southern and central Asia). However, *see* Mizrahim.

Shah: Pers. for "king"; title of royal rulers of Iran until 1979.

Shariah: complex Muslim religious law and code of sociopolitical conduct and relations, derived primarily from the Quran and sunnah and secondarily from other traditions and opinions.

Shaykh (sheikh): lit. "elder," but specifically a term of respect and rank given to an Arab tribal leader; extended to the ruler of smaller states, which are then referred to as shaykhdoms (e.g., Bahrain, Qatar, also sometimes called amirates [q.v.]); further, by extension, a learned Muslim.

Shield: rigid mass of stable, ancient (Precambrian) rocks, usually greatly metamorphosed, forming the nucleus of a continent or subcontinent—e.g., the Nubian-Arabian Shield of the southwestern Middle East (see Chap. 3).

Shii (Shiite): from Ar. for "partisan," i.e., partisan of Ali, Muhammad's kinsman and son-in-law. Shiis believe Ali should have succeeded to leadership of the *ummah* (q.v.) upon Muhammad's death and that Ali and his several successors (Shii imams) are the only true heads of the *ummah*. See also Sunni.

Steppe: grassland, especially land of short grasses, thus indicating subhumid or semiarid climate (Koeppen BS); in the Middle East, transitional between desert and Mediterranean climate areas or other more humid areas.

Sultanate: realm of a sultan, a secular ruler equivalent to a king or other dynastic ruler.

Sunnah: *see* Sunni.

Sunni (Sunnite): Muslim who accepts the legitimacy of Muhammad's successors. So-called after "sunnah," the admonitions and examples of Muhammad regarding proper Muslim belief and conduct. *See also* Shii.

Suq: Ar. for "marketplace," comparable to Pers. "bazaar."

Tectonism (tectonic, tectonics): internal earth forces that build up, form, or deform the earth's surface or subsurface. *See* plate tectonics.

Tell: Ar. for "hill" or "mound," specifically a characteristic surface mound made up of accumulated layers of debris from successive human occupations of a settlement site over many centuries (see Chap. 2).

Transform fault: a fault zone involving mostly horizontal displacement along an edge of a tectonic plate, e.g., the San Andreas fault in California and the North Anatolian and East Anatolian transform faults; displacement along such faults periodically involves disastrous earthquakes.

Ulama (ulema): Ar. collective term for learned Muslim legal and religious leaders; theoretically, the ultimate repository of power in Saudi Arabia.

Umayyad (Omayyed): Arab Muslim dynasty of the Quraysh tribe and the empire it ruled from Damascus AD 661–750; also the dynasty's continued rule in Spain until 1030.

Ummah: Ar. for the community of Muslims, an especially important concept pertaining to Arab Muslims in the early decades of the Muslim conquests.

UNRWA: United Nations Relief and Works Agency, which since 1949 has operated emergency housing and food distribution for hundreds of thousands of registered Palestinian Arab refugees, usually in UNRWA-operated camps.

Vilayet: a province under the administrative pattern of the Ottoman Empire; term became crucial in post–World War I territorial settlements in the Levant.

Viticulture: cultivation of grapevines, almost a way of life in some specialized agricultural areas.

Volcanism (vulcanism): igneous activity processes in general, not just those associated with volcanoes; especially the processes by which molten materials and associated solids and gases are forced into the lithosphere or onto the earth's surface through craters or fissures. *See* basalt.

Wadi: widely used Ar. term for arid area stream basin (and, by extension, the stream), including major valleys and broad, hardly perceptible linear depressions, whether stream flow is perennial or periodic. Ar. for a major river (Nile, Tigris) is *nahr*.

Wahhabi: often misused term pertaining to reform puritan Muslim movement and group that evolved from the preachings of Muhammad ibn Abd al-Wahhab in the mid–1700s in central Arabia. Wahhabi puritanism is still strong in much of Arabia.

Waqf (**wakf, vakf**): Muslim religious endowment or trust involving land or other property; widespread in Islamic world but decreasing in more secular states such as Syria.

Xerophytic: pertaining to specialized vegetation of arid lands. Special adaptations include deep or long roots, waxy leaves, and tough bark (see Chap. 5).

Zionism: Jewish nationalism stressing unity of Jews and creation and maintenance of a Jewish state in Eretz Yisrael (Land of Israel) in greater Palestine as a territorial base for Jewry.

Geological Time Chart

EON	PERIOD		EPOCH	AGE	MILLIONS OF YRS AGO
CENOZOIC	QUATERNARY		Holocene (Recent)		0.01
			Pleistocene		1.6
	TERTIARY	Neogene	Pliocene		11.2
			Miocene		23.7
		Paleogene	Oligocene		36.6
			Eocene		57.8
			Paleocene		66.4
MESOZOIC	CRETACEOUS		Late	Maastrichtian	74.5
				Campanian	84.0
				Santonian	87.5
				Coniacian	88.5
				Turonian	91.0
				Cenomanian	97.5
			Early		144
	JURASSIC		Late		163
			Middle		187
			Early		208
	TRIASSIC		Late		230
			Middle		240
			Early		245
PALEOZOIC	PERMIAN				286
	CARBONIFEROUS				360
	DEVONIAN				408
	SILURIAN				438
	ORDOVICIAN				505
	CAMBRIAN				570

PRECAMBRIAN

	ERA				
PROTEROZOIC	Late				900
	Middle				1600
	Early		·		2500
ARCHEOZOIC	Late				3000
	Middle				3400
	Early				3800

In this simplified geological time chart, *Ages* are shown only for the late Cretaceous, although *Age* subdivisions exist for all *Epochs* after the Middle Cambrian. The Middle East surface geology is dominantly Mesozoic and Cenozoic, although the Nubian-Arabian Shield is Precambrian. Western Gulf oil fields are mainly Jurassic and Cretaceous, whereas Iranian and Kirkuk fields are Paleogene.

BIBLIOGRAPHY

Bibliographical Note

The following list of references includes virtually all the works cited in the Notes, a few other sources in English utilized in this book, and several additional works in English that are especially useful for a mid-level student or general reader. Most listings are reasonably available. More advanced sources and materials in languages other than English may be found in the bibliographies mentioned below. In addition to Web sites given in the Notes, several of the most useful URLs are included in the references below. The Encyclopaedia Britannica yearbook's *Britannica World Data* section includes useful Web sites for virtually every country and for a number of relevant topics.

The simplest way to stay abreast of the explosion of new literature on the Middle East is to refer to the listings in the quarterly *Middle East Journal (MEJ)*, which includes reviews, short notices, listings of literature received, and a bibliography of periodical materials. The autumn issue has an annual index and lists the periodicals regularly surveyed for the bibliography. The *MEJ* entries may omit specialized geographical materials, most of which can be noted in one or another of the standard academic geographical journals (*Annals* of the Association of American Geographers, *Geographical Review*, *Professional Geographer*, *Geographical Journal*, and others). References and articles in both the *International Journal of Middle East Studies* and the *Middle East Studies Association Bulletin* are useful. The weekly *Economist* (London) and the daily *Christian Science Monitor* report regularly on Middle East affairs, as does the *New York Times*. More partisan but still useful are the *Jerusalem Post*, North American Edition (weekly, in English) *Israel Economist*, *Journal of Palestine Studies*, and *Middle East Policy*, called *American-Arab Affairs* before March 1992. Every issue of *Aramco World* magazine covers some aspect of the Middle East. Several of the book references listed below have especially good bibliographies. Statistics may most easily be found in the Encyclopaedia Britannica yearbook's *Britannica World Data* and, more fully, in the standard United Nations yearbooks or other UN periodical statistical volumes.

Three especially useful bibliographical works are:

ABC-Clio Information Services. *The Middle East in Conflict: A Historical Bibliography*. Clio Bibliography Series no. 19 [annotated]. Santa Barbara, CA: ABC-Clio Information Services, 1985. 302p.

Atiyeh, George N., comp. *The Contemporary Middle East, 1948–1973: A Selective and Annotated Bibliography*. Boston: G.K. Hall, 1975. 664p.

Collison, Robert L., ed.-in-chief (individual compilers for each volume). *World Bibliographical Series*. Includes no. 2, *Lebanon*; no. 5, *Saudi Arabia*; no. 27, *Turkey*; no. 28, *Cyprus*; no. 29, *Oman*; no. 36, *Qatar*; no. 42, *Iraq*; no. 43, *UAE*; no. 49, *Bahrain*; no. 50, *The Yemens*; no. 55, *Jordan*; no. 56, *Kuwait*; no. 58, *Israel*; no. 73, *Syria*; no. 81, *Iran*; and no. 86, *Egypt*. Santa Barbara, CA: ABC Clio Press, 1979–1991. Pages variable, from 162p. to 330p.

References

Abdullah, Muhammad Morsy. *The United Arab Emirates: A Modern History*. New York: Barnes & Noble, 1978. 365p.

Abercrombie, Thomas J. "Bahrain: Hub of the Persian Gulf." *National Geographic*, Sept. 1979, 300–329.

———. "Arabia's Frankincense Trail." *National Geographic*, Oct. 1985, 474–512.

Abu-Dawood, Abdul-Razzak S., and P. P. Karan. *International Boundaries of Saudi Arabia*. New Delhi: Galaxy Publications, 1990. 95p.

Abu-Izzedin, Najla M. *The Druzes: A New Study of Their History, Faith and Society*. Leiden: E. J. Brill, 1984. 259p.

Abu-Lughod, Janet L. *Cairo: 1001 Years of the City Victorious.* Princeton: Princeton Univ. Press, 1971. 284p.

Abu Odeh, Adnan. "Two Capitals in an Undivided Jerusalem." *Foreign Affairs* 71, no. 2 (Spring 1992): 183–188.

———. *Jordanians, Palestinians, and the Hashemite Kingdom in the Middle East Peace Process.* Washington, DC: U.S. Institute of Peace Press, 1999. 322p.

Abu-Hakima, Ahmad Mustafa. *The Modern History of Kuwait, 1760–1965.* London: Luzac and Company, 1983. 226p.

Adamec, Ludwig W., ed. *Historical Gazetteer of Iran.* Vol. 1, *Tehran and Northwestern Iran;* vol. 2, *Meshed and Northeastern Iran;* vol. 4, *Zahidan and Southeastern Iran.* Graz: Akademische Druck-u Verlagsanstalt, 1976–1988. Vol. 1, 734p. + 62p. maps; vol. 2, 708p. + 150p. maps; vol. 4, 480p. + 48p. maps.

Adams, Linda S. "Political Liberalization in Jordan: An Analysis of the State's Relationship with the Muslim Brotherhood." *Journal of Church and State* 38, no. 3 (Summer 1996): 507–528.

Agricultural Situation Report. Foreign Agricultural Service (FAS), U.S. Department of Agriculture. Web site: <http://www.fas.usda.gov/>

Aharoni, Yohanan. *The Land of the Bible: A Historical Geography.* Trans. A.F. Rainey. London: Burns and Oates, 1974. 409p.

Ahmad, Feroz. *The Making of Modern Turkey.* New York: Routledge, 1993. 252p.

Airport Operators Council International (AOCI). "Worldwide Airport Traffic Report." Published periodically by AOCI, Washington, DC.

Ajami, Fouad. *The Arab Predicament: Arab Political Thought and Practice Since 1967.* Updated ed. Cambridge: Cambridge Univ. Press, 1993. 279p.

Akins, James E. "The New Arabia." *Foreign Affairs* 70, no. 3 (Summer 1991): 36–49.

Akins, James E., et al. *Oil and Security in the Arabian Gulf.* New York: St. Martin's Press, 1981. 48p.

Akurgal, Ekrem. *Ancient Civilizations and Ruins of Turkey: From Prehistoric Times Until the End of the Roman Empire.* 2d ed. Trans. John Whybrow and Mollie Emre. Istanbul: Mobil Oil Türk, 1970. 375p. + 112p. photographs.

Ali, Sheikh Rustum. *Oil and Power: Political Dynamics in the Middle East.* New York: St. Martin's Press, 1987. 173p.

Allen, Calvin H., Jr. *Oman: The Modernization of the Sultanate.* Profiles: Nations of the Contemporary Middle East. Boulder, CO: Westview Press, 1987. 154p.

Allen, Richard. *Imperialism and Nationalism in the Fertile Crescent: Sources and Prospects of the Arab-Israeli Conflict.* New York: Oxford Univ. Press, 1974. 686p.

al-Ansary, A. R. *Qaryat al-Fau: A Portrait of the Pre-Islamic Civilization in Saudi Arabia.* London: Croom Helm, 1982. 147p.

AlSayyad, Nezar. *Cities and Caliphs: On the Genesis of Arab Muslim Urbanism.* Westport, CT: Greenwood Press, 1991. 196p.

Altorki, Soraya, and Donald P. Cole. *Arabian Oasis City: The Transformation of Unayzah.* Austin: Univ. of Texas Press, 1989. 266p.

Amirahmadi, Hooshang. *Revolution and Economic Transition: The Iranian Experience.* Albany: State Univ. of New York Press, 1990. 420p.

Amuzegar, Jahanir. "The Iranian Economy Before and After the Revolution." *MEJ* 46, no. 3 (Summer 1992): 413–425.

———. "Islamic Fundamentalism in Action: The Case of Iran." *Middle East Policy* 4, no. 1–2 [Issue 51–52] (Sept. 1995): 22–33.

———. "Khatami's Iran, One Year Later." *Middle East Policy* 6, no. 2 [Issue 60] (Oct. 1998) : 76–94.

———. "Khatami and the Iranian Economy at Mid-Term." *MEJ* 53, no. 4 (Autumn 1999): 534–552.

Andersen, Roy R., Robert P. Seibert, and Jon G. Wagner. *Politics and Change in the Middle East: Sources of Conflict and Accommodation.* 3d ed. Englewood Cliffs, NJ: Prentice-Hall, 1990. 331p.

Anthony, John Duke. *Historical and Cultural Dictionary of the Sultanate of Oman and the Emirates of Eastern Arabia.* Historical and Cultural Dictionaries of Asia no. 9. Metuchen, NJ: Scarecrow Press, 1976. 136p.

Antoniou, Jim. *Islamic Cities and Conservation.* Paris: Unesco, 1981. 109p.

Antonius, George. *The Arab Awakening: The Story of the Arab National Movement.* New York: Hamilton, 1938. 471p.

Arabian American Oil Company (R. O. Williams, oceanographer). *Aramco Meteorologic and Oceanographic Data Book for the Eastern Province Region of Saudi Arabia.* Dhahran: Arabian American Oil Co., n.d. (ca. 1978).

Aronson, Geoffrey. *Israel, Palestinians and the Intifada: Creating Facts on the West Bank.* London: Kegan Paul International (with the Institute of Palestine Studies, Washington, DC), 1990. 376p.

Askari, Hossein, and John Thomas Cummings. *Middle East Economies in the 1970s: A Comparative Approach.* Praeger Special Studies in International Economics and Development. New York: Praeger, 1976. 581p.

Assiri, Abdul-Reda. *The Government and Politics of Kuwait: Principles and Practice.* Shaab, Kuwait: Al Watan Printing Press, 1996. 235p.

Atherton, Alfred L. "The Soviet Role in the Middle East: An American View." *MEJ* 39, no. 4 (Autumn 1985): 688–715.

Attalides, Michael A. *Cyprus: Nationalism and International Politics.* New York: St. Martin's Press, 1979. 226p.

Avineri, Shlomo. *The Making of Modern Zionism: The Intellectual Origins of the Jewish State.* New York: Basic Books, 1981. 244p.

Ayubi, Nazih N. *Over-stating the Arab State: Politics and Society in the Middle East.* London: I. B. Tauris, 1995. 514p.

Bachrach, Jere L. A *Middle East Studies Handbook.* Rev. and exp. ed. Seattle: Univ. of Washington Press, 1984. 160p.

Background Notes. U.S. Department of State. Published periodically for each country. Web site: <http://www.state.gov/www/background_notes/>

Ball, George W. *The Passionate Attachment: America's Involvement with Israel, 1947 to the Present.* New York: W. W. Norton, 1992. 382p.

Baly, Denis. *The Geography of the Bible: A Study in Historical Geography.* New York: Harper, 1957. 303p.

———. *Basic Biblical Geography.* Philadelphia: Fortress Press, 1987. 80p.

Barakat, Helim. *The Arab World: Society, Culture, and State.* Berkeley: Univ. of California Press, 1993. 348p.

Bard, Mitchell Geoffrey. *The Water's Edge and Beyond: Defining the Limits to Domestic Influence on United States Middle East Policy.* New Brunswick, NJ: Transaction Publishers, 1991. 313p.

Barkey, Henri J. *The State and the Industrialization Crisis in Turkey.* Boulder, CO: Westview Press, 1990. 220p.

Barkey, Henri J., and Graham E. Fuller. *Turkey's Kurdish Question.* Lanham, MD: Rowman and Littlefield Publishers, 1998. 238p.

Basson, Philip, et al. *Biotopes of the Western Arabian Gulf: Marine Life and Environments of Saudi Arabia.* Dhahran: Aramco [Arabian American Oil Co.], 1979. 284p.

Batanouny, K. H. *Ecology and Flora of Qatar.* Doha: Univ. of Qatar, 1981. 245p.

Bates, Daniel, and Amal Rassam. *Peoples and Cultures of the Middle East.* Englewood Cliffs, NJ: Prentice-Hall, 1983. 288p.

Batuta, Hanna. "Some Observations on Social Roots of Syria's Ruling Military Group and the Causes for Its Dominance." *MEJ* 35, no. 3 (Summer 1981): 331–344.

El-Baz, Farouk. "Preliminary Observations of Environmental Damage Due to the Gulf War." *Natural Resources Forum* (Feb. 1992): 71–75.

Bean, George E. Turkey's *Southern Shore: An Archaeological Guide.* London: Ernest Benn, 1968. 188p.

Beaumont, Peter, and Keith McLachlan, eds. *Agricultural Development in the Middle East.* New York: John Wiley, 1985. 349p.

Beaumont, Peter, Gerald H. Blake, and J. Malcolm Wagstaff. *The Middle East: A Geographical Study.* 2d ed. New York: Halsted Press, 1988. 623p.

Begin, Menachem. *The Revolt.* New York: Nash Publishing Co. 1977. 386p.

Belt, Don. "Petra: Ancient City of Stone." *National Geographic,* Dec. 1998, 117–133.

———. "Lawrence of Arabia: A Hero's Journey." *National Geographic,* Jan. 1999, 38–61.

Ben-Dor, Gabriel, and David B. Dewitt, eds. *Conflict Management in the Middle East.* Lexington, MA; Lexington Books, 1987. 323p.

Benedick, Richard Elliot. "The High Dam and the Transformation of the Nile." *MEJ* 33, no. 2 (Spring 1979): 119–144.

Ben-Meir, Alon. "Why Syria Must Regain the Golan to Make Peace." *Middle East Policy* 5, no. 3 [Issue 57] (Sept. 1997): 104–112.

Bengio, Ofra, and Gabriel Ben-Dor, eds. *Minorities and the State in the Arab World.* Boulder, CO: Lynne Rienner Publishers, 1999. 223p.

Benvenisti, Meron. *The West Bank Data Projects: A Survey of Israel's Policies.* Washington, DC: American Enterprise Institute, 1984. 97p. Updated periodically.

———. With Ziad Abu-Zayed and Danny Rubenstein. *The West Bank Handbook: A Political Lexicon.* Boulder, CO: Westview Press, 1986. 228p.

———. *The Hidden History of Jerusalem.* Berkeley: Univ. of California Press, 1996. 274p.

Benvenisti, Meron, and Shlomo Khayat. *The West Bank and Gaza Atlas.* West Bank Data Base Project. Boulder, CO: Westview Press, 1988. 140p.

Berkoff, Jeremy. *A Strategy for Managing Water in the Middle East*. Washington, DC: The World Bank, 1994. 72p.

Betts, Robert Brenton. *The Druze*. New Haven: Yale Univ. Press, 1988. 161p.

Bibby, Geoffrey. *Looking for Dilmun*. New York: Knopf, 1969. 383p.

Bickerton, Ian J., and Carla L. Klausner. *A Concise History of the Arab-Israeli Conflict*. Englewood Cliffs, NJ: Prentice-Hall, 1991. 276p.

Bidwell, Robin Leonard. *The Two Yemens*. Boulder, CO: Westview Press, 1983. 350p.

Bill, James A. *The Eagle and the Lion: The Tragedy of American-Iranian Relations*. New Haven: Yale Univ. Press, 1988. 520p.

Biswas, Asit K., et al. *Core and Periphery: A Comprehensive Approach to Middle Eastern Water*. New Delhi: Oxford Univ. Press: Middle East Water Commission, 1997. 160p.

Black, Ian, and Benny Morris. *Israel's Secret Wars: A History of Israel's Intelligence Services*. New York: Grove Weidenfeld, 1991. 603p.

Blake, G. H., and Richard I. Lawless, eds. *The Changing Middle East City. Croom Helm Series on the Arab World*. London: Croom Helm, 1980. 273p.

Blake, Gerald H., and Richard N. Schofield, eds. *Boundaries and State Territory in the Middle East and North Africa*. Cambridgeshire, UK: Middle East and North African Studies Press, 1987. 167p.

Blake, Gerald, et al. *The Cambridge Atlas of the Middle East and North Africa*. New York: Cambridge Univ. Press, 1987. 132p.

Bleier, Ronald. "Will Nile Water Go to Israel? North Sinai Pipelines and the Politics of Scarcity." *Middle East Policy* 5, no. 3 [Issue 57] (Sept. 1997): 113–123.

Bobek, H. "Vegetation [of Iran]." Chap. 8 in Fisher, William B., ed., 1968.

Bolukbasi, Suha. "Behind the Turkish-Israeli Alliance: A Turkish View." *Journal of Palestine Studies* 29, no. 1 (Autumn 1999): 21–35.

Bonine, Michael E. "From Uruk to Casablanca: Perspectives on the Urban Experience in the Middle East." *Journal of Urban History* 3 (Feb. 1977): 141–180.

———. "The Morphogenesis of Iranian Cities." *Annals* (Association of American Geographers) 69, no. 2 (June 1979): 208–224.

Bonine, Michael E., ed. *Population, Poverty, and Politics in Middle East Cities*. Gainesville: Univ. Press of Florida, 1997. 361p.

Bonine, Michael E., and Nikki R. Keddie, eds. *Modern Iran: The Dialectics of Continuity and Change*. Albany: State Univ. of New York Press, 1981. 464p.

Boustani, Rafic, and Philippe Fargues. *The Atlas of the Arab World: Geopolitics and Society*. New York: Facts on File, 1990. 144p.

Brand, Laurie A. *Jordan's Inter-Arab Relations: The Political Economy of Alliance Making*. New York: Columbia Univ. Press, 1994. 350p.

Brice, William C., ed. *An Historical Atlas of Islam*. Leiden: E. J. Brill, 1981. 71p.

Brinkmann, R. *Geology of Turkey*. New York: Elsevier Scientific Publishing Co., 1976. 158p.

Brockelmann, Carl. *History of the Islamic Peoples*. Trans. by Joel Carmichael and Moshe Perlmann. New York: Putnam, 1949. 566p.

Brown, Glenn F. "Tectonic Map of the Arabian Peninsula." Map AP-2. Jiddah: Kingdom of Saudi Arabia, Directorate General of Mineral Resources, 1972.

Brown, Glenn F., and R. G. Coleman. "The Tectonic Framework of the Arabian Peninsula." *Proceedings of the 24th International Geological Congress*, 1972. Section 3: 300–304.

Brown, Harry. "The Iraq-Kuwait Boundary Dispute: Historical Background and the UN Decisions of 1992 and 1993." *International Boundaries Research Unit Boundary and Security Bulletin*, Univ. of Durham (1994): 66–80.

Brunsden, Denys, et al. "The Bahrain Surface Materials Resource Survey and Its Applications to Regional Planning." *Geographical Journal* 145, no. 1 (Mar. 1979): 1–35.

Brynen, Rex. *Sanctuary and Survival: The PLO in Lebanon*. Boulder, CO: Westview Press (with Pinter Publishers, London), 1990. 255p.

Bulliet, Richard W. *The Camel and the Wheel*. Cambridge: Harvard Univ. Press, 1975. 327p.

———. "Twenty Years of Islamic Politics." *MEJ* 53, no. 2 (Spring 1999): 89–200.

Burenhult, Goran, ed. *People of the Stone Age: Hunter-Gatherers and Early Farmers*. New York: HarperCollins, 1993.

———. *Old World Civilizations: The Rise of Cities and States*. New York: HarperCollins, 1994. 239p.

Burrell, Alison, ed. *Agricultural Policy in Jordan*. London: Ithaca Press, 1986. 147p.

Burrowes, Robert D. *The Yemen Arab Republic: The Politics of Development, 1962–1986*. Westview Special Studies on the Middle East. Boulder, CO: Westview Press (with Croom Helm, Kent, UK), 1987. 173p.

Butzer, Karl W. *Early Hydraulic Civilization in Egypt: A Study in Cultural Ecology.* Chicago: Univ. of Chicago Press, 1976. 134p.

Caldwell, Dan. "Flashpoints in the Gulf: Abu Musa and the Tunb Islands." *Middle East Policy* 4, no. 3 [Issue 53] (Mar. 1996): 50–57.

Calotychos, Vangelis, ed. *Cyprus and Its People: Nation, Identity, and Experience in an Unimaginable Community, 1955–1997.* Boulder, CO: Westview Press, 1998. 344p.

Canby, Thomas Y. "After the Storm." *National Geographic,* Aug. 1991, 2 32.

Central Intelligence Agency (CIA). *Issues in the Middle East: Atlas.* Washington, DC. U.S. Government Printing Office, 1973. 40p.

———. *Atlas of the Middle East.* Washington, DC: U.S. Government Printing Office, 1993. 76p.

———. *World Factbook.* Published annually. Web site: <http://www.odci.gov/cia/publications/factbook/index.html>

Christaller, Walter. *The Central Places of Southern Germany.* Trans. C. W. Baskin. Englewood Cliffs, NJ: Prentice-Hall, 1966.

Chubin, Shahram, and Charles Tripp. *Iran and Iraq at War.* Boulder, CO: Westview Press, 1988. 318p.

Clapp, Nicholas. *The Road to Ubar: Finding the Atlantis of the Sands.* New York: Houghton Mifflin, 1998. 342p.

Clarke, Angela. *Bahrain Oil and Development 1929–1989.* Boulder, CO: International Research Center for Energy and Economic Development, 1990. 432p.

Clarke, Duncan L. "US Security Assistance to Egypt and Israel: Politically Untouchable?" *MEJ* 51, no. 2 (Spring 1997): 200–214.

Clawson, Marion, Hans H. Landsberg, and Lyle T. Alexander. *The Agricultural Potential of the Middle East.* Rand Corporation and Resources for the Future. New York: American Elsevier Publishing Co., 1971. 312p.

Cobban, Helena. *The Palestinian Liberation Organization: People, Power, and Politics.* Cambridge Middle East Library. Cambridge: Cambridge Univ. Press, 1984. 305p.

———. *The Making of Modern Lebanon.* Boulder, CO: Westview Press, 1985. 248p.

———. "Thinking About Lebanon." *American-Arab Affairs* no. 12 (Spring 1985): 59–71.

Cockburn, Andrew, and Leslie Cockburn. *Dangerous Liaison: The Inside Story of the U.S.-Israeli Covert Relationship.* New York: HarperCollins, 1991. 416p.

Cohen, Avner. *Israel and the Bomb.* New York: Columbia Univ. Press, 1998. 470p.

Cohen, Saul. *The Geopolitics of Israel's Border Question.* Jerusalem: *Jerusalem Post,* for the Jaffee Center for Strategic Studies, Tel Aviv Univ. Distributed by Westview Press, Boulder, CO, 1988. 124p.

Collins, Frank. "The True Cost of Israel." *Washington Report on Middle East Affairs* 8, no. 9 (Jan. 1990): 21, 55.

Congressional Quarterly: The Middle East. Washington, DC: CQ Press, 2000. 596p.

"Contemporary Oman and U.S.-Oman Relations: A Symposium." *Middle East Policy* 4, no. 3 [Issue 53] (Mar. 1996): 1–29.

Cooper, Mark N. *The Transformation of Egypt.* Baltimore: Johns Hopkins Univ. Press, 1982. 278p.

Cordesman, Anthony H. *The Gulf War.* Vol. IV, Lessons of Modern War. Boulder, CO: Westview Press, 1996. 1,040p.

———. *Bahrain, Oman, Qatar, and the UAE: Challenges of Security.* Boulder, CO: Westview Press, 1997. 448p.

———. *Kuwait: Recovery and Security after the Gulf War.* Boulder, CO: Westview Press, 1997. 176p.

———. *Saudi Arabia: Guarding the Desert Kingdom.* Boulder, CO: Westview Press, 1997. 220p.

Cordesman, Anthony H., and Ahmed S. Hashim. *Iraq: Sanctions and Beyond.* Boulder, CO: Westview Press, 1997. 394p.

Cottam, Richard W. *Nationalism in Iran.* Pittsburgh: Univ. of Pittsburgh Press, 1979. 376p.

Cottrell, Alvin, gen. ed. *The Persian Gulf States: A General Survey.* Baltimore: Johns Hopkins Univ. Press, 1980. 695p.

Country Studies: Area Handbook Series. Prepared for the Department of the Army by the Library of Congress, with various editors. A study is available on every Middle East country (combined volume on *Persian Gulf States*), with fourth and fifth editions of studies of major Middle East countries published 1988–1991. Washington, DC: U.S. Government Printing Office. Web site: <http://www.lcweb2.loc.gov/frd/cs/>

Country Commercial Guide. U.S. Department of State. Annual. Web site: <http://lcweb2.loc.gov/x-ds-com.html>

Cressey, George B. "Qanats, Karez, and Foggaras." *Geog. Rev.* 48, no. 1 (Jan 1958): 27–44.

———. *Crossroads: Land and Life in Southwest Asia.* Chicago: Lippincott, 1960. 593p.

Crystal, Jill. *Oil and Politics in the Gulf: Rulers and Merchants in Kuwait and Qatar.* Cambridge Middle East Library, no. 24. Cambridge: Cambridge Univ. Press, 1990. 210p.

———. *Kuwait: The Transformation of an Oil State.* Boulder, CO: Westview Press, 1992.

Cullen, Robert. "The Rise and Fall of the Caspian Sea." *National Geographic,* May 1999, 2–35. With excellent map.

Curtis, Michael, ed. *Religion and Politics in the Middle East.* Westview Special Studies on the Middle East. Prepared under the auspices of the American Academic Association for Peace in the Middle East. Boulder, CO; Westview Press, 1981. 406p.

Curtiss, Richard. *Stealth PACs: Lobbying Congress for Control of U.S. Middle East Policy.* 4th ed. Washington, DC: American Educational Trust, 1996. 278p.

Danielsen, Albert L. *The Evolution of OPEC.* New York: Harcourt Brace Jovanovich, 1982. 305p.

Daum, Werner. *Yemen: 3000 Years of Art and Civilisation in Arabia Felix.* Innsbruck, Austria and Frankfurt/Main, Germany: Pinguin-Verlag and Umschau-Verlag, [1987]. 485p.

Davison, R. H. "Where Is the Middle East?" *Foreign Affairs* 38 (1960): 665–675.

Day, Alan J., ed. *Border and Territorial Disputes.* Harlow, Essex, UK: Longman, 1982. Middle East boundaries 178–233. 406p.

Defense Mapping Agency, U.S. Department of Defense. *Gazetteer of Iran:* Names Approved by the United States Board on Geographic Names, 2d ed. 2 vols. Washington, DC: U.S. Government Printing Office, 1985. 1,827p.

Dekmejian, R. Hrair. "Saudi Arabia's Consultative Council." *MEJ* 52, no. 2 (Spring 1998): 204–218.

Denktash, Rauf. *The Cyprus Triangle.* Boston: Allen and Unwin, 1982. 224p.

Devlin, John F. *Syria: Modern State in an Ancient Land.* Profiles: Nations of the Contemporary Middle East. Boulder, CO: Westview Press, 1983. 140p.

Dewdney, John C. *Turkey: An Introductory Geography.* New York: Praeger, 1971. 214p.

Dickson, H. R. P. *The Arab of the Desert: A Glimpse into Badawin Life in Kuwait and Saudi Arabia.* London: George Allen and Unwin, 1949. 668p.

———. *Kuwait and Her Neighbors.* London: Allen and Unwin, 1956. 627p.

Dillman, Jeffrey D. "Water Rights in the Occupied Territories." *Journal of Palestine Studies* 19, no. 1 (Autumn 1989): 46–71.

Dixon, J. E., and A. H. F. Robertson, eds. *The Geological Evolution of the Eastern Mediterranean.* Published for the Geological Society. Oxford: Blackwell Scientific Publications, 1984. 824p.

Doran, Charles F., and Stephen W. Buck, eds. *The Gulf, Energy, and Global Security: Political and Economic Issues.* Boulder, CO: Lynn Rienner Publishers, 1991. 275p.

Dresch, Paul. Tribes, *Government, and History in Yemen.* Oxford: Clarendon Press, 1989. 440p.

Drysdale, Alasdair, and Gerald Blake. *The Middle East and North Africa: A Political Geography.* New York: Oxford Univ. Press, 1985. 340p.

Dunbar, Charles. "The Unification of Yemen: Process, Politics, and Prospects." *MEJ* 43, no. 6 (Summer 1992): 456–476.

Dunn, Michael Collins. "The Wrong Place, the Wrong Time: Why Yemen Unity Failed." *Middle East Policy* 3, no. 2 [Issue 48] (1994): 148–156.

Dutton, R., and N. Winser. "The Oman Wahiba Sands Project." *Geographical Journal* 153, no. 1 (Mar. 1987): 48–58.

Earle, Sylvia A. "Persian Gulf Pollution: Assessing the Damage One Year Later." *National Geographic,* Feb. 1992, 122–134.

Economic Policy and Trade Practices: Country Reports. Department of State. Annual. Web site:<http://www.state.gov/www/issues/economic/trade_reports/>

Edwards, Mike, and Michael Yamashita. "Eyewitness Iraq." *National Geographic,* Nov. 1999, 2–27.

"Egypt: Open Economy, Closed Politics." *Economist,* June 12, 1999, 40.

EIA. Energy Information Administration, U.S. Department of Energy. Web site: <http://www.eia.doe.gov/emeu/international/>

Eickelman, Dale F. *The Middle East: An Anthropological Approach.* Englewood Cliffs, NJ: Prentice-Hall, 1981. 336p.

Eickelman, Dale F., and James Piscatori. *Muslim Politics.* Princeton, NJ: Princeton Univ. Press, 1996. 235p.

Elazar, Daniel J. *The Other Jews: The Sephardim Today.* New York: Basic Books, 1989. 236p.

Elhance, Arun. *Hydropolitics in the Third World: Conflict and Cooperation in International River Basins.* Washington, DC: U.S. Institute of Peace Press, 1999. 296p.

Ellis, Marc H. "The Future of Israel/Palestine: Embracing the Broken Middle." *Journal of Palestine Studies* 26, no. 3 (Spring 1997): 56–66.

Elmusa, Sharif S. "Faust without the Devil? The Interplay of Technology and Culture in Saudi Arabia." *MEJ* 51, no. 3 (Summer 1997): 345–357.

———. *Water Conflict: Economics, Politics, Law and the Palestinian-Israeli Water Resources.* Washington, DC: Institute for Palestine Studies, 1997. 408p.

Emmett, Chad F. "The Capital Cities of Jerusalem." *Geog. Rev.* 86, no. 2 (April 1996): 233–258.

Encyclopaedia Britannica, Inc. *Britannica World Data.* Part 2 of *Britannica Book of the Year.* Chicago: Encyclopaedia Britannica, Inc. Published annually.

Engineer, Asghar Ali. *The Rights of Women in Islam.* New York: St. Martin's Press, 1996. 188p.

English, Paul Ward. *City and Village in Iran: Settlement and Economy in the Kirman Basin.* Madison: Univ. of Wisconsin Press, 1966. 204p.

Entessar, Nader. *Kurdish Ethnonationalism.* Boulder, CO: Lynn Reinner Publishers, 1992, 207p.

Erinç, Sirri, and Necdet Tunçdilek. "The Agricultural Regions of Turkey." *Geog. Rev.* 42, no. 2 (Apr. 1952): 179–203.

Esman, Milton J., and Itamar Rabinovich, eds. *Ethnicity, Pluralism, and the State in the Middle East.* Published in cooperation with the Dayan Center for Middle Eastern and African Studies, Tel Aviv Univ. Ithaca, NY: Cornell Univ. Press, 1988. 296p.

Esposito, John L., ed. *The Iranian Revolution: Its Global Impact.* Miami: Florida International Univ. Press, 1990. 346p.

———, ed. *The Oxford Encyclopedia of the Modern Islamic World.* 4 vols. New York: Oxford Univ. Press, 1995. 1,920p.

———, ed. *Political Islam: Revolution, Radicalism, or Reform?* Boulder, CO: Lynne Rienner, 1997. 280p.

Exxon Corporation, Public Affairs Department. *Middle East Oil and Gas. Exxon Background Series.* New York: Exxon Corp., Dec. 1984. 40p.

Facey, William. *The Story of the Eastern Province of Saudi Arabia.* London: Stacey International, 1994. 160p.

Fahim, Hussein M. *Dams, People and Environment— The Aswan High Dam Case.* New York: Pergamon Press, 1981. 187p.

Fairbanks, Stephen C. "A New Era for Iran?" *Middle East Policy* 5, no. 3 [Issue 57] (Sept. 1997): 51–56.

Falah, Ghazi. "Land Fragmentation and Spatial Control in the Nazareth Metropolitan Area." *Professional Geographer* 44, no. 1 (Feb. 1992): 30–44.

———. "The 1948 Israeli-Palestinian War and its Aftermath: The Transformation and De-Signification of Palestine's Cultural Landscape." *Annals* (Association of American Geographers) 86, no. 2 (June 1996): 256–285.

Fall, Patricia L., Lee Lines, and Steven E. Falconer. "Seeds of Civilization: Bronze Age Rural Economy and Ecology in the Southern Levant." *Annals* (Association of American Geographers) 88, no. 1 (Mar. 1998): 107–125.

Farah, Tawfic E., ed. *Pan-Arabism and Arab Nationalism: The Continuing Debate.* Foreword by James A. Bill. Boulder, CO: Westview Press, 1987. 208p.

Farid, Abdel Majid, ed. *The Red Sea: Prospects for Stability.* Published in association with the Arab Research Centre. New York: St. Martin's Press, 1984. 173p.

Farouk-Sluglett, Marion, and Peter Sluglett. *Iraq Since 1958: From Revolution to Dictatorship.* London: I. B. Tauris Paperbacks, 1991. 336p.

Farsi, Zaki M. A. *National Guide and Atlas of the Kingdom of Saudi Arabia.* Jiddah: Zaki M. A. Farsi, 1989. n.p.

Farsoun, Samih K., and Christina E. Zacharia. *Palestine and the Palestinians.* Boulder, CO: Westview Press, 1998. 400p.

Fathi, Schirin H. *Jordan: An Invented Nation? Tribe-State Dynamics and the Formation of National Identity.* Hamburg, Germany: Deutsches Orient-Institut, 1994. 296p.

Al-Farsy, Fouad. *Modernity and Tradition: The Saudi Equation.* London and New York: Kegan Paul International, 1990. 337p.

Fernea, Elizabeth Warnock, and Basima Qattan Bezirgan, eds. *Middle Eastern Muslim Women Speak.* Austin: Univ. of Texas Press, 1977. 402p.

Fernea, Elizabeth Warnock, and Robert A. Fernea. *The Arab World: Personal Encounters.* New York: Anchor Press, Doubleday and Co., 1985. 354p.

Ffrench, Geoffrey E., and Allan G. Hill. *Kuwait: Urban and Medical Ecology.* Geomedical Monograph Series no. 4, New York: Springer-Verlag, 1971. 124p.

Findley, Paul. *They Dare to Speak Out: People and Institutions Confront Israel's Lobby.* 2d ed. Westport, CT: Lawrence Hill, 1989. 390p.

Finnie, David H. *Shifting Lines in the Sand: Kuwait's Elusive Frontier with Iraq.* Cambridge, MA: Harvard Univ. Press, 1992. 221p.

Fisher, Sydney Nettleton, and William Ochsenwald. *The Middle East: A History.* New York: McGraw-Hill, 1997. 741p.

Fisher, William B., ed. *Cambridge History of Iran.* Vol. 1, *The Land of Iran.* Cambridge: Cambridge Univ. Press, 1968. 782p.

Fisk, Robert. *Pity the Nation: The Abduction of Lebanon.* New York: Atheneum, 1990. 678p.

Friedlander, Dov, and Calvin Goldscheider. *The Population of Israel.* New York: Columbia Univ. Press, 1979. 240p.

Friedman, Thomas L. *From Beirut to Jerusalem.* New York: Farrar, Straus, Giroux, 1989. 525p.

Frisch, Hillel. *Countdown to Statehood: Palestinian State Formation in the West Bank and Gaza.* Albany: State Univ. of New York Press, 1998. 221p.

Fuller, Graham, and Ian O. Lesser. *Turkey's New Geopolitics.* Boulder, CO: Westview Press, 1993. 197p.

Gabriel, Erhard F. *The Dubai Handbook.* Ahrensburg, Germany: Institute for Applied Economic Geography, 1988. 243p.

Galnoor, Itzak. *The Partition of Palestine.* Albany: State Univ. of New York Press, 1995. 384p.

Gause, F. Gregory III. *Oil Monarchies: Domestic and Security Challenges in the Arab Gulf States.* New York: Council on Foreign Relations Press, 1994. 236p.

Gavin, Angus, and Ramez Maluf. *Beirut Reborn: The Restoration and Development of the Central District.* London: Academy Editions, 1996. 148p.

Geddes, Charles L., ed. *A Documentary History of the Arab-Israeli Conflict.* New York: Praeger, 1991. 461p.

Gerges, Fawaz A. *America and Political Islam: Clash of Cultures or Clash of Interests?* New York: Cambridge Univ. Press, 1999. 282p.

Gerner, Deborah J. *One Land, Two Peoples: The Conflict over Palestine.* 2d ed. Boulder, CO: Westview Press, 1994. 256p.

Ghabra, Shafeeq. "Kuwait and the Dynamics of Socio-Economic Change." *MEJ* 51, no. 3 (Summer 1997): 358–372.

Gharaibeh, Fawzi A. *The Economies of the West Bank and Gaza Strip.* Westview Special Studies on the Middle East. Boulder, CO: Westview Press, 1985. 182p.

Ghareeb, Edmund. *The Kurdish Question in Iraq.* Contemporary Issues in the Middle East. Syracuse: Syracuse Univ. Press, 1981. 223p.

Goldscheider, Calvin. *Israel's Changing Society: Population, Ethnicity, and Development.* Boulder, CO: Westview Press, 1997. 271p.

Goldschmidt, Arthur, Jr. *A Concise History of the Middle East.* 6th ed. Boulder, CO: Westview Press, 1998. 464p.

Goode's World Atlas. 20th ed. Chicago: McGraw Hill, 1999. 250p.

Gordon, David C. *The Republic of Lebanon: Nation in Jeopardy.* Profiles: Nations of the Contemporary Middle East. Boulder, CO: Westview Press, 1983. 171p.

Gradus, Yehuda, and Gabriel Lipshitz, eds. *The Mosaic of Israeli Geography.* Beer Sheva: Ben-Gurion Univ. of the Negev Press, 1996. 516p.

Grant, Michael. *The History of Ancient Israel.* New York: Scribner's, 1984. 317p.

Gresh, Alain. "Turkish-Israeli-Syrian Relations and their Impact on the Middle East." *MEJ* 52, no. 2 (Spring 1998): 188–203.

Graicer, Iris. "Spatial Integration of Arab Migrants in a Jewish Town." *Professional Geographer* 44, no. 1 (Feb. 1992): 45–56.

Grill, N. C. *Urbanisation in the Arabian Peninsula.* Durham, Eng.: Centre for Middle Eastern and Islamic Studies, Univ. of Durham, 1984. 113p.

Grimes, Barbara F., et al. *Ethnologue: Languages of the World.* 13th ed. Dallas, TX: Summer Institute of Linguistics, 1996. 966p. Web site: <http://www.sil.org/ethnologue>.

Gubser, Peter. *Jordan: Crossroads of Middle Eastern Events.* Profiles: Nations of the Contemporary Middle East. Boulder, CO: Westview Press, 1983. 139p.

Gulick, John. *Tripoli: A Modern Arab City.* Cambridge, MA: Harvard Univ. Press, 1967. 253p.

———. *The Middle East: An Anthropological Perspective.* Washington, DC: University Press of America, 1983. 244p.

Gunter, Michael M. *The Kurds and the Future of Turkey.* New York: St. Martin's Press, 1997. 184p.

Gürün, Kamvran. *The Armenian File: The Myth of Innocence Exposed.* New York: St. Martin's Press, 1985. 323p.

Haddad, Wadi D. *Lebanon: The Politics of Revolving Doors.* Washington Papers no. 114, published with the Center for Strategic and International Studies, Georgetown Univ. New York: Praeger, 1985. 154p.

Al-Haj, Abdullah Juma. "The Politics of Participation in the Gulf Cooperation Council States: The Omani Consultative Council." *MEJ* 50, no. 4 (Autumn 1996): 559–571.

Halliday, Fred. *Revolution and Foreign Policy: The Case of South Yemen 1967–1987.* Cambridge Middle East Library, no. 21. Cambridge: Cambridge Univ. Press, 1990. 315p.

Hammond Atlas of the Middle East: Geography, History, and Peoples. Maplewood, NJ: Hammond, 1991. 48p.

Hanna, Samir S. *Field Guide to the Geology of Oman.* Vol. 1: Western Hajar Mountains and Musandam. Ruwi, Oman: Historical Association of Oman, 1995. 178p.

Harris, George S. *Turkey:* Coping with Crisis. Profiles: Nations of the Contemporary Middle East. Boulder, CO: Westview Press, 1985. 240p.

Harris, Lillian Craig, ed. *Egypt: Internal Challenges and Regional Stability.* Chatham House Papers, no. 39. London and New York: Royal Institute of International Affairs and Routledge and Kegan Paul, 1988. 116p.

Hart, Parker T. *Saudi Arabia and the United States: Birth of a Security Partnership.* Bloomington: Indiana Univ. Press. 1998. 383p.

Hartshorne, Richard. "The Functional Approach in Political Geography." *Annals* (Association of American Geographers) 40, no. 2 (June 1950): 95–130.

Haynes, Kingsley E., and Dale Whittington. "International Management of the Nile—Stage Three?" *Geog. Rev.* 71, no. 1 (Jan. 1981): 17–32.

Heard-Bey, Frauke. F*rom Trucial States to United Arab Emirates: A Society in Transition.* New ed. London: Longman, 1996. 540p.

Held, Joanne D. [Cummings]. "The Effects of the Ottoman Land Laws on the Marginal Population and Musha Village of Palestine, 1858–1914." Master's thesis, Univ. of Texas, Austin, 1979. 225p.

Heller, Mark A. *A Palestinian State: the Implications for Israel.* Cambridge, MA: Harvard Univ. Press, 1983. 190p.

Helms, Christine Moss. *Iraq: Eastern Flank of the Arab World.* Washington, DC: The Brookings Institution, 1984. 215p.

Hersch, Seymour M. *The Samson Option: Israel's Nuclear Arsenal and American Foreign Policy.* New York: Random House, 1991. 354p.

Hershlag, Z. Y. *The Contemporary Turkish Economy.* London: Routledge, 1988. 178p.

Hertzberg, Arthur, ed. *The Zionist Idea: A Historical Analysis and Reader.* Rev. ed. New York: Atheneum, 1969. 638p.

Heun, Manfred, et al. "Site of Einkorn Wheat Domestication Identified by DNA Fingerprinting." *Science* 278, no. 5341 (1997): 1312–1314.

Hewison, R. Neil. *The Fayoum: A Practical Guide.* 2d ed. Cairo: American Univ. of Cairo Press, 1989. 115p.

Hills, E. S., ed. *Arid Lands: A Geographical Appraisal.* London: Methuen; Paris: UNESCO, 1966. 461p.

Hiro, Dilip. *Lebanon—Fire and Embers: A History of the Lebanese Civil War.* New York: St. Martin's Press, 1992. 274p.

Hitchens, Christopher. "Struggle of the Kurds." *National Geographic,* Aug. 1992, 32–61.

Hitti, Philip K. *The Near East in History: A 5000 Year Story.* Princeton, NJ: Van Nostrand, 1961. 574p.

Hobbs, Joseph J. *Bedouin Life in the Egyptian Wilderness.* Austin: Univ. of Texas Press, 1989. 165p.

———. "Speaking with People in Egypt's St. Katherine National Park." *Geog. Rev.* 86, no. 1 (Jan. 1996): 1–21.

———. "Sinai's Watchmen of the Wilderness." *Aramco World,* May/June 1999, 12–21.

Hof, Frederic C. "The Water Dimensions of Golan Heights Negotiations." *Middle East Policy* 5, no. 2 [Issue 56] (May 1997): 129–141.

Holden, David, and Richard Johns. *The House of Saud: The Rise and Rule of the Most Powerful Dynasty in the Arab World.* New York: Holt, Rinehart and Winston, 1982. 569p.

Holm, Donald August. "Desert Geomorphology in the Arabian Peninsula." *Science* 132, no. 3437 (1960): 1369–1379.

Hopwood, Derek. *Egypt: Politics and Society, 1945–1981.* London: Allen and Unwin, 1982. 194p.

———. *Syria, 1945–1986: Politics and Society.* London: Unwin Hyman, 1988. 193p.

Hourani, Albert H. *Minorities in the Arab World.* London: Oxford Univ. Press, 1947. 140p.

———. *The Emergence of the Modern Middle East.* Berkeley: Univ. of California Press, 1981. 243p.

———. *A History of the Arab Peoples.* Cambridge, MA: Belknap Press of Harvard Univ. Press, 1991. 551p.

Howard, Harry N. *The King-Crane Commission.* Beirut: Khayat, 1963. 369p.

———. *Turkey, the Straits, and U.S. Policy.* Baltimore: Johns Hopkins Univ. Press, in cooperation with Middle East Institute, 1974. 337p.

Hudson, James. "The Litani River of Lebanon." *MEJ* 25, no. 1 (Winter 1971): 1–14.

Hudson, Michael C., ed. *Middle East Dilemma: The Politics and Economics of Arab Integration.* New York: Columbia Univ. Press, 1999. 319p.

Hughes, Hugh. *Middle East Railways.* Harrow, Eng.: Continental Railway Circle, 1981. 128p.

Hunter, Shireen T. *Iran and the World: Continuity in a Revolutionary Decade.* Bloomington: Indiana Univ. Press, 1990. 254p.

El Hussini, Mohrez Mahmoud. *Soviet-Egyptian Relations, 1945–85.* New York: St. Martin's Press, 1987. 276p.

International Petroleum Encyclopedia (IPE). Published annually. Tulsa, OK: PennWell Publishing Co.

Israel: The Historical Atlas. By New York Times Correspondents. New York: Macmillan, 1997. 208p.

Israel Pocket Library. *Geography.* Compiled from material originally published in the *Encyclopaedia Judaica.* One of several volumes in this series *(Society; Religious Life and Communities; Immigration and Settlement; Economy;* and others). Jerusalem: Keter, 1973. 263p.

Issawi, Charles. *An Economic History of the Middle East and North Africa.* New York: Columbia Univ. Press, 1982. 304p.

———. *The Fertile Crescent 1800–1914; A Documentary Economic History.* Studies in Middle Eastern History. New York: Oxford Univ. Press, 1988. 502p.

Jabbur, Jibrail S. *The Bedouins and the Desert: Aspects of Nomadic Life in the Arab East.* Trans. Lawrence I. Conrad. Ed. Suhay J. Jabbur and Lawrence I. Conrad. Albany: State Univ. of New York Press, 1995. 670p.

Jaber, Hala. *Hezbollah: Born with a Vengeance.* New York: Columbia Univ. Press, 1997. 240p.

Janzen, Jörg. *Nomads in the Sultanate of Oman.* Westview Special Studies on the Middle East. Boulder, CO: Westview Press, 1986. 315p.

Jernazian, Ephraim K. *Judgment unto Truth: Witnessing the Armenian Genocide.* New Brunswick, NJ: Transaction Publishers, 1990. 163p.

Jones, Stephen B. "A Unified Field Theory of Political Geography." *Annals* (Association of American Geographers) 44, no. 4 (Dec. 1954): 111–123.

Joseph, John, *Muslim-Christian Relations and Inter-Christian Rivalries in the Middle East: The Case of the Jacobites in an Age of Transition.* Albany: State Univ. of New York Press, 1983. 240p.

Kadri, Ali. "A Survey of Commuting Labor from the West Bank to Israel." *MEJ* 52, no. 4 (Autumn 1998): 517–530.

Kahan Commission. *The Beirut Massacre: The Complete Kahan Commission Report.* With an introduction by Abba Eban. Princeton, NJ: Karz-Cohl, 1983. 107p.

Kahan, David. *Agriculture and Water Resources in the West Bank and Gaza, 1967–1987.* Boulder, CO: Westview Press, 1987. 181p.

Kahane, Meir. *They Must Go.* New York: Grosset and Dunlap, 1981. 282p.

Kaikobad, Kaiyan Homi. *The Shatt al-Arab Boundary Question.* Oxford: Oxford Univ. Press, 1988. 184p.

Kark, Ruth, ed. *The Land That Became Israel: Studies in Historical Geography.* New Haven; also Jerusalem: Yale Univ. Press; also Magnes Press, Hebrew Univ., 1989. 332p. + plates.

Karouzis, George, and Christina G. Karouzis. *Touring Guide of Cyprus.* Rev. ed. Nicosia, Cyprus: Selas, 1997. 304p.

Karpat, Kemal H. *The Gecekondu: Rural Migration and Urbanization.* Cambridge: Cambridge Univ. Press, 1976. 291p.

Karsh, Efraim. "Geopolitical Determinism: The Origins of the Iran-Iraq War." *MEJ* 44, no. 2 (Spring 1990): 256–268.

———. *Fabricating Israeli History: The "New Historians".* London: Frank Cass and Co., 1997. 210p.

Kaufman, Burton I. *The Arab Middle East and the United States: Inter-Arab Rivalry and Superpower Diplomacy.* New York: Twayne Publishers, 1996. 291p.

Kechichian, Joseph A. *Oman and the World: The Emergence of an Independent Foreign Policy.* Santa Monica, CA: Rand, 1995. 409p.

———. "Trends in Saudi National Security." *MEJ* 53, no. 2 (Spring 1999): 232–253.

Keddie, N. R. "Is There a Middle East?" *International Journal of Middle East Studies* 4 (1972): 255–271.

Kedourie, Elie. *Politics in the Middle East.* Oxford: Oxford Univ. Press, 1992. 366p.

Kelly, J. B. *Arabia, the Gulf and the West.* New York: Basic Books, 1980. 530p.

Kemp, Geoffrey, and Robert E. Harkavy. *Strategic Geography and the Changing Middle East.* Washington, DC: Carnegie Endowment for International Peace/Brookings Institution Press, 1997. 493p.

[Kennan, George F.] "The Sources of Soviet Conduct." *Foreign Affairs* 65, no. 4 (Spring 1987): 852–868. (Originally published in this journal in July 1947, includes Kennan's updated comments.)

Kennedy, David, and Derrick Riley. *Rome's Desert Frontier from the Air.* Austin: Univ. of Texas Press, 1990. 256p.

Kessler, Martha, Helena Cobban, and Hisham Melhem. "What about Syria?" *Middle East Policy* 7, no. 1 [Issue 63] (Oct. 1999): 101–112.

Keyder, Caglar, and Frank Tabak, eds. *Landholding and Commercial Agriculture in the Middle East.* Albany: State Univ. of New York Press, 1991. 260p.

Khadduri, Majid. *The Gulf War: The Origins and Implications of the Iraq-Iran Conflict.* New York: Oxford Univ. Press, 1988. 236p.

Khadduri, Majid, and Edmund Ghareeb. *War in the Gulf, 1990–1991.* New York: Oxford Univ. Press, 1997. 299p.

Khader, Bichara, ed. *The Economic Development of Jordan.* London: Croom Helm, 1987. 246p.

Khalidi, Walid. *Conflict and Violence in Lebanon: Confrontation in the Middle East.* Harvard Studies in International Affairs no. 38. Cambridge, MA: Center for International Affairs, Harvard Univ., 1979. 217p.

———. "Lebanon: Yesterday and Tomorrow." *MEJ* 43. no. 3 (Summer 1989): 375–387.

Khalidi, Walid, ed. *From Haven to Conquest: Readings in Zionism and the Palestine Problem Until 1948.* Beirut: Institute for Palestine Studies, 1971. 839p.

Khalifa, Ali Mohammed. *The United Arab Emirates: Unity in Fragmentation.* Boulder, CO: Westview Press, 1979. 235p.

al-Khalil, "Lebanon and Its Future Development." *American-Arab Affairs* 37 (Summer 1991): 57–60.

Khalil, Samir. *Republic of Fear: Saddam's Iraq.* Reprinted with new introduction 1990. New York: Pantheon Books, 1990. 310p.

el-Khawas, Mohamed, and Samir Abed-Rabbo. Foreword by Rabbi Elmer Berger. *American Aid to Israel: Nature and Impact.* Brattleboro, VT: Amana Books, 1984. 191p.

el Khazen, Farid. "The Lebanese Economy After a Decade of Turmoil." *American-Arab Affairs* no. 12 (Spring 1985): 72–84.

Kheirabadi, Masoud. *Iranian Cities: Formation and Development.* An Iran-American Foundation Book. Austin: Univ. of Texas Press, 1991. 160p.

Khoury, Rami G. *The Antiquities of the Jordan Rift Valley.* Amman, Jordan: Al Kutba, 1988. 151p.

Khoury, Phillip. *Syria and the French Mandate: The Politics of Arab Nationalism, 1920–1945.* Princeton, NJ: Princeton Univ. Press, 1987. 698p.

Kimmerling, Baruch, ed. *The Israeli State and Society: Boundaries and Frontiers.* Albany: State Univ. of New York Press, 1989. 301p.

Kingdom of Saudi Arabia. *Statistical Year Book.* Riyadh: Central Dept. of Statistics, published annually.

Klieman, Aaron S. *Foundations of British Policy in the Arab World: The Cairo Conference of 1921.* Baltimore, MD: Johns Hopkins Press, 1970. 322p.

Kolars, John. *Tradition, Season, and Change in a Turkish Village.* Research Paper no. 82, Department of Geography. Chicago: Univ. of Chicago, 1968. 205p.

———. "The Course of Water in the Arab Middle East." *American-Arab Affairs* 33 (Summer 1990): 57–68.

Kolars, John F., and William A. Mitchell. *The Euphrates River and the Southeast Anatolia Development Project.* Carbondale: Southern Illinois Univ. Press, 1991. 325p.

Korany, Bahgat, Ali E. Hillal Dessouki, et al. *The Foreign Policies of Arab States: The Challenge of Change.* 2d ed. Boulder, CO: Westview Press, 1991. 449p.

Korn, David A. *Stalemate: The War of Attrition and Great Power Diplomacy in the Middle East, 1967–1970.* Boulder, CO: Westview Press, 1992. 326p.

Kreiger, Barbara. *Living Waters: Myth, History, and Politics of the Dead Sea.* New York: Continuum, 1988. 226p.

Krimly, Rayed. "The Political Economy of Adjusted Priorities: Declining Oil Revenues and Saudi Fiscal Policies." *MEJ* 53, no. 2 (Spring 1999): 254–267.

Krinsley, Daniel B. *A Geomorphological and Paleoclimatological Study of the Playas of Iran.* Part I and Part II. Prepared for Air Force Cambridge Research Laboratories, U.S. Air Force, Bedford, MA. Washington, DC: U.S. Geological Survey, Department of the Interior, August 1970. Pt. 1, 329p.; Pt. 2, 486p.

Lacey, Robert. *The Kingdom.* New York: Harcourt Brace Jovanovich, 1981. 631p.

Lawless, Richard, ed. *The Middle Eastern Village: Changing Economic and Social Relations.* London: Croom Helm, 1987. 304p.

Lawson, Fred H. *Bahrain: The Modernization of Autocracy.* Profiles: Nations of the Contemporary Middle East. Boulder, CO: Westview Press, 1989. 150p.

Le Troquet, Yann, and Rozenn Hommery al-Oudat. "From Kuwait to Jordan: The Palestinians' Third Exodus." *Journal of Palestine Studies* 28, no. 3 (Spring 1999): 37–51.

Lees, G. M., and N. L. Falcon. "The Geographical History of the Mesopotamian Plains." *Geographical Journal* 118 (1952): 24–39.

Lefebvre, Jeffrey A. "Red Sea Security and the Geopolitical-Economy of the Hanish Islands Dispute." *MEJ* 52, no. 3 (Summer 1998): 367–385.

Lenczowski, George. *American Presidents and the Middle East.* Durham, NC: Duke Univ. Press, 1990. 321p.

Lesch, Ann M. "Palestinians in Kuwait." *Journal of Palestine Studies* 20, no. 4 (Summer 1991): 42–54.

Lesch, Ann Mosely, and Mark Tessler. *Israel, Egypt, and the Palestinians: From Camp David to Intifada.* Foreword by Richard B. Parker. Indiana Series in Arab and Islamic Studies, Bloomington: Indiana Univ. Press, 1989. 298p.

Lesch, David W. *The Middle East and the United States: A Historical and Political Reassessment.* 2d ed. Boulder, CO: Westview Press, 1999. 496p.

Leslie, S. Clement. *The Rift in Israel: Religious Authority and Secular Democracy.* London: Routledge and Kegan Paul, 1971, 185p.

Levins, John. *Days of Fear: The Inside Story of the Iraqi Invasion and Occupation of Kuwait.* Dubai, UAE: Motivate Publishing, 1997. 672p.

Lewis, Bernard. *The Emergence of Modern Turkey.* 2d ed. New York: Oxford Univ. Press, 1968. 530p.

Lewis, Norman N. "Lebanon—The Mountain and Its Terraces." *Geog. Rev.* 43, no. 1 (Jan. 1953): 1–14.

———. *Nomads and Settlers in Syria and Jordan, 1800–1980.* Cambridge Middle East Library. Cambridge: Cambridge Univ. Press, 1987. 249p.

Lewis, Peter G. "The Politics of Iranian Place-Names." Geographical Record. *Geog. Rev.* 72, no. 1 (Jan. 1982): 99–102.

Lewis, Samuel W. "The United States and Israel: Evolution of an Unwritten Alliance." *MEJ* 53, no. 3 (Summer 1999): 364–378.

Limbert, John W. *Iran: At War with History.* Profiles: Nations of the Contemporary Middle East. Boulder, CO: Westview Press, 1987. 186p.

Little, Douglas. "Cold War and Covert Action: The United States and Syria, 1945–1958." *MEJ* 44, no. 1 (Winter 1990): 51–75.

Long, David E. *The Persian Gulf: An Introduction to Its Peoples, Politics, and Economics.* Rev. ed.

Westview Special Studies on the Middle East. Boulder, CO: Westview Press, 1978. 174p.

———. *The Kingdom of Saudi Arabia.* Gainesville: Univ. Press of Florida, 1997. 154p.

Long, David E., and Bernard Reich, eds. *The Government and Politics of the Middle East and North Africa.* 2d ed., rev. and updated. Boulder, CO: Westview Press, 1986. 479p.

Lorenz, Joseph P. *Egypt and the Arabs: Foreign Policy and the Search for National Identity.* Boulder, CO: Westview Press, 1990. 184p.

Lorimer, J. G. *Gazetteer of the Persian Gulf, Oman, and Central Arabia.* 4 vols. Calcutta: Superintendent of Government Printing, 1915.

Lustick, Ian. *Arabs in the Jewish State: Israel's Control of a National Minority.* Modern Middle East Series no. 6. Austin: Univ. of Texas Press, 1980. 385p.

———. *For the Land and the Lord: Jewish Fundamentalism in Israel.* [New York]: Council on Foreign Relations Press, 1988. 256p.

———. "Has Israel Annexed East Jerusalem?" *Middle East Policy* 5, no. 1 [Issue 55] (Jan. 1997): 34–45.

McDowall, David. *A Modern History of the Kurds.* Rev. ed. London: I. B. Tauris, 1999. 504p.

McGowan, Daniel A., and Marc Ellis. *Remembering Deir Yassin: The Future of Israel and Palestine.* New York: Olive Branch Press, 1998. 150p.

McKee, Edwin D., ed. *A Study of Global Sand Seas.* U.S. Geological Survey Professional Paper 1052. Prepared in cooperation with the National Aeronautics and Space Administration. Washington, DC: U.S. Government Printing Office, 1979. 429p.

McLachin, Keith, ed. *The Boundaries of Modern Iran.* New York: St. Martin's Press, 1994. 150p.

Mackinder, Sir Halford J. "The Geographical Pivot of History." *Geographical Journal* 23 (1904): 421–444.

———. *Democratic Ideals and Reality: A Study in the Politics of Reconstruction.* New York: Holt, 1919. 266p.

Makiya, Kanan. *Republic of Fear: The Politics of Modern Iraq.* 2d ed. Berkeley: Univ. of California Press, 1998. 323p.

Makram-Ebeid, Mona. "Political Opposition in Egypt: Democratic Myth or Reality?" *MEJ* 43, no. 3 (Summer 1989): 423–436.

el Mallakh, Ragaei. *The Economic Development of the United Arab Emirates.* New York: St. Martin's Press, 1981. 215p.

Malville, J. M., et al. "Megaliths and Neolithic Astronomy in Southern Egypt." *Nature* 392, no. 6675 (1998): 488–491.

Mandaville, James P., Jr. "Plants [of the Oman Mountains]." In *The Scientific Results of the Oman Flora and Fauna Survey 1975*. A Journal of Oman Studies Special Report. Published by the Ministry of Information and Culture, Sultanate of Oman. n.d. 229–267.

———. "Studies in the Flora of Arabia, XI: Some Historical and Geographical Aspects of a Principal Floristic Frontier." *Notes from the Royal Botanic Garden, Edinburgh* 42, no. 1 (1984): 1–15.

———. *Flora of Eastern Saudi Arabia*. London: Kegan Paul International, 1990. 482p.

Manners, Ian R. "Problems of Water Resource Management in a Semi-Arid Environment: The Case of Irrigation Agriculture in the Central Jordan Rift Valley." Chap. 5 in Brian S. Hoyle, ed., *Spatial Aspects of Development*. Chichester, Eng.: John Wiley, 1974.

Marlowe, John. *The Persian Gulf in the Twentieth Century*. London: Cresset Press, 1962. 278p.

Marr, Phebe. *The Modern History of Iraq*. Boulder, CO: Westview Press, 1985. 382p.

Mastney, Vojtech, and R. Craig Nation, eds. *Turkey between East and West: New Challenges for a Rising Regional Power*. Boulder, CO: Westview Press, 1997. 296p.

Matheson, Sylvia A. *Persia: An Archaeological Guide*. Park Ridge, NJ: Noyes Press, 1973. 330p.

Mauger, Thierry. *The Bedouins of Arabia*. Trans. Khia Mason and Igor Persan. Paris: Souffles, 1988a. 139p.

———. *Flowered Men and Green Slopes of Arabia*. Trans. Khia Mason. Paris: Souffles, 1988b. 189p.

Mazzawi, Musa. *Palestine and the Law: Guidelines for the Resolution of the Arab-Israel Conflict*. Ithaca, NY: Ithaca Press, 1997. 433p.

Mehr, Farhang. *A Colonial Legacy: The Dispute Over the Islands of Abu Musa and the Greater and Lesser Tumbs*. Lanham, MD: Univ. Press of America, 1997. 215p.

Melamid, Alexander. *Oil and the Economic Geography of the Middle East and North Africa: Studies*. Ed. C. Max Kortepeter. Princeton, NJ: Darwin Press, 1991. 320p.

Middle East Research Institute (MERI), University of Pennsylvania. Reports on most major Middle East states, titles with respective state names. London: Croom Helm, mostly mid-1980s.

Mikesell, Marvin W. "The Deforestation of Mount Lebanon." *Geog. Rev.* 59, no. 1 (Jan. 1969): 1–28.

Miller, Judith, and Laurie Mylroie. *Saddam Hussein and the Crisis in the Gulf*. New York: Times Books Division of Random House, 1990. 268p.

Minerals Yearbook. U.S. Geological Survey, Bureau of Mines. Published annually. Web site: <http://minerals.er.usgs.gov/minerals/pubs/myb.html>

Ministry of Agriculture and Water [Saudi Arabia]. In cooperation with the Saudi Arabian–United States Joint Commission on Economic Cooperation. *Water Atlas of Saudi Arabia*. Riyadh: Saudi Arabian Printing Co., 1984. 112p.

Mitchell, William A. "Reconstruction After Disaster: The Gediz Earthquake of 1970." *Geog. Rev.* 66, no. 3 (July 1976): 296–313.

Monshipouri, Mahmood. "Iran's Search for the New Pragmatism." *Middle East Policy* 6, no. 2 [Issue 60] (Oct. 1998): 95–112.

Montaigne, Fen. "Iran: Testing the Waters of Reform." *National Geographic*, July 1999, 2–33.

Moore, Clement Henry. "Money and Power: the Dilemma of the Egyptian Infitah." *MEJ* 40, no. 4 (Autumn 1986): 634–650.

Moore, John Norton, ed. *The Arab-Israeli Conflict*. 3 vols.: 1 and 2, *Readings*; 3, *Documents*. Sponsored by the American Society of International Law. Princeton: Princeton Univ. Press, 1974. Vol. 1, 1,067p.; vol. 2, 1,193p.; vol. 3, 1,248p.

Moorehead, John. *In Defiance of the Elements*. With photographs by Robin Constable. London: Quartet Books, 1977. 160p.

Morris, Benny. *The Birth of the Palestinian Refugee Problem, 1947–1949*. Cambridge: Cambridge Univ. Press, 1989. 380p.

Mortimer, Edward. *Faith and Power: The Politics of Islam*. New York: Random House, 1982. 432p.

Moscati, Sabatino. *The World of the Phoenicians*. Trans. Alastair Hamilton. New York: Praeger, 1968. 281p.

Mostyn, Trevor. *Major Political Events in Iran, Iraq, and the Arabian Peninsula 1945–1990*. Ed. Thomas S. Arms. New York: Facts on File, 1991. 308p.

Mufti, Malik. "Daring and Caution in Turkish Foreign Policy." *MEJ* 52, no. 1 (Winter 1998): 32–50.

Nabir, Mordechai. *Saudi Arabia in the Oil Era*. Boulder, CO: Westview Press, 1988. 247p.

Nachmani, Amikam. "The Remarkable Turkish-Israeli Tie." *Middle East Quarterly* 5, no. 2 (June 1998): 19–29.

Nakhleh, Emile A. *A Palestinian Agenda for the West Bank and Gaza.* Washington, DC: American Enterprise Institute, 1980. 127p.

———. "The West Bank and Gaza: Twenty Years Later." *MEJ* 42, no. 2 (Spring 1988): 209–226.

Nassar, Jamal R. *The Palestine Liberation Organization: From Armed Struggle to the Declaration of Independence.* New York: Praeger, 1991. 256p.

Nassar, Jamal R., and Roger Heacock, eds. *Intifada: Palestine at the Crossroads.* New York: Praeger, 1990. 347p.

National Atlas of United Arab Emirates. Al-Ain: UAE University, 1993.

National Geographic Atlas of the World. 7th ed. Washington, DC: National Geographic Society, 1999. 137 double pages plus index.

National Geographic Society. *Exploring Our Living Planet.* Washington DC: National Geographic Society, 1983. 366p.

Naval Intelligence Division [UK]. *Palestine and Trans-jordan.* Geographical Handbook Series B.R. 514. Oxford: Oxford Univ. Press for H.M. Stationery Office, 1943. 621p.

Netton, Ian Richard, ed. *Arabia and the Gulf: From Traditional Society to Modern States.* Totowa, NJ: Barnes & Noble, 1986. 259p.

"Next Steps with Iran: A Debate." *Middle East Quarterly* 5, no. 2 (June 1998): 63–77.

Niblock, Tim, ed. *Social and Economic Development in the Arab Gulf.* New York: St. Martin's Press, 1980. 242p.

———. *Iraq: The Contemporary State.* New York: St. Martin's Press, 1982. 277p.

Norton, Augustus Richard. *Amal and the Shi'a: Struggle for the Soul of Lebanon.* Austin: Univ. of Texas Press, 1987. 238p.

———. "Lebanon After Taif: Is the Civil War Over?" *MEJ* 45, no. 3 (Summer 1991): 457–473.

Norton, Augustus R., et al. "Gender, Politics and the State: What Do Middle Eastern Women Want?" *Middle East Policy* 5, no. 3 [Issue 57] (Sept. 1997): 155–189.

Norwich, John Julius. *A Short History of Byzantium.* New York: Knopf, 1997. 431p.

Nugent, Jeffrey B., and Theodore Thomas, eds. *Bahrain and the Gulf: Past Perspectives and Alternative Futures.* New York: St. Martin's Press, 1985. 221p.

O'Ballance, Edgar. *Civil War in Lebanon, 1975–92.* New York: St. Martin's Press, 1999. 240p.

O'Reilly, Marc J. "Omanibalancing: Oman Confronts an Uncertain Future." *MEJ* 52, no. 1 (Winter 1998): 70–84.

Olson, Robert. *The Kurdish Question and Turkish-Iranian Relations: From World War I to 1998.* Costa Mesa, CA: Mazda Publishers, 1998. 106p.

Olsson, Tord, Elisabeth Ozdalga, and Catharina Raudvere, eds. *Alevi Identity.* Istanbul, Turkey: Swedish Research Institute in Istanbul, 1998. 210p.

Organski, A. F. K. *The $36 Billion Bargain: Strategy and Politics in US Assistance to Israel.* New York: Columbia Univ. Press, 1990. 315p.

Orni, Efraim, and Efraim Efrat. *Geography of Israel.* 4th rev. ed. Jerusalem: Israel Universities Press, 1980. 556p.

"Overthrow Saddam? A Debate." *Middle East Quarterly* 6, no. 2 (June 1999) : 35–47.

Pampanini, Andrea. *Cities from the Arabian Desert: The Building of Jubail and Yanbu in Saudi Arabia.* Westport, CT: Praeger, 1997. 209p.

Pappe, Ilan. "Post-Zionist Critique on Israel and the Palestinians." *Journal of Palestine Studies* 26, no. 2 (Winter 1997): 29–41.

Parker, Richard B. *The Politics of Miscalculation in the Middle East.* Indiana Series in Arab and Islamic Studies. Bloomington: Indiana Univ. Press, 1993. 320p.

Parker, Richard B., ed. *The Six-Day War: A Retrospective.* Gainesville: Univ. Press of Florida, 1996. 345p.

Pearcy, G. Etzel. "The Middle East—An Indefinable Region." Department of State Publication 7684. Washington, DC: 1964. (Updated from an article in the Department of State Bulletin, Mar. 23, 1959.) 12p.

Peck, Malcolm C. *The United Arab Emirates: A Venture in Unity.* Profiles: Nations of the Contemporary Middle East. Boulder, CO: Westview Press, 1986. 176p.

Pelletiere, Stephen C. *The Kurds: An Unstable Element in the Gulf.* Boulder, CO: Westview Press, 1984. 220p.

Penrose, Edith, and E. F. Penrose. *Iraq: International Relations and National Development.* Nations of the Modern World. London: Ernest Benn, 1978. 569p.

Peretz, Don. *The West Bank: History, Politics, Society, and Economy.* Westview Special Studies on the Middle East. Boulder, CO: Westview Press, 1986. 173p.

———. *Intifada: The Palestinian Uprising.* Boulder, CO: Westview Press, 1990. 246p.

———. *The Middle East Today.* 6th ed. Westport, CT: Praeger, 1994. 593p.

———. "The Significance of Israel." *MEJ* 53, no. 3 (Summer 1999): 357–363.

Peretz, Don, and Gideon Doron. *The Government and Politics of Israel.* 3d ed. Boulder, CO: Westview Press, 1997. 308p.

Perthes, Volker. "The Syrian Economy in the 1980s." *MEJ* 46, no. 1 (Winter 1992): 37–58.

Peterson, J. E. *The Politics of Middle Eastern Oil.* Washington, DC: Middle East Institute, 1983. 529p.

Philby, H. St. John B. *Arabia of the Wahhabis.* London: Cass, 1977. (New impression of 1928 ed., with additions; one of Philby's several classic works on Arabia.) 422p.

Pipes, Daniel. *Greater Syria: The History of an Ambition.* New York: Oxford Univ. Press, 1990. 240p.

Pitcher, Donald Edgar. *A Historical Geography of the Ottoman Empire: From Earliest Times to the End of the Sixteenth Century.* Leiden: E. J. Brill, 1972. 171p. + 29 folded maps.

Purser, B. H., ed. *The Persian Gulf.* New York: Springer-Verlag, 1973. 471p.

al-Qasimi, Sultan Muhammad. *The Myth of Arab Piracy in the Gulf.* 2d ed. New York: Routledge, 1988. 244p.

Quandt, William B. *Camp David: Peacemaking and Politics.* Washington, DC: Brookings Institution. 1986. 426p.

Quandt, William B., ed. *The Middle East: Ten Years After Camp David.* Washington, DC: Brookings Institution. 1988. 517p.

Rabinovich, Itamar. *The War for Lebanon, 1970–1985.* Ithaca: Cornell Univ. Press, 1985. 262p.

———. *The Brink of Peace: The Israeli-Syrian Negotiation.* Princeton, NJ: Princeton Univ. Press, 1998. 283p.

Radwan, L. "Water Management in the Egyptian Delta: Problems of Wastage and Inefficiency." *Geographical Journal* 164, no. 2 (1998): 129–138.

Ragette, Friedrich, ed. *The Beirut of Tomorrow: Planning for Reconstruction.* Beirut: American Univ. of Beirut, 1983. 141p.

Rahman, H. *The Making of the Gulf War: Origins of Kuwait's Long-Standing Territorial Dispute with Iraq.* Berkshire, UK: Ithaca Press, 1997. 378p.

Rahman, Mushtaqur, ed. *Muslim World: Geography and Development.* Lanham, MD: Univ. Press of America, 1987. 190p.

Rajaee, Farhang. "A Thermidor of 'Islamic Yuppies?' Conflict and Compromise in Iran's Politics." *MEJ* 53, no. 2 (Spring 1999): 217–231.

Rajaee, Farhang, ed. *Iranian Perspectives on the Iran-Iraq War.* Gainesville: Univ. Press of Florida, 1997. 168p.

Ramazani, Rouhallah K. *The Persian Gulf and the Strait of Hormuz. International Straits of the World,* vol. 3. Alphen aan den Rijn, Netherlands: Sijthoff and Noordhoff, 1979. 180p.

———. "Iran's Foreign Policy: Both North and South." *MEJ* 46, no. 3 (Summer 1992): 393–412.

Ramazani, R. K. "The Shifting Premise of Iran's Foreign Policy: Towards a Democratic Peace." *MEJ* 52, no. 2 (Spring 1998): 177–187.

Randal, Jonathan C. *After Such Knowledge, What Forgiveness? My Encounters with Kurdistan.* Boulder, CO: Westview Press, 1998. 368p.

Raschka, Marilyn. "Beirut Digs Out." *Archaeology* 49, no. 4 (July-Aug. 1996): 44–50.

Al Rashoud, Claudia Farkas. *Kuwait: Before and after the Storm.* Kuwait: Kuwait Bookshops Co., 1992. 201p.

Reddaway, John. *Burdened with Cyprus: The British Connection.* London: Weidenfeld and Nicholson, 1986. 237p.

Redman, Charles L. *The Rise of Civilization: From Early Farmers to Urban Society in the Ancient Near East.* San Francisco: Freeman, 1978. 367p.

———. "Mesopotamia and the First Cities, 4000 BC–539 BC." *In Old World Civilizations: The Rise of Cities and States.* Ed. Goran Burenholt. New York: HarperCollins, 1994.

Reich, Bernard, and Gershon R. Kieval. *Israel: Land of Tradition and Conflict.* 2d ed. Boulder, CO: Westview Press, 1993. 236p.

Rempel, Terry. "The Significance of Israel's Partial Annexation of East Jerusalem." *MEJ* 51, no. 4 (Autumn 1997): 520–534.

Richards, Alan, and John Waterbury. *A Political Economy of the Middle East.* 2d ed. Boulder, CO: Westview Press, 1996. 464p.

Richardson, John P. *The West Bank: A Portrait.* Special Study no. 5. Washington, DC: Middle East Institute, 1984. 221p.

Riphenburg, Carol J. *Oman: Political Development in a Changing World.* Westport, CT: Praeger Publishers, 1998. 248p.

Ritter, Scott. *Endgame: Solving the Iraq Problem—Once and for All.* New York: Simon and Schuster, 1999. 240p.

Robinson, Andrew. *The Story of Writing.* London: Thames and Hudson, 1995. 224p.

Robinson, Glenn E. *Building a Palestinian State: The Incomplete Revolution.* Bloomington and Indianapolis: Indiana Univ. Press, 1997. 228p.

Rodenbeck, Max. *Cairo: The City Victorious.* London: Macmillan, 1998. 395p.

Rogers, Peter, and Peter Lydon, eds. *Water in the Arab World: Perspectives and Prognoses.* Cambridge, MA: Harvard Univ. Press, 1994. 376p.

Rouyer, Alwyn. "The Water Accords of Oslo II: Averting a Looming Disaster." *Middle East Policy* 7, no. 1 [Issue 62] (Oct. 1999): 113–135.

Roy, Olivier. "The Crisis of Religious Legitimacy in Iran." *MEJ* 53, no. 2 (Spring 1999): 201–216.

Roy, Sara. *The Gaza Strip: The Political Economy of De-development.* Washington, DC: Institute for Palestine Studies, 1995. 375p.

Rubin, Barry. *The Transformation of Palestinian Politics from Revolution to State-Building.* Cambridge, MA: Harvard Univ. Press, 1999. 277p.

Rudloff, Willy. *World Climates.* With tables of climatic data and practical suggestions. Stuttgart: Wissenchaftliche Verlagsgesellschaft mbH, 1981. 632p.

Rugh, William A. "The Foreign Policy of the United Arab Emirates." *MEJ* 50, no. 1 (Winter 1996): 57–70.

Runciman, Steven. *A History of the Crusades.* 3 vols. Cambridge: Cambridge Univ. Press, 1954.

Al-Sabah, Y. S. F. *The Oil Economy of Kuwait.* London and Boston: Kegan Paul, 1980. 166p.

Sachar, Howard M. *A History of Israel from the Rise of Zionism to Our Time.* Vol. 1. New York: Knopf, 1976. 932p. *A History of Israel from the Aftermath of the Yom Kippur War.* Vol. 2. New York: Oxford Univ. Press, 1987. 319p.

Saggs, H. W. F. *Civilization before Greece and Rome.* New Haven, CT: Yale Univ. Press, 1989. 322p.

———. *Babylonians.* Vol. I, *Peoples of the Past.* Norman: Univ. of Oklahoma Press, 1995. 192p.

Sahliyeh, Emile F. *The PLO After the Lebanon War.* Westview Special Studies on the Middle East. Boulder, CO: Westview Press, 1986. 286p.

Said, Edward W. *The Politics of Dispossession: The Struggle for Palestinian Self-Determination, 1969–1994.* New York: Pantheon Books, 1994. 450p.

Said, Edward W., and Christopher Hitchens, eds. *Blaming the Victims: Spurious Scholarship and the Palestine Question.* London: Verso, 1988. 296p.

Said, Rushdi. *The Geology of Egypt.* Amsterdam: Elsevier, 1962. 377p.

———. *The Geological Evolution of the River Nile.* New York: Springer-Verlag, 1981. 151p.

Salamé, Ghassan, ed. *The Foundations of the Arab State.* London: Croom Helm, 1987. 260p.

Salameh, Elias. "Jordan's Water Resources: Development and Future Prospects." *American-Arab Affairs* 33 (Summer 1990): 69–77.

Salabi, Kamal. *A House of Many Mansions: The History of Lebanon Reconsidered.* Berkeley: Univ. of California Press, 1988. 247p.

———. *The Modern History of Jordan.* 2d ed. New York: I. B. Tauris, 1998. 298p.

Sandler, Shmuel, et al. "The Religious-Secular Divide in Israeli Politics." *Middle East Policy* 6, no. 4 [Issue 62] (June 1999): 137–145.

Saqqaf, Abdulaziz Y., ed. *The Middle East City: Ancient Traditions Confront a Modern World.* New York: Paragon House, 1987. 393p.

Saudi Aramco and Its World: Arabia and the Middle East. Rev. ed. Dhahran: Saudi Arabian Oil Co., 1995. 291p.

Savir, Uri. *The Process: 1,100 Days That Changed the Middle East.* New York: Random House, 1998. 326p.

Sayari, Sabri. "Turkey and the Middle East in the 1990s." *Journal of Palestine Studies* 26, no. 3 (Spring 1997): 44–55.

Sayigh, Rosemary. *Too Many Enemies: The Palestinian Experience in Lebanon.* London: Zed Books, 1994. 369p.

Sayigh, Yezid. *Armed Struggle and the Search for State: The Palestinian National Movement, 1949–1993.* New York: Oxford Univ. Press, 1997. 953p.

Sayigh, Yusif A. *The Economies of the Arab World: Development Since 1945. The Economies of the Arab World,* vol. 1. New York: St. Martin's Press, 1978. 726p.

Schick, Irvin C., and Ertugrul Ahmet Tonak, eds. *Turkey in Transition: New Perspectives.* New York: Oxford Univ. Press, 1987. 405p.

Schiff, Zeev, and Ehud Yaari. *Intifada: The Palestinian Uprising—Israel's Third Front.* Ed. and trans. Ina Friedman. New York: Simon and Schuster, 1989. 356p.

Schmandt-Bessarat, Denise. "The Earliest Precursor of Writing." *Scientific American* 238 (1978): 50–59.

Schnell, Izhak, Itzhak Benenson, and Michael Sofer. "The Spatial Pattern of Arab Industrial Markets in Israel." *Annals* (Association of American Geographers) 89, no. 2 (June 1999): 312–37.

Schofield, Richard. *Kuwait and Iraq: Historical Claims and Territorial Disputes*. London: Royal Institute of International Affairs, 1993. 226p.

———. "Mending Gulf Fences." *Middle East Insight*, March/April 1996, 36–41.

Schulz, E., and J. W. Whitney. "Vegetation in North-Central Saudi Arabia." *Journal of Arid Environments* 10 (1986): 175–186.

Schwarzkopf, H. Norman. Written with Peter Petre. *It Doesn't Take a Hero*. New York: Bantam Books, 1992. 530p.

Scientific American. Special issue, The Dynamic Earth. 249, no. 3 (Sept. 1983).

Scott, Jamie, and Paul Simpson-Housley, eds. *Sacred Places and Profane Spaces: Essays in the Geographics of Judaism, Christianity, and Islam*. Contributions to the Study of Religion, no. 30. Westport, CT: Greenwood Press, 1991. 200p.

Scoville, Sheila A., ed. *Gazetteer of Arabia: A Geographical and Tribal History of the Arabian Peninsula*. Vol. 1, A-E. Graz, Austria: Akademische Druck- u. Verlagsanstalt, 1979. 742p.

Sela, Avraham, ed. *Political Encyclopedia of the Middle East*. New York: Continuum, 1999. 815p.

Selzer, Michael. *The Wineskin and the Wizard*. New York: Macmillan, 1970. 241p.

Serjeant, R. B., ed. *The Islamic City*. Paris: Unesco, 1980. 210p.

Shahir, Issa M., and Ayman H. Nasr. "Using Satellite Images to Detect Land-Use Change in Al-Ain City, United Arab Emirates." *Arab World Geographer* 2, no. 2 (Summer 1999): 139–148.

Shamekh, Ahmed A. *Spatial Patterns of Bedouin Settlement in al-Qasim Region, Saudi Arabia*. Lexington: Univ. of Kentucky, 1975. 315p.

Shaw, Stanford. *History of the Ottoman Empire and Modern Turkey*. Vol. I. Cambridge: Cambridge Univ. Press, 1976. 351p.

Shaw, Stanford, and Ezel Kural Shaw. *History of the Ottoman Empire and Modern Turkey*. Vol. II. Cambridge: Cambridge Univ. Press, 1977. 518p.

Shipler, David K. *Arab and Jew: Wounded Spirits in a Promised Land*. New York: Times Books, 1986. 596p.

Shlaim, Avi. *The Politics of Partition: King Abdullah, the Zionists and Palestine 1921–1951*. [New York]: Columbia Univ. Press, 1990. 465p.

Shohat, Ella. "The Invention of the Mizrahim." *Journal of Palestine Studies* 29, no. 1 (Autumn 1999): 6–20.

Sindelar, H. Richard, III, and J. E. Peterson, eds. *Crosscurrents in the Gulf: Arab, Regional and Global Interests*. For the Middle East Institute. London: Routledge, 1989. 256p.

Smith, Charles D. *Palestine and the Arab-Israeli Conflict*. 4th ed. Basingstoke: Macmillan, 2000. 358p.

Smith, George Adam. *The Historical Geography of the Holy Land*. 25th ed. London: Hodder and Stoughton, 1935. 744p.

Smith, Pamela Ann. "The Palestinian Diaspora, 1948–1985." *Journal of Palestine Studies* 15, no. 3 (Spring 1986): 90–108.

Soffer, Arnon. *The Conflict over Water in the Middle East*. Lanham, MD: Rowman and Littlefield, 1999. 303p.

Soffer, Arnon, and Julian V. Minghi. "Israel's Security Landscapes: The Impact of Military Considerations on Land Uses." *Professional Geographer* 38 (Feb. 1986): 28–41.

Spiegel, Steven L. *The Other Arab-Israeli Conflict: Making America's Middle East Policy, from Truman to Reagan*. Middle Eastern Studies, Monograph no. 1. Graduate School of International Studies, University of Miami. Chicago: Univ. of Chicago Press, 1985. 522p.

Spykman, Nicholas John. *The Geography of the Peace*. New York: Harcourt, Brace, 1944. 66p.

Stasis, Anastasios, and Michael Mavrocordatos. *Geography of Cyprus*. 3d ed. Larnaca: American Academy, 1989. 121p.

Steffen, Hans, et al. *Final Report on the Airphoto Interpretation Project of the Swiss Technical Cooperation Service, Berne*. Project carried out for the Central Planning Organisation, Sana. The major findings of the Population and Housing Census of February 1975. Zurich: Dept. of Geography, Univ. of Zurich, 1978. Two parts in 1 vol.: pt. 1, 164p; pt. 2, 231p. (Much of the same information appears in Hans Steffen, *Population Geography of the Yemen Arab Republic, Tubinger Atlas des Vorderen Orients, suppl. ser. B. [Geisteswissenschaften]*, no. 39 [Wiesbaden: Ludwig Reichert, 1979], 132p.)

Stein, Leonard J. *The Balfour Declaration*. Jerusalem: Magnes Press of Hebrew Univ., 1983. 681p.

Sternhell, Zeev. *The Founding Myths of Israel: Nationalism, Socialism, and the Making of the Jewish State.* Princeton, NJ: Princeton Univ. Press, 1998. 419p.

Stewart, Dona J. "Cities in the Desert: The Egyptian New-Town Program." *Annals* (Association of American Geographers) 86, no. 3 (Sept. 1996): 459–480.

Stookey, Robert W. *South Yemen: A Marxist Republic in Arabia.* Profiles: Nations of the Contemporary Middle East. Boulder, CO: Westview Press, 1982. 124p.

Stronach, David, and Stephen Lunsden. "The University of California Berkeley's Excavations at Nineveh." *Biblical Archaeologist* 55, no. 4 (Dec. 1992): 227–233.

Suleiman, Jaber. "The Current Political, Organizational, and Security Situation in the Palestinian Refugee Camps of Lebanon." *Journal of Palestine Studies* 29, no. 1 (Autumn 1999): 66–80.

Summers, W. M. "Proto-Elamite Civilization in Fars." In Uwe Finkbeiner and Wolfgang Rollig, *Gamdat Nasr: Period or Regional Style?* Wiesbaden: Ludwig Reichert, 1986. 199–211.

Survey of Israel. *Atlas of Israel.* 3d ed. Tel Aviv: Survey of Israel, 1985. Pages unnumbered.

Swagman, Charles F. *Development and Change in Highland Yemen.* Salt Lake City: Univ. of Utah Press, 1988. 200p.

Taha, M. F., et al. "The Climate of the Near East." Chap. 3 in K. Takahasha and H. Arakawa, eds., *Climates of Southern and Western Asia, World Survey of Climatology,* vol. 9. Amsterdam: Elsevier Scientific Publishing Co., 1981.

Al Taie, Hatim, et al. *Oman: A Comprehensive Guide to the Sultanate of Oman.* n.p., Oman: Al Roya Publishing, 1997. 464p.

Taryam, Abdullah Omran. *The Establishment of the United Arab Emirates, 1950–85.* London: Croom Helm, 1987. 190p.

Taylor, Alan R. *The Superpowers and the Middle East.* Contemporary Issues in the Middle East. Syracuse, NY: Syracuse Univ. Press, 1991. 212p.

Tekiner, Roselle, et al. *Anti-Zionism: Analytical Reflections.* Brattleboro, VT: Amana Books, 1988. 358p.

Telhami, Shibley. "From Camp David to Wye: Changing Assumptions in Arab-Israeli Negotiations." *MEJ* 53, no. 3 (Summer 1999): 379–392.

Tessler, Mark. *A History of the Israeli-Palestinian Conflict.* Bloomington: Indiana Univ. Press, 1994. 906p.

Theroux, Peter. "Syria: Behind the Mask." *National Geographic,* July 1996, 106–131.

———. "Beirut Rising." *National Geographic,* Sept. 1997, 100–123.

Thesiger, Wilfred. *Arabian Sands.* London: Longmans, 1959. 326p.

———. *The Marsh Arabs.* New York: Dutton, 1964. 242p.

Townsend, John. *Oman: The Making of a Modern State.* New York: St. Martin's Press, 1977. 212p.

Tubb, Jonathan N. *Canaanites, Peoples of the Past.* Norman: Univ. of Oklahoma Press, 1998. 160p.

Turkey. 3d ed. Insight Guides. Hong Kong: Apa Publications, 1989. 404p.

Twinam, Joseph Wright. *The Gulf, Cooperation and the Council: An American Perspective.* Washington, DC: Middle East Policy Council, 1992. 294p.

United Nations, Food and Agriculture Organization (FAO). *Production Yearbook.* Rome: FAO. Published annually.

United States Geological Survey (USGS). *Geology of the Arabian Peninsula.* Geological Survey Professional Paper 560. A review of the geology of Saudi Arabia as shown on USGS Miscellaneous Geologic Investigations Map I-270 A, "Geologic Map of the Arabian Peninsula" (1963). Washington, DC: U.S. Government Printing Office, 1966–1967, 1975, and 1989. (This study consists of nine USGS Professional Papers in the 560 series, Geology of the Arabian Peninsula: A, "Arabian Shield," B, "Yemen," C, "Aden Protectorate," D, "Sedimentary Geology of Saudi Arabia," E, "Bahrain," F, "Kuwait," G, "Southwestern Iraq," H, "Eastern Aden Protectorate and Part of Dhufar," and I, "Jordan.")

Vance, James E., Jr. *This Scene of Man.* New York: Harper, 1977. 437p.

van Dam, Nikolaos. "Sectarian and Regional Factionalism in the Syrian Political Elite." *MEJ* 32, no. 2 (Spring 1978): 201–210.

Van Dusen, Michael H. "Political Integration and Regionalism in Syria." *MEJ* 26, no. 2 (Spring 1972): 123–136.

Ventner, Al J. "The Oldest Threat: Water in the Middle East." *Middle East Policy* 6, no. 1 [Issue 59] (June 1998): 126–136.

Vidal, F. S. *The Oasis of al-Hasa.* Dhahran: Arabian American Oil Co. 1955. 216p.

Vita-Finzi, C. *Recent Earth Movements: An Introduction to Neotectonics.* London: Academic Press, 1986. 226p.

Voll, John Obert. *Islam: Continuity and Change in the Modern World.* Boulder, CO, and Essex, UK: Westview Press and Longman, 1982. 397p.

Wagstaff, J. M. *The Evolution of Middle Eastern Landscapes.* Totowa, NJ: Barnes & Noble, 1985. 304p.

Water for the Future. Washington, DC: National Academy Press, 1999. 226p.

Waterbury, John. *Hydropolitics of the Nile Valley.* Syracuse: Syracuse Univ. Press, 1979. 301p.

———. *The Egypt of Nasser and Sadat: The Political Economy of Two Regimes.* Princeton Studies on the Near East. Princeton: Princeton Univ. Press, 1983. 475p.

Weekes, Richard V., ed. *Muslim Peoples: A World Ethnographic Survey.* 2d ed., rev. and enl. 2 vols. Westport, CT: Greenwood Press, 1984. 953p.

Weinbaum, Marvin G., Politics and Development in Foreign Aid: US Economic Assistance to Egypt, 1975–82." *MEJ* 37, no. 4 (Autumn 1983): 636–655.

Wendorf, Fred, and Romuald Schild. *Prehistory of the Eastern Sahara.* New York: Academic Press, 1980. 414p.

Wenner, Manfred W., ed. *North Yemen: The Yemen Arab Republic After Twenty-Five Years.* Boulder, CO: Lynne Rienner Publishers, 1991. 185p.

Whalen, Norman M., and David W. Pease. "Early Mankind in Arabia." *Aramco World,* July–Aug. 1992, 16–23.

Whittlesey, Derwent. "Sequent Occupance." *Annals* (Association of American Geographers) 19 (1929): 162–165.

Wilkinson, John C. *Arabia's Frontiers: The Story of Britain's Boundary Drawing in the Desert.* London: I. B. Tauris, 1991. 422p.

Williams, Richard S., et al. "Environmental Consequences of the Persian Gulf War 1990–1991: Remote-Sensing Datasets of Kuwait and Environs." *Research and Exploration* (Special issue of National Geographic Society) 7 (1991): 1–48 (entire issue).

Wilson, Sir Arnold T. *The Persian Gulf: An Historical Sketch from the Earliest Times to the Beginning of the Twentieth Century.* London: George Allen and Unwin, 1928. 327p.

Wilson, Jeremy. *Lawrence of Arabia: The Authorized Biography of T. E. Lawrence.* New York: Atheneum, 1990. 1,188p.

Wilson, Mary C. King *Abdullah, Britain and the Making of Jordan.* Cambridge Middle East Library. Cambridge: Cambridge Univ. Press, 1987. 289p.

Wolf, Aaron T. *Hydropolitics along the Jordan River: The Impact of Scarce Water Resources on the Arab-Israeli Conflict.* New York: United Nations Univ. Press, 1995. 272p.

Wolffsohn, Michael. *Israel: Polity, Society, Economy 1882–1986: An Introductory Handbook.* Trans. Douglas Bobovoy. Atlantic Highland, NJ: Humanities Press International, 1987. 302p.

Woodward, Peter N. *Oil and Labor in the Middle East: Saudi Arabia and the Oil Boom.* New York: Praeger, 1988. 195p.

Yapp, Malcolm. *The Making of the Modern Near East, 1792–1923.* London: Longman, 1987. 404p.

———. *The Near East Since the First World War: A History to 1995.* 2d ed. London: Longman, 1996. 597p.

Yazbeck, Haddad, and John L. Esposito, eds. Islam, *Gender, and Social Change.* Oxford: Oxford Univ. Press, 1998. 259p.

Yehia, Mohamed Adel Ahmed. *Atlas of Qatar: From Landsat Images.* Doha: Centre of Scientific and Applied Research, Qatar Univ., 1983. 166p.

Yergin, Daniel. *The Prize: The Epic Quest for Oil, Money, and Power.* New York: Simon and Schuster, 1991. 917p.

Yiftachel, Oren, and Avinoam Meir, eds. *Ethnic Frontiers and Peripheries: Landscapes of Development and Inequality in Israel.* Boulder, CO: Westview Press, 1998. 337p.

Al-Yousef, Mohamed bin Musa. *Oil and the Transformation of Oman 1970–1995: The Socio-Economic Impact.* London: Stacey International, 1995. 144p.

Zahlan, Rosemarie Said. *The Creation of Qatar.* London: Croom Helm, 1979. 160p.

———. *The Making of the Modern Gulf States: Kuwait, Bahrain, Qatar, the United Arab Emirates, and Oman.* Rev. and updated ed. Reading, UK: Ithaca Press, 1998. 200p.

Zangeneh, Hamid. "The Post-Revolutionary Iranian Economy: A Policy Appraisal." *Middle East Policy* 6, no. 2 [Issue 60] (Oct. 1998): 113–129.

Zangwill, Israel. "The Return to Palestine." *New Liberal Review* 2 (Dec. 1901): 615–634.

Zohary, Michael. *Plant Life of Palestine: Israel and Jordan.* New York: Ronald, 1962. 262p.

al-Zoubi, Abdallah S., and Awni T. Batayneh. "Two Main Play Concepts Identified in Jordan's Basins." *Oil and Gas Journal,* July 26, 1999, 86–89.

EPILOGUE

At least one unchanging aspect of the contemporary Middle East is the certainty of rapid change. Just since the completion of the manuscript for this volume, three significant events have altered regional patterns: (1) the Israeli withdrawal from southern Lebanon, (2) the sudden death of Syrian President al-Asad, and (3) developments in the Israeli-Palestinian-Syrian peace process, especially the Camp David summit. Less dramatic but still significant have been (4) Iranian elections and the growing international acceptance of Iran, (5) the ripple effect of increased oil prices, and (6) Iraq's continuing isolation.

(1) During Israeli elections of mid-1999, Ehud Barak pledged that as the new prime minister he would withdraw Israeli forces from Lebanon by July 2000. Occupation of southern Lebanon after 22 years had become increasingly counterproductive and costly in Israeli lives. World opinion had become sharply critical of Israel's failure to abide by UN Resolution 425 of 1978 calling for Israel's withdrawal from Lebanon. More important internally, domestic public opinion, especially among mothers of young men, vigorously opposed continued occupation, since nearly 1,000 Israeli soldiers had been killed and many more wounded in the process. Hizballah guerrillas and other forces defending the area had become increasingly effective and made each week cumulatively painful for Israeli troops and their South Lebanon Army (SLA) proxies.

In frustration, Prime Minister Barak sent Israeli aircraft to bomb Lebanese targets, including power stations and guerrilla bases, for eleven straight days in February 2000 in punishment for Lebanon's failure to control Hizballah. Lebanese spokesmen complained that if Israel, the region's leading military power, could not control the guerrillas, it could hardly expect Lebanon, with the region's weakest military force, to do so. With the situation deteriorating and with members of the SLA defecting in large numbers, Israel speeded up its evacuation timetable and completed its withdrawal from the so-called "security zone" on May 24.

Israel's withdrawal left the remaining elements of the SLA without support and terrified of retribution from Hizballah and other former foes. Israel awarded SLA troops substantial severance pay, but thousands of them and their family members fled into Israel after mid-May. The Israeli government requested that the United States, Canada, Australia, and other countries accept SLA refugees.

Israel's withdrawal set off several days of enthusiastic celebrations by Hizballah and Lebanese civilians north of the border. Almost inevitable acts of minor violence included some individuals' taunting and throwing stones at Israeli troops several meters south of the border. Israeli soldiers fired at the demonstrators, wounding several during the summer months.

Despite some continuing contention about Israel's holding small areas of Lebanese territory after withdrawing, the UN certified on June 16 that Israel had, indeed, withdrawn from Lebanon. The confirmation opened the way for the UN to increase its peacekeeping forces (UNIFIL) from 4,400 to 5,600, thus helping stabilize an uncertain situation along the 72-mile/116-km border. Reestablishment of Lebanese sovereign control over the evacuated zone proceeded gradually, with troops and police forces taking charge in August. Even after Israeli withdrawal, Lebanon—along with its many socioeconomic and political problems—is still left with two major unwanted groups: more than 35,000 Syrian troops supporting the political domination by Syria, plus about 375,000 Palestinian refugees who have been present for half a century. Lebanon conducted peaceful elections for members of parliament in late summer.

(2) Syrian President Hafiz al-Asad died of a heart attack on June 10. Although his authoritarian methods of governance had been widely opposed in Syria, the death of the president was genuinely mourned nation wide. He had been in ill health for several years, following a serious heart attack in 1983, but his death was unexpected and had a powerful impact on the region. President al-Asad had been grooming his younger son, Bashar, to succeed him, in place of his older son, Basil, who died in an automobile accident in 1994. Bashar al-Asad, 34 years old, was trained in Britain in ophthalmology and computer technology. Within ten days after his father's death he was designated secretary general of the Baath Party and commander of the armed forces and was nominated for president after parliament hastily lowered the minimum age for a president-elect from 40 to 34. Parliament endorsed the nomination on June 25, and, as the only candidate, Bashar al-Asad was elected president in a national referendum on July 10 and was sworn in July 16. The new president is expected to move carefully but is almost certain to push for technological modernization in many sectors of Syrian society. He will probably maintain the same stance as that of his father on recovery of the Golan and on other aspects of peace arrangements with Israel.

(3) Now ten years in evolution, the "peace process" has taken on a life of its own and has absorbed a multiplicity of aspects of the "Arab-Israel problem." With at least two main tracks—the Palestinian-Israeli and the Syrian-Israeli—the process was pursued at several levels during the first half of 2000. Syrian-Israeli negotiations prior to the death of President al-Asad promptly reached stalemate and were broken off. In a later session with President al-Asad on March 26 in Geneva, President Clinton was unable to persuade him to restart discussions. Syria's young new president will need some time to consolidate his position before he feels confident enough to negotiate terms of a peace agreement with Israel.

On the Palestinian track, talks between Israelis and Palestinians in early 2000 were virtually continual at lower levels, although high-level discussions in March and June made only limited progress. Even so, the spring talks set the agenda for a later tripartite summit to grapple with the most serious "final status" problems. September 13 as the mutually agreed final status target date loomed ahead, and President Arafat twice expressed his intention to declare a Palestinian state if Israel continued to refuse to negotiate on equal terms.

When Israel withdrew from a promised 6.1 percent of the West Bank in March, the PA complained that the surrendered sectors comprised the poorest kinds of land, to which Israel replied that it had the sole right to select what areas to hand over. Also, when, for the first time, Israeli negotiators displayed detailed maps of how they envisioned the future borders between the two entities, the Palestinians were dismayed. They pointed out that Israel was offering to return only scattered, poor parcels and to leave Jewish settlements and roads in Israeli hands. In May, Palestinians demonstrated and rioted over their perception of Israeli intransigence in the peace process, throwing rocks and precipitating a brief exchange of gunfire between Palestinians and Israelis. These and other manifestations are indicative of the depth and breadth of disagreement and feeling between the two parties. Meanwhile, Prime Minister Barak and President Arafat have each been threatened with assassination by extremists among their respective citizens for negotiating with the other.

Summit talks began July 10 at Camp David, Maryland, with President Clinton attending and encouraging Prime Minister Barak and President Arafat to persevere and compromise. With both sides having declared certain immutable opposing positions, negotiations on final status issues were intense: Jerusalem, Palestinian state and its borders, scores of Jewish settlements in the West Bank, water rights, and refugee rights. The status of Jerusalem became the sticking point: Israel has often unilaterally declared that Jerusalem is its eternal and undivided capital, while the PA has stated that there can be no peace in the Middle East unless East Jerusalem becomes the capital of a Palestinian state. And meanwhile, observers recalled that in the 1947 Palestine Partition Plan Jerusalem was designated a *corpus separatum* under UN control and not under the sovereignty or control of either the Jewish state or the Arab state.

By July 26 the Camp David negotiators announced their inability to reach agreement but also stated that although the talks did not succeed they did not fail: The really tough decisions had finally been faced and grappled with. Moreover, despite some reciprocal recriminations, both sides now clearly recognized what had to be done and both faced the inevitability of having to live together willy-nilly.

Having agreed to delay declaration of a Palestinian state in late 1999, President Arafat indicated after Camp David that he might proceed with the declaration if negotiations with Israel failed to meet the agreed-upon September 13 deadline. Indicative of the long-standing U.S. bias toward Israel, President Clinton responded to a request from Prime Minister Barak by stating on Israeli television that Israel had been more forthcoming at Camp David than had the Palestinians; and he further declared that he would review his stance on not moving the American Embassy from Tel Aviv to Jerusalem, particularly if President Arafat did not withdraw his intention unilaterally to declare a Palestinian state. The embassy declaration raised a vigorous protest in the Middle East and also in Europe. Reports suggested that the decision might be made just before the November elections.

(4) In Iranian elections on February 18, reform candidates for parliamentary seats won their positions in overwhelming numbers, to an extent even greater than had been expected. The mood of the electorate, mostly young in age, has clearly been moving away from the ultraconservatism of the Islamist religious oligarchy as has been shown in their support of the moderate-liberal president, Muhammad Khatami. The shift in character of the new parliament is another step forward, but more moderate news print media were shut down in mid-2000, demonstrating that the ultimate power continues to be in the hands of the ultraconservative ayatollahs.

Another major aspect of Iranian developments in early 2000 is the improvement in relations between Iran and two of its most ardent recent opponents, the United States and Israel. In a major policy address March 17 to the Iranian-American Society, Secretary of State Madeleine Albright advocated a lowering of the level of hostility between the United States and Iran and expressed hope that Iran would respond in kind. She also announced a symbolic lifting of certain sanctions, such as prohibitions against importation of Iranian carpets, caviar, and pistachios; and she acknowledged mistakes in some U.S. actions regarding Iran, including the 1953 CIA support of the ouster of Prime Minister Muhammad Mossadegh. (Details of the plot, which had been murky for 47 years, were published in the *New York Times* in mid-April and again in mid-June.)

Israel likewise, during the spring of 2000, announced official desire for warmer relations with Iran, suggesting that the growing reform movement and the efforts of moderate-liberal President Khatami deserve encouragement. With Iran obviously easing prosecution of thirteen Jews (and several Muslims) accused of anti-state activities and of links with Israel, the Israeli government lowered its rhetoric against Iran. Emphasis was placed on the fact that Israel and pre-1979 Iran under the shah had had close secret relations, with Israel developing missiles for the shah and receiving compensation in oil quietly delivered to Elat. By cultivating coordination with Turkey and Iran, Israel can thereby develop a cordon around the Arab core and follow a "strategy of the periphery."

(5) During the first half of 2000, not only the OPEC members in the Middle East but also other exporters (Oman, Yemen, Egypt) enjoyed welcome relief from serious budget deficits of the recent past, especially 1997 to spring of 1999, by the rise in oil prices. The ripple effect also stimulated the economy of the entire Middle East. The prosperity resulted from action by OPEC countries and other petroleum exporters in March 1999 to reduce output and seek relief from the disastrously low prices of the previous 30 months. The price per barrel gradually rose from a low of $10 in December 1998 to a high of $34 on March 8, 2000. At the high point, OPEC sought a formula to keep the price in a band between $22 and $28 per barrel—the "target zone system": OPEC producers would increase

output (500,000–700,000 bpd) if the price exceeded $28/bbl for three weeks and would decrease output if the price fell below $22/bbl for three weeks. Because demand can vary greatly depending on weather, economic conditions, and downstream operations, any system is difficult to apply. Oil was selling for $28.63 per barrel in mid-2000 and had averaged $26.61 for the first half of the year, compared to $17.47 for 1999 and $12.28 for 1998.

The "special relationship" between the United States and Israel was ruffled in early 2000 when the United States took the unusual step of openly criticizing Israel for contracting to sell advanced military technology to China. The specific item was an advanced AWACS-type system, installed by Israel in a Russian aircraft for use by the Chinese military. U.S. concern also included reservations about "the entire developing defense relationship between Israel and China," pointing to China's J-10 aircraft based on an Israeli prototype developed a few years ago with U.S. financing. Israel reacted testily and refused for several months to halt the sale. Finally, comments by angry congressmen that included threats to cut aid to Israel induced Israel to cancel the sale. Meanwhile, the United States completed work on a laser weapon, successfully tested in June, that Israel plans to deploy along its northern border in September.

(6) Stalemate continues in Iraq, with President Saddam Husayn demanding that UN sanctions be lifted before weapons inspectors will be allowed to return. The UN has extended for another six months the oil-for-food program that earned $8.4 billion from sales of Iraqi oil in the previous six months. Iraq has also been allowed to import equipment and spare parts to enhance its oil industry, since others benefit from significant Iraqi oil production. For example, one-third of the income goes to Kuwait for reparations, and the UN itself gains certain compensations. In the north, the Kurds are enjoying virtual sovereignty and record economic well-being under their own currency and regulations.

Elsewhere, GCC states are enjoying a return to prosperity with the rise in oil prices, and some are cautiously seeking a return to normal relations with Iraq and Iran. Saudi Arabia is emerging from the economic downturn produced by the collapse of oil prices in 1997–1998 and has adopted a policy of greater economic openness, especially to aid its bid to join the WTO. In easing requirements for local partners in domestic enterprises, it is opening its markets to more foreign investments. In Jordan, the new king, Abdullah, is working hard to establish rapport with the divided Jordanian society and has been evaluated as being even more popular than was his father, the late King Husayn. Economic problems of the kingdom remain formidable. Despite one or two events of violence, Egypt has achieved admirable stability in early 2000, with the crucial tourism industry back to normal after the tragic massacre of tourists at Luxor in late 1997.

August 28, 2000

INDEX